THE ESSENTIAL ARTICLES SERIES

Bernard N. Schilling
University of Rochester
General Editor

Donald G. Adam
Bowdoin College
Assistant General Editor

Harry G. Rusche
Emory University
Assistant General Editor

Volumes Available

ESSENTIAL ARTICLES FOR THE STUDY OF ENGLISH
AUGUSTAN BACKGROUNDS

Ed. Bernard N. Schilling

ESSENTIAL ARTICLES FOR THE STUDY OF ALEXANDER POPE

Ed. Maynard Mack

Volumes in Preparation

ESSENTIAL ARTICLES FOR THE STUDY OF JOHN DRYDEN

Ed. H. T. Swedenberg, Jr.

ESSENTIAL ARTICLES FOR THE STUDY OF OLD ENGLISH
LITERATURE

Ed. Jess Bessinger and Stanley J. Kahrl

Essential Articles

for the study of
Alexander Pope

Edited by **Maynard Mack**

Professor of English
Yale University

ARCHON BOOKS   Hamden, Connecticut   1964

Library of Congress Catalog Card Number: 64-21623
Printed in the United States of America

CONTENTS

v

CONTENTS

vi

CONTENTS

*The first two of these (Sats. , II i and ii) were contained in the Works of 1735, but are here grouped with the other Imitations.

vii

CONTENTS

V. HOMER, SHAKESPEARE, AND THE LETTERS

VI. THE DUNCIAD

FOREWORD

Immense resources are now available for literary study in England and America. The contributions to scholarship and criticism are so numerous and often so valuable that the student preparing himself for a career in literary teaching and study may be embarrassed, not to say overwhelmed. Yet from this mass of commentary certain titles have emerged which seem to compel attention. If one offers a seminar in one of the standard areas or periods of English literature, the syllabus will show year after year some items which cannot be omitted, some pieces every serious student should know. And with each new offering of the course, one must face the task of compiling a list of these selections for the seminar's reserve shelf, of searching out and calling in the library's copies, and reserving space for the twenty or thirty or forty volumes the list may demand. As if this were not enough, one must also attempt to repair or replace the volumes whose popularity has had the unfortunate side effects of frequent circulation and the concomitant wear, abuse, and general deterioration.

We propose an alternative to this procedure. We propose to select from the many learned journals, scholarly studies, and critical books the best selections available, the selections which consistently reappear on graduate seminar shelves and on undergraduate honors program reading lists. Let us choose from those articles which time has sanctioned, those too from the best of more recent performances, and let us draw them into a single volume of convenient size. This offers a clear gain in simplicity and usefulness. The articles chosen make up a body of knowledge that cannot fail to be valuable, and they act as models of the kind of contributions to learning which we are training our students to make themselves. And if we can have ready to hand a concentration of such articles for each of the standard areas, and several individual authors, we may conduct the study of these subjects with greater confidence, knowing more fully the extent and kind of reading we can take for granted. And, while we benefit our classes and students, we can also allow the library to keep the original editions of the articles on its shelves and to fulfill its proper and usual function.

FOREWORD

We must add, finally, that each book in the series, and therefore the whole series, is the result of unselfish help from contributors and editors from all of Great Britain and the United States. We wish to acknowledge their help in rendering this useful service.

B. N. S.	Rochester, N. Y.
D. G. A.	Brunswick, Me.
H. G. R.	Atlanta, Ga.

PREFACE

Strictly speaking, no article is essential to the study of
Alexander Pope or any other author: the texts suffice. But once
this fact has been acknowledged, and set aside as counsel for
some other world than ours, the number of writings which can
be defended as essential to understanding one or other aspect
of an author's career mounts dizzily. I have tried in these pages
to contain the tide by establishing strict bounds. With one exception (the essay by Auden) — which I would gladly have made
two if Geoffrey Tillotson's essays on eighteenth-century diction
had been available to me — I have admitted no work which was
not in fact originally an article or essay in a literary periodical,
though of course some have subsequently reappeared in books;
I have limited the contribution of any single author to a single
piece; and I have once or twice preferred a sound treatment of
a work which could not otherwise be brought under discussion
here to a better treatment, by the same hand, of a work on
which good commentary abounds. Judgments will necessarily
differ as to the wisdom of certain inclusions and exclusions,
but I hope that most leaders of graduate seminars will agree
that the book offers in convenient format (subject to the "periodical" limitations already mentioned) much of the best that
has been said about Pope in our time.

Pope's critical history, so far as our century is concerned,
begins in the early thirties, following roughly forty years of
deprecation and neglect. (True, Pope's personality and work
were debated and revalued largely downward from the late
eighteenth century to the Elwin-Courthope edition and the Leslie
Stephen life; but this was inevitable in view of the height his
reputation had reached in his own time, and occurred at least
in part because his poetry was felt to be a force that could not
be ignored. In the Romantic backwater after 1890, he was con-
signed finally to the underworld of polished and empty triflers,
whence an effigy purporting to represent him could occasionally be haled, as by Lounsbury in 1915, to be hanged anew).
Eliot's homages to Dryden announced the new outlook during
the twenties, but the pioneering reconsideration of Pope by
Leavis did not appear till 1933, Sherburn's masterly Early

xi

<u>Career</u> not till 1934, Tillotson's first work on diction in 1935, and <u>Auden</u>'s tribute in 1937.

Twenty-five years later, in the sixties, the first phase of revaluation appears complete. The outlines of the man have been cut free of lies and legend to reveal a credible human mixture of faults and strengths, and the avenues to a balanced estimate of the work, considered quasi-absolutely, have been laid, often by the essays in this volume. What has yet to be consummated, or even very seriously undertaken, is the task of replacing Pope in his time, and his time in the larger history of European culture. The traditions his work incorporates, the presence in his achievement of the Latin authors at a deeper level than "imitation," and of Chaucer, Spenser, Jonson as well as Milton, Dryden, Donne; the discrimination of his style from the style of Dryden and other practitioners of the couplet mode in terms more relevant to our present lexical, metrical, and linguistic sophistication than those which Johnson uses with such skill at the conclusion of his life of Pope; the mastering of types of formal organization which we now only faintly understand, notable in the satires of the golden decade; the relating of his major poems not to quarrels of Catholic families, personal animus, literary entrepreneurship, and other efficient causes in Aristotle's sense, but to the psychic needs, hopes, anxieties, intuitions of human truth and destiny which the poet in every age makes manifest to his fellows; above all, perhaps, the reassimilation of the Augustan period as a whole, so long absurdly viewed as aberration (emotionless, mythless, poetless), into the main currents of English and European life and art: this is but a sampling of the lively enterprises which remain to try the mettle of the oncoming generation. Let no one imagine that the eighteenth century has been exhausted as a subject for serious study. As the essays in this collection show, we are just beginning to know how to ask the right questions.

M. M.

10 July 1963
1314 Davenport College
New Haven, Connecticut

I. BACKGROUNDS AND POINTS OF VIEW

POPE

F. R. Leavis

Pope has had bad luck. Dryden, fortunate in the timeliness
of Mr. Mark Van Doren's book, was enlisted in the argument
against the nineteenth century. It was an opportunity; the cause
was admirable and Homage to John Dryden admirably served it
(though Mr. Eliot, who -- or so it seems to me — has always
tended to do Dryden something more than justice, was incidentally, perhaps accidentally, unfair to Pope). The homage announcing, on the other hand, Pope's rehabilitation was left to
Bloomsbury, and Pope, though he has more to offer the modern
reader than Dryden and might have been enlisted in the argument with certainly not less effect, was taken over, an obvious
property, by the postwar cult of the dix-huitième — an opportunity for Lytton Strachey and Miss Sitwell.

Such attention as he has received from critics qualified to
appreciate him — an aside from Mr. Middleton Murry,[1] a note
by Mr. Edgell Rickword,[2] a paragraph or two of Empsonian
analysis[3] -- has been casual. It is true that what is offered by
these three critics (and there is not a great deal more to record) would, if considered, be enough to establish an intelligent
orientation to Pope. And Pope's achievement being so varied,
I can hardly pretend to attempt more than this. Keeping in view
the purpose of the book and the necessary limits of space, I can
aim at little more than to suggest coercively the re-orientation
from which a revaluation follows; if more, to indicate something of Pope's range and variety.

"Re-orientation," here, envisages in particular the classification "satirist." It may be no longer necessary to discuss

Reprinted from Revaluation by F. R. Leavis by permission of W. W. Norton & Company, Inc. Copyright 1947 by George W. Stewart, Publisher,
Inc. First published in the Norton Library 1963 by arrangement with
George W. Stewart, Publisher, Inc. This article appeared earlier in
Revaluation by F. R. Leavis, Chatto & Windus: London, 1935, pp. 68-91,
and is reprinted by permission of author and publisher. It also appeared
in Scrutiny, Vol. 2 (1933-4), pp. 268-284.

whether satire can be poetry, and we may have entirely disposed of Matthew Arnold; nevertheless, when Pope is classed
under "Satire" it is still with a limiting effect, as if he did only
one kind of thing, and that involving definite bounds and a re-
stricted interest. So there is point in considering to begin with
a poem of an excellence that is obviously not satiric.

The rare fineness of the Elegy to the Memory of an Unfortunate Lady has not had the recognition it deserves. It is praised
commonly (when praised) for a "pathetic" power distinguishing
it from the body of Pope's work, but this does not appear to
recommend it even to Miss Sitwell. In fact, though to condemn
the manner as declamatory is no longer the thing, there is something about it that is found unengagingly outmoded. I remember
to have heard, incredulously, a theory, purporting to come from
a critic of high repute, that is worth mentioning because it calls
attention to certain essential characteristics of the poem. The
theory was that Pope opened in all solemnity, but finding it impossible to continue in so high-flown a strain without smiling at
himself (he had, after all, a sense of humour), slipped in a
qualifying element of burlesque and achieved a subtle total effect analogous to that of Prufrock. The evidence? Well, for example, this:

> As into air the purer spirits flow,
> And sep'rate from their kindred dregs below;
> So flew the soul to its congenial place,
> Nor left one virtue to redeem her Race.

The percipient reader, one gathered, smiled here, and, if
it were pointed out that "dregs" turned "the purer spirits" into
a ludicrous metaphor, the less percipient would smile also.

Nevertheless, the reader who sees the relevance here of
remarking that Pope was born in the seventeenth century will
not be inclined to smile any more than at

> But ah! my soul with too much stay
> Is drunk, and staggers in the way

in Vaughan's The Retreat. If it had never even occurred to one
that the image could strike any reader as funny, it is not because of the lulling effect of Pope's orotund resonances, but

because, by the time one comes to the lines in question, one has
been so potently reminded of Pope's Metaphysical descent. The
preceding lines are actually those quoted by Mr. Middleton Murry as illustrating the Metaphysical element in Pope:

> Most souls, 'tis true, but peep out once an age,
> Dull sullen pris'ners in the body's cage:
> Dim lights of life, that burn a length of years
> Useless, unseen, as lamps in sepulchres;
> Like Eastern Kings a lazy state they keep,
> And close confin'd to their own palace, sleep.

Mr. Murry's observation is just. Pope is as much the last poet
of the seventeenth century as the first of the eighteenth. His
relationship to the Metaphysical tradition is aptly suggested by
his Satires of Dr. Donne Versified: bent as he was (with Dryden
behind him) on being the first "correct" poet, Metaphysical
"wit" — the essential spirit of it — was at the same time congenial to him, more so than to Dryden; and what is suggested in
the undertaking to "versify" Donne he achieved in his best work.
In it subtle complexity is reconciled with "correctness," his
wit is Metaphysical as well as Augustan, and he can be at once
polite and profound.

In the passage first quoted one is not merely solemnly impressed by the striking images; their unexpectedness and variety — the "heterogeneous ideas" that are "yoked together" — involve (on an adequate reading) a play of mind and a flexibility of
attitude that make such effects as that of "dregs" acceptable
when they come: there is an element of surprise, but not the
shock that means rejection (complete or ironically qualified) of
the inappropriate. Seriousness for Pope, for the Metaphysicals,
for Shakespeare, was not the sustained, simple solemnity it
tended to be identified with in the nineteenth century; it might
include among its varied and disparate tones the ludicrous, and
demand, as essential to the total effect, an accompanying play
of the critical intelligence. So in these lines of Pope: the associations of "peep" are not dignified, and one's feelings towards
the "souls" vary, with the changing imagery, from pitying contempt for the timorous peepers, through a shared sense (still
qualified with critical contempt, for one is not oneself dull
and sullen) of the prisoners' hopeless plight, and a solemn

contemplation in the sepulchral couplet of life wasted among
shrivelled husks, to that contempt mixed with humour and a
sense of opulence that is appropriate to the Kings lazing in their
palaces.

The Kings are at least dignified, and they make the transition to the complete dignity of the Lady, who enters again in the
next couplet:

> From these perhaps (ere nature bade her die)
> Fate snatch'd her early to the pitying sky.
> As into air the purer spirits flow, <u>etc</u>.

But her dignity is not a precarious one, to be sedulously guarded from all possibly risible associations. The "mean" element
in the texture of the previous passage can be safely carried on
in "dregs." The very violence of this, directed as it is upon her
contemptible family ("her Race"), draws the attention away
from the value it gives, retrospectively, to "spirits," though
enough of this value is felt to salt a little, as it were, the sym-
pathetically tender nobility that is opposed to "dregs."

Indeed, the successful reconciliation of so formally exalted
a manner with such daring shifts and blends is conditioned by
this presence of a qualifying, seasoning element. This presence
is wit. We have a clear sense of its being generated (to take the
process at its most observable) in the play of thought and image
glanced at above, from "Most souls" to "sleep." The changes
of tone and attitude imposed on the reader (consider, for instance, that involved in passing from "souls" to "peep" in the
first line) result in an alertness; a certain velleity of critical
reserve in responding; a readiness for surprise that amounts
in the end to an implicit recognition, at any point, in accepting
what is given, of other and complementary possibilities. It becomes plain, in the light of such an account, why we should
find ourselves describing as "mature" the sensibility exhibited
by verse in which wit is an element, and also why, in such
verse, a completely serious poetic effect should be able to contain suggestions of the ludicrous such as for Gray, Shelley or
Matthew Arnold would have meant disaster.

The use here of the term "wit" has its prompting, of course
in the seventeenty century, when wit was an established mode,
cultivated as such by the practitioner of verse. "An established

mode" — it is extremely difficult in compressed statement to
avoid misleading simplifications: the line running from Ben
Jonson was as important as that running from Donne. Yet, as
the first chapter of this book will have conveyed, to speak of
two is also misleading; what merging there was is suggested
well enough by the mention of Carew and Marvell. "Wit" com-
prehended not only the audacities of Donne, but also the urbane
critical poise of Ben Jonson. A like poise is an essential characteristic of Marvell's best Metaphysical work, and is developed, as it were, for inspection in the Horatian Ode, that perfect triumph of civilization, unique in English, beside which
the Augustanism of Pope appears to have a note of provinciality
(one may at any rate say that in comparison with Pope's, which
is strongly "period," Marvell's is timeless.)

It is, then, plain enough that Pope's reconciliation of Metaphysical wit with the Polite has antecedents.

> A Soul hung up, as 'twere, in Chains
> Of Nerves, and Arteries, and Veins.
> Tortur'd, besides each other part,
> In a vain Head, and double Heart.

— The familiar turn of that close, a turn not confined to Marvell,
of whom, however, the supreme representative of seventeenth-
century urbanity, it is most characteristic, surely has affinities
with a characteristic effect of Pope's longer couplet:

> First slave to Words, then vassal to a Name,
> Then dupe to party; child and man the same;
> Bounded by Nature, narrow'd still by Art,
> A trifling head, and a contracted heart.[4]

But such particularity of resemblance may hinder as much
as help; it may be better to adduce something as insistently
unlike anything Pope could have written as King's

> 'Tis true, with shame and grief I yield,
> Thou like the Vann first took'st the field
> And gotten hast the victory
> In thus adventuring to dy

> Before me, whose more years might crave
> A just precedence in the grave.

A certain crisp precision of statement, a poised urbanity of movement and tone, that relates this passage to the other two becomes very apparent in the last line. The effect is as of an implicit reference, even here in King where personal feeling is so indubitably strong, of the immediate feeling and emotion to a considered scale of values — a kind of critical "placing," as it were.

A kindred effect begins, in the latter half of the first paragraph, to make itself felt even in the rather histrionic exaltation of Pope's opening:[5]

> Is it, in heav'n, a crime to love too well?
> To bear too tender, or too firm a heart,
> To act a Lover's, or a Roman's part?
> Is there no bright reversion in the sky,
> For those who greatly think, or bravely die?

Enough at any rate is there to make possible the marvellously sure transition to the passage, quoted by Mr. Murry and examined above, which constitutes most of the second paragraph.

It is time now to consider the declamatory heightening characteristic of the poem. It compels attention to itself again at about the thirteenth line, leading as it does to those magnificent exaggeration-effects:

> But thou, false guardian of a charge too good,
> Thou, mean deserter of thy brother's blood!
> See on these ruby lips the trembling breath,
> These cheeks now fading at the blast of death:
> Cold is that breast which warm'd the world before,
> And those love-darting eyes must roll no more.
> Thus, if Eternal justice rules the ball,
> Thus shall your wives, and thus your children fall;
> On all the line a sudden vengeance waits,
> And frequent hearses shall besiege your gates.
> There passengers shall stand, and pointing say,
> (While the long fun'rals blacken all the way)

> Lo these were they, whose souls the Furies steel'd,
> And curs'd with hearts unknowing how to yield.

The success of these effects depends, it is clear, upon the heightened tone and manner, or rather it is a matter of complementary manifestations.

No modern poet, of course, could adopt successfully so lofty and formal a decorum, though the modern reader should have no difficulty in living into it. Pope could find it natural because it was sanctioned by contemporary convention. So obvious a statement may seem not worth making, but there are implications that still, apparently, need insisting on. It is not a question of merely literary convention, any more than Pope's "correctness" is to be discussed as Lytton Strachey elegantly affects to discuss it,[6] in prosodic terms (one cannot say "technical"—technique in any serious sense does not exist for discussion at that level), as consummating a bent towards regularity and symmetry—a bent developing out of the recognition that the "possibilities" of blank verse were "exhausted." The development was in English life, and the "correctness" of Pope's literary form derives its strength from a social code and a civilization. With Dryden begins the period of English literature when form is associated with Good Form, and when, strange as it may seem to us, Good Form could be a serious preoccupation for the intelligent because it meant not mere conformity to a code of manners but a cultivated sensitiveness to the finest art and thought of the time.

The Augustans could be so innocently unaware of the conventional quality of the code — it was "Reason" and "Nature" — because they were in complete accord about fundamentals. Politeness was not merely superficial; it was the service of a culture and a civilization, and the substance and solid bases were so undeniably there that there was no need to discuss them or to ask what was meant by "Sense." Augustanism is something narrower, less fine and less subtle, than what Marvell stands for, but it has a corresponding strength of concentration and single-mindedness.

If Pope too, then, could be both elegant and insolent, the elegance and the insolence were not inane. How firmly he realized the substance, and how habitually present to him were the positive bases, one is apt to find most strikingly evidenced in the neighbourhood of his most spirited satiric passages. For instance, there is the culminating passage, in Epistle IV (Of the Use of Riches, to Richard Boyle, Earl of Burlington), of the attack on Canons:

> But hark! the chiming Clocks to Dinner call;
> A hundred footsteps scrape the marble Hall:
> The rich Buffet well-colour'd Serpents grace,
> And gaping Tritons spew to wash your face.
> Is this a dinner? this a Genial room?
> No, 'tis a Temple, and a Hecatomb.
> A solemn Sacrifice, perform'd in state,
> You drink by measure, and to minutes eat.
> So quick retires each flying course, you'd swear
> Sancho's dread Doctor and his Wand were there.
> Between each Act the trembling salvers ring,
> From soup to sweet-wine, and God bless the King.
> In plenty starving, tantaliz'd in state,
> And complaisantly help'd to all I hate,
> Treated, caress'd, and tir'd, I take my leave,
> Sick of his civil Pride from Morn to Eve;
> I curse such lavish cost, and little skill,
> And swear no Day was ever past so ill.

After the sneering, destructive gusto of this one can for a moment hardly credit that the next four lines are unironically solemn, so complete is the change of tone:

> Yet hence the Poor are cloth'd, the Hungry fed;
> Health to himself, and to his Infants bread
> The Lab'rer bears: What his hard Heart denies,
> His charitable Vanity supplies.

If there were any doubt it would be settled at once by what follows. This is a passage that occasions some of the finest criticism in Mr. Empson's Seven Types of Ambiguity (pp. 161-2):

> Another age shall see the golden Ear
> Embrown the Slope, and nod on the Parterre,
> Deep Harvests bury all his pride has plann'd,
> And laughing Ceres re-assume the land.

Mr. Empson's subtle commentary, which is immediately relevant and should be looked up, ends with a hope for agreement
on the part of the reader that there is conveyed in these lines
a feeling for nature, called forth "by a conception of nature in
terms of human politics"; "that there is some sense of the im-
mensity of harvest through a whole country; that the relief with
which the cripple for a moment identifies himself with something so strong and generous gives these two couplets an extraordinary scale."

The qualification and addition that I would make are that the
cripple may be over-stressed and that there is a more general
significance. The relevant commentary for my argument is offered implicitly by Pope himself in the lines that come next:

> Who then shall grace, or who improve the Soil?
> Who plants like Bathurst, or who builds like Boyle.
> 'Tis Use alone that sanctifies Expense,
> And Splendour borrows all her rays from Sense.
> His Father's Acres who enjoys in peace,
> Or makes his Neighbours glad, if he increase:
> Whose cheerful Tenants bless their yearly toil,
> Yet to their Lord owe more than to the soil;
> Whose ample Lawns are not asham'd to feed
> The milky heifer and deserving steed;
> Whose rising Forests, not for pride or show,
> But future Buildings, future Navies, grow:
> Let his plantations stretch from down to down,
> First shade a Country, and then raise a Town.
> You too proceed! . . .

— And so it goes on, in fourteen more lines of hortatory grandeur, to the end.

Formal compliment in the Grand Style, some one may remark, was in order in such a piece, particularly in the close;
it was in the convention of the period. It was. The period was
one that could support such a convention, and Pope here (that
is the point) has the strength of his period. That the positives
so magnificently asserted are asserted more than conventionally we know from the force and life of the passage, which is
essentially continuous with those superb prelusive lines appraised in Mr. Empson's analysis. The same inspiration

informs the whole: the ideal (generally shared and not hopelessly removed from the actual) of a civilization in which Art and
Nature, Beauty and Use, Industry and Decorum, should be reconciled, and humane culture, even in its most refined forms,
be kept appropriately aware of its derivation from and dependence on the culture of the soil. The aesthetic, the moral and
the utilitarian are characteristically associated in the "milky
heifer and deserving steed," which graze the "ample lawns" of
an eighteenth-century landscape, itself a work of art.

From the supply-varying, continually surprising, play of
satiric ridicule to these resonant and decorous elevations (where
"steed" comes naturally) Pope can pass with perfect ease and
sureness of transition -- a testimony not only to the stable poise
that makes the elevations safe, but, reciprocally, to something
in the satire.

The commentary called for by the exalted decorum of the
Elegy is, then, implicitly provided by Pope himself:

> 'Tis Use alone that sanctifies Expense,
> And Splendour borrows all her rays from Sense.[7]

Pope was at one with a society to which these were obvious but
important truths. So supported, he could sustain a formal dignity such as, pretended to, would make a modern ridiculous.
"Use" represents robust moral certitudes sufficiently endorsed
by the way of the world, and "Sense" was a light clear and unquestionable as the sun.

There is no need to illustrate further the variety of tone
from passage to passage of the Elegy, or the sureness of the
transitions. After various tones of declamation, we pass through
the passage anticipating (or furnishing) an eighteenth-century
mode, associated with Collins and Gray,[8] of conventional elegiac sentiment to the deeply moving final paragraph, in which the
strong personal emotion, so firmly subdued throughout to the
"artificial" form and manner, insists more and more on its
immediately personal intensity.

It is time now to turn to the satirist. What in the foregoing
page or two may have appeared excessively elementary will be
recognized, perhaps, in its bearing on the satire, to serve at
least some purpose. For, granting Pope to be pre-eminently
a satirist and to enjoy as such what favour he does enjoy, one

cannot easily find good reasons for believing that an intelligent appreciation of satiric poetry is much commoner to-day than it was among the contemporaries of Matthew Arnold. Elementary things still need saying. Such terms as "venom," "envy," "malice" and "spite" are, among modern connoisseurs, the staple of appreciation (it is, at any rate, difficult to find anything on Pope in other terms): ". . . we are in the happy position of being able, quite imperturbably, to enjoy the fun. . . . We sit at our ease, reading those Satires and Epistles, in which the verses, when they were written, resembled nothing so much as spoonfuls of boiling oil, ladled out by a fiendish monkey at an upstairs window upon such of the passers-by whom the wretch had a grudge against — and we are delighted." The Victorians disapproved; Bloomsbury approves: that is the revolution of taste.

It is, in some ways, a pity that we know so much about Pope's life. If nothing had been known but the works, would "envy," "venom," "malice," "spite" and the rest have played so large a part in the commentary? There is, indeed, evidence in the satires of strong personal feelings, but even — or, rather, especially — where these appear strongest, what (if we are literate) we should find most striking is an intensity of art. To say, with Leslie Stephen and Lytton Strachey, that in the character of Sporus Pope "seems to be actually screaming with malignant fury" is to betray an essential inability to read Pope.

But one has to conclude from published criticism that the nature of Pope's art is very little understood. Just as I reach this point there comes to hand the following, by an American critic:[9] "A familiar charge often brought against Shelley is lack of discipline, but in such charges one must always know what the poet is trying to control. If, as in the case of Pope, it is the mere perfection of a regulated line of verse, the problem becomes one of craftsmanship." A "mere perfection of a regulated line of verse" is not anything as clearly and precisely indicated as the critic, perhaps, supposes; but that he supposes Pope's technique ("craftsmanship" being plainly depreciatory) to be something superficial, some mere skill of arranging a verbal surface, is confirmed by what he goes on to say: Pope's "recitation of the dogmas of his day is hollow," and "in his day as in ours it is a relatively simple matter to accept a ritual of devotion as a substitute for an understanding of basic moral values."

An "understanding of basic moral values" is not a claim one need be concerned to make for a poet, but that Pope's relation to the "basic moral values" of the civilization he belonged to was no mere matter of formal salute and outward deference has been sufficiently shown above, in the discussion of the close of Epistle IV. When Pope contemplates the bases and essential conditions of Augustan culture his imagination fires to a creative glow that produces what is poetry even by Romantic standards. His contemplation is religious in its seriousness. The note is that of these lines, which come in Epistle III not long after a vigorous satiric passage and immediately before another:

> Ask we what makes one keep and one bestow?
> That Pow'r who bids the Ocean ebb and flow,
> Bids seed-time, harvest, equal course maintain,
> Thro' reconcil'd extremes of drought and rain,
> Builds life on Death, on Change Duration founds,
> And gives th' eternal wheels to know their rounds.

The order of Augustan civilization evokes characteristically in Pope, its poet, when he is moved by the vision of it, a profound sense of it as dependent on and harmonious with an ultimate and inclusive order. The sense of order expressed in his art when he is at his best (and he is at his best more than most poets) is nothing merely conventional or superficial, explicable in terms of social elegance and a pattern of verse. His technique, concerned as it is with arranging words and "regulating" movements, is the instrument of a fine organization, and it brings to bear pressures and potencies that can turn intense personal feelings into something else. "His 'poetic criticism of life,'" says Lytton Strachey, gibbeting solemn fatuity, "was simply and solely the heroic couplet." Pope would have found it hard to determine what precisely this means, but he certainly would not have found the fatuity Arnold's, and if the Augustan idiom in which he expressed much the same commonplaces as Arnold's differed from the Victorian, it was not in being less solemn.

> Ask you what Provocation I have had?
> The strong Antipathy of Good to Bad[10]

14

— we may not accept this as suggesting adequately the moral
basis of Pope's satire, but it is significant that Pope could offer such an account: his strength as a satirist was that he lived
in an age when such an account could be offered.

The passages of solemnly exalted imagination like those
adduced above come without incongruity in the midst of the
satire — the significance of this needs no further insisting on.
What does need insisting on is that with this capacity for poised
and subtle variety goes a remarkable command of varied satiric
tones.[11] The politeness of the Atticus portrait is very different
from that of the Rape of the Lock (a work that, in my opinion,
has enjoyed more than justice); the intense destructive vivacity
of the Sporus portrait is different from that of the attack on
Timon; the following (which is very far from an exception) is
enough to dispose of the judgment that "Pope was witty but not
humorous" — the theme is Paper Credit:

> Had Colepepper's whole wealth been hops and hogs,
> Could he himself have sent it to the dogs?
> His Grace will game: to White's a Bull be led,
> With spurning heels and with a butting head.
> To White's be carry'd, as to ancient games,
> Fair Coursers, Vases, and alluring Dames.
> Shall then Uxurio, if the stakes he sweep,
> Bear home six Whores, and make his Lady weep?

The story of Sir Balaam at the end of Epistle III is, again,
quite different — but one cannot by enumerating, even if there
were room, do justice to Pope's variety. Indeed, to call attention to the satiric variety as such is to risk a misleading stress.

Even Mr. Eliot, in Homage to John Dryden, manages to
limit Pope very unjustly. Some accidental unfair suggestion one
might expect in such casual reference. But there is decidedly
more than that to complain of. For instance:

> But the effect of the portraits of Dryden is to
> transform the object to something greater, as were
> transformed the verses of Cowley quoted above.

> A fiery soul, which working out its way,
> Fretted the pigmy body to decay:

> And o'er informed the tenement of clay.

> These lines are not merely a magnificent tribute. They
> create the object which they contemplate; the poetry
> is purer than anything in Pope except the last lines of
> the Dunciad.

This is a judgment that Matthew Arnold would have understood — or thought he understood; for one knows that Mr. Eliot
is not appealing here to the prejudices that it is the general aim
of his essay to destroy. Yet the judgment is perplexing. The
end of the Dunciad was admired in the Victorian age as approaching nearer to "pure poetry" than Pope does characteristically;
but no one could have better pointed out than Mr. Eliot its
strength and subtlety of wit. The passage seems to me finer
than anything in Dryden; decidedly finer, for instance, than the
comparable part of Mac Flecknoe. It has a greater intensity
(an intensity that Dryden, with his virtues of good humour and
good nature, was incapable of), and this is manifest in the very
much tauter and more sensitive verse, the finer life of the
movement.
    As for "comic creation," it seems to me easy to find pas-
sages of Pope that have a like advantage over the lines of Dryden quoted by Mr. Eliot:

> The country rings around with loud alarms,
> And raw in fields the rude militia swarms;
> Mouths without hands; maintained at vast expense,
> In peace a charge, in war a weak defence;
> Stout once a month, they march, a blust'ring band,
> And ever, but in times of need, at hand;
> This was the morn, when issuing on the guard,
> Drawn up in rank and file they stood prepared
> Of seeming arms to make a short essay,
> Then hasten to be drunk, the business of the day.

Repeated re-readings of both passages only convince me the
more that this of Dryden's is much inferior to the following,
which starts twenty lines before the final paragraph of the
Dunciad:

> More had she spoke, but yawn'd — all Nature nods:
> What mortal can resist the Yawn of Gods?
> Churches and Chapels instantly it reach'd;
> (St. James's first, for leaden Gilbert preach'd)
> Then catch'd the Schools; the Hall scarce kept awake;
> The Convocation gap'd, but could not speak:
> Lost was the Nation's Sense, nor could be found,
> While the long solemn Unison went round:
> Wide, and more wide, it spread o'er all the realm;
> Ev'n Palinurus nodded at the Helm:
> The Vapour mild o'er each Committee crept;
> Unfinish'd Treaties in each Office slept;
> And Chiefless Armies doz'd out the Campaign;
> And Navies yawn'd for Orders on the Main.

Dryden, says Mr. Eliot, "bears a curious antithetical resemblance to Swinburne. Swinburne was also a master of words, but Swinburne's words are all suggestion and no denotation; if they suggest nothing, it is because they suggest too much. Dryden's words, on the other hand, are precise, they state immensely, but their suggestiveness is almost nothing." These lines of Pope seem to me to have all the strength of Dryden's, and to have, in addition, a very remarkable potency of suggestion.

We feel the enveloping, thickening, drowsy vapour spread irresistibly and take on, even, something of a rich romantic glamour — a quality concentrated in

> Ev'n Palinurus nodded at the Helm.

This is certainly poetic creation, even by Romantic standards, and yet it is, at the same time, "comic creation." The suggestive richness is blended with something quite un-Romantic:

> Lost was the Nation's Sense, nor could be found,
> While the long solemn Unison went round.

The effect of the first of these lines is, to nineteenth-century taste, intrinsically unpoetical, but in the second line the "long solemn Unison" is, though ludicrous, at the same time truly solemn. The "Chiefless Armies" doze in an immensely fantastic

17

dream-comedy, and the Navies yawn vastly on an enchanted sea.

Beside the passage of Mac Flecknoe in which Dryden uses Cowley may be set, not to Pope's disadvantage, this from the fourth book of the Dunciad:

> When Dullness, smiling, — "Thus revive the Wits!
> But murder first, and mince them all to bits;
> As erst Medea (cruel, so to save!)
> A new Edition of old Aeson gave;
> Let standard-authors, thus, like trophies born,
> Appear more glorious as more hack'd and torn.
> And you, my Critics! in the chequer'd shade,
> Admire new light thro' holes yourselves have made.
> Leave not a foot of verse, a foot of stone,"
> A Page, a Grave, that they can call their own.

A commentary like that which Mr. Eliot makes on Dryden's borrowings ("only a poet could have made what Dryden makes of them") is applicable to Pope's, except that there seems to be even more point in Pope's use of his, and a greater intensity of surprise in his poetry. The ragged squalor of the Critics in their dark garrets ("batter'd and decay'd") is ironically enhanced by contrast with Milton's

> many a youth and many a maid
> Dancing in the chequered shade.

But it is the use of Waller that is most felicitous:

> The soul's dark cottage, battered and decay'd
> Lets in new light through chinks that Time hath made.

There is nothing merely flippant in Pope's sardonic play upon "light"; the solemnity of Waller's theme is present in the indignant observation that it was not Time that made these holes. Indeed, the seriousness of the original is intensified, for Waller is rather easily conventional in his solemn sentiment. The weight makes itself felt in the next couplet, the last of those quoted:

> Leave not a foot of verse, a foot of stone,
> A Page, a Grave, that they can call their own.

The recognition of inevitable death, decay and oblivion charges the bitterness of this -- of the pun in the first line and the sardonic concentration of the second.

The Metaphysical descent here is plain, but no plainer than in abundance of other passages. The following, in its satiric mode, has in the opening the deep note of those lines in the Elegy ("Most souls, 'tis true," etc.), and the ironical fantasy of the whole has a poetic intensity extraordinarily rich in beauty, oddness and surprise:

> The common Soul, of Heaven's more frugal make,
> Serves but to keep fools pert, and knaves awake:
> A drowsy Watchman, that just gives a knock,
> And breaks our rest, to tell us what's a-clock.
> Yet by some object, ev'ry brain is stirr'd;
> The dull may waken to a humming-bird;
> The most recluse, discreetly open'd, find
> Congenial matter in the Cockle-kind;
> The mind, in Metaphysics at a loss,
> May wander in a wilderness of Moss;
> The head that turns at super-lunar things,
> Pois'd with a tail, may steer on Wilkins' wings.

An element that in the close of the Dunciad blends with the sublime here associates naturally with quite other effects:

> With that, a Wizard Old his Cup extends;
> Which whoso tastes, forgets his former friends,
> Sire, Ancestors, Himself.[12] One casts his eyes
> Up to a Star, and like Endymion dies;
> A Feather, shooting from another's head,
> Extracts his brain; and Principle is fled;
> Lost is his God, his Country, ev'ry thing;
> And nothing left but Homage to a King!
> The vulgar herd turn off to roll with Hogs,
> To run with Horses, or to hunt with Dogs;
> But, sad example! never to escape
> Their Infamy, still keep the human shape.

19

> But she, good Goddess, sent to ev'ry child
> Firm Impudence, or Stupefaction mild;
> And straight succeeded, leaving shame no room,
> Cibberian forehead, or Cimmerian gloom.

But illustration might go on indefinitely. A representative selection of passages would fill a great many pages. A selection of all Pope that one would wish to have by one for habitual re-reading would fill a great many more. Is it necessary to disclaim the suggestion that he is fairly represented in short extracts? No one, I imagine, willingly reads through the Essay on Man (Pope piquing himself on philosophical or theological profundity and acumen is intolerable, and he cannot, as Dryden can, argue interestingly in verse); but to do justice to him one must read through not merely the Epistles, but, also as a unit, the fourth book of the Dunciad, which I am inclined to think the most striking manifestation of his genius. It is certainly satire, and I know of nothing that demonstrates more irresistibly that satire can be great poetry.

An adequate estimate of Pope would go on to describe the extraordinary key-position he holds, the senses in which he stands between the seventeenth and the eighteenth centuries. Communications from the Metaphysicals do not pass beyond him; he communicates forward, not only with Johnson, but also (consider, for instance, Eloïsa to Abelard) with Thomson and Gray. It was not for nothing that he was so interested in Milton.

NOTES

1 See the essay on Collins in Countries of the Mind.

2 In a review of The Oxford Book of Eighteenth Century Verse reprinted in Towards Standards of Criticism (edited by the present writer).

3 Seven types of Ambiguity, pp. 161-2.

4 The Dunciad, Bk. IV, 1. 501.

5 The first part of the paragraph runs:
> What beck'ning ghost, along the moon-light shade
> Invites my steps, and points to yonder glade?
> 'Tis she! -- but why that bleeding bosom gored,

> Why dimly gleams the visionary sword?
> Oh ever beauteous, ever friendly! tell, <u>etc.</u>

6   See his Leslie Stephen lecture on Pope.

7   Cf. See! sportive fate, to punish awkward pride,
    Bids Bubo build, and sends him such a Guide:
    A standing sermon, at each year's expense,
    That never Coxcomb reach'd Magnificence!
    You show us, Rome was glorious, not profuse,
    And pompous buildings once were things of Use.
                        (From the same epistle.)

8   See p. 108, <u>Revaluation</u>.

9   Horace Gregory: <u>A Defense of Poetry</u> in <u>The New Republic</u>,
    11th October 1933.

10 <u>Epilogue to the Satires, Dialogue II</u>.

11 See Note, <u>Revaluation</u>, pp. 92-100.

12 These first two and a half lines, by themselves, would be
    taken for Tennyson.

ALEXANDER POPE

W. H. Auden

About 1705 Wycherley's visitors began to "meet a little
Aesopic sort of animal in his own cropt hair, and dress agreeable to the forest he came from -- probably some tenant's son
of Wycherley's making court for continuance in his lease on the
decease of his rustic parent — and were surprised to learn that
he was poetically inclined and writ tolerably smooth verses." As
is so often the case, just as Proust was a Jew, and Hitler is an
Austrian, the man who was to epitomize Augustan culture was
not of it by birth. The invalid self-educated son of a Roman
Catholic linen merchant, it was not a very promising beginning
for the man who was to become the friend of dukes, the gardener and gourmet, the poet to whom a mayor was to offer £4000
for a single couplet.

If Pope's social advantages were few his physical charms
were even less. Only four feet six in height, he was already a
sufferer from Pott's disease, "the little Alexander whom the
women laugh at," and in middle age was to become really repulsive. ". . . so weak as to stand in perpetual need of female
attendance; extremely sensible of cold, so that he wore a kind
of fur doublet, under a shirt of a very coarse warm linen with
fine sleeves. When he rose, he was invested in a bodice made
of stiff canvas, being scarce able to hold himself erect till they
were laced, and he then put on a flannel waistcoat. One side
was contracted. His legs were so slender, that he enlarged their
bulk with three pairs of stockings, which were drawn on and off
by the maid; for he was not able to dress or undress himself,
and neither went to bed nor rose without help. His weakness
made it very difficult for him to be clean. His hair had fallen
almost all away. . . ."

Nor, it must be admitted, even if not as sublimely odious

Reprinted from Essays in Criticism, Vol. 1 (1951), pp. 208-224, by permission of author and publisher. This article appeared earlier in From
Anne to Victoria, ed. Bonamy Dobrée, Cassell and Company: London,
1937, and is reprinted by permission of editor and publisher.

as Addison, was he a prepossessing character. He was a snob
and a social climber, who lied about his ancestry and cooked
his correspondence; he was fretful and demanded constant attention, he was sly, he was mean, he was greedy, he was vain,
touchy, and worldly while posing as being indifferent to the
world and to criticism; he was not even a good conversationalist.

As a poet, he was limited to a single verse form, the end-
stopped couplet; his rare attempts at other forms were failures.
To limitation of form was added limitation of interest. He had
no interest in nature as we understand the term, no interest in
love, no interest in abstract ideas, and none in Tom, Dick and
Harry. Yet his recognition was immediate, and his reputation
never wavered during his lifetime.

If we are to understand his contemporary success, if we
are to appreciate the nature of his poetry and its value, we
must understand the age in which he lived.

At the beginning of the eighteenth century, although one
quarter of the population was in receipt of occasional parish
relief, England was the most prosperous country in Europe.
According to Gregory King, out of a population of about 5 mil-
lion, the two largest classes were cottagers and paupers, and
the labouring people and outservants, both of which the Act of
Settlement of the Poor prevented from leaving the parishes in
which they were born; about a quarter were tenant farmers or
freeholders; an eighty-seventh small landed gentry with an income of from £250 to £450 a year; and the remainder the large
landowners. One tenth of the population lived in London, which
was more than fifteen times larger than her nearest rival,
Bristol. The relative prosperity of the country was due, partly
to colonies and Britain's favourable position on the Atlantic
seaboard, partly to her export of cloth to Europe, partly to her
free internal trade and partly to the comparative lack of friction,
compared, for example, with France, between the landed aristocracy and business. Though the former professed to look
down on the latter, they were ready to profit from them; the
younger sons of the poorer gentry were frequently apprentices
to business houses, and successful business men could and did
become landed gentry. The Act of Toleration prevented religious difference from interfering with trade; and the establishment of the Bank of England and the National Debt drew financial
and political interests close together.

The dependence on air and water for motive power preserved the balance between town and country; indeed, through
the wish to escape obsolete borough restrictions, industry was
less urban than in earlier times. There was therefore no emotional demand for "nature" poetry.

If a large number of the population were illiterate; if, by
our modern liberal standards, their amusements of drinking,
gambling, and cock-fighting were crude, their sanitation prim-
tive, their politics virulent and corrupt, there had nevertheless been an improvement. There were more educated people
than ever before, a greater interest in education -- charity
schools were being built everywhere -- and England's increasing
importance in, and ties with, Europe, gave her culture a breadth
and balance hitherto unknown. The arts have hitherto flourished
best where cultured society was large enough to provide variety
and small enough to be homogeneous in taste. The eighteenth
century in England fulfilled both these conditions. There was a
growing consciousness of the value of refinement and good manners -- a society for the Reformation of Manners is a symptom
of a social rather than a Puritan conscience — and the age saw
the development of these typical modern amusements -- smoking
-- tea- and coffee-drinking -- shooting birds on the wing instead
of sitting -- horse-racing -- and cricket. Whether intentional or
not, the wearing of wigs helped to delouse the upper classes,
and in politics bribery may not be desirable but it is an improvement upon imprisonment and political murder.

You have, then, a society which, in spite of very wide
variations in income and culture varying from the cottager with
his bible and peddler's ballads, through the small squire with
his Hudibras and Foxe's Book of Martyrs, through the Squire
Westerns and the Sir Roger de Coverleys, up to the Duke with
his classical library, his panelled room, his landscape garden,
his china and mahogany furniture, and his round of London,
Bath and his country estate, was at no point fundamentally
divided in outlook and feeling. Owing to the fusing of landed
and trade interests, owing to the fact that England was still rural, was a genuine economic unit, and rising in power, there
was little clash between politics and economics, no apparent
class conflict.

In studying the ideas and art of this period, therefore, we
are studying firstly those of any rising class which has recently

won power and security for itself -- (perhaps the surest sign of
victory in a political struggle is the removal of the Censorship;
this happened in 1695) -- and secondly those of a particular example of such a class in a small European island shortly before
the Industrial Revolution. In consequence we may find certain
characteristics which seem likely to recur through history, and
others which are peculiar to the particular circumstance of the
time, and can never happen again.

To take the more universal characteristics first; what
should we expect to find? Those who have risen from a subordinate to a dominant position are, firstly, pleased with themselves, and, secondly, anxious to preserve the status quo. No
one is so ready to cry Pax and All's well as he who has just got
what he wants. They are optimistic, full of vitality, pacific,
within their circle, and conservative.

> All Nature is but Art, unknown to thee;
> All Chance, Direction, which thou canst not see;
> All Discord, Harmony not understood;
> All partial Evil, universal Good;
> And, spite of Pride, in erring Reason's spite,
> One truth is clear, WHATEVER IS, IS RIGHT.

Secondly, they bring with them a sense of social inferiority;
they are anxious to possess and develop the culture and social
refinements of the class they have replaced. Contempt for art
and manners is a symptom of a rising class that has not yet
won power. When they have, they will welcome and reward
handsomely art which teaches them refinement, and proves
them refined. Because they have been successful, they are interested in themselves. The art of their choice will celebrate
their activities, flatter their virtues, and poke fun at their
fables.

Certain qualities of Augustan poetry, then, its air of well
being, its gusto, its social reference,

> Correct with spirit, eloquent with ease.

are those which might occur after any social revolution. Others
are more unique.

The Reformation split the conception of a God who was both

25

immanent and transcendental, a God of faith and works, into
two, into the Inner light to be approached only through the private conscience, and the Divine Architect and Engineer of the
Physical Universe and the laws of Economics, whose operations
could be understood but not interfered with. The religious life
tended to become individualized, and the social life secularized.
The evil effects of what a Catholic writer has described as

> Sundering the believer from his laicized body
> Sundering heaven from an earth evermore hireling,
> secularized, enslaved,
> tied down to the manufacture of the useful.

are more apparent now than then, but of the importance of such
an attitude to nature and historical law in the development of
the physical sciences, there can be no doubt, and the secular-
ization of education hastened the growth of culture among others
than those in orders, and the creation of a general reading
public.

At first the emphasis was all on the liberty of the individual
conscience, and the Renaissance glorification of the individual,
on anti-authoritarianism and anti-popery. But when those who
believed in private illumination gained political and public power,
they became, as they were bound to become, tyrants. After the
Restoration, therefore, there was a swing over to the other pole,
to a belief, equally one-sided, in reason against inspiration, in
the laws of nature against enthusiastic private illumination, in
society against the individual fanatic.

> For Forms of Government let fools contest;
> Whate'er is best administered is best:
> For Modes of Faith let graceless zealots fight;
> His can't be wrong whose life is in the right:
> In Faith and Hope the world will disagree,
> But All Mankind's concern is Charity:
> All must be false that thwart this one great end;
> And all of God, that bless Mankind or mend.

Anti-popery remained, reinforced by the events of 1688,
Louis XIV's power in Europe, and his persecution of the Hugue-
nots, but to it was added Anti-Dissent. Neither were violent

enough to lead to real persecution or to prevent social intercourse; they were the natural distrust that people who are doing
very nicely as they are, have for those who might interfere with
them, with their social order, their pleasures, and their cash,
but are in point of fact powerless.

The appreciation of law extended itself naturally enough to
literature, and literary criticism became for the first time a
serious study. Suspicious of enthusiasm and inspiration, Dryden
and his successors based their psychology of creative work on
Hobbes:

> Time and education beget experience.
> Experience begets Memory.
> Memory begets Judgement and Fancy.
> Memory is the world in which the Judgement, the
> severer sister, busieth herself in a grave and rigid
> examination of all the parts of Nature, and in register-
> ing by letters their order, causes, uses, differences,
> and resemblances; whereby the Fancy, when any work
> of Art is to be performed, finding her materials at
> hand and prepared for her use, needs no more than a
> swift motion over them.
> Imagination is nothing else but sense decaying or
> weakened by the absence of the object.

Such a theory reduces imagination to a recording device,
and makes creative work a purely conscious activity. It has no
place for the solar plexus or the Unconscious of modern writers,
nor for the divine inspiration of the Ancients. Poetry becomes
a matter of word-painting of the objective world.

The difference is apparent if we compare Pope's invocation
at the beginning of his philosophical poem with those of a Catholic like Dante, or a puritan like Milton.

> O good Apollo . . .
> Into my bosom enter thou, and so breathe as when
> thou drewest
> Marsyas from out what sheathed his limbs.

> And chiefly thou, O spirit, that dost prefer
> Before all temples the upright heart and pure,

Instruct me, for thou knowest . . .
. . . What in me is dark
Illumine; what is low, raise and support.

Awake, my St. John! leave all meaner things
To low ambition and the pride of Kings.
Let us (since life can little more supply
Than just to look about us and to die)
Expatiate free o'er all this scene of Man;
A mighty maze! but not without a plan.

But it would be a mistake to say that the best poetry of
Dryden or Pope or any of the Augustans was deliberately written to their theories. The writing of poetry is always a more
complex thing than any theory we may have about it. We write
first and use the theory afterwards to justify the particular kind
of poetry we like and the particular things about poetry in general which we think we like. Further, like most theories, it
has its points. We, who have been brought up in the Romantic
tradition, are inclined to think that whenever the Augustans
wrote bad poetry, they were using their own recipe, and whenever they wrote good poetry they were using the Romantic recipe by mistake. This is false. Without their ideas on nature
and the Heroic poem, we should miss The Rape of the Lock and
the Dunciad just as much as we should be spared Eloisa to
Abelard or Darwin's Loves of the Plants. The gusto, objectivity
and perfection of texture of the one, owe quite as much to their
theories, as does the bogus classicalism of the other.

All theories are one-sided generalizations; and are replaced
by their opposite half-truths. When society has become too big
to manage, when there is a class of persons whose incomes are
drawn from investments without the responsibilities of landowners or employers, when the towns are congested, we shall
hear other voices. Instead of Hobbes's psychology, we shall
have Blake's "Natural objects deaden and weaken imagination
in me." Instead of Pope's modest intention to please, the poets
will proclaim themselves, and be believed in so far as they are
listened to at all, as the Divine legislators of the world.

We, again, fancy we know better now; that the writing of
poetry is a matter of neither a purely unconscious inspiration,
nor purely conscious application, but a mixture of the two, in

proportions which vary with different kinds of verse; that it is rarely the tortured madness which some of the Romantics pretended it was, and certainly never the effortless and thoughtless excitement the cinema public imagines it to be.

If the Augustans had the defects of their qualities, so did the Romantics. If the former sometimes came down, according to the late Professor Housman, to "singing hymns in the prison chapel," the latter sometimes went off into extempore prayers in the county asylum.

And on the whole, yes, on the whole, I think we agree with Byron "Thou shalt believe in Milton, Dryden and Pope. Thou shalt not set up Wordsworth, Coleridge and Southey." But then we know better now.

During the two centuries preceding Pope, the literary language had undergone considerable change. We cannot tell how far Shakespeare's conversations in The Merry Wives of Windsor is a realistic transcript, but it is remote from us in a way that the dialogue of the Restoration dramatists is not. In Dryden's essay on The Dramatic Poesy of The Last Age he gives as the reason, "the greatest advantage of our century, which proceeds from conversation. In the age wherein these poets lived, there was less of gallantry than in ours; neither did they keep the best company of theirs."

The change in social status is important. It is doubtful if the Elizabethan dramatists would have been received in the best drawing-rooms. The poets of a later age certainly were, and if poetry lost that complete unity of language and sensation which the Elizabethans at their best achieved,

in her strong toil of grace

the rise of the writer into society was at least partly responsible. A classical education and the company of ladies and gentlemen may have advantages, but they make an instinctive vocabulary very difficult.

But it is the mark of a great writer to know his limitations. Had Dryden attempted to continue the Elizabethan traditions, he would have been no greater than Massinger. Instead, he did what Nature has usually done in evolutionary changes, he turned to a form which, though it had once been important, during the last age had played second fiddle to blank verse.

29

The couplet had nevertheless had a continuous history, parallel to and influenced by blank verse. The couplet of Chaucer's time degenerated with the dropping of the final "e," and with the exception of Dunbar's Freiris of Berwik, is hardly seen, till it turns up again in Spenser's Mother Hubbard's Tale.

> To such delight the noble wits he led
> Which him relieved as their vain humours fed
> With fruitless follies and unsound delights.

Its principal use was for narrative, as in Marlowe and Chapman's Hero and Leander, with enjambement and spreading of sentences over several couplets, a feature which developed in Donne and Cowley to a point where the feeling of the couplet is almost lost.

> Seek true religion, O where? Mirreus,
> Thinking her unhoused here and fled from us,
> Seeks her at Rome, there, because he doth know
> That she was there a thousand years ago;
> And loves the rags so, as we here obey
> The state-cloth where the prince sate yesterday.
> Crants to such brave loves will not be enthrall'd,
> But loves her only who at Geneva's call'd
> Religion, plain, simple, sullen, young,
> Contemptuous yet unhandsome; as among
> Lecherous humours, there is one that judges
> No wenches wholesome, but coarse country drudges.
> Graius stays still at home here, and because
> Some preachers, vile ambitious bawds, and laws,
> Still new, like fashions, bid him think that she
> Which dwells with us, is only perfect, he
> Embraceth her, whom his godfathers will
> Tender to him, being tender; as wards still
> Take such wives as their guardians offer, or
> Pay values. Careless Phrygius doth abhor
> All, because all cannot be good; as one,
> Knowing some women whores, dares marry none.

But side by side with this, through the use of rhyming tags to round off dramatic scenes, through the conclusions of the

sonnets, and occasional addresses, there is a development of
the end-stopped epigrammatical couplet. Lytton Strachey in
his essay on Pope has drawn attention to a series of couplets
in Othello, ending,

> She was a wight if ever such wight were
> To suckle fools and chronicle small beer.

And there are plenty of other instances. Fairfax's Tasso
and Sandys's Metamorphoses are no sudden new developments.

The evolution of the end-stopped couplet from Spenser
through Drayton to them and Waller and Denham, and on to Dryden and Pope is continuous. It is only the pace of the development that alters.

The choice of a verse form is only half conscious. No form
will express everything, as each form is particularly good at
expressing something. Forms are chosen by poets because the
most important part of what they have to say seems to go better
with that form than any other; there is generally a margin which
remains unsaid, and then, in its turn, the form develops and
shapes the poet's imagination so that he says things which he
did not know he was capable of saying, and at the same time
those parts of his imagination which once had other things to
say, dry up from lack of use.

The couplet was not Dryden's only instrument — the Ode on
St. Cecilia's Day, Annus Mirabilis, the Threnodia Augustalis
succeed in expressing things that the couplet could not have
expressed — but it was Pope's.

Nor is the heroic couplet the only tune of the eighteenth
century. There are the octosyllabics of Swift, the blank verse
of Thomson, the odes of Gray and Collins. There is Prior:

> Now let us look for Louis' feather,
> That used to shine so like a star:
> The generals could not get together,
> Wanting that influence, great in war.

There is Gay, forestalling Byron.

> See generous Burlington with goodly Bruce
> (But Bruce comes wafted in a soft sedan),

> Dan Prior next, beloved by every Muse,
>> And friendly Congreve, unreproachful man!
> (Oxford by Cunningham hath sent excuse;)
>> See hearty Watkins come with cup and can,
> And Lewis who has never friend forsaken,
>> And Laughton whispering asks "Is Troytown taken?"

or Dr. Johnson, forestalling Housman,

> All that prey on vice and folly
>> Joy to see their quarry fly;
> There the gamester light and jolly,
>> There the lender grave and sly.

and a host of popular songs and hymns.

> Come cheer up, my lads, 'tis to glory we steer
> To add something more to this wonderful year.

No, the poetry of the eighteenth century is at least as varied as that of any other, but Pope is labelled as the representative Augustan poet, and as he confined himself to the couplet, the couplet is labelled as the medium of Augustan poetry. As far as Pope personally was concerned, his limitation of form — he even denied himself the variety of an occasional Alexandrine — had its advantages. "Of this uniformity the certain consequence was readiness and dexterity. By perpetual practice, language had in his mind a systematical arrangement, having always the same use for words, he had words so selected and combined as to be ready at his call."

With this limit of form went a limit of interest. Pope was interested in three things, himself and what other people thought of him, his art, and the manners and characters of society. Not even Flaubert or Mallarmé was more devoted to his craft. "What his nature was unfitted to do, circumstance excused him from doing"; and he was never compelled to write to order, or to hurry over his work. He missed nothing. If he thought of something in the midst of the night, he rang for the servant to bring paper; if something struck him during a conversation, he would immediately write it down for future use. He constantly altered and rewrote, and always for the better.

32

ALEXANDER POPE

The introduction of sylphs and gnomes into the Rape of the Lock, and the conclusion of the Dunciad were not first thoughts.

> Let there be Darkness (the dread power shall say),
> All shall be Darkness, as it ne'er were day:
> To their first chaos Wit's vain works shall fall
> And universal Dullness cover all.
> No more the Monarch could such raptures bear;
> He waked, and all the Vision mixed with air.
>
> (1728)

> Lo! the great Anarch's ancient reign restored
> Light dies before her uncreating word . . .
> Thy hand, great Dullness! lets the curtain fall,
> And universal Darkness covers all.
> Enough! enough! the raptured Monarch cries;
> And through the ivory gate the Vision flies.
>
> (1729)

and finally,

> Lo! thy Dread Empire, Chaos! is restored,
> Light dies before thy uncreating word.
> Thy hand, great Anarch! lets the curtain fall,
> And universal darkness buries all.

The beauties and variety of his verse have been so brilliantly displayed by others, notably Miss Sitwell, that I shall confine myself to considering two popular ideas about Pope. That his language is either falsely poetic, or "a classic of our prose," and that his poetry is cold and unemotional. The question of poetic diction was the gravamen of the Romantic's charge. The answer is that Pope and his contemporaries were interested in different fields of experience, in a different "nature." If their description of cows and cottages and birds are vague, it is because their focus of interest is sharp elsewhere, and equal definition over the whole picture would spoil its proportion and obscure its design. They are conventional, not because the poets thought that "the waterpudge, the pilewort, the petty chap, and the pooty" were unpoetic in their naked nature and must be

33

suitably dressed, but because they are intended to be conventional, a backcloth to the more important human stage figures. When Pope writes in his preface to the Odyssey, "There is a real beauty in an easy, pure, perspicuous description even of a low action," he is saying something which he both believes and practises.

> To compass this, his building is a Town,
> His pond an Ocean, his parterre a Down:
> Who but must laugh, the Master when he sees,
> A puny insect, shivering at a breeze!
> Lo! what huge heaps of littleness around!
> The whole, a laboured Quarry above ground;
> Two Cupids squirt before; a Lake behind
> Improves the keenness of the Northern wind.
> His Gardens next your admiration call,
> On every side you look, behold the Wall!
> No pleasing Intricacies intervene,
> No artful wildness to perplex the scene;
> Grove nods at grove, each Alley has a brother,
> And half the platform just reflects the other.
> The suffering eye inverted Nature sees,
> Trees cut to Statues, Statues thick as trees;
> With here a Fountain, never to be played;
> And there a Summer-house, that knows no shade;
> Here Amphitrite sails through myrtle bowers;
> There Gladiators fight, or die in flowers;
> Un-watered see the drooping sea-horse mourn,
> And swallows roost in Nilus' dusty Urn.
>
> Now lap-dogs give themselves the rousing shake,
> And sleepless lovers, just at twelve, awake:
> Thrice rung the bell, the slipper knocked the ground,
> And the pressed watch returned a silver sound.

There is no vagueness here. These are the images of contemporary life. This poetry, not Wordsworth's, is the ancestor of "the patient etherized on the table," of Baudelaire's,

> On entend ça et là les cuisines siffler,
> Les théâtres glapir, les orchestres ronfler;

ALEXANDER POPE

> Les tables d'hôte, dont le jeu fait les délices,
> S'emplissent de catins et d'escrocs, leur complices,
> Et les voleurs, qui n'ont ni trêve ni merci,
> Vont bientôt commencer leur travail, eux aussi,
> Et forcer doucement les portes et les caisses
> Pour vivre quelques jours et vêtir leurs maîtresses.

Those who complain of Pope's use of periphrasis, of his refusal to call a spade a spade, cannot have read him carefully. When he chooses he is as direct as you please.

> So morning insects that in muck begun
> Shine, buzz, and flyblow in the setting sun.

And when he does use a periphrasis, in his best work at least, it is because an effect is to be gained by doing so.

> While China's earth receives the smoking tide.

To say that Pope was afraid to write, as Wordsworth might have written,

> While boiling water on the tea was poured

is nonsense. To the microscopic image of tea-making is added the macroscopic image of a flood, a favourite device of Pope's, and the opposite kind of synthesis to Dante's "A single moment maketh a deeper lethargy for use than twenty and five centuries have wrought on the emprise that erst threw Neptune in amaze at Argo's shadow."

There are places in Pope, as in all poets, where his imagination is forced, where one feels a division between the object and the word, but at his best there are few poets who can rival his fusion of vision and language.

> Chicane in furs, and casuistry in lawn

> Bare the mean heart that lurks beneath a star.

> How hints, like spawn, scarce quick in embryo lie,
> How new-born nonsense first is taught to cry,

Maggots half-formed in rhyme exactly meet,
And learn to crawl upon poetic feet.
Here one poor word an hundred clenches makes,
And ductile Dulness new maeanders takes;
There motley images her fancy strike,
Figures ill paired, and Similes unlike.
She sees a Mob of Metaphors advance,
Pleased with the madness of the mazy dance;
How Tragedy and Comedy embrace;
How Farce and Epic get a jumbled race;
How Time himself stands still at her command,
Realms shift their place, and Ocean turns to land.
Here gay Description Egypt glads with showers,
Or gives to Zembla fruits, to Barca flowers;
Glittering with ice here hoary hills are seen,
There painted valleys of eternal green;
In cold December fragrant chaplets blow,
And heavy harvests nod beneath the snow.

You will call this Fancy and Judgement if you are an Augustan, and the Imagination if you are a Romantic, but there is no doubt about it.

Like Dante, Pope had a passionate and quite undonnish interest in classical literature. The transformation of the heroic epic into The Rape of the Lock and the Dunciad, is not cheap parody; it is the vision of a man who can see in Homer, in eighteenth-century society, in Grub Street, similarities of motive, character and conduct whereby an understanding of all is deepened. Rams and young bullocks are changed to folios and Birthday odes, and

Could all our care elude the gloomy grave,
Which claims no less the fearful than the brave,
For lust of fame I should not vainly dare
In fighting fields, nor urge thy soul to war

becomes

O if to dance all night and dress all day,
Charmed the small pox, or chased old age away;

> Who would not scorn what housewife's cares produce,
> Or who would learn one earthly thing of use?

Literature and life are once more happily married. We laugh
and we love. Unlike Dryden, Pope is not a dramatic poet. He
is at his best only when he is writing directly out of his own
experience. I cannot feel that his Homer is anything but a set
task, honourably executed: the diction gives it away. But show
him the drawing-rooms where he longed to be received as a
real gentleman, let him hear a disparaging remark about himself, and his poetry is beyond praise. The Essay on Man is
smug and jaunty to a degree, until we come to Happiness and
Fame

> All that we feel of it begins and ends
> In the small circle of our foes or friends;
> To all beside as much an empty shade
> An Eugene living, as a Caesar dead.

Pope knew what it was to be flattered and libelled, to be
ambitious, to be snubbed, to have enemies, to be short, and
ugly, and ill and unhappy, and out of his knowledge he made
his poetry, succeeded, as Rilke puts it, in

> transmuting himself into the words.
> Doggedly, as the carver of a cathedral
> Transfers himself to the stone's constancy.

and won his reward as he perceived

> . . . how fate may enter into a verse
> And not come back, how, once in, it turns image
> And nothing but image, nothing but ancestor,
> Who sometimes, when you look at him in his frame
> Seems to be like you and again not like you.

"A GRACE BEYOND THE REACH OF ART"

Samuel Holt Monk

In a famous passage in the <u>Essay on Criticism</u>, Pope admits the inadequacy of rules to produce the highest poetic effects; and consequently he makes room within his critical system for originality and poetic license.

> Some beauties yet no precepts can declare,
> For there's a happiness as well as care.
> Music resembles poetry; in each
> Are nameless graces which no methods teach
> And which a master hand alone can reach. . . .
> Great wits sometimes may gloriously offend,
> And rise to faults true critics dare not mend;
> From vulgar bounds with brave disorder part,
> And snatch a grace beyond the reach of art,
> Which, without passing through the judgment, gains
> The heart, and all its ends at once attains.
>
> (I, 141-145; 152-157)

Plainly these lines are a <u>pastiche</u> of critical commonplaces, for which there are many sources: Quintilian, Horace, Boileau, Rapin, Davenant have obviously contributed to the phrasing as well as to the content; Longinus and Dryden have helped Pope to an understanding of the inadequacy of rules and formulae in the creating of art. Indeed, the general point of view characterized English criticism from its beginning. It has not been generally recognized, however, that when Pope wrote of "nameless graces" and "a grace" he was using the technical language of criticism and aesthetics, not merely inventing a neat phrase; and that he must have been aware of the fact that the term had a well-defined history, some of which he surely knew. It is the purpose of this paper to trace the history of <u>grace</u> as a critical

Reprinted from <u>Journal of the History of Ideas</u>, Vol. 5 (1944), pp. 131-150, by permission of author and publisher.

term before Pope used it in 1711.

A good starting point is Roger de Piles' L'Idée de Peintre Parfait, 1699. I quote from the English translation of 1706. Pictures, says de Piles, will not be entirely perfect "if beauty be not accompany'd with Grace," which supports and perfects genius, but which can never be demonstrated by rules. It is a mysterious quality that a painter derives from nature alone and that he possesses without understanding. "It surprises the Spectator, who feels the effect without penetrating into the true Cause of it; . . . We may define it thus, 'Tis what pleases, and gains the Heart, without concerning itself with the Understanding. Grace and Beauty are two different things, Beauty pleases by the Rules only, and Grace without them. What is beautiful is not always Graceful; but Grace join'd with Beauty is the height of Perfection."[1]

Phraseology and general ideas are so close to Pope's that the two passages belong to the same tradition. It is notable that de Piles and Pope agree (1) that grace is a distinct aesthetic quality; (2) that it is a gift of nature; (3) that it is to be distinguished from those beauties that rules make possible; (4) that its effect is sudden and surprising; (5) that it defies analysis; (6) that it appeals rather to the heart than to the head; (7) that it is especially the mark of genius. Here, evidently, is a well-developed aesthetic and critical concept applicable alike to both literature and painting.

In Pope's day, of course, most critical and aesthetic ideas were felt to be equally applicable to painting and to poetry, thanks to the hold that Horace's phrase ut pictura poesis had on the minds of cultivated men. Dryden's Parallel of Poetry and Painting, 1695, is a familiar example of how men thought about the "sister arts."[2] But it is equally true that poetry and rhetoric went hand in hand. The importance of ancient and renaissance rhetorical theory and practice to both poetry and painting is only now being fully realised by literary scholars. Literary criticism from antiquity was both scanty and fragmentary; and criticism of the fine arts was even more so. The humanists supplied the deficiency by turning to the rhetoricians, whose rules they applied to poetry, the theatre, and even painting. It would be difficult to over-emphasize the influence of Quintilian and Cicero on renaissance and post-renaissance taste. Any neoclassical critical term is likely to have a complicated genealogy and to be the off-spring of literary critics, critics of the fine arts, and rhetoricians. The idea of grace illustrates this fact.

Its obvious origin, so far as Pope's world is concerned is the Elder Pliny's account of Apelles in his Historia Naturalis, a passage that renaissance writers never tired of repeating.

> The grace of his art remained quite unrivalled, although the very greatest painters were living at that time. He would admire their works, praising every beauty and yet observing that they failed in the grace, [venustas] called χάρις in Greek, which was distinctively his own; everything else they had attained, but in this alone none equalled him. He laid claim to another merit; when admiring a work of Protogenes that betrayed immense industry and the most anxious elaboration, he said that, though Protogenes was his equal or even his superior in everything, yet he surpassed the painter in one point — namely in knowing when to take his hand from a picture; . . . showing that too much care may often be hurtful.[3]

It should be observed that Pliny translates venustas by Greek χάρις, and that he associates venustas and χάρις with ease of execution and lack of effort and care. He has removed grace beyond the reach of art.[4]

The term χάρις is somewhat elusive in Greek criticism, but we can discover enough to prove Pliny's use of the word normal.[5] Demetrius of Phalerum, discussing elegance of style, found that elegance includes grace and geniality, and that "the very first grace of style is that which results from compression, when a thought which would have been spoiled by dwelling on it is made graceful by a light and rapid touch."[6] This, of course, suggests Apelles' dissatisfaction with the labored care of Protogenes.

Dionysius of Halicarnassus regarded charm (ἡ ἡδονή) and beauty (τὸ καλόν) as separate though related qualities of literature and the fine arts, and made grace (ἡ χάρις) one of the attributes of charm. Among the qualities that made up charm are "freshness, grace (χάρις), euphony, persuasiveness, and all similar qualities"; and "grandeur, impressiveness, solemnity, dignity, and mellowness" make up beauty.[7] This definition

and separation of beauty and charm curiously suggest the distinction between beauty and sublimity that we find in the critical
thought of the eighteenth century.

Dionysius did not stop with merely isolating grace as a
quality of style. He found a supreme example of this quality in
the style of Lysias, who became for Greek and Roman critics
a stock instance of grace in literature, just as Apelles was an
example of grace in painting. In the tenth and eleventh chapters
of De Lysia, Dionysius discussed grace, the distinguishing
trait of Lysias: it is inexpressible, altogether marvelous, very
difficult to define, and even the most eloquent attain it only with
labor. A formal explication of grace is as difficult as is one of
charm, harmony, and other qualities that are felt rather than
known rationally. Grace is the result of a mixture of art and
nature.[8]

Known and named among the Greeks, grace was an aesthetic quality familiar also to Roman rhetoricians, as Cicero and
Quintilian, the most authoritative writers for future times,
plainly show. Cicero's writings on oratory contain frequent
references to such allied concepts as venustas, lepor, and
suave, all related to the idea of grace or charm. One can piece
together enough from scattered passages in the Orator and the
De Oratore to discover that by these terms Cicero intended to
designate the quality that the Greeks called χάρις.

Among the requirements of an orator, he says, are "grace
and wit," terms that apply alike to mind, speech, and delivery.[9]
This quality Lysias especially had, venustas being a particular
attribute of Attic eloquence, which was distinguished for its
"studied negligence of Attic simplicity," as some women are
more beautiful because they neglect all ornament.[10] Finally,
grace and aptness in speaking render eloquence "productive of
the utmost delight," making it "penetrate effectually into the
inmost hearts of the audience." Nor can this grace be acquired
through the rules of the rhetoricians.[11]

Quintilian was equally aware of venustas and gratia. "The
meaning of venustas," he says, "is obvious; it means that which
is said with grace and charm."[12] Too much attention to niceties
of style will make the orator self-conscious and will therefore
prevent his attaining grace.[13] For Quintilian grace is found in
the simple and unaffected tone of Lysias, the writings of Horace,
the diction of Terence, and the paintings of Apelles — all of

course critical commonplaces.[14] Most important of all, perhaps, is Quintilian's admission that rules can be broken, because they are not laws, but the children of expediency. Too great a dependence on rules in a picture, as in a statue, begets stiffness and lack of grace. "A similar impression of grace and charm is produced by rhetorical figures, whether they be figures of thought or figures of speech, for they involve a certain departure from the straight line and have the merit of variation from the ordinary usage. . . ."[15]

It can readily be seen from the foregoing that the ancients recognized in χάρις , venustas, gratia, a quality that distinguishes a certain style in oratory, literature, and the plastic arts. Though no one discussed it as thoroughly as Longinus discussed elevation, grace acquired in classical antiquity, if not a very precise meaning, at least a group of definite connotations and associated ideas. It was recognized as being an indefinable perfection that accompanies simplicity, naturalness, ease; it was felt to be rather the product of nature and genius than of art and the rules; and its effect was attained by appealing not to the reason, but to the emotions, the heart. Though no ancient critic would or could have written Pope's lines, it is none the less true that everything that Pope said had been said or implied by the ancients. We shall see now how renaissance critics modified and transmitted these ideas to Pope's generation.

In 1613 Cesare Ripa published at Siena his Iconologia, one of the many emblem books whose importance in the study of renaissance thought and art is becoming clear to us through the work of such scholars as Mario Praz and Erwin Panofsky. These emblem books gave visible and allegorical treatment to abstract ideas, and are extremely useful in such a study as the present one. Among Ripa's emblems is one for Gratia. He describes it thus:

> A smiling and beautiful young girl, dressed in a lovely costume, and crowned with jasper and precious stones. In her hand she holds thornless roses of many colors, which she is about to toss playfully. She has a necklace of pearls around her neck.
>
> The jasper is worn to signify grace, in accordance with the opinion of natural philosophers, who say that he who wears jasper gains the favor of men.

The thornless roses signify the same thing, as do
the pearls which shine and please as a rare and secret
gift of nature, like grace, which is a certain special
charm in men that moves and ravishes the mind to
love, and by stealth engenders liking and benevolence.16

Ripa was expressing in an image much of what renaissance
writers had been saying for a century. They had taken over
grace from classical antiquity and extended the idea to personal charm; at the same time they added a typically renaissance
touch in the word ravish, which has neo-platonic overtones,
since the principal effect of the Divine Beauty, according to
neo-platonic aesthetics, is to commit a pleasing rape on the
soul. When grace can be said to ravish, it has been removed
far beyond right reason and the rules.

Little interest in grace is found among literary critics of
the renaissance, chiefly because the main current of critical
thought flowed in Aristotelian channels, where the important
ideas were rules, imitation, and the kinds. The inadequacy of
rules without genius, of art without nature, was a truism with
even the most thorough-going Aristotelians, but their emphasis
remained on the rules. Such anti-formalists as Patrici (Patrizi)
and Bruno, both influenced by neo-platonism, protested against
rules and insisted on the recognition of poetic madness.17

Neo-platonism not only supported original genius against
Aristotelianism; it also, through Ficino and his immediate followers, profoundly influenced the concept of beauty. The neo-
platonist especially associated beauty with grace, ignoring the
attempt of the ancients to separate them.18 To the neo-platonist
beauty is a divine attribute, eternal, immutable, and independent of earthly forms. Shining from the countenance of God, it
is reflected in three "mirrors": in angels, where it becomes
patterns, ideas; from angels it is reflected in the souls of men,
becoming knowledge; from mind it is reflected in matter, becoming images and forms. But beauty can descend into bodies
only if they are prepared to receive it, through having the various parts harmoniously and fittingly disposed.19 For Ficino
beauty is "the splendor of God's countenance (la Belleza è lo
Splendore del Volto di Dio), and the grace of his countenance
(Et noi chiamiamo Belleza quella grazia del volto divino. . .19a),
and "a certain vital and spiritual grace," infused by the divine

ray into angels, souls, and bodies. This grace, "by means of reason and sight, and hearing, moves and delights our minds, and in delighting it ravishes, and in ravishing it inflames with ardent love."[20]

It would be false to assume that this neo-platonic mysticism survived intact in the colder atmosphere of the Enlightenment, but it is, I believe, a vaguely felt presence, re-emphasizing the relationship between grace and the loftiest aesthetic experience, which, by its very nature, was felt to lie beyond the reach of merely rational rules. So cartesian a mind as that of Nicholas Poussin could echo the very language of Ficino, when he wrote of the idea of Beauty, that incorporeal Idea, that descends into material forms when they are properly prepared to receive it.[21]

A characteristically renaissance appendage to the neo-platonic conception of grace can be found in Firenzuola's Della Bellezza delle Donne, 1541. A typical instance of renaissance feminist literature, it is oddly compounded of medieval chivalry, Platonism, and neo-platonism. For Firenzuola, grace is a part of beauty, a "splendor . . . born of a secret proportion and a measure which is not in our books, which we do not know, nor even imagine, and it is, as one says of things that we do not know how to express, un non so che." This non so che is, of course, the je-ne-sais-quoi of the next century in France and England.[22]

An interesting and influential treatment of the idea of grace is found in the first book of Castiglione's Il Cortegiano, 1528, much of which is devoted to a discussion of that supreme ease of manner and pleasing demeanor which Castiglione called grace and which is descended not only from Cicero's decorum (De Officiis, I, 35) but from Greek χάρις and Latin venustas as well.

It is almost a proverb, says Castiglione, that grace cannot be taught, for it is the gift of nature and of heaven, but diligence can improve it.[23] The great enemy of grace is affectation; it arises from negligence or careless ease (sprezzatura), which conceals art and gives the impression that things are done without effort and almost without forethought. One should use art, as did the ancient orators, to conceal art, avoiding the forced, which always lacks grace.[24] The story of Apelles' criticism of Protogenes is recounted to support the idea that, in manners as in painting, sprezzatura is the source of grace. As a single line not labored, a single stroke of the brush taken easily without being guided by study or art often attests the excellence of the painter, so the excellence of the courtier is apparent if, in everything that he does and says, he avoids affectation.[25]

 Likewise women fail of grace when they take too great pains to be beautiful, since in personal beauty, as in manners and the arts, sprezzatura is essential.[26] We are reminded of Ben Jonson's song on this theme:

> Give me a look, give me a face
> That makes simplicity a grace;
> Robes loosely flowing, hayre as free:
> Such sweet neglect more taketh me
> Than all th' adulteries of art;
> They strike mine eyes, but not my heart.

Il Cortegiano took these ideas into every part of Europe; by the end of the sixteenth century the word grace with its associated ideas was common to all cultures, and there can be no doubt that Castiglione had a part in its dissemination.[27]

 Against this background of neo-platonic aesthetics and courtesy books, the theory of grace was being applied once more to painting. Thanks to Pliny and to the authority of the ancients, writers on painting during the Italian renaissance used the word grace frequently, although only a few attempted to give it a full or very precise meaning. Of these we shall consider three from the latter part of the sixteenth century: Dolce, Vasari, and Lomazzo.

 Dolce's notorious attack on Michelangelo in his dialogue on painting, L'Aretino, 1557, developed the idea (to become a commonplace in the seventeenth and eighteenth centuries) that Raphael like Apelles was the master of ease and grace, a quality that Dolce identified with the non so che and with χάρις. Dolce declared Michelangelo's design and terribilità to be qualities inferior to Raphael's grace and softness (la maniera leggiadra e gentile di Raffaello) since "facility is the principal evidence of excellence in any art, and the most difficult to attain."[28] Thus painters who draw their figures with excessive care and exactness fall into affectation and do not achieve sprezzatura. Inevitably Dolce cited Apelles' disapproval of Protogenes'

studied care, a disapproval that he extended to writers whose
works reveal an over-labored diligence.[29] In contrast to Michelangelo Raphael, like Apelles, had grace, which Aretino in
the dialogue identifies with the non so che and Fabrini with
Greek χάρις.[30]

These ideas, already familiar to us, were given a more
thorough analysis by Vasari, who applied to painting the whole
theory of grace as it had been developed by Castiglione and the
neo-platonist writers on feminine beauty. Le Vite de' più ec-
cellenti Architetti, Pittori, et Scultori Italiani, first published
in 1550 and much expanded in the second edition of 1568, contains scattered references to grace which Mr. Anthony Blunt has
recently gathered together and discussed.[31]

As the renaissance disintegrated and as painting passed
into the Manneristic phase, both painters and theorists abandoned the rational, almost scientific attitude toward painting
and the technique of the painter that had characterized the fifteenth century. Alberti, for example, whose Della Pittura
dates from 1436, knew and used the term grace, but could conceive no other way of attaining it except by the most diligent
study and the careful imitation of nature -- in short through the
use of intellect and the following of rules.[32] Vasari made his
final aesthetic appeal to what he termed the judgment, which
Mr. Blunt interprets correctly as "an instinct, an irrational
gift, allied to what we call taste, and residing not so much in
the mind as in the eye," a faculty more capable of attaining
grace than is mathematical measurement of the sort that Alberti had recommended.[33] Aware that correctness cannot produce grace, Vasari made a clear distinction between beauty,
"a rational quality dependent on the rules," and grace, "an indefinable quality dependent on judgment and therefore on the
eye." He also related grace to facility, a quality much admired
by the Mannerists. He therefore condemned the painters of the
fifteenth century as "dry," because they labored their works
too diligently in order to attain exactness. And of course he
found the source of grace in nature and held that grace and
facility cannot be taught.[34]

Vasari's opinions were influential during the next century,
but another Mannerist painter and theorist, Giovanni Paolo
Lomazzo, was also an important source for seventeenth- and
eighteenth-century writers on painting. His two books, Trattato

dell' Arte della Pittura, Scultura et Architettura, (1585) and
Idea del Tempio della Pittura (1590) were quoted, paraphrased,
and pilfered throughout the seventeenth century.[35]

The word grace came readily to Lomazzo, just as it did to
Vasari; and it had much the same meaning for both writers.
All facility and grace, Lomazzo maintains, are born of genius,
and the best painters have a natural bent which they must follow.
Not to do so is to miss grace, no matter what efforts the painter
may make or how learned he may be.[36] For Lomazzo grace is
a quality of beauty, as he states in a passage taken almost ver-
batim from Ficino.[37] Although he added nothing to renaissance
thought on the subject, he certainly served to transmit that
thought to the French academicians, and through them to eighteenth-century Europe. For Lomazzo, as for many writers of
the next two centuries, Raphael was the example of grace and
charm in painting, having been especially gifted in expressing
comeliness, charm, loveliness.[38] And he continued Vasari's
comparison of Raphael and Apelles, which was to become trite
during the next century, but which helped to keep alive Pliny's
story, with all of its meaning for the idea of grace.[39]

The most interesting discussion of grace in the early seventeenth century is found in Franciscus Junius' De Pictura Vete-
rum, published at Oxford in 1637. It was translated into English
by its author in the following year. A typical example of late
humanistic scholarship, the book is learned, eclectic, pedantic,
exhaustive. Almost all that could be known in 1637 about Greek
and Roman painters and aesthetic theory is found in it. What
Junius lacked in subtlety and insight he made up in thoroughness.

After discussing the traditional five parts of painting (Invention, Proportion, Color, Motion, and Disposition), Junius
turns in Book III, Chapter 6, to the subject of grace. A painting
perfect in the five parts may yet "want that comely graceful-
nesse, which is the life and soule of Art," if the parts do not
combine into a harmonious whole. As in the human body, so in
a painting, beauty does not charm "unlesse there bee . . . that
same ayre and comely Grace, which is made up by the concord
and agreement of severall accomplished parts. . . ." And he
continues:

> This is questionless that grace, which readily and
> freely proceeding out of the Artificer's spirit, cannot

> be taught by any rules of art: no more can assiduity
> of importunate studies helpe us to it. Too much care
> therefore is rather like to spoyle the comely sweet-
> nesse of this Grace, than to advance it; and where-
> soever we do but begin to streighten the freenesse of
> it by an unseasonable and over curious niceness of
> studying, the decent comeliness of the work is in-
> stantly gone and lost.

Grace, therefore, is "the worke of a wisely dissembled arte."[40]
    With Quintilian and Longinus Junius maintains that grace,
the perfection of beauty, and elevation are the products not of
mere natural genius, but of nature and art. But he immediately
quotes Apelles' judgment on Protogenes as a warning against
excessive care and polishing, and recommends on the authority
of Plutarch and Cicero, ease and facility as making grace more
graceful. He quotes Cicero's De Oratore to support the contention, reminiscent of Castiglione, that "there is a certaine kind
of negligent diligence"; and he mentions the charm of unadorned
feminine beauty as an example of avoiding over-curious affectation. In short he repeats virtually all that had been said about
grace by writers of both classical antiquity and the Italian renaissance.[41]
    For Junius the effect of grace on spectators is amazement:
it "carries them into an astonished extasie, their sense of
seeing bereaving them of all other senses"; and it also "doth
sweetly enthrall and captivate the hearts of men with the lovely
chain of due admiration and amazement." He cites both Cicero
and Quintilian as authorities for the fact that no precept can
teach it.[42] Finally grace is the height of art, the product of
"the unaffected facility of an excellent art and forward nature,
equally concurring to the worke; . . . this inimitable grace,
equally diffused and dispersed through the whole worke, as it
is not had so easily cannot be discerned so easily."[43]
    The raw material of Pope's lines is evident in Junius.
There is no doubt about the importance of Junius to neo-classical criticism of painting. Both Fréart de Chambray and Roger
de Piles acknowledged him as a source; and as late as George
Turnbull's Treatise on Ancient Painting and Lessing's Laokoon
he was still a recognized authority.[44] His ideas are too conventional to be easily identified in the plethora of platitudes that

make up academic writing on painting, but his importance as a
transmitter of renaissance ideas to the early eighteenth century
is indisputable.[45]

Fréart's Idée de la Perfection de la Peinture, 1662, leans
heavily on Junius, as well as on Dolce and the other detractors
of Michelangelo. It exalts Raphael as an example of the "just
and regular" in contrast to the capriciousness, violence, and
unnatural quality of such a work as the Last Judgment. Raphael
is the Apelles of modern painters.[46] But Fréart did not develop
the idea of Grace, although in another work he defined it, not
very interestingly, as "a certain free Disposition in the whole
Draught, answerable to that unaffected Frankness of Fashion
in a Living Body, Man or Woman, which doth animate Beauty
where it is, and supply it where it is not."[47]

It is rather surprising that the French Academicians had
so little to say on grace. The Conférences are devoid of interest
in the subject, and it remained for de Piles, as we have seen,
to give the perfect definition in 1699. But meanwhile literary
critics were taking up the term and applying it to the problem
of rules and beauty.

Bouhours' Les Entretiens d'Ariste et d'Eugène, 1671, contains a dialogue devoted wholly to the je ne scay quoy in which
ideas traditionally associated with grace are used to describe
the French version of the Italian non so che. It is said to be
more easily felt than known, its nature being incomprehensible
and inexplicable; the heart instinctively perceives it; without it
all attractive qualities are lifeless; it is, in short, charm or
grace.

> . . . it is something so delicate and imperceptible
> that it escapes the most penetrating and subtle intel-
> ligence. The intellect does not know what it is that
> charms when the heart is touched by a sensible object.

It is all a matter of feeling, not of reason.[48] This quality is
found in art as well as in nature. It is that inexplicable quality
which charms us in paintings and statues, though the artist
takes pains to conceal the art that he uses to please us. In literary works it consists in that urbanity that Cicero could not
define. Bouhours distinguishes grace from beauty (the calculated effect of regularity) as follows:

> There are great beauties in Balzac's books; they
> are regular beauties that please a great deal; but it
> must be said that the works of Voiture which have
> those secret charms, those fine hidden graces of
> which we speak, please infinitely more.[49]

The discussion ends with the interesting suggestion that
there is a relationship between grace in art and nature and
grace in theology, itself an inexplicable mystery about which
it is best to be silent, but which triumphs over the heart and
which may be described as the je ne scay quoy of the supernatural and the divine.[50]

In this dialogue Bouhours was merely restating in terms
of French thought and society in the grand siècle the ideas that
had clustered round the word grace since classical antiquity.
His reference to the non so che of the Italians indicates the
source of most of his thoughts.[51] His contemporary René Rapin,
one of the French critics most revered by the Augustans, gave
the concept grace its final expression in the seventeenth century.

In discussing the qualities that make an oration pleasing,
Rapin says that besides propriety

> . . . there is yet a secret grace in saying things which
> is no less inexplicable [than decorum], though it is also
> necessary if eloquence is to persuade, for one persuades
> almost only as one pleases. That gift comes of a happy
> nature that knows how to give to things a turn that ren-
> ders them agreeable. A discourse may have proportion,
> precision, ornaments, beauties, without being agree-
> able, because the material is not turned with that cer-
> tain air which pleases and charms. For there is a dif-
> ference between grace and beauty.

But what this charm is Cicero himself could not tell. "There
are precepts for speaking well; but there is none at all for
teaching that easy turn of which I speak." This is the effect of
genius as opposed to art in eloquence.[52] Rapin acknowledges
that Dionysius of Halicarnassus is the source for his distinction
between beauty and grace, an interesting example of how ancient rhetoric helped to shape neo-classical theory. Beauty is
found in grandeur, nobility, majesty, weightiness; grace in

harmony, elegance, clarity, sweetness, brilliance, and propriety Grace comes from genius and nature; beauty often from
art alone: one is the gift of heaven, the other a reward of labor.[53]

    Having based eloquence on genius, a natural gift for lan-
guage, "without which one cannot succeed, and with which one
always succeeds," he goes on:

> Eloquence which touches only the mind and does not
> reach the heart is not true eloquence. . . . Thus all
> those beauties that go to the mind without touching the
> heart are not true beauties. . . .[54]

These scattered passages give more or less casual expression
to the ideas that Rapin phrased perfectly in the well known words:

> There are yet in poetry, as in the other arts, certain
> ineffable qualities which cannot be explained: those
> things are like mysteries. There is no precept at all
> to teach those secret graces, those imperceptible
> charms, and all those hidden and agreeable qualities
> of poetry which move the heart, as there is no method
> for teaching someone to please. It is entirely an effect
> of nature.[55]

    Elwin and Courthope cited this passage as the immediate
source for Pope's "Some graces yet no precepts can declare."
And indeed Pope's phraseology suggests Rapin, just as certain
phrases in his passage on the grace beyond the reach of art
suggest the words of de Piles, quoted early in this paper. There
is every likelihood that Pope knew de Piles; there is no doubt
that he knew Rapin. Whether he took from them the particular
turns of expression that he used is unimportant; the point is that
he could scarcely have escaped including grace in his critical
theory and interpreting it as he did. The word was well established in English criticism, as we shall now briefly demonstrate.
    Until Pope wrote out the full implications of the word grace
in 1711, English critics had been content to use the term without
analysing its content. From the sixteenth century on it is common
in English critical essays, where it seems to have the rather vague
meanings of "charm" or appeal." There is no single use of the
word in Elizabethan criticism that merits quotation.[56]

During the seventeenth century, grace assumed some of the meanings that we have found in Italian and French criticism. Jonson, of course, knew the word and gave it some content. Affectation, he says, destroys the grace of metaphors; it will confer grace on letters if on occasion letter-writers "use (as ladies doe in their attyre) a diligent kind of negligence."

Davenant's Preface to Gondibert, 1650, illustrates the manner in which the arts could be confused in the seventeenth century; for after using the terms of the drama to explain the method and structure of the epic Gondibert, he employs terms from the criticism of painting when he states that "all the shadowings, happy strokes, sweet graces, and even the drapery" have been observed. And there is something of the idea of grace in Davenant's famous definition of wit:

> And Wit is the laborious and the lucky resultances of
> thought, having towards its excellence, as we say of
> the strokes of Painting, as well a happiness as care . . .

Hobbes, too, knew grace as ultimate charm, the power of pleasing.

The long survival of Apelles' χάρις and Castiglione's sprezzatura is apparent in Sprat's praise of Cowley: "He perfectly practices the hardest secret of good Writing, to know when he has done enough." Of Cowley's style Sprat wrote (illustrating aesthetic by social grace):

> And the same judgment should be made of men's styles
> as of their behaviours and carriage: wherein that is
> most courtly and hardest to be imitated, which consists
> of a Natural easiness and unaffected Grace, where
> nothing seems to be studied, yet everything is extra-
> ordinary.

Similarly Wolseley praised Rochester because "the loosest Negligence of a great Genius is infinitely preferable to that obscura diligentia of which Terence speaks," and because his style is "natural and easy" and thus lacks "too nice a Correctness," which makes a piece stiff and dead. He continues:

"A GRACE BEYOND THE REACH OF ART"

> To conclude this Point, his Poetry has everywhere
> a Tincture of that unaccountable Charm in his Fashion
> and Conversation, that peculiar Becomingness in all
> he said and did, that drew the Eyes and won the Hearts
> of all who came near him.

Temple contrasts Homer's "Spirit, Force and Life" with
Virgil's grace. He regards rules as inimical to grace:

> The truth is, there is something in the Genius of
> Poetry, too Libertine to be confined to so many
> Rules; and whoever goes about to subject it to such
> Constraints loses both its spirit and Grace, which are
> ever Native and never learnt. . . .

Finally John Hughes, in 1699, identified grace with the
curiosa felicitas of Horace, which is due to natural and happy
strokes, rather than to pains and study.[57]

This paper has tried to show that when Pope admitted the
limitations of the rules and provided in his critical system for
the free play of originality and license, he was not, as is often
said, showing the bold and liberal taste of the Englishman; nor
was he showing the liberalising influence of Longinus on English
criticism. He was expressing traditional critical ideas in traditional language: whence his use of the word grace and his interpretation of its meaning.

From the beginning, critical theory had taken into account
both the beauty that derives from regularity and the beauty that
derives from irregularity. No system ever excluded the one in
favor of the other. Art is a world that revolves on the two poles
of reason and imagination; regularity and irregularity; restraint
and spontaneity; conformity and originality. It is this fact that
gives any meaning at all to our use of the terms classic and
romantic. All theories of art and all practice of art acknowledge
at least tacitly the validity of both methods, although from age
to age emphasis may shift toward one or the other pole. Categories must be found to contain these two opposing sets of values: the opposition of beauty and grace long served critics as a
convenient device for discussing these values. Up to Pope's time
those elements in a work of art which were not due to correctness were usually categorized under grace.

In the eighteenth century, however, the sublime supplanted grace as a repository for the irregular and irrational elements in art. And as the romantic period drew nearer, the concept of sublimity became increasingly important.[58] The new antithesis, beauty and sublimity, supplanted the old renaissance dichotomy of beauty and grace; and Longinian ideas began to obscure the fact that from its inception neo-classical aesthetics had provided an important place for original genius under the category of grace. Pope, of course, was aware of the Longinian sublime as well as of grace, as was his contemporary, the painter, Jonathan Richardson.[59] But as the century wore on, grace took on an increasingly specialised meaning and dropped out of general use in the sense in which Pope had employed it. Its later association with the idea of beauty in motion has been discussed by W. G. Howard in his article "Reiz ist Schönheit in Bewegung."[60] That aspect of the subject is of no concern to this article, which must end where it began -- with Pope's grace beyond the reach of art: lines that perfectly illustrate another phrase of Pope's, "What oft was thought but ne'er so well expressed."

NOTES

1 Roger de Piles, The Art of Painting, etc., London (1706), 8. It is not necessary to this paper to maintain that Pope's immediate source for the lines on grace was this passage, but the verbal resemblances are remarkably close. It seems likely that Pope would have known de Piles' book in view his interest in painting. He studied painting with Jervas during the years just preceding the publication of the Essay on Criticism and addressed to that painter the beautiful epistle, prefixed to the second edition of Dryden's translation of Du Fresnoy's De Arte Graphica. It is notable that Dryden had translated not the original Latin, but de Piles' French version of Du Fresnoy's poem, and that both the first and the second editions of The Art of Painting contained de Piles' commentary on Du Fresnoy. Jervas corrected Dryden's translation for the second edition, in which Pope's Epistle to Mr. Jervas was printed. (C. A. Du Fresnoy, The Art of Painting, etc. Second Edition, Corrected and Enlarg'd, London [1716], 6-8).

2 This complex and difficult subject has at last been thorough-
   ly studied in Professor Rensselaer W. Lee's essay "Ut
   Pictura Poesis: The Humanistic Theory of Painting," Art
   Bulletin XXII (1940), 197-269. I am greatly indebted to
   Professor Lee in the present study for bibliographical hints
   and helpful advice.

3 XXXV, 36, 79, cf. The Elder Pliny's Chapters on the History of Art, (tr. by K. Jex-Blake, London, 1896), 121. Cf.
   a similar and equally famous story of Apelles told by Plutarch in his "Demetrius," Lives, (ed. and tr. B. Perrin,
   London and New York), IX, 53.

4 When Quintilian referred to Pliny's account of Apelles, he
   used the word gratia for Pliny's venustas: ". . . ingenio
   et gratia, quam in se ipse maxime iactat, Apelles est
   praestantissimus." (Institutio, XII, 10, 6.) Thus the word-
   cluster χάρις, venus, venustas, gratia was established in
   ancient criticism. Other less important words attached
   themselves to this group also, but the shades of meaning
   that they express are of no importance to this study. It is
   interesting, in view of Quintilian's words just quoted, to
   notice that when Carlo Dati paraphrased Pliny's account of
   Apelles in his Vite de' Pittori Antichi, 1667, he spoke of
   "quella vaghezza e venustà, la quale i Greci e noi Toscani
   chiamiamo Grazia." (Vite, Milano [1806], 155.) Similarly
   in his letter prefixed to Vasari's Lives Giovanni Battista
   Adriani, remarking on Apelles' grace, paraphrased Pliny:
   ". . . nondimeno a tutti diceva Apelle mancare quella leggiadria, la quale da' Greci e da noi è chiamata grazia . .
   . ." (Vasari, Vite, etc., Milano [1807], 11, 29, 30.) From
   Italian grazia to French grâce and English grace the path
   is obvious.

5 The article on χάρις in Lidell and Scott's A Greek-English
   Lexicon (New Edition, Revised and Augmented, Oxford,
   1940) gives an idea of the scope and varied meaning of the
   word and provides sufficient evidence of its frequent use
   in relation to literature and the fine arts.

6 Demetrius, On Style (ed. W. Rhys Roberts, Cambridge,
   1902), paragraphs 128, 132, 137.

7 Dionysius of Halicarnassus, On Literary Composition (ed. W. Rhys Roberts, London, 1910), 119-121.

8 Denys d'Halicarnasse, Jugement sur Lysias (ed. and tr. by A. M. Desrousseaux and Max Egger, Paris, 1890), 21-23.

9 De Oratore (ed. A. S. Wilkins, Oxford, 1892), I, 5, 17; pp. 90-91.

10 Orator (ed. H. M. Hubbell, Cambridge, 1939), IX, 29; p. 324; XXIII, 78, 79; p. 362.

11 Orator, XXV, 84, p. 366; XXVI, 87, p. 368; and De Oratore, I, 31, p. 148; I, 32, p. 155.

12 Institutio, VI, 111, 18. (My references here and in the following notes are to the edition of H. E. Butler, London, 1920.)

13 Ibid., VIII, Proem, 23.

14 Ibid., IX, iv, 17; X, 1, 96; X, 1, 100; XII, x, 6.

15 Ibid., II, xiii, 6-17. Quintilian's suggestion that grace is found in the curved line is interesting in view of the re-emergence of this idea in eighteenth-century aesthetics. This aspect of the subject has been sketched by W. G. Howard's "Reiz is Schönheit in Bewegung," PMLA, NS., XVII (1909), 286-293.

16 P. 302.

17 Francesco Patrici, Della Poetica, Deca Disputata, Ferrara (1586), pp. 1-30. I refer to the chapter entitled "Del Furore Poetico." Tracing the idea of poetry as divine madness back to Plato and Aristotle, Patrici maintained the irrelevance of rules to the poet, who does not know what he is saying. "And if the greatest poets could compose in such great numbers without any rule of art, it seems possible to argue that art is either entirely vain or of so little help to poetry that the poet can compose his works without it. Hence comes perhaps the saying of Aristides the Rhetorician, "Everything great is without art" (p. 25). The passage from Bruno is almost too familiar for quotation: "You conclude rightly that poetry is not born of the rules, unless

slightly or accidentally so; but the rules are derived from the poetry; and there are as many kinds and sorts of true rules as there are kinds and sorts of true poets." De Gli Eroici Furori (ed. Francesco Flora, Torino, 1928), p. 34.

18   Instances of the close association of the two words can be found in Spenser's poems, where the word grace occurs frequently, especially when he thinks platonically, as in the description of Una's unveiled countenance (F.Q., I, iii, 4) and the Fowre Hymnes. See also Ded. Son., XV, 12, and XVI, 7; F.Q., I, vi, 18, 5; III, vi, 52, 2; III, vii, 23, 5; IV, x, 44, 1; VI, viii, 2, 2; Am., xxi, 2; Epith., 170; H.B., 17, 57, 167; H. H. B., 208.

19   Marsiglio Ficino, Sopra lo Amore, etc. Firenze (1544), Ch. VI. See also Nesca Robb, Neoplatonism of the Italian Renaissance, London (1935), Ch. III.

19a Ibid., Oration, V, Ch. IV.

20   Ibid., Ch. VI. The original is: Belleza [è] una certa grazia vivace e spiritale, laquale per il raggio divino prima si infonde negli Angeli, poi nelle anime degli uomini, dopo questo nelle figure e voci corporali; e questa grazia per mezo della ragione e del vedere e dello udire muove e diletta lo animo nostro, e nel dilettare rapisce, e nel rapire d'ardente amore infiamma." Cf. Pietro Bembo, Gli Asolani, 1505 (ed. Carlo Dionisotti-Casalone, Torino, 1932), p. 129; Giovanni Della Casa, "Il Galateo," 1561, in Rime et prose, Fiorenza (1572), pp. 49 ff.; Ripa, op. cit., "Bellezza," pp. 67-69. In all these works grace and beauty are regarded as intimately related.

21   The passage is interesting since it suggests Platonic influence on the neo-classical doctrine of belle nature or beau idéal. See Giovanni Pietro Bellori, Le Vite de' Pittori, Scultori, ed Architetti (Edizione Seconda, Roma, 1728), pp. 301, 302. Poussin probably derived his terminology not directly from Ficino but from Lomazzo, for whom see below. For the presence of Platonism in neo-classical critical thought see Louis Bredvold, "The Tendency toward Platonism in Neo-Classical Esthetics," E. L. H., I (1934), 91-119.

22 Agnolo Firenzuola, Opere, Milano (1802), I, 52-54. See
    further his description of the highly irrational effect of
    beauty, "this celestial grace," on the beholder. Ibid., I,
    16. ". . . questo splendore nasca da una occulta propor-
    zione, e da una misura, che non è ne' nostri libri, la quale
    noi non conosciamo, anzi non pure immaginiamo, ed è
    come si dice delle cose che noi non sappiamo esprimere,
    un non so che." Ibid., 54.

23 Baldassar Castiglione, Il Cortegiano (ed. Vittorio Cian,
    Firenze, 1910), 59, 60.

24 Ibid., 63, 64.

25 Ibid., 67-69.

26 Ibid., 99-101.

27 Kenneth Orne Myrick's Sir Philip Sydney as a Literary
    Craftsman, Cambridge (Mass.), 1935, is largely concerned
    with the importance of sprezzatura in Sidney's art. See par-
    ticularly pp. 25, 26; 298-315.

28 Lodovico Dolce, L'Aretino: Dialogo della Pitture, Lancia-
    no (1913), 7.

29 Ibid., 63, 64. In questo mi pare, che ci si voglia una certa
    convenevole sp[r]ezzatura, in modo che non ci sia nè trop-
    pa vaghezza di colorito, nè troppa politezza di figure; ma
    si vegga nel tutto una amabile sodezza. Perciocchè sono
    alcuni pittori, che fanno le lor figure sì fattamente pulite,
    che paiono sbellettate, con acconciature di capelli ordinati
    con tanto studio che pur uno non esce dell' ordine. Il che
    è vizio e non virtù; perchè si cade nell' affettazione, che
    priva di grazia qualunque cosa. . . . Bisogna sopratutto
    fuggire la troppa diligenza che in tutte le cose nuoce. . . .
    Oh quanto la soverchia diligenza è anco dannosa negli scrit-
    tori! Perciocchè ove si conosce fatica, ivi necessariamente
    è durezza ed affettazione, la quale è sempre abborrita da
    chi legge.

30 Ibid., 80. ". . . e questa è, la venustà, che è quel non so
    che, che tanto suole aggradire, così ne' pittori, come ne'
    poeti, in guisa che empie l'animo altrui d'infinito diletto,
    non sapendo da qual parte esca quello che a noi tanto

piace. . . . Questa, che voi dite venustâ, è detta dai Greci
charis che io esporrei sempre per grazia."

31 Anthony Blunt, Artistic Theory in Italy 1450-1600 (Oxford,
1940), 86-98. I have borrowed from this book for my discussion of Vasari, but I cannot agree with the author when
he credits Vasari with originating a new aesthetic quality
in his treatment of grace.

32 Leon Battista Alberti, Della Architettura, della Pittura,
e della Statua, Londra (1726), v. III, fol. 15ᵛ (Della Pittura,
Bk. II). Dal componimento delle superficie ne nasce quella
leggiadria e quella grazia che costoro chiamano bellezza.
Conciosinachè quel Viso che avrà alcune superficie grandi,
e alcune piccole, che in un luogo escano troppo in fuori e
nell' altro si nascondano troppo addentro, come si vede ne'
visi delle Vecchie; sarà questo a vedersi certamente cosa
brutta: mà in quella Faccia, nella quale le superficie saranno di maniera congiunte insieme, che i dolci lumi si con-
vertano a poco a poco in ombre soavi, e non vi saranno
alcune asprezze di angoli; questa chiameremo a ragione
Faccia bella e venusta. Adungue in questo componimento
delle superficie bisogna andar investigando grandemente
le grazie e la bellezza. Ma in che modo noi possiamo ot-
tener questo, io non ò trovata via più certa, che andare a
considerar la natura stessa: e però guardiamo diligentis-
simamente, e per lunghissimo tempo, in che modo la
natura maravigliosa artefice delle cose abbia composte le
superficie nelle bellissime membra: nello imitar la quale
bisogna esercitarsi con tutti i pensieri e diligenze nos-
tre. . . .

33 Blunt, op. cit. , 90, 91.

34 Ibid. , 96, 97.

35 The Trattato was published in an English version as A
Tracte Containing the Artes of Curious Paintinge, etc.
(tr. R. H[aydocke]), London, 1598.

36 Idea del Tempio della Pittura (Milan, 1590), 9. Perciocchè
essi stentano più mentre che riuolti tutti ad imitar altri,
niente intendendo il genio proprio, onde nasce tutta la

facilità & la gratia del operare, non sanno mai leuar la
mano dalla tauola, nè mai trouano il fine di polire le opere,
che all'vltimo gli riescono senza alcuna forza come essi
ben il prouano, & se n'auegono.
Cf. Lomazzo's definition of grace: La quale non s'acquisita
ferò con forza di studio, & d'arte solamenta, ma si ha
principalmente per dono di natura. Ibid., 46.

37 Ibid., 83-85.

38 Ibid., p. 55. See also p. 43 and p. 146. Ha hauuto particolar
talento, & gratia d'esprimere nelle faccie la venustà, la
gentilezza, la leggiadria, & i garbi douuti ne i giovanni, e
d'esprimere in loro le vere Idee, . . .

39 Ibid., p. 146. Similar ideas were touched on by Giovanni
Battista Adriani in his letter to Vasari, prefixed to Vite;
by Giovanni Battista Armenini in his De' Veri Precetti
della Pittura, Ravenna (1586), pp. 143, 144; and by Feder-
igo Zuccaro in his L'Idea de' Pittori, Scultori, ed Architetti, Roma (1768), pp. 83, 102, 103. The book was first
published in 1607.

40 Franciscus Junius, The Painting of the Ancients in three
Books: Declaring by Historicall Observations and Examples,
the Beginning, Progresse and Consummation of that most
Noble Art, etc., London (1638), 321-324. It is worth noticing that a second edition was called for in 1694.

41 Ibid., 324-327.

42 Ibid., 329 and 332.

43 Ibid., 334, 335.

44 See Roland Fréart de Chambray, Idea of the Perfection of
Painting, etc. (tr. J[ohn] E[velyn], London, 1668), p. 10;
C. A. Du Fresnoy, The Art of Painting with Remarks (tr.
John Dryden, London, 1716), p. 115; Turnbull, Treatise
on Ancient Painting, London (1740), xxv; Laokoon (ed. W.
G. Howard, New York, 1910), 32.

45 Another book that helped to popularize the idea of grace and
the parallel of Apelles and Raphael is the already mentioned
Vite de' Pittori Antichi (1667), of Carlo Dati. See edition

printed in Milano, 1806: 151; 152; 156; 257; 258. This book
was one of the sources used by Richard Graham when he
added his "Short Account of the Most Eminent Painters" to
the second edition of Dryden's Du Fresnoy, 1716. See p.
229.

46   Fréart, op. cit., 3 and 8.

47   Fréart de Chambray, Parallel of the Ancient Architecture
with the Modern, etc. (tr. John Evelyn, London, 1733),
xxiv. A few passages in Du Fresnoy's De Arte Graphica,
1667, with the comment of de Piles, bear on the subject:

> sit Nobilitas, charitumque Venustas
> Rarum homini munus, Coelo, non Arte petendum.

(11.222,223)

De Piles' comment is an early attempt on his part to define
grace: "It is difficult enough to say what this Grace of Painting is: 'tis to be conceiv'd and understood much more easily
than to be explain'd by words. It proceeds from the illumination of an excellent Mind, which cannot be acquir'd, by
which we give a certain turn to things which makes them
pleasing, and have all its parts regular, which notwithstanding all this, shall not be pleasing, if all these parts
are not put together in a certain manner, which attracts
the Eye to them, and holds it fix't upon them: For which
reason there is a difference to be made betwixt Grace and
Beauty." (Du Fresnoy, op. cit., 149.) Of course Apelles
and Raphael are linked as painters whose fame rests upon
their grace. (Ibid., 150.) See also de Piles' remarks on
the inability of any man to give rules for attaining the
"greatest beauties." (Ibid., 101.)

48   [Dominique Bouhours], Les Entretiens d'Ariste et d'Eugène,
Paris (1691), pp. 246-257. Similar ideas are to be found
in the same author's La Manière de Bien Penser, etc.,
Seconde Edition, Amsterdam (1692), pp. 130, 131; 157-159.
See also [Baltasar Gracián y Morales], The Complete
Gentleman (tr. T. Saldkeld, Dublin, 1776), Ch. XII; also
his The Hero (tr. by a Gentleman of Oxford, London, 1726),
Ch. XIII. Gracián repeats many of Bouhours' ideas on the
je ne scay quoy.

49 Ibid., 260, 261.

50 Ibid., 262, 263. The analogy between aesthetic and theological grace suggested by Bouhours is implicit in the fact that χάρις is the Greek word for both. The subject is touched on by James Moffat in his Grace in the New Testament, New York (1932), 7-21.

51 Ibid., 253, 254. The phrase is at least as old as Petrarch. In Aretino (p. 80) Dolce quoted Petrarch's line: "E un non so che negli occhi."

52 "Comparaison de Démosthène et de Cicéron," 1670, Oeuvres, La Haye (1725), I, 46-48. Cf. Bouhours, Entretiens, p. 260.

53 "Comparaison de Thucydide et de Tite-Live," 1681, Ibid., I, 199.

54 "Réflexions sur l'Usage de l'Éloquence de ce Tems en Général," 1672, Ibid., II, 20.

55 "Réflexions sur la Poétique d'Aristote," 1674, Ibid., II, 130.

56 See Gregory Smith, Elizabethan Critical Essays, Oxford (1904): Ascham, 1570, I, 2: Gascoigne, 1575, I, 52; Sidney, 1583, I, 168, 202; Webbe, 1586, I, 230, 256, 257, 267, 299; Puttenham, 1589, II, 85, 117, 143, 165, 173; Harington, 1591, II, 206; Harvey, 1593, II, 248, 260; Carew, 1595, II, 293; Meres, 1598, II, 312; Daniel, 1600, II, 360.

57 See J. E. Spingarn, Critical Essays of the Seventeenth Century, Oxford (1908): Jonson, I, 37, 47; Davenant, II, 17, 20; Hobbes, II, 71; Sprat, II, 130, 136-137; Wolseley, III, i, 8, 9; Temple, III, 82, 83, 84. John Hughes, "Of Style," in W. H. Durham, Critical Essays of the XVIII Century, New Haven (1915), 82, 83.

58 See the present writer's The Sublime, New York, 1935.

59 Richardson discussed "Grace and Greatness" as one of the seven parts of painting. Works, London (1773), pp. 93-116.

60 Loc. cit., 286-293. There is room for a further study of the idea of grace in the eighteenth century. Among other writers on the subject are Shaftesbury, Turnbull, Spence, Hogarth, Reynolds, Kames. A useful summary of the idea may be found in Giogri Bertóla, Saggio sopra la Grazia nelle Lettere ed Arti, Ancona, 1823.

ONE RELATION OF RHYME TO REASON: ALEXANDER POPE

W. K. Wimsatt, Jr.

I

The view of rhyme which I wish to discuss in this essay has been formerly advanced but has never, I believe, been widely entertained. I am aware of statements of it by French prosodists[1] and of theoretical discussions by German aestheticians,[2] but to my knowledge the view has never been expounded in English and has never become a part of English literary theory[3] in the sense of being illustrated from English poetry. It is a view which is worth expounding because it relates to the more radical metaphysical problem of unity and diversity in art, or the universal and the concrete, a problem posed implicitly by Aristotle and still at the heart of metaphysical aesthetics. The last chapter of John Crowe Ransom's book The New Criticism is entitled "Wanted: An Ontological Critic";[4] and here with a stroke of brilliant candor he points out that poetry is a double performance in which the verse makes concessions to the sense and the sense to the verse. The poet does two things simultaneously as well as he can, and thus he produces a certain particularity or irrelevance of sense, and further a heterogeneity of structure by which the phonetic effect serves to give thickness or texture to the meaning. The total is a concreteness which makes the difference between poetry and science. In the discussion of verse, and more particularly of rhyme, which follows, I wish to develop the idea that verse gives to poetry a quality of the concrete and particular not merely in virtue of being a simultaneous and partly irrelevant performance, but in virtue of a studiously and accurately alogical character by which it imposes upon the meaning a counterpattern and acts as a fixative or preservative of the sensory quality of words. In a very abstract way I suppose this is believed by almost every theorist. I wish to apply the theory in detail to English rhyme, especially to the neo-classic

Reprinted from Modern Language Quarterly, Vol. 5 (1944), pp. 323-338, by permission of author and publisher.

rhyme of Pope, and thus to bring out a basic relation of rhyme to reason or meaning. Traditional prosodists have discussed rhyme as a degree of likeness in word sounds and have catalogued its approximations, alliteration, assonance, slant rhyme, eye rhyme, analyzed rhyme, dissonance, and so forth. But about the meaning of rhyme words they have had little to say. At least one ought to point out that the meanings of two words composing a rhyme pair are usually quite different -- and that they thus create a contrast which gives point to the likeness of sound[5] and which is characteristic of verse, where parallels of form do not, as in prose, support parallels of stated meaning, but run counter to meaning.

II

It would be only an exaggeration, not a distortion, of principle to say that the difference between prose and verse is the difference between homoeoteleuton and rhyme. "Non modo ad salutem ejus exstinguendam sed etiam gloriam per tales viros infringendam," says Cicero, and Quintilian quotes[6] it as an example of homoeoteleuton or like endings. Here the -endam and the -endam are alike, logically and legitimately alike; each has the same meaning, or is the same morpheme, and each supports the logic of the sentence by appearing in analogous places in the structure. Stylistic parallels[7] or forms of meaning of this and of other sorts seem to come fairly to the aid of logic; they are part of the normal framework of prose. The difference between these and rhyme in prose may be illustrated by the following examples from St. Augustine: "Lingua clamat, cor amat"; "Praecedat spes, ut sequatur res."[8] Here not only the endings but also the roots rhyme, and the result is an effect of alogicality, if not of excess and artificiality. It is not really to be expected that the roots should rhyme. The same may be said for all parallels of sound which do not inhere in some parallel meaning of the words themselves, but acquire their parallel merely through being placed in parallel structures. Such, for example, is the transverse alliteration of Lyly,[9] where the series of parallel consonants has logically nothing to do with the antithetic parallel of the words. Of somewhat the same character is the cursus or metrical ending.[10] And if a prose writer were to reënforce a pair of parallel or antithetic clauses by making each

one an iambic pentameter, we should say that this was decidedly
too much, that the metrical equality was hardly interesting unless it combined with a vein of logic that ran differently.

III

It is possible to point out examples, in balladry and in other
primitive types of poetry, where the equalities of verse coincide
with the parallels of meaning. Even in sophisticated poetry such
as Tennyson's In Memoriam one may find some stanzas where
a high degree of parallel is successful.[11] But on the whole the
tendency of verse, or certainly that of English verse, has been
the opposite. The smallest equalities, the feet, so many syllables, or so many time units, are superimposed upon the linear
succession of ideas most often without any regard for the equalities of logic. Two successive iambs may be two words, or one
word, or parts of two words, and so on. The larger units, the
lines, also are measured without reference to logically parallel
sections of sense. Even in heavily end-stopped verse, such as
that in Shakespeare's early plays, the complete phrase of which
each line is formed stands in oblique relation to the lines before
and after. The lines do not parallel one another but spring
ahead, one from another, diversely.

The more primitive and forthrightly emotional the poetry,
as in balladry, the less it may demand the sensory resistance
of verse non-parallel to logic. The more sophisticated and intellectualized the poetry, the more it will demand such resistance. The point is worth illustrating from the blank verse of
Paradise Lost — one of the most artful verse forms in the range
of English literature. An important phrase in Milton's own prescription for blank verse is "sense variously drawn out from
one verse into another." This various drawing out he accom-
plishes for the most part by his ever various, subtly continuous,
confused and tenuous syntax, by which the sense drips down
from line to line and does not usually run parallel in any successive lines. But if it does run parallel, there will be certain
careful and curious dislocations that prevent the lines from
seeming to be the unit of logical measure.

> Abhorred Styx, the flood of deadly hate;
> Sad Acheron of sorrow, black and deep;

> Cocytus, named of lamentation loud
> Heard on the rueful stream; fierce Phlegethon,
> Whose waves of torrent fire inflame with rage.[12]

It is I who have italicized the names of the four infernal rivers. These are the four heads of the parallel -- moving back toward the front of the line, from Styx to Cocytus, then leaping to the end with Phlegethon. The modifiers of the first two are of about the same length and place in the line; that of the third is longer and runs through two lines; that of the fourth fills just one line. Thus comes the sense of weaving back and forth, of intellect threading complexity, in place of a cool, simplifying triumph of classification.[13] The same handling of parallel can sometimes be seen in single lines.

> Un^x re´ spit^x ed´, un^x pit´ ied^x, un´ re^x prieved´
>
> Un^x sha´ ken^x, un´ se^x duced´, un^x ter´ ri^x fied´
>
> Thou´ art´ my^x fa´ ther^x, thou´ my^x au´ thor^x, thou´
> My being gavest me.[14]

The italicized syllables escape a prosaic parallel by falling in different metrical positions, now in thesis, now in arsis. The third "thou" is thrust out alone at the end of the line. The verse runs sinuously, intertwining with the sense and making a tension and resilience.

IV

We come then to rhyme, the subject of our argument. And first it must be admitted that in certain contexts a high degree of parallel in sense may be found even in rhyme. Even identical words may rhyme. In the sestina, for example, the same set of rhyme words is repeated in six different stanzas. But here the order changes and so does the relation of each rhyme word to the context. That is the point of the sestina. Somewhat the same may be said for a refrain when it does not rhyme with any other line of the context. In the broadest sense, difference of meaning in rhyme words includes difference of syntax. In fact, words have no character as rhymes until they become points

in a syntactic succession. And rhyme words (even identical
ones) can scarcely appear in a context without showing some
difference of meaning. The point of this essay is therefore not
to prove that rhyme words must exhibit difference of meaning,[15]
but to discuss the value of the difference and to show how a
greater degree of difference harmonizes with a certain type of
verse structure.

Under certain conditions (much more common than the
sestina or refrain mentioned above) the opportunity and the demand for difference of meaning in rhyme may be slight.

> Scogan, that knelest at the stremes hed
> Of grace, of alle honour and worthynesse,
> In th'ende of which strem I am dul as ded,
> Forgete in solitarie wildernesse,--
> Yet, Scogan, thenke on Tullius kyndenesse;
> Mynne thy frend, there it may fructifye!
> Far-wel, and loke thow never eft Love dyffye.[16]

The three identical "nesse" rhymes could be very flat, mere
prosy homoeoteleuton, if the three words occurred in positions
of nearly parallel logic or syntax. But Chaucer's sense, meandering like the stream through the stanza, makes no great demand upon these rhymes, and weak though they are, they are
strong enough. Even in Chaucer's couplets the same continuity
of sense through the verse may be discovered, and the same
tendency in rhyming,[17] as we shall illustrate in the comparison
which follows.

Pope is the English poet whose rhyming shows perhaps the
clearest contrast to Chaucer's. Chaucer found, even in Middle
English, a "skarsete" of rhyme.[18] There would come a day
when an even greater scarcity of easy rhymes would create a
challenge to the English poet and at the same time indicate one
of his most subtle opportunities. In the course of three hundred
years English lost many of its easy rhymes, stressed Germanic
and Romance endings, y, ing, ere, esse, and able, age, al,
aunce, aile, ain, esse, oun, ous, ure,[19] so that Pope perforce
rhymed words differing more widely in meaning. The characteristics of Pope's couplet, as opposed to Chaucer's, are, of
course, its closure or completeness,[20] its stronger tendency
to parallel, and its epigrammatic, witty, intellectual point.

One can hardly imagine such a couplet rhyming "wildernesse" and "kyndenesse," or "worthynesse" and "hethenesse," as Chaucer does in one couplet of the knight's portrait.

Most likely it is neither feasible nor even desirable to construct a scale of meaning differences to measure the cleverness of rhyme. The analysis which I intend is not in the main statistical. But an obvious, if rude, basis for classification is the part of speech. It may be said, broadly, that difference in meaning of rhyme words can be recognized in difference of parts of speech and in difference of functions of the same part of speech, and that both of these differences will be qualified by the degree of parallel or of oblique sense in the pair of rhyming lines. We may distinguish (I) lines of oblique relation having (a) rhymes of different parts of speech, (b) rhymes of the same part of speech; (II) lines of parallel relation having (a) rhymes of different parts of speech, (b) rhymes of the same part of speech. The tenor of the comparison which follows will be to suggest that Pope's rhymes are characterized by difference in parts of speech or in function of the same parts of speech, the difference in each case being accentuated by the tendency of his couplets to parallel structure.

Class Ia includes a large number of rhymes in both Pope and Chaucer, or indeed in any English poet, which statistically are rather neutral to our inquiry.

> Whan that Aprille with his shoures soote
> The droghte of March hath perced to the roote . . . .[21]

Here the rhyme makes its contribution to difference of sense against equality of verse, but because the oblique phrases themselves make a fundamental contrast to the metrically equal lines, and the rhyming parts of speech are a function of the phrases, the rhyme is not likely to be felt as a special element of variation. There is a higher proportion of these rhymes in Chaucer than in Pope.[22] Class Ib also includes a higher proportion of rhymes in Chaucer than in Pope,[23] and for the same reason, that in general Chaucer relies for variation more on continuous sense and syntax than on rhyme. But in rhymes of Class Ib, since the rhyme words are the same part of speech, there is some opportunity for comparing the effect of the rhyme itself. Chaucer is apt to give us a dullish rhyme:

ONE RELATION OF RHYME TO REASON

> Me thynketh it acordaunt to resoun
> To telle you al the condicioun. . . .[24]

Pope is apt to find some quaint minor contrast in length and quality of words:

> What guards the purity of melting maids,
> In courtly balls, and midnight masquerades?[25]

It is in Class IIa and Class IIb, however, that the rhyming of Pope is seen to best advantage. Because of the parallel in sense between the lines, the difference in parts of speech of rhymes in Class IIa is much more noticeable than in Class Ia. And not only are there more of these rhymes in Pope than in Chaucer,[26] but their effect is more pronounced in Pope because the parallel within the closed couplet of Pope is likely to be more intellectual and pointed. Chaucer will write:

> And everemoore he hadde a sovereyn prys;
> And though that he were worthy, he was wys.[27]

Similarly but more often Pope will write:

> The light coquettes in Sylphs aloft repair,
> And sport and flutter in the fields of air.[26]

Or he will write:

> Oft, when the world imagine women stray,
> The Sylphs thro' mystic mazes guide their way.

> When Florio speaks, what virgin could withstand,
> If gentle Damon did not squeeze her hand.[29]

In the last two examples the syntax is oblique but the sense is antithetic and hence parallel. It is a subtlety which is frequent in Pope (whose couplets, no matter what their syntax, tend to hover on the verge of parallel) but is rarely to be found in Chaucer. Here the structure of Pope's couplet forces more of the burden of variety on the rhyme.

In Class IIb one might expect to find that the parallel of

general sense and of rhyming parts of speech would produce a quality of flatness, a sort of minimum rhyme such as we found in St. Augustine — "Lingua clamat, cor amat" — the first step beyond homoeoteleuton. One thing that prevents this and often lends the rhyme a value of variation is that through some irregularity or incompleteness of parallel the rhyming words have oblique functions. Thus Chaucer:

> No deyntee morsel passed thurgh hir throte;
> Hir diete was accordant to hir cote.[30]

And Pope:

> From each she nicely culls with curious toil,
> And decks the Goddess with the glitt'ring spoil.[31]

There are more of these couplets in Pope than in Chaucer,[32] and with Pope the rhyme difference is more likely to seem the result of some deft twist or trick.

> Some are bewilder'd in the maze of schools,
> And some made coxcombs Nature meant but fools.[33]

There is a kind of inversion (from pupils to schools and back to the pupils in a new light) which in some couplets appears more completely as chiasmus, an effect concerning which I shall have more to say.

The two types of rhyme difference which characterize Pope's poetry (that of different parts of speech and that of the same part of speech in different functions) are a complement, as I have suggested, of his tendency to a parallel of lines. To recognize this may affect our opinion about how deliberately or consciously Pope strove for difference of rhyme, but it should not diminish the impression which the actual difference of rhyme makes upon us. Such rhyme difference may be felt more clearly as a characteristic of Pope if we examine the rhymes in a passage where the parallel is somewhat like that which Chaucer at times employs. It is difficult to find passages of sustained parallel in Chaucer. The usual narrative movement of his couplets is from then to then to then, with the oblique forward movement of actions in a sequence. But in the character sketches of the Canterbury Prologue a kind of loose parallel often prevails for ten or twenty lines, as one feature of a pilgrim after another is enumerated. The sense is continuous, in that the couplets tend to be incomplete, but the lines are all members of a parallel bundle. A clear example may be seen in the yeoman's portrait.

> And he was clad in cote and hood of grene.
> A sheef of pecock arwes, bright and kene,
> Under his belt he bar ful thriftily,
> (Wel coude he dresse his takel yemanly:
>
> .   .   .   .
>
> Upon his arm he baar a gay bracer,
> And by his syde a swerd and a bokeler,
> And on that oother syde a gay daggere
> Harneised wel and sharp as point of spere;
> A Cristopher on his brest of silver sheene.
> A horn he bar, the bawdryk was of grene.[34]

"Thriftily" and "yemanly," "bracer" and "bokeler," "sheene" and "grene," rhymes like these (aside even from the use of final syllables, "ly" and "er") I should call tame rhymes because the same parts of speech are used in closely parallel functions. To see the difference in this respect between Chaucer and Pope we may turn to the classic lines of another portrait:

> Bless'd with each talent and each art to please,
> And born to write, converse, and live with ease;
> Should such a man, too fond to rule alone,
> Bear, like the Turk, no brother near the throne;
> View him with scornful, yet with jealous eyes,
> And hate for arts that caus'd himself to rise;
> Damn with faint praise, assent with civil leer,
> And without sneering teach the rest to sneer;
> Willing to wound, and yet afraid to strike,
> Just hint a fault, and hesitate dislike;
> Alike reserv'd to blame or to commend,
> A tim'rous foe, and a suspicious friend; . . .[35]

The parallel of lines is continuous, but the rhymes are always different parts of speech. The portrait continues:

> Dreading ev'n fools; by flatterers besieged,
> And so obliging that he ne'er obliged;
> Like <u>Cato</u>, give his little Senate laws,
> And sit attentive to his own applause.

Here the same parts of speech are rhymed, but one verb is passive, one active; one noun is plural, one singular. The functions are different, in each case what he does being set against what he receives.

It is to be noted that in the yeoman's portrait such rhymes as "grene" and "kene," "thriftily" and "yemanly" fall into Class IIb and are of the sort which we described above as minimum rhyme, only one step away from homoeoteleuton. Class IIb often escapes this extreme, as we saw, by some irregularity of parallel. But it is significant to add now that even when Pope does not escape the extreme he has resources of piquancy.[36] Here and there he will be guilty of a certain flatness:

> Each motion guides, and every nerve sustains,
> Itself unseen, but in th'effects remains.[37]

Very often, however, he conveys some nice contrast in the parallel.

> True wit is Nature to advantage dress'd,
> What oft was thought, but ne'er so well express'd.[38]

Here the two rhyme verbs are not merely parallel examples. One is literal, one is figurative, and in being matched with each other they express in brief the metaphor on which this classic critical doctrine is based, that to express is to dress.

> Th' adventurous Baron the bright locks admired;
> He saw, he wish'd, and to the prize aspired.[39]

Here the difference between "admired" and "aspired," the swift ascent of the Baron's aspiration, is precisely the point. In other parallel rhymes Pope finds an opportunity for brisk irony.

ONE RELATION OF RHYME TO REASON

> One speaks the glory of the British Queen,
> And one describes a charming Indian screen.

> Do thou, Crispissa, tend her fav'rite Lock;
> Ariel himself shall be the guard of Shock.[40]

From "British Queen" to "Indian screen," from "Lock" to
"Shock," here is the same bathos he more often puts into one
line — "When husbands, or when lapdogs breathe their last."[41]

V

But what I conceive to be the acme of variation occurs in
a construction to which I have already alluded, chiasmus. The
basis of chiasmus will be a high degree of parallel, often antithetic. The rhyme may be of the same part of speech or of
different parts. If it is of the same part, the chiastic variation
will be a special case of the "schools" — "fools" rhyme already
quoted, where a twist in the meaning gives different functions
to the rhyme words. If the rhyme is of different parts, the variation will be a special case of that already discussed, where
different parts of speech rhyme in parallel lines.

> $\quad\quad\quad\quad$ 1 $\quad\quad$ 2
> Whatever Nature has in worth denied
> $\quad\quad$ 2' $\quad\quad\quad\quad\quad\quad\quad\quad\quad\quad$ 1'
> She gives in large recruits of needful Pride.[42]

> $\quad\quad\quad\quad\quad$ 1 $\quad\quad\quad\quad$ 2
> Whether the nymph shall break Diana's law,
> $\quad\quad\quad\quad$ 2' $\quad\quad\quad$ 1'
> Or some frail China jar receive a flaw.[43]

In the first line the breakage, then the fragile thing (the law);
in the second line another fragile thing (the jar) and then its
breaking (the flaw). The parallel is given a kind of roundness
and completeness, and intellectual lines are softened into the
concrete harmony of "law" and "flaw."

73

$$\overset{\displaystyle 1 \qquad\qquad 2}{\text{What dire offence from am'rous causes springs,}}$$
$$\underset{\displaystyle 2' \qquad\qquad 1'}{\text{What mighty contests rise from trivial things.}}^{44}$$

What dire offence from am'rous causes springs,
What mighty contests rise from trivial things.[44]

Love, Hope, and Joy, fair Pleasure's smiling train,
Hate, Fear, and Grief, the family of Pain. . . .[45]

Fear to the statesman, rashness to the chief,
To kings presumption, and to crowds belief.[46]

Thus critics of less judgment than caprice,
Curious, not knowing, not exact, but nice, . . .[47]

In the fourth example the antithesis is tripled, and the order being successively chiastic, returns upon itself, which is sufficient complication to make "caprice" and "nice" a surprise. Then one is an adjective and one a noun, and "caprice" has two syllables.[48]

The contemplation of chiastic rhyme, the most brilliant and complex of all the forms of rhyme variation, leads me to make a brief general remark upon the degree of Pope's reputation for rhyme. I have relied heavily upon examples of rhyme from Pope because he takes clearer advantage of the quality of difference in rhyme than other poets that I know. To that extent, and it seems to me a very important extent, he is one of the greatest English rhymers. Yet a critic of Pope's rhyme has spoken of "true" rhymes and "false" rhymes and "rimes to the eye" and has been concerned to discover that of 7874 rhymes in Pope 1027 are "false."[49] Another has approved of Pope's "correctness" in excluding polysyllables from his rhymes, but has found Pope's repeated use of the same rhyme words "monotonous in a high degree and a very serious artistic defect." The same critic has actually spoken of Pope's "poverty of rhyme."[50] One of the purposes of my argument is to cut the

ground from under such judgments as far as they are value
judgments. They can spring only from a very limited view of
rhyme as a kind of phonetic harmony, to be described and appraised in terms of phonetic accuracy, complexity, and variety
-- in other words, from a failure to connect rhyme with reason.

In more recent years Robert K. Root has pointed out that
Pope usually makes the rhyme fall on significant words and has
added a caution to readers against overstressing the rhyme
word.[51] Geoffrey Tillotson, in his progressive essay, On the
Poetry of Pope, has recorded his impression that Pope prefers
"a verb for at least one of the rime-words in a couplet" and that
"a verb at the end of the first line is often followed by its object
in the next line."[52] These are glances in the right direction.
Mr. Tillotson's remark is clearly one that I may quote in support of my own analysis of Pope's rhyme.

In this essay I have not pretended to explain all the rhetorical values that may be found in rhyme or in Pope's rhyme.
Nevertheless, the principle on which I am intent is one that
concerns rhyme as a fusion of sound and sense; and, as it is
a broad principle, it is rather a starting place for many analyses than the conclusion of any one. In the examples already
quoted from Pope I have shown several modes of its operation.
In my next section I shall suggest another or obverse aspect of
the whole.

VI

We have so far considered rhyme as it makes variation
against the parallels of verse. If we think now of the meaning
of the words as the basis of comparison, thus beginning with
variation or difference, we can discuss the sameness of the
rhyme sound as a binding force. Rhyme is commonly recognized
as a binder in verse structure. But where there is need for binding there must be some difference or separation between the
things to be bound. If they are already close together, it is su-
pererogatory to emphasize this by the maneuver of rhyme. So
we may say that the greater the difference in meaning between
rhyme words the more marked and the more appropriate will
be the binding effect. Rhyme theorists have spoken of the "surprise" which is the pleasure of rhyme, and surely this surprise

is not merely a matter of coming upon a similarity which one
has not previously anticipated. It cannot be a matter of time.
Even after the discovery, when the rhyme is known by heart
and said backwards, the pleasurable surprise remains. It must
depend on some incongruity or unlikelihood inherent in the co -
pling. It is a curious thing that "queen" should rhyme with
"screen"; they are very unlike objects. But Pope has found a
connection between them, has classified them as topics of chat,
and then the parallel of sound comes to his aid as a humorous
binder.[53] The principle is well illustrated in Pope's penchant
for proper-name rhymes. What more illogical than that a proper name should rhyme with any thing? For its meaning is unique.

> Poor Cornus sees his frantic wife elope,
> And curses Wit and Poetry, and Pope.[54]

> Yet ne'er one sprig of laurel graced these ribalds,
> From slashing Bentleys down to piddling Tibbalds.[55]

> The hero William, and the martyr Charles,
> One knighted Blackmore, and one pension'd Quarles.[56]

"Elope" and "Pope" suggest there is some connection between
the two; the joke is that we know very well there is not. Poor
"Tibbald" was not a "ribald," nor did "Charles" pension
"Quarles," but we are well on the way to believing both things;
the rhyme at least is a fait accompli.
  The most extreme examples of this kind of humor are the
extravagant double or triple rhymes of a Butler, a Swift, a
Byron, or a Browning. One stanza from Byron will do.

> He was a Turk, the colour of mahogany;
> And Laura saw him, and at first was glad,
> Because the Turks so much admire philogyny,
> Although their usage of their wives is sad;
> 'Tis said they use no better than a dog any
> Poor woman, whom they purchase like a pad:
> They have a number, though they ne'er exhibit 'em,
> Four wives by law, and concubines "ad libitum."[57]

If Byron had rhymed "philogyny" and "misogyny," it would not be very funny, for one expects these two words to sound alike; they are formed alike from the Greek and make the end words of a very natural antithesis. They are mere homoeoteleuton. "Mahogany" makes a comic rhyme with "philogyny" because of the wide disparity in meaning between the words. Mahogany, the Spanish name of a reddish hardwood, is not a likely companion for the learned Greek abstraction, but once an ingenious affinity in meaning is established, the rhyme sounds a triple surprise of ratification. Then comes "dog any," and difference of meaning in rhyme has proceeded to the point of disintegration and mad abandon. Rhymes of this sort are not distant relations of the pun and the "mixt Wit" which Addison defined as consisting "partly in the Resemblance of Ideas, and partly in the Resemblance of Words."[58] I mean that what convinces us that "dog any" belongs in this stanza is not so much its inevitable or appropriate meaning as the fact that it does rhyme.

VII

"Rime," says Henry Lanz, "is one of those irrational satellites that revolve around reason. It is concerned not with the meaning of verse but only with its form, which is emotional. It lies within the plane of the a-logical cross-section of verse."[59] It is within the scope of my argument to grant the alogical character of rhyme, or rather to insist on it, but at the same time to insist that the alogical character by itself has little, if any, aesthetic value. The music of spoken words in itself is meagre, so meagre in comparison to the music of song or instrument as to be hardly worth discussion. It has become a platitude of criticism to point out that verses composed of meaningless words afford no pleasure of any kind and can scarcely be called rhythmical -- let them even be rhymed. The mere return to the vowel tonic (the chord or tone cluster characteristic of a vowel[60]) will produce not emotion but boredom. The art of words is an intellectual art, and the emotions of poetry are simultaneous with conceptions and largely induced through the medium of conceptions. In literary art only the wedding of the alogical with the logical gives the former an aesthetic value. The words of a rhyme, with their curious harmony of sound and distinction of sense, are an amalgam of the sensory and the logical, or an arrest and precipitation of the logical in sensory form; they are the ikon in which the idea is caught. Rhyme and other verse elements save the physical quality of words -- intellectualized and made transparent by daily prose usage.[61] But without the intellectual element there is nothing to save and no reason why the physical element of words need be asserted. "Many a man," says Dr. Lanz at the close of his book, "was cruelly put to death for a 'daring rhyme.' " And he regards it as a "triumph of modern science that, instead of marveling at the mystery of this force, we can 'dissect it as a corpse.' "[62] There is more truth than malice in my adding that men are cruelly put to death not for melodies but for ideas, and that it is only when reduced to a purely "physical basis" that rhyme becomes a "corpse."

> When Adam dalf and Eve span,
> Who was then a gentilman?[63]

If there is something daring in this rhyme of John Ball's, it is certainly not in the return to the overtone of 1840 vibrations per second characteristic of ă [ae],[64] but in the ironic jostle by which plebeian "span" gives a lesson in human values to aristocratic "gentilman."

NOTES

1 Cf. notes 15 and 58.

2 The most formal statement seems to be that of J. S. Schütze, Versuch einer Theorie des Reimes nach Inhalt und Form (Magdeburg, 1802). I have been unable to consult this work and owe my knowledge of it to a summary in Dr. Henry Lanz's Physical Basis of Rime (Stanford University, 1931), pp. 162-66. I have on the whole found Dr. Lanz's survey of rhyme theory of great assistance — though I disagree with his central thesis.

3 Cf. Louis Untermeyer, "Rhyme and Its Reasons," Sat. Rev. Lit., Aug. 6, 1932, pp. 30-31; "The Future of Rhyme," Sat. Rev. Lit., Nov. 15, 1924, p. 278; Theodore Maynard, "The Reason for Rhyme," Freeman, VIII (1924), 469-70; E. E. Kellett, "Rhyme and Reason," Spectator, CXLV (1935), 544-45; J. W. Rankin, "Rime and Reason," PMLA, XLIV

(1929), 997-1004. Cf. notes 5, 11, and 19.

4 The New Criticism (Norfolk, Conn. , 1941), pp. 294-330.

5 "Mice most assuredly sounds like mice," says a recent critic. "But, the ear asks, what of it?" (T. Walter Herbert, "Near-Rimes and Paraphones," Sewanee Review, XLV [1937], 437). Rather, one might say, the mind asks, what of it? Cf. note 58.

6 Pro Milone, II, 5; Institutio Oratoria, IX, iii, 73 ff. Cf. Aristotle, Rhetoric, III, 9.

7 I have discussed such parallels in my Prose Style of Samuel Johnson (New Haven, 1941), pp. 15-43.

8 Richard C. Trench, Sacred Latin Poetry (London, 1864), p. 28 n. Cf. F. J. E. Raby, A History of Secular Latin Poetry in the Middle Ages (Oxford, 1934), 1, 49. Cf. Quintilian on verbal resemblances (op. cit. , IX, iii, 73ff.); Ad Herennium on the figure "similiter desinens."

9 "Althoughe hetherto Euphues I have shrined thee in my heart for a trustie friende, I will shunne thee heerafter as a trothles foe" (Euphues, in Works, ed. R. Warwick Bond [Oxford, 1902], I, 233; cf. I, 123).

10 Cf. Eduard Norden, Die antike Kunstprosa (Leipzig, 1898), II, 950-51.

11 Cf. C. Alphonse Smith, Repetition and Parallelism in English Verse (New York, 1894); Charles F. Richardson, A Study of English Rhyme (Hanover, 1909), p. 16.
    The parallels of Hebrew poetry are, of course, the outstanding exceptions to the generality which I propose, but in this connection I believe it ought to be observed that the lines and half lines of Hebrew poetry are not equal with the metrical exactitude of classical and modern European verse. The number of accents is the same, the number of syllables indeterminate, and the parallel of sense (as in looser English verse like Whitman's) plays an important rôle in strengthening the equality and pattern of the verse. Cf. W. O. E. Oesterley, Ancient Hebrew Poems Metrically Translated (New York, 1938), pp. 3-7; W. O. E. Oesterley and Theodore H. Robinson, An Introduction to the Books

of the Old Testament (New York, 1934), pp. 140-45.

12 Paradise Lost, II, 577-81.

13 Cf. the morning laudate of Adam and Eve — recited in "holy rapture" and "various style" (Paradise Lost, V, 146-47, 192-99). This passage affords an instructive comparison with the King James version of Psalm cxlvii, 2-4, 8-10, where the Hebrew parallel of sense and rhythm is largely preserved.

14 Paradise Lost, II, 185; V, 899; II, 864.

15 The most positive statement that I know is that of Théodore de Banville, Petit Traité de Poésie Française (Paris, 1894), pp. 75-76; "Vous ferez rimer ensemble, autant qu'il se pourra, des mots très-semblables entre eux comme SON, et très-différents entre eux comme SENS. Tâchez d'accoupler le moins possible un substantif avec un substantif. . . ."

16 Lenvoy de Chaucer a Scogan, lines 43-49.

17 Cf. the Rhyme Indexes of the Chaucer Society; Max Kaluza, Chaucer und der Rosenroman (Berlin, 1893), pp. 65-81; Edward P. Morton, "Chaucer's Identical Rimes," MLN, XVIII (1903), 73-74; Gustav Vockrodt, Reimtechnik bei Chaucer als Mittel zur chronologischen Bestimmung seiner im Reimpaar geschriebenen Werke (Halle, 1914), pp. 13, 26, 35-37.

18 Complaint of Venus.

19 Cf. Max Kaluza, Englische Metrik in historischer Entwicklung (Berlin, 1909), §§ 140, 149, pp. 162-64, 172-73. It is beyond the scope of this essay to consider the history of rhyme meaning-differences by languages and periods. That seems to me a field where research may yield some interesting results. Cf. Jakob Schipper, A History of English Versification (Oxford, 1910), p. 11; Norden, op. cit., II, 825, 839-40; Kaluza, op. cit., § 145, p. 168. In a limited sense rhyme apparently does originate in parallel of syntactic construction and identity of endings (cf. Norden, op. cit., II, 819-24, 867-68; Lanz, op. cit., pp. 127, 184), but certainly the step to the more difficult rhyming of roots

and of words in non-parallel positions is the most important which rhyme takes in its development.

20 The difference is far greater than is shown by the statistics
of William E. Mead, The Versification of Pope in its Relations to the Seventeenth Century (Leipzig, 1889), pp. 31-33.
Mead gives Chaucer's Canterbury Prologue a percentage
of 10.7 unstopped lines against 5.41 for the Rape of the Lock.
But he does not take into account the various degrees of
end-stopping nor the difference between stopping the first
line of a couplet and stopping the second. Cf. Friedrich
Klee, Das Enjambement bei Chaucer (Halle, 1913), pp.
19-22, 33, and Table II; Mary A. Hill, "Rhetorical Balance
in Chaucer's Poetry," PMLA, XLII (1927), 845-61.

21 Canterbury Prologue, line 1.

22 I base my statement on a general impression which is borne
out in a line-by-line analysis of four passages from each
author: Chaucer (Works, ed. F. N. Robinson [Boston, 1933]),
Legend of Good Women, Prologue F, lines 1-148; Canterbury Prologue, lines 1-148; Knight's Tale, Part II, first
148 lines, 1355-1502; Nun's Priest's Tale, first 148 lines,
2821-2968; Pope (Complete Poetical Works, ed. H. W.
Boynton [Boston, 1903]), Essay on Criticism, I, 1-148;
Rape of the Lock, I, 1-148; Epistle to Dr. Arbuthnot, lines
1-148; Dunciad, Book IV, lines 1-148.
The numbers for the first type of couplet described
above, by passages, in the order named, are: Chaucer,
41, 23, 33, 34; Pope, 26, 24, 29, 27. (I should hardly expect another tabulator to arrive at exactly the same results.)
T. Walter Herbert's "The Grammar of Rimes," Sewanee Review, XLVIII (1940), 362-77, is a statistical investigation which seems to me to test not so much the
rhyme as the line-ending. It would apply almost as well to
blank verse. Franz Beschorner, Verbale Reime bei Chaucer (Halle, 1920), studies the number of finite verbs and
infinitives used as rhymes by Chaucer. Unlike Mr. Herbert,
he finds Chaucer's "Tendenz" in this direction "ausseror-
dentlich stark" (p. 1).

23 The numbers are: Chaucer, 18, 15, 24, 16; Pope, 11, 10,
20, 8.

24 Canterbury Prologue, line 37.

25 Rape of the Lock, I, 71.

26 The numbers are: Chaucer, 0, 13, 8, 11; Pope, 21, 22, 12, 22.

27 Canterbury Prologue, line 67.

28 Rape of the Lock, I, 65.

29 Rape of the Lock, I, 91, 97.

30 Nun's Priest's Tale, line 2834.

31 Rape of the Lock, I, 131.

32 The numbers are: Chaucer, 5, 6, 5, 6; Pope, 9, 10, 9, 10.

33 Essay on Criticism, I, 26.

34 Canterbury Prologue, lines 103-116. Another clear example is the knight's portrait, lines 47-58.

35 Epistle to Dr. Arbuthnot, lines 195-206.

36 Since examples within this sub-classification differ so widely, the numbers have little significance: Chaucer, 10, 17, 4, 6; Pope, 9, 8, 4, 7.

37 Essay on Criticism, I, 78.

38 Essay on Criticism, II, 97.

39 Rape of the Lock, II, 29.

40 Rape of the Lock, III, 13; II, 115.

41 Rape of the Lock, III, 158.

42 Essay on Criticism, II, 5.

43 Rape of the Lock, II, 105.

44 Rape of the Lock, I, 1.

45 Essay on Man, II, 117.

46 Essay on Man, II, 243.

47 Essay on Criticism, II, 85.

48 For three exquisite examples of chiasmus from three other

poets, see the rhyme of "dust" and "lust" in Andrew Marvell's "Coy Mistress," "thrush" and "bush" in Christina Rossetti's "Spring Quiet," and the double chiasmic rhyme of "leaping" and "sleeping," "laid" and "fade" in A. E. Housman's "With rue my heart is laden."

49 L. Mary McLean, "The Riming System of Alexander Pope," PMLA, VI (1891), 134-60.

50 Mead, op. cit., pp. 48, 140.

51 Robert K. Root, The Poetical Career of Alexander Pope (Princeton, 1938), p. 37.

52 Geoffrey Tillotson, On the Poetry of Pope (Oxford, 1938), p. 124.

53 In this respect the relation between rhyme and alliteration may be readily seen. It is the very disparity of the words brought into one web of sense which gives virtue to the alliterative binding. "Fed with soft Dedication all day long" (Epistle to Arbuthnot, line 233). "Through pain up by the roots Thessalian pines" (Paradise Lost, II, 544).

54 Epistle to Arbuthnot, line 25.

55 Epistle to Arbuthnot, line 163.

56 Epistle to Augustus, line 386.

57 Beppo, stanza LXX.

58 Spectator, No. 62. For the relation of rhyme to pun see Léon Bellanger, Études Historiques et Philologiques sur la Rime Française (Angers, 1876), pp. 1-26, on the early sixteenth-century rhyming school of Molinet and Crétin. For identical rhyme (reicher Reim, rime riche) in Middle English, see Max Kaluza, op. cit., §§ 144-49, pp. 167-73; Jakob Schipper, op. cit., p. 273. Cf. Lowell's Fable for Critics (Works [Boston, 1910], X, 16, 29).

59 Henry Lanz, The Physical Basis of Rime, An Essay on the Aesthetics of Sound (Stanford University, 1931), p. 293.

60 Lanz, op. cit., pp. 10-13.

61 Cf. G. W. F. Hegel, The Philosophy of Fine Art, trans.

F. P. B. Osmaston (London, 1920), IV, 7-10, 84, 90-91, Part III, Subsection III, chap. iii.

62   Lanz, op. cit., p. 342.

63   Lanz, op. cit., pp. 121, 342.

64   Lanz, op. cit., pp. 18, 20, 22, 243.

POPE

Austin Warren

Neoclassical theory of poetry and neoclassical poetry imperfectly agree. This discrepancy is most simply accounted for by remembering that the period called, in literary and aesthetic history, "neoclassical" is, in philosophical and cultural history, the age of the Enlightenment -- the age, that is, of rationalism. Some bold spirits, impatient of adjustment, were willing to enter heaven at the loss of an eye: in the celebrated quarrel over the relative merits of the Ancients and the Moderns, the modernists firmly took their stand on the achievements of the natural sciences and on social progress, rejecting much ancient literature, notably Homer, as obsolete, childish stuff, compounded of immoral gods, absurd miracles, and primitive manners. The classicists -- likely to be either men of letters or churchmen — were necessarily less neat in their position; for, though sharing with their contemporaries the desire to be sensible, enlightened, and modern, they also genuinely admired the achievements of ages unlike their own. Hence their creed often formalizes past moments in literary history, while their practice is very much of their own time.

Thus, while the Enlightenment reinforces the impetus of the Georgics and the Horatian epistles toward literature as instruction, the orthodox neoclassical creed still runs: the epic and the tragedy are the highest genres. Dryden praises the Georgics for showing what virtuosity can do in making poetry out of the most unpromising stuff ("opus superbat materiam"); but in his own works he distinguishes between the sermo pedestris of such ratiocinative essays as Religio laici and his "poetry," a distinction not invalidated by the customary real superiority of his "lower" over his "higher" style. When Pope says, I "stoop to truth and moralize my song," he is not wholly ironic.

Reprinted from Rage for Order by Austin Warren by permission of The University of Michigan Press and of the author. Copyright 1959 by The University of Michigan Press. This article is a revision of "The Mask of Pope," Sewanee Review, Vol. 54 (1946), pp. 19-33.

Neoclassical poems are likely to conform to Cartesian criteria for truth — clarity and distinctness; and the poet is likely to be a well-educated, methodical, and elegant expositor of accepted ethical generalizations. But neoclassical criticism continues to employ a terminology important parts of which are ultimately referable to Plato: words like "invention" (creative imagination), "inspiration," "fire," and "poetic fury." Like Enlightened Christians who, though retaining the word "revelation," are centrally concerned to show that theirs is a reasonable religion, the poet-critics use language difficult to reconcile with their performance or thin down and rationalize the old terms. Thus Johnson dismissed, as mere commonplace, Young's conjectural exhortation to literary originality; and Pope's preface to Homer exalts "invention" and "fire" above all the strategies of literary intelligence; yet neoclassical poetry lacks that large boldness it praises. It praises what it cannot really imitate.

The poets and critics were partially aware of this situation. Unlike the simpler modernists, they found a characteristic adjustment in a double standard of loss and gain, progress and decadence, an advance in refinement, a diminution of vigor. "Our numbers were in their nonage till Waller and Denham" has to be reconciled with the humble acknowledgment of "giant wits before the Flood." Walsh's famous advice to Pope must not be taken too simply; it really means: the great things are done; the age of myth-making is over; what remains to be done is to achieve that "correctness," that nicety of detail, which bolder writers and bolder ages perforce neglect.

Attempting to reconcile Homer and Shakespeare with Hobbes and Locke, the poets found themselves handicapped. The dramatists — Wycherly, Congreve, Dryden (in All for Love, which, and not Cato, gives us a conception of good neoclassical tragedy) — fared best, though English classicism suffers for want of a tragic genius comparable to Racine's. Milton's epic is not easy to locate in literary history; but, written by a poet versed in the Italian and French critics, praised as well as "tagged" by Dryden, demonstrated by Addison to be a "regular" epic, admired by Pope as well as by Dennis and Gildon, Paradise Lost may be regarded as England's neoclassical epic. After Paradise Lost, however, epic poetry loses virtue in both France and England, though it is still to be essayed by the ambitions of Blackmore,

Glover, and Voltaire. As Pope's ironic recipe for writing on
epic implies, a series of technical devices drawn by generalization from the accredited masterpieces is inadequate unless
there is an epic spirit -- perhaps he would have added, if properly questioned, "and a heroic age."

The idea of the Great Poem, of the Great Genius, of the
(often correlated) Grand Style intimidated many Augustan poets,
"froze the genial current" of their souls. Only, it seems, if
they could say to themselves, "This is of course not poetry,
or not really great poetry," could they have a fair chance of
writing it. Thus Prior, though himself proud of his epic-didac-
tic Solomon, his certification that he is a "major" poet, is
really sure of his tone, really poetic only in his fables and songs
and mock-didactic Alma. "Rural Elegance: An Ode" and its
companion odes and elegies are negligible exercises; but let
Shenstone suppose himself to be writing "levities," and he moves
toward poetry. Intending a burlesque of Spenser, he is free to
write imaginatively of his childhood. More violent ways of em-
ancipating one's self from the censorship of reason were those
of Chatterton and Macpherson, both of whom found pseudonymous personalities through which to express their censorable
selves. Chatterton, whose public self held the atheist and re-
publican views of a "man of reason" and wrote able satire ("Kew
Gardens"), created, for his more imaginative self, the persona
of a fifteenth-century Catholic priest. The two kinds of verse
written by Christopher Smart, in and out of his mind, instance
another split.

The most successful reconciliation of classicism and rationalism, or poetry and philosophy, or the incorrect, great
past and the neater, thinner present, took place in terms of
burlesque. Burlesque is often mask, often humility. The mock-
epic is not mockery of the epic but elegantly affectionate homage,
offered by a writer who finds it irrelevant to his age. As its signal advantage, burlesque (with its allied forms, satire and irony)
allows a self-conscious writer to attend to objects, causes, and
persons in which he is deeply interested yet of which, in part or
with some part of him, he disapproves. "Interest" is a category
which subsumes love and hate, approval and disapproval; very
often it is an unequal, an unsteady mixture. Burlesque covers
a multitude of adjustments; and each specimen requires to be
separately scrutinized and defined.

Gay's Shepherd's Week is one of the clearer cases. Written at Pope's request, it was intended to exhibit the disgustingly crude manners and speech of genuine rustics and so, by reverse, to vindicate Pope's "Vergilian" pastorals against Phillips' wobblingly "natural" ones. Actually, however, it exhibits the unsteadiness of Gay's own feelings. We have Johnson's testimony that contemporary readers felt, like us, that most of Gay's shots had hit an unintended target. Without meaning to betray Pope's cause — indeed imagining that he indorsed it -- he discovered in the writing the division of his emotional loyalties and discovered, in that division, his attachment to folkways and rural pieties.

In the mock-genres (as well as in the satire and the epistle) it was possible to escape the stylistic restrictions of Great Poetry -- its avoidance of "low" terms, its aim at consistent dignity and elegance. It was possible to shift, honorably, from the Beautiful to the Characteristic.

Pope's development followed, in general, this line — from the elegantly decorative to the richly -- even the grotesquely — expressive. His poetry is not so homogeneous as its virtual confinement to couplets has often suggested. We should differentiate the Pastorals, the Homer, Eloisa (which is not only an Ovidian "heroic epistle" but a soliloquy from tragedy, in the manner of Racine), the essays on Criticism and on Man, the satires and epistles, and the mock-epics. Pope's contemporaries did not confuse them or like them equally. Joseph Warton was not the only reader to think that in Eloisa and the Elegy Pope showed himself capable of the Pathetic and to regret his turning from this mode to satire. Nor did Coleridge, in the next "age," fail to distinguish between the Homer (to which he assigned the chief responsibility for the poetic diction of the eighteenth century) and the satires (composed in such words as a Lake Reformer might have used).

The two pieces, early and late, which give the measure of Pope's development are the Pastorals, written before he was eighteen, and the Dunciad, which appeared in its enlarged and final form the year before his death.

The Pastorals once seemed a monument to poetic "progress." In testimony to his admirer, Spence, Pope judged them "the most correct in the versification and musical in the numbers" of all his works; and Warton, in an estimate echoed by

Johnson, finds their merit in their "correct and musical versification, musical to a degree of which rhyme could hardly be
thought capable, and in [their] giving the first specimen of that
harmony in English verse which is now become indispensably
necessary." These are technical estimates, specifically of
prosody. The Pastorals offer evidence of other care and contrivance: they combine as many traditional motifs as possible
(e.g., the elegy, the singing match); they profess — in contraction and enrichment of Spenser's precedent — to traverse the
four seasons, the four times of day, the four ages of man. De-
monstrably superior to Phillips' rival pieces — now turgidly
elegant, now rustically English, now plain childish -- Pope's
stylized pastorals consistently exclude realism.

> See what delight in sylvan scenes appear!
> Descending Gods have found Elysium here.
> In woods bright Venus with Adonis strayed,
> And chaste Diana haunts the forest-shade.

In an early letter Pope explains his prosodic aims in terms
suggestive of a "pure" poetry. The principle of delightful variation is conceived of syllabically and as one might conceive of
it if one were writing a string quartet. Indeed Pope's initial aim
amounts to a precise working within strict quasi-musical forms.
Characteristic canons concern the artful shifting of the caesura,
the prohibition of the Alexandrine and the triplet rhyme — indul-
gences which weaken, by relaxing, the triumph of variation
within the confines of twenty syllables. The rules sound mechanical; but the poet who wrote them trusted, confidently, to his
ear: "One must," he said to Spence, "tune each line over in
one's head to try whether they go right or not."
That the "great rule of verse is to be musical" Pope would
never deny — assuming, however, that there are more kinds of
music than the sweetness of pastoral verse and the majesty of
heroic; he could even distinguish "softness" from "sweetness."
Whether in blame or praise, eighteenth-century critics often
tagged Pope as "sweet" or "smooth," or "melodious," as though
his work were all of a texture. But Pope claimed: "I have followed the significance of the numbers, and the adapting them
to the sense, much more even than Dryden; and much oftener
than any one minds it" — that is, not only in the set pieces. He

liked to recollect a showy couplet from his juvenile and discarded epic:

> Shields, helms, and swords all jangle as they hang
> And sound formidinous with angry clang.

Such an instance, however, makes Pope's notion of "representative harmony" appear limited to the stunt-effects of Poe's "Bells" or Lindsay's "Congo" or his own and Dryden's Cecilian correlations of poetry and music. Nor is Pope helpful to a subtle cause in the Essay on Criticism, where his four specimens appear to restrict the phonetic expressiveness of verse to the categories of the loud-harsh, the smooth-soft, the slow, and the rapid. Yet it is not onomatopoeia exclusively or primarily which he is commending; in modern terminology, he wants to say that the meaning of a poem is inclusive of its sound as well as its paraphrasable statement. The "echoes to the sense" either are rhythmical (accelerating or prolonging the line, interrupting it into staccato effect, or letting it flow in a legato) or they are phonative (euphonic or cacophonous — according to ease or difficulty of articulation); often these devices work together:

> Behold yon Isle, by Palmers, Pilgrims trod,
> Men bearded, bald, cowled, uncowled, shod, unshod,
> Peeled, patched, and pie-bald, linsey-woolsey brothers,
> Grave mummers! sleeveless some, and shirtless others.

Except for allowing himself the extra syllable in the feminine rhyme, Pope restricts himself to his decasyllabics; but though neoclassical doctrine allows for no further metrical variation than an occasional trochaic substitution, Pope's ear evades the rule by counting, as unstressed, syllables which any intelligent reading (including his own) must certainly have stressed, so permitting himself such a seven-stress line as has been cited. The excess of stressed syllables slows up the lines; the serried syntax gives an irregular, staccato movement; the dominance of plosives helps, with abruptness, in the total intended tone or "meaning" of grotesqueness.

The neoclassical theory of serious diction called for a thinly honorific vocabulary, for adjectives which singled out

an obvious attribute implicit in the noun -- the "verdant" mea-
dow, the "blue" violet -- or were devised as loosely decorative
epithets -- the "pleasing" shades, the "grateful" clusters, the
"fair" fields: all examples from the Pastorals. The inhibitions,
imposed upon the joint authority of Philosophy and the Ancients,
are stringent. Words must not be ambiguous or multiple-mean-
inged (for then they become puns, and puns are forms of verbal
wit, and verbal wit is "false wit"); they must not be homely or
technical (since poetry addresses men as such -- gentlemen, not
specialists in science or laborers); they must be lucid (for poetry owes its kinship with philosophy to its universality).

These inhibitions are removed or greatly mitigated, however, when the poet does not profess poetry but only an epistle
or a burlesque imitation. The difference is notable in the Moral
Essays, the Rape, the Dunciad.

> But hark! the chiming clocks to dinner call;
> A hundred footsteps scrape the Marble Hall;
> The rich buffet well-colored serpents grace,
> And gaping Tritons spew to wash your face.
>
> .   .   .   .
>
> Whether the nymph shall break Diana's law,
> Or some frail China jar receive a flaw;
> Or stain her honor, or her new brocade;
> Forget her prayers, or miss a masquerade;
> Or lose her heart, or necklace, at a ball.

Zeugma, the joining of two unlike objects governed by a single
verb, is of course a form of pun; yet this verbal play constitutes
one of Pope's most poetic resources in the Rape: it is this device, one might say, which gives the tone to the whole.

Burlesque are both Pope's masterpieces, the Rape and the
Dunciad. Of the mock-epic, we may provisionally say that it
plays form against matter, a lofty and elaborate form against
a trivial situation or set of persons or theme. But "form against
matter" is too simple a naming. The real failure of the post-
Miltonic epic lay, surely, in the supposition that the heroic
poem could be written in an unheroic age; that a poem which,
generically, involved the interrelation of the human and the
divine, the natural and the supernatural, could be written in

an age when "thinking people" had grown too prudent for heroism, too sophisticated for religion. John Dennis, whose taste among the Ancients was for Homer, Pindar, and Sophocles, and among the Moderns for Milton, was not unsound in his critical contention that great poetry like that of his favorites must be religious. So we might restate the incongruity as between heroic things and refined, between an age of faith and an age of reason. The mock-epic reminds an unheroic age of its own nature: by historical reference, it defines the "civilized" present.

Is Pope, then, satirizing Belinda's world? Yes, but lightly. His intent is rather to juxtapose contrasting modes than to decide how far his aristocracy has gained by its elegance, how far lost by its safe distance from war, politics, poverty, and sin. The poem is in nothing more dexterous than in its controlled juxtaposition of worlds. In another context we should find ominous those brilliant lines which couple by incongruity the worlds of the bourgeoisie and the proletariat with that of the leisure class:

> The hungry Judges soon the sentence sign,
> And wretches hang that jury-men may dine;
> The merchant from the Exchange returns in peace,
> And the long labors of the Toilet cease.

The Rape owes its richness and resonance to its overstructure of powerful, dangerous motifs. What keeps it from being that filigree artifice which the romantics saw (and praised) is its playing with fire, especially the fires of sex and religion. Though Pope was scarcely a "good Catholic," his parents were devout; and he is writing of an "old Catholic" society; and many of his effects involve the suggestion of blasphemous parallels: the linking of English folklore and the Lives of the Saints, and of both to his gentle mythology of urbane "machines." He links the nurse's moonlit elves and fairy ring with the priest's tales of "virgins visited by Angel-powers"; the visions of the Cave of Spleen are

> Dreadful as hermit's dreams in haunted shades,
> Or bright as visions of expiring maids,

visions which may or may not be reducible to physiological

disturbances; the Baron and Belinda have their altars to Pride and Love, their real religions.

What, for religion, is got by parody parallel is, for sexual morality, managed by insinuation. Though it is admitted that nymphs may break Diana's law, we see none do so; the titular Rape is but of a lock. The opening of Canto III (a preview for the School for Scandal) shows the chorus at work ("At every word a reputation dies"); but we do not hear the death. A characteristic passage of double-entendre retails the difficulty of preserving a "melting maid's" purity at such a time and place of temptation as the midnight masquerade, while assuring us that her male companions' Honor, or her sylph, preserves her virtue.

Without doubt the specific perspectives through parody and irony are purposed. But there may be doubt whether these effects are not local and episodic, unsubject to central design and all-governing tone; for, though silly things have been said about Pope's work of composition (as if "closed couplets" must all be equally discrete and unreconciled), he was, of course, so intent on making every verse exciting and finished as to make it difficult for the poem to subordinate them. In the case of the Rape he is often in danger but, I think, unvanquished. What organizes the poem is not exclusively the narrative, with its chronological and dramatic sequence of scenes (including two battles); it is yet more its tone — the steadiness with which it holds, against heroic and religious perspectives, to its seriocomic view of a little elegant society.

Not to the manor born, Pope makes the drawing-room seem an achievement. He so treats a woman's day, says Johnson, that "though nothing is disguised, everything is striking; and we feel all the appetite of curiosity for that from which we have a thousand times turned fastidiously away." Pope had not turned fastidiously away; like Proust, another "outsider," he was fascinated by the ritual which gave — or signified — the aristocratic status. He has practiced, on other matter, the Wordsworthian formula of giving to the unmarvelous the light of wonder. Society is a wonder, we are made to feel; convention a triumph of happy contrivance; coffee a luxury; a card game a crisis. This effect is in large measure the result of the "machinery" of sylphs, who not only contrast with Homer's and Milton's "machines" but parallel Pope's women — those coquettes, termagants, dociles, and prudes whose natures they abstract and stylize.

The burlesque of the Rape provides, then, an elaborate stratification of attitudes and effects: amusement at trifles taken seriously; delight at elegance; recollections of earlier literature (Homer and Spenser) in counterpoint against the current literary mode; juxtaposition of corresponding worlds (Achilles' shield, the great petticoat); reminders of the economic and political structures which make possible this leisure-class comedy, of the moral and religious structures which make possible a society at all.

In the Dunciad, the mock-heroic frame is intermittent. There are frequent local parodies of passages from Homer, Virgil, and Milton; there are classical devices like the Homeric games, the descent into the lower world, the preview of future history from the mount of vision; but there is no plot, no "fable." The loose organization is expressively loose. The poem tenders some recent episodes in a long contest between stupidity and intelligence, anarchy and culture, barbarism and civilization. In this long contest, stupidity and its allies win out, not because of their superior plans, designs, or purposes — for there is no real war of opposed strategies — but because of their sheer multitudinous mass, their dead weight. The poem, a kind of anti-masque, is a series of ritual tableaux and pageants and processions, chiefly sluggish of movement and visually dusky. There are occasional light reliefs, like the episode of the dilettanti, fresh from the grand tour, where (in lines which, for satiric effect, return to Pope's old Pastoral "sweetness") one looks back

> To happy Convents, bosomed deep in vines,
> Where slumber Abbots, purple as their wines:
> To Isles of fragrance, lily-silvered vales,
> Diffusing languor in the panting gales.

But the general tone, prefigured in the brilliant Canto IV of the Rape, is somber and grotesque.

Time has assisted rather than damaged the poem. Though Pope's friends warned him against keeping alive his lampooned enemies, the warning was futile. Outside of literary circles, even in Pope's own time, most of the names must have been meaningless. And today it is certainly not the case that one

need master footnotes to understand the poem Pope wrote; for
the context provides the categories, which are permanent, while
the proper names are annually replaceable. If one is confused
by the blur of names, that too serves the purpose: these are not
the names of the few masters but of the many applicants. As for
the applicants: Pope is satirizing not bad men or poor men as
such but bad poets and commercial publishers and undiscrimin-
ating patrons and pedantic professors. To relax one's critical
standards is to be literarily immoral.

The finale is seriously epic because Pope credits the dia-
bolical power of stupidity. In the myth of Book IV, civilization
dies. According to Pope's view of history, brief episodes of
enlightenment had all along alternated with far longer sequences
of darkness: the primitive golden age gave way to barbarism;
Roman civilization yielded to Gothic monkery and mummery;
the Renaissance of Leo and Raphael and the Enlightenment of
Newton and Locke and Bolingbroke were now threatened by extinction. What there is of the mythic and the dramatic in Pope
comes from this sense. He felt the precariousness of civilization.

If this is a comic poem, it is comic only as Volpone is
comic, by virtue of a grim extravagance, a grim grotesqueness;
for it is not without reminder of the Inferno with its moral categories, its wry jokes, and its smoky lighting. The method involves not only "representative harmony" but visual imagery of
a correspondent sort: the clumsiness and ugliness of the dull,
the filthy foulness of their games, in which moral horror turns
physical.

> Slow rose a form, in majesty of Mud;
> Shaking the horrors of his sable brows,
> And each ferocious feature grim with ooze.

Pope was not a metaphysician; and it is unlikely that in another age he would have attempted to be, though he might well
have been something else -- a "metaphysical poet." His "views"
are flat and tiresome when he expresses them in general terms,
when (as in his letters) he undertakes to moralize like a noble
Roman. If he could turn a maxim, it was not this which made
him, and keeps him, a poet but his power to see and hear what
he felt, to find correlatives for his feelings toward people and

doctrines. He images Hervey as a bug, a spaniel, a puppet, a toad; the scholars as grubs preserved in amber; the bad poet as a spider; the virtuosi as "locusts blackening all the land"; he sees Chaos regain its dominion.

> Light dies before Thy uncreating word;
> Thy hand, great Anarch! lets the curtain fall,
> And Universal Darkness buries all.

POPE'S GROTTO: THE MAZE OF FANCY

Frederick Bracher

I

Long after the death of Alexander Pope, his grotto at
Twickenham continued to be one of England's major literary
shrines, and a popular resort of tourists and sightseers. Horace Walpole used to take parties over from Strawberry Hill,
and pious disciples of the great Augustan poet came from all
parts of England to admire and pay homage. For twenty years
Pope had enlarged and embellished it, spending, according to
Martha Blount,[1] over a thousand pounds on it. Robert Dodsley
expressed a fairly common opinion in his verses on "The Cave
of Pope": "Thy sacred grot shall with thy name survive."[2]

Yet today the grotto, though some of it still survives in
the physical sense,[3] is almost forgotten, and is mentioned by
scholars and critics only in passing. The garden, to which the
grotto was an entrance, is still justly famous, and its diminutive mounts, serpentine walks, shell temple, and wild-wood
have been fully discussed as a stage in the development of the
natural garden.[4] But a garden is ephemeral and temporary at
best, and Pope's frequent replanting and redesigning of his garden seem to reflect little more of his personality than his restlessness and love of pottering.

An artificial grotto, however, especially one as large as
Pope's, is a relatively permanent construction, not to be dug
up and replanned overnight or in the course of a dull winter.
During the twenty-odd years in which Pope was working on it,
the grotto did not so much alter as grow; and the slow changes
it underwent are significant of a strong and continuing interest.
The purpose of this paper is to determine, so far as possible,
exactly what the grotto was like, how it compared with what
may be called the traditional grotto -- that ubiquitous eighteenth-
century garden ornament -- and what it reveals of the taste and

Reprinted from Huntington Library Quarterly, Vol. 12 (1949), pp. 140-162,
with corrections by the author, by permission of author and publisher.

personality of Alexander Pope.

Garden-grottoes were common enough in Pope's day, as
they had been since the Renaissance. Ultimately, the grotto
goes back to the classical nymphaeum, a natural cave with a
spring, supposedly the home of a nymph.[5] The essential elements were overhanging rock and running water, though moss,
trailing vines, and shining minerals are often added, especially
in literary tradition. Greek and Roman gardeners, lacking a
natural cavern, often built artificial grottoes, sometimes in
imitation of nature but sometimes expanded into halls which became dedicated to the Muses and were used for philosophical
discussions. The tradition that grottoes and springs are a haunt
of the Muses is a poetic fiction which has flourished since Greek
and Roman times, and it was particularly prevalent among the
poets of the seventeenth and eighteenth centuries. Milton invokes the sisters of the sacred well that from beneath the seat
of Jove doth spring, and Thomas Warton the elder, though he
does not claim such honors for himself, refers, in "A Farewell
to Poetry," to the solemn grot where Homer first conceived his
mighty scheme.

Whatever the poets might pretend, the garden-grotto, during the Renaissance, became primarily a show-place: the rude
rock was often replaced by colored tiles and mosaics, and the
spring was elaborated into fountains and intricate water-works.
The fountains of the Pratolino Villa in Florence were especially
famous,[6] but England also had some notable examples of Renaissance exuberance and ingenuity in the management of running
water. Perhaps the most famous was the grotto of the Earl of
Pembroke in his garden at Wilton, mentioned approvingly by
Evelyn.[7] It is, according to Celia Fiennes,[8] "garnished with
many fine ffigures of ye Goddesses, and about two yards off the
doore is severall pipes in a line that with a sluce spouts water
up to wett the strangers." The inner rooms also contained damp
surprises for visitors: "by the turning their wires ye water
runnes in ye rockes — you see and hear it and also it is so contrived in one room yt it makes ye melody of Nightingerlls and
all sorts of birds." But when spectators went to look more
closely, they were squirted from concealed pipes. The Duke of
Devonshire's house near Chesterfield also boasted elaborate
water-works -- two stone nymphs with water pouring from
pitchers in their hands, and a brass willow tree which could

drip rain from each leaf. The grotto here, according to Celia
Fiennes,[9] was "all stone pavement Roofe and sides, . . .
designed to supply all ye house wth water, besides severall
ffanceyes to make diversion." It also contained a sunken bath tub.
    Most Renaissance and seventeenth-century grottoes, both in
England and on the Continent, seem to have been highly formal
and artificial, often constructed above ground, lined with finished stone or tile, and furnished with statues and urns. The
Grotto of Thetis at Versailles was a large building with a triple-
arched portico, in which almost the only remaining hint of the
aquatic rusticity of a nymphaeum was the shells with which the
interior was finished.[10] This represents perhaps an extreme in
artificiality, though Merlin's Cave, which Stephen Duck tended
for Queen Caroline in London, was likewise a far cry from the
Egerian grot of the classical poets.
    But the original tradition of sylvan ruggedness persists
even in the midst of baroque splendor. On the Continent, about
the middle of the sixteenth century, tufa was used for its picturesque effect in grottoes, and began to replace colored tile
and mosaic.[11] In England, natural caves were popular with
travelers and sightseers. Celia Fiennes[12] calls Poole's Hole
near Buxton in Derbyshire "a wonder," and she speaks with enthusiasm of the dripping water, craggy rocks, and glittering
minerals. She was also impressed by another "wonder" — the
Devil's Arse, near Casleton, a natural cave with an underground
river, and by the "glistering rocks" of Oakley Hole, near Bristol (from which Pope later secured a piece of petrified wood for
his own grotto). Evelyn, too, had a feeling for the aesthetic
possibilities of natural rock and water. He says of Sir Guy of
Warwick's cave, " 'Tis a squalid den made in the rock, crown'd
yet with venerable oakes and looking on a goodly streame, so
as, were it improv'd as it might be, 'twere capable of being
made a most romantiq and pleasant place."[13] And he was impressed by the sublimity of Cliveden, whose "proud alcove,
The bower of wanton Shrewsbury and love" was known to Pope:
"I went to Clifden, that stupendous natural rock, wood, and
prospect, of ye Duke of Buckingham's. . . . The grotts in ye
chalky rock are pretty: 'tis a most romantic object, and the
place altogether answers the most poetical description. . . ."[14]
    Thomas Burnett in 1684 thought that "it would be very
pleasant to read good descriptions of these Subterraneous places,

and of all the strange works of Nature there; how she furnish-
eth these dark neglected Grottoes; they have often a little
Brook runs murmuring through them, and the roof is commonly
a kind of petrifi'd Earth or Icy fret-work; proper enough for
such rooms."[15] Burnett is speaking of natural caves, but his
description might also do for the grotto Pope actually constructed. The kind of romantic cavern upon which Shaftesbury placed
his seal of approval in 1711[16] not only anticipates the taste of
the later eighteenth century, but marks a return to the classical
conception of the nymphaeum:

> I shall no longer resist the passion growing in me
> for things of a natural kind; where neither art, nor the
> conceit or caprice of man has spoil'd their genuine
> order, by breaking in upon that primitive state. Even
> the rude rocks, the mossy caverns, the irregular un-
> wrought grotto's, and broken falls of water, with all
> the horrid graces of the wilderness itself, as repre-
> senting Nature more, will be the more engaging, and
> appear with a magnificence beyond the formal mockery
> of princely gardens.

Here the wheel has come full circle: Shaftesbury's budding romantic taste, rejecting the truly pseudo-classic grotto of the
Renaissance, has returned to the sweet water and living rock
celebrated by Virgil. In his grotto at the Leasowes, Shenstone
carved the following quotation from the Aeneid, which, according to Robert Dodsley,[17] he considered the very definition of a
grotto:

> Intus aquae dulces, vivoque sedilia saxo;
> Nympharum domus.
> > Book I, 167.

If we turn for a moment from the actual form of the traditional seventeenth- and eighteenth-century grotto to the motives
behind it, we find a similar diversity of intentions. Some of the
purposes of the garden-grotto have already been mentioned:
the home of the muses and hence a source of poetic inspiration;
the show-place, for the pleasure and astonishment of friends;[18]
the occasion of a romantic thrill, induced by the shock of darkness

and rugged rock-faces, as in a natural cave. To these must be
added some more characteristically eighteenth-century uses.
   The grotto was cultivated as a cool summer retreat, a
"place of shade, or estivation," as Bacon put it in his essay
"Of Building." Bacon's attitude toward the grotto was strictly
practical: he was less concerned with appearances than with
making sure that it be "level upon the floor, no whit sunken
under ground, to avoid all dampishness." But many of the poets
joined with Akenside in ignoring the dampishness and longing

> . . . beneath
> Some grotto's dripping arch, at height of noon
> To slumber, shelter'd from the burning heaven.[19]

This sentiment would seem to be more proper to the original
Mediterranean home of the muses than to England, as Dr. Johnson grumpily pointed out to the Lincolnshire lady who in defense
of her grotto asked "Would it not be a pretty cool habitation in
summer, Mr. Johnson!" "I think it would, Madam (replied he),
-- for a toad."[20] But James Thomson and the Wartons felt differently:

> Thrice happy he! who . . .
> . . . in the gelid caverns, wood-bine wrought,
> And fresh bedewed with ever-spouting streams,
> Sits coolly calm.[21]

   The quiet, secluded grotto served also, at least in literature, as a place of retirement — a "twilight, solemn cell for
musing Melancholy made," as Thomas Warton the elder put it.
Gay's Panthea longs for "some melancholy cave . . . where I
may waste in tears my hours away," and later in the century
the grotto becomes established as part of the conventional setting for the poetry of withdrawal and white melancholy.
   Finally, the ornamentation of grottoes served as an opportunity for the exercise of the builder's taste — a lesser art, to
be sure, but one in which the artist might yet take pride. Anthony Whistler, in "To Lady Fane, on her Grotto at Basilden,"[22]
1746, praises

> The beauties of this grott divine;

> What miracles are wrought by shells,
> Where nicest taste and fancy join.

Pope himself in his "Inscription on a Grotto of Shells at Crux-easton, the Work of Nine Young Ladies" describes "this radiant pile" as

> The glittering emblem of each spotless dame,
> Clear as her soul and shining as her frame.

Addison, to be sure, pokes mild fun at literary ladies who dabble in grotto-building. Leonora, whose "reading has lain very much among romances," has shaped the rocks around her country seat "into artificial grottoes covered with woodbines and jessamines. . . . The springs are made to run among pebbles, and by that means taught to murmur very agreeably."[23] Later, he comments

> There is a very particular kind of work which of late
> several ladies here in our kingdom are very fond of,
> which seems very well adapted to a poetical genius:
> it is the making of grottos. I know a lady who has a
> very beautiful one composed by herself; nor is there
> one shell in it not stuck up by her own hand.[24]

But there is no trace of irony in most of the verse eulogizing grottoes. Soame Jenyns (Dodsley's Collection, 1782, III, 149), wrote a poem "To a Lady, Sent with a Present of Shells and Stones designed for a Grotto." He describes his shells and stones as "the lovely sportings of a hand divine," but adds that they will be even more pleasing when "in your Grotto plac'd, They plainly speak the fair disposer's taste."

Many of Pope's early critics agreed with Warburton that "the beauty of his poetic genius in the disposition and ornaments of this romantic recess [the grotto], appears to as much advantage as in his best contrived Poems."[25]

William Mason, like Dodsley, regarded the grotto as one of Pope's major works. The edition of Musaeus printed for Robert Dodsley in 1747 has on the title page an engraving by F. Hayman showing Pope slumped in a chair of stone, dying in his grotto. He is consoled by a female figure, Virtue, and by

three poets. Chaucer and Spenser compliment him on his smooth
rhymes and his pastorals. Milton praises him for "countless
graces," and cites, as a particular example of these, the grotto:

> Various this peaceful scene; this mineral roof;
> This 'semblage meet of coral, ore, and shell;
> These pointed crystals fair, mid each obscure
> Bright glist'ring; all these slowly dripping rills,
> That tinkling stray amid the cooly cave.

Pope rejects the tribute, as recalling

> . . . the toys of thoughtless youth,
> When flow'ry fiction held the place of truth,
> When fancy rul'd . . .

But it is clear that Mason considered the grotto a major manifestation of Pope's taste and genius.

II

What was Pope's grotto really like? Aside from the incidental comments of men who, like Mason, Dodsley, and the
Wartons, might have visited the spot, there are four principal
sources of information: 1. Pope's letter to Edward Blount,
June 2, 1725.[26] 2. A floor-plan of the grotto drawn by Pope
himself in December, 1740. The original sketch is in the Harvard Library, but it has been reproduced in Robert Carruthers,
The Life of Alexander Pope (London, 1857), p. 175. 3. "An
Epistolary Description of the Late Mr. Pope's House and Gardens at Twickenham," by an anonymous correspondent to The
Newcastle General Magazine, January, 1748.[27] 4. A Plan of
Mr. Pope's Garden (London, 1745), by J. Serle [sic], Pope's
gardener.
This last is a small volume containing a "Plan of the Grotto," delineated by Searle, and an engraved illustration of the
interior, as well as some description of the grotto. Searle was
more interested in detailing the sources of the mineral ornaments in each room — the marble from the Grotto of Egeria
near Rome, the gold and silver ore from Mexico and Peru, the

spar and minerals from Mr. Borlase, etc. — than in describing
the grotto's over-all effect. But his map of the grotto is invaluable, and the key, in which the various minerals are located
on the map, enables one to get a fairly clear picture of the
grotto as it was at Pope's death. The Hoe copy of Searle's Plan
(now at the Huntington Library) has bound with it three sepia
and two wash drawings which apparently depict parts of the
grotto -- the entrances and some of the interior. It has also
bound with it a page from an unidentified book -- an engraved
"Plan of the Grotto of the late Alexr. Pope Esqr. at Twickenham. Sixty four feet long. 1785."

The grotto one reconstructs from these sources is a very
ornate and elaborate piece of work. Pope's house was on the
bank of the Thames, with a lawn running down to the water. But
the garden area to the rear was separated from the house by
the main highway to London, and for the sake of privacy and
easy access, Pope dug a tunnel under the house and the highway.
This simple tunnel, from river-lawn to garden, was, however,
only a beginning. By 1745, when Searle published his Plan, the
grotto consisted of five caverns, a lateral connecting passage,
a tunnel under the highway, and two galleries, or "porches" as
Pope called them, at either end of the main tunnel.

Facing the lawn and river was a long porch, at right angles
to the tunnel, with a door and two windows opening on the lawn.
This gallery was light and airy; the walls were finished with
crystals, blood-stone, amethyst, and ores. A statue stood at
either end, and the porch was furnished with curios -- coral,
petrified moss, a hummingbird's nest, two stones from the
Giant's Causeway, and the like. Behind this gallery, the central
tunnel had been hollowed out to make a sizable cavern dedicated
to the Rev. D. William Borlase, who had contributed most of the
minerals with which the walls were furnished -- purple, yellow,
black, and white spars and ores, with "large clumps of Cornish
diamonds."

On either side of the Borlase chamber were two small
caverns, about eleven feet square, if one can trust the scale
of the plans. The one to the left is labeled, on the 1785 Plan,
"The Cave of Pope"; it is shown as roughly octagonal in shape,
with busts and urns around the wall.[28] The walls were finished
with the usual marbles, spars, fossils, and gems, but the roof
was made of "small stones, incrusted over, out of the river

Thames." Just outside the Cave of Pope was an exit from the grotto, and stairs leading up to the house. This, presumably, was the room

> Where, nobly-pensive, ST. JOHN sate and thought;
> Where British sighs from dying WYNDHAM stole,
> And the bright flame was shot thro' MARCHMONT's Soul.[29]

when these and others of the Opposition (including the Prince and Princess of Wales) met in 1739 to plot the downfall of Walpole.[30] The opposite chamber, to the right of the central Borlase room, contained a large pool (Pope calls it a "bagnio" on his sketch), built up of rock-work and planted with fern, hart's-tongue, and other plants. The roof was of purple and yellow spar; the walls were finished with marble, mundics, and various petrifactions.

All three of these rooms opened into a lateral hall, at right angles to the main tunnel; this hall runs "to the house" on the left and "to the Cold Bath" on the right (1785 Plan). Immediately behind the intersection of main tunnel and lateral hall, the main tunnel widened out into the largest chamber of all -- the one with pieces of mirror and the orbicular lamp of alabaster in the ceiling. It was finished, according to Searle, with yellow and red spars and masses of Cornish diamonds. Beyond this room the tunnel contracted into a narrow twenty-foot passage leading under the highway to the garden, but even this was finished with flints, moss of many sorts, and "flakes of gold clift."

There was one more chamber — small, but in one sense probably the most romantic of the entire grotto. It was to the right of the large central room, but it opened on the dark hall leading to the cold bath. It seems to have been a winding cul-de-sac, described on the 1785 Plan as "a dark cavern," and by Searle as containing "some very natural Rock-work, compiled of flints and cinders from the glass-houses, furnaces, etc." There were no windows, no lamps, no shining mirror fragments -- only a twisting passage ending abruptly in a rock-face of dark stone. Here a person unable to visit Poole's Hole or the Devil's Arse might enjoy the thrill of imagining himself in the very bowels of the earth.

Near the garden end of the tunnel was a door, and beyond it a very small square porch with statues, opening into the garden. The walls were finished with fossils, snakestones, verd antique from Egypt, amethysts, and petrified moss. In the middle of this ante-chamber was a spring, which trickled down through the various chambers to the river.

The correspondent of The Newcastle General Magazine was particularly struck by the elaborateness of the water-works. His account of the general plan of the grotto is vague and impressionistic: "In passing it (the main tunnel) along, we are presented with many Openings and Cells, which owe their Forms to a Diversity of Pillars and Jambs, ranged after no set Order or Rule. . . . They seem as roughly hew'd out of Rocks and Beds of mineral Strata, discovering in the Fissures and angular Breaches, Variety of Flints, Spar, Ores, Shells, &c." But when the correspondent describes the "Stream issuing from the Spring of Water," he becomes lyrical and rhapsodic:

> Here it gurgles in a gushing Rill thro' fractur'd Ores and Flints; there it drips from depending Moss and Shells; here again, washing Beds of Sand and Pebbles, it rolls in Silver Streamlets; and there it rushes out in Jets and Fountains; while the Caverns of the Grot incessantly echo with a soothing Murmur of aquatick Sounds. To multiply this Diversity, and still more increase the Delight, Mr. Pope's poetic Genius has introduced a kind of Machinery, which performs the same Part in the Grotto that supernal Powers and incorporeal Beings act in the heroick Species of Poetry: This is effected by disposing Plates of Looking glass in the obscure Parts of the Roof and Sides of the Cave, where a sufficient Force of Light is wanting to discover the Deception, while the other Parts, the Rills, Fountains, Flints, Pebbles, &c. being duly illuminated, are so reflected by the various posited Mirrors, as, without exposing the Cause, every Object is multiplied, and its Position represented in a surprizing Diversity. Cast your eyes upward, and you half shudder to see Cataracts of Water precipitating over your Head, from impending Stones and Rocks, while saliant Spouts rise in rapid Streams at your Feet: Around, you are equally surprized with flowing Rivulets and rolling Waters, that rush over airey

Precipices, and break amongst Heaps of ideal Flints
and Spar. Thus, by a fine Taste and happy Management of Nature, you are presented with an undistin-
guishable Mixture of Realities and Imagery.31

Here is rock and water, with a vengeance. And there was
more of it outside. Searle describes the entrance from the garden as being composed of "various sorts of Stones thrown
promiscuously together, in imitation of an old Ruine." The
sketches in the Hoe copy of Searle's Plan include four rustic
entrances to a grotto. One of these is very likely the garden
entrance: the others may be the side entrances shown on the
1785 plan. Over the entrance was carved a quotation from Horace, suggesting Pope's probably imaginary desire to withdraw
from life into the sober retirement of these rocks and ruins:
"Secretum iter, et fallentis semita vitae."32

III

The composite picture drawn from these sources goes far
to justify Montague Summers' judgment: "No whole-hearted or
single-minded Classicist -- using the word strictly in the Augustan sense -- could have conceived and builded that delicious 'Aegerian grot' at Twickenham. . . . Here we have a baroque
romanticism no genuine Augustan would have tolerated for a
moment."33 Moreover, it must be remembered that this picture
of the grotto represents only one of its stages -- the final stage,
but only in the sense that Pope did not survive to carry the work
further. For over twenty years the grotto, like the garden, was
in process of construction and alteration, growing always more
extensive and more ornate. In his letters Pope is continually
announcing that he has put the finishing touches to his grotto
and then, a few months later, speaking enthusiastically of new
building or asking for more minerals and ore. Pope's grotto,
in short, does not represent a mere passing fancy or idle whim;
it reflects an active and continuing interest throughout Pope's
mature years. Through his correspondence, it is possible to
trace roughly the development of the grotto, and to get some
clues to the motives and tastes behind this extraordinary building program.

The mood in which Pope began is essentially that of "Windsor Forest," or "Eloisa to Abelard." In December, 1713, Pope is revising "Windsor Forest," and he writes, "I am endeavouring to raise up around me a painted scene of woods and forests in verdure and beauty. . . . I am wandering through bowers and grottoes in conceit."[34] The references to grottoes in his translations suggests that he had the classical nymphaeum in mind: "The rocks around . . . with native moss o'ergrown" ("Sappho to Phaon," 164), "The grots that echo to the tinkling rills" ("Eloisa to Abelard," 158). But in these early works and letters the neo-classic spirit — the restraint and decorum of the Augustans -- is notably absent. In a letter to Lady Mary Wortley Montagu, November, 1716 (Works, IX, 361), Pope describes himself as "romantic," and defends romantics as being in the right. In 1719 Pope sent Bishop Atterbury a collection of Arabian tales, which Pope obviously admired, though Atterbury damned them with the adjectives "romantic, wild, and absurd." The word "romantic" appears rather frequently in Pope's correspondence between 1716 and 1720.[35] It seems to mean, most often, reckless, fervent, or unrestrained, but it is also used to characterize the landscape around Stonor: "woody hills stumbling upon one another confusedly . . . with some mounts and waterfalls."[36] Professor Root[37] has pointed out that, during the years just preceding the construction of the grotto, Pope was deep in Fancy's maze, indulging his native "romantic" taste; and though he later stooped to truth and moralized his song, he did not impose a similar Augustan discipline on himself in the enlargement and ornamentation of the grotto.

During the winter of 1718 Pope seems to have established himself at Twickenham and busied himself with "draughts, elevations, profiles, perspectives, etc., of every palace and garden proposed."[38] A letter of December 31, 1718 (Works, VIII, 41), urges Broome to come for a visit: "I will tell Mrs. Betty Marriot such wonders of the enchanted bowers, silver streams, opening avenues, rising mounts, and painted grottos that her very curiosity shall bring her to us." By the spring of 1720 he is dividing his time between Homer and masons and gardeners (Works, VI, 271), and in the spring of 1722, Lady Mary Wortley Montagu writes to the Countess of Mar:

POPE'S GROTTO: THE MAZE OF FANCY

> Mr. Pope . . . continues to embellish his house at
> Twickenham. He has made a subterranean grotto,
> which he has finished with looking glass, and they
> tell me it has a very good effect.[39]

This effect must have been a strange mixture of nature and
art, but Pope had only contempt for consistency of style in gardens and building. In a letter to Bathurst, September 23, 1719
(Works, VIII, 329), he goes out of his way to criticize the narrowness of those gardeners who admire only one kind, or style,
and he adds, "I have lately been with my Lord * *, who is a
zealous yet a charitable planter, and has so bad a taste as to
like all that is good." A letter to Martha Blount in 1722 (Works,
IX, 300 f.) includes a long account of the gardens at Sherborne.
Pope stresses their natural landscaping (the beauty of the gardens, he says, arises from their irregularity); but he also
praises the urns in the bower, and proposes the addition of
some octagonal beds. On the whole, however, what he chiefly
admired was the picturesque rusticity of the place: "those views
which are more romantic than imagination can form them . . .
venerable wood, overarched by Nature, . . . natural cascade
. . . rustic seat of stone . . . this whole part inexpressibly
awful and solemn . . . the ruins, to complete the solemnity of
the scene."
Pope's taste in gardening was eclectic, beyond question,
and what could be more romantic (at least in Pope's sense of
the term) than an unrestrained eclecticism of personal taste?
The dominance of whim and fancy over consistency and decorum
is apparent also in the lengthy description of his grotto which
Pope wrote to Edward Blount on June 2, 1725 (Works, VI,
383 f.). He stresses the natural rusticity of the place and the
fact that it owes little to art, but he exhibits an almost childish
pleasure in the glitter of his alabaster lamp reflecting a thousand pointed rays from the pieces of looking glass in the ceiling.[40] The passage has often been reprinted, but since it is
Pope's fullest account of the grotto, it is worth quoting once
more:

> I have put the last hand to my works of this kind,
> in happily finishing the subterraneous way and grotto.
> I there found a spring of the clearest water, which

falls in a perpetual rill, that echoes through the cavern
day and night. From the river Thames, you see through
my arch up a walk of the wilderness, to a kind of open
temple, wholly composed of shells in the rustic manner;
and from that distance under the temple you look down
through a sloping arcade of trees, and see the sails on
the river passing suddenly and vanishing as through a
perspective glass. When you shut the doors of this
grotto it becomes on the instant, from a luminous
room, a Camera obscura, on the walls of which all the
objects of the river, hills, woods, and boats, are forming a moving picture in their visible radiations; and
when you have a mind to light it up, it affords you a
very different scene. It is finished with shells inter-
spersed with pieces of looking-glass in angular forms;
and in the ceiling is a star of the same material, at
which when a lamp, of an orbicular figure of thin alabaster, is hung in the middle, a thousand pointed rays
glitter, and are reflected over the place. There are
connected to this grotto by a narrower passage two
porches with niches and seats, -- one toward the river,
of smooth stones, full of light, and open; the other
toward the arch of trees, rough with shells, flints,
and iron-ore. The bottom is paved with simple pebble,
as the adjoining walk up the wilderness to the temple
is to be cockle-shells, in the natural taste, agreeing
not ill with the little dripping murmur, and the aquatic
idea of the whole place. It wants nothing to complete it
but a good statue with an inscription. . . .

> Hujus Nympha loci, sacri custodia fontis,
> Dormio, dum blandae sentio murmur aquae . . .

You will
think I have been very poetical in this description, but
it is pretty near the truth. I wish you were here to
bear testimony how little it owes to art, either the
place itself, or the image I give of it.

It is fairly certain that this, the first major stage of the
grotto, for all its ornate rusticity, is considerably simpler

than the elaborate system of chambers pictured by Searle. In 1725 the grotto seems to have been a simple tunnel widened out in the center to form a room. The tunnel was continued into the garden itself by an arch of trees running to the shell temple. The "luminous room," with looking glass and lamp is pretty certainly the large central chamber numbered 3 on Searle's plan. At either end of the tunnel are the two porches, one at the river entrance, roomy, and smooth, and one at the garden entrance, small and rustic. The central room must have been quite dark (hence the lamp of thin alabaster), and it must have been used largely as a show place — a mere stopping point on the way to the garden.

During the next six years, Pope's letters contain few references to the grotto.[41] Presumably, little work was done on it, and it remained essentially a wayside shrine, dedicated to the muses and to the astonishment of friends and visitors. Pope was busy during this period. Two of the summers (the best time for building) were taken up with visits from Swift, and Pope was at first working on the Dunciad and later waging war against the outraged dunces.

But during the ten years from 1731 to 1741 there are fairly frequent references in the letters to building and to the grotto. Swift may have started it. On April 20, 1731, he wrote urging Pope to repair his health by recreation: "Learn to play at cards, or tables, or bowls; . . . contrive new tramgams in your garden, or in Mrs. Howard's, or my Lord Bolingbroke's" (Works, VII, 226). Pope seems to have taken the last of this advice to heart: in November, 1732, he is "engaged in building" (Works, IX, 499), and the following spring he is constructing a "triumphal arch" leading into the garden (Works, VI, 341). On November 13, 1733 (Works, X, 51), Pope acknowledges an "agreeable present to my grotto" from Aaron Hill — shells "to embellish your marine temple." During the summer of 1734, Pope is advising Lord Bathurst on the ornamentation of his grounds, and drawing sketches and plans for him (Works, VIII, 345, footnote). In the spring of 1735, he is building the stone obelisk, in honor of his mother, at the far end of the garden, and adding "two new ovens and stoves, and a hot-house for ananas" (Works, IX, 129). By mid-winter the shell-temple has fallen down and must be rebuilt, Pope has been planting, and "my alterations are what you would not conceive" (Works, IX, 134). Next spring

Pope writes to Swift (Works, VII, 343) "my house is enlarged, and the gardens extend and flourish." In the fall of 1736 he complains half-seriously of "workmen in my garden" (Works, IX, 457).

On December 29, 1740, Pope drew his sketch of the grotto for Dr. Oliver at Bath, and on September 3, 1740, he wrote the letter to Bolingbroke containing the verses "On His Grotto at Twickenham":

> Next to patching up my constitution, my great
> business has been to patch up a grotto (the same you
> have so often sat in in times past under my house) with
> all the varieties of nature under ground, spars, min-
> erals, and marbles. I hope yet to live to philosophise
> with you in this museum, which is now a study for
> virtuosi, and a scene for contemplation [Works, VII,
> 406].

A month later he writes to Ralph Allen, "My grotto is now fin-ished . . . though still I could improve, had I more fine stone. It has cost infinitely more time and pains that I could have con-ceived."[42] On October 8, 1740, in a letter to Dr. Oliver, Pope announces that he has "entirely finished all except the outward façade." He also refers to the grotto as "my present pride and my pleasure," and confesses "I am so fond of it, that I should be more sorry to leave it unfinished, than any other work I at present can think of."[43]

The grotto was, in fact, never really finished. During the summer of 1741, Pope was writing to various acquaintances for more stone and minerals, and requesting a "hogshead of scallop shells" from Judge Fortescue.[44] There is some indica-tion that he had still further excavation in mind. On July 30, 1741, Thomas Edwards wrote to Richard Cambridge to explain a request for an additional shipment of stone: "I yesterday re-ceived an account that he [Pope] has enlarged his design intend-ing to add two rooms, which have windows into each wing of the Grotto, one to be covered with shells, and the other with min-erals."[45] These proposed rooms do not appear on any of the plans of the grotto, but the references to them indicate Pope's strong urge to go on building.

POPE'S GROTTO: THE MAZE OF FANCY

There is evidence in the letters that Pope continued to dec-
orate and embellish until 1743 at least, but his own sketch shows
conclusively that the major expansion of the grotto to the size
depicted by Searle had been completed by 1740. Moreover, the
reference in Pope's "Verses on His Grotto" (1740) to the

> . . . shadowy Cave
> Where ling'ring drops from min'ral Roofs distill,
> And pointed Crystals break the sparkling Rill

suggests that the water-works, described so enthusiastically by
the correspondent of The Newcastle General Magazine, were
also in operation by this time.

The letter to Bolingbroke, besides recording the completion
of the second stage in the building of the grotto, also marks a
new stage in its utilization. It is now being fitted out with "all
the varieties of nature under ground," and has become a museum, "a study for virtuosi," as well as a scene for contemplation. The references in the letters which follow bear out the
conclusion that Pope had turned collector. His old love for mere
glitter persists; he writes to the Duchess of Marlborough in
1741 (Works, V, 410)

> I must add, to my shame, I am one of that sort who
> at his heart loves bawbles better (than riches), and
> throws away his gold and silver for shells and glitter-
> ing stones, as you will find when you see . . . my
> Grotto.

But most of the references are requests for, or thanks for,
more minerals and mundics.[46]

Pope's standing as a virtuoso collector in the last years
of his life is strongly suggested by the tone of his correspondence with Sir Hans Sloane. He writes as an amateur, and with
proper deference to the great collector whose assortment of
natural curiosities was later to become part of the original
British Museum, but still on terms of equality, as one collector to another. In a letter of March 30, 1742 (Works, IX, 514),
he speaks deprecatingly of "the minerals and fossils which I
have gathered," and with appropriate respect of Sloane's collection — "so extensive a view of Nature in her most curious

113

works." But he is now well enough established as a collector to receive and gracefully acknowledge the gift from Sloane of "two joints of the Giant's Causeway" for his grotto, which, he adds not altogether truthfully, "consists wholly of natural productions, owing nothing to the chisel or polish."

IV

What are we to make of the spectacle of the greatest poet of the Augustan age digging a cave like any small boy, and for twenty years enlarging it and decorating it with "bawbles" and shining ore? Dr. Johnson, at least, had no doubt of the answer. He could be superciliously tolerant of Shenstone's enthusiasm for gardening:

> Whether . . . to make water run where it will be heard and to stagnate where it will be seen . . . demands any great powers of mind, I will not enquire: perhaps a sullen and surly speculator may think such performances rather the sport than the business of human reason. But it must be at least confessed, that to embellish the form of nature is an innocent amusement . . .[47]

But he sternly reproves Pope's vanity and frivolity:

> . . . being under the necessity of making a subterraneous passage to a garden on the other side of the road, he adorned it with fossile bodies, and dignified it with the title of a grotto, a place of silence and retreat, from which he endeavoured to persuade his friends and himself that cares and passions could be excluded.
>
> A grotto is not often the wish or pleasure of an Englishman, who has more frequent need to solicit than exclude the sun; but Pope's excavation was requisite as an entrance to his garden, and, as some men try to be proud of their defects, he extracted an ornament from an inconvenience, and vanity produced a grotto where necessity enforced a passage. It may

be frequently remarked of the studious and speculative, that they are proud of trifles, and that their
amusements seem frivolous and childish. . . .[48]

Other critics echo Dr. Johnson's disapproval. In the later
stages of her unhappy relations with Pope, Lady Mary Wortley
Montagu wrote a satirical fragment, "The Court of Dullness,"
in which the grotto -- that "palace plac'd beneath a muddy road"
— is ridiculed:

> Here chose the goddess her belov'd retreat,
> Which Phoebus tries in vain to penetrate,
> Adorn'd within with shells of small expense,
> (Emblems of tinsel rhyme and trifling sense).
> Perpetual fogs enclose the sacred cave;
> The neighbouring sinks their fragrant odors gave . . .[49]

Lady Mary refuses to accept the pretense which for Pope and
his friends turned a dank, unwholesome cavern into a rocaille
fairyland, and her realistic comments throw, by contrast, a
revealing light on the imaginative effort which lay behind Pope's
twenty years of building and ornamentation.

Not that Pope was solemn about his Villa. His letters make
it clear that he realized the absurdity of crowding all the paraphernalia of a large manor house and park into his five acres
of ground. He writes to the Earl of Strafford in 1725 (Works,
X, 183)

> I am as busy in three inches of gardening as any man
> can be in threescore acres. I fancy myself like the
> fellow that spent his life in cutting ye twelve apostles
> in one cherry stone. I have a Theatre, an Arcade, a
> Bowling-green, a Grove, & what not? in a bit of
> ground that would have been but a plate of sallet to
> Nebuchadnezzar, the first day he was turnd to graze.

And he was evidently used to joking about his diminutive estate
with Bathurst, whose tremendous grounds at Cirencester Pope
knew and loved. Bathurst's invitation for a visit sets the tone
(Works, VIII, 337):

If you refuse coming I will immediately send one of
my wood carts and bring away your whole house and
gardens, and stick it in the midst of Oakley wood,
where it will never be heard of any more, unless some
of the children find it out in nutting season and take
possession of it, thinking I have made it for them.

Such light-hearted banter merely proves that Pope knew
what he was doing. He was deliberately playing a part — pretending, or feigning; and the ability to feign (and to make other people accept the figments of one's imagination) is an essential
element of the poet's gift. Pope had early announced the importance, to the man of genius, of a strong and active imagination.[50] And all his early poetry shows clear evidence of his
gift in this respect. The contrast with Swift is instructive. The
Dean's fantasy, however extravagant it may become in Gulliver's Travels, is always realistic and wide-awake. If Swift constructed imaginary gardens, he placed real toads in them, and
the reader always feels the firm ground beneath his feet, as
a true Augustan liked to feel it. But in "The Rape of the Lock"
even the passages of brilliant social satire have something of
the unreal, fairy-land quality of the sylphs --

Transparent forms, too fine for mortal sight,
Their fluid bodies half dissolved in light.

Like Congreve, Pope could body forth an imaginary world and
make his friends and readers accept its brilliant artificiality.
Pope's ability to feign (fancy, invention, imagination --
whatever we call it) was well recognized by his contemporaries
and his nineteenth-century critics were not so apt to reproach
him for the overuse of this faculty as for his deficiencies in
taste. Bowles says flatly, "The taste of Pope was perhaps the
best of his age; but nothing can appear more puerile and affected
at this time, than what Warton calls his 'romantic grotto.' "[51]
Carruthers offers an apology ("Some degree of embellishment
was necessary to relieve the gloom and blankness of a subterranean passage"), but on the whole deplores: "There appears an excess of decoration here -- shells, spars, pieces of looking glass,
. . . which must have made the grotto appear out of keeping with the
chaster style of the garden and ornamental grounds."[52]

POPE'S GROTTO: THE MAZE OF FANCY

It is curious to find nineteenth-century editors and critics complaining of a lack of restraint in the author of the "Essay on Criticism," but they may be only underlining a side of Pope's personality which more recently has been too much ignored in the interest of easy generalization. Today most scholars are willing to admit that the "neo-classic" writers were not always restrained by decorum and the Golden Mean. There is much in Pope's life and writing to suggest a fundamental split between his spontaneous preferences and impulses and the neo-classic code which, at least in theory, he accepted. Professor Root has discussed at length the change which Pope himself referred to in the "Epistle to Dr. Arbuthnot" — the turning away from Fancy's maze to the more serious adult business of writing his Moral Essays. Such a change in direction is seldom complete. Remnants of the old impulses and habits inevitably persist; and the grotto would seem to have been a continuing expression of Pope's old delight in wandering in the maze of fancy.

I should be inclined to agree with Professor Havens[53] that ". . . the classicism of the time was a cult, a fad, an artificial taste which grew up under French influence among the more critical." But I should disagree with his judgment that

> Pope was an extreme classicist, a classicist not mere-
> ly because of a theory or fad but thru instinct and
> native feeling. It is impossible to conceive him as
> anything else. Accordingly he fixt extreme classicism
> as the fashion; so that his admirers, classicists them-
> selves but of a milder type, tried to curb their freer
> fancies and be correct.[54]

It seems to me more probable that the influence was the other way round -- that Pope's friends (particularly Bolingbroke and Swift) finally persuaded him that, as England's foremost poet, he ought to put away childish things and write serious poetry. Bolingbroke was urging him, as early as 1724, not to "look on your translations of Homer as the great work of your life. You owe a great deal more to yourself, to your country, and to posterity. Prelude with translations if you please, but after translating what was writ three thousand years ago, it is incumbent upon you that you write, because you are able to write, what will deserve to be translated three thousand years hence into languages as yet perhaps unformed."[55] In any case, Pope did accept his responsibilities as a major poet; as early as 1729 he had told Broome of his intention henceforth to write Horatian epistles,[56] and the Epistle to Dr. Arbuthnot records the change in subject matter which actually had taken place. The great expansion and ornamentation of the grotto took place between the years 1731 and 1740 — the period in which Pope was moralizing his song. His native impulse toward the feigned and extravagant, diverted from expression in his writing, now seems to have turned to his gardens and grotto. Here he could let himself go — pretending to be a Muse-inspired dreamer beside his trickling spring, a shepherd luxuriating in a cool shelter from the sun's scorching rays, a contemplative solitary escaping from the crude confusions of real life, or a virtuoso studying the glittering varieties of Nature underground. If the weight of Augustan opinion forbade the free expression of his fancy in literature, he had ample precedent, in both classical and Renaissance building, for following his own eclectic taste and turning the grotto into a combination of nymphaeum, rococo fairyland, and museum for virtuosi.

NOTES

1   Robert Carruthers, Poetical Works of Alexander Pope (London, 1853), I, 125.

2   Robert Dodsley, A Collection of Poems in Six Volumes by Several Hands (London, 1782), III, 360.

3   Cf. R. W. Babcock, "Pope's Grotto Today," South Atlantic Quarterly, 42 (1943), 292 f. The tunnel, still with fragments of mirror in the ceiling, now leads into the garden of a Catholic school for girls.

4   Cf. in particular B. Sprague-Allen, Tides in English Taste (Harvard University Press, 1937), II, 130 f.

5   Marie Luise Gothein, A History of Garden Art (London, 1928), I, 88.

6   Ibid., I, 248, 285.

7   Diary, July 20, 1654.

8 Through England on a Side Saddle in the Time of William and Mary, being the Diary of Celia Fiennes, edited by Mrs. Griffiths (London, 1888), pp. 4, 5. For this source and the reference to Burnett's The Theory of the Earth, I am indebted to Robert A. Aubin, "Grottoes, Geology, and the Gothic Revival," Studies in Philology, XXXI (1934), 408 f.

9 Ibid., p. 80.

10 Gothein, op. cit., II, 63.

11 Gothein, op. cit., I, 286.

12 Op. cit., p. 84.

13 Diary, Aug. 3, 1654.

14 Diary, July 23, 1679.

15 The Theory of the Earth (The Two First Books) (London, 1684), pp. 115-6.

16 "The Moralists, a Rhapsody," in Characteristicks (London, 1732), II, 393.

17 "A Description of the Leasowes," in Works in Verse and Prose of William Shenstone, Esq., (London, 1777), II, 317.

18 Evelyn (Diary, Oct. 20, 1664) gives us an amusing glimpse of the master of Bushell's Wells at Entstone, proud possessor of two mummies and a "grott where he lay in a hammock like an Indian."

19 "Hymn to the Naiads," in Robert Dodsley's A Collection of Poems in Six Volumes by Several Hands (London, 1782), VI, 4.

20 Hester Lynch Piozzi, "Anecdotes of the Late Samuel Johnson," in Johnsoniana, ed. Robina Napier (London, 1884), p. 83.

21 James Thomson, The Seasons, "Summer," 461 f. Cf. also Thomas Warton I, "An Ode written in a grotto near Farnham in Surrey, call'd Ludlow's Cave" and Thomas Warton II, "On the Approach of Summer."

22 Dodsley's Collection (1782), V, 68.

23 Spectator, No. 37, Apr. 12, 1711.

24 Spectator, No. 632, Dec. 13, 1714.

25 The Works of Alexander Pope (London, 1751), VI, 77.

26 Works, ed. W. Elwin and W. J. Courthope (London, 1871-89), VI, 383 f. All references to Pope's letters, unless otherwise specified, are to this edition.

27 I am indebted for this source to Professor George Sherburn, who, in turn, had it from Dr. T. C. D. Eaves. Dr. Sherburn also kindly supplied information about Pope's sketch of the grotto.

28 Pope's will (William Roscoe, The Works of Alexander Pope, Esq. [London, 1847], I, 491) verifies the existence of these busts. In specific bequests Pope mentions busts of Spenser, Shakespeare, Milton, Dryden, Homer, and Newton. To Martha Blount he leaves "all the furniture of my grotto, . . . urns in my garden . . . whatever is not otherwise disposed of in this will." According to Joseph Warton (The Works of Alexander Pope [London, 1822], I, xxii) some of the urns were the gift of Frederic, Prince of Wales.

29 Pope, "On His Grotto at Twickenham, Composed of Marbles, Spars, Gems, Ores, and Minerals," lines 10-12.

30 Elwin-Courthope, Works, V, 321.

31 The Newcastle General Magazine, Jan., 1748, p. 26.

32 Ibid., p. 27.

33 Montague Summers, The Gothic Quest (London, n.d.), p. 20.

34 Works, VI, 178.

35 Works, IX, 22, 274 n., 359, 361, 365. Cc. also the letter to Martha Blount, Sept. 4, 1728, IX, 312.

36 Works, IX, 312.

37 R. K. Root, The Poetical Career of Alexander Pope (Princeton, 1938).

38 Letter to Jervas, Works, VIII, 27. Since this letter was

rewritten for publication, the date is probably inexact.

39 Correspondence (Everyman ed.), p. 213.

40 Pope's enthusiasm for glitter was lifelong. In an undated letter to Dr. William Oliver, written between 1740 and 1743 (Works, X, 243), he requests more ore from Mr. Borlase — "some of the metallic kind that are most common. So they do but shine and glitter it is enough . . . ."

41 Swift saw and approved it on his visit to England in the summer of 1726. Works, VII, 54, 72.

42 George Paston, Mr. Pope, His Life and Times (London, 1909), II, 633, footnote.

43 Carruthers, The Life of Alexander Pope (London, 1857), pp. 173-74.

44 Helen S. Hughes, "Mr. Pope on His Grotto," Modern Philology, XXVIII (1930), 103.

45 Richard D. Altick, "Mr. Pope Expands His Grotto," Philological Quarterly, XXI (1942), 430.

46 Works, VII, 385; IX, 199, 530-31; X, 113, 243 f.

47 The Lives of the Poets, ed. Napier (London, 1890), III, 287.

48 Ibid., III, 106 f.

49 Works (London, 1803), V, 181.

50 Letter to Jervas, December 12, 1718, Works, VIII, 27.

51 Elwin-Courthope, Works, VI, 384 n.

52 Life (1857), p. 172.

53 R. D. Havens, "Romantic Aspects of the Age of Pope," PMLA, 27 (1912), 298.

54 Ibid., p. 302.

55 Works, VII, 394.

56 Works, VIII, 154-55.

AN ALLUSION TO EUROPE: DRYDEN AND POETIC TRADITION

Reuben Brower

> He professed to have learned his poetry from Dryden,
> whom, whenever an opportunity was presented, he
> praised through his whole life with unvaried liberality;
> and perhaps his character may receive some illustra-
> tion if he be compared with his master.
>
> (Samuel Johnson, Life of Pope)

Any talk of Pope's achievement as a poet or of his relation
to poetic tradition must begin with the tradition of Dryden. Like
Dryden he was catholic in his tastes, and he enjoyed an easy
commerce with the poetry of the past and present. From his
early reading and imitations and translations, it is clear that
Pope had direct and lively contact with Homer and the greater
Roman and English poets and with many lesser English and
French poets of his own generation and of the century before
him. Feeling no nineteenth-century compulsion to be merely
original, he took pleasure in imitating the poets he read and
admired, one and all. Speaking years later of his youthful epic
Alcander, he remarked to Spence,

> I endeavoured, [said he, smiling] in this poem, to
> collect all the beauties of the great epic writers into
> one piece: there was Milton's style in one part, and
> Cowley's in another: here the style of Spenser imitated,
> and there of Statius; here Homer and Virgil, and there
> Ovid and Claudian.

Although it is highly probable that without Dryden's example Pope would have discovered a voice of his own and a way of

Reprinted from R. A. Brower, Alexander Pope, Poetry of Allusion,
Clarendon Press: Oxford, pp. 1-14, by permission of author and publisher. This article appeared earlier in English Literary History, Vol.
19 (1952), pp. 38-48.

mastering this embarrassment of poetical riches, the fact remains that he "learned his poetry" from Dryden and that as Johnson also says,

> By perusing the works of Dryden, he discovered the most perfect fabric of English verse, and habituated himself to that only which he found the best . . .

From Dryden he learned how to imitate without loss of originality, how to make use of the resources of other poets and other poetic modes and yet remain himself and the same. The poetic education he received was more than technical training in versification and practice in the ancient literary art of skilful borrowing. While searching "the pages of Dryden for happy combinations of heroic diction" or more musical cadences, he was also finding his relation to the poetry of the European past and to the mind of Europe. By following Dryden and surpassing him, Pope became after Chaucer, Shakespeare, and Milton the most European of English poets. Reduced to its simplest terms, his problem was how to connect the old world of Homer and Virgil and Horace, or of Spenser and Milton, with the actual society of eighteenth-century London in which he and his readers were living. His success as a poet depended directly on Dryden's achievement in solving a similar problem for the very different society and literary public of the Restoration.

As literary histories of the neo-classical period remind us far too often, it is easier to bury Dryden than to praise him. So much depends on the tradition we choose to place him in and on the standards by which we measure poetic success. If we follow Dr. Johnson and set Dryden in the succession of Waller and Denham, we arrive at a pious tribute to the "reformer of our numbers." If we follow F. R. Leavis and trace "the line of wit," we bring out Dryden's undeniable limitations as compared with Donne or Marvell. (Leavis' strategy was justified in relation to his aims and results: he has made us aware that "serious wit" did not end with the Metaphysicals.) But if we are to make a positive estimate of Dryden's achievement, we should include in his ancestry English poets of the earlier and later Renaissance and their ancient predecessors, and we need to maintain a keen sense of what Dryden accomplished for his contemporaries. So viewed, Dryden marks the reaffirmation of "Europe" in English poetry and culture after an experiment in insularity and at a time of artificial essays in continental "Classicism."

Again, it would be easy to arrive at a rather tepid estimate of Dryden's career -- true enough, but hardly of much concern to readers with a live interest in either history or poetry. Dryden's reaffirmation matters -- aesthetically and historically -- because it is a poet's affirmation, realized in the shaping of new modes of expression and in the writing of poetry which is imaginatively various and unified. His direct critical propaganda for French and Latin literary standards counts for relatively little in the continuing life of the Renaissance tradition. A more adaptable Arnold, like Pope,

> He won his way by yielding to the tyde.

By "indirection," by creating his unique satirical mode, Dryden reaffirmed important European values, while engaging the most lively concerns of his readers. It is to this poetic feat that I want to draw attention.

Dryden's accomplishment is more remarkable in view of the situation in which he wrote. Charles had been "restored," and with him an audience that was alien to the most vigorous of the surviving older poets. Milton withdrew; Cowley retired without producing much of the "wit" he prescribed. Marvell dived as a Metaphysical and came up as a satirist; but as a poet he belonged to another world. Although Dryden talked sentimentally of "retiring," he was unequivocally the "first" man of this

> Laughing, quaffing, and unthinking time.

His success lay in his ability to draw on a wide range of English and European literary traditions while "speaking home" to this audience of Court and City. A glance at his development as a dramatist will suggest how he attained a style which had this twofold effectiveness.

In the period between Astraea Redux and Absalom and Achitophel, while Dryden was mightily pleasing his auditors in the theatre, he struck out two more or less distinct styles which were blended in the successes of his maturity: one, the "heroic"; and the other, the style of public address which he somewhat scornfully regarded as Horatian. Whatever we call

them, both styles bear traces of their mixed European and
English origin. In the process of making his outrageous exper-
iments in drama, the Heroic Plays, Dryden invented a style
that gave an impression of ancient epic grandeur; at times, in
narratives of quite incredible exploits, the impression became
almost convincing, thanks to the skill with which Dryden combined Virgilian allusions with rather obvious echoes of Virgilian
rhythm.

In the last and best of these plays, Aureng-Zebe, we first
hear distinctly what Mark Van Doren calls Dryden's "grouping"
of couplets, an enlargement of rhythm which comes when he
had been reading Shakespeare, and, more significantly, soon
after his reworking of Paradise Lost. Milton's example, along
with Sylvester's and Cowley's, helped fix the Old Testament-
ecclesiastical strain in Dryden's mature heroic style, as it
finally emerged in Absalom and Achitophel. In tone the style is
unmistakably a "translation out of the original tongues."

While Dryden was cultivating a manner that had almost no
appropriateness to his auditors -- except by a law of literary
contraries -- he was learning to speak to them with directness
and ease in his prologues and epilogues. Here he acquired his
mastery of more varied tones; and here "the great reform" of
language and rhythm was most happily realized. The language
is "such words as men did use" (in an age less polished than
our own); and the moulding of speech idiom to the patterns of
the couplet is admirable. After the tepid velleities of Waller —
the "crooner" of the couplet -- Dryden's prologues mark a partial recovery of the toughness and "juice" of Jonsonian English.
But though they are highly original, they are linked via Jonson
with an earlier tradition. The prologue, as used by Jonson to
give instruction in literary taste, is a theatrical form of the
Roman epistle. Dryden's later blend of the prologue-satirical
style with the heroic is anticipated in the insolent debates of
the plays and in the prologues themselves. Given a very slight
excuse, Dryden will sound off with an ancient literary parallel,
or a debased parody of one. Part of the game of amusing his
listeners consisted in deliberately talking over their heads.

The "huddled notions" of Dryden's satiric mode lay in
readiness when the Monmouth "conspiracy" offered the occasion
his genius had been waiting for. He could now compose heroic
narrative and dialogue while talking to his familiar audience.

BROWER

What is remarkable is that in scoring a journalistic and political
success he produced poetry of a high order. Here is a representative passage, the commemoration of Titus Oates, the
Presbyterian "weaver's issue" who testified that the Jesuits
were plotting to murder Charles II:

> Yet, Corah, thou shalt from oblivion pass:
> Erect thyself, thou monumental brass,
> High as the serpent of thy metal made,
> While nations stand secure beneath thy shade.
> What tho' his birth were base, yet comets rise
> From earthly vapours, ere they shine in skies.
> Prodigious actions may as well be done
> By weaver's issue, as by prince's son.
> This arch-attestor for the public good
> By that one deed ennobles all his blood.
> Who ever ask'd the witnesses' high race,
> Whose oath with martyrdom did Stephen grace?
> Ours was a Levite, and as times went then,
> His tribe were God Almighty's gentlemen.
> Sunk were his eyes, his voice was harsh and loud,
> Sure signs he neither choleric was nor proud:
> His long chin prov'd his wit; his saintlike grace
> A church vermilion, and a Moses' face.
> His memory, miraculously great,
> Could plots, exceeding man's belief, repeat;
> Which therefore cannot be accounted lies,
> For human wit could never such devise.
> Some future truths are mingled in his book;
> But where the witness fail'd, the prophet spoke:
> Some things like visionary flights appear;
> The spirit caught him up, the Lord knows where;
> And gave him his rabbinical degree,
> Unknown to foreign university.

(632-59)

To see the imaginative unity of these lines is to see the
blending of Dryden's earlier styles and to feel the active pressure of older literary traditions. As in most satirical verse,
the lines are held together in part by the broad illogic of irony:

126

Dryden makes a series of triumphant assertions every one of
them the opposite of the truth from the Court point of view. But
it is Dryden's "intonation" that sets his mark on the lines and
gives them life and singleness of effect. His note is clearly
heard in "arch-attestor," with its upper level of churchly associations, and in "prodigious," which nicely combines Latin
solemnity with the literal Latin meaning of "monstrous." Dryden has anticipated the high level of this commemoration by
suggesting that it belongs to a Homeric catalogue; he then addresses Oates in a line so nobly reminiscent of Virgil that it
is hardly recognizable as parody:

> Yet, Corah, thou shalt from oblivion pass . . .

The occasionally Latin flavour of the diction is also vaguely
suggestive of Virgilian epic, while at many points the language
is more or less Biblical, ranging from near-quotation to expressions with religious or churchly associations. Working within
a fairly narrow range of allusion Dryden maintains a declamatory tone that is both Biblical-ecclesiastical and Roman-heroic.
But the "venom" of the address depends on the contrast of
another tone which is unmistakably the voice of the prologues,
insolently vulgar and knowingly unliterary:

> Ours was a Levite, and as times went then,
> His tribe were God Almighty's gentlemen.

The blend of manners is most subtle in the lines of greatest
imaginative variety:

> Yet, Corah, thou shalt from oblivion pass:
> Erect thyself, thou monumental brass,
> High as the serpent of thy metal made,
> While nations stand secure beneath thy shade.

The focus of the ironies is also the focus of opposing styles and
of the widest range of literary and religious associations, the
ironies arising mainly from the double references of "monumental" and "brass." Taking "monumental" on its high Latinate
side, in a Virgilian address, we feel that this beneficent hero
is "monumental" in greatness. Or we may read the whole line

as a preposterous parody of Horace's

> Exegi monumentum aere perennius . . .

But Biblical and ecclesiastical connotations of "brass" and "monuments" suggest that our hero is worthy of a "monumental brass" in an English church, the rude command implying that this monument, contrary to decent custom and the laws of gravity, will rise of its own power. Finally, "brass" in its vulgar sense reminds us that such effrontery is otherwise "monumental."

In these lines Dryden's satirical mode appears at its characteristic best. There are the black-and-white oppositions of irony with rhetorical and metrical emphasis striking in unison. There is the smack of life and vulgarity in a word from "Jonsonian" London, the word which imparts the ironic intention and gives force to Dryden's thrust. But the irony is most concentrated in a word of classical origin which is rich in literary and historical connotations and which suggests the Roman oratorical tone.

These features appear in close combination in many of the best lines in Dryden's satirical verse:

> A fiery soul, which, working out its way,
> Fretted the pigmy body to decay,
> And o'er-informed the tenement of clay.

(The reminiscences of Aristotle and Plato, Bishop Fuller, and Carew have often been pointed out.) Or consider:

> Besides, his goodly fabric fills the eye
> And seems design'd for thoughtless majesty;
> Thoughtless as monarch oaks that shade the plain,
> And, spread in solemn state, supinely reign.
> Heywood and Shirley were but types of thee,
> Thou last great prophet of tautology.

or

> But gentle Simkin just reception finds
> Amidst this monument of vanish'd minds:

DRYDEN AND POETIC TRADITION

or

>   Thou leap'st o'er all eternal truths in thy
>   Pindaric way!

Finally, a delicious blend of neo-Platonic fancy and shrewd
analysis in these lines on the Church of England:

>   If, as our dreaming Platonists report,
>   There could be spirits of a middle sort,
>   Too black for heav'n, and yet too white for hell,
>   Who just dropp'd halfway down, nor lower fell;
>   So pois'd, so gently she descends from high,
>   It seems a soft dismission from the sky.

From these examples and from our analysis, it is clear that
"allusive irony" is a more adequate term than "mock-heroic"
for Dryden's satirical mode, whether in Absalom and Achitophel
and Mac Flecknoe or in passages of incidental satire in his argumentative verse. His mode is allusive in a wide variety of
ways: in close imitation or parody of other writers, in less exact references to language, styles, and conventions of other
literatures — Classical, Biblical, and French — in drawing on
the large materials of philosophy and theology, in playing on
popular parallels between contemporary religious and political
situations and those of ancient history, sacred and secular.
Through this mode Dryden makes his "affirmation of Europe."
     A solemn claim and a preposterous one, if we think of the
mode as devices for heightening style. The difference between
allusive irony and the heroic trimmings added to the Annus
Mirabilis lies in the imaginative union of tones and levels of
meaning that I have been describing: "thou monumental brass"!
The vulgar thrust is inseparable from the reference to high
literary styles and to heroic behaviour and ecclesiastical splendour.
     That the union of styles was more than an academic trick is
further shown by the success of the poem with contemporary
readers. As compared with Restoration plays or lampoons and
gazettes, Absalom and Achitophel spoke to more of the interests
of the reading public in 1681, and, as Beljame observed, to
more of the public. Although the Classical heroic was especially

flattering to the aristocrats' view of themselves, Latin culture
was the common possession of educated men, whatever their
political and religious allegiances might be. Dryden, Milton,
and Marvell have at least this in common. The Old Testament
flavour, satirically amusing to the Court, was richly meaningful and insidiously attractive to Nonconformists. And the colloquial idiom brought the high talk down to the level where Court
and City lived. By responding so naturally to the double claims
of both his audience and his development as a poet, Dryden
"made himself heard" and created a fresh form of art in English
poetry.

By this fact alone, he affirmed an important European value
to his audience: that poetic craft matters. Dryden's admiration
for what Boileau had done for French satire is a sign of his
belief that he had performed a similar service for English satire. Boileau would have recognized as art of a high order the
poise and finish of Dryden's mode:

> At his right hand our young Ascanius sate,
> Rome's other hope, and pillar of the State.
> His brows thick fogs, instead of glories, grace,
> And lambent dulness play'd around his face.

The poise is evident in the balance between crude burlesque in
"thick fogs" and the subtle gravity of "lambent dulness"; the
finish is felt in the melodious and resilient verse. But the
smoothness is not merely fashionable: it functions poetically
in the strategy of civilized irony. The reader is momentarily
beguiled into taking the lines as an exquisite compliment. Dryden had a right to claim that like Boileau he was bringing into
modern satire a Virgilian refinement of "raillery." In the fine
Latin wit of "lambent dulness" or "spread in solemn state,
supinely reign," Dryden is "alluding" to a culture and the fineness of response which it fostered.

It is no great compliment to describe Dryden's achievement
as a triumph of neo-classicism, if we mean by neo-classicism
mechanical use of conventions borrowed from Boileau or Rapin.
Dryden's achievement is not one of "meeting requirements";
the conventions "at work," as in the lines just quoted, are expressive of larger aesthetic and cultural values. In writing verse
which combined the normality and vigour of good talk with a

musical pattern that was the apt accompaniment of ironic wit and in using language which was equally alive in its reference to immediate interests and to literary tradition, Dryden expressed a community in attitude and standards of art with European poets and critics. Some of these attitudes and standards -- the detachment, the refinement of ironic censure, the insistence on design and precise mastery of language — were particularly salutary for readers too well pleased with Hudibras and for writers who mistook ease for art. But Dryden did not sacrifice the vigour of Butler to "correctness." The Augustan reform as initiated by Dryden, unlike that of Addison, kept close contact with a masculine audience. Dryden's allusive mode shows a positive strength in neo-classicism which the odious term and its theories completely conceal.

Let us consider more particularly how this mode worked, how and why epic allusions offered Dryden a way of expressing important values. In ironic contexts, the more or less close imitations of epic introduced a standard of manners and actions by which the exploits of politicians and poetasters might be measured. Fomenters of Popish plots and rash rebellions and slipshod writers were exposed to ancient and Biblical ideals of prince and prophet, and their operations were socially and intellectually "placed." In contexts less purely ironic, as in parts of the Shaftesbury and Monmouth "characters," the allusions to Classical and Biblical heroic had another effect. The magnificence imparted by the Miltonic flavour was not merely literary. For Shaftesbury had great abilities as a judge and diplomat; Monmouth had noble looks and manners, and Dryden himself confessed a "respect" for "his heroic virtues." By granting their loftiness some degree of pride the satirist, too, attained a largeness of temper: "Preposterous plottings, but rather splendid persons!" Nevertheless, as Dr. Johnson observed, there are limits in heroic allegory: "Charles could not run continually parallel with David." But though the David-Aeneas incarnation cannot be taken seriously, the tone adopted in addressing Charles and attributed to him and his courtiers did have a certain validity. The parallel between state manners and Roman aristocratic manners was justified, even in Restoration England. In public discourse, the English aristocracy, like the Roman, had a hereditary right to high oratory. And heroic poetry had been by a long tradition an aristocratic possession.

The grand yet lively eloquence that characterizes and satirizes Shaftesbury and Buckingham is thus quite different from the
inflated and dully insistent rant of the Heroic Plays, for Dryden
had found the one kind of situation in which a Restoration poet
might adopt the heroic style. As spokesman for aristocracy,
Established Church, and monarchy, he could rightly assume
the Roman dignity of Renaissance epic. As the critic of the
King's enemies, he could parody his own heroic style and so express still another true relationship between contemporary
events and the heroic ideal. The discovery of relationships which
were true for Dryden both as poet and citizen made it possible
for him to use his accumulated literary skills with a new freedom. His satirical poetry exhibits a fluidity and force and a
concentrated range of reference which his earlier verse had
rarely shown.

Why may we reasonably describe this success as "European"? Not simply because Dryden's satiric mode was widely
and often precisely allusive to European writers and styles and
to English writers who were most consciously European in their
styles and critical standards. Nor simply because he satisfied
a continental standard of literary craft, although this is significant. But rather because he brought the larger light of European literature and a European past into verse of local public
debate. He invited his readers, including Nonconformists, to
take a less parochial attitude toward the persons and events of
contemporary history. We have only to compare Absalom and
Achitophel or The Medal with Marvell's satires to appreciate
the imaginative value of linking these smaller and greater worlds.
The Marvell of the Ode on Cromwell had brought to political
history a similar largeness of scene and a poise of values much
finer than Dryden's. But breadth of vision and sureness of rhythm are missing in Last Instructions to a Painter, although the
poem has some of the obvious ear-marks of epic satire. The
spectacle is rather painful: the earlier Marvell could not address this world without sacrificing many of his virtues as a
poet. Dryden could; with losses, too, if his poetry is measured
by the standard of the Cromwellian Ode; but he managed to
translate to his audience something of the larger historic vision,
the noble manner, and the justness of style of the Renaissance
tradition in which the younger Marvell wrote. He was a vigorous civilizer among the sons of Belial.

DRYDEN AND POETIC TRADITION

Dryden did something else for his generation that Marvell and Milton, much less Cowley, could not do: he reaffirmed the public role of the poet, the Graeco-Roman conception of the poet as the voice of a society. It is true that Dryden succeeded only too well in fixing the public tone as the Augustan norm; but the voice we hear is not solely that of the party or class or church. Thanks to Dryden the tone of Augustan poetry is less parochial than it might have been: it is resonant with echoes of other literary worlds, of larger manners and events. Minor Augustan poetry is dead for modern readers not because it was too "general," but because it was too local.

In praising Dryden for reaffirming the European tradition in his satirical mode, it is well to recall the conditions of our praise. The eighteenth century is littered with epics, odes, and philosophical poems that are traditional in the academic sense; the "forms" and the "diction" are too often reminiscent of the best writers of Greece and Rome. Dr. Johnson's remark on Gray's Odes is the appropriate comment on such products: "They are forced plants raised in a hotbed; and they are poor plants; they are but cucumbers after all." Dryden's achievement matters because the verse through which he draws on the European tradition satisfies us as other poetry does by offering concentrated and surprising richness of relationship: we feel that language is being "worked" for all its worth. (The allusive mode is for Dryden what the symbolic metaphor was for the Metaphysicals.) But Dryden's use of tradition satisfies also a condition of another sort. In the act of writing poetry that was far from provincial in implication, Dryden engaged the most active political and intellectual interests of his immediate audience. The particular issues are of little concern for us at present; but we can recognize their importance in the late seventeenth century, and see that the general issues involved are of a sort that is central in any conceivable society. There are local successes in literature that are instructive to later generations: Dryden's is one of them.

But Pope and the poets who were contemporary with him were not prepared to take instruction from Dryden the controversialist, since they quite consciously removed themselves from the field of public debate. Although political pamphleteering of a violent sort continued throughout the age of Anne, the typical watchwords of the new world of belles lettres were

"politeness" and "retirement." That Pope could inhabit this
Addisonian world of well-bred amenities and moderate enthusiasms and yet rise above it to a serious criticism of life, he
owes in part to Dryden's forceful example.

Dryden's most valuable gift to Pope was the creation of his
generously allusive mode with all of its wider cultural implications. (I am not overlooking "the couplet": the style is inseparable from its rhythmic form.) With his shrewd flair for craft,
Pope realized the principle within the mode, and possessing a
finer responsiveness to the poetry of the past, both Classical
and English, he enriched his satire with more subtle and more
various kinds of reference. His obvious imitations of epic in
the Rape of the Lock and the Dunciad are of less importance
than his blending of the heroic with other literary styles and
non-literary idioms into the complex modes appropriate to his
two very different "mock-epics." Although some single traditional style or genre is dominant in each of Pope's major works,
from the Pastorals and the Rape of the Lock to the satirical
epistles and the Dunciad, his poetry is freshly and variously
allusive to poets of many traditions and many periods. At random one can think of allusions to Spenser, Ovid, Catullus, to
Shakespeare, Milton, and Crashaw, to Rochester, Denham,
and Addison. From Dryden Pope also learned the art of self-
parody, which he exploited with amusing thrift. He alludes with
overtones of wit to his own pastoral insipidities, to the land-
scape-painting of Windsor Forest, to the Ovidian theatrical
rhetoric of Eloisa to Abelard, and of course to the heroics of
his Iliad.

As in Dryden, the Roman heroic is always breaking in; and
though the modulation of tone is infinitely various in the Moral
Essays and the Satires, the tone of Roman cultivation — more
refined and more truly Horatian, less downright and less pompous than in Dryden — still prevails. With the changes in state
and society that had been taking place since the Glorious Revolution, the tone had acquired a validity which it could hardly
have had in the Restoration. It might well be argued that the
actual society in which Pope wrote was considerably nearer to
the ideal of the original Augustan Age than that of Charles II.
Burlington, Bolingbroke, and Bathurst, in public and private
life were certainly less unlike their ideal literary selves than
Charles and Rochester. But if the society was not more Augustan

Pope was: his work taken as a whole shows that he had mastered
the intellectual and aesthetic ideals which for the Age of Anne
were embodied in the Age of Augustus and Virgil and Horace.
In Pope's verse, the cultivated tone and the oblique reference
to Roman grandeur and decorum symbolize an ideal of culture
which he is frequently expressing by other more explicit means.
The symbolic force of the allusive mode which he had first
learned from Dryden can be felt wonderfully in his address to
Burlington in the fourth Moral Essay:

> You show us, Rome was glorious, not profuse,
> And pompous buildings once were things of Use.
> Yet shall (my Lord) your just, your noble rules
> Fill half the land with Imitating Fools;
> Who random drawings from your sheets shall take,
> And of one beauty many blunders make;
> Load some vain Church with old Theatric state,
> Turn Arcs of triumph to a Garden-gate;
> Reverse your Ornaments, and hang them all
> On some patch'd dog-hole ek'd with ends of wall,
> Then clap four slices of Pilaster on't,
> That, lac'd with bits of rustic, makes a Front;
> Or call the winds thro' long Arcades to roar,
> Proud to catch cold at a Venetian door;
> Conscious they act a true Palladian part,
> And, if they starve, they starve by rules of art.

(23-38)

After that, the tradition of Dryden needs no further justification;
renewed and refined, it speaks for itself.

ON POPE'S "HORTICULTURAL ROMANTICISM"

A. L. Altenbernd

In the "Epistle to Richard Boyle, Earl of Burlington," the fourth of the Epistles to Several Persons, Alexander Pope's discussion of taste — or of false taste — includes a section on gardening which is his fullest expression of a theory he had developed during a period of almost twenty years. As a child at Binfield, Pope was exposed to his father's enthusiasm for gardening,[1] and when the poet leased his own tiny estate at Twickenham in 1718, he laid out a grotto and gardens with such success that friends seeking to improve their own grounds frequently sought his advice. To the end of his life, Pope continued to expand and embellish his grotto, to revamp his grounds, to plan gardens for his friends, and to advise such professional gardeners as Charles Bridgman and William Kent, two of a succession of notable designers who developed the famous gardens at Stowe. In addition, Kent was Burlington's protégé, so that he was chiefly responsible, apparently with some suggestions from Pope, for the grounds which the poet praised for their good taste in the fourth Epistle.

During the period of his interest in gardening, Pope made a number of statements which taken together constitute a reasonably consistent theory of the garden art. This theory called for the abandonment of the excessive artifice of the formal garden and for the adoption of a simpler, more "natural" style in gardening. Pope's precepts on the subject and his example at Twickenham have been credited with popularizing a revolution in garden design leading to the widespread growth of the natural landscape garden.[2]

More recently, a number of writers have considered Pope's gardening to be a romantic contradiction to the prevailing neoclassicism of his poetry. Thus Professor Bracher sees the grotto at Twickenham as an outlet for submerged romantic tendencies during the years of "moralized song."[3] This attitude

Reprinted from Journal of English and Germanic Philology, Vol. 54 (1955), pp. 470-477, by permission of author and publisher.

parallels the tendency to label Pope's earlier, obviously more exuberant poetry "romantic," as against the later satiric and didactic work, which is presumed to be typically neoclassic.[4] Arthur O. Lovejoy, on the other hand, speaks of the "horticultural romanticism" of Pope's later years as leading "to a revulsion against the strait-laced regularity and symmetry of the heroic couplet, to a general turning from convention, formality, artifice in all the arts."[5] While there is little room for doubt that Pope was influential in spreading the gospel of the naturalistic landscape garden, I believe that there is no real contradiction between his neoclassicism as a poet and his theory and practice as a gardener. This point of view can best be demonstrated by considering Pope's theory against the background of English gardening as it had developed to the time of his first comment on the matter.

Early in the seventeenth century, Inigo Jones, influenced by Palladio, the great sixteenth-century Italian neoclassic architect, had introduced into England a style of building emphasizing horizontal lines and perfect symmetry. The stateliness and formality of the Palladian style seemed to demand a comparable treatment of the grounds about the building. Like neoclassic architecture, formal gardening followed distinct principles. Its most prominent feature was an axial design reflecting the precise symmetry of the building and extending its vistas through the grounds. The garden axis was marked by an avenue cut through the woodland or by symmetrically planted trees or shrubs accurately spaced and trimmed to geometric precision. The distant end of the vista was often closed by a piece of statuary, a perspective scene painted on a wall, or even by artificial ruins.

The extreme of garden formalism was achieved in a number of artificial devices. "Knots," inherited from the English medieval garden and developed with great intricacy throughout the Renaissance, were symmetrical designs composed of interlaced bands of close-cropped cover plants such as carpet bugle. A French development of the same technique produced the parterre de broderie, an intricate pattern worked out on a flat surface in colored earth or gravel. Small square or octagonal beds of low-growing flowers arranged in geometric patterns were duplicated at precise intervals throughout a regular area to give the scene all the natural wildness of a tile floor. And by the early

years of the eighteenth century, formal gardening had reached
a summit of absurdity in topiary work, sculpture representing
animals and geometric figures, using yew, privet, or boxwood
as a medium.[6]

Topiary work provided Pope with his first opportunity to
comment on gardening, for in The Guardian, No. 173, September 29, 1713, he satirized the "various tonsure of greens." An
eminent town gardener, Pope reported, planned to dispose of
a collection of carved shrubs including such items as: " 'Adam
and Eve in yew; Adam a little shattered by the fall of the tree
of knowledge in the great storm: Eve and the serpent flourishing.
'St. George in box; his arm scarce long enough, but will be in a
condition to stick the dragon by next April.' "[7] More important
for our consideration of Pope as poet is the comment with which
he introduced this bit of whimsy:

> There is certainly something in the amiable simplicity
> of unadorned nature that spreads over the mind a more
> noble sort of tranquility and a loftier sensation of pleas-
> ure, than can be raised from the nicer scenes of art.
> . . . I believe it is no wrong observation, that persons
> of genius, and those who are most capable of art, are
> always most fond of nature: as such are chiefly sensible,
> that all art consists in the imitation and study of nature.[8]

The idea that art is the imitation of nature persisted in
Pope's utterances on gardening; in 1722, writing to Martha
Blount, he described Robert Digby's estate at Sherborne in
these terms:

> The gardens are so irregular, that it is very hard to
> give an exact idea of them, but by a plan. Their beauty
> arises from this irregularity; for not only the several
> parts of the garden itself make the better contrast by
> these sudden rises, and falls, and turns of ground; but
> views about it are let in.

Yet Pope also noted a colonnade of lime trees, six terraces,
and a T-shaped canal — all formal features -- as beauties of the
Sherborne scene. He suggested that the open courts between
buildings of the ruined castle that adorned the grounds be "throw

into circles or octagons of grass or flowers," and a little temple, he thought, might well be built on a neighboring hill.[9] In the same vein is the remark attributed to Pope by Joseph Spence in 1728: "Arts are taken from nature; and after a thousand vain efforts for improvements, are best when they return to their first simplicity." Again Spence reports Pope to have said, "In laying out a garden, the first thing to be considered is the genius of the place." While this remark has sometimes been taken to mean that the gardener should make the most of the terrain by adapting his design to it, the rest of the sentence makes clear that this was not Pope's intention: "thus at Riskins, for example, Lord Bathurst should have raised two or three mounts; because his situation is all a plain, and nothing can please without variety."[10]

Later Pope made further specific suggestions which find an echo in the "Epistle to Burlington." The influence of the Italian landscape painters is evident in the comment reported by Spence for September, 1739:

> The lights and shades in gardening are managed by disposing the thick grove work, the thin, and the openings, in a proper manner. . . . You may distance things by darkening them, and by narrowing the plantation more and more towards the end, in the same manner as they do in painting.[11]

Thus the landscape painter's techniques of chiaroscuro and perspective may be used by the gardener. Spence later reports a conversation of 1742 in which Pope expressed a summary and (as the date indicates) mature view of gardening: "All the rules of gardening are reducible to three heads: — the contrasts, the management of surprises, and the concealment of the bounds." Pope then quoted lines fifty-five and fifty-six of the "Epistle to Burlington" as a concise statement of his aesthetic view: "He gains all points, who pleasingly confounds, / Surprises, varies, and conceals the bounds."[12]

What Pope objected to, then, was the artificiality of the formal garden. In the "Epistle to Burlington" Timon's offensive garden is bounded by a wall and patterned in tiresome symmetry. Topiary work and statuary abound, while the fountain and the summer house are placed without regard for the functions they might be expected to perform. Pope's remedies would consist of improving upon the natural beauties of the terrain, introducing intricate variety in design, and opening vistas into the natural landscape beyond the garden by "concealing the bounds," that is, by eliminating walls or hedges that marked the limits of the garden. Thus Pope undoubtedly advocated a garden design more natural than that of the seventeenth-century formal garden. After his time the relaxation of garden formality was carried even further by such professional designers as Kent and "Capability" Brown.[13] But that there is any serious split in Pope's mind on the subjects of gardening and poetry may be doubted. Several considerations show that the discrepancy is less serious than has been supposed.

First, I would suggest that the contrast between the poems before and after 1717 has been exaggerated. An Essay on Criticism, surely the English epitome of neoclassic poetics, belongs to the earlier period.[14] In addition, as Professor B. Sprague Allen points out, such a poem as "Windsor Forest" (1704, 1713), while it does discuss nature, does so in the rather formal conventions of neoclassicism rather than in the intimate, affectionate manner of the romantics, who drew on first-hand knowledge of field, river, and forest.[15] Pope is not approving the wildness of untamed nature here, for he describes the scene as

> Not chaos-like together crushed and bruised,
> But, as the world, harmoniously confused:
> Where order in variety we see,
> And where, though all things differ, all agree.[16]

These lines are in accord with both the neoclassic view of the cosmos, and the view of nature as the model for poets expressed in An Essay on Criticism. If there was more exuberance and more outdoor scenery in the early work than in the later satires, there is, nevertheless, no need to label this tendency romantic, or to suppose that Pope suppressed romantic tendencies after he turned to the satires.

Secondly, too much has undoubtedly been made of Pope's "correctness" as a poet. It should be remembered that in An Essay on Criticism, Pope struck out not only at poetry "where nothing's just or fit; / One glaring chaos and wild heap of wit," but also at dullness in "such lays as neither ebb nor flow, /

Correctly cold, and regularly low."[17] In addition, the endless
variety of effect Pope achieved throughout his own poetry by
variation in meter, tone color, caesura position, and weight
of syllable, and by the imaginative daring of many of his lines
suggests that for him there was nothing "strait-laced" about the
regularity and symmetry of the heroic couplet. Indeed he would
undoubtedly — and with justice, I think — have rejected the comparison between his verse and the monotonous orderliness of
an unimaginative formal garden. The parterres, hedges, and
topiary work which Pope ridiculed in Timon's Villa may more
justly be compared to Euphuistic than to Addinsonian prose, to
the dull, rule-bound neoclassic poetry which Pope ridiculed
than to his own.

Another matter that needs attention is the significance of
the term "nature." The neoclassicists in poetry had appealed to
nature as their ultimate authority, just as the rebels against
formalism in gardening did after them. Pope had, in fact, coun-
selled his readers to follow nature in both poetry and gardening.
Professor Lovejoy holds that the ultimate effect of the advice
was very different in the two cases, however, for Pope and
others had shifted the "aesthetic connotation of 'conformity to
nature' from simplicity to complexity and from regularity to
irregularity."[18] Yet Pope's earliest extant comments on gardening, in the Guardian paper of 1713, referred to nature as the
desirable norm in much the same way that An Essay on Criticism had used the term only a few years earlier. If the Guardian
paper had found less regularity in nature than in the artificial
garden, it had nevertheless found greater simplicity. And all
of Pope's subsequent remarks on the garden art were essentially
harmonious with this earliest statement. In gardening and poetry
alike, Pope recommended the emulation of nature by the use of
surprise instead of monotony, variety instead of rigid regularity,
and subtle concealment — but not overthrow -- of the rules governing the composition.

A final body of evidence helps us evaluate both the extent
of Pope's "romanticism" as a gardener, and the signification
which he attached to such terms as "regular," "wild," "intricate," and "natural." His own garden, considered as an exem-
plification of his theories, shows him to be less a rebel than
his manifestoes alone might indicate. The layout of Pope's
grounds as they appeared at the time of his death has been

preserved in a plan by John Searle, his gardener.[19] The design
does not forget nature, but it seems to remember her through
the mists of a dream. While some pleasing intricacy appears
in the far corners of the plot, a symmetry of straight lines and
a balanced arrangement of statuary dominates the central area.
The main structural characteristic of the plan is an axial vista
terminated by an obelisk in memory of the poet's mother. Several mounds with spiral walks leading to the apex improve on the
genius of the place. Here is "nature methodized"; to find "nature
to advantage dressed" we need only turn to Pope's beloved grotto
Pope's house was separated from his garden by the Hampton
Court-London road, so that he found it advantageous to build a
tunnel giving access to the garden. Expanding the tunnel and
extending rock structures at each end, Pope developed a grotto
in the style then popular in English gardens. Shells, minerals,
bits of looking-glass, busts of poets, and an alabaster lamp
contributed to what Pope conceived to be a garden ornament in
the "rustic" or "natural" taste.[20] In his own garden Pope retained many of the characteristics of the earlier formal plan,
and employed a sort of wildness which was at best "artful"
indeed. The grounds at Twickenham represented not so much
a reaction against the formal garden itself as against its excesses; Pope's garden was a half-way stage in the development
toward the later landscape garden which became a fully developed reality only after the middle of the eighteenth century.

Pope was, then, neither the most strait-laced of neoclassic
poets nor the most unbridled of romantic gardeners, so that
there is no real discrepancy between his theories of the two arts
For Pope, poetry, gardening, painting, and architecture were
all expressions of a whole mind.

The real difficulty, I believe, lies in our tendency to sim-
plify the history of the arts by establishing arbitrary criteria
for "periods" or "movements" — criteria to which sometimes
even the most prominent figures of the time cannot be made to
conform. The work of the cultural historian should be descriptive rather than normative, so that we need show neither delighted surprise nor irritation when we discover that Pope, of
all people, does not fit our definitions of neoclassicism. Our
understanding of neoclassicism should be broadened to accommodate the actual Pope, who will not fit an a priori idea of
eighteenth-century rigidity. In addition, metaphorically

representing the development of aesthetic standards as a series of revolutions or swings of the pendulum or alternations of the tides leads us to expect, without warrant, that all the standards of a previous age will be dislodged in an upheaval that wholly reshapes the cultural landscape. This aesthetic catastrophism needs to be modified, I think, by a concept which, while taking full account of those moments in history when tastes in all the arts are sufficiently in harmony to permit a description and a name, will recognize the essentially evolutionary character of aesthetic standards.

NOTES

1   George Sherburn, The Early Career of Alexander Pope (Oxford, 1934), p. 35.

2   Isabel Wakelin Chase, Horace Walpole: Gardenist (Princeton, N. J., 1943), pp. 28-29, 107; Christopher Hussey, "The Aesthetic Background of the Art of William Kent," in The Work of William Kent . . . by Margaret Jourdain (London, 1948), pp. 21-22.

3   Frederick Bracher, "Pope's Grotto: The Maze of Fancy," Huntington Library Quarterly, XII (1949), 141-62.

4   Émile Montégut, "Heures de lecture d'un critique: Pope," Revue des deux mondes, LXXXVI (1888), 274-323; Robert K. Root, The Poetical Career of Alexander Pope (Princeton, N. J., 1938), pp. 69ff.; Bracher, op. cit.

5   "On the Discrimination of Romanticisms," PMLA, XXXIX (1924), 241. B. Sprague Allen, Tides in English Taste (Cambridge, Mass., 1937), II, 125: "It is ironic . . . that Addison and Pope, who from many points of view symbolized the age of classical authority in its more brilliant moments, were chiefly instrumental in dislodging from its position in popular esteem the garden of axial design, which impressively embodied the Renaissance ideal of order." Montague Summers, The Gothic Quest (London [1938]), pp. 20-21: "No whole-hearted or single-minded Classicist . . . could have conceived and builded that delicious 'Aegerian grot' at Twickenham. . . . Here we have a baroque romanticism no genuine Augustan would have tolerated for a moment."

Chase, p. 171: "Pope, whose poetry represents the epitome of neo-classic polish, was a romantic in his garden at Twickenham."

6   For the foregoing discussion, I am largely indebted to Allen, op. cit.

7   Thomas Babington Macauley, ed., The Tatler and Guardian (Cincinnati, 1884), p. 233.

8   Ibid., p. 231. Pope seems to be echoing here ideas advanced by Joseph Addison in The Spectator, No. 414, June 25, 1712, and No. 477, September 6, 1712. Addison summarized No. 414 in this manner: "Contents: The works of nature more pleasant to the imagination than those of art. The works of nature still more pleasant, the more they resemble those of art. The works of art more pleasant, the more they resemble those of nature. . . ." Addison then went on to praise French and Italian gardens for their "artificial rudeness" as against the trim neatness of English formal gardens. The Spectator (London, 1808), VI, 75-79.

9   The Works of Alexander Pope, ed. Rev. Whitwell Elwin and W. J. Courthope (London, 1871-89), IX, 300. This edition is hereafter referred to as Works.

10 Joseph Spence, Anecdotes, Observations, and Characters of Books and Men, ed. S. W. Singer (London, 1820), pp. 11-12. I wish to express my thanks to Dr. James M. Osborn of Yale University, who has verified the dates of the quotations from Spence. This quotation will be part of item 609 in Dr. Osborn's forthcoming edition of Spence's Anecdotes enlarged from the original manuscript.

11 Ibid., pp. 209-10; item 610 in Dr. Osborn's text. See also Elizabeth Manwaring, Italian Landscape in Eighteenth Century England (New York, 1925). For the possible influence of Pope's experience as an amateur painter, see Robert J. Allen, "Pope and the Sister Arts," Pope and His Contemporaries, ed. James L. Clifford and Louis A. Landa (Oxford, 1949), pp. 78-88.

12 Spence, p. 260; item 612 in Dr. Osborn's text.

13 Margaret Jourdain, "Landscape Gardening," The Work

of William Kent . . . (London, 1928), pp. 74-81.

14 Although published in 1711, An Essay on Criticism was
written even earlier. Professor Root places the poem in
the "maze of fancy" because it shows Pope's "power of
terse and witty epigram" — a quality hardly lacking in the
later satires — but he recognizes its neoclassic aesthetics.
Root, op. cit., p. 70.

15 Allen, I, 129.

16 Works, I, 340; ll. 13-16.

17 Works, II, 50, 48; ll. 291-92; 239-40.

18 "The First Gothic Revival and the Return to Nature," MLN,
XLVII (1932), 442.

19 John Serle [sic], A Plan of Mr. Pope's Garden (London,
1745).

20 Pope's letter to Edward Blount dated June 2, 1725, from
Twickenham gives the poet's own description of the grotto.
See Works, VI, 383-84. A more detailed description is
contained in Professor Bracher's article cited in Note 3,
above. The perspective view of the grotto appearing in
Searle's Plan may be more readily found by many readers
in [Robert Dodsley], A Collection of Poems . . . by Several
Hands, 5th ed. (London, 1758), III, [I], where it appears
as a headpiece over Pope's "On a Grotto near the Thames,
at Twickenham. . . ."

II. POEMS PUBLISHED IN THE <u>WORKS</u> OF 1717

POPE'S ODE FOR MUSICK

Earl R. Wasserman

That repetition of inherited opinion which gradually fixes a poem's public status has long since assigned Pope's "Ode for Musick. On St. Cecilia's Day" to the class of the respectable poor. The ode still persists in making its appearance alongside its betters in anthologies and volumes of selections, but it is popularly known to be, in the words of a distinguished critic, one of Pope's "least successful" poems. Ever since John Dennis it has been seemly to complain that "Pantomimical" Pope merely emulated Dryden's two odes on the subject, fell far short of his models, and completely failed to capture their rich representational harmonies. The ode is "painfully imitative" of Dryden, writes Pope's most recent critic — who, incidentally, feels that its saving grace is a brief anticipation of the "romantic mythological style" of Collins and the early Keats. That the poem lacks Dryden's sonorities, displays some clumsiness of style, and is in a metrical form in which Pope was not proficient is probably as unquestionable as its surface reflection of Dryden's Cecilian odes. But the sanctioned criticism of the poem also protests against its structural disorder: the first three stanzas, we are told, stagger about instead of preparing for the Orpheus myth, and the story of Orpheus occupies disproportionate attention and does not lead to the brief stanza on St. Cecilia, who, presumably, should be the main subject. Even Professor Dobrée, who senses that it is a much better piece of work than is usually conceded, laments that it "does not hang together with the inevitability that we associate with the fully developed Pope."[1]

The last is the most damaging complaint, for an undistinguished effort to represent qualities and emotional moods by verbal sound may distress only our affective responses, and an "imitation" may be a new creation; but since poetic significance resides in the total articulation of the materials, structural

Reprinted from English Literary History, Vol. 28 (1961), pp. 163-186, by permission of The Johns Hopkins Press and the author.

chaos denies the poem any significant reason for existing. Art, however, cannot wear its structure on its sleeve, and it is always conceivable that we have not brought the proper anatomy to bear or have not penetrated deeply enough into Pope's ode to discover the course of its arteries.

Students of the Middle Ages and the Renaissance are now fully aware of an extensive and complex theory of macrocosmic-microcosmic harmony that once gave vitally and profoundly symbolic value to all aspects of music. But our habit of thinking in terms of strict cultural eras has lowered an impenetrable curtain somewhere around the Restoration that hinders our seeing the important continuity of thought and learning. Even Gretchen Lee Finney, whose studies of Renaissance theories and symbolism of music are invaluable, has agreed that with the advent of science and rationalism the musical symbolism familiar to the Elizabethans disappeared "in the years after 1650," save for some dreary fag ends.[2] Yet it is not difficult in fact to see that Dryden, at least, not only was still drawing for his symbolism upon the earlier systems which held that the laws of music are also the basic laws of God, nature, and man; he could also significantly organize a poem by means of harmonies analogously drawn from that radical art, music, and could, with metre, rhyme, and structure, "play" the words of a poem as notes and phrases in a musical composition.

Dryden's interest in the sisterhood of poetry and music was lifelong, and an occasion like the death of Henry Purcell gave him the obvious opportunity to experiment with the representational and musical possibilities of language, just as contemporary composers had been representing the meanings of words with sounds. The opening line of his "Ode on the Death of Mr. Purcell," for example, assigns to the lark two identical back vowels and to the linnet two similar front vowels: "Mark how the lark and linnet sing." Since music was defined as a concordia discors, a harmonious wedding of contraries, the duet or alternate singing of these birds is a "mutual spite"; or, more properly, they sing with "rival notes," since "rivalry" is the technical musical term for a concert of voices[3] and, moreover, joins in the diphthong of its stressed syllable an approximation of both the back vowel assigned the lark and the front vowel assigned the linnet. A somewhat different version of musical concordia discors probably is being enacted symbolically by the

chiastic arrangement of the s and w sounds in the two lines that
then follow:

> They strain their warbling throats
> To welcome in the spring.

Certainly the complementary but necessarily simultaneous acts
of listening and being silent are audibly contained in the repeated
inversion of the s and l sounds in "And list'ning and silent, and
silent and list'ning, and list'ning and silent obey." And, equally
certain, the consistent recession of vowels, "They sung no
more," which enacts the growing silence, is exactly inverted in
the second hemistich, which also inverts the sense of the first:
"or only sung his fame."

Yet this is only a highly wrought union of music and sense
appropriate to a poet's tribute to a musician and is but a token
of Dryden's interest in the poetic exploitation of music and its
symbolism. His encomium musicae, "A Song for St. Cecilia's
Day," shows him more comprehensively organizing as though
he were composing a piece of music which, in turn, takes its
shape from the tradition of musical symbolism. Since, according to this tradition, all disorder is cacophony and all order
symphony, God is the Musician, and the universe is the song
He sang into existence. St. Basil, for example, wrote that at
creation God brought into one perfect accord all the clashing
elements in order to make "a harmonious symphony result from
the whole"[4]; and Clement of Alexandria recorded that God "composed the entire creation into melodious order and tuned into
concert the discord of the elements."[5] This of course is the
symbolism on which Dryden's first strophe is built: God's "tuneful Voice" sings the jarring atoms into successive musical harmonies through all the successive notes of the instrument
("compass," "Diapason"), the complete harmony, or diapason,
ending in that "perfect" cadence, man ("closing full").

The first stanza, then, is the customary rendering of the
hexaemeron as the perfect act of music — the musica mundana
and the musica humana derived from "heav'nly Harmony" and
presented in terms of musica instrumentalis. The theme had
been run into the ground long before Dryden. However, the essence of neoclassic art lies not in the creation of new materials,
but in the special ordering of traditional materials (which we

falsely call clichés), saturated with their accumulated values and significances, into fresh structures that more intrinsically and organically embody the topic than could a discursive statement. Here we might find our clue to Dryden's organizational procedure by observing a peculiarity in his seventh strophe. The penultimate line of that stanza fails to rhyme with the others; and this is the line expressing the drearily conventional theme that an angel, misled by Cecilia's divine song, mistook earth for heaven. Since the angel is not part of musica mundana, the line does not rhyme with the others; but angels, perpetually singing around God, are their own harmony, and hence the line, sequestered from the others, rhymes internally: "An Angel heard, and straight appear'd." What this expressive structural device suggests is that in this poem on music the very organization of its "musical" features — metre and rhyme — may be a performance of its theme.

Because of the apparent irregularity of Dryden's stanzas the poem has been assumed to be a pseudo-Pindaric ode, that form that requires wildness and abrupt disorder; and on this quality of the first stanza Verrall has built all it can tolerate:

> "Pindaric" verse is not really appropriate to anything except Chaos, and the structure is a sort of jest upon this point: for harmony — the actual word "harmony" — brings the delayed rhyme. The first two rhymes of the section, "harmony" and "began," are left suspended . . . while all the irregularly accented lines that follow one after another find their re-echoing rhymes. Only with the repetition of the two opening lines is the expectant ear fully satisfied.[6]

The proposal is admirably ingenious, finding in the supposed Pindaric disorder a kind of irony that joins the original Chaos with the subsequent harmonious Creation. Yet, it places undue emphasis on both irregularity and the expectations of the ear. In fact, the remarkably complex prosody of the stanza is entirely coherent, as the following analysis will make evident:

From Harmony, from heav'nly Harmony   5A
  This universal Frame began.   4B
When Nature underneath a heap   4C
  Of jarring Atomes lay,   3D
And cou'd not heave her Head,   3E
The tuneful Voice was heard from high,   4F

  Arise ye more than dead.   3E'
Then cold, and hot, and moist, and dry,   4F'
In order to their stations leap,   4C'
  And MUSICK'S pow'r obey.   3D'
From Harmony, from heav'nly Harmony   5A
  This universal Frame began: 4B

From Harmony to Harmony   4A
Through all the compass of the Notes it ran,   5B'
The Diapason closing full in Man.   5B''

That is, after six unrhymed lines the rhymes begin in perfectly systematic order, picking up first the fifth and sixth lines, then the third and fourth, and finally the first and second. Each of the second six lines, moreover, has the same metrical form as its fellow rhyme-line among the first six.

Clearly this poetic account of the six days of Creation as an act of musical harmony is itself a structural hexaemeron, and the poet is the microcosmic Creator who uses the harmonic devices available to him to create his analogous verbal world. The "jarring Atomes" of Chaos are figured by the first six disordered lines, unrhymed and of irregular lengths. Only with the fiat of the "tuneful Voice" — "Arise ye more than dead" — do the rhymes begin, for this creative command is the beginning of harmony, whose poetic counterpart is rhyme; and the lines then proceed through the six successive acts of creative harmonizing that occupied the first six days of God's creative week, suggesting Athanasius Kircher's account of each day of Creation as the Arch-Musician's opening one of the stops of the organ-universe.[7] Since Creation in Genesis is God's symphony of the already-existing or previously created jarring atoms of Chaos, each of Dryden's six rhyme-lines has the metrical form of its fellow in the first six lines and therefore harmonizes precisely that which had previously been irregular and inharmonious. But although each creative act was a musical concordia discors whose poetic counterpart is the fusion of that difference and similarity, or dissonance and consonance, of which rhyme consists, the total Creation, like God, is a perfect unity, the circle without beginning or end. Consequently although Creation was a progress from one harmonizing rhyme to another, the prosodic arrangement of the first twelve lines is circular, and the last two lines of the second six-line unit do not rhyme but are identical throughout with the two lines that begin the poem: "From Harmony, from heav'nly Harmony / This universal Frame began." The poet has brought the twelve hexaemeral lines full circle to form that perfection which corresponds to God and his Creation.

The three-line coda which then ends the strophe is devoted to man, for he not only is the product of the sixth day but also is the microcosm. Consequently he is the perfect cadence, or ending ("closing full") of the "compass," or range of the scale of Creation; and correspondingly the rhymes perform a cadence, falling from the A to the B rhyme. But since he is also a little world analogous to the universe, the rhymes of the coda depend upon the A and B lines that both open and close the first twelve lines, making them a perfect and self-containing circle; and the mere analogy of the relationship is established by inverting the lengths of the original A and B lines (4A, 5B) and by introducing rhymes instead of identical terminal words for the B-lines (ran, Man).

Undoubtedly there are other symbolic structural features in the poem. Undoubtedly Dryden was careful to phrase the divine fiat, "Arise ye more than dead," in language that suggests the Last Day and foreshadows the penultimate line of the poem, "The Dead shall live, the Living die"; for thereby he not only car rest both the creation and destruction of the world on music, but also can make Creation and the Resurrection of man analogous musical acts, each being a summons from death to life. It is significant, moreover, that the second strophe and the final "Grand Chorus" are nine-line stanzas, for this probably represents the ninefold harmony of the spheres and their governing Muses, or angelic orders, whom the Platonist Macrobius reported to be "the tuneful song of the eight spheres and the one predominant harmony that comes from all of them."[8] And it is at least highly suggestive, in view of the hexaemeral nature of the first stanza, that after stanzas of successively four, five, and six lines the poem reaches its climax in a seven-line stanza whose subject is the heavenly music of St. Cecilia. It is most unlikely that any of these significances can be heard by the ear or were expected to be. Dryden is not playing program music but is structurally enacting his theme by analogy with the iconology of sound, appearance, and form that can be found in baroque music. Just as Bach represents snakes by a succession of notes sinuously arranged on the page, or night by a black note, or the ten-ness of the Ten Commandments by ten repetitions of a melody — and, indeed, as Draghi, in setting this song by Dryden, represents "heaven" with the highest note of his composition, and "jarring" by a rapid, irregular run of notes[9] — so Dryden has embodied significances in the non-assertive visible features of language. At least it is evident that Dryden was not merely repeating the stale topics of the encomium musicae and the Boethian analogy of musica mundana, humana, and instrumentalis. These systems, together with all their symbolic ramifications, are still vital enough to give shape and energy to his poem; and we might justifiably ask whether there may not be, beneath the apparent conventionality and discontinuity of the surface of Pope's Cecilian ode, a shaping force that derives from the same kind of musical symbolism.

Pope's opening strophe conventionally invokes the Muses to inspire music and then traces the consequent musical composition through the orchestrated instruments to its climax and final cadence. This overt statement is pursued with consistency throughout the stanza, and much of the language is drawn from the technical vocabulary of music. For example, "broken Air" (17) reflects an acoustical theory long entertained;[10] and "dying Fall" (21), like Dryden's "closing full," is a technical term for "cadence" and very fittingly brings the musical composition and the stanza to an end as its lines break and grow short.[11] The stanza is self-sufficient as a description of a piece of music, and we might therefore be content that the technical meaning of such a term as "dying Fall" is its exclusive sense, were it not that later approximately the same words become the means of describing the irretrievable loss of Eurydice: "Again she falls, again she dies, she dies!" (94). If now we add the existence in the public domain of both a parallelism and a causal connection

155

among the music of the universe, of man, and of musical instruments, it becomes necessary to question whether the "dying Fall" of the first strophe is to be read not only as the final phrase of a musical composition but also as the death that closes that other piece of music, man -- the death he inherits from the Fall. For man, like the macrocosm, is a musical instrument whose earthly music God brings to an end with a final cadence.

The topos that man is a musical instrument and that not only his song but even his speech is a music created to praise and glorify his Maker is too widespread and well-known to require evidence here. It permitted a popular pun on "organ"; and since speech was thought of as a kind of music, the vocal organs were compared to plectrum and stringed instrument, the plectrum linguae having been given man to praise his Creator. For theorists like Athanasius Kircher who took music as the archetype of order it was customary to translate every aspect of man, even his passions, shape, and pulse-rate into the proportions and mechanics of instrumental music. The theme is, of course, recurrent in such poets as Shakespeare, Donne, and Herbert. Consequently it is at least consistent with the tradition to read Pope's first strophe as containing within its external assertions about musica instrumentalis the creation, earthly course, and death of man; and the possibility is further hinted at by the poet's requesting that the stringed instruments be awakened, not into musical sound, but "into Voice" (3). The prayer that the Muses "inspire" the "breathing Instruments" (2) is, then, only superficially the threadbare request for divine artistic aid; and the words distantly echo those of Clement of Alexandria, who wrote that "The Lord fashioned man a beautiful, breathing instrument (ὄργανον ἔμπνουν) . . . an all-harmonious instrument of God, melodious and holy."[12] Pope's "breathing Instrument" is not only a wind instrument but also man, and the etymological sense of "inspire" operates here to recall the manner in which Adam was given life: "And the Lord God formed man of the dust of the ground and breathed into his nostrils the breath of life; and man became a living soul" (Genesis ii. 7). In the Vulgate, incidentally the "breathed" of the A.V. appears, not unexpectedly, as "inspiravit." Indeed, the passage in Genesis is even more precisely the control over Pope's opening lines, for, as almost all Scriptural commentators pointed out, the Targum of Onkelos here reads, not "et factus est homo in animam viventem," but, as it was translated, ". . . in animam loquentem" -- and man became a speaking soul. Usually this variant was interpreted as not inconsistent with the Vulgate, since speech is a manifest sign of human life and implies reason, the distinctive property of man. In this sense, the breathing of life into the dust of the ground was the awakening of man "into Voice." Pierre de la Primaudaye also had written that man's speech is possible only because he is an organ through which God the Organist has blown His breath;[13] but perhaps the most pertinent commentary on Pope's lines as a translation of the Genesis account of man's creation into terms of the creation of music is supplied by Cowley, who, having described the formation of the macrocosm as God's musical harmony, turns to His other "Harmonie," the microcosm Man -- that "single Quire! / Which first Gods Breath did tunefully inspire!"[14]

Through such verbal clues Pope's stanza reveals that by means of the design of a musical composition it is metaphorically outlining the course of man's life. In one sense the nine Muses, who govern the nine heavenly spheres and collectively produce the unheard harmony of the universe, are asked to descend and inspire the analogous instrumental music. In another, the divine creative spirit descends to "inspire" man to life and awakens his passions, the two poles of which are the concupiscent and the irascible: "sadly-pleasing" love, represented by the lyre, and war, the musical symbol of which is the trumpet.[15] But man is also soul, the "solemn" organ; and in his spiritual course the orchestration of his three instruments reaches its climax when his music fills "with spreading Sounds the Skies; Exulting in Triumph" (15-16), only to tremble in "broken Air" (his vital breath failing),[16] decay, and end in a dying fall. For man aspires, or spiritually leaps to heaven but, in his earthly life, suffers the breaking of his vital spirits and dies.

Depending on the analogy of musica humana and musica instrumentalis, the stanza has traced both the form of music and man's life as the descent of a power (or spirit) that inspires (or animates), and as a crescendo to a climax (or spiritual height) and a diminuendo (or decay) into a "dying Fall." If now we consider this stanza in the context of the entire poem we can recognize that this configuration is also precisely that of the Orpheus myth and that the identity of the two patterns -- intimated

by the analogy of the musical strains that "decay . . . In a dying, dying Fall" and Eurydice's doom, "Again she falls, again
she dies, she dies!" -- further demands the reading of the first
stanza as metaphoric of man's mortal career. For just as the
Muses are asked to "descend and sing" to arouse the music
which ascends to the skies and sinks in dissolution — or just as
a spirit descends to animate man, who then aspires to heaven
and decays in death — so Orpheus descends into hell with song
to "restore Eurydice to Life" (81) and makes "the tortur'd
Ghosts respire" (64), nearly achieves Eurydice's resurrection,
but fails as she sinks down again to her final death. The similarity of outline suggests that this may be the larger syntactical
organization of the poem's materials and demands that we ask
how the similarly structured materials are meaningfully related.

For this pattern of descent and ascent is everywhere the
internal organizational control over the poem and is responsible
for the coherence of the apparently random topics of the encomium musicae. The second stanza, still depending on the relation of musica humana and musica instrumentalis, and still
alluding to both areas by means of such equivocal words as
"Temper" and "Airs," elaborates the three established "effects,"
or ethea, of music: "serrer, deserrer, acoyser les espritz."17
Pope has assigned these effects to three different faculties,
mind, breast, and soul: ideally the rational mind should keep
"an equal Temper" (22), neither rising nor falling, the naturally
tumultuous passions should be suppressed, and the soul, which
tends to be pressed down in the temporal world, should be exalted heavenward. Indeed, the words "Or when the Soul is
press'd with Cares / [music] Exalts her in enlivening Airs"
(26-27) might equally well have been used to describe Orpheus'
raising of the fallen Eurydice by means of music. Similarly,
in the third stanza Orpheus' martial music raises even higher
those who were already demi-gods and raises mere mortals to
heroes, half-mortal and half-divine, just as his music falls
short of raising Eurydice entirely from hell, and just as the
music of the first stanza, though reaching to the skies, fails to
sustain its "Triumph." And finally the poem will close with
angels leaning down from heaven to hear the mortal Cecilia's
divine music, and with the contrast between Orpheus' and Cecilia's power to exalt:

POPE'S ODE FOR MUSICK

His Numbers rais'd a Shade from Hell,
Hers lift the Soul to Heav'n.

The pattern of ascent and descent, then, pervades the entire
poem and serves as the compositional means of correlating the
mortal life of man, the three "effects" of music on his earthly
conduct, the myth of Orpheus the Argonaut and that of Orpheus
the lover of Eurydice, and the spiritual power of the patron
saint of music.

This, however, supplies us only with the configuration that
artistically unifies these otherwise disparate topics of the theme
of music, and not the organized end that the configuration is
working to bring about. The poetic significance to which the internal compositional pattern is the means can best be grasped
by understanding the role of the Orpheus myth, which dispropor-
tionately and irrelevantly, it would seem, occupies the bulk of
the poem.

That Orpheus was a type of Christ is, of course, as ancient
a theme as Christianity itself, and one of the major Medieval
and Renaissance interpretations of the classical myth devotes
itself to elaborating the parallelism.[18] Of this tradition the
Metamorphosis Ovidiana attributed to Thomas Walleys and
probably by Berchorius may be taken as characteristic: Orpheus,
son of the sun, is Christ, son of God, and was conjoined with
Eurydice, the human soul, "per specialem praerogativam a
principio." When the human soul was stung by sin and carried
off to hell, "Orpheus Christus" personally descended to rescue
it, Orpheus' song being the divine word, and his lyre the
Cross.[19] The identification of Orpheus with Christ was made
on the same grounds by Giles Fletcher[20] and was a recurrent
theme in seventeenth-century Spanish drama.[21]

Yet of course if this interpretation of Orpheus as Christ is
relevant, it certainly is not explicit in Pope's version of the
myth, and it appears that he has offered no more than a fairly
exact adaptation of the Orpheus episode in Vergil's fourth
Georgic, detail for detail. Indeed, the words that do dislocate
the Orpheus myth from its merely classical source and assimilate it to the Christian typological interpretation make their
appearance most casually as Pope's narrative opens:

> But when thro' all th'Infernal Bounds
> Which flaming Phlegethon surrounds,
> Love, strong as Death, the Poet led
> To the pale Nations of the Dead.   (49-52)

In no way has Pope altered Vergil's sense or details; but the words "Love, strong as Death" derive, not from Vergil, but from the Song of Songs (viii. 6): "Set me as a seal upon thine heart, as a seal upon thine arm: for love is strong as death; jealousy as cruel as the grave." In that firmly established Christian tradition which read Canticles as the divine love-dialogue of the bridegroom Christ and his bride Ecclesia, these words are assigned to Christ; and their almost universally accepted meaning, as reported by Cornelius à Lapide, is that "amor sponsi per crucem liberavit sponsam a morte et inferno cui ob peccatum addicta erat."[22] The consequence of Pope's passing allusion to Canticles is to intimate the similarity of Orpheus to Christ, since both descended to hell to rescue their brides from sin and death. The relation of the Orpheus legend to the Christian interpretation of Canticles is an obvious one; and in describing how "Orpheus Christus" raised Eurydice from hell it was to Canticles that Berchorius turned for the words he assigned to the Bridegroom: "Surge, propera amica mea, et veni" (ii. 10).

Recognition that, at least at the beginning of his Orpheus myth, Pope has assimilated it to the typological reading of Canticles unfolds the Christian sense he has also infused into the passage that closes this first phase of his Orpheus narrative — the only phase that parallels the life of Christ. Orpheus' rescue of Eurydice was

> O'er Death and o'er Hell,
> A Conquest how hard and how glorious.
> Tho' Fate had fast bound her
> With Styx nine times round her,
> Yet Musick and Love were Victorious.   (88-92)

The details fit the classical myth perfectly, and it is likely that the reference to the "hard" conquest reproduces the words of the Sibyl to Aeneas when, in reply to his protest that Orpheus was able to call up the ghost of his wife, the Sibyl informs him

that the descent into hell is easy, but the return to upper air,
"hoc opus, hic labor est."[23] But the martial language Pope has
chosen, while it echoes the momentary "Triumph" of the music-
soul as it moves toward the skies in his first stanza, also suggests Christ's triumph over hell, rather than Orpheus'; for it
calls up the language of many Easter and Ascentiontide hymns:
"Victor surgit de funere . . . Gloria tibi, Domine, / qui sur-
rexisti a mortuis"; "Aeterne Rex altissime, / redemptor et
fidelium, / cui mors perempta detulit / summae triumphum
gloriae"; or "Victor, subactis inferis, / trophaea Christus ex-
plicat."[24] Even more significant, in the very act of describing
Orpheus' accomplishments in terms suggesting Christ's, Pope
is incorporating in this passage the same verse from the Song
of Songs with which he began his story of Orpheus and with
which he associated Orpheus with Christ. For, whereas the
A.V. reads, "love is strong as death; jealousy is cruel as the
grave," the Vulgate has, "fortis est ut mors dilectio, dura
sicut infernus aemulatio"; and such exegetes as Cornelius à
Lapide went to considerable lengths to explain why both terms,
death and hell, were necessary, the phrase running like a refrain through their commentaries: "amor Christi fuit fortis
sicut mors et infernus, quia amor eum coegit mori et descen-
dere in infernum."[25] Pope's lines therefore ostensibly translate
Vergil's fourth Georgic, even in mentioning the nine circuits
of the Styx. But by echoing the language of the hymns he cor-
relates his narrative with Christ's ransom of man; and by referring to the conquest "O'er Death and o'er Hell" he surrounds
this unit of the classical myth with borrowings from Canticles
which identify Orpheus with the Christ who rescued the church
by His crucifixion.

Yet, however much Pope may have directed the Orpheus
myth to evoke the acknowledged parallel with the sacrifice of
Christ for the salvation of the human soul, the fact remains
that Orpheus failed where Christ succeeded, and the allusion
to Christ cannot be Pope's whole purpose. Those commentators
who had connected Orpheus and Christ had found it necessary,
of course, to omit Orpheus' ultimate failure, and Pope tells
the myth to its tragic end. Rather, in suggesting Christ, Pope
is evoking the parallel for the more customary purpose of making it evident that Orpheus, whatever the similarity, is not
Christ. For example, George Wither, protesting against the

popularity of pagan stories, asked:

> Can we be delighted to heare a Heathen Poet sing a
> fabulous story of Hercules, their great Champion
> (whose valour never benefitted us) how hee went down
> to hell, and by force brought thence the Lady Proser-
> pina, whom the Prince of that infernall Region had
> ravished? And can we not take as great pleasure to
> heare the divine Muse of this heavenly Poet, sing in a
> true Historie, how for the benefit of all men (even for
> us) Christ our farre more victorious Captaine descend-
> ed into the lowest depths, for the salvation of our
> soules; and having subdued death, and hell, delivered
> that faire Ladie the Church from being ravished by the
> Prince of Darknesse? Doth it affect us to heare but
> the bare relation, how Orpheus, the Thracian Poet,
> so prevailed among the unmerciful Inhabitants of Hell,
> that by the power of his Charmes, he brought his Wife
> Euridice from those unpleasant shades? And can we
> sit when the thrice excellent of Poets repeats unto
> us the very songs themselves, wherewith the inspirer
> of all excellencie did himself ravish heaven, earth,
> and hell? and in spight of the strongest manacles of
> sinne, death, and the Divell, brought his Spouse, our
> Mother, from the tyranny of Sathan?[26]

Despite the similarity of Orpheus and Christ, only Christ is the
true Orpheus, wrote Alexander Ross:

> it was he onely who went down to hell, to recover the
> Church his spouse who had lost her selfe, by running
> away from Aristeus, even goodness itselfe; and de-
> lighting her selfe among the grasse and flowres of
> pleasure, was stung by that old serpent the Devil.
> What was in vain attempted by Orpheus, was truly
> performed by our Saviour, for he alone hath deliv-
> ered our soules from the nethermost Hell.[27]

Similarly Pope has contrived that his version of the Orpheus
myth call up the reader's sense of the relation to Christ, and
yet by recounting Orpheus' failure he has denied the full identity.

162

To be like Christ is only Orpheus' unfulfilled potentiality. For Pope's purpose, in part, is to play off the possibility of an allegory of Christ against the customary moral interpretation of the myth. By this means he can set Orpheus' moral failure into the context of Christian spiritual values, since the narrative that begins by intimating Christ's sacrifice develops into an account of Orpheus' spiritual lapse.

The Medieval and Renaissance moral interpretation normally identified Eurydice as the human soul, or reason. She is wedded to Orpheus when the soul is joined with the body, and is sent to hell when she is trapped in sensual pleasures and stung by sin. Orpheus' music, which represents the harmony of actions whence virtue springs, raises her from hell, or the vices; but he fails at last because, violating the commandment, he mentally looks back upon the sensual delights of the world.[28] The variants of this interpretation have comparatively little effect on the eventual moral purport of the myth. To Boccaccio, for example, Orpheus represents the eloquence of wisdom, and his wife natural desire; for, the commentators agreed, no mortal is without these appetites. Eurydice's death and descensus ad inferos are therefore to be understood as the total lapse of man's natural desires into earthly concerns; and Orpheus, the prudent orator, retrieves Eurydice with his songs, or true arguments, leading her back to virtue and directing the appetites to laudable things and the higher good. But he cannot resist the temptations of fervent desires and, instead of confining himself to meditation, glances back upon temporal things.[29] The central sense of all the moral glosses, however variously Orpheus and Eurydice may have been identified, remained constant and was most succinctly expressed in Boethius' De consolatione (III, meter 12) and by the commentaries on it by the Pseudo-Aquinas: the theme of the myth is man's need to contemplate steadily the highest good and throw off the bondage of the world and the body; and the hell from which Eurydice is temporarily rescued is not the Christian hell, but the lust for temporal things.[30]

But Pope has disturbed the texture of the Orpheus myth even less to call up this moral meaning than he did to assimilate Orpheus to Christ; for the moral reading is neither explicit nor implied in his verbal formulations. What does generate it is not the language but the stationing of the legend of St. Cecilia after that of Orpheus. Their adjacency is a syntactical device that

conjures up their similarities, and Pope's final contrast of
Orpheus and Cecilia causes the two legends to interact and un-
fold their opposition as two modes of conduct and devotion. Both
legends center around the relation of husband and wife, but
whereas Orpheus was consumed by love of Eurydice, Cecilia,
directly after her wedding to Valerian, pledged him to preserve
her virginity because she was betrothed to an angel. It is for
the purpose of this contrast that Pope has underscored and
heightened Vergil's account of Orpheus' single-minded devotion
to Eurydice, even after his death, when we might expect his
thoughts to be on heavenly things:

> — Ah see, he dies!
> Yet ev'n in Death Eurydice he sung,
> Eurydice still trembled on his Tongue,
>   Eurydice the Woods,
>   Eurydice the Floods,
> Eurydice the Rocks, and hollow Mountains rung.[31]

> (112-17)

Against this uxoriousness and the carnis concupiscentia implied
by Orpheus' singing only of his wife, Pope poses Cecilia's total
dedication to God, for her legend tells that during her wedding
she "to her Maker's Praise confin'd the Sound" (125). Whereas
Orpheus, destroyed by the mad, chaotic frenzy that the Bac-
chantes represent, confined his thoughts to earthly desires
"ev'n in Death," Cecilia accepted her union with Valerian in this
world as her spiritual marriage to God. And whereas the pagan
Orpheus, however Christ-like his actions, finally failed to raise
Eurydice, the converted pagan Cecilia converted Valerian to
Christianity and so lifted his "Soul to Heav'n."

The line on which these two similar and yet contrasting
legends pivot and through which they become thematically connected is Pope's gratuitous addition to the Orpheus myth. Pope
has emphasized that earthly love is the sole force in this myth,
for he attributes Orpheus' momentary success in raising Eurydice not only to music but also to love (92), and he is careful to
say that it is "the Lover" (93) who looks back upon Eurydice,
instead of antedating "the Bliss above" (123) as Cecilia does
even during her marriage to her mortal lover. When, therefore,

Eurydice suffers the dying fall because of Orpheus' excessive love, Pope addresses to Orpheus a seeming consolation:

> No Crime was thine, if 'tis no Crime to love.   (96)

But the line is strangely equivocal, and its theme is strangely recurrent in Pope's poetry: his Cleopatra vehemently protests, "No guilt of mind the rage of Heav'n cou'd move; / I knew no crime, if 'tis no crime to love"; his Unfortunate Lady is asked, "Is it, in heav'n, a crime to love too well?"; and Eloisa complains that Abelard's religious instructions too soon "taught me 'twas no sin to love."[32] So phrased, the theological point is indeed an ambiguous one, and the ambiguity comments equally on Orpheus and Cecilia. Orpheus' desire for Eurydice as naturalis concupiscentia is no sin, the moral interpreters explain, since "Nemo . . . absque sua naturali concupiscentia est,"[33] and natural love, when purified, is the means to love of God. It is therefore a good and, in this sense, can know no excess. Yet it degenerates into tragic luxuria because Orpheus cannot rise to a superior love and, even after his mortal life, yearns for Eurydice alone. The saintly Cecilia, on the other hand, could sublimate earthly love and perform her human wedding as a marriage to God. Therefore, whereas Orpheus' song, representing the virtuous power of human love, could, Christ-like, raise momentarily "a Shade from Hell" (133), or sin, but could not raise the fallen soul to the vita nuova, her song, representing divine love, lifts "the Soul to Heav'n." And it is significant not only that Pope has opposed shade and soul, hell and heaven, but also that he tells whence human love can raise the soul and whither divine love can exalt it.

Slight though the exposed surface of the poem may be, then, Pope has expanded his encomium musicae into a statement that embraces the whole of man. By means of the metaphor of music the first two stanzas present man in his human and earthly perspective, graphing the curve of his mortal life as a musical composition and, within the same artistic design of ascent and descent, and through the metaphor of the therapeutic power of music over his faculties, prescribing his earthly conduct. These stanzas lay the groundwork for Pope's main concern and are prefatory to it: the relation of man's conduct to his spiritual welfare and his future existence, expressed as a similar pattern of ascent and descent, triumph and failure. The Orpheus who does not sustain his Christ-like role reveals that he is a pagan and the natural man after all and that the virtuous resources available to him, although not wrong, are inadequate and insecure. His natural love and natural reason are Christ-like, since they can raise the soul out of sin; but reason can at length be overpowered by love, and natural desires can become their own end. By contrast, Cecilia is the Christian consummation of Orpheus as the state of grace is the consummation of the state of nature, and she transcends the partial success of the natural man by purifying natural into divine love. The theme of Pope's two legends is that of the Apostle: "He that loveth his life shall lose it; and he that hateth his life in this world shall keep it unto life eternal" (John xii. 25); and the religious purpose of the poem, like that of the customary sermons on St. Cecilia's day, is "the fixing our Attention, and enflaming our Affections" in our undistracted devotions to God.[34] Orpheus' secular song finally binds him to the mortal world, but "Nothing so raises the soul and gives it wings and frees it from earth," wrote St. Chrysostom, "as music and divine song." In this sense, then, Pope's encomium musicae is the contrast of the Old Song of Orpheus with the New Song of Cecilia, "the new music with its eternal strain that bears the name of God." Hence the change of tense in the final lines: Orpheus' numbers "rais'd a Shade," Cecilia's "lift the Soul." The songs of Orpheus, wrote Clement of Alexandria, led men to idolatry. By contrast, "See how mighty is the New Song! . . . They who were otherwise dead, who had no share in the real and true life, revived when they but heard the song. . . . This is the New Song, namely, the manifestation which has but shined forth among us, of Him who was in the beginning, the pre-existing Word."[35]

But there is another and larger sense in which Orpheus, not Cecilia, is the center of the poem; and Pope was right to devote most of his space and attention to him. For although Cecilia is the martyr and saint, Orpheus is Man. It is significant that the pattern of ascent and descent in the Orpheus-Eurydice myth is exactly that of Pope's first stanza, which outlines man's life as it is seen in its human, earthly perspective. The analogy identifies Orpheus as man's natural condition, including the possibility inherent in that condition of man's sharing in the incarnate God and being Christ-like. Just as even secular music is more than earthly because it can correct the mind's, breast's, and soul's disorders that are the consequence of the Fall, so Orpheus' earthly love of Eurydice is more than earthly since it can raise the soul above the world of sin and mortality. But in the end his failure shows, not that this is wrong, but that this heroic much is not enough and must conclude in the answerless despair of the human condition, must conclude with Orpheus "Despairing, confounded" (107). Cecilia -- whose song lifts the soul to Heaven and who is customarily portrayed rapturously looking up -- is symbolized diagrammatically by only the upward movement that counterbalances the descent, aspiration, and fall of human life; and thereby she provides the answer to Orpheus' despair, to which otherwise there had been no answer. Cecilia therefore does not necessarily displace Orpheus in the poem, nor does she merely supplement him. She does if we read Orpheus and Cecilia only in the context of chronological time: Christianity succeeds and displaces paganism. But what Orpheus and Cecilia symbolize also coexists at every moment in time after the Incarnation: nature and grace, death and salvation. Man must love greatly the worldly things of God, must lose them, must fail in his spiritual aspiration, however heroic, and must die; and at the same time, if he is to resolve that desperate condition, must to his "Maker's praise" confine his song. The mysterious paradox of human limitation and human glory has been contained in the ambiguity of "No Crime was thine, if 'tis no Crime to love."

The poem therefore gradually and coherently swells to its final triumph. But Pope has not merely deposited disjunctive blocks into which the reader is to read their implied relationships and the growing development. This disjunctiveness is certainly there on the surface, and much of the artistry resides not in any explicit integration of the materials and their shapes, but in the subtle, characteristically neoclassic ways in which they evoke larger areas of reference -- man's mortal career, the allegorical and moral meanings of the Orpheus myth, the legend of St. Cecilia, for example -- and array these in a significant syntactical order. Yet beyond this Pope has further integrated all the apparently diverse segments of his poem by consistently weaving through it two threads that climactically become one in the closing stanza on St. Cecilia.

It will be recalled that in the first stanza the range of man's

passions was represented by its extremes, love and war, symbolized by the "sadly-pleasing" lyre and the trumpet, while the
"solemn" organ implied the soul. Correspondingly, in the next
stanza, after the presentation of the three ethea of music as
modes of ascent and descent, Pope describes the effect of music
on warrior and lover; and on the basis of the tradition that love
is a kind of war, he interchanges their attributes:

> Warriors she [music] fires with animated Sounds;
> Pours Balm into the bleeding Lover's Wounds. (28-29)

The Orpheus myth also conforms to this pattern, since Pope has
chosen to deal with two separate phases of Orpheus' career: not
only his tragic love for Eurydice but also his part in the martial
adventures of the Argonauts. Since one of the psychological
powers of music is to purge the "Intestine War" of the passions,
the stanza on the three ethea leads directly to the contrasting
stanza on Orpheus' martial music and the adventures of the
Argonauts, which Pope presents as a virtuous war in "our Country's Cause." Even Orpheus' pleading song in hell returns to the
themes of love and war, for he prays equally to the two groups
who inhabit the Elysian Fields:

> By the Heroe's armed Shades,
> Glitt'ring thro' the gloomy Glades,
> By the Youths that dy'd for Love,
> Wandring in the Myrtle Grove.   (77-80)

And Orpheus' momentary defeat of hell by music and love, like
the exulting of the soul in the first stanza as it aspires to heav-
en, is described as a conquest, victory, and triumph. In other
words, throughout the poem there is a consistently evolving
dialectic of love and war. In the first stanza they are merely
descriptive of the range of man's passions and are not evaluated.
War is then condemned when it is intestine conflict, but praised
when it is in "our Country's Cause" -- and in view of Pope's frequent equivocal use of "home" as this world and the soul's dwelling place in heaven, we might well suspect a double sense in
the words "our Country." Similarly, the story of Orpheus and
Eurydice, we have seen, distinguishes between virtuous and
vicious love, the naturalis concupiscentia needful to all men

and the carnis concupiscentia to which Orpheus succumbs. But when Orpheus is successful in redeeming Eurydice and before he falls victim to carnal love, the two strands we have been tracing are brought together, and virtuous love and war are united: "A Conquest how hard and how glorious. . . . Musick and Love were Victorious." But since Orpheus then fails, this is an unstable fusion, and it remains for St. Cecilia to bring the two themes together into a true and permanent union. Throughout, war has been associated with warmth and fire, and therefore has become nearly synonymous with zeal. By Orpheus' martial music, for example, the Argonauts were "Enflam'd with Glory's Charms"; and, in view of the theme of the entire poem, we might justifiably wonder in what sense we are to understand "Glory," whether it is merely human or possibly divine. But the entire process of the poem has worked to transform this martial zeal, or flame of glory, into Cecilia's religious zeal, or "sacred Fire" (120), which, in a glaring play on words, is fanned by the "solemn Airs." For her love of God, which transcends Orpheus' earthly love and her own earthly wedding, is identical with her militant religious zeal, and the "sacred Fire" is indiscriminately a virtuous love and a virtuous war. Through divine music, wrote Bishop Atterbury, we raise and inflame "that most heavenly Passion of Love, which reigns always in pious Breasts" and "make the Devotions of this our Church Militant here on Earth, the lively Image of those of the Church Triumphant in Heaven."[36]

The final stanza, then, both contains and transcends the rest of the poem. The summary of the "effects" of music, with which it begins, repeats the theme of the second stanza; but just as Pope followed that theme with an account of Orpheus' nearly successful redemption of Eurydice, so the "effects" in the final stanza are transcended by the power of music to "antedate the Bliss above" (123), and the Orpheus who, even in death, confined his song to Eurydice is replaced by Cecilia, who "to her Maker's Praise confin'd the Sound" (125). In the first stanza, while the lute and trumpet represented the human passions, the "solemn" organ figured the soul, and it is now because of the music of this instrument that "Born on the swelling Notes our Souls aspire" (128), just as in the first stanza the symphony of the passions and the soul rose and filled "with spreading Sounds the Skies; / Exulting in Triumph now swell the bold Notes" (15-16).

And yet, for all the scope and grandeur of its purpose, and for all the complex intensity of its art, it must be confessed that the poem is not wholly sound at center and falls short — but not immeasurably short — of Pope's best. It is not that Pope lacks sincerity where it matters most; on the contrary, he is too exclusively devoted to his religious theme, and the materials of the occasion will not support its weight. The poem demands that the metaphor of music carry a very great theme indeed, and Pope's world is not truly musical in the sense that it was to Shakespeare or Herbert or Donne or Milton. If one superficially reads the poem as only a tribute to music on the occasion of St. Cecilia's day, it is a trite exercise in juggling stale materials, a cento of the common musical topics. If one reads it for its total thematic purpose, the musical metaphor sinks beneath the load and disappears from attention because it is not a reality, but only a convenient vehicle. To test its inadequacy one need only contrast the insincerity of the musical metaphor here with the reality, aliveness, and immediacy of Horace's poems and the Horatian vision when, in poems like the epistles to Bolingbroke, Bathurst, and Augustus, Pope similarly uses them as a kind of metaphoric base on which to climb to religious truth.

NOTES

1 English Literature in the Early Eighteenth Century (Oxford, 1959), p. 201.

2 "A World of Instruments," ELH, 20 (1953), 87-120. Other studies of musical symbolism in the Renaissance relevant to this paper are Mrs. Finney's "Ecstasy and Music in Seventeenth-Century England," JHI, 8 (1947), 153-86, and " 'Organical Musick' and Ecstasy," JHI, 8 (1947), 273-92; Leo Spitzer, "Classical and Christian Ideas of World Harmony," Traditio, 2 (1944), 409-64 and 3 (1945), 307-64; James Hutton, "Some Poems in Praise of Music," English Miscellany, 2 (1951), 1-63; and John Hollander, The Untuning of the Sky (Princeton, 1961).

3 Spitzer (op. cit., III, 340-41) has dealt with the relation of "rivalry" and "concert" (concertare: to contend, to fight with someone).

4   Homily I. 7, in Nicene and Post Nicene Fathers, 2nd series, ed. Schaff and Wace (New York, 1895), VIII, 56.

5   Exhortation to the Greeks (Loeb trans.), I, 3.

6   Lectures on Dryden (Cambridge, 1914), pp. 194-95.

7   Musurgia universalis (Rome, 1650), chap. x.

8   Commentary on the Dream of Scipio, trans. W. H. Stahl (New York, 1952), p. 193.

9   M. Bukofzer, "Allegory in Baroque Music," Journal of the Warburg and Courtauld Institutes, 3 (1939), 1-21; Ernest Brennecke, "Dryden's Odes and Draghi's Music," PMLA, 49 (1934), 1-36.

10 Chaucer, Hous of Fame, II, 257: "Soun is noght but air y-broken." John Oldham's ode for St. Cecilia's day: "Hark! how the waken'd strings resound, / And sweetly break the yielding air!" See also John Arthos, The Language of Nature Description in Eighteenth-Century Poetry (Ann Arbor, 1949), pp. 135, 310-15.

11 Cp. Twelfth Night. I. i. 4: "That strain again! It had a dying fall."

12 Op. cit., p. 13.

13 L'Academie Françoise (Paris, 1584), p. 65b; see also 59b and 62b.

14 Davideis, Bk. 1.

15 Servius, who at one point (on Aeneid VI, 645) identified the nine spheres with cosmic music, elsewhere (on Aeneid VI, 439) wrote of them, ". . . dicunt intra novem hos mundi circulos inclusas esse virtutes, in quibus et iracundiae et cupiditates. . . ."

16 In his Second Anniversary Donne urges that we contemplate "our state in our death-bed":

> Thinke thy selfe labouring now with broken breath,
> And thinke those broken and soft Notes to bee
> Division, and thy happyest Harmonie. (90-92)

Cp. Oldham ode for St. Cecilia's day: "Without the sweets of melody, / To tune our vital breath, / Who would not give it up to death."

17 See F. A. Yates, French Academies of the Sixteenth Century (London, 1947), p. 45 n.

18 See, e.g., Eusebius, Panegyric to Constantine (P. G. , XX, 1409-12).

19 (1509), fol. lxxiii.

20 Christs Triumph over Death, stanza 7. See also Gawin Douglas, Poetical Works, ed. J. Small, II, 18, and Antonio Bosio, Roma sotterranea (Rome, 1710), p. 630.

21 See Pablo Cabañas, El mito de Orfeo en la literatura española (Madrid, 1948).

22 Commentarius in Canticum Canticorum (Lugduni, 1732), p. 250.

23 Aeneid VI, 129.

24 See The Hymns of the Breviary and Missal, ed. Dom Matthew Britt (New York, 1955).

25 The commentators also correlated this verse with appearances of the term "mors et infernus" in the Book of Revelation.

26 A Preparation to the Psalter (1619), pp. 77-78. Note the application of the words "death and hell" to Hercules, Christ, and Orpheus; and also the similarity of Wither's theme to Pope's conclusion: "Of Orpheus now no more let Poets tell, / To bright Cecilia greater Pow'r is giv'n" (131-32).

27 Mystagogus Poeticus (1653), pp. 338-39. See also Clement of Alexandria, op. cit. , pp. 9-13.

28 This is essentially the interpretation offered by Philomusus (in Fulgentius, Mythologiarum libri tres, Augsburg, 1521), Landino (Opera Virgiliana, 1529), J. Badius (in Boethius, De consolatione, Venice, 1524, fols. 58b-59b; and in Opera Virgiliana, 1529, p. cclxiii), Sperone Speroni (Opera, Venice, 1740, pp. 43-44), Giovanni F. da Fighine (L'Opera

di Virgilio, Venice, 1615), Natalis Comes (Mythologiae, Patavii, 1616, p. 402), and Thomas Heywood (Dialogue betwixt Earth and Age, in Dramatic Works, 1874, VI, 149-50). Many of these merely repeat each other's words without acknowledgment. According to an interpretation offered by Berchorius (Metamorphoses Ovidiana, 1509, fol. lxxiii), Orpheus is "peccator," and his songs in hell are his repentance, which, through grace, reclaims his soul.

29 Genealogia deorum gentilium, V. xii. This is very close to the interpretations by Bernardus Silvestris (Commentarum . . . Eneidos, ed. William Riedel, 1924, p. 54), Guillaume de Conches (see E. Jeauneau in Archives d'histoire doctrinale et littéraire du Moyen Age, 24 [1957], 40-50), Salutati (De laboribus Herculis, IV, i, 7), and G. A. dell'Anguillara and Gioseppi Horologgi (Ovid, Le metamorfosi, Venice, 1584, pp. 357, 387). See also Fernando de Herrera, Anotaciones a las obras de Garcilaso, 1580 (quoted in Pablo Cabañas, op. cit., p. 28). The similarity of the myth to the story of Adam and Eve is obvious, and the prototype of this moral interpretation probably is to be found in Philo Judaeus' identification of Adam as mind and Eve as the senses or the body: " . . . in us mind corresponds to man, the senses to woman. . . . Reason is forthwith ensnared and becomes a subject instead of a ruler" (Loeb trans., I, 131).

30 Or, according to Thomas Heywood, loc. cit., "dull and deepe melancholy, with the trouble of a perplext conscience." All the commentators were agreed that a pagan reference to a descensus ad inferos can only be an allusion to the mortal world, temporal things, carnal desires, and vices. Hence, in translating Boethius' meter on Orpheus, Chaucer felt it necessary to gloss Boethius' references to hell with "that is to seyn, who-so sette this thoughtes in erthely things" and "that is to seyn, in-to lowe thinges of the erthe." Similar additions appear in the 1556 translation by George Colville and in the 1695 translation by Lord Preston. That this is the sense in which we are to read Pope's references to hell is not destroyed by his description of

Eurydice "With Styx nine times round her," a direct translation from Vergil's fourth Georgic. For Servius, whose commentary was included in most of the early editions of Vergil and whose gloss on the river Styx was much discussed, especially by Badius, explained that "et novies Styx interfusa coercet" refers to the earth, which is surrounded by the nine spheres (on Aeneid VI, 127, 439): ". . . circulos Stygis, quae inferos cingit, id est terram. . . ." Elsewhere Servius relates the nine spheres to music and Orpheus (VI, 645), and in the Platonic tradition, we have seen, they become identified with the nine Muses, whom Pope invoked at the beginning of his poem. For a similar interpretation of the nine circuits of the Styx as the spheres about the earth, see Favonius Eulogius, Disputatio de somnio Scipionis, ed. A. Holder (Leipzig, 1901), p. 13.

31   Te, dulcis coniunx, te solo in litore secum,
       te veniente die, te decendente canebat. . . .
       tum quoque, marmorea caput a cervice revulsum
       gurgite cum medio portans Oeagrius Hebrus
       volveret, Eurydicen vox ipsa et frigida lingua,
       ah miseram Eurydicen! anima fugiente vocabat;
       Eurydicen toto referebant flumine ripae.

                                   (Georgic IV, 465-66, 523-27)

32   "On the Statue of Cleopatra," 61; "Elegy to the Memory of
       an Unfortunate Lady," 6; "Eloisa to Abelard," 68.

33   Bernardus Silvestris, loc. cit.; also Boccaccio.

34   Francis Atterbury, "The Usefulness of Church Musick:
       a Sermon Preached on St. Cecilia's Day, 1698," in Sermons
       and Discourses (1745; third ed.) IV, 238.

35   Op. cit. , pp. 11, 17.

36   Op. cit. , pp. 250, 263.

POPE ON WIT: THE ESSAY ON CRITICISM

Edward Niles Hooker

Since the publication of Tillotson's admirable study we have become increasingly aware of the extraordinary art of Pope's verse. That awareness, however, has not led us insistently enough to suspect that the Essay on Criticism has something to say, something neither trivial nor commonplace, and worthy of the artistry with which the ideas are set forth. Supposing that Pope never could make up his mind about certain crucial terms such as wit and nature, we are tempted to regard the poem as a mélange of confused and sometimes contradictory assertions or as a potpourri of Augustan clichés. Poor addled Pope (one recent editor intimates) employed the word wit throughout the Essay on Criticism in seven different senses; and we can conclude, if we like, that he knew no better.

To the acute and subtle mind of Empson we stand indebted for the explicit recognition that the Essay has a solid core of intelligible meaning, or perhaps a complex of meanings, coherent and applicable, and revolving around what he regards as the key word, wit.[1] A close reading of the poem leaves no room for doubting that Pope intended to convey what seemed to him the significant facts about the place of wit in literature, and that for some reason it struck him as particularly desirable to do so. To understand the Essay, therefore, we should address ourselves to three questions. Why, in an essay devoted to the principles of criticism, does Pope lavish space and attention on wit rather than on taste? Second, what controversies being agitated at the time he was composing the poem would have led Pope to take a stand, and how is that stand established in the Essay? And third, what body of contemporary thought, more or less parallel to his own, was available to him as he wrote, and how

Reprinted from The Seventeenth Century by Richard Foster Jones and others, pp. 225-246, with the permission of the publishers, Stanford University Press. Copyright 1951 by the Board of Trustees of the Leland Stanford Junior University. This article appeared earlier in The Hudson Review, Vol. 2 (1950), pp. 84-100.

can it illumine the direction and implications of his thinking?

In the first place, Pope at the start, after describing the highest form of artistic talent in the poet as true genius, and the highest gift of the critic as true taste, proceeds to the principle that the best critics are those who excel as authors (lines 15-16).[2] True taste, therefore, is best revealed in the operations of genius. That genius and taste "have so intimate a Connection" is not an idea peculiar to Pope; as one of his contemporaries remarked, "there are Cases where they cannot be . . . separated, without almost taking away their Functions."[3] A discussion of the art of criticism would be idle unless it expounded taste by revealing the ways and standards of genius.

Or, since genius is distressingly rare, one may, like Pope, examine the ways of wit, that more inclusive thing, conceived of as literary talent or as the distinguishing element in literature, the breath of life informing the dull clay. As Dryden had proclaimed, "The composition of all poems is, or ought to be, of wit . . ."[4] He meant, not ingenuity, but a spark. The special gift of those who create literature is to "invigorate their conceptions, and strike Life into a whole Piece"; what would otherwise remain leaden or sluggish is magically transformed by Flame and Strength of Sense.[5] Nothing could be more natural than that Homer and Virgil, authors who possessed such qualities in the highest degree, should be called "these Two supreme Wits."[6] Fire, invention, and imagination became inextricably associated with wit; they were the life-giving forces -- so David Abercromby meant when he said that "we never write wittily, but when our Imagination is exalted to a certain degree of heat, destructive to our cold dulness."[7] In the words of John Oldmixon, a minor contemporary of both Dryden and Pope: "Every Thing that pleases in Writing is with us . . . resolved into Wit, whether it be in the Thought or the Expression."[8] When John Sheffield, Duke of Buckingham, said in his Essay upon Poetry, " 'Tis Wit and Sence that is the Subject here,"[9] he had in mind much the same idea that Blackwall owned when he remarked of Horace, "His Sprightliness of Imagination is temper'd with Judgment; and he is both a pleasant Wit, and a Man of Prudence."[10] Sense and judgment are the solid, useful stuff with which the writer works, but wit is the magic that lifts the stuff to the plane of belles-lettres. A critic must understand wit if he is to talk of literature. And in an essay on literary criticism we should expect Pope to deal in generous measure with the problem of wit.

But in 1711 there were additional reasons why he had to confront the subject, reasons general and reasons personal. As for the general reasons, no one at the time could have forgotten that outburst of hostilities in 1698-1700, in which the righteous had beset the wits -- and had driven them to cover. It is true, of course, that the attack had been directed overtly against specific forms of wit, the facetious varieties which played with sex and trifled with religion and morality. But underneath lay an impulse more sinister, more dangerous, which denied the worth of literature itself (or what we think of as creative writing).

The psychological basis for the hostility can be found in Dryden's friend Walter Charleton, who observed that in works of wit "Phansie ought to have the upper hand, because all Poems, of what sort soever, please chiefly by Novelty."[11] How this remark becomes significant will appear when it is set beside Charleton's definition of Fancy as the faculty by which we conceive similarities "in objects really unlike, and pleasantly confound them in discourse: Which by its unexpected Fineness and allusion, surprizing the Hearer, renders him less curious of the truth of what is said."[12] In an age when the utilitarian and scientific movement had grown to giant size, an art which pleased by confounding truth and deceiving men was bound to be viewed with hostility. All wit came under attack.

The philosophic and moral basis for the hostility was well stated by Malebranche, who wrote:[13]

> But that which is most opposite to the efficacy of the Grace of Christ, is that which in the Language of the World is call'd Wit; for the better the Imagination is furnish'd, the more dangerous it is; subtilty, delicacy, vivacity and spaciousness of Imagination, great qualities in the Eyes of Men, are the most prolifick and the most general causes of the blindness of the Mind and the corruption of the Heart.

Without intending to betray her own cause Margaret, Duchess of Newcastle, made this humble request:[14]

> Give me a Wit, whose Fancy's not confin'd;
> That buildeth on it self, with no Brain join'd. . . .

Exactly what many had suspected! The current prejudice against
wit was vigorously put by Ferrand Spence, who viewed it as nothing but the froth and ferment of the soul, beclouding reason
and sinking rational pursuits into the miasma of fantasy.[15]
In the few years preceding the publication of Pope's Essay
the agitation concerning wit was intensified, partly because of
the appearance of the Letter concerning Enthusiasm (1707) and
Sensus Communis (1709), both of which, by pleading for the
complete freedom of wit and raillery, even in the most serious
matters, sent shivers of horror down the spines of some English
and Continental readers. Both were speedily translated into
French, and both reviewed in 1709 by the indefatigable Jean Le
Clerc, who warned concerning the former: "Le livre mérite
d'être lû avec attention, pour ne pas lui donner un sens et un
but, qu'il n'a point."[16] But whether they read attentively or not,
many readers detected the sense and aim which was not really
present (to Le Clerc). There soon issued a long and bitter retort called Bart'lemy Fair: or, an Enquiry After Wit; In Which
Due Respect is Had to a Letter Concerning Enthusiasm (1709).
This work takes Shaftesbury's Letter to be primarily an assault
on religion, and sees wit as a mode of enquiry that would un-
settle everything, morals and government alike. Of the terrible
menace lurking in wit the anonymous author bitterly remarks:
"To be Witty, if a Man knows how, is the only way to please.
Wit is the Salt that gives a goût to any Carrion: Nothing so Pro-
fane, or Lewd, but shall be relish'd if it pass for Wit."[17]
Such objections are obviously directed against, not true
wit, but the abuse of it. Yet wit easily lent itself to abuse, and
the contemporary mind distrusted it as a likely enemy to all
goodness. With almost uncanny prescience the learned Dr.
Samuel Clarke answered part of Shaftesbury's contentions a
few years before they were printed. In a series of sermons
preached at St. Paul's in 1705, he denounced the sort of men
who pretend to seek for truth and to explode falsehood by means
of wit:[18]

> . . . whatsoever things are profane, impure, filthy,
> dishonourable and absurd; these things they make it

their business to represent as harmless and indifferent, and to laugh Men out of their natural shame and abhorrence of them; nay, even to recommend them with their utmost Wit. Such Men as these, are not to be argued with, till they can be persuaded to use Arguments instead of Drollery. For Banter is not capable of being answered by Reason: not because it has any strength in it; but because it runs out of all the bounds of Reason and good Sense, by extravagantly joining together such Images, as have not in themselves any manner of Similitude or Connexion; by which means all things are alike easy to be rendered ridiculous. . . .

Wit appeared to many good men as a threat to decency because it walked regularly with irreligion and vice. Thus James Buerdsell, fellow of Brasenose College, complained in 1700 that "the prevailing Humour of Scepticism" had become "so extreamly Modish, that no Person can be that self-admir'd thing, a Wit, without it."[19] In the same year young Samuel Parker, of Trinity College, Oxford, deplored the sad fact that "Dissoluteness and Irreligion are made the Livery of Wit, and no body must be conscious of good parts, but he loses the credit of them unless he take care to finish 'em with Immoralities."[20]

Because wit, having become fashionable, began to appear as the natural ally of the scoffer, undermining religion and morals, it seemed to constitute a menace to society -- a menace that must be understood if one is to feel the force of Swift's digressions on wit in the Tale of a Tub (1704). The threat, obvious to large numbers of intelligent men, was aggravated by the appearance of Shaftesbury's essays, at the very time when Pope meditated on the problems of wit and criticism.

One must not forget that the publication of the Tatler and the Spectator, both by their nature and their purpose, affected the debate: by their nature, for they were seen to follow in the footsteps of Montaigne, one of the greatest of modern wits; and by their purpose, for they proposed to temper wit with morality and to enliven morality with wit. Wit could be made an ally of goodness, they demonstrated forcefully — and so successfully that it was possible two decades later for the author of the Preface to the Plain Dealer to assume general agreement when he remarked that periodical essays are composed in the finest taste when they cloath good Sense with Humour, and embellish good Morals with Wit; when they instruct Familiarly, and reprove Pleasantly; when they don't swell above Comprehension, nor sink below Delicacy: In short, when they adapt the Wisdom of the Antients to the Gust of the Moderns, and constrain Montaigne's Pleasantry within Bickerstaffe's Compass.

Much of the Tatler and Spectator papers was devoted to exposing false wit in social life, discrediting the antics of the unseemly biters and banterers, the scatterbrained and volatile, the uncouth leapers and slappers, the hollow laughers, the pert coxcombs. False wit in literature was attended to by Addison in the Spectator. Underlying these endeavors is the assumption that wit needed to be defended, and that it could be restored to its rightful place by stripping it of the gaudy and unclean adornments which thoughtless admirers had forced upon it. And at least since the time of Cowley's ode "Of Wit," the separation of true from false wit had been a regular mode of defending literature itself.

But besides these general reasons Pope had a personal stake in the argument over wit. The subject had interested him for years before the Essay on Criticism was published, as the correspondence with Walsh shows. It was in his correspondence with Wycherley, however, that the subject became crucial — and almost necessarily so. For in the late years of Dryden and the early years of Pope, Wycherley had become the very symbol of the poet of wit.

The trouble began with Wycherley's belated urge for recognition as a nondramatic poet, signalized by the publication in 1704 of his Miscellany Poems. Preceding the poems is a Preface that remains one of the unreadable wonders of our language. It is wit gone mad, an avalanche of simile and metaphor, a breathless flow of whim and fancy, out of which, now and then, there half emerges, here and there, a globule of meaning; after which a cloud of darkness settles, and the reader gropes his way blindly toward the poems that follow (where he is not to fare much better).

Little enthusiasm greeted the Miscellany Poems. But Wycherley, undaunted, commenced almost immediately to plan a new collection which should contain some unpublished verses and some revised and corrected versions of poems already printed. This time, however, he showed no unseemly haste in afflicting printer and public. Instead, he passed copies around to his friends for advice and correction. Among others so honored was Alexander Pope.

Pope, as we know, took this responsibility seriously. In Wycherley's letter dated February 5, 1705/6,[21] we discover that our bold youth was already pruning excrescences from the elder bard's disorganized fancies. On April 10, Pope was explaining with admirable candor that some of the poems were so wretched that "to render them very good, would require a great addition, and almost the entire new writing of them." Wycherley's chaos sprang from a false conception of wit. For great wits such as John Donne, said Pope, like great merchants take least pains to set out their valuable goods, whereas the "haberdashers of small wit" spare no decorations to present their little wares as seductively as possible.[22] As the business of lopping and grafting proceeded, Wycherley's assumed meekness wore thin, until a minor explosion occurred in 1707. Pope had set about to produce a semblance of logical order in the poem on Dullness, subjecting it to radical alterations; such amiable helpfulness provoked Wycherley to this response on November 22:[23]

And now for the pains you have taken to recommend
my Dulness, by making it more methodical, I give
you a thousand thanks, since true and natural dulness
is shown more by its pretence to form and method,
as the sprightliness of wit by its despising both.

Here was a home-thrust, impelled by some resentment and hostility. Pope's letter, dated one week later, shows that he was aware of the resentment; nevertheless he replied patiently: "To methodize in your case, is full as necessary as to strike out; otherwise you had better destroy the whole frame, and reduce them into single thoughts in prose, like Rochefoucauld, as I have more than once hinted to you."[24] As for the alleged incompatibility of wit and method, Pope urged that this is true only for the trivial forms of wit embodied in fancy or conceit; but as for true wit, which is propriety, why, that requires method not only to give perspicuity and harmony of parts, but also to insure that each detail will receive its increment of

meaning and beauty from the surrounding elements.
This strange contest of wills lasted from 1706 until 1710
at least. In the latter year, on April 11, Wycherley wrote to
Pope in protest against the extent to which the younger man was
improving his verses. By your tuning of my Welsh harp, he
said, my rough sense is to become less offensive to the fastid-
ious ears of those finicky critics who deal rather in sound than
in meaning.[25] Wit shines with a native luster that defies the
need of polish.

As Wycherley saw it, there was a generous, libertine spirit
in wit, too free to be confined, and too noble to be sacrificed for
smoothness or regularity. Taking form as a novel simile, a
brilliant metaphor, a dazzling paradox, or a smart aphorism,
wit is its own justification wherever it happens to appear. Some
of Wycherley's contemporaries were wont to say of great wits
that their "careless, irregular and boldest Strokes are most
admirable."[26] For wit in writing is the sign of a fertility of
mind, of multitudinous thoughts crowding in upon one or flying
out toward the most sublime and exalted objects, of a capacity
for wide-ranging speculation that soars above man's necessities
and desires, of a flame and agitation of soul that little minds
and men of action cannot comprehend.[27] To sacrifice such
flashes of wit to an ordered design, to a carefully conceived
framework, is to sacrifice poetry itself. Even the feebler manifestations of wit are sacred; we recall that Wycherley had composed a Panegyrick upon Puns.

Pope's artistic conscience told him that such scintillation,
when it failed to fit into its proper place and contribute to the
effect of the whole, was false wit because it was bad art. And
he must have understood that such irresponsible, uncontrolled
flashes, lacking any relationship with artistic purpose and solid
sense, had contributed to the disrepute into which wit had fallen.
As he was driven to correct and revise Wycherley's manuscripts,
he was impelled to defend himself, and true wit as well, by
reaching a coherent view of literature that would justify his own
practice. It was a bold step for a virtually unknown young author
to set himself against the most famous wit surviving from the
glamorous court of Charles II. But he might draw comfort and
support from the fact that a few of the distinguished men of the
time had expressed concepts of wit similar to his own. Little
by little his ideas take form; we can see them developing in his

correspondence, especially that with Wycherley. He told Spence later that he had formulated the substance of the Essay on Criticism in prose before he undertook the poem.

One passage in the poem that would seem to have Wycherley in mind is that contained in lines 289-304, where he speaks of the writers addicted to conceits and glittering thoughts, specious prodigalities which are valued by their creators not because they are essential parts of the meaning or because they fit into the places where they are thrown, but because they startle and surprise or raise admiration for their makers' liveliness. These are diseases. Works so constructed are "One glaring Chaos and wild heap of wit" — an extraordinarily apt description of Wycherley's Miscellany Poems of 1704.

But there is a clearer and more specific connection between the correspondence and the poem visible in the passage comprising lines 494-507. Here Pope describes the unhappiness that wit brings to those who possess it by stirring up malice and envy in the dull and ignorant. This, as we learn from a letter dated November 20, 1707,[28] was a subject which he had treated in his reorganization of Wycherley's poem on Dullness. If his distinguished correspondent failed to appreciate the addition, nothing prevented the use of it in a new poem.

By an interesting association of ideas Pope proceeds from here, through a short transitional passage (lines 508-25) dealing with the shame and disgrace that wit suffers at the hands of its friends, to the conclusion of Part II. This concluding section (lines 526-55) completes the subject of Dullness and likewise fulfills the thought developed in lines 408-51, where Pope describes two types of false wit, one caused by servile dullness and the other by modes and current folly. In the closing lines of Part II two more kinds of false wit are exposed: that which grows out of the union of dullness with bawdry, and that which springs from dullness and irreligion. The interesting feature of Pope's strategy in this passage is that these two abuses of wit are made to appear as temporary phases in a historical process, the first brought about by the dissoluteness, luxury, and idleness in the reign of Charles II, and the second, by the license and impiety allowed in the reign of William III. These particular manifestations of false wit (both of them "modes in wit" and "current folly") are sharply dissociated from true wit by artfully fixing them in past reigns, which Pope had no need to defend, especially as, out of the Wit's Titans who flourished in these two reigns, the last surviving member and champion was none other than William Wycherley.

It would take a monograph to show in detail how the analysis of false wit (with which Part II of the Essay is largely concerned) responds to particular literary developments in Pope's age, and this is not the point where such an investigation could be most profitable. We must still ask ourselves, what did Pope mean by true wit, and what Augustan writers whose thoughts were taking a similar direction can help us to comprehend the import of his view?

In the course of exposing false wit, Pope suggests two criteria by which true wit may be determined. First, it belongs not to the part but to the whole. It is the master idea which informs every portion of the body and gives life and energy; it is the joint force of all components, and not the beauty, regularity, or brilliance of any one feature. It unites the parts, and prevents undue attention from falling on any one; and no part has goodness or badness in itself except in its relation to the whole. And if the whole is properly informed with wit, it gives a generous pleasure, warming the mind with rapture so that we are delighted though we know not why, so delighted that we cannot be disturbed by trivial faults in the execution.

The second test is, that it must take its course from nature, that is, from truth. But not necessarily from the worn or commonplace; enough that we recognize, when we encounter it in art, its essential agreement with the frame of our minds, with universal human experience. So far from being commonplace, the whole piece gives the effect of boldness, not because of style or artifice but because new life, energy, and insight have been added. It comes with the graces of expression, which tend to heighten the outlines of truth rather than to disguise or conceal them. The expression, in fact, should be as modestly plain as the subject and form permit; and sprightly wit is so far from adhering to it that the expression may rather be said to set off the wit. Nature alone is not true wit until it becomes animated and is drawn into a unity by the shaping spirit.

It is in Part I of the Essay, however, where we must look for a fuller account of the relationship of wit and art in the production of poetry.

POPE ON WIT: THE ESSAY ON CRITICISM

Pope begins by specifying genius as the quality necessary in the poet, and taste in the critic, but notes that the two functions ideally should coincide. Genius is a synonym for wit, and after the first sixteen lines the former word is discarded in favor of the latter. Wit, then, is a quality that must be present at birth, and it is apportioned to men in varying measure and strength. If it is the genuine poetic gift, it may be fitted for only one type of poetry. Each man must discover his own special strength and cultivate only that for which he is specially fitted.

Along with genius (or taste) we can expect to find at least a rudimentary sense, or judgment, which is just as much the gift of heaven as wit. This sense needs developing; otherwise it is easily perverted, either by the formulas of academic learning or by the distortions of fashion. But nature, to protect us, herself provides the standard of good judgment: an impulse that leads us to prefer the lasting and universal over the ephemeral and local.

This thought is first suggested in lines 19-27, and is taken up again for further development in lines 68-87. Again we are assured that nature furnishes us with a just and universal standard of judgment. But nature also provides the life, force, and beauty that a work of genius requires; it is the source and end as well as the test of art. From this fund art draws its supplies, and proceeds quietly, unobtrusively, to endow all parts of the body with spirit and vigor.

At this point it is easy for the reader to become confused, for the principle of control, which at the start of the passage was called judgment, has now become art; a few lines later it appears as wit, and by the end of the passage it has been transformed back to judgment again. Perhaps the most perplexing lines are the oft-quoted:

> Some, to whom Heaven in wit has been profuse,
> Want as much more to turn it to its use. . . .

The lines lend themselves to ridicule, and Pope knew all too well that they left him open to banter. Yet, with his marvelous gift of lucidity to aid him, he left the couplet as we see it. Why? Presumably because it seemed to be the best way of putting something that was very difficult to express.

He found it difficult because it involved a question on which the credit of literature depended. For Pope's contemporaries, encouraged by Locke, were erecting a wall between wit and judgment and attempting to deposit the most valued achievements of mankind on the side of the wall occupied by judgment. This way of thinking is well described by Sir William Temple in his essay "Of Poetry." In the usual acceptation, he says, man's goal is taken to be profit or pleasure. The faculty of the mind conversant with profit is wisdom; that conversant with pleasure is wit (or the vein that produces poetry). To wisdom is attributed "the Inventions or Productions of things generally esteemed the most necessary, useful, or profitable to Human Life"; and to wit, "those Writings or Discourses which are the most Pleasing or Entertaining."[29] Wit may borrow from wisdom, of course, but its own proper role is to dazzle the eyes and tickle the ears and cut capers; it has no insight of its own, no peculiar way of thinking, nothing to offer but toys.

Into this pitfall Pope had no desire to plunge. Nor was he tempted by the compromise that seduced many of his contemporaries: to say that the essence of poetry is fable, design, or structure (product of the faculty to which we assign reason, judgment, and wisdom).[30] If the core of literature is provided by the plain rational faculty, then it is conceivable that whatever is valuable in it could be conveyed more profitably in another way (say, in plain didactic prose), without the fuss and feathers of literary art. But apart from that, the compromise effectively disinherits most of the kinds of poetry, for only epic, tragedy, and comedy necessarily have fables.

To Pope, wit and judgment, as they operate in literature, are married. In this union, so long as they are in a healthy state, they work together as a single faculty. As for the meaning of wit in the perplexed couplet, we must go back to the early lines in the poem, where we are told that genius and taste must ideally coincide; or, as the thought is expanded, that wit is accompanied by a rudimentary sense, potentially excellent, which requires development by experience. However great the gifts of heaven, wit, without that development, falls short of its perfection: natural wit needs training for its proper expression in art. But such training does not propose to foster an alien power, at odds with wit. Pope tries to make himself clear in the following passage (lines 88-140). The training designed to perfect the rudimentary sense is an experience of the great wit

of the past, first through a study of the rules, in which the
principles underlying the mighty achievements of past art are
set forth in simple abstraction; and second by a detailed study
of "each Ancient's proper character" in every page of his work.
Out of such experience should come literary judgment, literary
taste, which is the accomplished phase of wit; or, to put it in
another way, wit in the writer is not merely the power to conceive of objects and endow them with "Life, force, and beauty,"
but also the ability to find an appropriate style and form in which
to express them; the latter ability, developed by knowledge of
the rules and of masterpieces of literature, serves as taste and
judgment. In the writer it is also art, invisibly guiding the energy of the conception so that it permeates the form and language,
and achieves its desired end. Thus, if this sense (call it taste,
judgment, or art) guides the creative energy and, in a way,
contains it, nature is still the test of art, for this judgment must
be constructed on the foundation of a natural artistic gift. And
because this gift comes originally from Heaven, or nature, it
may at times conduct the creative impulse to its objective by a
route not recognized by the rules and untried by past masterpieces — so snatching a grace beyond the reach of art.

The important point is that Pope believed there was a special way of thinking peculiar to literature, a way called wit,
which possessed unique values; he saw that wit (in the narrower
sense) and judgment in the artist are but two aspects of a single
way of thinking, and that judgment (or art) is not a churlish,
rational censor but a natural literary sense cultivated by a wide
acquaintance with literary masterpieces. Literature therefore
is good, not because it charms eye or ear with sparkle and
melody nor because it borrows wisdom from philosophy or
science, but because wit, the unique mode of the literary artist,
provides an insight into nature, endows it with "Life, force,
and beauty," and conveys it directly to our hearts, charming us
as it makes us wiser.

The Essay on Criticism, then, had something to say. There
is much more in it than we have either time or space to examine.
But if we can follow what Pope says of wit, we can grasp his
primary purpose. He had difficulty in expressing his ideas concerning wit because there existed no adequate critical vocabulary for him to draw upon. There did, however, exist a body
of thought concerning wit, some expressions of which Pope was

certainly acquainted with, and some part of which could serve
to strengthen and clarify his own views. To the consideration
of that body of thought it is reasonable that we proceed.
The first fact about wit that struck observers was that it
made for a lively mind. Hobbes himself defined it as celerity of
imagining, and thought of it as a tenuity and agility of spirits,
which, as it distinguished its possessors from the dull and
sluggish of soul, must to that extent have seemed to him as a
virtue.[31] If wit meant nothing more than liveliness, it would
have its value. Welsted, who liked to take an extreme position,
remarked years later, partly out of admiration for sheer life
and animation, that even the sprightly nonsense of wit is preferable to the dull sense of plodding, earth-bound creatures.[32]
   A number of writers, however, refused to confine the liveliness of wit to sprightly nonsense. Liveliness, indeed, was
the first quality that impressed the author of Remarques on the
Humours and Conversations of the Town (1673), who described
wit as "properly the vivacity, and the agreeableness of the
fancy"; nevertheless he adds immediately, "yet there ought to
belong something more to that high quality, than a little flash
and quibble."[33] "Something more," as he explains in the following pages, meant to him an intelligent subject, delivered "sweet
and pleasantly, in the native beauties of our Language." In that
high quality, true wit, we see, sense, liveliness, and worthy
expression might coalesce. So likewise it appeared in the opinion of the great Robert Boyle, who remarked that wit, "that
nimble and acceptable Faculty of the Mind," involves both a
readiness and subtlety in conceiving things, and a quickness and
neatness in rendering them[34] — a way of putting the idea that
neatly anticipates Pope's phrasing in a letter to Wycherley dated
December 26, 1704: true wit is "a perfect conception, with an
easy delivery."[35]
   The vivacity of wit could be valuable for one of two reasons:
either because it naturally operated to charm other minds, or
because it was the mark of a soul capable of unusual powers,
beyond the reach of ordinary men. There is a point at which
vivacity and subtlety melt into swiftness and acuity. To the
soon-to-be-duncified Fleckno, wit appeared to have an extraordinary force; it was, he said, a spiritual fire that rarefies
and renders everything spiritual like itself.[36] To Margaret,
Duchess of Newcastle, it seemed unearthly, mysterious, "the

purest Element, and swiftest Motion of the Brain: it is the Essence of Thoughts; it incircles all things: and a true Wit is like
the Elixir, that keeps Nature always fresh and young."[37] And,
lest we smile at this, let us remind ourselves that the mysterious power of wit to penetrate to the heart of darkness is attest-
ed by the greatly influential La Rochefoucauld, whose Augustan
translator (perhaps Stanhope) rendered him thus:[38]

> The making a Difference between Wit and Judgment,
> is a Vulgar Error. Judgment is nothing else but the
> exceeding Brightness of Wit, which, like Light,
> pierces into the very Bottom of Things, observes
> all that ought to be observed there, and discovers
> what seemed to be past any bodies finding out: From
> when we must conclude, that the Energy and Extension
> of this Light of the Wit, is the very Thing that pro-
> duces all those Effects, usually ascribed to the Judg-
> ment.

The comparison between wit and light appealed strongly to
a few writers of the age, who reveal something of the mystic's
fervor when they address themselves to it. Thus an unknown
author wrote at the turn of the century:[39]

> Wit is a Radiant Spark of Heav'nly Fire,
> Full of Delight, and worthy of Desire;
> Bright as the Ruler of the Realms of Day,
> Sun of the Soul, with in-born Beauties gay. . . .

And at the time when the ideas of the Essay on Criticism were
beginning to take form in Pope's mind, another author, rejecting the notion that wit consists of merely exotic language,
satire, floridity, quibbles or trifles, banter, or smart repar-
tee, insisted:[40]

> No, 'tis a Thought sprung from a Ray Divine,
> Which will through Clouds of Low'ring Criticks shine:
> When in a Clear, Innubilous Serene,
> The Soul's Abstracted, Purg'd from Dross and Spleen. . . .

These mystic utterances are interesting but rather less

189

important than the remarks of men like La Rochefoucauld, who
looked upon wit as a natural instrument for probing the secrets
of nature, and apparently as a mode of thinking unlike the rational method operating in mathematics. As representative of
this group we may take Joseph Glanvill, who instructed his
readers that true wit might be useful even in sermons:[41]

> . . . For true Wit is a perfection in our Faculties,
> chiefly in the Understanding, and Imagination; Wit
> in the Understanding is a Sagacity to find out the
> Nature, Relations, and Consequences of things; Wit
> in the Imagination, is a quickness in the phancy to
> give things proper Images. . . .

And in another work he castigates those who debase wit, which
is truly fitted for "great and noble Exercises of the Mind." It
is in reality, he remarks, "a Faculty to dive into the depth of
things, to find out their Causes and Relatives, Consonancies
and Disagreements, and to make fit, useful, and unobvious
Applications of their respective Relations and Dependencies."[42]
The simile and metaphor of literature, therefore, may become,
not the trifling ornaments laid upon the truth, but instruments
of the profoundest thinking, the natural way of revealing the
discovery of hidden relationships. A second representative of
this group is Francis Atterbury, later a friend of Pope's, who
discussed the subject in a sermon printed in 1708, while Pope
was establishing his defenses against Wycherley. Atterbury
wrote, "Wit, indeed, as it implies a certain uncommon Reach
and Vivacity of Thought, is an Excellent Talent; very fit to be
employ'd in the Search of Truth, and very capable of assisting
us to discern and embrace it . . ."[43] His subsequent remarks
show clearly that wit was not to be employed, as Shaftesbury
proposed, in banter and raillery, to strip the mask from falsehood and thus arrive, indirectly, at truth; rather, it plunged
straight to its object by virtue of its own range, acuity, and
vivacity.

Even though Addison accepted Locke's definition of wit,
thereby splitting off wit from judgment and demoting wit to the
role of a mild spice serviceable in making morality pleasing
to the palate, there were enough others who refused to be so
misled. They persisted in thinking of wit as "a high quality,"

fitted for "great and noble Exercises of the Mind," as a special
and valuable mode of apprehending nature and truth -- not the
plain and obvious, but the depth of things, where the complex
relationships, the consonancies and disagreements, among the
parts of nature lay open to wit alone. Some thought of judgment
as a phase of wit; some thought of fancy as that part of wit which
provided appropriate images and expression to deliver wit's
discoveries. Wit and art are eternally wedded, and true wit is
"a perfection in our Faculties."

This lofty conception of wit, making it possible to claim
for literature a noble rank among human activities and a value
far greater than can be granted that which merely entertains
and pleases, was overshadowed in the early eighteenth century
by the ideas of Locke and of men like him. And yet, sanctioned
as it was by such formidable names as Robert Boyle, La Rochefoucauld, and Atterbury (some of whom were known to Pope),
it offered an easily tenable position from which to defend literature from the assaults of those intent on debasing it.

There was one other type of answer to those engaged in de-
preciating wit, and it is worth examining because Pope was evidently attracted by it. At least from the Renaissance, men had
been familiar with the idea that strangeness is an essential element in all excellent beauty. So Bacon had said. Wit and strangeness seemed inextricably connected in Davenant's mind, for he
explained the wit of <u>Gondibert</u> to lie "in bringing Truth, too
often absent, home to mens bosoms, to lead her through un-
frequented and new ways, and from the most remote Shades
. . ."[44] Likewise Leonard Welsted defined wit as "some uncommon Thought or just Observation, couch'd in Images or Allusions, which create a sudden Surprize"— a definition which admits the just Observation but stresses the uncommon and surprising.[45] In actual practice, wit became increasingly associated after 1690 with the strange, novel, and surprising.

But because novelty was so often connected with the ephemeral, with whim or fashion, and because subtle, uncommon
ideas were often suspected of heresy, or the kind of enthusiasm
which had led to the logic-chopping and violence of the Civil
War, the charge was constantly made that wit depended on a
love of quaintness and paradox, of novelty rather than truth,
and was therefore offensive to the wise and good.[46] To meet
this charge certain writers began to stress the sound content of

the product rather than the swiftness and acuity of mind that wit
signified. Thus David Abercromby in 1685 defined wit as "either
a senceful discourse, word, or Sentence, or a skilful Action."[47]
Not "dead, and downright flat Sence" would do, but good sense
properly animated. Something similar appears to have been in
Boileau's mind when he remarked that "Wit is not Wit, but as it
says something every Body thought of, and that in a lively, delicate, and New Manner"[48] -- an observation that probably lays
more stress on style and manner than the author intended; even
as Pope's

> True wit is Nature to advantage dressed,
> What oft was thought, but ne'er so well expressed . . .

is easily misinterpreted to mean that any old saw will do as wit
so long as it is well groomed and elegantly turned out. Actually
Pope was far from desiring to confine wit to expression. His
thinking at the time was close to that of William Walsh, who observed to him in a letter dated September 9, 1706, that nature
alone is to be followed, and that we must carefully eschew similes, conceits, and all kinds of "fine things." And as for what
you remark concerning expression, said Walsh, it is truly in
the same relation to wit as dress is to beauty.[49]

Certainly Pope intended to oppose any idea of wit that separated subject matter from style. It is significant that in a letter
dated November 29, 1707, he defined wit, in "the better notion
of it," as propriety.[50] This, of course, was Dryden's definition,
stated as early as 1677, and rephrased as "thoughts and words
elegantly adapted to the subject."[51] It was Dryden's idea of wit
to the end of his career, a definition which, as he says, "I im-
agin'd I had first found out; but since am pleasingly convinc'd,
that Aristotle has made the same Definition in other Terms."[52]
That Dryden's conception of wit interested other men than Pope
at this time is strongly suggested by the Tatler's article from
Will's Coffee-house which begins, "This evening was spent at
our table in discourse of propriety of words and thoughts, which
is Mr. Dryden's definition of wit . . ."[53]

The term propriety conveys no very clear idea to us when
it is applied to literary criticism, and for that reason Dryden's
definition has been taken much less seriously by modern scholars than it was by the Augustans. It deserves to be understood.

POPE ON WIT: THE ESSAY ON CRITICISM

The Tatler supposed, incorrectly, that it involved a relationship between thoughts and words only. In reality Dryden was urging a threefold relationship, between thoughts, words, and subject, effected in such a way that the three elements appear to belong to one another (propriety conveyed the sense of ownership); and the words "elegantly adapted" point to the need of an active literary intelligence to produce the work of wit.

This account of wit as propriety bears a resemblance to an Augustan theory concerning the artistic process which may help to explain it. The theory, in brief, supposed that objects produce in genius (the artistic mind raised to a high degree of emotion and sensibility) certain thoughts which, in the very instant of their generation, take on forms and expression adequate to convey them and completely appropriate to them. A form of the theory can be found in the works of Dryden's young friend, John Dennis. In the genius, says Dennis, "as Thoughts produce the Spirit, the Spirit produces and makes the Expression; which is known by Experience to all who are Poets . . ."[54] The expression (which includes style, harmony, rhythm, etc.), then, is not the result of a separate act but exists in the most intimate and necessary relationship with the ideas, emotions, and attitudes of the artist, being engendered along with them. The thoughts do not become wit until they are animated and transfused by the shaping spirit which gives them expression -- and all elements take form in perfect propriety.

To define wit, therefore, as "What oft was thought, but ne'er so well expressed," does not say or imply that wit is a stale or commonplace thought nicely tricked out. The definition rather supposes that the writer, starting with a common and universal experience, sees it in a new light; and his sensitive spirit, endowing it with life and fresh meaning, provides it with form, image, language, and harmony appropriate to it. It presupposes the liveliness and insight of the creative mind; and it demands propriety, the perfect agreement of words, thoughts (as reshaped by the artist), and subject. The result is nature, and it is wit.[55]

When Pope composed the Essay on Criticism, there was need for a defense of wit — and that is to say, of literature as well. His own circumstances, involved as he was in a controversy with the most famous writer surviving from the court of Charles II and what was understood to have been the golden age of wit, demanded that he should justify his bold and rash treatment of Wycherley. Locke's conception of wit was of no use to him; in fact, it served the enemy better. But there were other ideas available which were consistent with a conviction of the high dignity and noble function of literature. Through this maze Pope attempted to thread his way. If he was not entirely successful in conveying his meaning with utter clarity, the fault lay partly in the lack of a critical vocabulary. But he had something important to say, and there are good clues to his intention. Pope saw, thought, felt, and wrote as the complete artist. Those who would like to understand his views of the literary art (and of criticism, its complement) must read the Essay on Criticism with a fuller awareness of its historical setting.

NOTES

1 "Wit in the Essay on Criticism," Hudson Review, Vol. II, No. 4 (Winter 1950), pp. 559-77.

2 References to and quotations from the Essay on Criticism are based on George Sherburn's edition, Selections from Pope (New York: Nelson and Sons, n. d.).

3 Anon., The Polite Arts (1749), p. 15.

4 Preface to Annus Mirabilis, in Essays of Dryden, ed. W. P. Ker, I, 14.

5 Antony Blackwall, An Introduction to the Classics (6th ed., 1746), p. 12.

6 Ibid., p. 18.

7 Discourse of Wit (1685), p. 180.

8 Essay on Criticism (1728), p. 44.

9 In Critical Essays of the 17th Century, ed. Spingarn, II, 288.

10 Introduction to the Classics, p. 21.

11 Brief Discourse concerning the Different Wits of Men (1669), p. 25.

12 Brief Discourse, pp. 20-21.

13 A Treatise of Morality, trans. James Shipton (1699), p. 114.

14 Poems, or, Several Fancies in Verse (3d ed. , 1668), p. 224.

15 Preface to trans. of St. Évremond, Miscellanea (1686), sig. A9v-A10r.

16 Bibliotheque Choisie, XIX (Amsterdam, 1709), 431.

17 P. 18.

18 Works of Samuel Clarke (4 vols. , 1738), II, 603-4.

19 Discourses and Essays on Several Subjects (Oxford, 1700), p. 205.

20 Six Philosophical Essays (1700), p. 18.

21 Pope, Works, ed. Elwin-Courthope, VI, 26.

22 Elwin-Courthope, VI, 28.

23 Ibid. , VI, 33.

24 Ibid. , VI, 34-35.

25 Ibid. , VI, 44.

26 Cf. John Dennis, Critical Works, II (Baltimore, 1943), 381.

27 Ibid. , II, 383. Thus Dennis wrote to Wycherley, knowing he was addressing a sympathetic spirit.

28 Elwin-Courthope, VI, 32.

29 In Spingarn, III, 73-74.

30 For a rather typical expression of the idea, see Mary Astell (?), Bart'lemy Fair (1709), p. 80: "Colouring is the least of the Matter, both in Wit and Painting; a few bold Strokes never made an Artist; the Attitudes, Proportions, and above all the Design, shew the Masterly Genius." Cf. also Dennis, Critical Works, II, 46.

31 Leviathan, I, viii.

32 Epistles, Odes, &c (1724), Dedication, p. xli.

33 P. 93.

34 Occasional Reflections (1665), p. 37.

35 Elwin-Courthope, VI, 16.

36 "Of Wit," in A Farrago (1666), pp. 58-59.

37 The Worlds Olio (2d ed., 1671), p. 11.

38 Maxim 98, in La Rochefoucauld, The Moral Maxims and Reflections (2d ed., 1706), as reprinted in the edition of George Powell (New York: F. A. Stokes Company, n. d.).

39 A Satyr upon a Late Pamphlet Entitled, A Satyr Against Wit (1700).

40 The British Apollo, September 1-3, 1708.

41 Essay Concerning Preaching (2d ed., 1703), pp. 71-72.

42 A Whip for the Droll (1700), pp. 4-5.

43 "A Scorner Incapable of True Wisdom" (preached, 1694), in Fourteen Sermons (1708), pp. 158-59.

44 Preface to Gondibert, in Spingarn, II, 23.

45 Epistles, Odes, &c (1724), Dedication, p. lx.

46 Thus Atterbury, in Fourteen Sermons (1708), pp. 158-59, describing the forms most commonly taken by wit in his day, wrote: "Men of Quick and Lively Parts are apt to give themselves a loose beyond plain Reason and Common Sense; and to say many things not exactly Right and True, in order to say somewhat New and Surprizing." For this reason Wycherley himself remarked that wit is generally false reasoning -- a remark that was pounced upon gleefully by Warburton in the Divine Legation (2d ed., 1738), I, xiv. The excellent author of the Whole Duty of Man, in Works (1726), Part II, pp. 47, 82, 85, 248, anticipates one of Swift's most brilliant essays in irony by observing that a great deal of wit depended on reversing universally accepted judgments on the most serious and sacred subjects and that if the Bible were taken away, the wit of many men would forthwith dry up.

47 Discourse of Wit (1685), p. 7.

48 Works, trans. Ozell (2d ed., 1736), I, iii.

49 Elwin-Courthope, VI, 55.

50 Ibid., VI, 34-35.

51 Essays of Dryden, ed. W. P. Ker, I, 190; cf. also I, 270, and II, 9.

52 "Life of Lucian," in Works of Lucian (1711), I, 42.

53 Tatler, No. 62 (September 1, 1709).

54 Advancement and Reformation of Modern Poetry (1701), in Critical Works, I (Baltimore, 1939), 222.

55 The tendency to define wit in terms of the thoughts produced, or to emphasize the necessary presence in wit of common sense, is well illustrated by Bouhours, who in Les Entretiens d'Ariste et d'Eugene (Paris, 1737), p. 258, defined wit as: "C'est un corps solide qui brille . . ." It is no accident that Bouhours, after a neglect of three decades, was becoming influential in England by 1710. Garth had recommended him to Oldmixon, as he probably had to Pope; and Addison in the Spectator was to proclaim him the greatest of the French critics. Although Bouhours in La Maniere de Bien Penser seemed to lay heavy stress on common sense and the logical element in wit, he made it clear that he was really concerned not with thought but with the turn given the thought by the ingenious mind and with the appropriateness of the style and language to that turn or attitude. Common sense did not strike him as wit until it was vivified and illuminated by the author. This much Pope and Bouhours had in common; in what remains, Pope's superior artistic sense is obvious.

WIT IN THE ESSAY ON CRITICISM

William Empson

I have been trying to build a theory about the way complex meanings are fitted together in a single word, especially the "key word" of a long poem, in which one would expect to find something worth examining. I thus approached the Essay on Criticism rather coolly, as a specimen likely to provide crude examples; but I now think that the analysis improves the poem a great deal, and lets us recover the way it was meant to be read. Critics may naturally object that the Augustans did not deal in profound complexities, and tried to make the words as clear-cut as possible. This is so, but it did not stop them from using double meanings intended as clear-cut jokes. The performance inside the word wit, I should maintain, was intended to be quite obvious and in the sunlight, and was so for the contemporary reader; that was why he thought the poem so brilliant; but most modern readers do not notice it at all, and that is why they think the poem so dull.

On my theory, a double meaning "A. B. " in a word often forms a covert assertion "A = B," called an equation; it is read "A is B" and can be interpreted in various ways, such as "A is like B," "A is part of B," and "A entails B." Thus the order of terms make a difference, and equations are classified according to which way round they go. The equations in Pope, I think, are of the simplest type, as a critic who emphasizes the Augustan simplicity would expect; that is, the subject of the equation is the sense demanded by the immediate context, and the predicate is a "head" meaning of the term which easily pokes itself forward in any context. But to decide what the head meaning was likely to be, for the intended reader, one needs to consider the history of the word. One has also to consider how far the

Reprinted by permission of author and publisher from The Hudson Review, Vol. 2, No. 4, Winter, 1950, pp. 559-577. Copyright 1949 by The Hudson Review, Inc. This article has also appeared in William Empson, Structure of Complex Words.

covert assertions are really meant and how far they appear as ironical jokes.

The word appears on an average every sixteen lines of the Essay, and by these frequent uses of it, I should maintain, Pope was in effect building a system on what was almost a slang word; this is already a kind of assertion, that one can think best in the fashionable language of the moment. The covert assertions of the word seem to me to go neatly into formulae, but the effect is comic and somewhat unjust to Pope; the interesting thing is not that the Essay asserts the notions but that by seeming to accept them it uses them to imply a hierarchy, and thus puts them in their place. Pope continually plays off different kinds of people so as to make himself look better than either, and in the same way the smart flat little word wit seems meant to make Pope himself look something more important. "And are, besides, too moral for a wit," he makes an opponent say of him in the Satires; very possibly, we are to feel, but not too moral for a great poet. The personal trick was a useful piece of machinery, but the final effect is less trivial; Pope and his rules are above the wits, but smaller than such poets as can be conceived, even though all poets are called wits. Thus my equations are not supposed to show Pope's final opinions, only the basis of common assumption that he accepted and played upon. The cleverness of the thing is that the epigrams are irrefutable if you stretch the meanings of the words far enough and give what the age demanded if you let them slip back. Yet to play this trick on such a scale comes at last to suggest more dignified notions; that all a critic can do is to suggest a hierarchy with inadequate language; that to do it so well with such very inadequate language is to offer a kind of diagram of how it must always be done.

Whether there are other key words with important tricks ought also to be considered. Nature is an obvious candidate, but I think Nature here is simply everything, however diverse, that is outside wit; a source of wit as well as in various ways a contrast to it. Sense is an important word, though not used very often; but has not I think much variety of meaning here; its function is to give a solid basis for the convolutions of wit above it. That word treats genius with a certain playfulness out of deference to the democracy of the polite drawing room, but such a view could only be made plausible if the drawing room were assumed to have a high standard; the strategy of Pope therefore made large demands on the "common sense" which was to be made adequate to the task of criticism. Pope also tries to connect it with the good humor of a reasonable man ("Good humor and good sense must ever join," 523) which gives it another claim as part of the general outlook he thought he was recommending. But I do not think either word is used, as wit is, for elaborate byplay.

What is now the most prominent and common meaning of the term, something like "power to make ingenious (and critical) jokes," was I think already the most prominent one for the smart milieu which Pope was addressing. It was more than a century old (e. g. Falstaff says: "I am not only witty in myself, but the cause that wit is in other men") but the prominence was a novelty. Also it is agreed that the special form "a wit" for a man possessing wit had taken on a new meaning some time after the Restoration. I say "agreed" chiefly because it is in the N. E. D. , which gives an older use of the form as "9 (trans. from 5) A person of great mental ability" etc. as in the Sonnets, "The wits of former days / To subjects worse have given admiring praise," and then "10 (trans. from 7) A person of lively fancy, who has the faculty of saying smart or brilliant things, now always so as to amuse; a witty person," for which the first example is dated 1692. This example and the following Augustan one under the same head both show wits as quarreling with one another. "5" begins "good or great mental capacity" and extends to "acumen," apparently a critical power, whereas "7" begins "quickness of intellect or liveliness of fancy" and includes the Falstaff example. Thus "a wit" for a person possessing the modern "wit" is given as a novelty for Pope, not yet invented when he was born. This seems rather improbable, but I think the great dictionary is right to assume an important change around that date. The sense no doubt became more frequent then, even if not then first introduced, but the reason for what one feels to be a novelty, I suspect, is something different; the form "a wit" acquires a Mood.

I use this term for any stock feeling in a word which needs to be translated, for listing, into a sentence relating the speaker to someone else. Originally it is put in by the tone of voice, but a stock use of it need not be always self-conscious. Here the Mood, the real novelty in the word, which incidentally makes for a narrower sense of it, is "I have placed him; I am an individual and he is a type." This of course, if you were yourself a wit, could not be logically sustained, and anyway the type itself was not a very clear one. The idea of a Mood I think is needed to show why there was so much play of personal implication. It seems to have been put into many class-names of that rather schoolboyish period, for example into the queer word "parson." The implication is that of the Comedy of Humors, that one belittles a man merely by classifying him; his Humor is supposed to be a Ruling Passion, so that all his actions are explained by it: he is regarded as a mechanical toy. Pope himself makes much play with this claim in the Satires. It makes the speaker superior if only because it gives him a feeling of social power -- he can manage people easily now that he has "placed" them. Thus the appearance of the Mood at this date does not need explaining for this word in particular. But one could maintain, taking a historical view, that the word wit had been sinking in dignity, partly because of the gradual rise of sense to take over many of its functions, and that this might give a feeling of belittlement to the word in the functions it still had. Pope did not fully accept this; as was said in effect by Warburton, he set out to combine the seventeenth and nineteenth century notions of wit, range of imaginative power and bright social criticism. The view of him as tied to a blind "classicism" is of course quite wrong; he imagined he was striking a balance between Longinus' "The true sublime thrills and transports the reader" and Horace's "Fools admire but men of sense approve." It is a mistake to suppose that his use of the word could not come near Coleridge's Imagination.

> In a true piece of wit all things must be
> Yet all things there agree
> . . . as the primitive forms of all
> (If we compare great things with small)
> Which without discord or confusion lie
> In that strange Mirror of the Deity.

This is Cowley's Ode to Wit, and it was in easy reach; he if no other metaphysical poet was still read. What it makes the word mean, after laboring to cut out the idea of jokes, is almost exactly Coleridge's divine coadunative power. This view indeed

had become suspected in favor of the rationalism of Locke's theory of wit (opposing it to judgment) but one could get at a decent distance from Locke by insisting that the kind of wit now in hand was True.
A wit, then, or man who displays wit, may be a
    1. bright social talker
    2. critic of the arts or of society
    3. poet or artist,
and in each class he may be divided into similar heads;
    a. mocking
    b. acting as judge
    c. giving aesthetic pleasure or expressing new truths.
These divisions are perhaps only a matter of how he is applying his wit, and in all of them there is a doubt about what qualities of mind are so called. This is decided in a given case mainly by emotions of admiration or satirical amusement, expressed somehow by the context or tone of voice, and the resulting change in the Sense of the word is I think best expressed by plus and minus signs. (The usual technical terms for this are Appreciative and Depreciative Pregnancy.) No doubt in themselves Fancy and Imagination, or whatever the pair may be, are radically different and ought not to be symbolized in this way, but by doing it we imitate the pretense of Pope that they are similar. It is also convenient to introduce a sense "4" to cover the grammatical form "wit" as apart from "a wit"; the plus and minus signs are originally attached to that, but they can be called in to qualify the persons possessing wit as well.

    4+ conceptual force, range of imaginative power
    4- power to make neat jokes or ornament an accepted structure.

Because of the Mood, there is a rule that a wit must not have all these advantages at once.
    We have now to decide how the equations go between these meanings, and no doubt it depends a good deal how you interpret the style. After I had written down my version I found an excellent school edition of the poem with notes by J. Churton Collins. His first note on the word wit, after saying that the various shades of meaning should be carefully distinguished, goes like this:

Its derivation is from the A.-S. <u>witan</u>, 'to know' so that its primary meaning is (a) the knowing power, pure intellect, mental capacity as in [line 17] and in lines 53, 61, 210 and elsewhere; then (b) in a slightly wider sense, genius, as in line 657; then (c) as a synonym for ingenious or gifted writers, as in line 36; next (d) it comes to mean knowledge, learning, or ingenuity, as in 259, 447, 468, 494, 508, particularly 'polite learning,' 652. Next it is a synonym (e) for imagination or fancy, as in 292, 590, 717, 722. Then (f) it is employed for judgement, as in [the couplet 80-81], where it is employed in a double sense, imagination, and the control of imagination, i. e., judgement. Lastly, it is employed in the sense in which it was occasionally used in Pope's time and is generally used now; namely, as "a combination of heterogeneous images, the discovery of occult resemblances between things apparently dissimilar," as in line 28.

"Primary" at the beginning of this passage is a pun, carrying the equation "historically first, and therefore the chief meaning in Pope's time." ("The first is the chief.") The preface says that the edition is designed mainly for the use of students both in England and in the Colonies. It seems to me that this otherwise excellent note is likely to give a foreign student an entirely wrong idea about the tone of the word, and indeed of the whole poem. Even when it gets to "lastly" the definition of a joke is so scarifying as to be quite unrecognizable, and at best this idea is at the bottom of the pile. I had been taking for granted, and I still do, that there is not a single use of the word in the whole poem in which the idea of a joke is quite out of sight. Indeed I think that the whole structure of thought in the poem depends on this. It was the deliberate policy of Pope to start from the slang meaning of the word, because it gave the tone of society:

> Without good breeding truth is disapproved;
> That only makes superior sense beloved. (576)

and indeed because

The current folly proves the ready wit.   (449)

Wit as joke could be relied upon as the "head meaning," because the flippant reader could be trusted to think of it in any
context; the context in the poem often makes it very unsuitable
and the other meaning which is required then appears as the
subject of the equation, the thing "meant by the word," but the
idea of the joke or the smart joker will still crop up as a predicate of it. To be sure this could not be done unless the other
meanings were in fairly easy reach; if the use had too much
feeling of strain, so as to give an effect of metaphor, the meaning "joke" would appear as subject because it would be felt as
"what the word really means." But the other meanings were
still in regular use; the point is merely that the term "a wit"
made a false claim to simplicity. I take it then that "1" the
bright social talker never appears as subject in an equation; if
the term is definitely used about such a man it appears flat. But
when it is used about a poet or critic the word will compare
either of these to the smart joker, and I think the critic is close
enough to the idea of the coffeehouse wit to appear as predicate
in some equations on his own. It seems to me that if you write
down the more pointed equations, on this general principle, you
get a fairly complete parody of the Augustan critical position.

3 = 1, 2 = 1.	Both poet and critic are social entertainers and must keep to the tone of polite society, since that is the final judge of the arts.
3 = 2	The poet is a critic; he should judge his work coolly, not rely on enthusiasm.
3c = 3a	The normal mode of poetry, in itself merely a cultivated pleasure, is satire.
a = b	The satirist is a judge; he tells the truth about life and upholds wisdom and virtue.
4+ = 4-	The field of imaginative writing is limited and simple; one can go ahead and give the correct rules.

3b+ = 1a-   Even in authoritative writers one
                 must expect a certain puppyishness.

II

I had better begin the examples with one that shows "a wit" being treated with some contempt, as apparently there is a doubt whether this happens. The form comes in Mr. Churton Collins' list only as "(c) a synonym for ingenious or gifted writers," with a reference to the following passage:

> Some have at first for wits, then poets passed,
> Turned critics next, and proved plain fools at last.
> Some neither can for wits nor critics pass,
> As half-formed mules are neither horse nor ass.
> These half-formed witlings, numerous in our isle
> As half-formed insects on the banks of Nile;
> Unfinished things, one knows not what to call,
> Their generation's so equivocal;
> To tell them would a hundred tongues require,
> Or one vain wit's, which might a hundred tire.   (36-45)

Certainly Pope does not say, and could not say, that a wit as such is always contemptible; but it is made clear that an inferior kind of wit (a witling) is very common, so that we expect him to be referred to when we hear more about wits; and the final turn of contempt is a kick at some type of person who it seems is really a wit, though a vain one. You might even read vain as a sort of Homeric stock epithet, implying that all wits may be assumed to be vain; and indeed these witlings are being satirized, however unfairly, for just that combination of functions which the term "a wit" seems designed to recommend. The whole passage is something like an attack on the idea of "a wit" in general. It comes early in the poem and helps to set the tone. But this of course is not a complete account of the thing; Pope is involved in the business of being "a wit" himself, and on the other hand there is no suggestion that all good writers are contemptible in the same way that "wits" are. He is kicking at his own vocabulary, and can hardly avoid kicking at himself; and our chief impression after recognizing this picture

of the bad writers is that the good writers are something different and yet something to which it would not be sensible to give
another name.

As a rule, indeed, the poem uses a limitation of one counter
merely as the only way to exalt another one;

> One science only will one genius fit,
> So vast is art, so narrow human wit,   (61)

or contrariwise

> Great wits may sometimes gloriously offend
> And rise to faults true critics dare not mend;
> From vulgar bounds with brave disorder part
> And snatch a grace beyond the reach of art.   (159)

It is only by narrowing wit and art each in turn that he contrives
to elevate the concepts they might be supposed to name. Incidentally wit in the abstract is given the negative role in this couple,
and "wits" are given the positive one; there is no animus against
the form "a wit" as such. The only effect of the process, which
does not feel at all like a contradiction, is to imply that there
is a hierarchy which ordinary language cannot be expected to
describe directly.

However even the "great wits" of this quatrain, if you took
it alone, might still be rather lightweight writers; cavalier love
poets writing with the ease of gentlemen, perhaps. Pope in this
kind of use meant to include any poet, however impressive,
among his wits, and I must now try to give convincing enough
examples of the high use of the term; most readers perhaps will
have more easily believed in the low one, unlike Mr. Churton
Collins. As he pointed out, the term is used for "the knowing
power" taken in general:

> Nature to all things fixed the limits fit
> And wisely curbed proud man's pretending wit.   (53)

Of course there is still a joke in it; the thinker is dwarfed when
he pits himself against heaven, and can therefore be compared
by implication to the coffeehouse atheist making blasphemous
quips. But the meaning imposed on the term as the relevant one

for the context is as high as any human mental power.

> He who, supreme in judgement, as in wit,
> Might boldly censure, as he boldly writ,
> Yet judged with coolness though he sung with fire;
> His precepts teach but what his works inspire.   (657)

There is no trace here of a desire to sneer at Horace by speaking of his wit; the antithesis seems to make it mean his imagination, which was so strong that it needed strong judgment to control it. But there is still room for the simpler idea; when he came to criticism, his "fire" might have expressed itself in making very rude jokes about bad authors; but instead of this boldness he judged coolly and "talked us into sense."

A more definite, though less warm, example is therefore given by the following antithesis:

> Authors are partial to their wit, tis true,
> But are not critics to their judgement too?   (18)

Judgment being the main function of a critic, the wit of an author can hardly be less than his creative power. This gives a firm definition of the sense required by the context, even though the secondary meaning is also particularly clear. What the author likes best are the flashy parts, the jokes or the purple passages; he is always puppyish.

The passage about Aristotle is nearly an unambiguous use of the high sense of wit.

> Poets, a race long unconfined, and free,
> Still fond and proud of savage liberty,
> Received his laws; and stood convinced twas fit
> Who conquered Nature, should preside o'er Wit. (652)

Mr. Churton Collins says that this means "polite learning," part of his group "d" which includes knowledge and ingenuity. I found this a puzzling unit till I realized that he was claiming a logical distinction between "products of wit" and "the capacity to produce them," and that this was meant to subdivide any specified sense of wit. He had much better have said so; his Colonial students will have to be on their toes here if they are to guess his meaning. But in any case I think Aristotle might preside over both these logical entities. A more interesting question is whether there is any joke about wit here. It is against the poets rather than against Aristotle; the shaggy barbarians, as they droop before their conqueror, seem unlikely to have a very great supply of the polished facetiousness of which they are so proud. Or rather (as we should interpret this picture) the smart fellow who thinks he can give a quick answer on questions of taste is really more of a barbarian than he supposes, and ought to be thankful that Aristotle took the trouble to make laws for him. This I think is the suggestion intended; but none the less the main statement intended is that Aristotle does preside over wit, and indeed is a wit, the chief one.

> No longer now that golden age appears
> When patriarch-wits survived a thousand years;
> Now length of fame (our second life) is lost,
> And bare three-score is all even that can boast. (470)

I take it this is a much more definite joke; Methusaleh is absurd in himself, and the idea of his being witty for a thousand years is positively depressing. We are to feel that Homer (who has just been mentioned) cannot really be placed as a wit, because this points the contrast with the contemporary scene. The very name of a modern artist proves that he cannot stand up to immortality. But Homer is unflinchingly called a wit, and no doubt would prove to have the frailties of the species if Pope could meet him. There is an idea that he was a moralist, as Methusaleh presumably was, and as Pope is, but it is not elaborated. Pope here is in effect satirizing his own key term, but without any hint that some other would be better; indeed no other would suggest so clearly that there is a hierarchy of literature which it would be ridiculous to peg down by terms.

> Some to conceit alone their taste confine
> And glittering thoughts struck out at every line;
> Pleased with a work where nothing's just or fit,
> One glaring Chaos and wild heap of wit. (292)

No doubt this is a smack at Cowley and any other metaphysicals not yet forgotten, but the grandeur of the suggestions in the background prevents it from seeming an unfair one. There is perhaps an idea that great powers are seen most clearly in a tragically suicidal freedom; they create their destruction. There is a doubt, as usual in the form "A and B of C," whether "chaos" is qualified by "of wit"; a heap of jokes is a trivial kind of chaos, but if we choose to read "a chaos of wit" there is a certain note of doom. The two readings are related, I think, by the idea behind MacFlecknoe and the Dunciad, that there is an ominous mystery in the way the lowest and most absurd things make an exact parallel with the highest. For this idea you invert the conventional equation and read "4- = 4+"; Pope made fuller use of it later in life. I have taken this example last of the "high" uses of wit, and will now go on to what might be called the social applications of the standing contrasts in the word.

We have already seen that wit in the abstract is alternately opposed to judgment and identified with it:

> Some, to whom Heav'n in wit has been profuse
> Want as much more, to turn it to its use;
> For wit and judgement often are at strife,
> Though meant each other's aid, like man and wife. (80)

Warburton makes an amusing attempt to clear this up, but had little right to be surprised, because the process of alternately identifying and separating a key pair of opposites is a fundamental one for the style.

> Here the poet (in a sense he was not, at first, aware of) has given us an example of the truth of his observation itself. . . . In the first line, Wit is used, in the modern sense, for the effort of Fancy; in the second it is used, in the ancient sense, for the result of Judgement. This trick, played on the reader, he endeavoured to keep out of sight . . . (by making a trivial change in the second line). . . . The truth is, the Poet had said a lively thing, and would, at all hazards, preserve the reputation of it, though the very topic he is on obliged him to detect the imposition; in the very next lines, which show he meant two very different things, by the same term, in the two preceding.

Man and wife are allowed the same surname; in the same way, Pope had every right to choose a term covering both his allied ideas and allowing a generalization to be expressed about them together; and it was graceful to choose an unassuming one. The writer unwilling to face the labors of correction is to be exhorted to do so, and the best exhortation is to tell him that this is only another part of the straightforward (the humanly vain) impulse to display his wit. This was the main use of identifying the poet and the critic, creation and polish, in the one key term; and indeed Blake himself, with his hundreds of corrections in the poems dictated to him by the Holy Spirit, could hardly deny that inspiration and revision are part of the same process. Pope, I think, in making wit his general term, felt not only that it was persuasive to adopt the tone of polite society but that he was working against "the very thing that gives modern Criticism its character; whose whole complexion is abuse and censure." The good humor of the thing was meant to exhort the reader against pettiness. Here, I suppose, as so often, his method betrayed him, and the effect of the identity was rather the other way.

> True wit is Nature to advantage dressed,
> What oft was thought, but ne'er so well expressed;
> Something, whose truth convinced at sight we find
> That gives us back the image of our mind. (297)

"True" is of course an invocation to the god in the machine of the term "wit." It may be Imagination "+" or simply "wit that tells truth" "b", perhaps only in personal satire "a", which would reduce wit to jokes "-". The image of our mind is chiefly what we had already felt about the matter in hand, from our previous experience of it; but it may also be something in the structure of the mind itself, not corresponding to anything in the outer world, a taste for myths for example (that is, "true" can mean only beautiful, true to the facts of aesthetics), and this would let us approve of any degree of unreality in the wit. Pope clearly means to praise some kind of truth, but the usual drag towards the drawing room has a powerful effect here. I think that the strongest resultant meaning is to impute a queer sort of democracy to the work of the gentleman poet; the essential fact about a true, as apart from a vain, wit is that he is not a bore.

WIT IN THE ESSAY ON CRITICISM

Dr. Johnson, from whom sympathy might have been expected, thought the definition both false and foolish; novelty was not as unwelcome as all that; such an account of wit "depresses it below its natural dignity, and reduces it from strength of thought to happiness of language." This interpretation I think simply followed from having less respect for polite drawing rooms. For a really solemn treatment of the couplet we must go to Warburton, whose note on it makes a bold attempt to keep Locke at bay and decides that it really means to recommend Optimism, or flattery towards Nature.

> Mr. Locke had defined Wit to consist in "the assemblage of ideas, and putting those together, with quickness and variety, wherein can be found any resemblance or congruity, whereby to make up pleasant pictures and agreeable visions in the fancy." But that great Philosopher, in separating Wit from Judgement, as he does here, has given us (and he could therefore give us no other) only an account of wit in general; in which false Wit, though not every species of it, is included. A striking Image of Nature, is therefore, as Mr. Locke observes, certainly Wit; but this image may strike on several other accounts, as well as for its truth and beauty; and the Philosopher has explained the manner how. But it never becomes that wit which is the ornament of true Poesy, whose end is to represent Nature, but when it dresses that Nature to advantage, and presents us to her in the brightest and most amiable light.

This interpretation would not have occurred to me, but it is adopted by Mr. Churton Collins, and certainly helps to illustrate the rich confusion of these apparently simple couplets. However, the main purpose of Warburton's note is to claim that the opposites have been reconciled: "whenever Wit corresponds with Judgement, we may be sure that it is true."

It seemed worth looking at this old puzzle because it serves to show what irrelevant problems arise if you do not interpret the poem in the light of its social tone, and this is largely a matter of getting the right play out of wit. I hope this view will not be taken to imply that all the uses of the word are facetious

211

or contemptuous. Neither of these two last examples was so intended, and many uses are intended definitely the other way, to provide an escape from the harshness of the criteria that Pope was laying down.

> As men of breeding, sometimes men of wit
> To avoid great errors, will the less commit;
> Neglect the rules each verbal critic lays,
> For not to know some trifles is a praise.   (259)

The tenderness of Pope towards a real poet has something touching about it; he feels that such a person is sure to need protection, and adopts rather the same tone towards him as towards young ladies. The real gentleman is expected to be a help in getting him treated decently; it would I suppose be fussy to separate the wit of Sense "1", the social talker, into two classes only one of which has "breeding," but the distinction is fairly well marked. Incidentally it is clear here that the antitheses are not meant to be exclusive; the first line opposes gentlemen to writers, but Pope certainly did not intend to say that a writer cannot be a gentleman; the terms name functions of the complete man rather than types, and even the functions are called similar. The only way to make the head meaning "1" appear as predicate inside wit, in this example, is to distinguish the polite man from the joker, but even if you regard the man of breeding as one who makes jokes tactfully the head meaning "1" is still prominently in view.

What is perhaps the finest line about wit brings in "generous," a key word for Pope though not a frequent one.

> A perfect judge will read each work of wit
> With the same spirit that its author writ;
> Survey the WHOLE, nor seek small faults to find
> Where Nature moves, and rapture warms the mind,
> Nor lose, for that malignant dull delight
> The generous pleasure to be charmed with wit.   (233)

How are we to get away from Horace and "Fools admire, but men of sense approve"? Can we sometimes forgive authors who do not copy Homer exactly? This background of stupid and frightened nagging, I think, gives the last couplet great power.

WIT IN THE ESSAY ON CRITICISM

It is generous, that is, indulgent and forgiving, of a superior
critic to put up with mere "wit"; what he likes is Homer. Also
in a way it is noble (generous as well-born) to enjoy calmly
what is available; the best in this kind are but shadows, as a
Duke said of Bottom. Only as a third alternative does the dangerous idea poke up; that no one but the broad, unspecialized
and in a way careless person (the well-born soul) can recognize
a new development of the imagination even when it is thrust
under his nose, and that even he only does it by rejoicing. The
whole world of the Rules and the "slight faults" is dwarfed and
trampled upon, and the bad rhyme is meant as a brave illustration of the virtues of carelessness which are being praised.
Generous indeed still meant "brave" (a dictionary of 1623 actually defines it as "valiant, noble"). There is again a certain
tenderness towards the reader who is capable of doing this; it
is really very good of him, because he is sure to make a fool
of himself quite often. What kind of wit he is admiring cannot
be known beforehand, and the pathos of the inadequacy of man
still hangs over the whole topic.
　　The feeling that there is something unpleasant about the
whole business of being a poet was expressed by Pope with great
dignity in his prefaces, and it is this touch of self-pity which
gives the more human side of his incessant play on the word.
There is a fine paragraph on the unpleasing fate of genius which
seems to reach beyond the stock comparison to the joker and
suggest rather the romantic view of the clown.

> Unhappy wit, like most mistaken things,
> Atones not for the envy that it brings.
> In youth alone its empty praise we boast,
> But soon the short-lived vanity is lost. . . .
> What is this Wit, which must our cares employ?
> The owner's wife, which other men enjoy;
> Then most our trouble still when most admired,
> And still the more we give, the more required . . .
> Tis what the vicious fear, the virtuous shun,
> By fools tis hated, and by knaves undone.　　(494-507)

Wit appears essentially mistaken in this passage, even the good
kind of wit which the vicious fear, and the reason must be that
all worthy labors are mistaken by comparison to an assault on

Heaven. This overriding religious sentiment allows of a high view of wit (and Pope is using the first person) but even here a lower view is allowed to be a natural one; why otherwise do the virtuous shun it? The poet-outcast idea is no less strong in Pope than in Byron; he must expect to be despised because of his merits, so if he is to use the language of the world he must at least pretend to despise himself. The idea that the young lyrical poet always arouses hatred seems to be made more plausible by dissolving it into the idea of the satirical "wit" who goads the mob; but even this figure seems to enjoy his duty only so far as he remains childish, a Shakespearean fool perhaps. "Yet then did Gildon draw his venal quill" in the early days of Pope's Pastorals "when pure description took the place of sense"; no doubt Pope would have denied that this opposition is a real one.

As the appeal goes on (it is the heart of the poem) the wit is urged to distinguish himself from the clown by behaving with good nature; as usual, the terms put into an antithesis are thereby made to overlap.

> And while self-love each jealous writer rules,
> Contending wits become the sport of fools.   (517)

Their vanity is the chief reason why they deserve the slang term wit; but if so, after all, it may well apply to many learned and profound thinkers. The next paragraph indeed recognizes that Pope is urging the impossible, and the writer is asked at any rate to make his clownishness respectable by venting his spleen upon vice or blasphemy. In the Restoration period this was not done:

> Jilts ruled the state, and statesmen farces writ,
> Nay wits had pensions, and young lords had wit;
> The fair sat panting at a courtier's play,
> And not a mask went unimproved away.   (539)

We are back in the normal double attitude. It would seem a good thing that the dashing aristocrat under the Restoration set out to write verse and often did it well; Pope can admit this without losing his tone of contempt, because the type of wit in view may be a merely social one, and besides, the lords of his own day

214

are despised for not showing it. The government of his own day is despised for not giving pensions. The wit in need of a pension he could also despise for not being a lord; so that the line gives him a full superiority all round.

> Encouraged thus, Wit's Titans braved the skies
> And the press groaned with licensed blasphemies. (552)

It may be either wits or Titans who are ridiculously inadequate for this purpose; wit may also have its gods, genuine good writers who are at home in the skies. There is again a touch of "4- = 4+," the ominous idea that the lowest is an exact parallel of the highest. Yet it is clear that the same machinery would allow him to despise any writer who deviated into infidelity; already a wit, such a man would automatically become a comic kind of wit.

It is difficult to analyze this satirist without satirizing him, but to say that his tricks were often used unfairly does not go very far. The contradictions of his self-contempt and self-justification are erected into a solid and intelligent humility before the triumphs and social usefulness possible to his art. And it is the same evasively contemptuous use of his formula which saves him from the abject reverence for rules and ancients of which he is commonly accused. The statements against the rules are, after all, very resounding:

> We cannot blame, indeed, but we may sleep. (242)

And in a later poem

> Reason raise o'er instinct as you can
> In this tis God directs, in that tis man.

He is always ready with his contempt for those who accept the rules he identifies himself with:

> The rules a nation, born to serve, obeys
> And Boileau still by right of Horace sways.
> While we, brave Britons, foreign laws despised,
> And kept unconquered and uncivilised. (714)

The "critic-learning" of the French does not seem to be called mistaken; there is only a possibility that Boileau's claim to be heir of Horace might be wrong. But while Pope despises the English for breaking the rules he contrives still more to despise the French for keeping them. The only final question about Pope, I think, since you cannot think him wrong after a full analysis of his meaning, is as to the quality of the contempt through whose action his meaning is imposed; whether you find this a nasty little view of human affairs or a nobly stern one.

THE UNITY OF POPE'S ESSAY ON CRITICISM

Arthur Fenner, Jr.

This paper will undertake to defend the novel proposition that Pope's Essay on Criticism, quite apart from its character as a piece of critical writing, is a rather admirably unified poem in its own right.

Certainly few critics in two centuries and a half have thought that it is. From Addison and Johnson (who admire it), through De Quincey, Leslie Stephen, and Saintsbury (who do not), critics have casually noted its lack of order and connection as an obvious fact. Our own times are more favorable again to Pope, but in this particular the standard opinion is still almost universal. Printed discussions of the Essay are usually not concerned with its structure as a poem;[1] half of those concerned with its structure as theory fail to find unity;[2] and of course all notices-in-passing take the established dogma on faith.

Unity of any kind would represent a singular triumph of form, on Pope's part, over materials which had baffled the efforts of virtually all his predecessors. The Ars Poetica of Horace, according to modern scholars, is not without a plan — though there is much disagreement on its details.[3] But until this century Horace has been considered rather formless, and certainly the series of verse manuals that follow his lead are unsystematic as "thought." The aim is not to analyze poetry, or anything else, and deduce precepts from the analysis; but rather to express, as charmingly and memorably as possible, those scraps of observation and precept, assembled from every possible source, which good sense or authority has certified as true. Without a single theory as a framework for their poems, writers of verse "arts of poetry," from the Renaissance onward, have endeavored to achieve continuity of other kinds. A first step, of course, was to build verse paragraphs by grouping related sententiae together or by amplifying single points with details and examples. But cementing the paragraphs together

Reprinted from Philological Quarterly, Vol. 39 (1960), pp. 435-456, with corrections by the author, by permission of author and publisher.

was more difficult. Relationships of contrariety or consequence could be arranged only here and there, and the poets scarcely seem able to contrive any others. The main difficulty in such poems, as Geoffrey Tillotson observes,[4] is to make the transitions. In this difficulty poets very often seized upon two simple formal patterns which had been in vogue for critical treatises throughout classical and medieval times: a history, usually of poetry, and a catalogue, usually of tropes or literary genres. Each of these supplied a frame on which the poet could hang a great load of precept and observation, with an obvious — if somewhat artificial — show of continuity and structure. But until An Essay on Criticism these stratagems were only moderately successful, and Horace and most of his successors, as if in acknowledgment that they failed to practice the unity they preached, couched their manuals in an informal style, and published them as epistles or essays.[5] The original master of this genre had been eminently charming, eminently memorable, and (at least in men's minds) eminently disconnected. His pupils continued the tradition.

Vida opens Book III of his De Arte Poeticae (1527) by grandly announcing that he will, nunc autem, treat of Language and Style, "the last stage of my course"; but stage and course can mean in this context hardly more than page and book, and the conjunctions are the most perfunctory tag. The wandering path Vida has traveled over all kinds of territory in Books I and II could as well have led to any other place. Two hundred and fifty of his 1,750 lines comprise a sort of history (the education of the young poet), and some coherence is given to another two hundred lines by a catalogue of the figures of speech, though it disappears and reappears more than once. But at many other points Vida either fails to indicate any relation between "subject blocks" at all, or suggests that one subject has simply reminded him, somehow, of the next.

Boileau has four passages of history in his Art Poetique (1674), and when well into his course he abruptly and stiffly imposes the structure of the genre-catalogue on a long passage (almost one-half of the poem). Elsewhere he is somewhat more successful than Vida in connecting one subject with the next, but there is no sense of over-all progression, or of any other functioning of these parts in a master design.

THE UNITY OF POPE'S <u>ESSAY ON CRITICISM</u>

Three English lords attempted "Arts of Poetry" shortly before Pope: Mulgrave, Roscommon, and Lansdowne.[6] The poem by Lansdowne is an interesting exception. It does have unity, and it shows how a simple prose outline can give order to a short work — the poem is only one hundred and five lines in length. Lansdowne's catalogue of the three "parts" of poetry where extravagance is to be avoided -- metaphors, hyperboles, and fables — and his little history of the improvement of poetry in this regard, comprise all of his poem except the general introduction and the conclusion. But the two other verse manuals are much longer and have a much wider subject to cover, and they are both conspicuously faulty at the connections.

In <u>An Essay on Translated Verse</u> sixty lines are usually as many as Roscommon can weld together; between these larger units there is only the faintest connection, or none. His anecdote of a doctor, which he borrowed from Boileau and probably inserted while the poem was awaiting publication, is a lively picture of mistaken talents, but it would do just as well in another place, or another poem. This passage is abruptly followed by one on the faults of needy and of wealthy authors; then, again abruptly, a contrast between genuine inspiration and mere "possession"; then, the great ancients' license to seem to trifle, and so on.

If in Roscommon transitions are often lacking, in Mulgrave they are often all too evident. He moves from one topic to another with a self-conscious "Here rest, my Muse," or "Let's cast a view on. . . ." After opening on the theme that genius is divine, and fancy without judgment mad, he declares, without any warning whatever:

> Here I should all the differing kinds reherse
> Of <u>Poetry</u>, with various sorts of Verse.

The catalogue of genres which follows is pushed out of shape by the fact that the fifth on the list, drama, occupies more space than the preceding four put together. In fact this long fifth section makes us forget the catalogue framework, so that the sixth genre, the epic, appears as a surprise:

> By painfull steps we are at last got up
> <u>Pernassus</u> hill, upon whose Airy top

The <u>Epick</u> poets . . .

It is well that Mulgrave got up to the epic poets, for he can now close his poem in a paean to Homer and Virgil, but his reader has had little sense of his getting there "by steps," painful or otherwise.

The tradition, then, that leads to Pope is a series of failures in order. Minor local successes have been achieved by "prose" means: the cement of transition, the catalogue, and the history. But one cannot find a more vital dramatic or poetic organization in any of these poems, or even an expository order, that unifies the whole.

I

In the second section of <u>An Essay on Criticism</u> Pope employs the device of the catalogue — to list not poetic genres but kinds of bad critics (289-473),[7] and he hangs on this frame the usual load of aphorism and example. But there is a very great difference between his catalogue and those of his predecessors. For one thing it is less a static list of familiar entities (epic, drama, satire, etc.) than a procession of rather novel and interesting fools. More important, the catalogue is part of the whole organization of Section II. It follows logically from what precedes it: The perfect judge will survey the whole, for it is that, and not the exactness of peculiar parts, that we call beauty. But La Mancha's knight would advise sacrificing everything else in a play, just to get an armed tournament into it. Thus critics offend by a love of parts (233-288). Then the catalogue, opening with further examples of this last. And all of its items are articulated into a whole by the fact that there is a clear, even a grammatical continuity running through the "topic sentences" at the head of each:

Some to <u>Conceit</u> alone their taste confine,   289
Others for <u>Language</u> all their care express,   305
But most by <u>Numbers</u> judge a Poet's song.   337
[Avoid extremes of pleasure or offense at trifles.]   384
Some foreign writers, some our own despise;   394
Some . . . catch the spreading notion of the Town; 408-409

220

> Some judge of authors names, not works;   412
> The Learn'd . . . if the throng
> By chance go right, they purposely go wrong; 425-427
> Some praise at morning what they blame at night; 430
> Some . . . [value] those of their own side or mind. 452

Pope further organizes the series, and insures against tedium, by dividing bad critics into two kinds: those with specialties, and those with ulterior motives.[8] For these reasons the outlines of the catalogue simply do not obtrude themselves like a rack on which to hang the poet's remarks.

Pope does not need any such rack; elsewhere, he achieves continuity without it to a quite satisfactory degree. Each paragraph has the internal unity of its separate topic, but at the same time its first lines bear a close relation of some sort to those that precede them, and its last to those that follow. For all its distinctness, each paragraph assists and is assisted by its neighbors and forms a link between them.

Almost any passage might serve as illustration. Take two paragraphs from Section I, with the couplets coming before and after them:

> These leave the sense, their learning to display,
> And those explain the meaning quite away.
>> You then whose judgment the right course would steer,
> Know well each ANCIENT'S proper character;
> [study Homer day and night.] . . .
> Still with itself compar'd, his text peruse;
> And let your comment be the Mantuan Muse.
>> When first young Maro in his boundless mind
> A work t' outlast immortal Rome design'd,
> Perhaps he seem'd above the Critic's law,
> . . . [and drew only from Nature, but later he found
> Nature and Homer to be the same. Thereafter
> strict rules confined his work] . . . .
> Learn hence for ancient rules a just esteem;
> To copy nature is to copy them.
>> Some beauties yet no Precepts can declare,
> For there's a happiness as well as care.

The first paragraph, a block of advice to study the ancients, flows from the paragraph above it as a consequence ("You, then, . . ."); the advice is given to correct the abuses just noted. The second paragraph in the passage furnishes, of course, an example of the conduct which the first paragraph recommends. Thus each, as a unit, has its connection. But in addition, the edges of each block are cemented to the edges of those adjacent. At the head of the first paragraph Pope puts "you" in sharp and flattering contrast to the dull fools just described. At the head of the second, he concedes what might be said on the other side of the question he has raised: "True, young Virgil set out to be independent," and of course Virgil, as immediate subject, also carries across the gap. At the third paragraph juncture there is a sharper contrariety; Pope follows a firm commitment to the rules by a firm commitment to the je ne sais quoi, the beauty which no precepts can declare. This is not a clash, but the turning point in a pattern very frequent in Augustan didactic verse: a dialectical "zig-zag" across the golden mean, in which a doctrine is checked, and its limits firmly set, by the claims of the opposite doctrine. In the last line quoted Pope softens the sharpness of the turn by embracing both doctrines in a pair of terms: "For there's a happiness as well as care."

If the main difficulty in such poems is to make the transitions, then Pope is constantly solving it. Whole paragraphs may be considered transitions, and the poem moves along smoothly from point to point.

II

But does it go anywhere that is important? And is there transition between larger units than couplets and paragraphs? What is the movement through the three sections into which the poem is divided? Section I might be entitled "Principles of Criticism"; II, "Applying Criticism to Poetry"; and III, "Communicating Criticism to Poets." There is this orderly sequence of topics, and the poem has the kind of expository structure which might be represented in an outline with these three titles as its main heads. And these, incidentally, resemble the three-part division of classical treatises: Poesis, the general subject; Poema, technical details; and Poeta, the qualities and duties of the poet (in this case, the critic). But there is much in each section which these titles do not cover. Section III is intent on more than those good manners in the critic which will make his strictures palatable; the object is his morals, and his heart, in general. To put it more specifically than these sub-titles do: the first section proposes the general basis for right judgment, and the second offers concrete examples of right judgment and wrong. But the third abandons concern about whether the critic is right or wrong (though it assumes he is right), and dwells on his motives and actions as a moral being. Section III would seem to represent a radical shift in purpose, from one decidedly professional and intellectual to one decidedly moral. But Pope does not write at this point as if he were adding another purpose to his first, like a new subject, but as if he were drawing the consequences of premises he has already established. Section III opens with

LEARN then what MORALS Critics ought to show. (560)

Such an important "then" cannot be accounted for by the little four-line warning at the end of the previous section not to "mistake an author into vice."[9] The premises for this conclusion, and the transition from Section I to Section III, are embedded everywhere in Section II.

One way Pope builds up the proper "atmosphere" for turning to the critic's morals is to make a gradual shift in the view he affords us of modern poets -- from the ridiculous, to the admirable, to the valiant but shamefully beset. In the first two units of the catalogue (289-336) all we see of poets are their conceits and fantastic language. In the third unit, on "Numbers" (337-383), Pope first shows us other ridiculous writing, the pleasing murmurs that put us to sleep; then better writing, his own exercises in onomatopoeia; then that of Dryden, who equals the ancients themselves as a conqueror with sound. From this peak the typical modern poet gradually falls in fortunes, and rises as an object for solicitude. His verse is judged harshly because his social station is low (418-419), the approval of fools deludes him into thinking his reputation safe (450-451), and envy arises to obscure the fame, momentarily, even of the greatest (458-466). Here again Dryden is spoken of with the ancients, and again he triumphs like them (though now it is not "all our [willing] hearts" he conquers, but malicious criticism). But in the next paragraph a crueler enemy, the changing language itself,

223

defeats him, and now it is not Homer he resembles, but forgotten Chaucer (476-483). Finally, in a light thrown full on the poet's personal wretchedness, we see the fate of all creative talent at the hands of its public:

> Unhappy Wit, like most mistaken things,
> Atones not for that envy which it brings;
>
> . . . .
>
> 'Tis what the vicious fear, the virtuous shun,
> By fools 'tis hated, and by knaves undone!

(494-495; 506-507)

This swinging of attention to the plight of the poet effects a shift in one's conception of the duty of the critic. Earlier in the poem he was to judge correctly of literary merit; now he must deal kindly with a friendless man.

But there is another and more important development underlying the major transition from I to III. As the bad judgments are paraded past, the nature of the faults they stem from gradually changes from error to sin. At the opening of Section II pride, the chief cause of judging ill, is called a "vice," but it is presented without any moral implications. It is found in opposition to "right reason," and it "fills up all the mighty void of sense" in the weak heads of fools (201-212). A little later there is a hint of the moral viewpoint in "malignant" and "gen'rous" (237-238); but this aspect is submerged under the dominant impression of mere error and folly. La Mancha's knight is a harmless and possibly amiable specialist ass. Those who confine their taste to Conceit, Language, or Numbers (289-343) are only mistaken fools; and, significantly, their criteria are still literary and their judgments are still favorable: they are pleased with a wild heap of wit, they praise and value books for their dress of words, they admire the Muse's tuneful voice.

But the paragraph of summarizing precept between the two parts of the catalogue (384-393) refers to critics' being offended as well as pleased, and thus begins the transition to adverse judgments and the critic's morals. To continue the catalogue: when authors are judged on the basis of their time or nationality (394-401), personal elements enter and adulterate literary judgment; in the next paragraph only the personal motive is left, for

224

critics "Nor praise nor blame the writings, but the men" (413);
and in the final unit of the catalogue, party warfare combines
with personal quarrels to redouble "hate" (457). Traces of the
intellectual element might still be present, but the moral has
come steadily to the fore. A single line (452) points to both:
"Some, valuing those of their own side or mind," and each is
elaborated in turn; first "mind": "we but praise ourselves in
other men"; then "side": "And public faction doubles private
hate" (455, 457). The next three words restate all the themes
of Section II: "Pride, Malice, Folly, against Dryden rose"; but
now the poem concentrates for fifteen lines on malice alone
(459-473).

The catalogue is over, and it has done more than list and
illustrate types of bad judging. It has shifted the grounds of
criteria -- persuasively because by an intricate and gradual process -- from the intellectual and literary to the moral. The shift
is so successful that there is no jar of surprise when we read
in the next couplet a precept that is not, in the strictest sense,
literary or critical at all: "Be thou the first true merit to be-
friend; / His praise is lost, who stays, till all commend" (474-
475).

But the supreme point in the development is still to come.
Accompanied by a steady deepening of emotional tone -- there is
no more of the light humor that played about the metrical music-
makers and La Mancha's knight -- a sense of the evil behind attacks on poetry has been steadily growing. And now, piled on
top of the folly, partiality, and envy of dunces, there are the
sins among critics and poets who stand on Parnassus itself,
where "self-love each jealous writer rules" (516); and we reach
the climactic utterance toward which we have been moving from
the beginning of Section II:

> To what base ends, and by what abject ways,
> Are mortals urg'd thro' sacred lust of praise!
> Ah ne'er so dire a thirst of glory boast,
> Nor in the Critic let the Man be lost!
> Good-nature and good-sense must ever join;
> To err is human, to forgive, divine.   (520-525)

Section II concludes by telling the critic what faults in a writer
he need not forgive, and they are not poetic crimes: obscenity,

heresy, blasphemy (526-559). Section III, devoted to the ideally virtuous critic, now has behind it an enormous weight of justification.

Considering all of Section II once more, we find that a single theme runs through the transition from Section I to III. While Pope is shifting the criteria for judging, he is at the same time keeping rather well within the limits set by the statement which opens the section, that the chief cause of judging ill is pride. Too great love of a specialty — whether tournaments or smooth numbers, the literature of one's own country, one's momentary opinion, or the writer who shares it — can be considered love of self in disguise. Even the servile flatterer is called "proud dulness," the partial critic "praises himself in other men," and finally it is self-love and dire thirst of glory that urges men by abject ways to base ends (415, 455, 520-521). In Section II folly turns into vice, but both are the result of pride.

The idea of pride broods over the entire poem. Almost from the opening lines of Section I there are constant glances in that direction: each man believes his own watch (and his own judgment); critics are as partial to their taste as authors to their wit (10, 17), and through the remainder of Section I there is a crescendo of terms — "proud . . . pretending," "vain ambition," "bold," "presumptuous," and finally "sacrilegious" (53, 65, 110, 169, 182). In Section II, after the catalogue, and after the "shift" described above, the poet is moved to his highest pitch of compressed ironic intensity when he sees "Heaven's free subjects" dispute their rights with God, and when

> . . . Wit's Titans brav'd the skies
> And the press groan'd with licens'd blasphemies.

> (552-553)

The professed object of the poem is not, of course, to banish pride, but to establish proper criticism. Yet the first is so intensely conceived as the indispensable means to the second that when the poet is most explicit about his purpose in addressing his reader it is to make him humble:

> But you who seek to give and merit fame,
> And justly bear a Critic's noble name,

> Be sure yourself and your own reach to know,
> How far your genius, taste, and learning go;
> Launch not beyond your depth, . . .   (46-50)

And in what might be called the official invocation of the poem, he prays for inspiration "to teach vain Wits a science little known, / T' admire superior sense, and doubt their own!" (199-200)

For Augustans pride was the super-category in which most sins could be included, because any violation of God's law is a refusal to take one's proper (subordinate) place in the Chain of Being He has created. To try to be something one is not -- as does a bumpkin in regal purple, or an ape dressed like our grandsires (321, 332) — is to disrupt the hierarchy of Nature. Instead one must follow Nature (68), and not only where she has set standards for poetry, but where she has "fix'd the limits" to a critic's mental powers, "And wisely curb'd proud man's pretending wit" (52-53). Modern critics, the poem indicates several times, have not followed her, but have left their proper places in her hierarchy. False learning has turned some into coxcombs Nature meant but fools; others are not even a species at all -- unsuccessful poets turned critics, half-formed things which can pass for neither (27-43). In contrast to these, the critics of an earlier age, pointing out glories in older authors, and helping and encouraging those of their own day, are described as "gen'rous," meaning, in part, "pure bred" (92-103). Modern critics, a bastard kind, have abandoned their proper function and have turned on the poets in envy and spite (30-33, 104-107).

Thus the pride of the critic and his malice lie behind the poem at almost every point. The two together accomplish the transition from Section I to Section III, they give An Essay on Criticism a pronouncedly moral cast,[10] and they give it a great deal of dramatic "point" and unity as a poem.

But not all of its point and unity by any means, for the analysis here — confined chiefly to Section II, and to the negative side of its thought — is far from complete. Maynard Mack has made a brilliant little sketch of how analysis might proceed further, to a positive value behind the attack on pride and malice: the corporate ideal against which the critic's "love to parts" offends.[11] And another sort of analysis might reveal an interesting ambiguity in the notion of pride itself.[12] But incomplete as it is, my study shows, I hope, that as a poem An Essay on Criticism is not the string of commonplaces (or the mere string of pearls) it has been thought.

And it does one thing more. It indicates (as has E. N. Hooker from a different point of view)[13] another historical "background" for the poem besides the tradition of literary theory in which it takes its place. The Essay is Pope's contribution to a rather bitter warfare then raging between the "wits" and their critics, a warfare which had included the Ancients and Moderns controversy, Collier's Short View and the many replies to it, Blackmore's Satyr Against Wit, and several Spectator essays. This is the context, I think, for the opening lines. They do not quite enter the fray but appeal in a friendly, colloquial fashion to one who (like the speaker of the lines) remains urbanely above it. The voice is partisan, but conciliatory: It's hard to say which is a worse bungler, but surely a bad poet is less dangerous to us than a bad critic, and in recent years bad critics have become ten times more numerous (1-8). "Authors are partial to their wit 'tis true, / But are not Critics to their judgment too?" (17-18) The dramatic intention is already visible, and it is more than the merely technical purpose of the usual didactic "Ars." The Essay on Criticism does indeed organize and give memorable expression to a large body of critical judgments and injunctions, but it suspends them all, as it were, in an act of speech, a defense of poets against foolish and hostile critics in tones that shift gradually from banter to a passionate plea.

NOTES

1 Austin Warren deals with the doctrine and its antecedents, Alexander Pope as Critic and Humanist (Princeton, 1929), Chap. I; R. K. Root, with the doctrine, The Poetical Career of Alexander Pope (Princeton, 1938), Chap. I; and William Empson, with brilliant local effects, "Wit in the Essay on Criticism," Hudson Review, II (1950), 559-577. The single exception, a criticism of the poem as a whole which I shall discuss at the end of this paper, is by Maynard Mack, The Augustans (New York, 1950), pp. 20-23.

2 Against the charge that the poem is "a potpourri of Augustan
   clichés," E. N. Hooker finely demonstrates the coherence
   and profundity of the theory of wit it expresses. In doing so
   he leaves the implication that such coherence also belongs
   to the poem itself, but he does not pursue the idea. "Cliché"
   is the object of his attack, not "potpourri"; see "Pope on
   Wit: the Essay on Criticism" in The Seventeenth Century,
   R. F. Jones et al, (Stanford, 1951), pp. 225-246. G. Wilson
   Knight's rapid paraphrase is intended to indicate coherence
   in the doctrine, Laureate of Peace (New York, 1955), pp.
   40-43.
        On the other hand George Sherburn notes a lack of
   structure, though less than usual in Pope, The Best of
   Pope, rev. ed. (New York, 1940), p. 394. Emile Audra
   finds abrupt reversals of intention, confused development,
   and irresolution (flottement) in the thought, L'Influence
   française dans l'oeuvre de Pope (Paris, 1931), pp. 215-218.
   W. J. Bate summarizes "the topics discussed" in an outline,
   but fails to assimilate into it three considerable passages,
   and agrees with Samuel Johnson that paragraphs might
   easily exchange places, Criticism: The Major Texts (New
   York, 1952), pp. 172-173.

3 Several theories are described briefly by Allan H. Gilbert,
   Literary Criticism Plato to Dryden (New York, 1940), pp.
   125-127. But it still seems to me that Horace slips through,
   and rambles widely outside, any fences analysts can build
   for him.

4 On the Poetry of Pope, rev. ed. (Oxford, 1950), p. 48.

5 That poets sought so earnestly after method and connection
   is, strictly speaking, only an assumption, a convenient way
   of describing the results, which are my real concern. The
   poets may in fact have written this way because they thought
   truth and familiarity justified their dicta, however assembled, or because they were imitating Horace in structural
   negligence, or for other reasons.

6 John Sheffield, Earl of Mulgrave, An Essay upon Poetry,
   1682; Wentworth Dillon, Earl of Roscommon, An Essay
   on Translated Verse, 1684; George Granville, Baron Lansdowne, An Essay upon Unnatural Flights in Poetry, 1701.

All three are reprinted in Critical Essays of the Seventeenth Century, ed. J. E. Spingarn (Oxford, 1908), II, 286-296, 297-309, III, 292-295.

7 And of course the final hundred lines of the poem are a history of criticism.

8 Boileau — and Mulgrave, following him -- divide their catalogues between the lesser genres and the greater. The former does it with nothing but white space on his page and "Chant III"; the latter inserts an elaborate pause to let his muse rest and gather strength.

9 The warning is merely one of those qualifications (like the reversal of emphasis discussed above) which Pope has employed several times in the poem to save his doctrine from excess. As part of a "zig-zag" from vice to opposite vice, this warning attaches itself to the exhortation just above it, which it qualifies; it is obviously incapable of effecting the major transition to Section III.

10 The moral aspect has troubled critics. Audra finds passages like that on jealousy among writers, excrescences in a didactic poem on criticism. They are here, he says, because Pope imitates Boileau too closely — and Boileau was discussing poets, not critics. In his outline of the "thought" of the poem, Professor Bate simply omits the invocation on humility and a long passage leading up to it; lines 201-232 he brackets off from his outline as "Digression on the Need for Humility." On the other hand Professor Sherburn notes that "this poem has as its general office . . . the rehabilitation of the critic in good nature and good manners." A Literary History of England, ed. A. C. Baugh (New York, 1948), p. 843.

11 Cited in note 1 above.

12 At least in what is suggested, the dramatic speaker has it both ways: he is the humble poet ("the last, the meanest of your sons" -- 196) battling proud critics, even the plain man like any other, peering painstakingly thro' the gloom as the poem opens (" 'Tis hard to say. . . , our judgments as our watches none / Go just alike"); but at the same time he enjoys the detached view, the godlike ability to penetrate the

scene and judge the actors. This is implied not only in the fact that so many critical pronouncements are made, but in the doctrine that the poet — in lines 15-16 <u>only</u> the poet — has the authority to make them, and in the image of the poet of genius surrounded by insects and abortions who claim to be critics. Is the speaker this great man? The specifically poetic intelligence behind the parodies of sweetness and demonstrations of "sound echoing sense" (344-383), and the entire <u>Essay</u> as itself a poem, are his credentials. "Pride," like "wit" and even "Nature," appears on both sides of the ledger.

13 Cited in note 2 above, pp. 227-231.

WINDSOR FOREST AND WILLIAM III

J. R. Moore

On March 29, 1867, Sainte-Beuve wrote to M. Louis Dépret, "Je suis resté, malgré tout, de l'école classique, de celle d'Horace, du chantre de la fôret de Windsor, . . ."[1] But certain lines of Pope's poem reveal more of the Wasp of Twickenham than of the Singer of Windsor Forest.

It has been observed that in 1713 Pope "aspired to be nonpartisan and yet to please both parties."[2] However, the implicit attack on William III, whether it carried over from the earlier form of "Windsor Forest" (as I suspect) or was added in a later revision, was certainly partisan in tone. It could not conceivably have pleased those Whigs who continued to celebrate the birthday and to mourn the anniversary of the death of "William of Glorious Memory," who had come to England as a "Deliverer."

It is commonly observed that the poem has two distinct strands of thought; the account of the pastoral scene was "remade to fit the political situation" and thereby "to celebrate the conclusion of a Tory peace. . . ."[3] But Elwin, insensitive as he was to many of his author's purely literary qualities, made a shrewd remark on his political bias: "Pope did not stop with applauding the Peace; he denounced the Revolution."[4] I wish to call attention to Pope's denunciation of the Revolution only as it appears in his attack on the person of William III.

After the death of the late king in 1702 and the subsequent triumph of the Tories in the parliamentary election, it became an object of party policy to attach Queen Anne to the Tories more firmly by alienating her from the memory of William. A desperate effort was made to prove that he had sought to set aside her claim to the throne. He was stigmatized as a foreigner and a dissenter; she was "truly English" and "a daughter of the Church." He was a usurper, they said, or at best a king by parliamentary sanction; constant claims were made for her title as an hereditary one. When her army won a battle, she

Reprinted from Modern Language Notes, Vol. 66 (1951), pp. 451-454, by permission of the author.

was said to be putting an end to William's ruinous wars. Pope's own sympathies can hardly be in doubt. He must have remembered the restrictions on Catholic residence near the capital, which led his father to give up business in London and settle in Windsor Forest. As recently as 1711 ("An Essay on Criticism," l. 544) he had inveighed against the irreligious "licence of a Foreign reign." All the men whose names figure in the poem were Tories: Sir William Trumbull, who first suggested the topic; Ralph Bridges, who saw the poem in manuscript in 1707; and Lord Lansdowne, a Jacobite later imprisoned in the Tower for complicity in the rebellion of 1715, who urged the adaptation to the Peace of Utrecht and to whom the poem was dedicated. The Tory, especially the anti-Williamite, bias lies deeply rooted in the whole work.

The Tory charges that William had kept the nation in constant wars and that he had displaced the legitimate Stuart line, which run through scores of contemporary tracts, are brilliantly summed up in a single verse (l. 42):

> And peace and plenty tell, a STUART reigns.

William's passion for hunting was well known; it was often remarked that his face became animated only in the chase or on the field of battle. Luttrell's Brief Relation (v, 145) and The Dictionary of National Biography give the following accounts of the accident which hastened his death:

> . . . as his majestie was hunting a stagg near Kingston upon Thames, his horse fell with him and broke his collar bone; . . .

> On his return to England he had so far kept up the appearance of health as to ride and even hunt at Hampton Court; . . . . On this very day his favorite horse Sorrel, which he was riding through the park at Hampton Court, stumbled on a molehill, causing him to fall and break his collar-bone.

The extreme Tories could not be satisfied with any such dryly factual statement. For them, Sorrel was not only William's favorite horse, but he had formerly been owned by Sir John

Fenwick, who had been executed for conspiring against the life of the king. Even the mole which dug the fatal hill became a divine instrument of national salvation, and loyal toasts were drunk to "the little gentleman in velvet." This partisan view is perhaps most clearly stated by Sir Walter Scott's example of the violent Jacobite, the fatalistic Laird of Redgauntlet:

> The usurper, William of Nassau, went forth to hunt,
> and thought, doubtless, that it was by an act of his
> own royal pleasure that the horse of his murdered
> victim was prepared for his kingly sport. But Heaven
> had other views; and before the sun was high, a stum-
> ble of that very animal over an obstacle so inconsid-
> erable as a mole-hillock cost the haughty rider his
> life and his usurped crown.[5]

So too the death of William the Conqueror had been hastened by an injury from his horse:

> . . . upon leaping over a Ditch on Horse-Back, he so
> bruised the Rimm of his Belly against the Pummel of
> the Saddel, that he was soon thrown into a dangerous
> Distemper that ended his Days.[6]

More explicitly, the divine vengeance which later fell on William III had been meted out to the family of the Conqueror. According to the poem, he was "denied a grave"; and two of his sons (one of whom, Rufus, bore the fateful name of William) were killed in the chase.

In 1706, in advocating a general policy of deforestation,[7] an able writer urged that Windsor Forest should be spared because Queen Anne herself occasionally hunted there.[8] Such a fact must have been familiar to Pope, but it would not have suited his purpose; in his poem the royal hunters were men of violence and of usurpation.

In fact, one of the principal alleged resemblances between the two Williams was in their having come to the throne through military force. According to the anonymous Political Remarks on the Life and Reign of King William III, the new sovereign was crowned by a parliamentary title and was accepted by the general consent of his people:

yet these Pontifens must needs be giving him a new right, which forsooth was that of conquest. The Dutch at first were well enough pleased with the fancy, and the court itself shewed not much aversion to the ill grounded chimera: But the Parliament soon took up the quarrel, and shewed the vanity of these pretensions, and gave the world to understand, that England never submitted but once (if it did so) in the reign of William the Conqueror.[9]

Most of the events during the reigns of the early Norman kings which Pope sets forth so vehemently happened in the New Forest or in France, and so have little or nothing to do with Windsor Forest; but they are intimately concerned with another foreign tyrant named William, who came over from Normandy as William III came from Holland. The accidental recurrence of the royal name gave a chance to insinuate against the third foreign William all the other evils alleged against his namesake: hostility to the Church, contempt for the agricultural interests, heartless indifference to the rights of the people, callousness toward the shedding of human blood. Unhistorically enough, all subsequent Norman kings were represented by Pope as relaxing the strictness of the forest laws out of pity for the subjects, and as taking pleasure in seeing the displacement of royal forests by peaceful villages (ll. 85-86); only the first two Williams were, like "the butcher of Glencoe," men of blood.

These ideas are implicit in ll. 43-90 of the final version of the poem. But two rejected lines of the original (ll. 91-92) were so directly stated in favor of the Stuart succession that during the reign of William III or the later reign of George I a Tory reader might have taken them in a sense which was hardly short of treasonable:

> O may no more a foreign master's rage,
> With wrongs yet legal, curse a future age!

NOTES

1 Nouvelle Correspondance (Paris, 1880), p. 235.

2 George Sherburn, The Early Career of Alexander Pope (Oxford, 1934), p. 101.

3 Loc. cit.

4 The Works of Alexander Pope (London, 1871-89), I, 326.

5 Redgauntlet, chapter viii (Dryburgh ed. , p. 223).

6 Laurence Echard, The History of England (London, 1707-1718), I, 151.

7 This policy (especially for the New Forest in Hampshire) was urged in Tutchin's Observator (December 30-January 2, 1702/3) and in Defoe's Tour (Everyman ed. , I, 200-206) at a later date (1724).

8 The Meanes Of a most Ample Encrease of the Wealth and Strength of England In a few years. There are at least three copies of this manuscript extant (one in the Henry E. Huntington Library, HM 1264, U4Q4; one in the British Museum, Lansdowne MS. 691; and one in private hands). The first two of these are signed "Neh: Grew" and the third is signed "Daniel De Foe."

9 Harleian Miscellany, X, 554.

THE CASE OF MISS ARABELLA FERMOR:
A RE-EXAMINATION

Cleanth Brooks

Aldous Huxley's lovers, "quietly sweating, palm to palm," may be conveniently taken to mark the nadir of Petrarchism. The mistress is no longer a goddess — not even by courtesy. She is a congeries of biological processes and her too-evident mortality is proclaimed at every pore. But if we seem to reach, with Huxley's lines, the end of something, it is well to see what it is that has come to an end. It is not the end of a naïve illusion.

The Elizabethans, even those who were immersed in the best tradition of Petrarchism, did not have to wait upon the advent of modern science to find out that women perspired. They were thoroughly aware that woman was a biological organism, but their recognition of this fact did not prevent them from asserting, on occasion, that she was a goddess, nevertheless. John Donne, for instance, frequently has it both ways: indeed, some of the difficulty which the modern reader has with his poems may reside in the fact that he sometimes has it both ways in the same poem. What is relevant to our purposes here is not the occurrence of a line like "Such are the sweat drops of my mistress' breast" in one of the satiric "elegies," but the occurrence of lines like

> Our hands were firmly cemented
> With a fast balm, which thence did spring

in a poem like The Ecstasy. The passage quoted, one may argue, glances at the very phenomenon which Huxley so amiably describes; but Donne has transmuted it into something else.

But if Donne could have it both ways, most of us, in this

First printed in The Sewanee Review, Autumn 1943, pp. 505-524. Copyright ©1943 by The University of the South. Reprinted by permission of author and publisher. This article has also appeared in Cleanth Brooks, The Well-wrought Urn.

latter day, cannot. We are disciplined in the tradition of either-or, and lack the mental agility — to say nothing of the maturity of attitude — which would allow us to indulge in the finer distinctions and the more subtle reservations permitted by the tradition of both-and. Flesh or spirit, merely a doxy or purely a goddess (or alternately, one and then the other), is more easily managed in our poetry, and probably, for that matter, in our private lives. But the greater poems of our tradition are more ambitious in this matter: as a consequence, they come perhaps nearer the truth than we do with our ordinary hand-to-mouth insights. In saying this, however, one need by no means confine himself to the poetry of Donne. If we are not too much blinded by our doctrine of either-or, we shall be able to see that there are many poems in the English tradition which demonstrate a thorough awareness of the problem and which manage, at their appropriate levels, the same kinds of synthesis of attitudes which we associate characteristically with Donne.

Take Pope's Rape of the Lock, for instance. Is Belinda a goddess, or is she merely a frivolous tease? Pope himself was, we may be sure, thoroughly aware of the problem. His friend Swift penetrated the secrets of the lady's dressing room with what results we know. Belinda's dressing table, of course, is bathed in a very different atmosphere; yet it may be significant that Pope is willing to allow us to observe his heroine at her dressing table at all. The poet definitely means to give us scenes from the green room, and views from the wings, as well as a presentation "in character" on the lighted stage.

Pope, of course, did not write The Rape of the Lock because he was obsessed with the problem of Belinda's divinity. He shows, indeed, that he was interested in a great many things: in various kinds of social satire, in a playful treatment of the epic manner, in deflating some of the more vapid clichés that filled the love poetry of the period, and in a dozen other things. But we are familiar with Pope's interest in the mock-epic as we are not familiar with his interest in the problem of woman as goddess; and moreover, the rather lurid conventional picture of Pope as the "wicked wasp of Twickenham" — the particular variant of the either-or theory as applied to Pope — encourages us to take the poem as a dainty but rather obvious satire. There is some justification, therefore, for emphasizing aspects of the poem which have received little attention in the past and, perhaps, for neglecting other aspects of the poems which critics have already treated in luminous detail.

One further point should be made: if Pope in this account of the poem turns out to be something of a symbolist poet, and perhaps even something of what we call, in our clumsy phrase, a "metaphysical poet" as well, we need not be alarmed. It matters very little whether or not we twist some of the categories which the literary historian jealously (and perhaps properly) guards. It matters a great deal that we understand Pope's poem in its full richness and complexity. It would be an amusing irony (and one not wholly undeserved) if we retorted upon Pope some of the brittleness and inelasticity which we feel that Pope was inclined to impose upon the more fluid and illogical poetry which preceded him. But the real victims of the manoeuver, if it blinded us to his poem, would be ourselves.

Pope's own friends were sometimes guilty of oversimplifying and reducing his poem by trying to make it accord with a narrow and pedantic logic. For example, Bishop Warburton, Pope's friend and editor, finds an error in the famous passage in which Belinda and her maid are represented as priestesses invoking the goddess of beauty. Warburton feels forced to comment as follows: "There is a small inaccuracy in these lines. He first makes his heroine the chief priestess, then the goddess herself." The lines in question run as follows:

> First rob'd in white, the nymph intent adores
> With head uncover'd, the cosmetic pow'rs.
> A heav'nly image in the glass appears,
> To that she bends, to that her eyes she rears . . . .

It is true that Pope goes on to imply that Belinda is the chief priestess (by calling her maid the "inferior priestess"), and that, a few lines later, he has the maid "deck [Belinda] the goddess with the glittering spoil." But surely Warburton ought not to have missed the point: Belinda, in worshipping at the shrine of beauty, quite naturally worships herself. Whose else is the "heav'nly image" which appears in the mirror to which she raises her eyes? The violation of logic involved is intended and is thoroughly justified. Belinda is a goddess, but she puts on her divinity at her dressing table; and, such is the paradox of beauty-worship, she can be both the sincere devotee and the divinity herself. We shall certainly require more sensitive instruments than Bishop Warburton's logic if we are to become aware of some of the nicest effects in the poem.

But to continue with the dressing-table scene:

> The fair each moment rises in her charms,
> Repairs her smiles, awakens every grace,
> And calls forth all the wonders of her face:
> Sees by degrees a purer blush arise,
> And keener lightnings quicken in her eyes.

It is the experience which the cosmetic advertisers take with a dead level of seriousness, and obviously Pope is amused to have it taken seriously. And yet, is there not more here than the obvious humor? Belinda is, after all, an artist, and who should be more sympathetic with the problems of the conscious artist than Pope himself? In our own time, William Butler Yeats, a less finicky poet than Pope, could address a "young beauty" as "dear fellow artist."

In particular, consider the "purer blush." Why purer? One must not laugh too easily at the purity of the blush which Belinda is engaged in painting upon her face. After all, may we not regard it as a blush "recollected in tranquility," and therefore a more ideal blush than the actual blush which the spontaneous overflow of motion — shame or hauteur on an actual occasion — might bring? If we merely read "purer" as ironic for its opposite, "impurer" -- that is, unspontaneous and therefore unmaidenly — we shall miss not only the more delightful aspects of the humor, but we shall miss also Pope's concern for the real problem. Which is, after all, the mere maidenly blush? That will depend, obviously, upon what one considers the essential nature of maidens to be; and Belinda, we ought to be reminded, is not the less real nor the less feminine because she fails to resemble Whittier's robust heroine Maude Muller.

One is tempted to insist upon these ambiguities and complexities of attitude, not with any idea of overturning the orthodox reading of Pope's irony, but rather to make sure that we do not conceive it to be more brittle and thin than it actually is. This fact, at least, should be plain: regardless of what we may make of the "purer blush," it is true that Belinda's dressing table does glow with a special radiance and charm, and that

Pope, though amused by the vanity which it represents, is at
the same time thoroughly alive to a beauty which it actually
possesses.

There is a further reason for feeling that we shall not err
in taking the niceties of Pope's descriptions quite seriously.
One notices that even the metaphors by which Pope characterizes Belinda are not casual bits of decoration, used for a moment, and then forgotten. They run throughout the poem as if
they were motifs. For instance, at her dressing table Belinda
is not only a priestess of "the sacred rites of pride," but she
is also compared to a warrior arming for the fray. Later in the
poem she is the warrior once more at the card table in her conquest of the two "adventurous knights"; and again, at the end
of the poem, she emerges at the heroic conqueror in the epic
encounter of the beaux and belles.

To take another example, Belinda, early in the poem, is
compared to the sun. Pope suggests that the sun recognizes in
Belinda a rival, and fears her:

> Sol through white curtains shot a tim'rous ray,
> And oped those eyes that must eclipse the day.

But the sun's fear of Belinda has not been introduced merely in
order to give the poet an opportunity to mock at the polite
cliché. The sun comparison appears again at the beginning of
Canto II:

> Not with more glories, in th'ethereal plain,
> The sun first rises over the purpled main,
> Than issuing forth, the rival of his beams
> Launch'd on the bosom of the silver Thames.

Belinda is like the sun, not only because of her bright eyes,
and not only because she dominates her special world ("But
every eye was fix'd on her alone"). She is like the sun in another regard:

> Bright as the sun, her eyes the gazers strike,
> And, like the sun, they shine on all alike.

Is this general munificence on the part of Belinda a fault or a virtue? Is she shallow and flirtatious, giving her favors freely to all; or, does she distribute her largesse impartially like a great prince? Or, is she simply the well-bred belle who knows that she cannot play favorites if she wishes to be popular? The sun comparison is able to carry all these meanings, and therefore goes past any momentary jest. Granting that it may be overingenious to argue that Belinda in Canto IV (the Cave of Spleen) represents the sun in eclipse, still the sun comparison does appear once more in the poem, and quite explicitly. As the poem closes, Pope addresses Belinda thus:

> When those fair suns shall set, as set they must,
> And all those tresses shall be laid in dust;
> This lock, the Muse shall consecrate to fame
> And 'midst the stars inscribe Belinda's name.

Here, one notices, that the poet, if he is forced to concede that Belinda's eyes are only metaphorical suns after all, still promises that the ravished lock shall have a celestial eternity, adding, like the planet Venus, "New glory to the shining sphere!" And here Pope, we may be sure, is not merely playful in his metaphor. Belinda's name has actually been inscribed in the only heaven in which a poet would care to inscribe it. If the sceptic still has any doubts about Pope's taking Belinda very seriously, there should be no difficulty in convincing him that Pope took his own work very seriously indeed.

We began by raising the question of Belinda's status as a goddess. It ought to be quite clear that Pope's attitude toward Belinda is not exhausted in laughing away her claims to divinity. The attitude is much more complicated than that. Belinda's charm is not viewed uncritically, but the charm is real: it can survive the poet's knowledge of how much art and artifice have gone into making up the charm.

To pursue the matter of attitude farther still, what, after all, is Pope's attitude toward the irridescent little myth of the sylphs which he has provided to symbolize the polite conventions which govern the conduct of maidens? We miss the whole point if we dismiss the sylphs as merely "supernatural machinery." In general, we may say that the myth represents a qualification of the poet's prevailingly naturalistic interpretation. More specifically, it represents his attempts to do justice to the intricacies of the feminine mind. For in spite of Pope's amusement at the irrationality of that mind, Pope acknowledges its beauty and its powers.

In making this acknowledgement, he is a good realist — a better realist, indeed, than he appears when he tries to parade the fashionable ideas of the Age of Reason as in his <u>Essay on Man</u>. He is good enough realist to know that although men in their "learned pride" may say that it is Honor which protects the chastity of maids, actually it is nothing of the sort: the belles are not kept chaste by any mere abstraction. It is the sylphs, the sylphs with their interest in fashion notes and their knowledge of the feminine heart:

> With varying vanities, from ev'ry part,
> They shift the moving toy-shop of the heart;
> Where wigs with wigs, with sword-knots sword-knots strive
> Beaux banish beaux, and coaches coaches drive.

Yet the myth of the sylphs is no mere decoration to this essentially cynical generalization. The sylphs do represent the supernatural, though the supernatural reduced, of course, to its flimsiest proportions. The poet has been very careful here. Even Belinda is not made to take their existence too seriously. As for the poet, he very modestly excuses himself from rendering any judgment at all by ranging himself on the side of "learned pride:"

> Some secret truths, from learned pride conceal'd
> To maids alone and children are reveal'd:
> What, though no credit doubting wits may give?
> The fair and innocent shall still believe.

In the old wives tale of the child's fairy story may lurk an item of truth, after all. Consider the passage carefully.

"Fair" and "innocent" balance "maids" and "children." Yet they act further to color the whole passage. Is "fair" used merely as a synonym for "maids" — e. g., as in "the fair?" Or, is it that beauty is easily flattered? The doctrine which Ariel urges Belinda to accept is certainly flattering: "Hear and believe! thy own importance know / . . . unnumbered spirits round thee fly. . . ." Is "innocent" to be taken to mean "guiltless," or does it mean "naïve," perhaps even "credulous?" And how do "fair" and "innocent" influence each other? Do the fair believe in the sylphs because they are still children? (Ariel, one remembers, begins by saying: "If e'er one vision touch thy infant thought. . . .") Pope is here exploiting that whole complex of associations which surround "innocence" and connect it on the one hand with more than worldly wisdom and, on the other, with simple gullibility.

Pope, as we now know, was clearly unjust in suggesting that Addison's advice against adding the machinery of the sylphs was prompted by any desire to prevent the improvement of the poem. Addison's caution was "safe" and natural under the circumstances. But we can better understand Pope's pique if we understand how important the machinery was to become in the final version of the poem. For it is Pope's treatment of the sylphs which allows him to develop, with the most delicate modulation, his whole attitude toward Belinda and the special world which she graces. It is precisely the poet's handling of the supernatural -- the level at which he is willing to entertain it -- the amused qualifications which he demands of it — that makes it possible for him to state his attitude with full complexity.

The sylphs are, as Ariel himself suggests, "honor," though honor rendered concrete and as it actually functions, not honor as a dry abstraction. The sylphs' concern for good taste allows little range for critical perspective or a sense of proportion. To Ariel it will really be a dire disaster whether it is her honor or her new brocade that Belinda stains. To stain her honor will certainly constitute a breach of good taste — whatever else it may be -- and that for Ariel is enough. Indeed, it is enough for the rather artificial world of manners with which Pope is concerned.

The myth of the sylphs is, thus, of the utmost utility to Pope: it allows him to show his awareness of the absurdities of a point of view which, nevertheless, is charming, delightful, and filled with a real poetry. Most important of all, the myth allows him to suggest that the charm, in part at least, springs from the very absurdity. The two elements can hardly be separated in Belinda; in her guardian, Ariel, they cannot be separated at all.

In this connection, it is well to raise specifically the question

of Pope's attitude toward the "rape" itself. We certainly under-
estimate the poem if we rest complacently in the view that Pope
is merely laughing at a tempest in a teapot. There is such
laughter, to be sure, and late in the poem, Pope expresses his
own judgment of the situation, employing Clarissa as his mouthpiece. But the tempest, ridiculous though it is when seen in perspective, is a real enough tempest and related to very real issues. Indeed, Pope is able to reduce the incident to its true
importance, precisely because he recognizes clearly its hidden
significance. And nowhere is Pope more careful to take into
account all the many sides of the situation than just here in the
loss of the lock itself.

For one thing, Pope is entirely too clear-sighted to allow
that the charming Belinda is merely the innocent victim of a
rude assault. Why has she cherished the lock at all? In part
at least, "to the destruction of mankind," though mankind, of
course, in keeping with the convention, wishes so to be destroyed. Pope suggests that the Baron may even be the victim
rather than the aggressor — it is a moot question whether he
has seized the lock or been insnared by it. Pope does this very
skilfully, but with great emphasis:

> Love in these labyrinths his slaves detains
> And mighty hearts are held in slender chains.
> With hairy springs we the birds betray,
> Slight lines of hair surprise the finny prey,
> Fair tresses man's imperial race ensnare,
> And beauty draws us with a single hair.

Indeed, at the end of the poem, the poet addresses his heroine,
not as victim but as a "murderer:"

> For, after all the murders of your eye,
> When after millions slain, yourself shall die. . . .

After all, does not Belinda want the Baron (and young men
in general) to covet the lock? She certainly does not want to
retain possession of the lock forever. The poet naturally sym-
pathizes with Belinda's pique at the way in which the Baron obtains the lock. He must, in the war of the sexes, coax her into
letting him have it. Force is clearly unfair, though blandishment

is fair. If she is an able warrior, she will consent to the young man's taking the lock, though the lock still attached to her head -- and on the proper terms, honorable marriage. If she is a weak opponent, she will yield the lock, and herself, without any stipulation of terms, and will thus become a ruined maid indeed. Pope has absolutely no illusions about what the game is, and is certainly not to be shocked by any naturalistic interpretation of the elaborate and courtly conventions under which Belinda fulfills her natural function of finding a mate.

On the other hand, this is not at all to say that Pope is anxious to do away with the courtly conventions as a pious fraud. He is not the romantic anarchist who would abolish all conventions because they are artificial. The conventions not only have a regularizing function: they have their own charm. Like the rules of the card game in which Belinda triumphs, they may at points be arbitrary; but they make the game possible, and with it, the poetry and pageantry involved in it in which Pope very clearly delights.

The card game itself, of course, is another symbol of the war of the sexes. Belinda must defeat the men; she must avoid that debacle in which

> The Knave of Diamonds tries his wily arts,
> And wins (oh shameful chance!) the Queen of Hearts.

She must certainly avoid at every cost becoming a ruined maid. In the game as played, there is a moment in which she is "Just in the jaws of ruin and Codille," and gets a thrill of dangerous excitement at being in so precarious a position.

If the reader objects that the last comment suggests a too obviously sexual interpretation of the card game, one must hasten to point out that a pervasive sexual symbolism informs, not only the description of the card game, but almost everything else in the poem, though here, again, our tradition of either-or may cause us to miss what Pope is doing. We are not forced to take the poem as either sly bawdy or as delightful fantasy. But if we are to see what Pope actually makes of his problem, we shall have to be alive to the sexual implications which are in the poem.

They are perfectly evident — even in the title itself, and the poem begins with an address to the Muse in which the sexual implications are underscored:

> Say what strange motive, goddess! could compel
> A well-bred lord to assault a gentle belle?
> Oh say what stranger cause, yet unexplored,
> Could make a gentle belle reject a lord?

True, we can take assault and reject in their more general
meanings, not in their specific Latin senses, but the specific
meanings are there just beneath the surface. Indeed, it is hard
to believe, on the evidence of the poem as a whole, that Pope
would have been in the least surprised by Sir James Frazer's
later commentaries on the ubiquity of hair as a fertility symbol.
In the same way, one finds it hard to believe, after some of the
material in the "Cave of Spleen" section ("And maids turn'd
bottles call aloud for corks"), that Pope would have been too
much startled to come upon the theories of Sigmund Freud.

The sexual implications become quite specific after the
"rape" has occurred. Thalestris, in inciting Belinda to take
action against the Baron, cries:

> Gods! shall the ravisher display your hair?
> While the fops envy and the ladies stare?

Even if we take ravisher in its most general sense, still the
sexual symbolism lurks just behind Thalestris' words. Else
why should honor be involved as it is? Why should the Baron
desire the lock, and why should Belinda object so violently,
not as to an act of simple rudeness, but to losing "honor" and
becoming a "degraded toast?" The sexual element is involved
at least to the extent that Belinda feels that she cannot afford
to suffer the Baron, without protest, to take such a "liberty."

But a deeper sexual importance is symbolized by the whole
incident. Belinda's anguished exclamation --

> Oh hadst thou cruel! been content to seize
> Hairs less in sight, or any hairs but these!

carries on, unconsciously, the sexual suggestion. The lines
indicate, primarily, of course, Belinda's exasperation at the
ruining of her coiffure. The principal ironic effect, therefore,

is one of bathos: her angry concern for the prominence of the lock deflates a little her protests about honor. (Something of the bathos carries over to the sexual parallel: it is hinted, perhaps, that for the belle the real rape might lose some of its terrors if it could be concealed.) But though Belinda's vehemence gives rise to these ironies, the exclamation itself is dramatically appropriate; and Belinda would doubtless have blushed to have her emphasis on "any" interpreted literally and rudely. In her anger, she is obviously unconscious of the faux pas. But the fops whose admiring and envious comments on the exposed trophy Thalestris can predict — "Already hear the horrid things they say" — would be thoroughly alive to the unconscious double entendre. Pope's friend, Matthew Prior, wrote a naughty poem in which the same double entendre occurs. Pope himself, we may be sure, was perfectly aware of it.

In commenting on Pope's attitude toward the rape, we have suggested by implication his attitude toward chastity. Chastity is one of Belinda's most becoming garments. It gives her her retinue of airy guardians. As a proper maiden, she will keep from staining it just as she will keep from staining her new brocade. Its very fragility is part of its charm, and Pope becomes something of a symbolist poet in suggesting this. Three times in the poem he refers to the breaking of a frail china jar, once in connection with the loss of chastity, twice in connection with the loss of "honor" suffered by Belinda in the "rape" of the lock:

> Whether the nymph shall break Diana's law,
> Or some frail china jar receive a flaw. . . .
>
> Or when rich China vessels, fall'n from high,
> In glitt'ring dust and painted fragments lie!
>
> Thrice from my trembling hands the patch-box fell;
> The tott'ring china shook without a wind. . . .

Pope does not say, but he suggests, that chastity is, like the fine porcelain, something brittle, precious, useless, and easily broken. In the same way, he has hinted that honor (for which the sylphs, in part, stand) is something pretty, airy, fluid, and not really believed in. The devoted sylph who interposes

his "body" between the lock and the closing shears is clipped
in two, but honor suffers little damage:

> Fate urged the shears, and cut the sylph in twain,
> (But airy substance soon unites again).

It would be easy here to turn Pope into a cynic; but to try
to do this is to miss the point. Pope does not hold chastity to
be of no account. He definitely expects Belinda to be chaste;
but, as a good humanist, he evidently regards virginity as essentially a negative virtue, and its possession, a temporary
state. He is very far from associating it with any magic virtue
as Milton had in his Comus. The only magic which he will allow
it is a kind of charm -- a je-ne-sais-quoi such as the sylphs
possess.

Actually, we probably distort Pope's views by putting the
question in terms which require an explicit judgment at all.
Pope accepts in the poem the necessity for the belle to be chaste
just as he accepts the necessity for her to be gracious and attractive. But in accepting this, he is thoroughly alive to the
cant frequently talked about woman's honor, and most of all,
he is ironically, though quietly, resolute in putting first things
first. This, I take it, is the whole point of Clarissa's speech.
When Clarissa says:

> Since painted, or not painted, all shall fade,
> And she who scorns a man must die a maid,

we need not assume with Leslie Stephen that Pope is expressing
a smug masculine superiority, with the implication that, for
a woman, spinsterhood is the worst of all possible ills. (There
is actually no reason for supposing that Pope thought it so.) The
real point is that for Belinda perpetual spinsterhood is the worst
of all possible ills. In her own terms, it would be a disaster to
retain her locks forever -- locks turned to gray, though still
curled with a pathetic hopefulness, unclaimed and unpossessed
by any man. Belinda does not want that; and it is thus a violation
of good sense to lose sight of the fact that the cherished lock is
finally only a means to an end — one weapon to be used by the
warrior in the battle, and not the strongest weapon.

Clarissa is, of course, promptly called a prude, and the

battle begins at once in perfect disregard of the "good sense" that she has spoken. Pope is too fine an artist to have it happen otherwise. Belinda has been sorely vexed — and she, moreover, remains charming even as an Amazon. After all, what the poet has said earlier is sincerely meant:

> If to her share some female errors fall,
> Look on her face, and you'll forget them all.

Though Pope obviously agrees with Clarissa, he is neither surprised nor particularly displeased with his heroine for flying in the face of Clarissa's advice.

The ensuing battle of the sexes parodies at some points the combat in the great epic which Milton fashioned on the rape of the apple. But the absurdity of a battle in which the contestants cannot be killed is a flaw in Milton's great poem, whereas Pope turns it to beautiful account in his. In Paradise Lost, the great archangels single each other out for combat in the best Homeric style. But when Michael's sword cleaves the side of Lucifer, the most that Milton can do with the incident is to observe that Lucifer feels pain, for his premises force him to hurry on to admit that

> . . . th'Ethereal substance clos'd
> Not long divisible. . . .

Lucifer is soon back in the fight, completely hale and formidable as ever. We have already seen how delightfully Pope converts this cabbage into a rose in the incident in which the sylph, in a desperate defense of the lock, is clipped in two by the shears.

The absurdity of a war fought by invulnerable opponents gives an air of unreality to the whole of Milton's episode. There is a bickering over rules. Satan and his followers cheat by inventing gunpowder. The hosts under Michael retort by throwing the celestial hills at the enemy; and the Almighty, to put a stop to the shameful rumpus, has the Son throw the trouble-makers out. But if the fight were really serious, a fight to the death, why does the heavenly host not throw the hills in the first place? Or, why does not the Almighty cast out the rebels without waiting for the three days of inconclusive fighting to elapse? The

prevailing atmosphere of a game — a game played by good little
boys and by unmannerly little ruffians, a game presided over
by the stern schoolmaster, haunts the whole episode. The advantage is wholly with Pope here. By frankly recognizing that
the contest between his beaux and belles is a game, he fulfills
his basic intention.

The suspicion that Pope in this episode is glancing at Milton is corroborated somewhat by Pope's general use of his
celestial machinery. The supernatural guardians in The Rape
of the Lock are made much of, but their effectiveness is hardly
commensurate with their zeal. The affinities of the poem on
this point are again with Paradise Lost, not with the Iliad. In
Milton's poem, the angels are carefully stationed to guard
Adam and Eve in their earthly home, but their protection proves,
in the event, to be singularly ineffectual. They cannot prevent
Satan from finding his way to the earth; and though they soar
over the Garden, their "radiant Files, / Daz'ling the Moon,"
they never strike a blow. Even when they discover Satan, and
prepare to engage him in combat, God, at the last moment,
prevents the fight. Indeed, for all their numbers and for all
their dazzling splendor, they succeed in determining events
not at all. They can merely (for instance, Raphael) give the
human pair advice and warning. Milton, though he loved to call
their resonant names and evidently tried to provide them with
a realistic function, was apparently so fearful lest he divert
attention from Adam's own freely made decision that he succeeded in giving them nothing to do.

If this limitation constitutes another ironical defect, perhaps, in Milton's great epic, it fits Pope's purposes beautifully.
For, as we have seen, Pope's supernatural machinery is as
airy as gossamer, and the fact that Ariel can do no more than
Raphael, advise and warn — for all his display of zeal — again
fulfills Pope's basic intention. The issues in Pope's poem are
matters of taste, matters of "good sense," and the sylphs do
not violate the human limitations of this world which Pope has
elected to describe and in terms of which judgments are to be
made. Matters of morality -- still less, the ultimate sanctions
of morality — are never raised.

To return to the battle between the beaux and belles: here
Pope beautifully unifies the various motifs of the poem. The
real nature of the conventions of polite society, the heroic

pretensions of that society as mirrored in the epic, the flattering genial ragging. Indeed, the clichés of the ardent lover become the contention absurd and pompous, do indicate, by coming alive on another level, the true, if unconscious, nature of the struggle.

> No common weapons in their hands are found,
> Like Gods they fight, nor dread a mortal wound.

"Like Gods they fight" should mean in the epic framework "with superhuman energy and valor." And "nor dread a mortal wound" logically completes "Like Gods they fight" -- until a yet sterner logic asserts itself and deflates the epic pomp. A fight in which the opponents cannot be wounded is only a sham fight. Yet, this second meaning is very rich after all, and draws "Like Gods they fight" into its own orbit of meanings: there may be extra zest in the fighting because it is an elaborate game. One can make godlike gestures because one has the invulnerability of a god. The contest is godlike, after all, because it is raised above the dust and turmoil of real issues. Like an elaborate dance, it symbolizes real issues but can find room for a grace and poetry which in a more earnest struggle are lost.

I have said earlier that Pope, by recognizing the real issues involved, is able to render his mock-epic battle meaningful. For the beaux of Hampton Court, though in truth they do not need to dread a mortal wound, can, and are, prepared to die. "To die" had at this period, as one of its submeanings, to experience the consummation of the sexual act. (Donne, Dryden, and even Shakespeare use the term with a glance at this meaning; sceptics may consult the second song in Dryden's Marriage à La Mode.) Pope's invulnerable beaux rush bravely forward to achieve such a death; for the war of the sexes, when fought seriously and to the death, ends in such an act.

The elegant battleground resounds with the cries of those who "die in metaphor . . . and song." In some cases, little more is implied than a teasing of the popular clichés about bearing a "living death" or being burnt alive in Cupid's flames. But few will question the sexual implications of "die" in the passage in which Belinda overcomes the Baron:

> Nor fear'd the chief th'unequal fight to try,

Who sought no more than on his foe to die. . . .
"Boast not my fall, (he cried) insulting foe!
Thou by some other shalt be laid as low."

The point is not that Pope is here leering at bawdy meanings. In the full context of the poem, they are not bawdy at all
— or, perhaps we put the matter more accurately if we say
that Pope's total attitude, as reflected in the poem, is able to
absorb and digest into itself the incidental bawdy of which Pope's
friends, and obviously Pope himself, were conscious. The crucial point is that Pope's interpretation of Belinda's divinity does
not need to flinch from bawdy implications. The further meanings suggested by the naughty double entendres are not merely
snickering jibes which contradict the surface meaning: rather
those further meanings constitute the qualifying background
against which Belinda's divinity is asserted. Pope's testimony
to Belinda's charm is not glib; it is not thin and one-sided. It
is qualified, though not destroyed by a recognition of all the
factors involved — even of those factors which seem superficially to negate it. The touch is light, to be sure, but the poem is
not flimsy, not mere froth. The tone is ironical, but the irony
is not that of a narrow and acerb satire; rather it is an irony
which accords with a wise recognition of the total situation. The
"form" of the poem is, therefore, much more than the precise
regard for a set of rules and conventions mechanically apprehended. It is, finally, the delicate balance and reconciliation of
a host of partial interpretations and attitudes.

It was observed earlier that Pope is able to reduce the
"rape" to its true insignificance because he recognizes, as his
characters do not, its real significance. Pope knows that the
rape has in it more of compliment than of insult, though he
naturally hardly expects Belinda to interpret it thus. He does
not question her indignation, but he does suggest that it is,
perhaps, a more complex response than Belinda realizes. Pope
knows, too, how artificial the social conventions really are,
and he is thoroughly cognizant of the economic and biological
necessities which underlie them — which the conventions sometimes seem to mask and sometimes to adorn. He is therefore
not forced to choose between regarding them as either a hypocritical disguise or as a poetic and graceful adornment. Knowing their true nature, he can view this outrage of the conventions

with a wise and amused tolerance, and can set it in its proper
perspective.

Here the functional aspect of Pope's choice of the epic
framework becomes plain. The detachment, the amused patronage, the note of aloof and impartial judgment — all demand that
the incident be viewed with a large measure of aesthetic distance. Whatever incidental fun Pope may have had with the epic
conventions, his choice of the mock-epic fits beautifully his
general problem of scaling down the rape to its proper insignificance. The scene is reduced, and the characters become
small and manageable figures whose actions can always be plot-
ted against a larger background.

How large that background is has not always been noticed.
Belinda's world is plainly a charming, artificial world; but
Pope is not afraid to let in a glimpse of the real world which
lies all about it:

> Meanwhile, declining from noon of day,
> The sun obliquely shoots his burning ray;
> The hungry judges soon the sentence sign,
> And wretches hang that jurymen may dine;
> The merchant from th' exchange returns in peace,
> And the long labours of the toilet cease.
> Belinda now. . . .

It is a world in which business goes on and criminals are hanged
for all that Belinda is preparing to sit down to ombre. This momentary glimpse of the world of serious affairs, of the world
of business and law, of the world of casualness and cruelty, is
not introduced merely to chrivel the high concerns of polite
society into ironical insignificance, though its effect, of course,
is to mock at the seriousness with which the world of fashion
takes its affairs. Nor is the ironical clash which is introduced
by the passage uncalculated and unintentional: it is not that Pope
himself is unconsciously callous -- without sympathy for the
"wretches." The truth is that Pope's own perspective is so
scaled, his totality of view so honest, that he can afford to embellish his tempest in a teapot as lovingly as he likes without
for a moment losing the sense of its final triviality. A lesser
poet would either have feared to introduce an echo of the "real"
world lest the effect prove to be too discordant, or would have

254

insisted on the discord and moralized the contrast between the gay and the serious too heavily and bitterly. Pope's tart is perfect. The passage is an instance of the complexity of tone which the poem possesses.

THE RAPE OF THE LOCK AND POPE'S HOMER

William Frost

In a provocative article on "The Mode of Existence of a Literary Work of Art," Professor René Wellek has recently observed that a poem, or any work of literature,

> . . . has something which can be called 'Life.' It arises at a certain point of time, changes in the course of history and may perish. A work of art is 'timeless' only in the sense that, if preserved, it has some fundamental structure of identity since its creation, but it is 'historical' too. It has a development which can be described. This development is nothing but the series of concretizations of a given work of art in the course of history, which we may, to a certain extent, reconstruct from the reports of critics and readers about their experiences and judgments, and the effect of a given work of art on other works.[1]

Without recourse even to the reports of critics and readers it is now possible, on the basis of evidence presented in Professor Geoffrey Tillotson's admirable footnotes to Pope's Rape of the Lock, to reconstruct a neglected, and somewhat puzzling, chapter in the early development of that poem. It has become clear, from Professor Tillotson's citations, that The Rape of the Lock, as a parody-epic, was incomplete (at the time of publication) even in its five-canto incarnation, and that it would remain incomplete until certain examples of epic style, parodied in the Rape, should appear in print.

To be specific, the 1714, five-canto Rape of the Lock embodies in its satire lines and couplets decidedly mimicking Pope's own translation of Homer, which began appearing in

Reprinted from Modern Language Quarterly, Vol. 8 (1947), pp. 342-354, by permission of author and publisher.

1715 and was not completely before the public until 1726. After
a few words on the general method of mock-epic in the Rape,
I will present and analyze in detail instances of this unusual
poetic proceeding.

I

The rhetoric of The Rape of the Lock is not only based on
the rhetoric of the classical epic, but is based on it in such a
way that an attentive Augustan reader, even though he might be
unskillful in Greek and Latin, would instantly recognize Pope's
language as epical if he were fairly well read in the English literature of the age. For example, in Pope's day the most celebrated recent contribution to the epic in English had been Dryden's translation of the Aeneid (1697), a work which Pope takes
pains to echo unmistakably at a number of points in The Rape
of the Lock. In the sixth book of the English Aeneid – to glance
at one passage -- the hero, on a tour of the underworld, visits
the Elysian Fields, where he meets the souls of the blessed
disporting themselves; and, in the midst of a description of
their games, the following couplet occurs:

> The love of Horses, which they had, alive,
> And care of Chariots, after Death survive. (VI, 889 f.)

Early in the first book of The Rape of the Lock, Ariel describes
to Belinda in a dream the future immortal existence of woman:

> Think not, when Woman's transient Breath is fled,
> That all her Vanities at once are dead; . . .
> Her Joy in gilded Chariots, when alive,
> And Love of Ombre, after Death survive. (I, 51 ff.)

Belinda is to have her own mock-Elysian Fields; and, as Pope's
editor points out, the "Chariots" have acquired an effective
double meaning from the fact that London carriages of Pope's
own time were often so called.

Similarly, in the opening to Canto IV of The Rape of the
Lock Pope means his readers to recall the opening of a more
famous fourth book. "But anxious Cares the pensive Nymph

257

opprest," he writes; just as Dryden had written "But anxious cares already seiz'd the Queen" (IV, 1) — and Belinda becomes another queenly Dido.[2]

Dryden's Aeneid was not, of course, the only work whose English style Pope found suggestive of epic manner. The author of Genesis may not be strictly an heroic poet, but his famous sentence "And God said, 'Let there be light,' and there was light" (1:3) had been commended by Longinus as the very zenith of sublimity in literature -- a commendation Pope did not forget when he wrote "Let Spades be Trumps! she said, and Trumps they were" (III, 46). In like manner, the frivolous clutter of Belinda's dressing table -- "Puffs, Powders, Patches, Bibles, Billet-doux" (I, 138) -- has its dignified ancestor in the horrific confusion of Milton's Hell: "Rocks, Caves, Lakes, Fens, Bogs, Dens, and Shades of Death" (Paradise Lost, II, 621). Still other works and authors laid under contribution for Pope's heroic diction were: Virgil's Georgics, Cowley's Davideis, Dryden's The Hind and the Panther, Ovid in several translations, Dryden's Juvenal, Lucan, Statius, Shakespeare, Chaucer, Donne.[3]

Perhaps the most extended and sustained piece of epic parody in the whole poem, however, is based on a translation from ancient epic made by Pope himself: I refer to the famous speech of Clarissa at the beginning of the fifth canto of the Rape, which amounts to a delicate burlesque of the equally famous speech of Sarpedon, the Trojan captain, in the twelfth book of the Iliad. Before the appearance of The Rape of the Lock, this speech of Sarpedon to Glaucus had already been made familiar to eighteenth-century readers in three translations or adaptations: that of Motteux, the translator of Don Quixote, in The Muse's Mercury, Volume I (1707); that of John Denham, the author of Cooper's Hill, in 1668 (republished, as Professor Tillotson notes, in Miscellany Poems, The First Part, third edition, 1702); and that of Pope, in Tonson's Poetical Miscellanies: The Sixth Part (1709).

In view of the use which I shall show Pope to have made of certain passages in his as yet unpublished Iliad and Odyssey, it is interesting to note that of these three versions of Sarpedon's speech at hand, in print and familiar to him, it was his own which he chose as a model for Clarissa's phrasing.[4] The most important echoes are the following:

SARPEDON:
Why on those Shores are we with Joy survey'd . . .
Unless great Acts superior Merit prove . . . ?

(XII, 377, 379)

CLARISSA:
How vain are all these Glories, all our Pains,
Unless good Sense preserve what Beauty gains. . . .

(V, 15-16)

SARPEDON:
'Tis ours, the Dignity They [the Gods] give, to grace;
The first in Valour, as the first in Place.5. . .

(XII, 381-82)

CLARISSA:
That Men may say, when we the Front-box grace,
Behold the first in Virtue, as in Face!

(V, 17-18)

SARPEDON:
But since, alas, ignoble Age must come,
Disease, and Death's inexorable Doom. . . .

(XII, 391-92)

CLARISSA:
But since, alas! frail Beauty must decay,
Curl'd or uncurl'd, since Locks will turn to grey. . . .

(V, 25-26)

The second echo, involving as it does a surprise rime-word, is
particularly subtle. The ear that remembers Sarpedon's speech
-- and we may be sure that Pope's ear, at least, remembered
it clearly enough — expects "Behold the first in Virtue, as in
Place"; and "Place," of course, would be a perfectly fitting

word for Clarissa to use, in view of the "Front-box" of the preceding line. It would be more than fitting, in fact, it would be admirably satiric; for when Sarpedon speaks of his "Place," he is referring to his position among the generals and noblemen of Troy, whereas Clarissa is talking about a good seat at the theatre. But how much better, in the context of Clarissa's whole speech, is "Face"! Not only does it create the shock of surprise and of an unfamiliar, imaginative expression (in ordinary speech we do not customarily refer to a preëminent beauty as "the first in Face"), but it also throws Clarissa's emphasis precisely where Pope wants it: on <u>physical</u> beauty, the melancholy characteristic of which is its transitoriness:

> Curl'd or uncurl'd, since Locks will turn to grey,
> Since painted, or not painted, all shall fade. . . .

To call such writing as this a parody is almost to belittle it. Sarpedon's speech is predominantly heroic, Clarissa's elegiac; reminiscences of heroism blend into the elegy, forming one strain of its melancholy music. This is particularly true of the third parallel cited above.

II

An examination of Professor Tillotson's footnotes to <u>The Rape of the Lock</u> reveals some fifty-odd citations of Pope's translations of Homer, most of them[6] citations from his Iliad. Some of these references have nothing to do with diction,[7] and might just as well have been made to the text of the original; others seem to involve only the poetic small change of the time (phrases like "distinguish'd Care," I, 27; and "giddy Motion," II, 134), and thus constitute, at most, vague, rather than precise, echoes of heroic rhetoric. But some, I feel sure, are intentional parallels to specific lines in Pope's Homer, meant to elevate <u>The Rape of the Lock</u> by their verbal echoes of a loftier argument, and to diminish by contrast the people and the activities that make up Belinda's story.

For the student of the poem, such a situation raises three sets of problems. First of all, in the case of any given parallel, can we be sure that the parody is directed at Pope's translation of Homer, and not at the original Greek or some earlier English version of it? Secondly, assuming that a given passage can be shown to parallel Pope's translation specifically, rather than the original Greek or an earlier English version, have we established a date of composition not later than the publication of the Rape, for certain parts of Pope's Homer? In other words, did Pope, in 1712 or 1714, already possess in manuscript (or in mind) the telling Homeric phrases he echoes in The Rape of the Lock? Or, conversely, is it more probable that, years after the Rape had seen the light, he deliberately enriched that poem by inventing, and weaving into Homer, passages for which parallels in the Rape already existed? Which came first, in the poet's inventive soul — the poem or the parody? Thirdly, could not the echoes have been merely fortuitous — or rather, have they, whether fortuitous or intentional, a real artistic significance in the fabric of the Rape? And if so, what is that significance?

To give categorical answers to all these questions does not seem to me possible on the basis of existing evidence. What I shall attempt is a discussion of six such passages -- the six I believe to be the most crucial ones — and an indication of what some of the probabilities are in each instance.

(1) An exciting moment in the Ombre game of the enlarged, 1714, Rape of the Lock (Canto III, lines 61-64), comes when Belinda takes the jack of clubs; or, as Pope has it,

> Ev'n mighty Pam . . .
> Falls undistinguished by the Victor Spade!

Now the corpse of the mighty Pam (mighty because in the game of Loo he was the highest card), as it lies on the "velvet Plain" of the card-table top, recalls the corpse of the Trojan hero, great Sarpedon, who, in the sixteenth book of Pope's Iliad (1718), line 776,

> Lies undistinguish'd from the vulgar dead.

The consonants of the second half of each line are worth noticing: "the vulgar dead," "the Victor Spade" — this is a subtle type of poetic reminiscence, which Pope manages with infinite delicacy, and which occurs more than once in the Rape.

261

The name of the Trojan hero seems to furnish a clue to the problem of precedence in the composition of the two lines, for the speech of Sarpedon, discussed above, formed in Pope's first translation of it part of The Episode of Sarpedon, from Homer's twelfth and sixteenth books, published in Tonson's 1709 Miscellanies, the famous volume which opened with Ambrose Philips' Pastorals and closed with Pope's. This Episode as there published did not, it is true, actually contain the "vulgar dead" line: it comprised what were to be lines 345-424 and 435-562 of Pope's twelfth book of the Iliad, and lines 512-624 and 809-36 of his sixteenth; in other words, Pope did not include lines 624-809 of the sixteenth book in his version of the Sarpedon story -- and the "vulgar dead" line is number 776. But Pope may not have skipped this part when he was originally composing the translation; indeed, he may have wanted to print more than Tonson felt he could use: the publisher hints in his preface that he had more material for this collection than he was able to take care of.[9] Hence the line in question may well have existed in manuscript -- or in the poet's consciousness -- when he was preparing the 1714 Rape of the Lock.

The possibility remains that the "Victor Spade" line in the Rape might have been suggested by Homer's original Greek, or by a seventeenth-century translation of it; but this possibility vanishes upon investigation. The complete English translations of the Iliad before Pope's were those of Chapman (1611), Ogilby (1660), and Hobbes (1675).[10] None of these contains anything even close to Pope's "Lies undistinguish'd from the vulgar dead," and for a very good reason: there is nothing to correspond to it in Homer himself. I do not mean to suggest that Pope has been unfaithful to Homer's general sense in his rendering; he has merely rearranged matters and polished them up a bit. The entire passage in question, in Professor A. T. Murray's translation (which follows the Greek closely), is as follows:

> Nor could a man, though he knew him well, any more
> have discerned goodly Sarpedon, for that he was utterly enwrapped with darts and blood and dust, from his
> head to the very soles of his feet.[11]

Of the three seventeenth-century versions, Ogilby's is the one which, at this particular point, most closely approaches to what

Pope produced; Ogilby's is as follows:

> And now Sarpedon none could know, all o're
> From Head to Heel besmear'd with Dust and Gore,
> Trampled and dragg'd, with Arms and Truncheons hid;
> Whilst each to gain the Corps their utmost did.[12]

Pope's translation of the passage, in full, runs:

> Now great Sarpedon, on the sandy Shore,
> His heav'nly Form defac'd with Dust and Gore,
> And stuck with Darts by warring Heroes shed,
> Lies undistinguish'd from the vulgar dead.

(XVI, 773-76)

The only equivalent in the original for Pope's fourth line is Homer's remark that even a sagacious man would not have been able to identify Sarpedon. We are left with three possible hypotheses: (i) the echo in The Rape of the Lock is a chance coincidence, (ii) the "vulgar dead" line had already been composed when Pope wrote the longer Rape, or (iii) Pope deliberately put the "vulgar dead" line into his Homer in order to heighten the satiric effect of The Rape of the Lock, after the completion of the latter poem. Pope's usually minute methods of workmanship, as well as the fact that other instances of this kind occur in The Rape of the Lock, make hypothesis (i) seem the least likely. While I see no inherent objection against (iii), the fact that as early as 1709 Pope had been working with the Sarpedon story in the sixteenth book of the Iliad disposes me to accept (ii), tentatively, as the most probable theory about this particular passage. If (ii) be correct, we have evidence that at least part of the Iliad was composed several years before publication.

(2) The parallel between the Baron's oath in the fourth canto of the Rape and that of Achilles in the first book of the Iliad is a brilliant one, to which Pope himself called attention in a note to the 1714 edition of the former. (The Baron's oath, with an unimportant difference of one word, had already appeared in the 1712 version.) Since Pope himself did call attention to the matter before his own Iliad was out, we may assume he expected his readers to recall and compare the original

263

Greek (as well they might); but his own translation is closer to
the parody in one striking particular. I present the two for comparison; first the translation of Homer (1715):

> Now by this sacred Sceptre, hear me swear,
> Which never more shall Leaves or Blossoms bear,
> Which sever'd from the Trunk (as I from thee)
> On the bare Mountains left its Parent Tree;

(I, 309-12)

next the oath in The Rape of the Lock:

> But by this Lock, this sacred Lock I swear,
> (Which never more shall join its parted Hair,
> Which never more its Honours shall renew,
> Clipt from the lovely Head where late it grew). . . .

(IV, 133-36)

Pope's translation (except for his parenthetical "as I from
thee") varies from the original in no important particular; but
it is interesting to note that the word "sever'd," to which "clipt"
in the Rape satirically corresponds, has no basis in the Greek,
Homer having merely said (Iliad, I, line 235) that the staff left
(λέλοιπεν) its stump among the mountains. Thus Hobbes translates "hath left behind / The stock . . .";[13] and Chapman, "since
first it left the hills. . . ."[14]

In dealing with the first book of the Iliad, however, there
is yet another English version (Ogilby's having no relevance to
the "sever'd" —"clipt" parallel) to be considered: that of Dryden in his Fables (1700). Dryden handles the passage in question
as follows:

> But, by this Scepter, solemnly I swear
> (Which never more green Leaf or growing Branch shall bear
> Torn from the Tree, and giv'n by Jove to those
> Who Laws dispense and mighty Wrongs oppose). . . .[15]

The first two and a half lines here are sufficiently similar to
both Pope's translations and the Baron's oath to suggest that

264

they formed the model for both, Dryden's "Torn from the Tree" very likely having originally suggested Pope's "Clipt from the lovely Head where late it grew."[16] In this case, therefore, we do not need to suppose either that Pope wrote some of the first book of his Iliad before 1712, or that, writing it later, he derived this particular piece of diction from The Rape of the Lock — but I think it probable that he bore the latter poem in mind when he came to translate Achilles' oath.

(3) In the second book of Pope's Iliad (published 1715), the following line occurs in the course of Agamemnon's important speech in which, to test the temper of the Argive host, he craftily counsels retreat to Greece because of the supposed impossibility of taking Troy:

> And Troy prevails by Armies not her own. (160)

At the close of the first canto of the 1714 Rape of the Lock, Pope indicates how much Belinda's toilet owed to the Sylphs, and at the same time ironically compares the labors of her maid with the efforts of the Trojans:

> And Betty's prais'd for Labours not her own. (148)

It is hard to believe that this could have been a chance echo. In addition to the obvious similarities in structure, the two verbs, "prevails" and "prais'd," sound just enough alike to reinforce the parallel (compare "vulgar dead" and "Victor Spade"). The "Betty's prais'd" line is emphatic by virtue of being the final line of the canto. Furthermore, the "Troy prevails" line represents a deliberate change in both the word order and the emphasis of the original Greek, of which Professor Murray's more literal version runs: "But allies there be out of many cities, men that wield the spear, who hinder me mightily . . ." (lines 130 ff.) Nor did the early English translators of the Iliad give the passage a twist similar to Pope's:

HOBBES:
> But when upon their many aids I think,
> I wonder less that we no better speed. (115-16)

CHAPMAN:
> But their auxiliary bands, those brandishers of spears,
> From many cities drawn, are they that are our
>   hinderers. . . .   (111-12)

OGILBY:
> But their Auxiliars us far more annoy,
> Those mighty Nations which strong Javelins shake,
> Guarding the happy Bulwarks we would take (p. 36).

It seems clear to me, therefore, that either (a) Pope translated this part of the Iliad before he completed the five-canto Rape of the Lock or (b) Betty's "Labours not her own" suggested Agamemnon's rhetoric.

Of course, the two lines may well have been written about the same time. In December, 1713, Pope was finishing his additions to the Rape; and the following May found him "very busy in my grand undertaking" — that is, the translation of the Iliad.[17] The two lines could have sprung into being almost simultaneously; and the fact that the public would have to wait a year after The Rape of the Lock came out in order to appreciate the full force of the ending of its first canto need not have troubled the subtle poet in the least.

(4) A couplet in the "Moving Toyshop of the (Female) Heart" passage, in the first canto of The Rape of the Lock, occasions a veritable barrage of citations in the Twickenham edition footnotes; the couplet runs:

> Where Wigs with wigs, with Sword-knots Sword-knots strive,
> Beaus banish Beaus, and Coaches Coaches drive.

(100-01)

Of the parallels referred to, the closest seems to me to be the following, from the thirteenth book of Pope's Iliad (published 1717):

> Spears lean on Spears, on Targets Targets throng,
> Helms stuck to Helms, and Man drove Man along.

(181-82)

Another, however, from the fourth book (1715), is also very close:

> Now Shield with Shield, with Helmet Helmet clos'd
> To Armour Armour, Lance to Lance oppos'd. . . .

> (508-09)

These parallels seem different from the others that we have been considering. I do not think that Pope at any time intended readers of the Rape to make a specific reference of this couplet to any particular one in the epic; that is, I do not think he planned any comparison between the varying vanities in the heart of his tender maid and any particular battlefield of the Iliad -- such a comparison as he does seem to have planned between mighty Pam and great Sarpedon. The "Wigs with Wigs" couplet is intended, if I am correct, merely to suggest the atmosphere of classic poetry and heroic battlegrounds in general by means of a typically classical device of rhetoric -- a device well illustrated by the couplet Professor Tillotson cites from Statius' Thebaid (an epic with which Pope was familiar):

> Iam clipeus clipeis, umbone repellitur umbo
> Ense minax ensis, pede pes, et cuspide cuspis. . . .

> (VIII, 398-99)

Such rhetoric would be equally appropriate to a neo-classical translation of Homer; and therefore the close resemblance between the two passages in Pope's Iliad and the couplet in the Rape need be pressed for no further significance.

(5) The following couplet, referring to Achilles, comes in the twentieth book of Pope's Iliad (completed 1718, published 1720):

> But when the Day decreed (for come it must)
> Shall lay this dreadful Hero in the Dust. . . . (385-86)

It invites comparison with the following couplet, which appears in both the 1712 and the 1714 texts of The Rape of the Lock (at II, 189-90, and V, 147-48, respectively):

267

> When those fair suns shall sett, as sett they must,
> And all those Tresses shall be laid in Dust. . . .

Did Pope deliberately insert the former couplet into the Iliad
in order to sharpen the satire of the already published Rape of
the Lock finale? The six-year gap between publication of the
latter and completion of the former certainly suggests that he
did -- and a glance at the text of Homer's Iliad at this point
strengthens the conjecture. For the line in Homer which Pope
rendered by his "dreadful Hero" couplet merely reads "But
when Achilles has met his death and fate":

αὐτὰρ ἐπεί κ᾿ Ἀχιλεὺς θάνατον καὶ πότμον ἐπίσπῃ. . . (line 337)

Chapman translated it "But his fate once satisfied" (line 290);
Hobbes, "When he is gone" (line 310); and Ogilby, "But when
Achilles shall this Life forsake" (page 436). Only Pope, of the
early translators, makes much of the line; and the "Dust" on
which his Rape of the Lock echo partly depends is entirely his
own embellishment of Homer. In the absence of any evidence
that he had translated a part of the twentieth book of the Iliad
as early as 1712, the most probable explanation of this delayed-
action parody fairly clearly lies in an influence of The Rape of
the Lock on the Iliad.

    (6) The best parallel between The Rape of the Lock and
Pope's Odyssey, though a very close parallel indeed, is less
conclusive. Compare the following couplets, the first from the
seventeenth book of the Odyssey (a book which Pope himself
translated), the second from the first canto of the earlier Rape;
the first published in 1726, the second in 1712:

> 'Till now declining tow'rd the close of day,
> The sun obliquely shot his dewy ray (687-88).

> Now, when declining from the Noon of Day
> The Sun obliquely shoots his burning Ray. . . .(83-84)

Here again, Pope's rendering is a considerable elaboration of
Homer's Greek. Homer had merely said (line 606) "For late
afternoon had already arrived," but Pope's diction seems ultimately to derive from a passage (cited in the Twickenham

edition) in Ambrose Philips' much-mocked Pastorals of 1709,
published in the same volume of Tonson's Miscellanies that
contained The Episode of Sarpedon:

> The Sun, now mounted to the Noon of Day,
> Began to shoot direct his burning Ray.   (V, 7-8)

Possibly Pope's original couplet in the Rape was intended as a
thrust at Philips; but since such an intention could hardly explain its appearance in his Homer fourteen years later, its resemblance to the Odyssey couplet must be put down to coincidence, the result of subconscious memory. In contrast to
Philips, Pope seems to have taken his rays oblique, rather
than straight; compare the following line from the Odyssey,
Book VII:

> Nor 'till oblique he slop'd his ev'ning ray. . . . (372)

III

The evidence in the foregoing examples of Pope's methods
of composition cannot be said to lead to any one definite conclusion. Whether Pope wrote certain parts of his translations
years before the complete translations appeared, and mimicked
those parts in his heroi-comical poem; whether, conversely,
after writing the mock-epic in as heightened a style as he could
command, he later added to the allusiveness of certain of his
effects by surreptitious echoes newly dispersed through Iliad
and Odyssey; or whether, as he translated, he subconsciously
recalled to life old phrases which he once had used — which or
what combination of these alternatives, or what other alternative, may be true, we are not likely to determine with scientific
precision. For the biographer of Pope, the second and third
alternatives seem the most probable. For the reader and critic
of The Rape of the Lock, today or two centuries ago — any time
since the publication of his Homer — the second alternative is
literal truth: for the fact is that The Rape of the Lock is a
better parody because Pope later created (and by "created" I
mean wrote and printed) some of the effects he parodied in it.
To see how much this later creation added to the poem,

let us for a moment revert to the first of the six examples discussed above. What is the significance of Sarpedon? What did he mean to Pope and the Augustans? After all, he was the central figure in one of Pope's three earliest-published efforts — an effort which led, as far as Sir William Trumbull's encouragement had any effect (Sir William had seen the Episode in manuscript), to the translation of the entire Iliad, and to the fame and success that Pope derived from that translation.

Sarpedon, if not the noblest Trojan of them all (a title Hector perhaps better merits), was still sufficiently noble: the son, according to Homer, of Laodamia and Zeus himself; the king of Lycia,

> . . . predestin'd to be slain,
> Far from the Lycian shores . . . ,

a great fighter; the speaker of a lofty patriotic oration; and indeed a tragic hero of the Iliad. He fell at last by the lance of Patroclus, and his passing was bewept by the father of the gods, who sent Apollo to convey his body from the bloody field of battle. The reason this divine intervention was necessary was that, as the lines previously quoted suggest, in the general conflict ensuing on Sarpedon's death, his corpse had been mutilated and rendered unrecognizable in the blood and dust:

> His long-disputed Corpse the Chiefs inclose,
> On ev'ry side the busy Combate grows. . . .

So much for Sarpedon; now what of his opposite in The Rape of the Lock -- mighty Pam, the jack of clubs?

The passage in which this champion of the fights of Loo figures is an ostensibly playful one: Pam's conqueror, the spade facecard, has been introduced as "The hoary Majesty of Spades," who "Puts forth one manly leg to sight reveal'd," the other being hidden under his gaudy robe. The Augustan equivalent of contract bridge is certainly being given an elaborately pretentious treatment; but in the first couplet devoted to Pam little more appears on the surface than urbane tomfoolery:

> Ev'n mighty Pam, that Kings and Queens o'erthrew,
> And mow'd down Armies in the Fights of Lu. . . .

Then comes the second couplet, ending the first round of Belinda's battle, and suddenly a different note is struck:

> Sad Chance of War! now, dèstitute of Aid,
> Falls undistinguish'd by the Victor Spade!

For an instant the velvet plain of the card-table top becomes the sandy shore before Troy. The pasteboard knave is transformed into the heavenly form defaced with dust and gore. The shields and helmets rattle in our ears; the arms ring, the warriors fall. The permanence and the consequences of human conflict -- tragic or comic, heroic or trivial -- have been memorably asserted; and the trivial nature of Belinda's triumph over the Baron at the card table has, by one brief echo, been juxtaposed with the gigantic warring figures of the Homeric past.

NOTES

1   Southern Review, VII (1941-42). The passage quoted is on page 752.

2   In the shorter, 1712 Rape of the Lock, the "anxious Cares" line opens the second canto. The opportunity to have it begin the fourth canto (and more neatly) was doubtless one of the advantages Pope saw in expanding the poem. A minor point -- but with a workman like Pope we are not justified in assuming coincidence.

3   See the Twickenham edition footnotes, from which most of the citations in this article derive.

4   Here I am in disagreement with Professor Tillotson, who says in his note (p. 195) that "Clarissa's speech is in some ways a closer parody on Denham's version than on Pope's." I have found only one line of which this might be true: Clarissa's "Why Angels call'd, and Angel-like ador'd" is closer to Denham's "As Gods behold us and as Gods adore" than to Pope's corresponding "Admir'd as Heroes, and as Gods obey'd." There seems to be no other close verbal parody of Denham, however; and there are at least three sure echoes of Pope's version.

5   This line shows Pope's familiarity with Motteux' adaptation

of the speech (Motteux has "The First in Valour, as in Rank the First," p. 69), and thus perhaps indicates a date of composition for Pope's Episode of Sarpedon not earlier than 1707.

6   For the Odyssey, see the notes to Canto I, 27; I, 112; II, 32; III, 19 f.; III, 86; III, 101; III, 131 f.; IV, 82; IV, 140; V, 85 f.

7   Such as that to (Pope's) Iliad, III, 175 ff., in the note to the review of forces at the card table (Canto III, 37 ff.), where the parallel is of situation, rather than language.

8   Quotations are from the text of the Twickenham edition, Vol. II (London, 1940), for the Rape; and from the first edition of the Iliad and Odyssey translations (Griffith 39, 93, 112, 155, 166). The speech of Sarpedon, cited above, is from the text in Tonson's Miscellanies (Griffith 1).

9   See Tonson's "The Bookseller to the Reader" (at the beginning of the Miscellany): ". . . I have been forced to omit several of the copies sent, upon the publick Notice given, otherways this Volume would have swell'd beyond the Size of any of the former ones. I shall reserve those for another Volume. . . ." Evidently he was pressed for space.

10   Of the various translations of excerpts from Homer — such as those by Hall, Congreve, Maynwaring, Yalden, Dryden, and others — I have explained the available ones that bear on the passages discussed here. Thomas Grantham's first three books of the Iliad (1660) I have not seen.

11   Loeb Classical Library (London and New York, 1919); Iliad, XVI, 638-40. All quotations of Murray's version are from this edition.

12   John Ogilby's Homer his Iliads Translated (London: Printed by James Flesher, 1669), p. 336. All quotations of Ogilby are from this edition.

13   Thomas Hobbes' English Works, ed. Sir William Molesworth (London, 1844), Vol. X (the translation of Homer), Iliad, I, 222-23. I have used this edition for all quotations of Hobbes.

14 George Chapman's The Iliads of Homer, ed. Rev. Richard Hooper, 2nd ed. (London, 1865), I, 234. Quotations of Chapman are made from this text.

15 John Dryden's Poems, ed. John Sargeaunt (London, 1910), lines 348-51.

16 The appearance of this passage in the Rape influenced yet another translation of the first book of the Iliad — that of Thomas Tickell, which appeared in the same year as Pope's and partly occasioned Pope's quarrel with Addison. Compare with the last two lines quoted above from the Baron's oath the following couplet of Tickell's (The First Book of Homer's Iliad Translated [London, 1715]):

> Which never more its Verdure must renew,
> Lopp'd from the Vital Stemm, whence first it grew.

(pp. 16-17)

(Note especially the rime-words.) Pope, who made a minute analysis of Tickell's version, noticed this theft, which may have contributed to his irritation at Tickell. (See "Pope's Ms. Notes on Tickell's Homer," by Professor Conington, in Fraser's Magazine, LXII [1860].)

17 See Pope's letters to Caryll in Pope's Works, ed. Elwin-Courthope, VI (1871), 199, 207.

273

THE "FALL" OF CHINA AND THE RAPE OF THE LOCK

Aubrey Williams

In his Lectures on the English Poets, near the beginning
of his discussion of The Rape of the Lock, William Hazlitt cites
a passage from Shakespeare's Troilus and Cressida, opposes
it to the kind of poetry written by Pope, and remarks that, for
the Shakespearean "earthquakes and tempests," Pope typically
gives us the "breaking of a flower-pot or the fall of a china
jar."[1] Hazlitt's observation is, in its own way, remarkably
just — and apt, for Pope does deal, on occasion, in an extravagant amount of crockery in his poems. Yet if we are to compare
great things with small, it may be only fair to note that Pope
is now and again capable of raising his own kind of tempests,
even in his teapots.

In The Rape of the Lock a most important pattern of imagery is established by pervasive reference to a wide variety of
vessels: vases, bottles, pipkins, pots and China jars are signal
and memorable articles of the poem's furniture. There is the
array of jars on Belinda's dressing-table, the display of cups
and silver pots on the sumptuous buffet, the collection of containers in the lunar limbo, where

> Heroes' Wits are kept in pondrous Vases,
> And Beaus' in Snuff-boxes and Tweezer-Cases.

In the recesses of Belinda's own psyche, where they exist in
almost perfect pre-Freudian propriety, Pope reveals to us those
"Unnumber'd Throngs" of "Bodies chang'd to various Forms by
Spleen":

> Here living Teapots stand, one Arm held out,
> One bent; the Handle this, and that the Spout:
> A Pipkin there like Homer's Tripod walks;
> Here sighs a Jar, and there a Goose-pye talks;

Reprinted from Philological Quarterly, Vol. 41 (1962), pp. 412-425, by
permission of author and publisher.

> Men prove with Child, as pow'rful Fancy works,
> And Maids turn'd Bottels, call aloud for Corks.2

So much crockery in the poem can scarcely be ignored, and neither should the variety of special effects Pope obtains by its use. More particularly, awareness of the range of this vessel imagery serves to underscore its peculiar importance on three occasions when it relates most directly to the poem's central event. These three occasions, often remarked by critics, are, first, in Canto II, where, in a mood of gloomy anticipation, the sylph Ariel wonders

> Whether the Nymph shall break Diana's Law,
> Or some frail China Jar receive a Flaw;

second, in Canto III, where, after the lock has been cut, these lines occur:

> Not louder Shrieks to pitying Heav'n are cast,
> When Husbands or when Lap-dogs breathe their last,
> Or when rich China Vessels, fal'n from high,
> In glittring Dust and painted Fragments lie;

and, finally, in Canto IV, where Belinda recalls the morning omens:

> Thrice from my trembling hand the Patch-box fell;
> The tott'ring China shook without a Wind. . . .

Mr. Cleanth Brooks apparently first singled out these three special instances of the poem's vessel imagery, and he observed that at least one of them made a comment on chastity: "Pope does not say, but he suggests, that chastity is, like the fine porcelain, something brittle, precious, useless, and easily broken."3 Shrewd as the observation is, there yet seems to be occasion for amplification of Mr. Brooks' insight. For Pope's vessel imagery has a particularly rich background, and the association of "lasses and glasses" in his poem evidently had precise and subtle significances which must have been widely appreciated in the poet's own time.

I

For a number of years in the early 17th century the young James Howell travelled on the continent as agent for a London glass factory. In his Epistolae Ho-Elianae (1645-55), one of his letters, written from Venice on June 1, 1621, contains this passage:

> When I saw so many sorts of curious glasses made
> here I thought upon the compliment which a gentleman
> put upon a lady in England, who having five or six
> comely daughters, said he never saw in his life such
> a dainty cupboard of crystal glasses; the compliment
> proceeds, it seems, from a saying they have here,
> "That the first handsome woman that ever was made,
> was made of Venice glass," (which implies beauty, but
> brittleness withal. . . .

Howell's letter reveals a traditional use of "glass" imagery to suggest the lamentable fragility of feminine beauty. He may or may not be correct in assigning the origin of his particular saying to Venice,[4] but certainly the general terms of the comparison itself were part of the poetic and proverbial life of England much before his time. In The Passionate Pilgrim (1599), poem vii, Shakespeare (if indeed he is the author) has these lines:

> Fair is my love, but not so fair as fickle;
> Mild as a dove, but neither true nor trusty;
> Brighter than glass, and yet as glass is brittle. . . ;

and George Herbert, in his collection of Outlandish Proverbs (1640), includes this saying (no. 244): "A woman and a glasse are ever in danger." In such passages the implications of "brittleness" are uncomplimentary ones of weakness and inconstancy. As John Hall uses the image in his Paradoxes (1650), however, the very fragility of porcelain and feminine beauty serves only to heighten their value:

> And are not I pray you the best things ever in the great-
> est danger, Purselain and Venice Glasses are the most
> apt to be broke, the richest flowers are the soonest

> pulled, the goodliest Stag, wil be soonest shot, the
> best Faces doe the soonest decay. . . .[5]

To the examples given so far there must now be added a
special usage in which the implications already noted are usually
preserved, and have added to them a specific intensification. In
this new usage the breaking or cracking of a glass (sometimes
the "glass" is a mirror, sometimes a goblet) or piece of China
becomes specifically symbolic of a loss of virginity or chastity.
In Shakespeare's Pericles, IV. vi. 150-2, the bawd (speaking
of Marina) says to her man-servant:

> Boult, take her away; use her at thy pleasure. Crack
> the glass of her virginity, and make the rest malleable.[6]

This emphasis of the image also points up clearly the ambiguities residing within Herrick's little poem, The broken Christall:

> To Fetch me Wine my Lucia went
> Bearing a Christall continent:
> And making haste, it came to passe,
> She brake in two the purer Glasse,
> Then smil'd, and sweetly chid her speed;
> So with a blush, beshrew'd the deed.

In his Elegie on the Lady Marckham, ll. 41-4, Donne provides
a variation on this same theme by his exploitation of the super-
stition that a glass of purest crystal would not admit poison
without cracking:

> Of what small spots pure white complains! Alas,
> How little poyson cracks a christall glasse!
> She sinn'd, but just enough to let us see
> That God's word must be true, All, sinners be.

The exact nature of Lady Marckham's small spots of sin, the
"little poyson" in her character, is not entirely clear from
Donne's poem. He seems to be referring to some small and in-
escapable sexual taint[7] (perhaps the Hebrew/Miltonic idea of
"child-bed taint") she must have experienced as a wife and
mother. In any event, the notion that the utmost purity of glass

277

is flawed by the slightest poison seems to relate clearly to the idea that a loss of chastity can be vividly, and poignantly, expressed by a flaw in a very fine piece of China.

As one might expect, in much of this vessel imagery there is an emphasis on the irreparable nature of any damage done to fine glass or China, and an attendant emphasis on the irreparable nature of a loss of beauty, good name, or virginity. Ovid (Heroides, V. 103-4) had said, "By no art may purity once wounded, be made whole; 'tis lost, lost once and for all;[8] and The Passionate Pilgrim again, poem xiii, has these lines:

> As broken glass no cement can redress:
> So beauty blemish'd once, for ever lost,
> In spite of physic, painting, pain, and cost.[9]

The passages so far cited help to establish the sense of a line of imagery, mainly in terms of glass mirrors and fine crystal, susceptible of application to feminine beauty and frailty in a variety of ways. Perhaps it was a heightened and growing passion for fine China among women themselves[10] that led writers, in the course of the 17th century, to a substitution of China vases for crystal glasses in their imagery. At any rate, citation of a few more passages nearly contemporary with The Rape of the Lock may suggest not only that to readers of Pope's time such imagery was of traditional and commonplace import; it may also render more explicit to a modern reader exactly what some of these received implications were.

Near the end of Act I of John Crowne's Sir Courtly Nice (1685) there occurs this couplet:

> Women like Cheney shou'd be kept with care,
> One flaw debases her [sic] to common ware.

A few years later there occurs this passage in Steele's The Funeral: or Grief A-La-Mode (1701), II. iii:

> Lady Harriot. The fellow is not to be abhorred, if the forward thing did not think of getting me so easily. Oh! I hate a heart I can't break when I please. What makes the value of dear china, but that 'tis so brittle? Were it not for that, you might as well have stone mugs in your closet.[11]

And during the 1730's this song by Fielding was heard scores of times on the London stage:

> A Woman's Ware like <u>China</u>,
>   Now dear, now cheap is bought;
> When whole 'tis worth a Guinea,
>   When broke not worth a Groat.[12]

Perhaps the work most clearly revelatory of some of the nuances to be found in this imagery of China vessels, however, is John Gay's poem, <u>To a Lady on her Passion for Old China</u> (1725). The whole poem provides valuable comment on our theme, and seems peculiarly relevant to <u>The Rape of the Lock</u>. These lines are perhaps the most revealing:

> When I some antique Jar behold,
> Or white, or blue, or speck'd with gold,
> Vessels so pure, and so refin'd
> Appear the types of woman-kind:
> Are they not valu'd for their beauty,
> Too fair, too fine for household duty?
> With flowers and gold and azure dy'd,
> Of ev'ry house the grace and pride?
> How white, how polish'd is their skin,
> And valu'd most when only seen!
> She who before was highest priz'd,
> Is for a crack or flaw despis'd;
> I grant they're frail, yet they're so rare,
> The treasure cannot cost too dear!

The poem then concludes with this injunction:

> Love, <u>Laura</u>, love, while youth is warm,
> For each new winter breaks a charm;
> And woman's not like <u>China</u> sold,
> But cheaper grows in growing old;
> Then quickly chuse the prudent part,
> Or else you break a faithful heart.

Such imagery continued in use throughout the 18th century, and survived even into later times.[13] Thus Fanny Burney's

Evelina, Letter VIII of volume II, contains this passage: "Remember, my dear Evelina, nothing is so delicate as the reputation of a woman: it is, at once, the most beautiful and most brittle of all things." The sad fate of Phoebe Dawson, seduced and abandoned by her lover, is pathetically symbolized, in part two of Crabbe's The Parish Register, by the "broken pitcher" she takes to the pool for water.[14] And even Keats' Grecian urn, that "still unravish'd bride," may be in the same symbolic tradition, though of course it is a symbol of virginity still intact.

The ultimate sources for all this vessel imagery seem undiscoverable: Freud, indeed, sees all imagery of containers to be feminine, and thus attributes archetypal status to it. Yet some possible ancient sources should be noted, principally the general Biblical tendency to use vessels as an image of man,[15] and, more particularly, the passage in 1 Peter 3:7, which enjoins husbands to give "honour unto the wife, as unto the weaker vessel." The stress of the injunction should be observed: woman is accorded honor because she is the weaker vessel, and so the passage suggests that the very fragility of the vessel, as of feminine beauty and character in general, is somehow the source of the value and honor accorded it. And alongside such Biblical usage, there is the pagan classical tendency to see women as vessels. Thus Dryden translates Lucretius, III. 1008 ff.:

> This is the fable's moral, which they tell
> Of fifty foolish virgins damn'd in hell
> To leaky vessels, which the liquor spill;
> To vessels of their sex, which none could ever fill.[16]

But regardless of the ultimate sources for such imagery, we can now return to one of the crucial instances of its use in The Rape of the Lock, these lines,

> Whether the Nymph shall break Diana's Law,
> Or some frail China Jar receive a Flaw,

and perhaps more easily describe some of its implications. The first line of the couplet is relatively direct in its implications, and the harshness of "break" is admirably set off against the more subdued "receive" in the second line.[17] This second line, on the other hand, seems almost inexhaustible in its range of suggestions. First of all, there is the suggestion, here as in much of the poem's vessel imagery, that Pope is exploiting the Biblical image of woman as the weaker vessel, and that he is in some sense doing homage to this vessel: though Pope's view of her is laced with irony, Belinda's beauteous virginity is somehow rendered more precious, and our regard for it somehow more tender, by recognition of how easily it can be marred or shattered. At the same time, Pope's "frail" and brittle China jar humorously recalls the general view of women exemplified by Hamlet's exclamation, "Frailty, thy name is woman," or by George Herbert's saying that "A woman and a glasse are ever in danger." There is the hint of mortality inherent in all the imagery which likens women to something so frangible as fine glass or China: existing in a state of tremulous instability and inconstancy, the vessels seem to lean of themselves towards disaster. Made of the dust and clay of the earth, they seem destined for a shocking reversion to "glittring Dust and painted Fragments." Too, there are also all those inherent, as well as inherited, suggestions of loss — loss of perfection, beauty and virginity — so wittily engaged by the course of the poem and its central event. All three of the poem's crucial images of the "fall" of China, indeed, gather to themselves, and impart to the meaning of the poem at large, all of these suggestions, along with one more. This is the suggestion, made with varying degrees of emphasis by the three images, of the utter finality of the loss involved in the breaking of fine China, or of the frail bond of chastity.

II

Criticism of The Rape of the Lock in recent years has moved far from the 19th and early 20th century tendencies to approach the poem as a marvelous, but ultimately inconsequential, bit of filigree. The critical mood of our day will not suffer the poem to be "admirable in proportion as it is made of nothing,"[18] nor can it now be said that the poem has "no substance at all," that it is "nothing but grace; the astral body of an heroic poem, pure form, an echo of divine music . . . thin and clear!"[19] But in contrast to the mode of critical address represented by such declarations as these, yet another effort to describe the

more melancholy undercurrents of Pope's wit and humor in
The Rape of the Lock may well seem to wear a lamentable air
of too high seriousness. Still, there seems to be as much danger in taking the poem too lightly as there is in taking it too
seriously: the poem seems able to tease us into thought, as well
as out of it.

Recent discussions of The Rape of the Lock have been very
successful in focusing attention on some of the more ritualistic
aspects of the "war of the sexes" in the poem. Even so, some
of the emphases in these discussions seem to require adjustment. Mr. Brooks, for example, seems to insist too much that
the "issues in Pope's poem are matters of taste" and that "matters of morality . . . are never raised." In effect, he does not
seem to face directly enough the ultimate implications of the
imagery he explores so well: Belinda, after all, does undergo
a kind of "fall" in the poem; her "perfection" is shattered, and
she does lose her "chastity," in so far as chastity can be understood, however teasingly, as a condition of the spirit. Mrs.
Rebecca Price Parkin mainly follows Mr. Brooks, but in addition she regards Clarissa's speech as largely hypocritical, and
as essentially irrelevant to Belinda's situation.[20] And Mr. Hugo
Reichard, who establishes a number of valuable contexts for
events in the poem,[21] may encase Belinda too rigidly in an iron
maidenliness of "coquetry," with the result that she, and the
experience she undergoes, seem deprived of general significance.

Belinda's central experience can be approached by a wide
variety of ways, but there are two ways especially prepared for
by the foregoing discussion of the poem's vessel imagery. These
are provided, first, by the parallels to Paradise Lost, and,
second, by the parody of Sarpedon's speech in the Iliad. The
ethical discriminations insinuated by these two realms of reference are intimately related to, and strengthened by, the implications of the vessel imagery. Both realms of reference insist that Belinda undergoes one or another fall from "perfection,"
and to these other "falls" in the poem there are added the special heightenings furnished by Pope's imagery of the "fall" of
China.

The parallels to Paradise Lost in The Rape of the Lock are
numerous, and not all of them seem to have been remarked in
print. But the main direction and force of the Miltonic references can be illustrated by the sequence of three major parallels

alone. First, there is the dream of pride and vain-glory insinuated into Belinda's ear, which recalls the dream insinuated into
Eve's ear in Books V and VI of Paradise Lost. Second, there is
the parody of the Mass at Belinda's dressing table, where Belinda worships herself and which vividly recalls, as Mr. Reichard has noted, the new-born Eve's admiration of herself as
mirrored in the pool of Eden (P.L., IV. 460 ff.). But perhaps the
crucial parallel is the third, which occurs just before the cutting of the lock, when Ariel searches out the "close Recesses
of the Virgin's Thought." There he finds an "Earthly Lover lurking at her Heart," and Pope writes:

> Amaz'd, confus'd, he found his Pow'r expir'd,
> Resign'd to Fate, and with a Sigh retir'd.

The situation seems to echo clearly, as Mr. Reichard again has
noted, the moment in Paradise Lost when, after the fall of
Adam and Eve, the angelic hosts retire, "mute and sad," to
Heaven. The angels could have protected Adam and Eve from
any force attempted by Satan, but against man's own free choice
of evil they are as helpless as Ariel and his cohorts are in the
presence of Belinda's free choice of an earthly lover.
   The course of the Miltonic parallels makes it clear that
Belinda undergoes a "fall," at least in the eyes of Ariel. Yet
this fall is only a fall from the narcissistic self-love and arid
virginity which the sylphs, in one of their aspects, both represent and seek to preserve (this accounts for Pope's ability to
merge, in his parody, the actions of both Satan and the good
angels), and so in one sense it is merely a fall into a more
natural human condition and one best regarded, perhaps, as a
kind of "fortunate fall." Belinda simply falls in love, and thus
a situation is created whereby she can escape from the meaningless virginity and honor represented, on the poem's most serious level, by the sylphs. Here Pope further intensifies the
issues (and the element of free choice) by his hints, delicate
though they be, that Belinda actually acquiesces, however faintly, in the "rape." The sylphs warn her of the Baron's approach
by blowing back her hair and by thrice twitching "the Diamond
in her Ear." Thrice she looks back to the Baron, and it is noticeable that only after the warnings have been ignored does
Ariel search her heart. What he finds there (and the poem gives

us no reason to suspect that the "Earthly Lover" is anyone but the Baron[22]) suggests that Belinda is in some sense aware of the Baron's attempt on her, and that she does not turn from it.

Even so, Belinda's response to the rape is, from the viewpoint of her society (and perhaps of any society), perfectly natural: as critics have not tired of noting, the Baron's act is a rude violation of the rules of courtship. Too, Belinda does well to remember that, in John Gay's words, "She who before was highest priz'd, / Is for a crack or flaw despis'd." Yet the main point to be stressed is the fact that, after the rape and her immediate response to it (her tantrum), Belinda is faced now with the necessity of making a much more serious and deliberate decision: her immediate response, whatever its justification, had been marked, as the Cave of Spleen episode insists, by prudery, hypocrisy, and affectation, but she may now choose a course other than that which had placed her under the dominion of the gnome Umbriel. To make the alternatives before her emphatically clear, Pope presents her, and the reader, with the two points of view represented in the speeches of Thalestris and Clarissa. Thalestris, significantly given the name of an Amazonian queen, represents a kind of empty and vicious principle of female victory and dominance at all costs, and she also gives perfect expression to the prevailing moral chaos of the poem's world:

> Honour forbid! at whose unrival'd Shrine
> Ease, Pleasure, Virtue, All, our Sex resign.

But placed against the viewpoint of Thalestris, and her society, is the set of values voiced by Clarissa (the clarifier) and re-enforced by the whole weight of Sarpedon's speech in Book XII of the Iliad. Pope's translation of this speech, it should be remembered, was among the very first of his works to be published, for it appeared in 1709 in Poetical Miscellanies: The Sixth Part. This early translation of Sarpedon's speech passed, with only trivial revision, into Pope's full translation of the Iliad. Volume III of Pope's Iliad, containing Book XII, appeared in 1717, and in the same year Pope worked the speech of Clarissa into The Rape of the Lock, with the design, as he later noted, of opening "more clearly the Moral of the Poem."[23] Pope's own translation of the speech (exemplifying, one must

suppose, his own best understanding of Sarpedon's character)
provides, therefore, the best background against which to view
Clarissa's words. There is no need to cite here the full text
of Sarpedon's speech, but there is need perhaps to emphasize
its two concluding couplets, and to stress their relevance to
Belinda's situation:

> The Life which others pay, let us bestow,
> And give to Fame what we to Nature owe;
> Brave tho' we fall, and honour'd if we live,
> Or let us Glory gain, or Glory give!

Sarpedon's words are a glorious enunciation of the spirit of magnanimity (in the Preface to his Iliad, Pope distinguishes Sarpedon as "gallant and generous"). The admiration his speech elicits is the direct result of the utter generosity of spirit, the
supreme magnanimity of attitude, with which he faces the loss
of his life.

Pope's parody of his own translation of Sarpedon's speech
invokes an epic context which, from one point of view, may be
said to "trivialize" the mighty pother kept over the loss of a
lock. At the same time, it must also be recognized that Clarissa's speech offers to Belinda the possibility of adopting an attitude toward her loss quite at variance with the ugliness of
attitude endorsed by Thalestris. And in so far as the attitude
offered by Clarissa is at variance with the surrounding moral
chaos of the poem's world, this attitude is supported, even
corroborated and verified, by its Homeric antecedent. Moreover, Pope makes us aware of the fundamental validity of Clarissa's attitude by the grave and sobering currents in her speech:
the melancholy reminders of small-pox, housewifery and old
age, while perfectly subdued to the poem's gloss of wit, yet give
the whole speech a momentary air of mournful sobriety. At the
very least, Clarissa's speech opens up the possibility that Belinda may choose an attitude towards her loss in some way fully
analogous (however vastly different their spheres of experience
and action) to the attitude adopted by Sarpedon towards his loss.

One may well shrink from explicit exposition of the analogy
Pope has so discreetly and delicately imparted to his poem.
Baldly and briefly, however, the terms of the analogy would
seem to be something as follows: Sarpedon and Belinda enter

into different kinds of "war," and each kind of war imposes its attendant consequences. The consequence on the epic level of war between heroes is loss of life; on the level of war between the sexes it is loss of virginal innocence. Both Sarpedon and Belinda experience moments of victory, and both are called upon to face their moments of defeat and loss. The main difference between them (other than the extreme disparateness of contexts) is the difference in attitude with which loss is faced. A volunteer (like Sarpedon) in the lists, with the earlier victory over the Baron at Ombre (as well as countless other victories) under her belt, and with the "Earthly Lover" in her heart, Belinda is called upon to acknowledge and accept her defeat on one level, and yet, by virtue of the "good Humour" of such an acceptance, gain a different kind of victory on another level. For "good Humour" is here the perfectly appropriate analogy to the magnanimity of spirit displayed by Sarpedon, and when Clarissa says that

> good Humour can prevail,
> When Airs, and Flights, and Screams and Scolding fail,

she means essentially that the only victory possible to Belinda is that victory which gallantry and generosity of spirit in the face of defeat or loss always gain, whatever the level of experience. Having in some sense admitted an earthly lover to her heart and already separated herself from the virginal purity symbolized by the sylphs, Belinda is asked (and here we should recall the particular emphases in the last lines of Sarpedon's speech) to be "brave" though she "fall," that is, to "keep good Humour still whate'er . . . [she] . . . lose." Only thus might she be truly "Mistress of herself, tho' China fall."[24]

This interpretation of the purport of Clarissa's speech is confirmed, perhaps, by what may be another of the analogies to Paradise Lost in the poem. Here we are again indebted to Mr. Brooks, who suggested, though with quite another emphasis, that the advice offered to Belinda by Clarissa is analogous to that offered to Adam and Eve by Michael after their fall: "Michael promises that Adam can create within his own breast 'A Paradise . . . happier farr'," and "Clarissa's advice to Belinda makes the same point."[25] Separated from her state of innocence, no longer may Belinda enjoy familiar intimacy with her guardian

sylphs, just as Adam may no longer, after his loss, expect to
enjoy the familiar intimacy of "God or Angel Guest": now Belinda must rely, says Clarissa, on the support of a true and inner
virtue, not the mere face of virtue.

But Belinda, as the course of the game of Ombre had already implied and foretold, is not a good loser, and she does
not rise to the occasion afforded by her loss here. Instead, she
ratifies the course of prudery delineated earlier in the Cave of
Spleen episode, and persists in the ways of Ill-Nature and Affection. This is her real fall in the poem, and in this fall the
richest and fairest of the poem's many vessels is irreparably
shattered.

Given the world of Hampton Court, any attitude other than
that actually adopted by Belinda would have seemed to be a
violation of the poem's decorum. Yet it should also be recognized that, on the level of the poem where the humor becomes
a little stern and the examination of manners edges into an examination of morals,26 an opportunity is given to Belinda to
transcend the limitations of a world where "honor" and "virtue"
are equated with "reputation" and "appearance." Pope maintains
the decorum of his poem, but this should not obscure the fact
that Belinda fails to meet the test of her spirit proposed by
Clarissa.

Of course, as many critics have stressed, Pope's attitude
toward Belinda is very mixed and complicated: mocking and yet
tender, admiring and yet critical. This mixed and complicated
attitude, however, is at least partly the product of Pope's concern with a "type" of human experience which simultaneously
involves both loss and gain, one in which loss must be suffered
if the gain is to be at all achieved. The paradoxical nature of
Pope's attitude is thus intimately related to the paradox of
Belinda's situation, and to the sexual terms of that situation:
if Belinda is to find her role of woman, she must lose the role
of virgin, and the more graceful her acceptance of loss the
greater victory she achieves through it. Because Pope is dealing with this paradox, his attitude must be mixed and complicated. He can appreciate virginal perfection, however narcissistic, and "mourn" its loss; yet he can also give final honor to
a kind of perfection achieved on another level.

The loss of perfection and the marring of beauty, imaged
by the fall and shattering of rich China vessels, is seen in the

poem as an inevitable part of human experience. But in recompence for her particular losses, Belinda is offered the gain of a different kind of beauty and perfection: the kind Sarpedon achieved through simple generosity of spirit in the face of his loss, the kind Adam and Eve were offered after their loss, or the kind John Donne had in mind when, in the refrain to his Epithalamion made at Lincolnes Inne, he wrote of another maiden who, through loss of virginity, "To day puts on perfection, and a womans name."

Blinded by a false sense of shame and thinking only of reputation, Belinda can scarcely be expected to transcend the values of her society, but this does not mean that the reader, whatever his anxiety not to spoil the hilarious mockery of the occasion, is to ignore the ignominy of her real defeat, or the sadnesses of the poem at large. For amidst all the glitter and gaiety and irony, amidst all the shimmering brightness and lightness and sheer fun of the poem, there are insistent reminders of the shades just beneath and beyond the pale of paint and light. It is with such a reminder, indeed, that the poem approaches its close. There, in lines which recall other rich vessels which had fallen to lie in their own glittering dust, Pope looks forward, in a final suggestion of defloration, to the time when Belinda's eyes,

> those fair Suns shall sett, as sett they must,
> And all those Tresses shall be laid in Dust.

The awareness of these sadnesses in the poem, along with an awareness of Belinda's inability to turn defeat into victory, perhaps justifies the repetition again of another, the finest, of Hazlitt's responses to Pope's art: "You hardly know whether to laugh or weep."

NOTES

1 See Lecture IV, "On Dryden and Pope."

2 Even the "painted Vessel" of Canto II, 1. 47, may glance at Belinda.

3 "The Case of Miss Arabella Fermor," in The Well Wrought Urn (New York, 1947), p. 87. Mr. Brooks' essay first

appeared in The Sewanee Review, LI (1943), 502-24. Mrs. Rebecca Price Parkin, in The Poetic Workmanship of Alexander Pope (Minneapolis, 1955), pp. 86, 111, largely follows Mr. Brooks' interpretation of the vessel imagery.

4 The saying seems to have had widespread acceptance. Cf. Don Quixote, I. xxxiii.

5 P. 97.

6 See also The Winter's Tale, I. ii. 321-2, and Cymbeline, V. v. 206-7.

7 Cf. An Anatomie of the World: The first Anniversary, ll. 177-82. I owe the example in Donne to Professor Robert Bryan.

8 Loeb trans. The original reads: "nulla reparabilis arte / laesa pudicitia est; deperit illa semel."

9 Cf. Robert Sanderson, Twenty Sermons (London, 1656), p. 21: "I have sometimes . . . likened a flaw in the Conscience, and a flaw in the good name, to the breaking . . . of a Chrystal glass or China dish . . . no art can piece them so as they shall be either sightly or serviceable. . . ." Cf. Franklin, Poor Richard's Almanack (1750): "Glass, China and Reputation, are easily crack'd and never well mended."

10 The famous "China scene" in Wycherley's The Country Wife provides eloquent testimony for this passion.

11 Cf. this earlier passage in the same play (I. i): "We run, we strive, and purchase things with our blood and money, quite foreign to our intrinsic real happiness, and which have a being in imagination only, as you may see by the pudder that is made about precedence, titles, court favour, maidenheads, and china-ware."

12 The Welsh Opera (1731), Air XVII. The song also appears, with slight modifications, in The Grub-Street Opera (1731), Air XIX, and in The Mock Doctor (1732), Air VI. I owe these examples from Fielding, and the one from John Gay, to Professor Charles B. Woods.

13 The image survives into the 20th century. See the expression,

"crack a Judy's tea-cup," in Eric Partridge, A Dictionary of Slang and Unconventional English, 3rd ed. (1949), p. 187.

14 I owe this example to Professor E. S. Holden.

15 For a burlesque of the Biblical usage, see the sermon on The Dignity, Use and Abuse of Glass-Bottles, in The Prose Works of Alexander Pope, ed. Norman Ault (Oxford, 1936), I, 203 ff.

16 See ll. 218-21 of Dryden's trans. Geoffrey Tillotson, The Rape of the Lock (Twickenham Edition, vol. II), supplies the Lucretian source in a note to l. 54 of Canto IV.

17 For other discussion of these lines, see W. K. Wimsatt, "One Relation of Rhyme to Reason," in The Verbal Icon (University of Kentucky, 1954), p. 162.

18 Hazlitt, "On Dryden and Pope," in Lectures on the English Poets.

19 W. P. Ker, "Pope," in English Critical Essays: Twentieth Century, World's Classics ed. (Oxford, 1947), p. 112.

20 The Poetic Workmanship of Alexander Pope, pp. 126-7, 171-2.

21 "The Love Affair in Pope's Rape of the Lock," PMLA, LXIX (1954), 887-902.

22 Mr. Reichard's reasoning on this point seems valid.

23 Pope's Epistle to Miss Blount, With the Works of Voiture (1712) also has relevance to Clarissa's speech.

24 See Of the Characters of Women, 1. 268.

25 The Well Wrought Urn, pp. 91-2.

26 See the discussion of the poem by Maynard Mack, in his introduction to The Augustans, vol. V of English Master-pieces (New York, 1950), pp. 23-6.

TENSION IN ALEXANDER POPE'S POETRY

Rebecca Price Parkin

Poetry must not only communicate but communicate with
an urgency higher than that of prose. The most obvious attribute
differentiating poetry from prose, regularity of rhythm, helps
achieve this tension. So does rime and, when used as a line-
marker, alliteration. Once expectations of repetition in meter
and sound have been set up, the reader's ear remains alert to
have them satisfied.

This physical satisfaction is not, however, the only aspect
of rhythm and rime which helps produce tension. As soon as a
reader with even a little experience in poetry hears the first
measured lines of a new poem, he forms certain intellectual
expectations also. He knows that the realm of everyday prose,
whether written or spoken, is on the whole less taut intellectually than the realm of poetry. The tension existing objectively in
the art-form and arising in part from poetic attitude toward subject matter, creates a corresponding subjective "tension" in the
reader.

To both the physical and intellectual anticipations there are
exceptions. Good free-verse, for example, compensates for
lack of traditional metrical tension by special emphasis on tension secured in other ways — metaphor in particular. And some
metrical styles, such as the Victorian lyric — which thin, sentimental, and over-facile still haunts housewives' magazines
and middle-brow general magazines -- have become slacker than
good prose because of over-frequent, inept imitation. This happened historically to Pope's "own" heroic couplet. Less gifted
imitators -- unable to equal Pope's handling of closure, balance,
antithesis, compression, precision, and epigrammatic finish —
lowered the tension of his couplet.

Modern readers must make some effort to regain the expectation of brilliance and "nervous" energy Pope infused into
this form. Pope is not the only major poet whose style has been

Reprinted from The University of Kansas City Review, Vol. 19 (1953),
pp. 169-173, by permission of author and publisher.

vitiated by followers deficient in poetic ability. The Spenserian, Miltonic, and Shakespearean patterns have been similarly mishandled; and in our own day the little magazines are full of would-be Eliots.

Word meaning, however, is by far the most crucial element in creating tension. Since genre is broadly a categorizing of what and how a poem may mean, individual genres exhibit certain distinctive tensions. The tension proper to epic, for instance, arises primarily from the conflict of heroes with heroic adversaries and in some degree of both with fate. Achilles opposes Hector in the knowledge that hard upon the heels of victory will come the termination of his own brief life. Beowulf fights Grendel and the firedrake, but is himself overcome by man's mortality. Adam and Eve are set within a garden to combat the Devil himself, but within the framework of omnipotent God's — and the reader's -- foreknowledge that they will not combat successfully.

As for the fundamental tension of the mock-heroic, it resides in the constant comparison it promotes between this epic tension and low, frivolous, contemporary matters. As for the distinctive tension of satire, it lies in the pull between the norm of right conduct and the deviations from it.

Within the limits of each genre the individual poet may achieve certain characteristic modifications of the prevailing tension. Epics though they all are, we know that Beowulf, the Faerie Queene, and Paradise Lost are highly individual in degree and quality of tension. Likewise, Chaucer's Sir Thopas, Butler's Hudibras, Garth's Dispensary, and Pope's Rape of the Lock, though all mock-epics, operate at different levels of tension.

Of these mock-epics, the Rape of the Lock, in spite of its surface frivolity, offers the most serious and inclusive comment on human life. And the Dunciad in this respect surpasses the Rape; since public, general, "masculine" interests carry more weight than private, domestic, "feminine" interests. One poem is concerned with the relations of men to women; the other with the possibility of a whole civilization's slipping into a new Dark Age. Either of these subjects is more significant in its human import than criticism of pseudo-knighthood or even the question of free medicine for Londoners. And tension is in part a concomitant of seriousness of subject matter.

TENSION IN ALEXANDER POPE'S POETRY

Pope utilizes this truth in such a way that he very nearly turns mock-epic tension back into epic tension. The characteristic mock-epic tension between low subject and high style he does not maintain in a simple one-to-one fashion; he brings in a third dimension. For in neither of these mock-epics is Pope's real subject matter low. Belinda's boudoir and even Duncedom's games have a serious aspect. The two-way tension native to the genre is transformed by Pope into a three-way tension pointing back toward epic seriousness. Clarissa's speech in Canto V underlines several of the serious emphases of the Rape of the Lock:

> Oh! if to dance all night, and dress all day,
> Charm'd the smallpox, or chased old age away;
> Who would not scorn what housewife's cares produce,
> Or who would learn one earthly thing of use?
> To patch, nay, ogle, might become a saint,
> Nor could it sure be such a sin to paint.
> But since, alas! frail beauty must decay,
> Curl'd or uncurl'd, since locks will turn to gray;
> Since painted, or not painted, all shall fade,
> And she who scorns a man must die a maid;
> What then remains, but well our power to use,
> And keep good humor still whate'er we lose?
> And trust me, dear, good humour can prevail,
> When airs, and flights, and screams, and scolding fail.
> Beauties in vain their pretty eyes may roll;
> Charms strike the sight, but merit wins the soul.

Belinda, no less than Achilles, is cursed with a glorious but -- because curled or uncurled, locks will turn to gray -- brief dominion. The sun she personifies throughout the poem and the "suns of her eyes" will set. Old age for Belinda is the fire-dragon which will put an end to her proper career. The lack of applause with which Clarissa's speech is greeted makes it clear that to the belles virtue and useful skills are not acceptable alternatives for conquests of hearts.

Nor does Clarissa herself recommend virtue from the right motive. Her radically contorted female philosophy makes it appear that the typical belle, somewhat like Adam and Eve in the garden, is so enmeshed in fate that she has no reasonable

293

probability of rising above Clarissa's narrow and hypocritical opportunism. The seeds of something more serious underlie too the depiction of Belinda's dressing-table as an altar at which she worships the deity revealed in the mirror, herself. This does not make the Rape of the Lock an epic; but not very far beneath its amusing, lacquered surface there lurk graver issues, not ordinarily treated in mock-epic. Reacting with the more conventional mock-epic qualities, they produce a special type of tension very characteristic of Pope.

Another source of tension, notably exploited in the Dunciad and the Satires, is that derived from reference to particular people by name and to particular events. Pope's reliance upon this device has in the past received some adverse criticism. The following passages from Dialogue I, Epilogue to the Satires are typical. Pope's "friend" remonstrates with him:

> But Horace, sir, was delicate, was nice;
> Bubo observes, he lash'd no sort of vice:
> Horace would say, Sir Billy served the crown,
> Blunt could do business, Huggens knew the town;
> In Sappho touch the failings of the sex;
> In rev'rend bishops note some small neglects,
> And own the Spaniards did a waggish thing,
> Who cropt our ears, and sent them to the King.
>
> .   .   .   .
>
> Ye Gods! shall Cibber's son, without rebuke,
> Swear like a Lord; or Rich outwhore a Duke?
> A fav'rite's porter with his master vie,
> Be bribed as often, and as often lie?
> Shall Ward draw contracts with a statesman's skill?
> Or Japhet pocket, like His Grace, a will?
> Is it for Bond or Peter (paltry things)
> To pay their debts, or keep their faith, like Kings?

Reading of such passages is enriched by knowing the details of Bond's or Peter's perfidy, but such information is not necessary for understanding the satiric point. Sappho, Cibber, and Ward lived, and were poetically pilloried, in Horace's day; they live too in our own.

That this naming of names, however, increased the tension

of such passages for Pope's contemporaries is borne out by the protests they occasioned. Even in our time, merely realizing that Pope is referring not to fictional ghosts but to actual people and happenings augments the tension of the poem. The reader does not have to know personally the characters stigmatized or even to be acquainted with their biographies to recognize the heightening of satiric level Pope achieves by making "those not afraid of God afraid of him."

Wherever he can, Pope uses the rhetorical devices at his disposal to avoid a one-sided, narrow presentation of reality. Through irony, metaphor, paradox, layered meaning, and tonal variation he strives to gain an inclusiveness which will make his work comprehend the whole and not just a part of human experience. This inclusiveness, this attempt to do justice to many different facets of human experience at the same time, of itself powerfully increases tension. If the given subject of the poem be thought of as an animal body centered in a spider-web arrangement of ropes, then, tugging on many ropes simultaneously would cause more agony than tugging on just one rope -- and would keep the body in the center of the web instead of pulling it out to any one side.

In individual couplets and passages one of Pope's most effective ways of securing tension is to make syntax or meaning fight against form. A notable instance where this device provides the complete motivation of the poem is the Temple of Fame. The organizing concept of this poem is a logical inquiry into the nature and conduct of earthly fame. The ruling passion of the goddess is shown to be caprice. In instance after instance Pope demonstrates the complete irrationality of her behaviour. Even when she rewards the good with good fame and the bad with bad fame, it is the result of whim rather than of an attempt to do justice.

Fame is furthermore depicted as unreliable in her time aspect — as both fleeting and permanent. This is symbolized by the "rock of Ice" on which her temple stands. To substantiate this paradox, Pope in one of the outstanding comparisons of the poem asserts that ice does not melt — in Zembla:

> So Zembla's rocks (the beauteous work of frost)
> Rise white in air, and glitter o'er the coast;
> Pale suns, unfelt, at distance roll away,

> And on th'impassive ice the lightnings play;
> Eternal snows the growing mass supply,
> Till the bright mountains prop th'incumbent sky:
> As Atlas fix'd, each hoary pile appears,
> The gather'd winter of a thousand years.

This paradox of melting and not melting, fleeting and not fleeting, fights against the logical process of the inquiry and the firmly controlled couplets in which this analysis of the uncontrolled and illogical proceeds. In this connection, the controverted House of Rumor, sometimes said to detract from the unity of the poem, is seen to function logically. It stresses Fame's transience as Zembla's rocks stress her permanence.

Pope did not hesitate to make sweeping changes in Chaucer's unfinished original in order to secure for his own poem unassailable logic and unity of design. If Chaucer's whirling House of Rumor had been a distraction and a superfluity, it too would have been eliminated. But Rumor represents only a "stepping up" of the brief duration and fickleness of Fame herself. Rumor is another aspect of the same goddess. The ceaselessly whirling little house is appropriately and with climactic effect reserved for the end. In this way the contrast is made stronger between unstable earthly Fame and the just and enduring heavenly fame which Pope apostrophizes in the closing lines.

As a whole, Pope's poetry achieves and maintains a high level of tension. Because of the care he gave to minute questions of finish, his mature works contain very few passages where tension — though often varied in quality — is relaxed in degree.

POPE'S ELOISA TO ABELARD: AN INTERPRETATION

Henry Pettit

Anyone who wishes to find comfort for a philosophy of an-
archic literary taste, everyman to his own, should turn at once
to the critical tradition and current expression about Alexander
Pope's Eloisa to Abelard (1717). Here he will find the poem
condemned as "rhetorical"[1] and "theatrical"[2] or approved as
"moving"[3] and "dramatic."[4] He will find it dismissed as not
"successful"[5] and accepted as an "eloquent outpouring of a soul
in torment."[6] He will have it explained to him by an eminent
American scholar as "definitely out of the English tradition"[7]
and pronounced by no less an Englishman than Dr. Johnson as
"one of the most happy productions of human wit."[8] One need
not force these judgments to find a sufficient latitude of opinion
for further effort at interpretation.[9]

Pope himself is responsible for giving the poem an intellectual cast by characterizing it as a conflict between "grace
and nature."[10] In his own day, such a coloration may easily
have been overlooked or disregarded. Today, however, it tends
to give substance to dissatisfaction with the poem insofar as it
stresses the antitheses of emotion into which the heroine of the
poem is projected and gives no intimation of the evolution of a
maturing character within these constant eddies. It fits too
nicely a conception common enough of Pope as a robot turning
commonplaces of philosophy into quotable couplets on a piece-
work basis. "For Eloisa," Professor Root could say, "there is
no problem of conduct; her way of life, so far as the vita activa
is concerned, is irrevocably settled and rigorously ordered.
It is within the realm of vita contemplativa that the conflict
rages — 'rebel nature holds out half' the heart which entirely
'quit Abelard for God'."[11] Is there then no problem of conduct?

Dear fatal name! rest ever unreveal'd,

Reprinted from University of Colorado Studies: Series in Language and
Literature, No. 4 (1953), pp. 69-74, by permission of author and publisher.

> Nor pass these lips in holy silence seal'd.
> Hide it, my heart. . . .
> Oh write it not, my hand — The name appears
> Already written — wash it out, my tears!
> In vain lost Eloisa weeps and prays,
> Her heart still dictates and her hand obeys.
>
> (ll. 9-11, 13-16)

If this is in the realm of the vita contemplativa then the courts have no lawful right to subpoena a bundle of love letters in a breach of promise suit or even the account books of a corporation charged with evading the income tax. Try to pin Eloisa to the wall with a neat formula and she shrieks back at you: "Tears still are mine, and those I need not spare" (l. 45).

It is not that Professor Root has no truth in his analysis. The appeal to sympathy is undoubted. Eloisa is fixed as solidly as ever a Prometheus was riveted to a gneissic bastion. But she has none of the calm courage of Prometheus, inevitably suggested by Professor Root's formula and as violently contradicted by the poem. She cannot be compared with Prometheus because she is without his divine prescience of ultimate retribution. Plagued by an irreversible fate that has her entrapped, she fights back as relentlessly as a Wagnerian heroine, though with far more intelligence. My argument is simply that Eloisa's struggle is not satisfactorily stated as a conflict between grace and nature. Under her peculiar circumstances a choice between the two would be no choice at all, and anything like a will within her would amount only to a succumbing to inevitable consequences. " 'Tis the most beggarly Refuge imaginable," according to Pope's contemporary, the third Earl of Shaftesbury, "that they should strive to have Faith, and believe to the utmost: because if, after all, there be nothing in the matter, there will be no harm in being thus deceiv'd."[12] Such a unilateral decision as Eloisa would face, were it merely a choice between nature and grace, seems an underestimation of the extent of her involvement in human love and of the frank clarity with which Pope contrives for her to reflect on her fate.

What then is the choice before Eloisa? She is in love with Abelard. She cannot have him. She has no will to succumb to fate.

POPE'S ELOISA TO ABELARD

> Nature stands check'd; Religion disapproves;
> Ev'n thou art cold — yet Eloisa loves.   (ll. 259-260)

Her will is for the apparently unattainable. It is not conceivable
then that her choice is between denial or retention of her passion. Utterly devoted to love she has only the choice between
its inhibition or its exhibition. That she chose the latter goes
without saying. That she is indulged in more extravagant ex-
hibitionism by Pope than by any of his predecessors has been
amusingly pointed out by the French scholar Audra who counts
the sighs and tears used in various versions, observes their
steady increase, and finds in Pope "un déluge."[13] Seriously,
though, to appreciate the importance of this sentimental exhibition is to understand how it leads its lachrymose heroine to a
purgation of otherwise malignant bitterness. She actually ar-
rives at a higher conception of life than that from which she
starts. She has learned the irony of Sir William Temple's remark that "when [man] has looked about him as far as he can,
he concludes there is no more to be seen; when he is at the End
of his Line hs is at the Bottom of the Ocean."[14]

In his introduction to the text of the poem in the Twickenham edition of Pope's poetry, Professor Tillotson surveys the
undeniable influence of Ovid and adds: "Pope's passion, then,
derives from Nature and Ovid . . . newly flushed with the experience of the time in France and England."[15] At this point
Professor Tillotson chooses to illustrate the experiential pattern solely from the poets with no attention to the general philosophical temper. It is this more general concept with which
I should like to supplement an otherwise highly informative and
sensitive approach to the poem. To do this, let me quote at
length a student of philosophy on the peculiarly sharp dualism
of the time:

> The antithesis of matter and spirit is a resultant of
> a lengthy historical movement. And if we wish to see
> its source in Plato, we must see there only the be-
> ginning of a movement. There is good reason for
> looking upon St. Augustine as particularly influential
> in turning the distinction in the direction that culmi-
> nates in the Cartesian dualism of substances. But the
> fact that the concepts of matter and form are not simply

identifiable with the antithesis of matter and spirit is
demonstrated by the struggle between the sets of conceptions in the works of St. Thomas Aquinas. Stated
briefly, this struggle took the form of a competition
between a tendency to frank dualism, within man and
the universe, and the tendency to maintain the serial
arrangement of the hierarchy of forms. On the one
hand, there are many substances, and each is matter
and form (except the divine being); on the other, hierarchy shows signs of its instability, and it remained
for DesCartes to solve the internal conflict by precip-
itating the dualism.[16]

It is not necessary further to follow the involutions of philosophy
to accept the precipitation here remarked as characteristic of
the philosophical temper of Pope's day. Before Pope and Swift
had met, Swift had sensed this heightened dualism and lashed
out in A Tale of a Tub against the Lockean emphasis on sensational aspects of experience:

Whatever Philosopher or Projector [Swift wrote] can
find out an Art to sodder and patch up the Flaws and
Imperfections of Nature, will deserve much better of
Mankind, and teach us a more useful Science, than
that so much in present Esteem, of widening and exposing them.[17]

Pope could scarcely have been deaf to such an appeal, and it
may well be that he conceived of himself as just such a "Philosopher or Projector" to take on the whole academy of science.
In any event, he seems to have known well the language of the
new philosophy, for in the Eloisa to Abelard he individuated it
in the character of Eloisa.

The degree to which Eloisa comes to life as a sympathetic
character is very likely at the basis of critical disagreement
over the poem. In inviting attention to the impact of Cartesian
dualism, perhaps it is well to note that Eloisa is no Jacob
wrestling with an angel, no Laocoön writhing amidst snakes,
no Ovidian heroine crying in distress, any more than she is a
medieval figure out of the twelfth century. She is, though, a
highly intelligent English woman of the early eighteenth century,

devoted to love at a time when the god of love was being mate-
rialized into a mere physical passion. From this point of view
I dissent wholly from Professor Root's conclusion that "Pope
has not identified himself with his personage as Shakespeare
and Chaucer and Browning seem to do."18

Let us admit that Eloisa is essentially erotic. Without losing feminine delicacy,19 she is fundamentally sensational. She
is passionate in the most material sense. She has no fear and
no doubt of the value of life in itself. It is precious and to be
cherished,

> Till ev'ry motion, pulse, and breath, be o'er;
> And ev'n my Abelard be lov'd no more.   (ll. 333-334)

If she looks over her shoulder in a lyric moment that has always fascinated the romantic critics, it is well to realize that
she turns back better satisfied to have loved and lost than never
to have loved. It is this frankness and devotion to the world of
the Cartesian anatomist that endows her with a nature demanding compassion. Anything less frank and devoted than an Eloisa
would have been an uncharitable compromise on Pope's part.

The form of the Eloisa also enters into an understanding
of the poem. Deriving as it does from the letters of Eloisa and
Abelard it is almost inevitably bound in with the epistolary
tradition. But Pope modifies the epistolary form by what Professor
Tillotson terms a "tighter 'geometry' of situation," pitting one situation against another, and necessarily inviting comparison to the
heroic drama of the Restoration. Thus taking into account the two
evident relations of the formal structure of the Eloisa, Professor
Tillotson has brilliantly explained the scarified rhetoric of the
poem in terms of the two traditions of metaphysical poetry and
heroic drama. Such an explanation, not in itself remotely superficial, may seem nevertheless more appropriate to the superficial aspects of the poem than to its essential character. It may
be that Eloisa is neither pure epistle nor pure drama for the
same reason -- namely, that both forms customarily invoke an
opposition of two characters. The trouble with Abelard, at
least in Pope's poem, is that he is an incitant to action but no
more himself an agent of the first dimension than Paris in
Tennyson's Oenone — a poem which resembles the Eloisa in

more than this one point. Conflict in the Eloisa is entirely within the heroine. Thus the Eloisa should better be thought of as
an elegiac lyric, akin to the ode, excepting possibly in the pro-
jection of poetic personality into a dramatic character.[21]
    Such a conception of the poem has advantages. For one
thing, as has been suggested, instead of emphasizing an emotional stress aimed at a possible recipient of a letter, the
emotion is complete within the one character. Similarly, instead of positing a conflict personified in two characters, as
pure drama would demand, the conflict within the single character is thoroughly justified. Finally, without antagonist, either
actual or imagined, emotion is restrained only by the exigen-
cies of verbal expression. In other words, the purest form of
lyric is ecstasis to which all else is secondary. Pathetic fallacy
is supreme and sentiment surges for expression. Or, as an
English poet wrote just a few years before the Eloisa:

      The Poet here must be indeed inspir'd,
      With Fury too, as well as Fancy fir'd.[22]

    Consider then the Eloisa as an erotic lyric in an age of
sensational materialism. The poem falls into three clearly
marked parts, almost evenly dividing the poem into a time sequence of past, present, and future — the parts marked off by
the two appeals to Abelard to "come" (ll. 119 and 257). The
first part is historical, developing emotion through methodical
recollection. The second part deals with the immediate situation, climaxing the emotional stress as Eloisa faces her predicament. The third part is a vision of death, emotion slowly
relaxing in anticlimax.
    The poem begins with Eloisa asking why, when she has
retreated to the contemplation of eternal God, she is still
plagued by her temporal, corporal state (ll. 1-6). She is excited
by a letter from Abelard and by her act of writing his name
(ll. 7-16). She contrasts the inert substance of the convent with
her own suffering (ll. 17-28). It would appear that this is to be
an epistolary complaint, but no sooner does Eloisa begin to
complain (ll. 29-40) than she realizes the happiness in her grief
(ll. 41-50) and is grateful for language as an escape (ll. 51-58).
This recognition of happiness in sorrow in the first turning
point:

> No happier task these faded eyes pursue,
> To read and weep is all they now can do.   (ll. 47-48)

Having faced her predicament honestly and seen its poignant
emptiness and at the same time its exquisite agony, she indul-
ges in a straightforward exposition that at once supplies the
reader with the antecedent action and motivates her rising passion. She recalls the beginning of love in friendship (ll. 59-72),
her rejection of marriage as confining the instinctive freedom
of love (ll. 73-98), the mutilation of Abelard (ll. 99-106), and
their consequent resignation to celibacy (ll. 107-118):

> Not grace, or zeal, love only was my call,
> And if I lose thy love, I lose my all.   (ll. 117-118)

Here the first part ends with a plea for Abelard to come to help
her accept her fate (ll. 119-128).

Introducing the second part, the song changes to a momentary dishonesty when Eloisa pleads with Abelard to come to her
to minister to his flock ("Oh pious fraud of am'rous charity"
ll. 129-150), only to be checked by the recurring honesty of
realizing that she has a purely selfish interest in Abelard that
colors all her outlook on life (ll. 151-170). She asks for death
(ll. 171-176) and calls for aid from heaven, suddenly realizing
that only God can relieve her agony of frustrated love (ll. 177-
206). This is the turning point of the second part and the climax
of the poem. It comes in a flash of insight into religious experience. She cries out: "Assist me heav'n" and reflectively demands:

> But whence arose that pray'r?
> Sprung it from piety or from despair?   (ll. 179-180)

This is not as prolonged an occupation with ontology as Shakespeare allows a Juliet, but it is long enough for Pope to indicate
his awareness of a debate soon to have the extensive treatment
of Bishop Butler in Analogy of Religion Natural and Revealed
(1736). It is not important, of course, whether the idea of heaven has come to Eloisa by revelation or natural means, "from
piety or despair." It is important, however, that when she
calls on heaven she has arrived at a Platonic conception of

something superior to her love, something greater than even an
Abelard, something beyond the naturalistic cul-de-sac into which
she has entered. Before this point in the poem she can speak of
the confusion of her heart "where mix'd with God's his lov'd
Idea lies" (1. 12) and after this point she can make a clear distinction between God and man when Abelard's "image steals between my God and me" (1. 268). This sudden rationality is the
crucial point in the self-examination of Eloisa. The tension it
creates is relieved for an instant by Eloisa's vision of the happiness of women who have never been disturbed by love (ll. 207-
222) only to be restrung as the passage is followed by one in
which Eloisa contrasts her own condition when she dreams of
Abelard (ll. 223-248), who is himself removed from human passion (ll. 249-256):

> Then conscience sleeps, and leaving nature free,
> All my loose soul unbounded springs to thee.

(ll. 227-228)

The immediate context of these lines is a passage almost directly translated from Ovid's Laodamia to Protesilaus,[23] but
the psychology of dreams is that of Hobbes.[24] It is on this note
that the second part ends with a renewed plea for Abelard's
return, this time premised on the firmer base that love is part
of life (ll. 257-262) and that his sympathy can save her from
madness (ll. 263-288).

The last part, beginning here, is an anticlimax of detumes-
cent passion. One can almost hear the breathing of an operatic
soloist in the death song of Purcell's Dido when Eloisa bids
Abelard farewell, having faced the loss of her love in the dissolution of material substance in death (ll. 289-302), which she
envisages for herself (in the manner but not with the spectral
accompaniments of a medieval Juliet) as an eternal sleep (ll.
303-316) with Abelard paying the last rites (ll. 317-336) and
dying himself to enter into a kingdom of eternal if disconcert-
ingly generalized love (ll. 337-342).[25] She prays that one grave
may entomb them both (ll. 337-342), that the story of their love
may warn future lovers and bring their sympathy (ll. 345-358),
and finally that their story may be enshrined in verse by a poet
of tender sensibility (ll. 359-366). This coda permits a little

upward flip of the poet's coat-tails as he peers for a moment
from behind the scenes, mouthing his nasty little vulgarity about
his ability to express human emotions: "He best can paint 'em
who shall feel 'em most" (1. 366). The line brings us back to the
drawing-room society of eighteenth-century London and is not
inconsistent with a poem where human experience has been recorded as a sheer physical passion whose delightful lasting impression has permeated the most solitary cell of the recluse.

To read the <u>Eloisa</u> thus as a lyric expression of the transformation of personal values in a philosophically sensational
age is to identify the struggle with universal concepts, to enjoy
its peculiar eighteenth-century flavor, and at the same time to
become acquainted with one of the magnificent women of literature. It may even suggest certain tragic overtones in the pitifully circumscribed lives of Pope and Mary Wortley Montagu,
though one should not now indulge any tendency towards intentional reverie, so little do we know of these two. To adopt the
language of Mr. Cleanth Brooks, who has written charmingly
on the direct companion piece, <u>The Rape of the Lock</u>,26 the
"paradox" of the <u>Eloisa</u> is that of a wavering between the demands of theology and the insistence of an almost pagan conception of life. In terms of the eighteenth century it is an
understanding of the religious impulse as piously inspired or
desperately elaborated from experience. Eloisa's "paradox"
is, to give Professor Root a tardy assent, a conflict between
grace and nature. It seems important to add, however, that
Pope saw in Eloisa the potentiality of a woman capable of emotional transcendence of the gulf into which a casual and hasty
acceptance of Cartesian metaphysics threatened to plunge mankind. Passion is her paradox, as it was the paradox of Des
Cartes, mysteriously operating to join two disparate conceptions of reality. In so emphasizing the ideational depth of the
<u>Eloisa</u> there is of course danger of unwriting the poem, if not
of rewriting it far out of context. Professor Tillotson, in this
regard, is perhaps wise in by-passing philosophy to emphasize
a rhetorical tradition. Let us not, however, attempt to excuse
the violence of <u>Eloisa</u> as sheer literary convention. It has a
tragic understructure, which perhaps justifies Professor Sherburn's emphasis on its appeal to the French. After all, Des
Cartes was French but Pope was English. Eloisa may be clois-
tered, but she is far from fugitive; indeed she sallies out to

PETTIT

meet her adversary, whether it be a philosopher from Gresham or her own deceptive rationalizing, with all the courage and mental lucidity of a Scottish covenanter.

NOTES

1 Alan Dugald McKillop, English Literature from Dryden to Burns, New York: Appleton-Century-Crofts, Inc., 1948, p. 168.

2 Paul Robert Lieder, Robert Morss Lovett, Robert Kilburn Root (eds.), British Poetry and Prose (Revised Edition), Boston: Houghton Mifflin Co., 1938, I, 753.

3 Edith Sitwell, Alexander Pope, London: Faber and Faber Limited, 1930, p. 281.

4 Roger P. McCutcheon, Eighteenth-Century English Literature, New York: Oxford University Press, 1949, p. 47.

5 George Sampson, The Concise Cambridge History of English Literature, Cambridge: At the University Press, 1941, p. 461.

6 Emile Legouis and Louis Cazamian, A History of English Literature, New York: Macmillan Co., 1931, p. 756.

7 George Sherburn, The Early Career of Alexander Pope, Oxford: At the Clarendon Press, 1934, p. 203.

8 Samuel Johnson, Lives of the English Poets, ed. by George Birkbeck Hill, Oxford: At the Clarendon Press, 1905, III, 235.

9 An interesting study of imagery in the poem has been made by G. Wilson Knight (The Burning Oracle, Oxford: At the University Press, 1939), who says (p. 148): "This is certainly Pope's greatest human poem and probably the greatest short love poem in our language."

10 The Works of Mr. Alexander Pope, London: Bernard Lintot, 1717, p. 416. Pope actually speaks of "so lively a picture of the struggles of grace and nature," emphasizing the action in the situation.

11 Robert Kilburn Root, The Poetical Career of Alexander

Pope, Princeton: Princeton University Press, 1938, p. 100.

12   Anthony Ashley Cooper, Earl of Shaftesbury, Characteristicks of Men, Manners, Opinions, Times, second edition, London, 1714, I, 36.

13   E. Audra, L'Influence Française dans l'Oeuvre de Pope, Paris, 1931, p. 438. In view of what I shall urge about the lyric quality of the poem later, it is perhaps well to quote M. Audra here when he says the Eloisa "forme avec l'Élégie à une Dame infortunée le bagage lyrique, ou plutôt sentimental de Pope."

14   Sir William Temple, Works, London: A. Churchill, etc., 1720, I, 165. The quotation is from the Essay upon the Ancient and Modern Learning and appears to be a rewording of two lines from Abraham Cowley's To the Royal Society (ll. 101-2).

15   Geoffrey Tillotson (ed.), The Rape of the Lock and Other Poems (Vol. II of The Twickenham Edition of the Poems of Alexander Pope under the general editorship of John Butt), London: Methuen and Co., Ltd., 1940, p. 283 (italics are mine). All references to line numbers in the poem used in this article are according to this edition.

16   Albert G. A. Balz, Dualism in Cartesian Psychology and Epistemology (In Studies in the History of Ideas, ed. by the Department of Philosophy of Columbia University, New York: Columbia University Press, 1925, p. 87). A general acknowledgment of the universality of Cartesianism may be found in The Philosophy of the Enlightenment by Ernst Cassirer, translated by Fritz C. A. Koelln and James P. Pettegrove, Princeton: Princeton University Press, 1951, where the statement is made (p. 28) that "after the middle of the seventeenth century the Cartesian spirit permeates all fields of knowledge until it dominates not only philosophy, but also literature, morals, political science, and sociology, asserting itself even in the realm of theology to which it imparted a new form."

17   A. C. Guthkelch and David Nichol Smith (eds.), A Tale of a Tub, Oxford: Oxford University Press, 1920, p. 174.

18   Root, op. cit., p. 101.

19   Professor Tillotson (op. cit., p. 319) notices the withdrawal of a couplet following line 258 in his text in editions subsequent to that of 1720, probably as the result of a contemporary citation of it as evidence of Pope's prurience.

20   The passage opens with the line: "How happy is the blameless Vestal's lot!" (l. 207). In the first edition a question mark appears where in subsequent editions an exclamation point is used. Possibly this may be attributed not so much to a printer's error as to the failure of our punctuation system to supply a mark which would be ambiguous enough to include both.

21   There are two couplets, one early and one late in the poem, in which the speaker may be either the poet commenting on the heroine or the heroine commenting on herself objectively. The early one is this:

> In vain lost Eloisa weeps and prays,
> Her heart still dictates, and her hand obeys.   (ll. 15-16)

The later one is this:

> See in her Cell sad Eloisa spread,
> Propt on some tomb, a neighbour of the dead!
>
> (ll. 303-304)

The context of the second couplet seems more certainly to indicate Eloisa as speaking of herself. In discussing the "ideal" English Pindaric ode, Robert Shafer says: "The writer of such a poem should speak in his own person, not dramatically, or in a representative way." (The English Ode to 1660, Princeton: Princeton University Press, 1918, p. 26.)

22   John Sheffield, An Essay on Poetry, 1682; the text quoted is that of his Works of 1740, lines 119-120.

23   Inis Coon, The Influence of Ovid's Heroides on English Literature, 1930, an unpublished thesis at the University of Colorado, p. 82.

24 Sir William Molesworth (ed.), The English Works of
    Thomas Hobbes, Elements of Philosophy, London, 1839,
    I, 401 (Pt. IV, ch. 25, sec. 9).

25 Line 324 in all editions to 1736 referred to "the" soul of
    Eloisa. Later editions are more particular in substituting
    "my." Professor Tillotson (op. cit., p. 294) says: "This
    would seem a compositor's error of dittography inadver-
    tently retained in later texts, but in view of the similar
    variant at Rape of the Lock, i, 58, it must be a deliberate
    correction in the interests of theology."

26 Cleanth Brooks, "The Case of Miss Arabella Fermor," in
    The Well Wrought Urn, New York: Reynal and Hitchcock,
    1947.

VIRTUE AND PASSION:
THE DIALECTIC OF ELOISA TO ABELARD

Brendan O Hehir

There seems to be much to commend the familiar critical
strategy which has dealt with Pope's Eloisa to Abelard by applying to it the canons of Romantic appreciation. That strategy,
congenial to critics of such opposite personal taste as Byron
and Elwin, and illustrated in our time by John Butt in his essay
on "The Inspiration of Pope's Poetry,"[1] finds little trouble in
justifying itself by the text of the poem. Still more recently,
in a study of the poem conducted deliberately outside the Romantic framework, Henry Pettit nevertheless calls it "the purest form of lyric," in which "pathetic fallacy is supreme and
sentiment surges for expression."[2]

We do not have far to seek for specific instances of the sort
of pathetic fallacy Pettit no doubt has in mind. Butt, as a matter of fact, calls attention to two of them: "the shrines tremble
as Eloisa takes the veil; and later in that poem, when Eloisa
kneels before the altar in religious ecstasy . . . 'Altars blaze,
and Angels tremble round.' " The word tremble, Butt says,
"in each of these instances . . . is used to signify the uncon-
trollable reaction to some more than human activity, an essentially romantic effect." As each of these instances, we may be
sure, would be classed by Ruskin as pathetic fallacy, we may
safely forego independent attempts to define that emotionally-
charged term. Its emotional charge, however, may be illustrated by reference to the second phrase of Pettit's statement:
"sentiment surges for expression." I do not wish to be accused
of reading what was not written, but these critics seem to imply
at least that Pope was not entirely in control of his material.
Butt says explicitly that the effect of the passages he cites is
"most readily pleasing to the unsophisticated reader"; Pettit,
by using Ruskin's term, perhaps carries overtones of Ruskin's

Reprinted from Texas Studies in Literature and Language, Vol. 2 (1960),
pp. 219-232, with corrections by the author, by permission of author
and publisher.

judgment on the users of pathetic fallacy, the second order of poets, "men who feel strongly, think weakly, and see untruly." Whatever the cause, neither writer looks very closely at Pope's actual handling of "pathetic fallacy" in his poem. Let us therefore put assumptions aside, and proceed to examine a few of the more obvious occurrences.

The first of Butt's two instances occurs in a passage of which we may reproduce six lines:

> Canst thou forget what tears that moment fell,
> When, warm in youth, I bade the world farewell?
> As with cold lips I kiss'd the sacred veil,
> The shrines all trembled, and the lamps grew pale:
> Heav'n scarce believ'd the conquest is survey'd,
> And Saints with wonder heard the vows I made.

$$(109-114)[3]$$

Here, if anywhere, Pope's eye seems to be in a fine frenzy rolling from earth to heaven. Overmastered by violent emotion, the poet (or Eloisa) receives and records a highly distorted impression of external things — if we assume that the shrines did not literally tremble, nor the light of the lamps diminish sufficiently to be noticed by a casual bystander. The line, we may say, is a poetic heightening of "facts" to represent the effect on a woman's overwrought imagination of the realization of the enormity of her reluctant vows. But if we reconsider that the statement is phrased in the first person, and rule out the testimony of the bystander, we find much less reason to doubt the literal accuracy of Eloisa's words. Her vision is private and personal, but completely objective: it need only be remembered that her eyes are filled with tears, and her "taking the veil" is a gesture at once as literal as ritually significant. The moment the shadowing cloth falls before her eyes the lights quite naturally appear to dim and the outlines of the shrines to waver. None of the more "poetic" value of the scene is lost by recognizing that Eloisa is reporting accurately and naturalistically what in fact she saw.

For the second of Butt's examples we may also reproduce six lines:

> When from the Censer clouds of fragrance roll,
> And swelling organs lift the rising soul;
> One thought of thee puts all the pomp to flight,
> Priests, Tapers, Temples, swim before my sight;
> In seas of flame my plunging soul is drown'd,
> While Altars blaze, and Angels tremble round.

(271-276)

Here the crux is in the last line, but again it is evident that eyes suddenly filled with tears (to say nothing of the clouds of incense) account not only for the "Priests, Tapers, Temples" swimming before Eloisa's sight, but also for the smear of candle-blaze she sees across the marble altars, and the apparent trembling of the sculptured angels stationed around them. The "seas of flame" in the preceding line are products of the same optical illusion. Pope's wit provides him with all the melodramatic effects of pathetic fallacy without committing him to stating the absurd. (Of course the contrast of the rising and the plunging soul belongs to a different level of discourse that must be considered separately.)

Before trying to draw any conclusions from the evident fact that a natural reason underlies the "pathetic fallacy" in these two admittedly related instances, we should probably examine an instance or two selected independently from a more remote part of the poem. A passage of twelve lines just after the opening establishes the dramatic theme and setting in which, through the remainder of the poem, Eloisa struggles before achieving a resolution:

> Relentless walls! whose darksom round contains
> Repentant sighs, and voluntary pains:
> Ye rugged rocks! which holy knees have worn;
> Ye grots and caverns shagg'd with horrid thorn!
> Shrines! where their vigils pale-ey'd virgins keep,
> And pitying saints, whose statues learn to weep!
> Tho' cold like you, unmov'd, and silent grown,
> I have not yet forgot my self to stone.
> All is not Heav'n's while Abelard has part,
> Still rebel nature holds out half my heart;

Nor pray'rs nor fasts its stubborn pulse restrain,
Nor tears, for ages, taught to flow in vain.   (17-28)

Technically, this passage contains two examples of pathetic
fallacy. The relentlessness of the walls in the first line, however, is a relatively colorless attribute, a commonplace metaphoric extension of the adjective's range. The weeping statues,
on the other hand, present a strange and exorbitant image, the
secret rationale of which was exposed, however, as long ago
as 1794 by Gilbert Wakefield. "A puerile conceit," he called it,
"from the dew, which runs down stones and metals in damp
weather."[4] Puerile or not, this image, like those examined
previously, has a natural explanation. Wakefield, of course,
had not the use of Ruskin's melophonious terminology, but his
use of the word "conceit" may serve for modern tastes to turn
attention to seventeenth-century rather than to nineteenth-century analogs of the poem. Be that as it may, Pope in fact borrowed the conceit from Dryden's rendering of a line in the first
<u>Georgic</u>: "The weeping statues did the wars foretell / And holy
sweat from brazen idols fell." (647-48) The fact that this "pathetic fallacy" is a literary borrowing might in itself be pre-
sumptive evidence that Pope was not simply drunk with emotion
in writing these lines, but I think that we cannot doubt it was
the conceited wit of Dryden's verses that attracted Pope, nor
that the conceit was transparent to him.[5] The inference I wish
to draw is that our discovery of a natural basis for each of the
"pathetic fallacies" we have examined is not adventitious, that
Pope was perfectly well aware of what he was doing and as
much in control of his material as in any poem he had written
up to that time of his life (he had already published the revised
<u>Rape of the Lock</u>), and that the Ruskinian approach can only
serve to becloud our reading of the poem.
    It may still be objected that the poem is "hectic, feverish,
emotive," compared to most of Pope, but is there not the possibility of critical error, again based on preconceptions, in
this judgment? If we seek for a more descriptive and less eval-
uative means of discriminating <u>Eloisa to Abelard</u> from the remainder of Pope's poems we will notice that, with one nonde-
cisive exception,[6] it is his only major poem written in the first
person in which the speaker is not to be labeled as, in some
way, Alexander Pope the Poet. The question, therefore, we

are obliged to ask of the poem is whether the fever and the emotion belong to the poet or to the dramatic character of Eloisa. More than one reader has confused Gulliver with Swift.

If we return now to the contrast in our second specimen passage of the rising and the plunging soul (272; 275) it will be possible to extend our examination of Pope's use of language in Eloisa to Abelard. To paraphrase quite baldly Eloisa's statement in the lines under discussion, she tells us that she experiences some sort of spiritual exaltation from the incense and music of a religious service, but that one thought of Abelard obliterates the effect of the ritual, and makes her soul "plunge." The rising or the plunging of a soul is, however, a conventional way of talking about its salvation or damnation. Pope does not speak here of heaven or hell, but in a religious context he does have Eloisa say "In seas of flame my plunging soul is drown'd." Interpreted literally, that line could be read only as a conventional description of a soul in hell. But of course it is not to be read literally, although we have seen that the "seas of flame" do have a sort of literal reference to a visual experience. Yet in view of the calculated nature of the visual effects Pope has employed in this entire passage it seems more reasonable to assume that in the wording of this line, and in the contrast with the "rising soul" of line 272, he intends to convey a suggestion of the ultimate alternatives Eloisa is facing, than that he has lost control over his medium.

In his Advertisement to the poem Pope calls Eloisa's story a struggle of nature against grace, virtue against passion; and that struggle is, as Geoffrey Tillotson has said, "flushed . . . with Pope's own Roman Catholic devotion and the poetry of the mystics."[7] For Eloisa herself, moreover, the conflict is ineluctably confined to her heart and mind, the realm of devotion and mysticism, since, in the words of R. K. Root, "her way of life, so far as the vita activa is concerned, is irrevocably settled and rigorously ordered."[8] The world of the poem is the world of the convent in which Eloisa is a professed nun, and Eloisa's mental fight is carried out entirely within the confines of the convent, its furnishings, its rituals, and its religious significance. Yet paradoxically, within the purely contemplative world of the poem Eloisa finds herself at the apex of a traditional domestic triangle. By virtue of her vows, as we are reminded several times, Christ is her Mystical Spouse; Abelard,

of course, is the Adulterous Lover, though his physical mis-
fortune makes his role equally mystical. Another unusual feature of this triangle is the fact, as Eloisa several times informs
us, that she has some difficulty distinguishing between the ri-
vals. Upon first meeting Abelard she took him for "some ema-
nation of th'all-beauteous Mind" (62); within her heart "mix'd
with God's, his lov'd Idea lies" (12); his image "steals between
my God and me." (268) This confused rivalry is resolved in the
dialectic that forms the body of the poem, but further examination of Pope's verbal tactics, in the light of our awareness of
the existence of that rivalry, is a necessary antecedent to the
elucidation of that dialectic.

At this point a slight ambiguity in the wording of line 140
may profitably engage our attention. Eloisa recalls the found-
ing of her nunnery by Abelard ("You rais'd these hallow'd
walls," [133]) and concludes by remarking that its "plain roofs"
are "only vocal with the Maker's praise." (140) Tillotson glosses the word "Maker" as a reference to God -- what we should
expect -- but he also notes that Wakefield understood the reference as to Abelard. The ambiguity may have been inadvertent
on Pope's part, but it is not infelicitous, in view of Eloisa's
difficulties in making the same distinction. If we are willing to
go so far as to assume that such effects are conscious on Pope's
part, analogous to his manipulation of the pathetic fallacy conceits, we may gain confidence that in many similar instances
within the poem, of lack of specific reference, that the confusion is deliberately designed to reflect or imitate the confusion
in Eloisa's mind. Let us at any rate now consider a passage of
some length, and of perhaps inextricable rhetorical confusion:

> Let wealth, let honour, wait the wedded dame,
> August her deed, and sacred be her fame;
> Before true passion all those views remove,
> Fame, wealth, and honour! what are you to Love?
> The jealous God, when we profane his fires,
> Those restless passions in revenge inspires;
> And bids them make mistaken mortals groan,
> Who seek in love for aught but love alone.
> Should at my feet the world's great master fall,
> Himself, his throne, his world, I'd scorn 'em all:

> Not Caesar's empress would I deign to prove;
> No, make me mistress to the man I love.   (77-78)

The rhetorical confusion in fact envelops the entire verse-paragraph (73-98) from which these lines are excerpted. Eloisa's
use of tense in the opening line ("How oft . . . have I said")
seems to place her anti-matrimonial beliefs in the past, whereas at the close of the paragraph she is apparently of the same
persuasion still: "This sure is bliss . . . / And once the lot
of Abelard and me." (97-98) In this farrago we find the rather
unconventional equation of "true passion" with "Love" and un-
weddedness; "restless passions" with "fame, wealth, and
honour" and the wedded state — which nonetheless is characterized as "august" and "sacred." Further, the "restless passions"
(presumably for "fame, wealth, and honour") are inspired by
the "jealous God" (whom we are constrained to identify as
"Love") in revenge for profaning his fires (i. e. , presumably
for rejecting illicit love!). Lastly, Eloisa resolutely rejects
a purely \supposititious marriage-offer from the "world's great
master," whom we can with fair probability take to be the
"Caesar" of line 87. Such at least would be the minimal interpretation of these lines upon which most readers would probably
be able to agree.

Now, although it is no doubt a sound principle that in the
reading of poetry in general, and that of Pope in particular, the
literate plain reader's sense of the words, when determinable,
is to be preferred to any explication requiring learned ingenuity,
it remains true that the reading of these lines is far from
straightforward, and each interpretation suggested above depends upon a judgment of the greatest probability in each case.
There is no intent, however, to overthrow the "most probable"
interpretation as the fundamentally correct interpretation in
pointing out that that interpretation, alone, is intrinsically irrelevant to Eloisa's problems or to the discourse of the rest
of the poem. Extrinsically, the lines may illustrate the disordered state of Eloisa's reason, but intrinsically what do they
mean? No "wedded dame" has hitherto been introduced into the
drama; the only "restless passions" in evidence anywhere in
the poem are Eloisa's own; and if the importunings of a mar-
riage-bent emperor had ever been one of her serious problems
we have no other evidence for it. But if we are willing to make

the act of faith again that Pope did not share Eloisa's confusion of mind we can perhaps find the frame of reference in which these wild statements cohere.

The "jealous God" of line 81 is of course, as we have said, the "Love" of line 80 — that is, roughly speaking, the pagan deity known as Amor, Eros, or Cupid. But the identification is not specifically made, and at all its seven other occurrences in the poem, the word "God" refers exclusively to the Christian God whose nominal servant Eloisa is. And the latter God not only is Love, and a jealous God, but is prone to the very sort of behavior mentioned by Eloisa: "They have provoked me to jealousy . . . and I will move them to jealousy." (Deuteronomy xxxii. 21)[9] Insofar as the muddled tenses direct us to read this passage as referring to a period prior to the dramatic present, Eloisa's assumption that flouting the pagan God of Love would provoke restless passions proved to be an ironic prophecy of the restless passions she has now incurred in flouting the Christian God. And whomever Eloisa might have meant at one time by the "world's great master" whose marriage-offer she would disdain, she has since in fact accepted the marriage-offer of the world's great Master, albeit she is perhaps "the spouse of God in vain." (177) In taking the veil, however imperfect her motives, she had entered a marriage that allows no divorce. Still another tonal element of this passage derived from the unique requirement of celibacy attached to the type of marriage Eloisa has entered. Of these twelve lines, all but the last might have come unashamedly from the lips of the most irreproachable of nuns, one who had taken to heart St. Paul's rebuke that "she that is married careth for the things of the world, how she may please her husband." (I Corinthians vii. 34) Eloisa's words in fact, like her position in the convent, are equivocal.

That "happy state" of freedom to reject marriage proposals had of course come to an end in the brutal mutilation of Abelard, and the histrionic couplet in which Eloisa visualizes the event will also repay examination:

> Alas how chang'd! what sudden horrors rise!
> A naked Lover bound and bleeding lies!   (99-100)

The outcome of the attack was not alone to make impossible forever the continuance of the love affair between the two, but

also to precipitate Eloisa into the Convent of the Paraclete.
(How divided her feelings were upon that occasion of her reluctant marriage to Christ she confesses to Abelard a few lines
further on: "Not on the Cross my eyes were fix'd, but you."
[116]) But just as Eloisa's reports of the trembling Angels and
weeping statues have an objective basis in the furnishings of
the convent, so in all likelihood does this barbarous vision. Her
visualization of the attack on Abelard (which she did not witness)
is at the same time a lively representation of the horrid change
in her own life, the substitution for Abelard of a new naked lover, bound and bleeding in effigy upon the Cross. Since for
Eloisa the "lov'd Idea" of Abelard is inextricably intermingled
with the Idea of God, objects expressly designed to promote
pious meditation serve only to remind her of Abelard: the image
of the crucified Savior serves with special aptness to recall the
greatest calamity of her life. Pope, by avoiding specific reference here, as in the other passages we have looked at, leaves
open the avenue to recognition of the basis of Eloisa's confusion.
But our recognition of that basis is the product neither of imagination nor guesswork. We are told that the convent and its en-
vironment were designed to promote piety, (131-146) but that
for Eloisa they have failed their purpose: "no more these scenes
my meditation aid." (161) Much later the mechanics of that failure are clearly described:

> What scenes appear where-e'er I turn my view!
> The dear Ideas, where I fly, pursue,
> Rise in the grove, before the altar rise,
> Stain all my soul, and wanton in my eyes!
> I waste the Matin lamp in sighs for thee,
> Thy image steals between my God and me,
> Thy voice I seem in ev'ry hymn to hear,
> With ev'ry bead I drop too soft a tear.   (263-270)

Even the tears that Eloisa weeps are equivocal; though they
should be penitential tears — "taught to flow" — they remain "too
soft." Eloisa has not yet forgot herself to stone, so her tears
flow "in vain." Recognition at least of the fact that as Pope has
organized his poem, Eloisa's private cult of Abelard overlaps
and coincides at these points with her convent's official cult of
Christ, is a fundamental prerequisite to any attempt that hopes

to demonstrate successfully the dialectic of the poem. It is merely persistence of the critic in Eloisa's initial failure to see this partial identity of the opposite terms of her dilemma that results in a judgment that the dialectic of the poem embraces nothing "but the pattern of constant tossing to and fro and the recognition that only exhaustion (death) can bring it to an end — an end, not a solution."[10]

The drama of <u>Eloisa to Abelard</u> — the struggle of nature against grace, virtue against passion — takes the form of Eloisa's inability to reconcile with her spiritual duties as a nun her carnal memories of her former lover, Abelard. In her surges of passion the fact of Abelard's castration is at first overlooked, but as that fact (and others) comes to the foreground, an awareness of realities makes possible the ultimate resolution. As we have said, the dramatic setting and theme of the poem are established in an early passage already reproduced. (17-28) The setting is the Convent of the Paraclete, with its furnishings and rituals designed to promote the service of God, but serving for Eloisa chiefly to remind her of Abelard; the theme is Eloisa's thesis that "All is not Heav'n's while Abelard has part." (25)

Rebecca Price Parkin has formulated for the entire poem a "heat-light-life metaphorical group on the one hand and a cold-darkness-death group on the other."[11] In something like those terms we may recognize in the passage under discussion an emphasis upon the coldness and especially the stoniness of the convent setting. By a chiastic transposal of subject and adjunct Pope has even made the animate occupants of the convent seem less alive than the inanimate, attributing pity and tears to statues, the pale eyes of statues to immobile nuns, and in line 19 suggesting that "holy knees" are more adamantine than rocks. (The latter image is of course again based on a phenomenon observable at any much-frequented shrine, though Pope's Latinate syntax here makes it equally possible to read the line the other way around.) Though Eloisa has herself acquired the outward attributes of stone ("cold . . . unmov'd . . . silent"), she has not been able to submit to the final petrifaction she feels is required of her. So long as she continues to view her problem in this light rebel nature will continue to hold out half her heart, but it is essential for her nevertheless to subdue her "stubborn pulse." The reasons are at least two, the relative importance of which we may rank as we choose. One is the eschatological one, that her problem is not a mere abstract conflict between love and duty, but that her rejection of Christ will mean the damnation of her soul. The other is the practical one, that in any case she has no choice as between Abelard and Christ, for the former has been incapacitated as a lover.

It has been earlier noted that the image of the plunging soul drowned in seas of flame (275) hints at least at the peril of Eloisa's damnation, but explicit indications that she is aware of the possibility are by no means lacking. In recalling the joys of her liaison with Abelard, she also recalls her complacence at the time at the prospective consequence:

> Dim and remote the joys of saints I see,
> Nor envy them, that heav'n I lose for thee. (71-72)

Later she invites or dares Abelard to be the active agent of Hell: "Come, if thou dar'st, all charming as thou art . . . Assist the Fiends and tear me from my God!"(281-288) Finally, in imagining her death-scene, she offers a last chance for Abelard to damn her: "Suck my last breath, and catch my flying soul!" (324) Editors have noted that this line echoes Marlowe's Faustus xiii. 95 ("Her lips suck forth my soul; see where it flies!"), and perhaps it is unnecessary to emphasize that the echo is not erotic only.

Seclusion in the convent has not cured Eloisa of her passion, nor wrought the salvation of her soul. Unable to resolve her conflict, she comes eventually to regard death as the avenue to a resolution. Death itself cannot be the solution, however, for beyond death lies Hell or Heaven, and choice of one or the other is implicit in the problem. In fact that choice is her only real problem, for the alternatives she has constructed are otherwise illusory. Her choice lies not between Heaven (God) alone, and Hell with Abelard, but between Hell alone and Heaven with Abelard. Reunion with Abelard can come about only through reunion with her heavenly Spouse, because Abelard has already made his peace with God. Her obsession with the fact that Abelard first led her into sin blinds her for long to the fact that he is now on the side of the angels. She comes slowly and reluctantly to awareness of the truth — "Ev'n thou art cold — yet Eloisa loves" (260) -- but in the truth she finds at last the only resolution of her predicament.

VIRTUE AND PASSION: ELOISA TO ABELARD

The meaning of death for a nun, and therefore its potential
meaning for Eloisa, is set forth in the celebrated passage
(207 ff.) on the happiness of the blameless Vestal's lot. From
the description of the Vestal's death it becomes apparent that
the lifelong marriage of the nun to Christ is but a betrothal,
the consummation occurring only at death, which is the consummation:

> For her the Spouse prepares the bridal ring,
> For her white virgins Hymeneals sing;
> To sounds of heav'nly harps, she dies away,
> And melts in visions of eternal day.   (219-222)

Pettit's contention that here Eloisa merely "looks over her
shoulder in a lyric moment" implicitly denies any intrinsic
value to this display of the life and death of an exemplary nun,
but his belief that in the subsequent passage "she turns back
from looking over her shoulder better satisfied to have loved
and lost than never to have loved" seems to involve a misappre-
hension wider than simple failure to recognize the dialectic by
which at last Eloisa sublimates her passions. In contrast with
the heavenly nuptials of the blameless Vestal, Eloisa recollects
her own nocturnal sexual fantasies when "conscience sleeps":

> O curst, dear horrors of all-conscious night!
> How glowing guilt exalts the keen delight!
> Provoking Daemons all restraint remove,
> And stir within me ev'ry source of love.   (227-232)

Though Eloisa takes sensual delight in these visions, the words
"curst," "horrors," "guilt" and "Daemons" indicate that she is
something other than satisfied with their occurrence, and her
dreams end with the awareness not only that Abelard is out of
reach, but that he is moving toward heaven:

> Sudden you mount! you becken from the skies;
> Clouds interpose, waves roar, and winds arise.
> I shriek, start up, the same sad prospect find,
> And wake to all the griefs I left behind.   (245-248)

Admonition of this truth has occurred to Eloisa in her dreams, but not at once a waking realization of its meaning. From each subsequent intimation she recoils to an extreme, swinging back and forth from Virtue to Passion or from Abelard to God. But just as the extremes between which a pendulum swings are defined only by the length of the arc that separates them, so, as Eloisa's struggles deplete her energy, her postulated antitheses draw closer together to yield her finally the insight that in her death (stasis) she may be united both with Abelard and God.12

After her dream of Abelard's ascent Eloisa more coolly reflects that his castration has freed him from the undiminished ardor that continues to torment her. (249-262) In unconscious recognition of his present spiritual situation, she imagines his sexless state to be "Soft as the slumbers of a saint forgiv'n / And mild as opening gleams of promis'd heav'n." (255-256) Following the passage that ends with her soul plunged in seas of flame, (263-276) she pictures herself prostrate with repentance, but still challenges Abelard to snatch her from God (281-288).13 Without interval she recoils again, begging her lover to "fly me, fly me! far as Pole from Pole" (289) -- a suggestion quite redundant in view of the already great physical disjunction of the two. Now the resolution by death, implicit in the blameless Vestal's dying away, makes itself explicit as Eloisa hears a direct invitation from the spirit of a dead sister to join her in the calm of eternal sleep. (303-316) This second Vestal had been apparently less blameless than the first, her past having been not unlike Eloisa's present. But her career offers considerable hope for the latter: "Love's victim then, tho' now a sainted maid." (312) The tomb had resolved the dead nun's quandary, "for God, not man, absolves our frailties here." (316) Eloisa's response to the promise of forgiveness, in that realm where love and passion are no longer concealed or shameful, is instant and ardent (317-320) -- but once more she backslides. That particular formulation of the celestial solution to her problems does not mention Abelard, so she reverts to him again.

Her proposal is that Abelard be the priest who affords her the "last sad office" for the dying. But she has not yet learned how to synthesize Abelard with death and salvation, and an unregenerate motive betrays itself in her suggestion that he suck her last breath and catch her flying soul. But Virtue at once regains control, and the conjunction of Abelard, priesthood, and death-bed makes manifest the unity of the opposites she has been unable to reconcile. Abelard's absence is no longer a condition of her fidelity to God:

> Ah no — in sacred vestments may'st thou stand,
> The hallow'd taper trembling in thy hand,
> Present the Cross before my lifted eye,
> Teach me at once, and learn of me to die.   (325-328)

Since for Eloisa the struggle between Nature and Grace had been fought out in terms of a choice she was attempting to make between Abelard and Christ, her vision of Abelard as priest presenting to her the Cross of Christ is a revelation that with Christ both Nature and Grace, Passion and Virtue, are one. Death will effect for her a greater kindness than the quenching of the flames of earthly passion mutilation had effected for Abelard; it will in addition teach her the vanity of all worldly commitments. (311-336) No obstacles remain to the consummation of her marriage to Christ, and that consummation has also, paradoxically, a place for Abelard. But Eloisa no longer looks for a personal reunion in heaven with her earthly lover; the love to be experienced there is diffused and catholic, equally shared by all. When fate shall also have destroyed his fair frame, she prays, "From opening skies may streaming glories shine, / And Saints embrace thee with a love like mine." (341-342)

On earth, however, while Eloisa and Abelard achieve a sort of shadowy coitus in their legend (that will "graft my love immortal on thy fame," [344]) their dust may sinlessly mingle in a common grave in the chapel of the Convent of the Paraclete. But even in the grave their lifeless dust will commingle within sight of Christ's earthly presence at the "dreadful sacrifice" of the Mass, while <u>their</u> earthly presence will insert a note of humanity into the Divine solemnity:

> From the full quire when loud <u>Hosanna's</u> rise,
> And swell the pomp of dreadful sacrifice,
> Amid that scene, if some relenting eye
> Glance on the stone where our cold reliques lie,
> Devotion's self shall steal a thought from heav'n,
> One human tear shall drop, and be forgiv'n. (353-358)

By virtue of the dreadful sacrifice of the Atonement the sins of Abelard and Eloisa, like the "one human tear" of some sentimental worshipper, shall be forgiven, and they be made at one with God as with one another — Eloisa having at last forgot herself to the stone covering their "cold reliques." The confused identity of her "naked Lover bound and bleeding," at first impious, will have been sanctified. At a previous point in the poem Eloisa had recalled "that sad, that solemn day, / When victims at yon' altar's foot we lay," (107-108) but now by a willing yielding to her own dreadful sacrifice she can at last combine her love for Abelard with the consummation of her heavenly marriage — a consummation devoutly to be wished.

This present examination of Eloisa to Abelard cannot claim to involve a fundamental reappraisal of the poem's position either in the total corpus of Pope's work or in the body of English literature. Any study that pretended to a thorough revaluation of the work would need to cope with matters left here untouched -- the relationship between Pope's poem, for example, and John Hughes' 1714 version of Bayle's Letters of Abelard and Heloise, or the influence upon it of Crashaw and seventeenth-century devotional poetry in general. But if by recognizing here the deliberate and conscious nature of Pope's handling of hectic, emotive, and "romantic" language, we see the overwrought and hysterical Eloisa as the product of careful craftsmanship, less reason will appear to deny Pope credit for writing a poem imbued with the fundamental Christian irony that life must be lost to be gained. The ultimate victory of grace does not destroy nature, and virtue triumphant transfigures passion. Eloisa fights throughout the poem both not to recognize this truth and, ironically, to recognize it. Her defeat is victory.

What does require reappraisal, it seems to me, is the frame of mind that criticism has been bringing to this poem. Whether because, sixty years after Pope's death, a body of English poetry came to be written, composed on principles other than his but in language superficially resembling that of "Eloisa," or because of a posited unbalancing effect on Pope of his supposed infatuation with Lady Mary Wortley Montagu, it has been too casually assumed that the language of the poem is uncontrolled, its movement chaotic and undisciplined. Whatever construction we put upon Pope's remarks to Martha Blount about the composition of this poem ("The Epistle of Eloise grows

324

warm, and begins to have some Breathings of the Heart in it, which may make posterity think I was in love")[14] it is at least obvious that its effects are calculated, its confusion not without a plan.

NOTES

1 <u>Essays on the Eighteenth Century</u> presented to David Nichol <u>Smith</u> (Oxford, 1945), pp. 65-79.

2 "Pope's <u>Eloisa to Abelard</u>: an Interpretation," University of Colorado Studies, Series in Language and Literature, No. 4 (Boulder, 1953), pp. 67-74.

3 All quotations from the poem are from the Twickenham Edition, <u>The Poems of Alexander Pope</u>, Vol. II: <u>The Rape of the Lock and Other Poems</u>, ed. Geoffrey Tillotson (London, 1940), pp. 299-327. In the reset 3rd ed. of this volume (1962), the poem appears on pp. 318-349.

4 Cited by Tillotson, p. 300 (3rd ed. , p. 320).

5 Pope had but to compare Dryden's lines with Vergil's original: "Et maestum illacrimat templis ebur, aeraque sudant" (480) to note the degree to which the translator had pointed his source by the quasi-personification of <u>ebur</u> and <u>aera</u> to "statues" and "idols."

6 The exception is the epistle of <u>Sappho to Phaon</u>, a case parallel to <u>Eloisa to Abelard,</u> and also much more neatly a direct translation (of Ovid, Heroides xv).

7 Pope himself has called attention to a borrowing from Crashaw, (line 212) Warton to other influence from the same source. The present writer senses possible derivations from Southwell (esp. "Synnes Heavy Loade"), but thinks it inadvisable to press the likelihood.

8 <u>The Poetical Career of Alexander Pope</u> (Princeton, 1941), p. 100.

9 Cf. I John iv. 8, 16 (God is love); Deut. vi. 5, 15 (jealous God); Romans x. 19 (God provokes to jealousy).

10 Rebecca Price Parkin, <u>The Poetic Workmanship of</u>

Alexander Pope (Minneapolis, 1955), p. 73.

11 Ibid. , p. 101.

12 Cf. G. Wilson Knight, "The Vital Flame," The Burning
    Oracle (New York, 1939), p. 155. "Abelard, Christ, Death,
    each is all at the last, confusedly, mystically." (Reprinted
    in Laureate of Peace: on the Genius of Alexander Pope
    [London, 1954], p. 39.)

13 This challenge need by no means be read as an unequivocal
    wish on Eloisa's part to recapture the sinful past — there
    is something of mockery in her allusions to Abelard's
    cherished Schoolman's arts: "Come, if thou dar'st, all
    charming as thou art! / Oppose thyself to heav'n; dispute
    my heart." (281-282; italics mine)

14 Letter tentatively dated March 1716, in The Correspond-
    ence of Alexander Pope, ed. George Sherburn (Oxford,
    1956), I, 338.

III. POEMS PUBLISHED IN THE <u>WORKS</u> OF 1735

DOCTRINAL TO AN AGE: NOTES
TOWARDS A REVALUATION OF POPE'S ESSAY ON MAN

J. M. Cameron

> They support Pope, I see, in the Quarterly. Let
> them continue to do so: it is a Sin and a Shame, and
> a damnation to think that Pope!! should require it —
> but he does. Those miserable mountebanks of the day,
> the poets, disgrace themselves and deny God, in
> running down Pope, the most faultless of Poets, and
> almost of men.

BYRON.

The Essay on Man is a poem doctrinal to an age and a society if not to a nation. It is perhaps the most interesting example in English of a philosophical poem; and as such it has to
be considered in any discussion of the relation between poetic
form and intellectual content. Are we to discuss it as we should
an unornamented philosophical essay, as we should discuss,
say, Locke's Essay or Berkeley's Principles? It would plainly
be ridiculous so to discuss Lucretius. The De Rerum Natura
is a deeply moving poem for those who altogether reject its
philosophy and find the argument abstracted from the poem
shoddy. Are we to place it rather with Paradise Lost and with
The Prelude, as a work of the imagination which touches on
philosophical themes but of which it would not be sensible to
demand that it should exhibit logical consistency in a high degree? There is a respectable critical tradition against so placing this or any other of Pope's works. Arnold is the most distinguished representative of this tradition,[1] but it would not be
an exaggeration to say that, at least until fairly recently, most

Reprinted from The Dublin Review, Vol. 225 (1951), pp. 54-67, with
corrections by the author, by permission of author and publisher. This
article has also appeared in J. M. Cameron, The Night Battle, Burns &
Oates, Burns & Oates: London, 1962 and Helicon Press: Baltimore,
1962, pp. 150-168, and is reprinted by permission of the publishers.

English critics later than the Augustan age would have said that to apply the word poetry simultaneously to the work of Pope, and to the work of Shakespeare or Milton or Wordsworth, was almost to equivocate. Agreement with such an assertion would seem to throw us back upon the view that the Essay must be judged as rhymed philosophy. Judged in this way, it is not a remarkable piece of philosophy. And yet, after an attentive reading of the Essay, it is hard to say without hesitations and involuntary backward glances that the experience has been simply that of reading a poor philosophical essay embellished with rhymes and other ornaments. It is also true that the experience does not seem much to resemble the reading of Paradise Lost or of The Prelude. It is possible to argue that every poem is such that it differs in kind from every other poem and that it would therefore be unreasonable to approach An Essay on Man with expectations prompted by some other poem; but even if we agree that in some sense every poem is sui generis, it remains true that some have urged that the word poem cannot be used of the Essay except in the most trivial of its meanings. The publication of Mr. Maynard Mack's new edition of An Essay on Man in the Twickenham Edition[2] seems to offer an occasion for a reconsideration of the poem and of some of the critical issues thereby revealed.

If we examine Pope's own expressed intentions we find that he saw the Essay as "forming a temperate yet not inconsistent, and a short but not imperfect system of Ethics." He continues: "This I might have done in prose; but I chose verse, and even rhyme, for two reasons. The one will appear obvious; that principles, maxims, or precepts so written, both strike the reader more strongly at first, and are more easily retained by him afterwards: The other may seem odd, but is true, I found I could express them more shortly this way than in prose itself; and nothing is more certain, than that much of the force as well as grace of arguments or instructions, depends on their conciseness."[3]

This would seem to suggest that his principal intention was to exhibit a system of ethics and that its being cast in poetic form was a matter of convenience, much as we more readily remember the lengths of the months by reciting to ourselves, "Thirty days hath September. . . ." That this was what Pope thought himself to be doing does not tell us that this was what he did. Only from an examination of the poem itself can we decide upon this question. There is evidence that his attitude to the poem was somewhat less decided and more ambiguous than the words quoted above would suggest. When, partly through the influence of the Swiss philosopher Crousaz, the Essay began to acquire an evil reputation among the orthodox, Warburton strove to vindicate the orthodoxy of Pope's doctrine in a series of articles in The Republick of Letters. Pope was immensely gratified, and wrote that "you have made my system as clear as I ought to have done, and could not. It is indeed the same system as mine, but illustrated with a ray of your own, as they say our natural body is the same still when it is glorified. I am sure I like it better than I did before . . . I know I meant just what you explain; but I did not explain my own meaning so well as you. You understand me as well as I do myself; but you express me better than I could express myself."[4] Even if we allow for an excess of politeness, these admissions surely reveal a radical uncertainty over what exactly he was driving at in the Essay.

Pope's method of composing the Essay, so far as we can establish it,[5] supports the view that we are concerned with philosophy versified. He seems often to have prepared prose statements of arguments later to be turned into verse; and even though there is no longer any very good reason to take seriously the legend that in writing the Essay Pope simply cast into verse a prose argument supplied by Bolingbroke, it may be that the argument of the greater part of the Essay was first set down in prose. This does not mean that the structure of the Essay or of any one Epistle is a prose structure the sequence of which is determined by the development of a continuous argument. The units of which the poem is composed are, as Mr. Sherburn has shown, verse paragraphs, and it is arguable that the order of these paragraphs is up to a point arbitrary.[6] This Johnson perceived. "Almost every poem, consisting of precepts, is so far arbitrary and unmethodical, that many of the paragraphs may change places with no apparent inconvenience; for of two or more positions, depending upon some remote and general principle, there is seldom any cogent reason why one should precede the other."[7] Johnson appears to have thought that this was compatible with a sort of philosophical consistency, and so it may be; but the relevant comparison is with the philosophers

331

of Pope's own day, and it is hard to think of any contemporary
work of the first rank of which this would hold good — though it
might well be thought to hold good of the work of Shaftesbury or
Bolingbroke. In any case, Johnson, in rejecting as improbable
the story that Pope had put into verse a systematic argument
constructed by Bolingbroke, did so on the ground that "the Essay plainly appears the fabrick of a poet: what Bolingbroke supplied could be only the first principles; the order, illustrations,
and embellishments must all be Pope's."[8]

It would scarcely be worth while showing that, as philosophy,
the Essay is an unimpressive performance, unless one had some
further purpose in view.[9] But the inadequacies of the poem considered from this standpoint may bring out, by pointing to what
Pope has certainly not achieved, those characteristics of the
poem which may support a claim to another kind of achievement.
Two illustrations of what can be taken as incoherences of argument may be offered.

Epistle I is concerned to show that man is necessarily ignorant in two respects. In the first place, the cosmos in its
vastness and complexity escapes for the most part man's scrutiny because man's senses and intellectual powers are insufficient for the task.

> But of this frame the bearings, and the ties,
> The strong connections, nice dependencies,
> Gradations just, has thy pervading soul
> Look'd thro'? or can a part contain the whole?

> (Epistle I, ll. 29-32)

In the second place, man is unable to understand the rationale
of the cosmos considered as a scheme of things which is, both
in its particular operations and as a totality, good. That such
is the rationale of the cosmos Pope holds, simply by deduction
from the nature of God as infinite wisdom and infinite goodness,
to be certain. But how this can be is beyond the power of man
to determine.

> When the proud steel shall know why Man restrains
> His fiery course, or drives him o'er the plains;
> When the dull Ox, why now he breaks the clod,

> Is now a victim, and now Ægypt's God;
> Then shall Man's pride and dulness comprehend
> His actions', passions', being's, use and end;
> Why doing, suff'ring, check'd, impell'd; and why
> This hour a slave, the next a deity.

> (Epistle I, ll. 61-68.)

Now, the rest of the poem is simply inconsistent with this contention that man's ignorance is such that he is incapable of knowing the complex harmonies of the cosmos and of finding a justification of those detailed cosmic arrangements which seem inconsistent with the postulated Divine goodness. In the remaining three Epistles we are offered a variety of arguments designed to show precisely how the constitution of human nature and the situation of man vis-à-vis the forces of nature and the brutes are arranged with a view to the good of the individual and the whole.

Such appears to be one inconsistency of the poem taken as a whole. A failure of detail may be illustrated. In Epistle III Pope employs the conception, derived from Aristotle and brought home forcibly to the educated public of Pope's day by Locke, that the best form of state is that possessing a "mixed constitution." This fits in admirably with the Heraclitean thesis, advanced by Pope in several connexions, that order springs from a tension of opposing forces.[10]

> . . . jarring int'rests of themselves create
> Th'according music of a well-mix'd State.

> (Epistle III, ll. 293, 294.)

But within a few lines he can follow this with:

> For Forms of Government let fools contest;
> Whate'er is best administer'd is best. . . .

> (Epistle III, ll. 303, 304.)

If, then, we expect of the poem a system of ethics and a cosmic scheme notable for their internal coherence and capable

of being derived from plausible first principles, we are likely
to be disappointed. One has, all the same, to remember that,
judged by such tests, there are few philosophical works — perhaps none — that would be thought by all philosophers to be of
merit. Thomas Hobbes's Leviathan is without doubt a philosophical classic; but the first six chapters do not appear to be coherent with or even relevant to the rest of the argument, which
seems to be governed, not by the mechanistic anthropology of
the first chapters, but by a quite different anthropology derived
from introspection, historical learning, and acquaintance with
men and affairs. It is curious, and not altogether irrelevant to
our discussion of Pope's Essay, that Professor Oakeshott has
attempted to account for the distinction of Hobbes's work in
terms that in my judgement amount to a defence of the Leviathan
as an organic whole analogous to a great poem, and not as primarily a work of ratiocination.[11] Again, no philosophical work
has in modern times had a wider and deeper influence than the
Tractatus Logico-Philosophicus of Wittgenstein; and yet its
author has been so obliging as to indicate in the closing pages
its necessary — as he thinks — incoherence. I do not myself
find Pope's argument at all points quite so ludicrously bad as
Professor Laird found it.[12] If we are to have an argument for
"cosmic Toryism," Pope's is a great deal better than that of
Soame Jenyns, who argues that "our difficulties [with regard
to the existence of misery in the universe] arise from our wrong
notions of Omnipotence, and forgetting how many difficulties it
has to contend with. It is obliged either to afflict Innocence,
or be the cause of Wickedness; it has plainly no other Option:
what then could infinite Wisdom, Justice, and Goodness do in
this situation more consistent with itself, than to call into being
Creatures formed with such depravity, in their dispositions,
as to induce many of them to act in such a manner as to render
themselves proper subjects for such necessary sufferings. . . ."[13]
Nevertheless, we may agree that if we are to classify Pope as
a philosopher he belongs rather with Jenyns than with Locke or
Berkeley. Bolingbroke's flashy genius seems greatly to have
impressed him. This does not argue philosophic acumen in
Pope; but the very qualities which made him respond with such
ardour to Bolingbroke, the moving, breathing, eloquent, and
fetching man[14] — philosophy, so Pope thought, in the concrete —
are qualities which provide a partial explanation of a greatness

quite other than philosophical in the Essay on Man.

"The great poet, in writing himself, writes his time." So Mr. Eliot in a famous essay. He continues: ". . . it was [Shakespeare's] business to express the greatest emotional intensity of his time, based on whatever his time happened to think. Poetry is not a substitute for philosophy or theology or religion . . . [its] function is not intellectual but emotional, it cannot be defined adequately in intellectual terms."[15] It would be easy wilfully to misunderstand Mr. Eliot. Has "a time" a "greatest emotional intensity"? Are not the greatest emotional intensities of any time precisely those which transcend the time and are human rather than peculiar to a single time and culture? Is not the "function" of poetry too simply and too narrowly defined? These and other objections can be raised to the way in which Mr. Eliot has formulated his thought. If we go behind the formulation we find it suggested (or so I think) that there is an important sense in which, to take examples, Arnold's Dover Beach rather than Locksley Hall, Mr. Eliot's The Family Reunion rather than The Lady's Not for Burning, express with some degree of success an "emotional intensity" of their periods. Their importance, the extent to which they do perform their poetic function, lies in an ordering of feeling to expression and of expression to feeling, an ordering which is such that feeling and expression make up an organic rather than a casual and contrived unity. The quality and depth of the reverberation provoked by a reading of them carry with them a suggestion of authenticity that scarcely needs a precautionary analysis of the poem itself.

Such an analysis may all the same be necessary. We know that every culture has certain limitations making it difficult or impossible for those within it to enjoy poems or pictures or buildings which were enjoyed by earlier cultures and which will be enjoyed again by those still to come. These limitations make the distinctive "taste" of a period. The limitations were narrow enough in Pope's own day. The power and charm of the Gothic and of "primitive" art were on the whole inaccessible to the men of the period[16] — even Shakespeare we may suppose to have been less accessible than he was to the early seventeenth century or than he is to us. Where there was an expressed liking for the Gothic it was on account of its supposed fantasticality and was, so to speak, a species of fooling,

resembling in this respect the liking of Mr. Betjeman and his
disciples for certain examples of Victorian architecture. What
we have to show, if we are to vindicate the claim that An Essay
on Man is one of our greatest poems, is that an analysis of the
poem suggests that the general failure of the nineteenth century
— a failure which still overshadows us, making our response to
the poetry of Pope an embarrassed one — adequately to respond
to the Essay is simply a failure of taste, an inability to move
outside the narrowness imposed upon our literary culture by
the romantic movement. The making of the analysis will, if it
does seem to indicate a failure of taste in us, itself be a means
of modifying our taste in such a way as to liberate us from our
present narrowness.[17]

Mr. Mack's penetrating analysis of the poem is designed to
show that it has been enormously undervalued; that in it Pope
does "write his time"; and that the achievement in terms of his
accomplished union of expression with feeling is great both as
a formal structure and as being for us the possible occasion of
a deep and rich experience. But before I comment on what Mr.
Mack has to say, I should like to show from one example that
it is perhaps unjust to deride the failure of the nineteenth century to respond with pleasure to Pope as being simply a failure
of taste, a failure unfortified by any serious weighing of the
problem.

> . . . The relation between the three poems [i.e. The
> Faerie Queen, Paradise Lost, and An Essay on Man]
> is, indeed, characteristic. Milton and Spenser could
> utter their deepest thoughts about man's position in
> the universe and his moral nature by aid of a symbol-
> ism intelligible to themselves and their readers. But
> where was Pope to turn for concrete symbols suffi-
> ciently expressive of his thought? The legends of the
> Bible claimed too little reverence. Even in the majes-
> tic poetry of Milton we are unpleasantly reminded of
> the fact that the mighty expounder of Puritan thought
> is consciously devising a conventional imagery. The
> old romance which had fed Spenser's imagination was
> too hopelessly dead to serve the purpose. It had left
> behind a wearisome spawn of so-called romances; it
> had been turned into mere ribaldry by Butler; and

> Pope wisely abandoned his cherished project of an
> epic poem, though feebler hands attempted the task.
> The 'Essay on Man' is substantially a versification
> of the most genuine creed of the time; of that Deism
> which took various shapes. . . . But the thought had
> generated no concrete imagery. It remained of neces-
> sity what it was at first — a mere bare skeleton of
> logic, never clothed upon by imaginative flesh and
> blood. As in Clarke's sermons, we have diagrams
> instead of pictures; a system of axioms, deductions,
> and corollaries instead of a rich mythology; a barren
> metaphysico-mathematical theory of the universe,
> which might satisfy the intellect, but remained hope-
> lessly frigid for the emotional nature.
>   Pope's poetry is thus forced to become didactic,
> and not only didactic, but ratiocinative. . . .18

It may be that in this passage Leslie Stephen betrays a
partial failure of taste, a failure which has led him to neglect
some of the most striking features of the poem. It is a gross
simplification of the Essay to describe it as a versification of
Deism; this is to neglect the traditional elements that are, as
we shall see, both prominent in the poem and necessary to its
full effect. (We are not quite sure that Stephen may not also
have in mind a curious theory of poetry not at all coherent with
his main position; for shortly after the passage quoted above we
find him writing: "A consistent pantheism or a consistent scepticism may be made the sources of profoundly impressive poetry. Each of them generates a deep and homogeneous sentiment
which may utter itself in song. Pope, as the mouthpiece of Spinoza or of Hobbes, might have written an impressive poem. . . .)19
All the same, his comment is a shrewd one. He sees that if the
Essay fails it will be through the lack of a symbolism that can
be used with effect. The mythological cosmos which earlier
poets had used with effect has at last given way before the attack
which has raged with continual fury from Copernicus to Newton.
Poor Pope has thus no materials to build with: he is reduced to
"a barren metaphysico-mathematical theory of the universe."
     Now, I believe there is a perfectly serious and valid point
lying behind and accounting for Stephen's comment. But as the
comment stands it seems to indicate simply a failure on his

part to read the poem with the minimum degree of attention necessary for the understanding of it. Who but Pope has drawn attention to the bankruptcy of Newtonian physics, not indeed as descriptive, but as explanatory?

> Superior beings, when of late they saw
> A mortal Man unfold all Nature's law,
> Admir'd such wisdom in an earthly shape,
> And shew'd a NEWTON as we show an Ape.
> Could he, whose rules the rapid Comet bind,
> Describe or fix one movement of his Mind?
> Who saw its fires here rise, and there descend,
> Explain his own beginning, or his end?
> Alas what wonder! Man's superior part
> Uncheck'd may rise, and climb from art to art:
> But when his own great work is but begun,
> What Reason weaves, by Passion is undone.

> (Epistle II, ll. 31-42.)

Pope here shows that "a . . . metaphysico-mathematical theory of the universe" does not "satisfy the intellect"; and he is quite consciously setting himself against a prevailing climate of thought.[20] If it should be argued that, although he may see the limitation of the Newtonian physics as an explanatory hypothesis, he has nevertheless no other cosmic imagery upon which to draw, and must, if he does so draw, present us with sterile symbols having no power to fructify in the imagination, the answer can only be an appeal to the poem itself.

> Far as Creation's ample range extends,
> The scale of sensual, mental pow'rs ascends:
> Mark how it mounts, to Man's imperial race,
> From the green myriads in the peopled grass:
> What modes of sight betwixt each wide extreme,
> The mole's dim curtain, and the lynx's beam:
> Of smell, the headlong lioness between,
> And hound sagacious on the tainted green:
> Of hearing, from the life that fills the flood,
> To that which warbles thro' the vernal wood:
> The spider's touch, how exquisitely fine!

> Feels at each thread and lives along the line:
> In the nice bee, what sense so subtly true
> From pois'nous herbs extract the healing dew:
> How Instinct varies in the grov'ling swine,
> Compar'd, half-reas'ning elephant, with thine:
> 'Twixt that, and Reason, what a nice barrier;
> For ever sep'rate, yet for ever near!

(Epistle I, ll. 207-224.)

This is surely no "barren metaphysico-mathematical theory of the universe." It is in fact a far more primitive cosmological scheme than Newton's and one imaginatively realized with exquisite grace in these lines. Here Pope shows a fine sense of the connexion that must exist for poetry between the experience of living as a concrete process,

> Wild Nature's vigor working at the root[21]

and the conceptual schemes designed to universalize it. The notion of a "scale of being" is here triumphantly shown to be still a valid poetic symbol.

The surface meaning of Stephen's criticism, then, is not altogether supported by an examination of the poem. But I believe there is a point Stephen is trying to make, though he makes it very badly or perhaps not at all. This point, if it can be shown to be valid, by no means disposes of the Essay as a poem having pretensions to greatness; but it does suggest that there is a serious failure within it, and one which has to be attributed to a certain superficiality in the theology and philosophy upon which Pope has perforce to rely.

At the beginning of Epistle I Pope summons us to

> Expatiate free o'er all this scene of Man;
> A mighty maze! but not without a plan. . . .

(Epistle I, ll. 5, 6.)

The choice of the word "maze" as the apt symbol of the complex of relations within which man stands is of immense importance in governing our response to the poem as a whole.

339

A maze is a grouping of paths through which it is difficult to find one's way. But every maze is constructed on a plan which can in the end, given patience and ingenuity, be grasped. No doubt many of us, once within a maze, would be unable to find our way to the centre and thence to the point at which we entered, without the help of someone familiar with the construction of the maze. But this failure is not a radical one, springing from the insufficiency of our nature and a mysteriousness intrinsic to mazes; it denotes merely a failure on our part to observe, and to reason correctly. Again, the complexity of a maze exists, as it were, at a single level. It resembles the complexity of a game of chess or of a logical construction. It presents us with a problem; whereas, to employ the now familiar distinction of M. Marcel, the poetic cosmos must, if it is to draw from us an adequate response, present itself as mysterious rather than problematical. The Essay does not at all points fail to give us a sense of mystery; but the attitude often in control is that suggested by the word "maze."[22]

Again, what weight in reading do we give to "but not without a plan"? I submit that we are compelled to give it a certain lightness, almost jauntiness, indicating some complacency in our contemplation of the maze. It presents us with a teasing problem, certainly: but we are the men to solve it. Thus, although Pope specifically denies that men can do more than apprehend the most general features of the maze, the attitude created in us by the couplet disposes us not to take too seriously his professions of modesty. In his exposition in Epistle I of "the great scale," "Nature's chain," Pope plays with the supposition -- not conceived to be a real possibility — that the cosmic order should break down in one of its parts.

> And if each system in gradation roll,
> Alike essential to th'amazing whole;
> The least confusion but in one, not all
> That system only, but the whole must fall.
> Let Earth unbalanc'd from her orbit fly,
> Planets and Suns run lawless thro' the sky,
> Let ruling Angels from their spheres be hurl'd,
> Being on being wreck'd, and world on world,
> Heav'n's whole foundations to their centre nod,

And Nature tremble to the throne of God. . . .

(Epistle I, ll. 247-256.)

There is a parallel passage in Hooker.

> . . . Now if nature should intermit her course, and
> leave altogether though it were but for a while the
> observation of her own laws; if those principal and
> mother elements of the world, whereof all things in
> this lower world are made, should lose the qualities
> which now they have; if the frame of that heavenly
> arch erected over our heads should loosen and dissolve
> itself; if celestial spheres should forget their wonted
> motions, and by irregular volubility turn themselves
> any way as it might happen; if the prince of the lights
> of heaven, which now as a giant doth run his unwearied
> course, should as it were through a languishing faint-
> ness begin to stand and to rest himself; if the moon
> should wander from her beaten way, the times and
> seasons of the year blend themselves by disordered
> and confused mixture, the winds breathe out their last
> gasp, the clouds yield no rain, the earth be defeated
> of heavenly influence, the fruits of the earth pine away
> as children at the withered breasts of their mother
> no longer able to yield them relief: what would be-
> come of man himself, whom these things now do all
> serve? See we not plainly that obedience of creatures
> unto the law of nature is the stay of the whole world?[23]

If we take into account the advantages and limitations of
the poetic and prose forms -- the <u>intention</u> in each case seems
much the same — it seems to me plain that we have to say in
the end, not only that Hooker comes off in a way that Pope
does not quite come off, but also that there breathes through
the language and the images employed a different attitude to
the possibility which is being entertained. There is in Hooker
a <u>serious</u> attitude to the possibility, the same attitude that is
to be found in the parallel passage on "degree" in <u>Troilus and
Cressida</u>,[24] an attitude which (we may conjecture) springs
from a deep feeling of being involved in the strains and conflicts

of a revolutionary period. The attitude of Pope remains that of the spectator. The entities ordered within the cosmos are sys- tems — the choice of the abstract word is significant; I am con- fident, in face of Mr. Mack's telling us that the "ruling Angels" hurled from their spheres represent "a belief by no means wholly displaced in the Augustan age,"[25] that the "ruling Angels" are very far advanced on the way to becoming theatrical prop- erties. Perhaps the notion was not so idle a speculation as it would have seemed to a nineteenth-century agnostic; but there is no conceivable connexion with the Newtonian cosmos, which Pope takes perfectly seriously as a description, though he properly rejects it as an explanation; they are, in short, orna- ments. This attitude to imagery is strictly incompatible with the seriousness of the theme. That it is Pope's conscious atti- tude, however much he may from time to time rise above it, cannot be doubted. He expresses in "The Design" prefixed to the Essay, the hope that "these Epistles in their progress . . . will be less dry, and more susceptible of poetical ornament."[26]

Such, then, are some of the considerations which seem to make it important, for the sake of the credit of the poem itself, not to advance the highest claims for the Essay on Man. This granted, it remains to suggest that the unfavourable judgements which have beset the poem from its birth are at least in part misconceived.

NOTES

1   See Geoffrey Tillotson, "Matthew Arnold and Eighteenth-century Poetry," in Essays on the Eighteenth Century. Presented to David Nichol Smith, 1945.

2   Alexander Pope, An Essay on Man, edited by Maynard Mack, The Twickenham Edition, Vol. III, i. Methuen, 30s. This is hereafter referred to as Mack.

3   "The Design," Mack, pp. 7, 8.

4   Cited in Samuel Johnson, "Life of Pope," in Lives of the Poets (World's Classics, 1906, Vol. II, pp. 289, 290).

5   See George Sherburn, "Pope at Work," in Essays on the Eighteenth Century.

6   One may well suspect that in later days the Essay on Man would have been more favourably regarded by critics if the poet had printed his verse paragraphs frankly as such — if, in the manner of Traherne's Centuries of Meditations or of Tennyson's In Memoriam, he had been content to leave his verse units as fragmentary reflections on philosophic ideas that are bound to have recurrent interest." Ibid. , p. 61.

7   Johnson, op. cit. , p. 243.

8   Ibid. , p. 287.

9   The task of showing how bad as philosophy the Essay may be considered has been performed, without much sympathy and with little awareness that this is not the only relevant question, by the late Professor Laird. See John Laird, "Pope's Essay on Man," in Philosophical Incursions into English Literature, 1946.

10 Cf.   Passions, like Elements, tho' born to fight,
         Yet, mix'd and soften'd, in his work unite:
         These 'tis enough to temper and employ;
         But what composes Man, can Man destroy?
         Suffice that Reason keep to Nature's road,
         Subject, compound them, follow her and God.
         Love, Hope, and Joy, fair pleasure's smiling train,
         Hate, Fear, and Grief, the family of pain;
         These mix'd with art, and to due bounds confin'd,
         Make and maintain the balance of the mind:
         The lights and shades, whose well accorded strife
         Gives all the strength and colour of our life.

                   (Epistle II, ll. 111-122.)

11 Cf. "The coherence of [Hobbes's] philosophy, the system of it, lies not in an architectonic structure, but in a single 'passionate thought' that pervades its parts. The system is not the plan or key of the labyrinth of the philosophy; it is, rather, a guiding clue, like the thread of Ariadne. It is like the music that gives meaning to the movement of dancers, or the law of evidence that gives coherence to the practice of a court. And the thread, the hidden thought,

is the continuous application of a doctrine about the nature of philosophy. Hobbes's philosophy is the world reflected in the mirror of the philosophic eye, each image the representation of a fresh object, but each determined by the character of the mirror itself." Thomas Hobbes, Leviathan, edited with an Introduction by Michael Oakeshott, n.d., p. xix.

12 Immanuel Kant greatly esteemed the Essay. Cf. Mack, p. xli.

13 Soame Jenyns, "A Free Inquiry into the Nature and Origin of Evil," in Miscellaneous Pieces in Prose and Verse, Third Edition, 1770, pp. 306, 307.

14 Cf. Come then, my Friend, my Genius, come along,
Oh master of the poet, and the song!
And while the Muse now stoops, or now ascends,
To Man's low passions, or their glorious ends,
Teach me, like thee, in various nature wise,
To fall with dignity, with temper rise;
Form'd by thy converse, happily to steer
From grave to gay, from lively to severe;
Correct with spirit, eloquent with ease,
Intent to reason, or polite to please.

(Epistle IV, ll. 373-382.)

15 T. S. Eliot, "Shakespeare and the Stoicism of Seneca," in Elizabethan Essays, 1934, p. 50.

16 Cf. ". . . the grand distinction between Grecian and Gothic architecture, the latter being fantastical, and for the most part founded neither in nature nor in reason, in necessity nor use, the appearance of which accounts for all the beauty, grace, and ornament of the other." George Berkeley, Alciphron or the Minute Philosopher, Third Dialogue, in The Works of George Berkeley Bishop of Cloyne, Vol. III, edited by T. E. Jessop, 1950, p. 127. This state of affairs changes later in the century.

17 Two works may be mentioned as having done much to modify our sensibility and make the poetry of Pope more

accessible to us: Edith Sitwell, Alexander Pope, 1930; and
Geoffrey Tillotson, On the Poetry of Pope, 1938. Mr. Wilson Knight's "The Vital Flame: An Essay on Pope," in his
The Burning Oracle, 1939, should also be noted, especially
in connexion with the Essay on Man.

18 Leslie Stephen, History of English Thought in the Eighteenth
Century, Second Edition, 1881, Vol. II, p. 951.

19 Ibid., p. 352.

20 Cf. Marjorie Hope Nicolson, Newton Demands the Muse,
Princeton, 1946, pp. 135, 136. Pope was by no means
alone in this. See R. F. Jones, "The Background of the
Attack on Science in the Age of Pope," in Pope and His
Contemporaries. Essays presented to George Sherburn,
1949.

21 Epistle II, l. 184.

22 I do not know if it has been noticed that there may be some
significance in the professions of K. in Kafka's The Trial
and The Castle. In the former K. is a bank official, in the
latter a surveyor. In both professions we have to do with
measurement, the criterion of judgement is quantitative.
The failure of K. in both instances springs from an inability
to see that the relationship between man and the heavenly
powers is not problematical but mysterious. A mystery
cannot be solved: it can only be embraced in humility and
love. See my "Theological Fragments," The Downside
Review, Spring 1949, pp. 144 ff.

23 Richard Hooker, Of the Laws of Ecclesiastical Polity,
Book I, Ch. iii, 2, in The Works of Mr. Richard Hooker,
arranged by John Keble, Seventh Edition, revised by
R. W. Church and F. Paget, 1888, Vol. I, pp. 207, 208.
Hooker is here adapting a passage from Arnobius (fl. c.
A.D. 305).

24 I, iii.

25 Mack, p. 46.

26 Ibid., p. 8.

POPE'S ESSAY ON MAN:
                    THE RHETORICAL STRUCTURE OF EPISTLE I

R. E. Hughes

"The ESSAY ON MAN," wrote Joseph Warton, "is as close
a piece of argument, admitting its principles, as perhaps can
be found in verse."[1] This remark gives the clue to the structure
of the first epistle of Pope's Essay, which looks to be a deliberate use of the traditional oratorical framework. The phrase
"admitting its principles" is one way of getting at the basically
rhetorical structure of the first epistle, for the second, third
and fourth epistles are all built on the foundation of the first;
furthermore, each succeeding epistle contains an argument
first stated in the opening epistle. Thus, the first epistle establishes an epistemology which Pope focuses in the last fourteen
lines as "Know thy own point," "Submit," "All Nature is but Art
unknow to thee," "One truth is clear, 'Whatever is, is RIGHT.'"
The content of the second epistle, which is more or less the
establishment of a psychology, depends on the first: "Know then
thyself" is the transition between the theory of limitation in
Epistle I and the psychology of Epistle II, opening the way to
Pope's analysis of self and his argument for Passion and Reason
as the mainsprings of action. The third epistle develops this
psychology, in terms of Instinct and Reason, into a social philosophy ("Reason or Instinct operates alike to the good of each
individual. Reason or Instinct operates also to Society"[2]): Finally, in the fourth epistle comes a disquisition on Happiness
based on morality ("God intends Happiness to be equal; and, to
be so, it must be social"[3]). Each succeeding argument is a
logical or apparently logical extension of the argument in the
first epistle.

Secondly, in each of the last three epistles a principle of
the first epistle is made one of the terms in the new argument.
In Epistle II, Pope leads into his plea for empirical examination of human nature (an examination which results in seeing

Reprinted from Modern Language Notes, Vol. 70 (1955), pp. 177-181, by
permission of author and publisher.

Reason and Passion as constituting that nature) with the mocking exhortation to rise above the inherent limitations of the human mind, to "teach Eternal Wisdom how to rule."[4] This ridicule of suprahuman or pretentious learning is a repetition of the theme of Pride in the first epistle, pride being the vice through which "All quit their sphere, and rush into the skies."[5]

In the third epistle, "Of the Nature and State of Man With Respect to Society," in arguing that the relationship of man to nature demands a society, Pope asks whether all creation is appointed to man's needs, and whether or not brute creation has some important place in the scale of creation. In this section, Pope's final lines, "While Man exclaims, 'See all things for my use!' / 'See man for mine!' replies a pamper'd goose,"[6] almost reproduce a similar idea of Epistle I: "Ask for what end the heav'nly bodies shine, / Earth for whose use? Pride answers, ' 'Tis for mine.'"[7]

In the fourth epistle, there is a series of these repetitions: first, the argument that there is an external law of nature which is not to be disrupted for particular instances, stated in ll. 123-130 of Epistle IV and ll. 141-146 of Epistle I; second, the argument that to act his appointed part in the scale of being is man's truest virtue, stated in ll. 193-204 of Epistle IV and ll. 281-283 of Epistle I; finally, the argument that happiness consists, not in transitory triumphs, but in conforming to providence, stated in ll. 277-284 of Epistle IV and ll. 285-288 of Epistle I.

The argument of the second, third and fourth epistles, then, depends to a great extent on the principles Pope sets up in the first epistle. Recalling Warton's "admitting its princi-ples," it is revealing to recognize that the first epistle is a rhetorical persuasion drawn up along the lines of the classical oration;[8] for here is the exordium, preparing the minds of the audience to favor orator and oration, ll. 1-16; narratio, state-ment of the problem in brief, ll. 17-42; probatio, the bulk of the argument, setting up the terms, advancing the proofs, ll. 43-112; refutatio, objections to the argument and answers to those objections, ll. 113-280; peroratio, summation of the argument, ll. 281-294. Pope allows himself no variation on this scheme; it seems to be a conscious use of the rhetorical form. To examine it more closely:

From the first lines of the Essay, Pope shows himself aware of his audience and, like an accomplished orator, vies

for their favor. He makes use of a technique he uses heavily
in the Epistle to Dr. Arbuthnot and the Epilogue to the Satires,
aligning himself with a reputable figure, and adds to this a
series of ethical arguments: the notion that his is a noble undertaking ("Awake, my St. John! leave all meaner things"), that
the author is an admirable stoic ("since Life can little more
supply, / Than just to look about us and to die"), that his aim
is moral ("shoot folly as it flies"), that he is urbane ("Laugh
where we must") but also conscientious ("be candid where we
can") and virtuous ("vindicate the ways of God to Man") -- these
are all admirably suited to the demands of the classical exordium.

In ll. 17-42, we do see a fair statement of the main argument, not only of this epistle, but of the whole poem, namely,
that the universe is a "Vast chain of being,"[9] and "Where, one
step broken, the great scale's destroy'd."[10] We have, in other
words, the narratio of rhetorical argument, extended through
the twenty-six lines of the epistle in terms of empirical investigation, just gradations of the scale of being, and of man's
place in that graduated scale.

The specific parts of this argument, the principles which
proceed from it, are next treated. In ll. 43-50 Pope presents
the argument that man has an established place in the chain of
creation. Although the argument here is based on a supposition
("Of Systems possible, if 'tis confest / That Wisdom infinite
must form the best . . .[11]) once Pope moves beyond his con-
ditional clause, he is prepared for the succeeding position: if
the system is the best possible, there must be coherence; coherence means degree; there must be, therefore, a place for
man in his own degree; man must, therefore, be suited to his
place in the chain. Having "proved" (probit) his first conclusion
by inference from a supposition, Pope proves the second
("Man's as perfect as he ought"[12]) in ll. 51-90 by analogy to
brute creation which, like man, is not intended to know at what
goal he is pointed, this being the prerogative of the Creator.

The third step in Pope's argument, quite logically, is that
man must be contented with his limited state in the chain. This
he develops in ll. 91-112, again by analogy, this time to "the
poor Indian" who is satisfied with his own creed, asking no
angel's wing, no seraph's fire. These three sections form a
complete coverage of the main principles: all that is left is to

apply them to the state of man himself, to man in society, to man in respect to happiness. In other words, Pope has completed the probatio of a classical oration.

There follows the refutatio, the objections to such an argument, and the answering of those objections. These occur in ll. 113-130 (questioning of Providence which determines the scale of being), in ll. 131-172 (the argument that man is the focal point of creation, and that all creation ought therefore be subject to him) and in ll. 173-206 (the argument that man ought to have more highly developed faculties than he actually does have). Pope refutes these objections by a general statement of his position in ll. 207-280 (there is a gradation observed everywhere in the universe, matter extends far above and far below mankind, each step in this gradation is relative to another and to the whole) and by point-blank responses to the objections. He answers the first objection: "Go, wiser thou! and in thy scale of sense / Weigh thy Opinion against Providence. . . . Destroy all creatures for thy sport or gust. . . . Re-judge his justice, be the GOD of GOD!"[13] The second objection, that the universe is poorly suited to man's happiness, is answered, "If plagues or earthquakes break not Heav'n's design, / Why then a Borgia or a Catiline?"[14] The third objection, that man's faculties are unnecessarily limited, is answered in a series of startling images in ll. 193-206.

The peroratio, the summation, occurs in the final lines, reaching a climax in the manifesto, "Whatever is, is RIGHT." Exordium, narratio, probatio, refutatio, peroratio — Pope has advanced his argument, established his principles, and is free to move into the rational argument of epistle two, three and four, which build on the foundation Pope has theoretically persuaded us to accept.[15]

NOTES

1   Joseph Warton, An Essay on the Genius and Writings of Pope (4th ed. ; London: Printed for J. Dodsley, 1782), II, 58.

2   An Essay on Man, ed. Maynard Mack (Twickenham ed. ; London: Methuen, 1950), III, i, 91.

3   Ibid. , p. 127.

4 Ibid., pp. 56-59.

5 Ibid., p. 30.

6 Ibid., pp. 95-96.

7 Ibid., p. 31.

8 Cf. Quintilian, Institutio Oratoria, III, viii.

9 Essay on Man, p. 44.

10 Ibid., p. 45.

11 Ibid., pp. 18-19.

12 Ibid., p. 22.

13 Ibid., pp. 29-30.

14 Ibid., pp. 34-35.

15 That this rhetorical form has been overlooked or minimized
is partly due to Pope's suggestion that he is not attempting
to persuade us to anything; indeed, that his is a subject not
liable to debate. He writes in "The Design" of the poem:
"The science of Human Nature is, like all other sciences,
reduced to a few clear points; There are not many certain
truths in this world. It is therefore in the Anatomy of the
Mind as in that of the Body; more good will accrue to mankind by attending to the large, open, and perceptible parts,
than by studying too much finer nerves and vessels, the
conformations and uses of which will for ever escape our
observation. The disputes are all upon these last, and, I
will venture to say, they have less sharpened the wits than
the hearts of men against each other, and have diminished
the practice, more than advanced the theory, of Morality"
(Ibid., p. 7). The claim that he is here entering on matters
which involve no dispute is itself a rhetorical device, much
like Antony's "I am no orator," or Polonius' "Madam, I
swear I use no art at all."

ALEXANDER POPE'S UNIVERSAL PRAYER

R. W. Rogers

Alexander Pope first published his Universal Prayer in June, 1738, at a time when the orthodoxy of his Essay on Man was being seriously challenged in France and had been questioned, somewhat more hesitantly, in England. William Warburton, in his commentary upon the Universal Prayer, argued that Pope had published the poem in order to "shew that his system was founded in free-will, and terminated in piety."[1] Warburton also implied that Pope had composed the lines after the Essay had been "unjustly suspected of a tendency towards Fate and Naturalism." We now know, however, that the Universal Prayer was first written many years before the Essay on Man was conceived. The heading of one interesting transcript of it declares that it had been "Written by Mr. Pope at 15 Years Old." A more credible statement concerning the origin of the poem occurs in a letter which Pope sent Ralph Allen in September [1736].

> I've sent you the Hymn, a little alterd, & enlargd
> in one necessary point of doctrine, viz.: ye third stan-
> za, which I think reconciles Freedom & Necessity; &
> is at least a Comment on some Verses in my Essay on
> Man, which have been mis-construed. Mr Hooke tran-
> scribed this Copy, without having one himself; as I
> believe no man has, since I gave it twenty years ago,
> in its first State, to the Duke of Shrewsbury.[2]

Pope's statement that the poem was in existence in 1716 carries some weight, particularly since he was giving expression to sentiments in letters written between 1711 and 1717 which share the tolerant freethinking that produced the Universal Prayer.[3]
    I do not know of any manuscripts of the Universal Prayer in Pope's autograph; but there are four transcripts which purport

Reprinted from Journal of English and Germanic Philology, Vol. 54 (1955), pp. 612-624, by permission of author and publisher.

to be based on authoritative manuscripts. Taken together these give us a reasonably reliable picture of the way in which the poem developed before Pope published it and of the way in which Pope sought to justify himself in the light of criticism of his Essay on Man. One transcript, made in 1740 by Lady Mary Wortley Montagu and now among the Harrowby MSS at Sandon Hall, suggests an early state. There are two important transcripts in the University of Chicago Library. One of these was made by Nathaniel Hooke and enclosed by Pope in the letter to Ralph Allen of September, 1736, already referred to; it can be definitely traced to Pope, and it reflects the state which the poem had achieved at a specific time. The second transcript in the University of Chicago Library is perhaps the most interesting of all, especially since its existence has not previously been remarked. The note at the head of it reads: "A Hymn to God Written by Mr. Pope at 15 Years Old." The transcript was, however, made in the nineteenth century — the watermark is "I & E S 1811" — but because it includes corrections which are indicated as Pope customarily indicated corrections in his own manuscripts, and because the whole fits into the pattern set up by the other transcripts, it seems to have genuine authority. There is still a fourth transcript, or rather a report of one, by Mrs. Hester Lynch Thrale who described a transcript of the poem sent to her by the Rev. Michael Lort and based on "the first Copy of Pope's Universal Prayer."[4]

I am printing below the text of Lady Mary's transcript (designated A). The transcript reported by Mrs. Thrale (B) and that drawn up in the nineteenth century (C) follow it. The fourth text (D) is that found in Nathaniel Hooke's transcript; and the last (E) is the text of the poem in the first printed version (the folio edition of 1738, Griffith 492). They are presented in what I believe to be the order in which the manuscripts upon which they are based were written.

Lady Mary's transcript (A) is probably derived from the earliest manuscript, though not necessarily the one which Pope may have given the Duke of Shrewsbury about 1716.[5] It contains the stanzas later suppressed; and it lacks the stanza on free will that Pope composed about 1736 — as well as all three of the concluding stanzas appearing in the published version of the poem. Moreover, several lines in it (for example, ll. 9, 13, 15) lack the finish of comparable lines in the other transcripts.

B, C, and D are closely related to one another; and, despite the head-notes of the transcribers of B and C, both of these probably reflect efforts by Pope to refurbish his poem in 1735-36. D, we know, represents the state of the poem when Pope sent it to Ralph Allen in September, 1736. B and C represent states of the poem prior to D; but the number of different readings in them rules out the possibility that they may be derived from the same manuscript. To determine which one represents the earlier manuscript is, nevertheless, difficult. In important ways C is similar to A: it has the suppressed stanzas, it lacks the stanza on free will; it has two of the three concluding stanzas (but a note in the margin declares that these were added to the original text).

B is a puzzling text. Twice the phrasing in B is closer to A than is the phrasing in C (ll. 40, 41); but it is more often closer to D than C is to D (for example, ll. 18, 27, 36) — if we disregard the corrections to be found in C. B has the important stanza on free will, which C does not; and it also has, Mrs. Thrale says, all the concluding stanzas, which means that it has the last stanza of the printed version, which does not appear in A, C, or D. The presence of these stanzas would seem to lead unquestionably to the conclusion that B reflects a later state in the development of the poem than C; but examination proves that this seemingly compelling evidence is suspect. In stanza four the reading of l. 13 ("Yet gave me in this dark Estate") does not agree with that of the comparable line in D; it does agree with the line appearing in E and in all later printed editions. The reading of l. 16 ("Left free the human Will") occurs in neither D nor E; it does occur in the text of the poem printed in 1740, two years after first publication. Such evidence suggests that this stanza was introduced into the transcript, not from a manuscript, but from a printed text. One may also assume that the last stanza, which Mrs. Thrale says was in the transcript presented to her, came from a printed text rather than from a manuscript, since it appears otherwise only in printed texts. Thus the materials that seem to link B with D and E most closely show strong marks of being sophistications by a transcriber working with a printed text. C, on the other hand, is closely linked with D by the corrections occurring in it; many of them point directly to D. Because of the presence of these corrections, it seems juster to place the nineteenth-century transcript after B and immediately before D, though the reasons for doing so are admittedly open to argument.

Unless otherwise indicated in notes to the following texts, the material between brackets has been crossed out in the manuscript. Material between caret marks has been substituted for what has been crossed out or appears as an alternative reading to what precedes.

A. Transcript by Lady Mary Wortley Montagu.[6]

A Hymn

Father of All! in ev'ry Age
In ev'ry Clime ador'd
by Christian Saint, by Heathen sage,
Jehovah, Jove, or Lord.

O First of things! least understood! [5]
Who hast my Sense confin'd
To know but this, that thou art good,
And that my selfe am blind.

Who all dost see & all dost know
And all dost Love the best [10]
bidst Fortune [guide] ⟨rule⟩ ye World below
And Conscience guide ye Breast

W^{t}ever Conscience thinks not well
W^{t}ere it bids me do
That let me shun ev'n more than Hell [15]
This more than Heaven persu.

W^t pleasures thy free bounty gives
Let me not cast away
For Heav'n is paid w^n Man receives
To enjoy is to Obey. [20]

Can Sins of Moments claim ye Rod
Of Everlasting Fires?
Can those be Sins wth Natures God
W^{ch} Natures selfe inspires?

But if to Earths contracted span   [25]
Omnipotence I bound
Or think thee Lord alone of Man
W^n thousand Worlds are round.

If 'ere this weak [yet] unknowing Hand
presume thy Bolts to throw   [30]
And deal Damnation round ye Land
On each I judge my foe

If I condemn one Sect or part
of all y^t seek thy face
If Charity wthin this Heart   [35]
Hold not ye highest place

If 'ere my foolish breast knew Pride
for ought that thou hast given
If 'ere the Wretched I deny'd
Do thou deny me Heaven   [40]

As from my little I bestow
W^n I the needy see
That Mercy I to others show
That Mercy show to me

If I am right, thy Grace impart   [45]
still in ye right to stay
If I am wrong, Oh teach my Heart
to know ye better way

B. Transcript by Mrs. Thrale.[7]

"The first Copy of Pope's <u>Universal Prayer</u>"

Father of all, in every Age,
    In ev'ry Clime ador'd;
My Christian Saint, or heathen Sage
    Jehovah! Jove! or Lord!

Thou great first Cause least understood,   [5]

355

Who last my Sense confin'd;
To know but this, that thou art good,
And that myself am blind.

(Who all dost see, who all dost know,
And all dost love the best;   [10]
Bidst Fortune rule the World below,
And Conscience guide the breast.)

Yet gave me in this dark Estate,
To know the good from ill;
And binding Nature fast in Fate,   [15]
Left free the human Will.

What Conscience dictates to be done,
Or warns me not to do;
This teach me more than Hell to shun,
That — more than Heaven pursue.   [20]

(Can Sins of Moments claim the Rod
Of everlasting Fires?
Can those be Crimes to Natures God
Which Nature's Self inspires?)

What Pleasures thy free Bounty gives   [25]
Let me not cast away!
For God is paid when Man receives.
T'enjoy is to obey.

But if to Earth's contracted Span
Omnipotence we bound;   [30]
Or think thee Lord alone of Man
Whole Systems flaming round:

If e'er this weak unknowing hand
Presumes thy Bolts to throw;
And deal Destruction round the Land   [35]
Of each I judge thy foe.

(If I condemn one Sect or part
Of those that seek thy Face;

If Charity within this Heart
    Holds not the highest Place!   [40]

If e'er my foolish breast knew Pride
    For ought that thou hast given;
Or other's wants with Scorn deride
    Do thou deny me heaven.)

But if I feel another's Woe   [45]
    Or hide the Fault I see,
That Mercy I to others show,
    That Mercy shew to me.

"The rest of the Poem is as we read it in the common
Editions of Pope [Mrs. Thrale's concluding note]."

C. Transcript made in the nineteenth century.[8]

A Hymn to God Written by Mr. Pope
at 15 Years Old, from his own M. S.

Father of All in ev'ry Age
In ev'ry Clime ador'd,
By Christian Saint & Heathen, Sage,
Jehovah, Jove, or Lord.

Thou great first Cause, least Understood;   [5]
Who hast my Sense Confin'd
To know but this that Thou art God,
And that myself am Blind.

Who all dost see who all dost know
And all dost Love the best,   [10]
Bidst, Fortune rule the World below
And Conscience guide the Breast

What Conscience dictates to ⟨tells me shou'd⟩ be done
Or Whispers not to do;
This, teach me more than Hell to shun   [15]
That, more than Heav'n pursue

[Those] pleasures ⟨What Blessings⟩ thy free Bounty
    gives
Let me not cast away,
For Heav'n is paid when Man receives
T'Enjoy is to Obey —   [20]

[Can Sins of moment claim the Rod
Of everlasting Fire?
Can those be Crimes to Natures God,
Which Nature's self Inspires?]

But if to Earths contracted Span   [25]
[Omnipotence I] ⟨Thy Glory let me⟩ bound
Or think thee Lord alone of Man
When thousand Worlds are round ⟨whole systems
    flaming round⟩

If eer' ⟨let not⟩ this weak unknowing Hand
Presume thy Bolts to throw   [30]
And deal damnation round the Land
On each I judge my ⟨thy⟩ Foe

[If I condemn] ⟨Let me not name⟩ one Sect or part[9]
Of all who seek thy Face
3   [If] ⟨let⟩ Charity within this Heart   [35]
Still hold the highest Place

This   If e'er my foolish Breast knows Pride
first   For aught that thou hast given
       Or others wants with scorn [deny'd] ⟨deride⟩
       [Do thou] ⟨If so⟩ deny me Heav'n   [40]

       But if I feel anothers Woe
       Or hide [the Faults] ⟨a Fault⟩ I see
2   That Mercy I to others shew
       That Mercy shew to me[10]

If I am right thy Grace Impart   [45]
Still in the right to stay
If I am wrong O Teach my Heart
To know that better way

358

Mean tho' I am not wholly so
Since quicken'd by thy Breath   [50]
O Lead me wheresoe'er I go
Thro' this days Life or Death

This day, be Bread & Peace my Lot
All else beneath the Sun
Thou knowst if best bestow'd or not,   [55]
And let Thy will be done

This day
Whether tomorrows Sun
Shall Glitter in my eyes or not
O may thy

D. Transcript by Nathaniel Hooke.[11]

A
PRAYER TO GOD.
1715.

Father of All, in ev'ry Age,
    In ev'ry Clime ador'd,
By saint, by savage, and by Sage
    Jehovah, Jove, or Lord!

Thou Great First Cause, least understood,   [5]
    Who hast my sense confin'd,
To know but this, that Thou art Good,
    And that myself am blind.

Yet gav'st us in this dark Estate
    To know the Good from Ill;   [10]
And, binding Nature fast in Fate,
    Left'st Conscience free, and Will.

What Conscience dictates to be done,

Or warns me not to do,
This, teach me more than Hell to shun,   [15]
That, more than Heav'n pursue.

What Blessings thy free Bounty gives,
Let me not cast away,
For God is paid when man receives,
T'enjoy, is to obey.   [20]

But not to Earth's contracted span
Thy Goodness let me bound,
Not think Thee Lord alone of Man,
When thousand Worlds are round.

Let not this weak unknowing hand   [25]
Presume Thy Bolts to throw,
Or deal Damnation round the Land,
On each I judge Thy Foe.

Save me alike from foolish Pride,
Or impious Discontent,   [30]
At ought thy Wisdom has deny'd
Or ought thy Goodness lent.

Teach me to feel another's woe,
To hide the fault I see;
As I to others mercy show,   [35]
That mercy show to me.

If I am right, Thy Grace impart
Still in the right to stay,
If I am wrong, oh teach my heart
To find that better way.   [40]

Mean as I am, not wholly so,
Since quicken'd by Thy Breath,
O lead me wheresoe're I go
Thro' this day's Life or Death.

This day, be bread and peace my Lot,   [45]
All else beneath the Sun,

> Thou knowst if best bestow'd or not,
> And let Thy Will be done.

E. Text of the poem as first printed.

THE
UNIVERSAL PRAYER
DEO. OPT. MAX.

Father of All! in every Age,
  In every Clime ador'd,
By Saint, by Savage, and by Sage,
  Jehovah, Jove, or Lord!

Thou Great First Cause, least understood!   [5]
  Who all my Sense confin'd
To know but this, — that Thou art Good,
  And I my self am blind:

Yet gave me, in this dark Estate,
  To see the Good from Ill;   [10]
And binding Nature fast in Fate,
  Left Conscience free, and Will.

What Conscience dictates to be done,
  Or warns me not to doe,
This, teach me more than Hell to shun,   [15]
  That, more than Heav'n pursue.

What Blessings thy free Bounty gives,
  Let me not cast away;
For God is pay'd when Man receives,
  T'enjoy, is to obey.   [20]

Yet not to Earth's contracted Span,
  Thy Goodness let me bound;
Or think thee Lord alone of Man,
  When thousand Worlds are round.

Let not this weak, unknowing hand   [25]

Presume Thy Bolts to throw,
And deal Damnation round the land,
On each I judge thy Foe.

If I am right, thy Grace impart
    Still in the right to stay;   [30]
If I am wrong, oh teach my heart
    To find that better Way.

Save me alike from foolish Pride,
    Or impious Discontent,
At ought thy Wisdom has deny'd,   [35]
    Or ought thy Goodness lent.

Teach me to feel another's Woe;
    To hide the Fault I see;
That Mercy I to others show,
    That Mercy show to me.   [40]

Mean tho' I am, not wholly so
    Since quicken'd by thy Breath,
Oh lead me wheresoe'er I go,
    Thro' this day's Life, or Death:

This day, be Bread and Peace my Lot;   [45]
    All else beneath the Sun,
Thou know'st if best bestow'd, or not;
    And let Thy Will be done.

To Thee, whose Temple is all Space,
    Whose Altar, Earth, Sea, Skies;   [50]
One Chorus let all Being raise!
    All Nature's Incence rise![12]

    In comparing these texts, one will be struck by the fact
that major features of the poem remain constant. All versions
are addressed to a deity whom all rational minds may worship.
Discreet references are made to man's depravity; and the concept of grace is mentioned in each transcript (Warburton, after
Pope's death, gave it more emphasis by printing "grace"
in capitals).[13] Acquiescence in one's appointed role and the

cultivation of those attitudes of mind associated with charity are portrayed as the primary obligation of man; and in all four of the transcripts conscience rather than the promise of a future life of rewards and punishments is explicitly made the principal guide to virtue.

But while these major aspects of the poem remain virtually unchanged, interesting alterations were undertaken. The poem, originally a hymn, was recast as a prayer — Pope was still thinking of it as a hymn in his letter to Allen, although the accompanying transcript is definitely labelled a prayer. Other changes in the poem give it a more definitely Christian coloring. In A the "Father of All" is conceived as an omnipotent and stern judge denying heaven to one who fails in his moral and spiritual obligations. In D and E the character ascribed to the deity has been altered: He is a god of goodness and mercy who must provide the support, the aid necessary for the individual man to live up to his ideals. If Pope does not explicitly speak of supernatural revelation, these changes in his poem make him admit to something very like it. Verbal changes often involve the substitution of words and phrases more directly Christian in connotation than those they supplant. Pope altered the line, "Thy Omnipotence I bound" by substituting the word "Glory" (C), and then "Goodness" (D) for "Omnipotence." In the line, "What pleasures thy free Bounty gives" Pope substituted "Blessings" for "pleasures"; and he added two concluding stanzas in which occur direct echoes of the Lord's Prayer (ll. 43, 45, 48 of D).

Other changes were accomplished through the rewriting or elimination of stanzas. One of these (ll. 33-36 of A) pointed directly at factionalism among Christian sects:

> If I condemn one Sect or part
> of all y^t seek thy face
> If Charity wthin this Heart
> Hold not ye highest place.

Pope, perhaps remembering difficulties which a similar statement in the Essay on Criticism had occasioned, wrote a new and less pointed stanza:

> Save me alike from foolish Pride
> Or impious Discontent,

At ought they Wisdom has deny'd
Or ought thy Goodness lent.

Two other stanzas were dropped -- the third of A (ll. 9-12), in which the deity is portrayed as having bid "Fortune rule ye World below, and Conscience guide ye breast," and the sixth of A (ll. 21-24), in which Pope declared that Nature, not the abuse of free will inspires "Sins of Moments." Both of these stanzas were fatalistic in tone; and to prevent misunderstanding Pope not only eliminated them but also introduced a new stanza, expressly asserting the will to be free.

In recasting the Universal Prayer Pope obviously tried to secure more precise and effective phrasing, to improve the lyric tone of the poem. He also attempted to make his position regarding free will very clear and to outline a relationship between God and man generally consistent with basic points of Christian doctrine. In clarifying his views, the poet did not, however, alter main tendencies of the argument in the earlier version — a point that is often overlooked. The changes do eliminate important contradictions. The stanzas which imply necessity or fatalism appeared alongside other stanzas in which freedom of the human will is implicitly assumed. The stanzas in which Pope solicited damnation if he failed to perform his duties, were hardly consistent with the stanza in which he declared that conscience rather than the threat of hell should be the principal agent of virtue. Moreover, the stanza in which Pope condemned factional disputes in religious matters merely reiterated what had been said in the previous stanza. Its suppression may readily be explained in terms of an effort at greater conciseness. One can assert that the Universal Prayer would have been much less satisfactory than it is -- a much more confused undertaking -- if Pope had ventured to publish it before 1736.

NOTES

1   The Works of Alexander Pope (London, 1751), III, 155.

2   The original of the letter is in the University of Chicago Library. Attention was first called to its existence by George Sherburn, "Two Notes on the Essay on Man", PQ, XII (1933), 403.

3 Pope wrote Bishop Atterbury, November 21, 1717: "I verily
believe your Lordship and I are both of the same religion,
if we were thoroughly understood by one another; and that
all honest and reasonable Christians would be so, if they
did but talk together every day, and had nothing to do together, but to serve God, and live in peace with their
neighbour" (The Works of Alexander Pope, ed. Whitwell
Elwin and W. J. Courthope [London, 1871-89], IX, 11).
See also Pope to Lady Mary Wortley Montagu, August 20,
1716, (E-C, IX, 346-47); and Pope to John Caryll, July 19,
1711, (E-C, VI, 150).

4 Katherine C. Balderston (ed.), Thraliana (Oxford, 1951),
I, 405-407.

5 The circumstantial evidence supporting the thesis that Lady
Mary's transcript represents an early text has been summarized by Norman Ault and John Butt, Alexander Pope:
Minor Poems (New Haven, 1954), pp. 149-50: ". . . (i) it
does not follow any of the printed texts, although it was
copied out by her [Lady Mary] after the poem had become
easily accessible in three or four different editions; (ii)
it is entitled simply A Hymn, which is what . . . Pope calls
the poem in 'its first state'; whereas (iii) the 'alter'd' version which he sent Allen was entitled A Prayer to God, and
the published version was always called by its title The
Universal Prayer; (iv) Pope and Lady Mary were intimate
friends at or about the time the Hymn was originally written, and were also in the habit of exchanging poems with
each other in manuscript; whereas (v) they had long been
completely estranged when the poem came to be rewritten
and published . . ."

6 Printed here with the kind permission of the Earl of Harrowby.

7 The parentheses are those of Mrs. Thrale, who has used
them to distinguish suppressed stanzas. The text provided
here is drawn from Thraliana: The Diary of Mrs. Hester
Lynch Thrale, ed. Katharine C. Balderston (Oxford, 1951),
I, 405-407. Professor Balderston has been more than
gracious in replying to my minute queries about the text
which Mrs. Thrale gives.

8 Printed here with the permission of the trustees of the
University of Chicago Library. In the manuscript stanzas
two, nine, ten, and eleven are distinguished, in the left-
hand margin, by a bracket. The notes alongside stanzas
eight, nine, and ten point to a contemplated rearrangement
in the order of these three quatrains. The two dots between
stanzas twelve and thirteen are explained in a marginal
note: "By this Mark which is in the Orig: it should seem,
the two last Stanzas are added to what was at first design'd."

9 The following words appear in the right-hand margin, next
to this line: "Let not my"

10 The following words appear in the right-hand margin, next
to this line: "Let me not Blame."

11 Printed here with the permission of the trustees of the
University of Chicago Library. Crosses (x) appear in the
left-hand margins opposite lines twenty-eight and thirty-
seven.

12 I have collated this first printed text with the texts appear-
ing in the following later editions (copies in the University
of Illinois Library):
The Universal Prayer, 8vo (London, 1738; Griffith
493). Ref. 38a.
The Works of Alexander Pope, 8vo (London, 1738;
Griffith 507), vol. II, pt. ii. Ref. 38b.
The Works of Alexander Pope, sm. 8vo (London, 1740;
Griffith 523), vol. II, pt. i. Ref. 40.
The Works of Alexander Pope, sm. 8vo (London, 1743;
Griffith, 583), vol. II, pt. i. Ref. 43.
An Essay on Man, 8vo (London, 1745; Griffith 607).
Ref. 45.
An Essay on Man, sm. 8vo (London, 1748; Griffith
631). Ref. 48.
The Works of Alexander Pope, 8vo (London, 1751;
Griffith 645), vol. III. Ref. 51. This collation reveals some
effort to improve punctuation as well as the following ver-
bal variants:
1. 8. 1] that 38b, 40, 43, 45, 48, 51.
1. 12. Left . . . Will.] Left free the Human Will. 40,
43, 45, 48, 51.

1.29. thy Grace impart] oh teach my heart 40, 43, 45, 48.

1.31. oh teach my heart] thy grace impart 40, 43; thy GRACE impart 45, 48.

13 Pope evidently experienced some doubts about the most effective way in which to introduce the concept of grace. As first published the stanza read:

> If I am right, thy Grace impart
> Still in the right to stay;
> If I am wrong, oh teach my heart
> To find that better Way.

When the text was revised for publication in the octavo edition of the Works (1740), Pope, evidently believing that grace should more properly be associated with the sinner than the righteous man, altered the stanza to read:

> If I am right, oh teach my heart
> Still in the right to stay;
> If I am wrong, thy grace impart
> To find that better Way.

The stanza was allowed to remain in this form until after Pope's death and until the official edition of Pope's Works was published by Warburton in 1751. At this time Pope's editor reverted to the earlier reading, possibly because the change offered him another opportunity to display his dialectic skill: "As the imparting grace on the christian system is a stronger exertion of the divine power, than the natural illumination of the heart, one would expect that the request should have been expressed reversely; more aid being required to restore men to the right than to keep them in it. But as it was the poet's purpose to insinuate that Revelation was the right, nothing could better express his purpose than the making the right secured by the guards of grace" (Works [1751], III, 157). Warburton did not state that Pope had altered the reading.

THE PRINCE OF WALES'S SET OF POPE'S WORKS

V. A. Dearing

II

As already noted, Epistle II of "Ethic Epistles, the Second Book" in the second volume of the Prince of Wales's set is printed from the type of the quarto edition of Pope's Works . . . Volume II, 1735 (Griffith 372), except that two leaves, I1-2 (second count), pages 65-68, have been canceled and replaced by a full sheet, I1-4, pages 65-72. The type for the cancel sheet seems to have been set from a copy of the quarto printing in the margins of which Pope had written some revisions and two considerable passages for insertion.[1] Four small revisions occur in the last two leaves of the cancel sheet (indicated here by italics):[2]

> Our bolder talents in full light display'd,
> There none distinguish 'twixt your Shame or Pride,
> Yet hate to rest, and dread to be alone,
> 'Tis half their Age's prudence to pretend;

The quarto of 1735 reads: "view," "Where," "Repose," and "It grows." The folio printings of Pope's Works . . . Volume II, 1735 (Griffith 370-371) have "to rest" and " 'Tis half," but "light" and "There" are new with the cancel sheet.

A more striking revision, not found in any other printing, occurs in the first leaf of the cancel sheet:[3]

Quarto Works . . . Volume II

> Turn then from Wits; and look on Simo's Mate,
> No Ass so meek, no Ass so obstinate:
> Or her, that owns her faults, but never mends   85
> Because she's honest, and the best of Friends:

Reprinted from Harvard Library Bulletin, Vol. 4 (1950), pp. 325-336, by permission of author and publisher.

Or her, whose life the Church and Scandal share,
For ever in a Passion, or a Pray'r:
Or her who laughs at Hell, but (like her Grace)
Cries, oh how charming if there's no such place!
Or who in sweet Vicissitude appears
Of Mirth and Opium, Ratafie and Tears,   90
The daily Anodyne and nightly Draught
To kill those Foes to Fair-ones, Time and Thought.
Woman and Fool are two hard Things to hit,
For true No-meaning puzzles more than Wit.

Prince of Wales's Volume

Turn then from Wits to Issachar's dull Mate,
No Ass so meek, no Ass so obstinate:
True, that's her fault, and faults she never mends   85
Because she's honest, and the best of Friends.
See what a sweet Vicissitude appears
Of Mirth and Opium, Ratafie and Tears!
The daily Anodyne and nightly draught,
To kill those foes to Fair ones, Time and Thought.
At Hell she laughs; but like her simple Grace   91
Cries, O! how charming if there's no such place!
Woman and Fool are two hard things to hit,
For true No-meaning puzzles more than Wit.

It will be seen that in the Prince of Wales's volume the five
separate sketches of the quarto have been combined into a single more considerable portrait. The method makes one wonder
how frequently Pope's characters may have come into being
by mere synthesis or accretion rather than by development
from traits of a single person.

The additional passages in the cancel sheet occur between
the lines numbered in the quarto 99 and 100, and 105 and 106.[4]
When they were originally composed is uncertain, but while
some of the lines cannot have been written before 1735, others
may have been written at the same time as the rest of the poem,
for when Pope wrote to Swift in February 1733 that he had completed the poem, he added that it could not be published as written because the public was "so sore of satire" and so willing to

interpret Pope's examples of vice as attacks on specific persons.[5] He gave no indication that the poem was not complete as printed either in the separate publication of February 1735, entitled Of the Characters of Women: An Epistle to a Lady (Griffith 360-363), or in his quarto and folio Works . . . Volume II, published in April (Griffith 370-372); but in the octavo Works . . . Vol. II, published in July (Griffith 388-389), he added a note to the effect that "certain examples and illustrations" had been omitted between the lines numbered in the quarto 105 and 106.[6] The second of the two additional passages in the Prince of Wales's volume occurs at this point, but it is an argumentative passage (that outward appearance is no index to character); the examples, consisting of the characters of Philomede and Atossa, are found in the first of the passages, inserted six lines earlier.

When, at the end of 1742 or the beginning of 1743, Pope revised the poem, he included in it these two passages, altered and rearranged, and the character of Chloe, which had been first published as a separate poem in his Works . . . Vol. II. Part II, 1738 [1739] (Griffith 507).[7] He printed the revision in a new edition of the four poems which in his Works . . . Volume II had comprised "Ethic Epistles, the Second Book" and distributed a few copies to his friends just before he died (Griffith 591).[8] Warburton, who had compiled the notes for the edition and whose property it was under the terms of Pope's will, suppressed it, probably at the solicitation of some friends of the Duchess of Marlborough who feared that the character of Atossa might be identified as hers.[9] After her death, someone who had come into possession of a copy of the suppressed edition published, in 1746, the lines on Atossa as Verses upon the late D—— of M—— (Griffith 613).[10] Warburton then published the suppressed edition with a title-page: Four | Ethic Epistles | By | Alexander Pope, Esq. | With The | Commentary and Notes | Of | Mr. Warburton. | = | London, | Printed for J. and P. Knapton in Ludgate-Street. | – | MDCCXLVIII. The British Museum has what may be the only recorded copy distributed by Pope; it has no title-page, and is bound in the middle of a copy of the 1743 [i.e. 1744] edition of the Essay on Man with the Essay on Criticism (Griffith 589-590). Professor George Sherburn possesses a set of the sheets with the 1748 title-page.[11] Warburton reprinted the text of the suppressed edition in his large octavo edition of Pope's <u>Works</u>, 1751, with additional notes in which he supplied most of the lines found in the Prince of Wales's volume but omitted from the suppressed edition; these, he said, were taken from Pope's manuscript of the poem.[12] In this edition Warburton specifically denied that the character of Atossa had been suggested by that of the Duchess of Marlborough, pointing out that it was based upon that of Katherine, Duchess of Buckinghamshire.[13]

The second of the two passages added to the poem by the insertion of the cancel sheet in the Prince of Wales's volume was reprinted in the suppressed edition with little change beyond the omission of the last eight lines, and these Warburton supplied in his notes in 1751.[14] The whole passage exhibits four readings that differ from those of the later printings (italics mark the variants):[15]

> Th' <u>exacter</u> Traits of Body or of Mind,
> We <u>owe to</u> Models of an <u>humbler</u> kind.

> From honest <u>Schutz</u>,[16] <u>or that</u> plain Parson, Hale.

> As <u>H*e</u> and H**y preach, for Queens and Kings;

The suppressed edition, followed by Warburton, reads: "exactest," "humble," and "Mah'met, or"; Warburton's note gives only the asterisk of "H*e."

The first of the added passages was more considerably revised by Pope and less completely restored by Warburton.[17] The character of Philomede differs in the last line from the version in the suppressed edition:[18]

> And makes her hearty <u>banquet — on</u> a Dunce.

The suppressed edition reads: "meal upon." And the character of Atossa differs widely from the lines as printed by Pope in the suppressed edition and reprinted by Warburton, including also one important couplet that Warburton did not print in his notes in 1751:[19]

Prince of Wales's Volume

But what are these to great Atossa's mind?
That wild Epitome of Womankind!
Each hour at odds with other, from her birth, 120
And all her life one warfare upon earth:
No Thought advances, but her Eddy Brain
Whisks it about, and down it goes again.
Oppress'd with Wealth and Wit, Abundance sad!
One makes her poor, the other makes her mad. 125
Thus, while her Palace rises like a Town,
Atossa cheats the Lab'rer of a crown;
And while her Art excels in painting Fools,
Is ev'ry thing she blames or ridicules.
Who breaks with her, provokes Revenge from Hell,
But he's a bolder Man who dares be well: 131
Her ev'ry Turn with Violence persu'd,
Nor more a Storm her Hate than Gratitude.
In her, each Passion's Pride, or soon or late;
Love, if it makes her yield, must make her hate: 135
Superiors? death! and Equals? what a curse!
But an Inferior not dependant? worse.
Offend her, and she knows not to forgive;
Oblige her, and she'll hate you while you live.
Full sixty years the world has been her trade, 140
The wisest Fool much Time has ever made!
From loveless youth to unrespected age,
No Passion gratify'd except her Rage:
So much the Fury still outran the Wit,
The Pleasure miss'd her, and the Scandal hit. 145
Strange! by the Means defeated of the Ends,
By Spirit robb'd of Pow'r, by Warmth of Friends,
By Wealth of Follow'ers! without one distress.
Sick of her self thro' very selfishness!
Atossa, curs'd with many a granted pray'r, 150
And childless with three children, wants an Heir;
This Death decides, nor lets the blessing fall
On any one she hates, but on 'em all:
Curs'd chance! this only cou'd afflict her more,
If any part shou'd wander to the Poor. 155

Suppressed Edition

But what are these to great Atossa's mind?   115
Scarce once herself, by turns all Womankind!
Who, with herself, or others, from her birth
Finds all her life one warfare upon earth:
Shines, in exposing Knaves, and painting Fools,
Yet is, whate'er she hates and ridicules.   120
No Thought advances, but her Eddy Brain
Whisks it about, and down it goes again.
Full sixty years the World has been her Trade,
The wisest Fool much Time has ever made.
From loveless youth to unrespected age,   125
No Passion gratify'd except her Rage.
So much the Fury still out-ran the Wit,
The Pleasure miss'd her, and the Scandal hit.
Who breaks with her, provokes Revenge from Hell,
But he's a bolder man who dares be well: 130
Her ev'ry turn with Violence pursu'd,
Nor more a storm her Hate than Gratitude.
To that each Passion turns, or soon or late;
Love, if it makes her yield, must make her hate:
Superiors? death! and Equals? what a curse!   135
But an Inferior not dependant? worse.
Offend her, and she knows not to forgive;
Oblige her, and she'll hate you while you live:
But die, and she'll adore you — Then the Bust
And Temple rise — then fall again to dust.   140
Last night, her Lord was all that's good and great,
A Knave this morning, and his Will a Cheat.
Strange! by the Means defeated of the Ends,
By Spirit robb'd of Pow'r, by Warmth of Friends,
By Wealth of Follow'rs! without one distress   145
Sick of herself thro' very selfishness!
Atossa, curs'd with ev'ry granted pray'r,
Childless with all her Children, wants an Heir.
To Heirs unknown descends th'unguarded store
Or wanders, Heav'n-directed, to the Poor.   150

A note in <u>Verses upon the late D———ss of M———</u> explained that lines 139-140 of the later version alluded "to a

Temple she [the duchess] erected with a Bust of Queen Anne in it."[20] This bust was not placed in a temple, however, but in one of the rooms at Blenheim.[21] It follows that if "Temple" is not to be taken literally, then "the Bust" may be a reference to the Duke of Buckinghamshire's monument in Westminster Abbey, on which appear busts of his children in low relief,[22] or the whole phrase may be merely a figure of speech. Warburton noted that the concluding lines must refer to the Duchess of Buckinghamshire, who buried the last of her three sons in 1735;[23] the Duchess of Marlborough was survived by her youngest daughter.[24] Lines 141-142 of the later version, also, must refer to the Duchess of Buckinghamshire, who contested the provisions of her husband's will for his illegitimate children,[25] the Duchess of Marlborough took steps to ensure that the provisions of her husband's will would be carried out.[26] In short, every line of the later version may, and some lines must, be taken as referring to the Duchess of Buckinghamshire.

Courthope, then, may have been mistaken in supposing that Lord Bolingbroke wrote of the character to Lord Marchmont as having been modeled upon the Duchess of Marlborough and not merely as one that might be maliciously identified with her:

> Our friend Pope, it seems, corrected and prepared for the press just before his death an edition of the four Epistles, that follow the Essay on Man. They were then printed off, and are now ready for publication. I am sorry for it, because, if he could be excused for writing the character of Atossa formerly, there is no excuse for his design of publishing it, after he had received the favor you and I know; and the character of Atossa is inserted. I have a copy of the book. Warburton has the propriety of it, as you know. Alter it he cannot, by the terms of the will. Is it worth while to suppress the edition? or should her Grace's friends say, as they may from several strokes in it, that it was not intended to be her character? and should she despise it?[27]

Bolingbroke may have meant only that Pope had no reason when he wrote the character to be scrupulously careful to point it away from the Duchess of Marlborough. Warburton seems to have spoken of the lines to Joseph Spence as "his [i. e. , Pope's] character of the Duchess of Marlborough,"[28] but Spence's note of the conversation may be in his own rather than Warburton's words, and may reflect his acceptance of the evidence of the Verses (his note may have been written as late as 1755). The supposition that Pope's intimates were accustomed to think of the character of Atossa as an attack upon the Duchess of Marlborough finds perhaps its chief support in another entry in Spence's memorandum book: "In the Satire on Women there was a character of the old Duchess of Marlborough, under the name of Orsini, written before Mr. Pope was so familiar with her, and very severe. — Mrs. Arbuthnot, 1744."[29] No Orsini or Orsina (Courthope's conjecture)[30] is to be found in the poem, and it may be that Pope changed the name to Atossa — Atossa, the daughter of Cambyses, would suggest the Duchess of Buckinghamshire, the illegitimate daughter of James II -- and made enough other alterations so that the character would not be offensive to the Duchess of Marlborough.

Three lines in the earlier version of the character appear to support the conclusion suggested by the external evidence, but all three are capable of a contrary interpretation. Line 140 could not be literally applied to the Duchess of Buckinghamshire when it was printed (if the Prince of Wales's set was presented about 1738), for the duchess was only 61 when she died in 1743.[31] The Duchess of Marlborough came to court in 1673,[32] so that the line was literally applicable to her and would have been had it been composed in 1733 when Pope finished the rest of Epistle II. Similarly, lines 126-127 are not true of the Duchess of Buckinghamshire, who did not marry the Duke until after Buckingham House was built;[33] they fit the Duchess of Marlborough's law suits over the construction of Blenheim.[34]

Nevertheless, it seems clear from the concluding lines that Pope wrote this version of the character, also, as a portrait of the Duchess of Buckinghamshire.[35] He may have been using "sixty years" as a round figure; he may not have known precisely the Duchess of Buckinghamshire's age; he may not have anticipated the possibility that the line would be applied to the Duchess of Marlborough. Similarly, he may not have known that Buckingham House was built before she married the Duke. It is perhaps significant that he retained in the suppressed edition the "sixty years," which the passage of time had made literally applicable to the Duchess of Buckinghamshire, but removed the couplet on the palace. Presumably, he would have removed it also from the Prince of Wales's volume if he had recognized that it could not apply to the Duchess of Buckinghamshire. The Duchess of Marlborough has many admirers even in the twentieth century; the other duchess has practically none, and it might therefore please if one could demonstrate that this character by Pope referred only to the less amiable of the two haughty ladies; but it is still impossible to determine beyond all cavil which of the duchesses supplied the original inspiration for the character of Atossa.

One other circumstance connected with the character of Atossa remains to be discussed, namely, the incident -- if there needed an incident — that gave rise to the now discredited charge that the Duchess of Marlborough bribed Pope to suppress it.[36] The story is first found in a note on the verso of the last leaf of Verses upon the Late D———ss of M———:

> These Verses are Part of a Poem, entitled Characters of Women. It is generally said, the D———ss gave Mr. P. 1000l. to suppress them: He took the Money, yet the World sees the Verses; but this is not the first Instance where Mr. P.'s practical Virtue has fallen very short of those pompous Professions of it he makes in his Writings.

This note was written by an enemy of Pope, obviously, and its contents may be discounted. Not much more commanding of belief are the conflicting accounts of the Duchess of Portland. In a notebook written not earlier than 1750, the Duchess of Portland recorded that Pope read the character of Atossa to the Duchess of Marlborough while he was visiting her at Wimbledon, and that although she did not remark upon it at the time, she afterwards gave him £3000 in exchange for his manuscript. "This was told me by Lady Cowper, who had it from Hook," who, according to the Duchess of Portland, was the Duchess of Marlborough's agent in the affair.[37] This circumstantial story is weakened by a conflicting story that the Duchess of Portland told Joseph Warton. On her authority, Warton noted that when the lines were read, not by Pope, the Duchess of Marlborough burst out into abuse of the writer. Subsequently,

Warton tacked onto this account the remark that the Duchess
"gave him a thousand pounds to suppress this portrait, which
he accepted, it is said, by the persuasion of Mrs. M. Blount."[38]
Warton's story of the bribe, therefore, probably has as its
source, gossip aside, the note at the end of Verses upon the
late D——— ss of M———. The Duchess of Portland's story of
the bribe may also have derived eventually from the same
source, for she disliked Pope, and would not be inclined to
examine the veracity of an anecdote to his discredit.[39] The process of accretion to the original story represented in Warton's
reference to Martha Blount and in the duchess's £3000 is well
illustrated by Horace Walpole's version, in which he said that
Pope showed the lines to both duchesses, telling each it was a
portrait of the other.[40]

Warburton's version, recorded by Spence, is that the character was read to the Duchess of Marlborough as that of the
Duchess of Buckinghamshire — by whom is not clear -- and that
she afterwards "said she knew very well whom he meant."[41]
The one circumstance common to all these accounts is that the
Duchess of Marlborough knew of the lines before they were published. Had she wished them suppressed it is extremely unlikely
that Pope would have published them, for many of her friends
and political allies[42] were his friends, and she herself became
intimate with him. No bribe would have been necessary. It is
equally unlikely that anyone would risk her displeasure by reading to her a satire upon herself. But if Pope had read to her the
character as it stands in the Prince of Wales's volume, in good
faith supposing that she would accept it as a portrait of the
Duchess of Buckinghamshire, she would certainly have recognized that three lines in it, at least, would be immediately applied to her, and she would, perhaps through Hooke, have
represented the fact to Pope.[43] As before, however, the evidence provided by the Prince of Wales's volume is suggestive,
rather than conclusive.

NOTES

1 For an example of Pope's use of this method of revising
copy, see the facsimile in the third volume of Elwin-Courthope (facing the title-page).

2 Ll. 201, 204, 228, 236 in Elwin-Courthope (III, 109, 111); ll. 190, 193 (first count), 217, 225 in the Prince of Wales's volume (pp. 70, 72, second count); ll. 108, 111, 136, 144 in the quarto Works . . . Volume II (pp. 66, 68, second count).

3 Pp. 65-66 (second count) in the quarto Works . . . Volume II and the Prince of Wales's volume; ll. 101-114 in Elwin-Courthope, III, 102-103. The numbering of the lines in the quarto follows that of the folio editions of the Works . . . Volume II, which do not have the couplet, "Or her who . . . place!"

4 Ll. 114 and 151, and 156 and 199 in Elwin-Courthope (III, 103, 106, 109).

5 Elwin-Courthope, III, 76.

6 Ibid.; the lines are 102 and 103 in the octavo numbering.

7 Elwin-Courthope, III, 81-83. Mr. Ault (New Light on Pope, pp. 266-275) has disproved the previously accepted identification of Chloe as the Countess of Suffolk (Mrs. Howard).

8 Elwin-Courthope, III, 83. Griffith's title for Book 591 is of course conjectural.

9 See p. 374. Lords Bolingbroke and Marchmont were executors, the one literary, the other legal, of Pope; Lord Marchmont was an executor and considerable beneficiary of the Duchess of Marlborough.

10 Courthope's argument (Elwin-Courthope, III, 79) that the publisher was Lord Bolingbroke is suggestive, but not conclusive. For Bolingbroke's knowledge of the suppressed edition and animus toward Pope in 1744, see A Selection from the Papers of the Earls of Marchmont, ed. Sir George Henry Rose (London, 1831), II, 334-335, 338-339. Photostats of the volume referred to by Griffith as Book 614, evidently on the basis of the entry in the printed Catalogue of the British Museum, show it to be a copy of Book 613.

11 I am indebted to Professor Sherburn, at whose suggestion the last two parts of this essay were undertaken, for photostats of the title-page of his volume and of the text of

Epistle II in the British Museum volume.

12 Pope, Works, ed. Warburton (large octavo edition, 1751), I, v-vii (first count).

13 Warburton, VIII, 246.

14 Ll. 181-198 in Elwin-Courthope (III, 108-109), suppressed edition (pp. 33-34), and Warburton (III, 206), and footnote to line 199 in Elwin-Courthope (III, 109, n. 3) quoted from Warburton (III, 207, Variations); ll. 162-187 (first count) in the Prince of Wales's volume (pp. 69-70, second count).

15 Ll. 191-192, 198 in Elwin-Courthope, suppressed edition, and Warburton, and footnote to line 199 in Elwin-Courthope, and Warburton; ll. 172-173, 179, 185 (first count) in the Prince of Wales's volume.

16 Augustus Schutz, referred to by Pope as "honest S*z" in The First Epistle of the First Book of Horace Imitated, 1737 [i.e. 1738], l. 112; Imitations of Horace, ed. John Butt (The Twickenham Edition of the Poems of Alexander Pope, Vol. IV; London, 1939), pp. 286-287, 382.

17 Ll. 69-86, and 115-150 in Elwin-Courthope (III, 100-101, 103-106), suppressed edition (pp. 28-31), and Warburton (III, 199-203), and footnotes in Elwin-Courthope (III, 104, n. 1, 106, n. 2), quoted from Warburton (III, 202, 203, Variations); ll. 95-155 (first count) in the Prince of Wales's volume (pp. 66-68, second count).

18 L. 86 in Elwin-Courthope, suppressed edition, and Warburton; l. 117 in the Prince of Wales's volume. Elwin-Courthope (III, 100, n. 3) quotes from Warburton (III, 199, Variations) an additional reading found "in the MS." that does not appear in the Prince of Wales's volume.

19 The unrecorded couplet is ll. 126-127 in the numbering of the Prince of Wales's volume.

20 Verses, p. 4.

21 Sarah, Duchess of Marlborough, Letters of a Grandmother, 1732-1735, ed. Gladys Scott Thomson (London, 1943), pp. 152-153; Winston Churchill, Marlborough, His Life and Times (London, 1933-38), VI, 651.

22 There is an excellent photograph of the monument in Francis Bond, Westminster Abbey (London, 1909), p. 219. Pope, incidentally, had something to do with its execution; see Elwin-Courthope, X, 153.

23 Warburton, VIII, 246; G. E. Cokayne, The Complete Peerage, new ed. , ed. Vicary Gibbs and others (London, 1910-), II, 401.

24 Stuart J. Reid, John and Sarah, Duke and Duchess of Marlborough, 1660-1744 (London, 1914), p. 500.

25 Charles Wentworth Dilke, The Papers of a Critic (London, 1875), I, 284-285.

26 Katherine B. Thomson, Memoirs of Sarah, Duchess of Marlborough (London, 1839), II, 406-409, 564-565, 567.

27 Marchmont Papers, II, 334-335; Elwin-Courthope, III, 85.

28 Joseph Spence, Anecdotes, Observations, and Characters, of Books and Men, ed. Samuel Weller Singer (2nd ed. , London, 1858), p. 277, from Spence's first memorandum book, for 1755.

29 Spence, p. 278. Anne Arbuthnot, the daughter of the doctor, continued her father's intimacy with Pope; see Spence, p. 243.

30 Elwin-Courthope, III, 86.

31 Cokayne, II, 400.

32 Kathleen Campbell, Sarah, Duchess of Marlborough (London, 1932), p. 37.

33 Cokayne, II, 399 and note (c).

34 See William Coxe, Memoirs of the Duke of Marlborough, new ed. , rev. by John Wade (London, 1847-48), III, 409-416.

35 The Duchess of Buckinghamshire had five children by the Duke (Dilke, I, 286), two of whom were girls. Since Pope knew of all five — the busts of those who died before the duke are on his monument — he evidently counts only the boys, each of whom in turn was the duke's heir, and all of whom died before the duchess.

36 The evidence that the Duchess of Marlborough gave Pope £1000 outright, not as a bribe, rests upon the reported word of Lord Marchmont (Marchmont Papers, II, 334, note). Pope's correspondence with her shows that he received some sort of present from her about the end of 1742 (see Elwin-Courthope, V, 416-418), but neither its nature nor its value can be deduced. The inventory of Pope's estate made by George Arbuthnot shows that Pope had a bond of Slingsby Bethel for £1000 dated 27 March 1744, and a bond of Ralph Allen for £2000 dated 25 June 1743 (Robert Carruthers, The Life of Alexander Pope, 2nd ed., London, 1857, p. 456), but these are not proof of a gift of £1000.

37 Elwin-Courthope, III, 79; for the date of the anecdote, see p. 80.

38 Dilke (I, 226-228) pointed out this discrepancy between Warton's Essay on the Genius and Writings of Pope (1756-82, II, 202) and his note in his edition of Pope's Works (1797, III, 218).

39 See Elwin-Courthope, III, 77, n. 1.

40 Horace Walpole, "Reminiscences; Written in 1788," in The Letters of Horace Walpole, Earl of Orford, ed. Peter Cunningham (London, 1857-59), I, cxliv.

41 Spence, pp. 277-278.

42 See Campbell, pp. 264-266.

43 There is no assurance that Pope printed only one copy of the cancel sheet, and it might be assumed that before releasing a number he would have ascertained that the lines on Atossa would not offend the Duchess of Marlborough; but that he would have shown the lines to her, either himself or through another, if he had any suspicion that they were offensive, seems highly unlikely, and it is noticeable that the lines do not appear in the octavo editions of the Works published in the 1740's, which show Pope's revisions in other poems.

POPE AND "THE WEIGHTY BULLION
OF DR. DONNE'S SATIRES"

Ian Jack

Pope's debt to Dryden, which is at once immense and unmistakable, has tended to obscure his relation to earlier English satirists. But since in the Imitations of Horace and the
Moral Essays he was practising a genre untouched by Dryden —
satura, the formal verse satire without a plot — it is reasonable
to suppose that Pope owed something to other English satirists.
There is evidence that he regarded himself as having a place
in an English tradition of formal verse satire. When he came
on a copy of Hall's Satires late in life, "he wished that he had
seen them sooner";[1] and according to Warburton he intended
to imitate "two or three" of Hall's satires.[2] He was interested
in Rochester and Oldham. He read, of course, Love of Fame,
The Universal Passion; Young's "characteristical Satires" were
no doubt partly responsible for turning his own thoughts in the
direction of epistolary satire.

More than a decade before the first of Young's satires had
appeared, however, Pope had tried his hand at a formal satire.
About 1713 he wrote an imitation of Donne's Satyre II which has
recently been published for the first time. Twenty years later
he published an imitation of Donne's Satyre IV; and in 1735 he
printed an imitation of II much changed from his early version.

While the fact that Pope remembered Young and Boileau
and Horace as he wrote his own epistolary satires has not been
overlooked, little stress has been laid on Donne's position
among his models and predecessors. Yet a full understanding
of Pope's debt to Donne and of the aspects of the art of poetry
in which the two men agreed, as well as of those in which they
differed, should help to explain the course taken by English
poetry in a hundred and forty years of eventful development.
A study of the scope and nature of the changes which Pope made
when he imitated two of Donne's Satyres may afford some help

Reprinted from Publications of the Modern Language Association, Vol.
66 (1951), pp. 1009-1022, by permission of author and publisher.

towards this fuller understanding.

Since my main concern is with passages in which Pope follows Donne without alteration, or makes relatively slight changes, little in the way of introduction is necessary.[3] It is sufficient to notice that Pope followed Donne in subject and in the general development of his argument, much as he did with Horace. As in his Imitations of Horace he was obliged to modernise examples and allusions. Whereas in Donne the evil results of poetry are "dearth, and Spaniards" (II. 6) in Pope they are "Th'Excise and Army" (8).[4] In Donne boys play "at span-counter, or blow point" (IV. 108), while in Pope "Lad[s] . . . chuck [and] Lad [ies] vole" (146). Pope drops Donne's reference to "Maids pulling prime" (II. 86), no doubt because it would no longer be understood. Donne's famous liars, Jovius and Surius (IV. 48), make way in Pope for Oldmixon and Burnet (61). As authorities for language Beza, "some Jesuits, and two reverend men / Of our two Academies" (IV. 55-57) are succeeded by Onslow, Swift, and Ho[adl]y (71-73).

One minor change is of interest because it is so characteristic of Pope's satiric method: his introduction of real names in passages where Donne has none. An unscrupulous lawyer who is given no name in Donne or in Pope's early imitation, becomes "Coscus" in the first edition of his later version and "Peter" (Walter) in later editions (II. 66 et seq.). Similarly "wicked Waters" and "godly— [Hall?]" are mentioned at line 80 of the later version of his imitation of Donne's Satyre II, where no name occurs in Donne or in Pope's early version. Instances of this barbing of the satire with a personal point are particularly numerous in IV. Donne's Courtier, "Stranger than seven Antiquaries studies" (IV. 21), becomes "a verier Monster than . . . Or Sloane, or Woodward's wondrous Shelves contain" (30). Woodward is named again when Donne's statement that he sickens "like a Patient" (112) is expanded to: "As one of Woodward's Patients, sick and sore, / I puke, I nauseate . . ." (152-153). Another passage in which Pope introduces specific examples where none are given in Donne occurs at lines 50-53:

> Talkers, I've learned to bear; Motteux I knew,
> Henley himself I've heard, nay Budgel too:
> The Doctor's Wormwood Style, the Hash of Tongues,
> A Pedant makes: the Storm of Gonson's Lungs . . .

The principal alteration which Pope aimed at in his versions of Donne's satires is indicated by the quotation from Horace which he set on the title page of each of them:

> Quid vetat, ut nosmet Lucili scripta legentes
> Quaerere, num illius, num rerum dura negarit
> Versiculos natura magis factos, & euntes
> Mollius?   (Sat. I. x. 56-59)

"What poems [= genres] have not, with time, received an alteration in their fashion?" Dryden asked in the essay in which he summed up the Renaissance debate about satire.

> Has not Virgil changed the manners of Homer's heroes
> . . . ? Certainly he has, and for the better; for Virgil's age was more civilised, and better bred; and he writ according to the politeness of Rome, under the reign of Augustus Caesar, not to the rudeness of Agememnon's age, or the times of Homer. Why should we offer to confine free spirits to one form, when we cannot so much as confine our bodies to one fashion of apparel? Would not Donne's Satires, which abound with so much wit, appear more charming, if he had taken care of his words, and of his numbers?[5]

Pope agreed with Dryden's "censure"; agreed too that in the matter of versification, at least, "if we are not as great wits as Donne, yet certainly we are better poets." As Boileau had pointed out, "Le vers le mieux rempli, la plus noble pensée / Ne peut plaire à l'esprit, quand l'oreille est blessée."[6] That Lucilius had written harshly was no argument for Horace to do the same.[7]

There were passages in Donne, however, which did not offend the ear. Pope appreciated his self-contained single lines: "Sir, by your Priesthood tell me what you are?" (IV. 29).[8] Lines of this sort which Pope retained virtually unchanged include: "Of all our Harrys, and our Edwards talk" (IV. 77),[9] "More than ten Hollensheads, or Halls, or Stows" (IV. 97; Pope 131), and "And wooes in language of the Pleas and Bench" (II. 48).[10]

Such single-moulded lines Pope took over from Donne because they accorded with his own manner of composition: for

the same reason he retained a number of lines with a marked
medial pause, with or without antithesis:

>Carthusian Fasts, and fulsome Bacchanals
>
>>(II. 106; Pope 118)
>
>Make men speak treason, couzen subtlest whores
>
>>(IV. 46)[11]
>
>Jests like a licens'd fool, commands like law
>
>>(IV. 228; Pope 271)
>
>Like a Kings Favorite — or like a King
>
>>(II. 70; Pope 78)

At the opposite extreme from such lines, in Donne, is his
use of violent and apparently motiveless enjambements like
(IV. 106-107):

>>>egge-
>
>Shels.

Four lines from Donne's Satyre IV furnish a good example both
of the type of harshness that Pope was quick to remove and of
qualities in Donne which he was eager to retain and emphasize.
Donne had written (13-16):

>As prone to all ill, and of good as forget-
>full, as proud, lustful, and as much in debt,
>As vain, as witless, and as false as they
>Which dwell in Court, for once going that way.

Here Pope found an admirable climax in the third line, a fourth
line with little wrong with it, and in the first two lines a number
of incompletely developed antitheses wantonly spoilt by an un-
meaningly harsh enjambement. He rewrote the passage in this
way:

>As prone to Ill, as negligent of Good,
>As deep in Debt, without a thought to pay,

> As vain, as idle, and as false, as they
> Who live at Court, for going once that Way! [12]

More has been made of the antitheses, and simultaneously the "numbers" of the verse have been "reformed."

The basic fact is simply that while in Donne's time harshness of verse-movement was expected in a satire, in Pope's some measure of harmony was looked for, though less than in many other genres. This harmonizing could involve considerable changes, as in the passage quoted above; or it could be simply a matter of changing the order of one or two words, as when Donne's "A thing which would have pos'd Adam to name" (IV. 20) becomes "A thing which Adam had been pos'd to name" (25).

The avoidance of unnecessary "harshness" in the "numbers" of his verse was for Pope closely associated with certain preferences in rhetorical structure and syntax. While it would be an exaggeration to say that most sentences in Donne's Satyres are given their shape by bold enjambements, such sentences are relatively common. In the following passage slanting lines indicate the end of sentences and of clauses which are the equivalent of sentences:

> I more amaz'd than Circes prisoners, when
> They felt themselves turn beasts, felt my self then
> Becoming Traytor, / and methought I saw
> One of our Giant Statutes ope his jaw,
> To suck me in for hearing him: / I found
> That as burnt venemous Leachers do grow sound
> By giving others their sores, I might grow
> Guilty, and he free: / Therefore I did show
> All Signes of loathing; / but since I am in,
> I must pay mine, and my forefathers sin
> To the last farthing. /   (IV. 129-139)

Although these lines rhyme in pairs, the model is obviously dramatic blank verse. The distribution of major clauses and periods recalls that of Shakespeare's later plays. Pope rewrote the passage so that every major pause came at the end of a line:

> Not more Amazement seiz'd on Circe's Guests,

386

> To see themselves fall endlong into Beasts,
> Than mine, to find a Subject staid and wise,
> Already half turn'd Traytor by surprize. /
> I fear'd th'Infection slide from him to me,
> As in the Pox, some give it, to get free; /
> And quick to swallow me, methought I saw,
> One of our Giant <u>Statutes</u> ope its Jaw! /   (166-173)

"Nothing . . . can be more absurd," remarked William Melmoth, "than to write in poetical measure, and yet neglect harmony."[13] That would have been Pope's comment on lines 166-174 of Donne's <u>Satyre IV</u>:

> Hast thou seen,
> O Sun, in all thy journey, Vanity,
> Such as swells the bladder of our Court? I
> Think he which made your Waxen garden, and
> Transported it, from Italy, to stand
> With us at London, flouts our Courtiers; for
> Just such gay painted things, which no sap, nor
> Tast have in them, ours are; and natural
> Some of the stocks are, their fruits bastard all.

Rewritten, the passage becomes:

> Hast thou, O <u>Sun</u>! beheld an emptier sort,
> Than such as swell this Bladder of a Court?
> Now pox on those who shew a <u>Court in Wax</u>!
> It ought to bring all Courtiers on their backs.
> Such painted Puppets, such a varnish'd Race
> Of hollow Gewgaws, only Dress and Face,
> Such waxen Noses, stately, staring things,
> No wonder some Folks bow, and think them <u>Kings</u>.

> (204-211)

A quality inseparably associated with the "harshness" of Elizabethan satire was obscurity, darkness of "conceipt." This was largely due to the practice of Persius and Juvenal. By Pope's time, however, the example of Horace had become all-important. Believing as he did that "most little poems should

be written by a plan,"[14] Pope must have found Donne particularly culpable for not making the course of his argument sufficiently clear to the reader.[15] He took care to add transitions,
signposting the way in a manner very different from Donne's.
In Satyre IV, for example, Donne had written:

> Here
> He stopt me, and said, Nay your Apostles were
> Good pretty Linguists, so Panurgus was;
> Yet a poor Gentleman; all these may pass
> By travail. Then, as if he would have sold
> His tongue, he prais'd it . . .   (57-62)

Pope points the tendency of the passage more clearly with a
couplet:

> Thus others Talents having nicely shown,
> He came by sure Transition to his own.   (80-81)

While Donne's intentions cannot be certainly known, since he
did not print his Satyres, it is safe to say that no paragraphs
are obvious; and Grierson prints them without paragraphing.
Essentially they are long outbursts, impassioned soliloquies
which do not fall into any obvious parts. Pope's use of the
verse-paragraph marks him off clearly from Donne. His Imitations follow the sectional arrangement of all his epistolary
verse. Transitions are clearly marked, and the whole builds
itself up as the sum of a number of clearly interrelated parts.
    Another species of "harshness" in Donne which Pope avoids
may be seen in a line which is reminiscent of the "terrible sonnets" of Hopkins: "Shall I, none's slave, of high born or rais'd
men / Fear frowns?" (IV. 162-163). Yet the desire for conciseness which led Donne to such language was shared by Pope.
"Pope's talent," Shenstone remarked, "lay remarkably in . . .
the condensation of thoughts. I think no other English poet ever
brought so much sense into the same number of lines."[16] Although his other objects of "smoothness [and] ease" led Pope
to expand Donne's laconic "Mean's blest" (II. 107) into a whole
line — "And all mankind might that just mean observe" (119) —
there is no doubt that Donne's gift for brevity was one of the
aspects of his "wit" which Pope most admired.[17] The benefit

that he received from the example of such a master can be examined in many of the brilliantly epigrammatic lines which
occur in these Imitations even where he is not following Donne's
text closely. Such a line as this: "Whom Crimes gave wealth,
and wealth gave impudence" (II. 46) is a reminder that conciseness is a quality which links Pope and the best of the Augustans
(including, conspicuously, Swift and Matthew Green) with the
"strong" writers of a century before.

Since the essence of good writing was in Pope's view flexibility, the adaptation of the poet's manner to the demands of
his material and his purpose, he did not reject all enjambements on principle. In the index to his translation of the Iliad
he drew attention to the fact that he had used run-on lines where
he considered them appropriate. And two of the occasions on
which he retains Donne's enjambements are of interest because
they show him keenly perceptive of the dramatic possibilities
of this device. Donne's Court-bore knows

> When the Queen frown'd, or smil'd, and he knows what
> A subtle States-man may gather of that. (IV. 99-100)

Pope keeps this highly expressive use of the metre:

> When the Queen frown'd, or smil'd, he knows; and what
> A subtle Minister may make of that? [18]

The same acceptance of a metrical device turned to brilliant
rhetorical effect may be seen in Pope's retention of Donne's
enjambement at IV. 158-159:

> Than as a licens'd Spy, whom nothing can
> Silence, or hurt . . . [19]

One aspect of Donne's satiric style which the modern reader might expect an Augustan to have regarded as part of his
"harshness" is his daring and trenchant imagery. "Who but
Donne would have thought that a good man is a telescope?" [20]
Did Pope look on the strange metaphors and similes of Donne's
Satyres as part of the dross to be purged away from an old
outmoded poet? By no means. When the passages are marked
in which Pope takes over Donne's phrasing exactly or follows

him fairly closely, one finds that a large proportion contain
surprising imagery. Pope retains without significant alteration
the image in which Donne describes the rapacity of a dishonest
lawyer:

> Shortly (as th'sea) he'll compass all the land,
> From <u>Scots</u> to <u>Wight</u>, from <u>Mount</u> to <u>Dover</u> strand.[21]

Again, Pope takes over the hyperbolical imagery with which
Donne describes the immense Articles in which legal men are
adept at "fencing ill-got wealth by law." Donne had written:

> In parchment then, large as the fields, he draws
> Assurances, big as gloss'd civil laws,
> So huge, that men (in our times forwardness)
> Are Fathers of the Church for writing less. (II. 87-90)

Pope keeps the imagery:

> Large as the Fields themselves, and larger far
> Than Civil Codes, with all their glosses, are:
> So vast, our new Divines, we must confess,
> Are Fathers of the Church for writing less.   (95-98)

The comparisons describing the very different behaviour of
lawyers when they are drawing up deeds for their clients are
also taken over from Donne. He had written:

> But when he sells or changes land, h'impaires,
> The writings, and (unwatch'd) leaves out, <u>ses heires</u>,
> As slily as any Commenter goes by
> Hard words, or sense; or, in Divinity
> As controverters in vouch'd Texts, leave out
> Shrewd words, which might against them clear the doubt.

> (II. 97-102)

Pope wrote:

> But let them write for You, each Rogue impairs
> The Deeds, and dextrously omits, <u>ses Heires</u>:

> No Commentator can more slily pass
> O'er a learned, unintelligible place;
> Or, in Quotation, shrewd Divines leave out
> Those words, that would against them clear the doubt.

(99-104)

There is an old notion that Augustan poets preferred hackneyed imagery. But it is evident that Pope takes over some of the most out-of-the-way images in Donne. Although he changes the wording, he retains Donne's image of "the tender labyrinth of a Maids soft ear."[22] He follows him in comparing unfashionable "good works" to "old rich Wardrobes" (II. 110-111; Pope 122); and keeps an image which is reminiscent of medieval preaching and of such writers as George Herbert and Bunyan:

> [Shall I] . . . my mistress Truth, betray thee
> For th'huffing, braggart, puft Nobility?[23]

Pope modifies the first line but retains the second virtually unchanged.

"In the Satyres," Sir Herbert Grierson has remarked, "Donne is always, though he does not state his position too clearly, one with links attaching him to the persecuted Catholic minority."[24] Pope must have been quick to notice this characteristic of the poems; and he follows Donne in most of the images which suggest a Catholic background. When Donne said that the condition of poets "Is poor, disarm'd, like Papists, not worth hate" (II. 10), he was making a comparison that must often have occurred to Pope, who reproduced the line with slight changes.[25] Pope also retained the image in which Donne compares a lawyer who does not worry about the length of a document because he does not have to copy it out himself to Luther:

> In those first dayes
> When Luther was profest, he did desire
> Short Pater nosters, saying as a Fryer
> Each day his beads, but having left those laws,
> Adds to Christs prayer, the power and glory clause.

(II. 92-96)

So Donne. Pope "versified" the passage in this way, retaining the basic image and the striking final line unchanged:

> So Luther thought the Paternoster long,
> When doom'd to say his Beads and Evensong:
> But having cast his Cowle, and left those laws,
> Adds to Christ's prayer, the Pow'r and Glory clause.

(105-108)

Donne strikingly describes wicked men "Who with sins all kinds as familiar be / As Confessors" (II. 34-35). Pope gives the same image a sharper point: "Sins which Prisca's Confessor scarce hears" (40).

Sometimes Pope makes considerable changes in the wording of a passage, while still retaining the fundamental comparison. This is true of an unusual image which has again a Catholic background. Donne had described a fantastic courtier who

> call[s] his clothes to shrift,
> Making them confess not only mortal
> Great stains and holes in them, but venial
> Feathers and dust, wherewith they fornicate.

(IV. 200-203)

The rhythm of Pope's lines is different, but they contain the same remarkable comparison:

> and to Confession draw
> Those venial sins, an Atom, or a Straw:
> But oh! what Terrors must distract the Soul,
> Convicted of that mortal Crime, a Hole! (242-245)

Similarly the basic image with which Donne's Satyre IV and Pope's Imitation conclude is the same, though the wording is different. Donne has:

> Although I yet
> (With Maccabees modesty) the known merit
> Of my work lessen, yet some wise men shall,

POPE AND DONNE'S SATIRES

> I hope, esteem my Writs Canonical.

Pope rewrote this as follows:

> Howe'er, what's now <u>Apocrypha</u>, my Wit,
> In time to come, may pass for <u>Holy Writ</u>.

The <u>ordering</u> effect of Pope's couplets sometimes appears to lessen the shock of an image, which is yet just as remarkable as its prototype in Donne. Where Donne wrote

> As Itch
> Scratch'd into smart, and as blunt Iron grown'd
> Into an edge, hurts worse: So, I (fool) found,
> Crossing hurt me. (IV. 88-91)

Pope rewrote:

> But as coarse Iron, sharpen'd, mangles more,
> And Itch most hurts, when anger'd to a Sore;
> So when you plague a Fool, 'tis still the Curse,
> You only make the Matter worse and worse. (118-121)

A similar effect may be noticed when one compares lines 11-16 of Donne's <u>Satyre II</u> with lines 13-20 of Pope's Imitation. Here is the Donne:

> One, (like a wretch, which at Barre judg'd as dead,
> Yet prompts him which stands next, and cannot read,
> And saves his life) gives Idiot Actors means,
> (Starving himself) to live by his labour'd scenes.
> As in some Organs, Puppets dance above
> And bellows pant below, which them do move.

Here is the Pope:

> Here a lean Bard, whose wit could never give
> Himself a dinner, makes an Actor live:
> The Thief condemn'd, in law already dead,
> So prompts, and saves a Rogue who cannot read.
> Thus as the pipes of some carv'd Organ move,

> The gilded Puppets dance and mount above,
> Heav'd by the breath th'inspiring Bellows blow;
> Th'inspiring Bellows lie and pant below.[26]

In a letter which Pope wrote to Cromwell on 12 July 1707 there occur the following lines:

> I know you dread all those who write,
> And both with mouth and hand recite;
> Who slow and leisurely rehearse,
> As loath t'enrich you with their verse;
> Just as a still, with simples in it,
> Betwixt each drop stays half a minute.
> That simile is not my own,
> But lawfully belongs to Donne.[27]

This makes it clear that Pope was familiar with Donne's Satyres by his twentieth year, long before his version of Satyre IV was written, and four years or so before he tried his hand at II. But the importance of the passage is much greater than that. Taken in conjunction with Pope's remark to Spence, that "Donne had no imagination, but as much wit, I think, as any writer can possibly have,"[28] it points clearly to the fact that it was Donne's imagery, more than anything else, that Pope admired. He admired the "wit" which enabled Donne to describe his feelings on leaving the Court, "pleas'd so / As men from gaols t'execution go" (IV.230; Pope 273). He admired the command of language and image which inspired the lines:

> He like to a high-strecht Lute-string squeakt, O sir,
> 'Tis sweet to talk of Kings.[29]

If the imagery of Pope's own satire is subtler and richer than has usually been acknowledged, it is due in large measure to the example of Donne.[30]

It has sometimes been supposed that the reason for Pope's "refining" on Donne was that he found the "realism" of the earlier poet unacceptable. In his provocative book The Personal Principle, for example, D. S. Savage quotes this passage:

> But he is worst, who (beggerly) doth chaw

> Others wits fruits, and in his ravenous maw
> Rankly digested, doth those things out-spue,
> As his own things; and they're his own, 'tis true,
> For if one eat my meat, though it be known,
> The meat was mine, th'excrement's his own. (II. 25-30)

Following this with the corresponding passage from Pope, which ends with the lines:

> Sense, past thro' him, no longer is the same,
> For food digested takes another name,   (33-34)

Savage comments (pp. 62-63): "Pope's version reveals how too squeamish a refinement results in a sensuous impoverishment of the actual verse-texture. In Donne, the words seem to have been chewed over physically. In Pope, the verse has been refined of its physical grossness in its passage through the versifier's more civilised mentality, and concreteness of epithet is readily sacrificed for a conceit and an epigram." The difference in verse-texture is undeniable; but the word "squeamish" suggests a confusion of rhetorical and non-rhetorical criteria. In this species of writing it is unlikely that Pope would have refused to use the word "excrement," though here (as with "Drug" at IV. 135, in place of Donne's "poyson," 101) he finds it more effective to be oblique.

Another line which Savage might well have quoted to establish the contrast between Donne and Pope is this: "Worse than imbrothel'd strumpets prostitute" (II. 64). Pope rewrites this as: "Paltry and proud, as drabs in Drury-lane" (64). One should be cautious in relating the difference in verse-texture between such passages to differences in "sensibility." Such alterations Pope was obliged to make, taste quite apart, to avoid a heavy air of "period" which would have blunted the contemporary force of his satire. Donne's line is powerful; but so is Pope's. In spite of the difference of idiom Pope is neither mealy-mouthed[31] nor inferior to Donne in the management of the pattern of sound and sense made by the verse.

Is not the truth that Pope is writing in as "low" a style as Donne, but according to the criteria of a different age? Some of his images are of the lowest: he retains Donne's

> Like a big wife, at sight of loathed meat,
> Ready to travail: so I sigh, and sweat[32]

without significant alteration, and keeps the vivid metaphor in
"the bladder of our Court" (IV. 168; Pope 205). He retains many
of Donne's most colloquial turns of expression, merely changing "Grogaram" to "Padua-soy" in the line, "Your only wearing
is your Grogaram" (IV. 86; Pope 113). He retains "Tufftaffaty"
and "plain Rash."[33] In a passage not closely modelled on Donne
he has the phrase "some Folks."[34] He catches with admiration
at the echo of familiar speech in Donne's "And unto her protests,
protests, protests" (IV. 212).[35] A cursory glance at Pope's Imitations reveals such words as "sweat," "Whore," "Gewgaws,"
"the Pox," "Clap," the line

> Damn him, he's honest, Sir, -- and that's enuff,

"Bastardy," "puke," and "rank Widows."[36] Differences of versification being admitted, "squeamish" is not the word for
Pope's Imitations, which offer the reader as authentic an example of the middle-to-low idiom considered appropriate to
Horatian satire in the Augustan age as Donne's Satyres do of
that of the Elizabethan age.

Pope used to be portrayed as a reformer in strong revolt
against most English poetry before Dryden. To study him as
an imitator of Donne is to see him in a different perspective.
It is clear that the man who admired Donne's vivid homeliness
of phrase, his witty conciseness, and his bold satiric imagery
can be summed up as "correct" only if a very full historical
significance is given to that word. What has to be understood
is the connotation of "decorum" when it is applied to Horatian
satire.

It was thoroughly consonant with Pope's understanding of
the nature of tradition that he should "versify" the Satyres of
Donne, just as he had done with those of Horace. For the tradition from which he drew nourishment and inspiration was one
in which Horace and Donne were both his predecessors. The
English element so prominent in the originally classical genre
of formal satire deserves emphasis because in this form, more
than most, the continuity from the late Elizabethan to the Augustan age may be discerned.

POPE AND DONNE'S SATIRES

The idiom one tends to think of as characteristically Donne's — that of the Songs and Sonets — is naturally very different from that of the Epistle to Arbuthnot (which comes first to mind when Pope is mentioned). But if one compares the idioms of the two men in the same genre one finds, indeed, considerable differences, but less of a chasm than one might expect.[37] Diction and imagery differ less than might have been supposed: it is above all in "numbers" that the difference between the satiric idioms of the two men lies. It is because the versification of Augustan poetry has received a disproportionate amount of critical attention, at the expense of other aspects of poetic art, that Pope has been supposed to have little or nothing in common with Donne. But there is a sense in which the two men may be set together, and contrasted sharply with all poets after the middle of the eighteenth century: they are both poets of the Renaissance.[38]

NOTES

1   Johnson's Lives of the English Poets, ed. G. Birkbeck Hill, III, 251.

2   Works (1770), IV, 240. Not in the ed. of 1751.

3   Elwin-Courthope comment that the fact that line 78 in Pope's final version of Donne's second satire, together "with two or three others in the Satire, is transferred unaltered from Donne, . . . shows how firmly Pope's style is rooted in the genius of the English language" (III, 430 n. 2). I agree with this conclusion. But the number of lines which Pope takes over is larger than this. In his early version of II Pope retains 22 of Donne's 112 lines either unchanged or with very slight alterations (e. g., "That 'scuse for writing, and for writing ill," l. 24, is changed to "Excuse for writing and for writing ill," l. 32. In the later version he retains 12/112. In his imitation of IV he keeps 18/244. The evidence of retained rhymes, for what it is worth, confirms the relations to Donne suggested by these numbers. In his early version of II Pope keeps 30/56 of Donne's pairs of rhymes: in the later version 20/56. In his version of IV he has 16/122. Clearly the early version of II is the nearest to Donne of the three, while IV is much further from its original than even the later version of II. It is because

evidence of this sort is not of very great value, however, that I have written this paper to make the comparison in a more illuminating way.

4   All my quotations are from Vol. IV of the Twickenham edition, ed. John Butt. I cite Pope's text of Donne, as given by Butt, without mention of differences between it and Grierson. Unless otherwise mentioned, all references to Pope's imitation of II are to the later version.

5   Essays, ed. W. P. Ker, II, 101-102.

6   L'art poétique, I, 111-112.

7   "Most of the pieces which are usually produced upon this plan [that of the moral epistle], rather give one an image of Lucilius, than of Horace: the authors of them seem to mistake the aukward negligence of the favorite of Scipio, for the easy air of the friend of Maecenas." The Letters of Sir Thomas Fitzosborne [by William Melmoth], 4th ed. (1754), Letter xxxvii.

8   Pope 37 ("Cry" for "Sir").

9   Pope 105 ("all our Edwards").

10 Pope 60 ("wooe").

11 Pope 59 ("Scots" for "men").

12 20-23. As often, Pope here uses italics to emphasize the pattern of his rhetoric.

13 The Letters of Sir Thomas Fitzosborne, Letter xxxvii.

14 Spence's Anecdotes, ed. Singer (1820), p. 1.

15 Compare the severe judgment which Pope passed on gentle-men-poets in general, thinking particularly of Crashaw: "All that regards design, form, fable, which is the soul of poetry; all that concerns exactness, or consent of parts, which is the body, will probably be wanting . . ." Elwin-Courthope, Works, VI, 116.

16 "On Writing and Books," xxxiv, in the Works (1764), II, 178.

17 He retained Donne's concise "Wants reach all states" (IV. 184; Pope 224).

18   132-133. I have italicized the last word.

19   My italics. Donne has: "He like a privileg'd spie, whom nothing can / Discredit . . ." (121-122).

20   Johnson's Lives, I, 26.

21   II. 77-78. Pope has: "Till like the Sea, they compass all the land, / From Scots to Wight, from Mount to Dover Strand" (85-86).

22   II. 58. Pope: "The soft lab'rinth of a Lady's ear" (55).

23   IV. 163-164. Pope: "O my fair Mistress, Truth! Shall I quit thee, / For huffing, braggart, puft Nobility?" (200-201).

24   The Poems of John Donne (Oxford, 1912), II, 117.

25   "Yet like the Papists is the Poets state, / Poor and dis-arm'd, and hardly worth your hate" (11-12). Cf. The Second Epistle of the Second Book of Horace, imitated by Mr. Pope, p. 67.

26   Cf. An Epistle to Dr. Arbuthnot, 318.

27   Elwin-Courthope, Works, VI, 62. Cited by Butt in a note to IV. 126-129, where Pope takes the image over from Donne 94-96.

28   Anecdotes, p. 136.

29   IV. 73-74. Pope:

> Squeaks like a high-stretch'd Lutestring, and replies:
> "Oh 'tis the sweetest of all earthly things
> To gaze on Princes, and to talk of Kings! (99-101)

30   Warburton printed Parnell's version of Donne's Satyre III (Works, 1751, IV, 247-253) to show the superiority of Pope's versions. In nothing is Parnell's inferiority more evident than in his unwillingness to retain Donne's auda-cious imagery unweakened. He has also a tendency to step into too high a style. It is interesting to note that Warbur-ton, writing in the middle of the eighteenth century, calls Donne's Satyre III "the noblest Work not only of This, but perhaps of any satiric Poet" (p. 247). The subject of the

Satire is no doubt largely responsible for his enthusiasm.

31 He uses the word "Strumpet" at IV. 148.

32 IV. 117-118. Pope: "Like a big Wife at sight of loathsome Meat, / Ready to cast, I yawn, I sigh, and sweat" (156-157).

33 IV. 33-34; Pope 42 and 45.

34 IV. 211. Johnson says that the singular "Folk" is now used only in familiar or burlesque language" (Dictionary). The plural is yet more familiar.

35 Pope: "Prodigious! how the Things Protest, Protest" (255).

36 IV. 278; IV. 213; IV. 171; II. 47; IV. 263; II. 82; IV. 153; II. 87.

37 In judging that Donne's "Epistles, Metempsychosis, and Satires" were "his best things" (Spence, p. 144) Pope was obviously influenced by the fact that these were the poems most similar in intention to his own work.

38 I wish to thank my wife for helping me to arrange the materials in this paper. The phrase quoted in the title occurs in Joseph Warton's Essay on the Genius and Writings of Pope, 4th ed. (1782), II, 353.

THE COUNTRY HOUSE POEM
OF THE SEVENTEENTH CENTURY

G. R. Hibbard

I

Through the poetry of the early seventeenth century there
runs a thin but clearly defined tradition of poems in praise of
the English country house and of the whole way of life of which
the country house was the centre. Once the line is recognized,
there emerges a homogeneous body of poetry which is not only
a considerable achievement in its own right, marked, as it is,
by strong ethical thought and by a certain sobriety and weight
of utterance, but which is also of peculiar interest to all who
are concerned about the relation of poetry to the society from
which it springs, and which throws a good deal of light on what
the seventeenth century understood by "nature" and on the whole
concept of "use" as the accepted basis for a civilized human
existence. This tradition begins with Ben Jonson's poems To
Penshurst and Sir Robert Wroth, is continued through two
poems by Thomas Carew, To Saxham and To my Friend G. N.
from Wrest, through two poems by Herrick, A Country-life:
to his Brother Mr. Thomas Herrick and A Panegerick to Sir
Lewis Pemberton, and finally comes to an end in Marvell's
Appleton House which begins from well within the tradition,
though it ultimately grows into something very different from
any of the other poems.

In all these poems there is a considerable debt to Latin
poetry, especially to the work of Horace and Martial, but it is
a debt which can easily be overstated. It is only necessary to
place them beside Martial's epigram Baiana nostri villa, Basse,
Faustini (Book III, No. LVIII), or beside Horace's Beatus ille
(Epodes II), and it is at once apparent how thoroughly English
they are. The main business of using and adapting the Latin
model was done by Ben Jonson, and it was his work, rather

Reprinted from Journal of the Warburg and Courtauld Institutes, Vol. 19
(1956), pp. 159-174, by permission of author and publisher.

than that of Martial and Horace, which mattered most to those
who followed him. The marks of his influence are to be seen
in the constant references to architecture which occur in most
of these poems (something that is not found in the Latin models),
in the deep concern with the social function of the great house
in the life of the community, and in the understanding of the
reciprocal interplay of man and nature in the creation of a good
life. What the Latin poets provided was not an attitude which
could be taken over and used by the poets I want to consider,
but rather the general framework for a poem which lent itself
to the critical examination of certain aspects of life. It is here
that the importance of this body of poetry lies. It is truly Augustan in the sense that it voices and defines the values of a
society conscious of its own achievement of a civilized way of
living, and conscious also of the forces that threatened to under-
mine and overthrow that achievement. The function of the poet
in this society was to make it aware of itself; and because the
poet had a function the relation between poet and patron in these
poems is sound and wholesome. The poet is not a menial or a
hanger-on, but an honoured friend and guest, welcomed for
himself and for what he has to contribute to the life of the great
house. There is nothing "patronizing" in the patronage of Sir
Robert Sidney or Lord Fairfax, and nothing servile in the gratitude of Ben Jonson or Andrew Marvell; both poet and patron
are parts of an organic whole, each recognizes the importance
and place of the other in the life of the community.

After 1660 this kind of poem was no longer written, because
the way of life that it reflects, and out of which it grows, was
on the decline. The function of the great house changed, and to
this change in function there corresponded a new style of architecture. Even among the aristocracy, however, despite their
passion for building and rebuilding, most people continued to
live in houses erected during the sixteenth century, and this
helped to keep the old way of life alive as a potent idea, if nothing more. And so, while the country house poem as a distinct
form comes to an end with Marvell's Appleton House, the view
of life on which it rests is still present in Pope's Epistle to
Burlington, where the scale of values stated with such strength
and conviction in To Penshurst is used as a standard of sense
and taste against which to weigh the aberrations and excesses
of Timon. Pope's attitude is in fact fundamentally the same as

that of Ben Jonson, but the society he looks at is a very different one. For Ben Jonson Penshurst represents the norm, slightly idealized, perhaps, but still the norm; the values he believes in are embodied in it, and, while he is very much alive to the threat to those values evident in such a piece of self-glorification as Wollaton Hall, the poem remains a positive statement rather than a satirical attack. For Pope, Timon's villa is the norm, a house whose sole function is to minister to the pride of its owner; the values Pope believes in are no longer to be found in the great houses being built at the time, but in Burlington's designs, and in a way of life that had already largely disappeared among the upper class.

II

The century that lies between Ben Jonson and Pope saw a great change in English domestic architecture, which altered the whole character and function of the large country house. Most of the great houses built before the beginning of the Civil War followed a traditional pattern. No architect was employed in their construction, in fact no architect existed before about 1580. The usual method was to build by rough contract between owner and master workman, one or the other of whom supplied the plan which might undergo considerable alteration while the house was actually in course of erection.[1] The essential element in this plan was the great hall which was central. The kitchen, which was at one end of the hall, and the parlour or parlours, which were at the other, frequently took the form of two wings. The hall was the centre of the house not only because the house had grown out of it, but also because, as J. A. Gotch points out, "the household was in the nature of a large family."[2] The great hall was the common meeting ground for members of the family and their servants and, very often, their tenants as well. It was in fact the heart of a self-contained community and, as such, it continued to dictate the design of the house so long as the relation of the lord to his dependants was that of the father to a family, and so long as the sixteenth-century custom of "housekeeping" continued. In this kind of house all the rooms were, to quote Gotch, "intended for daily use."

Not all the great houses built during Elizabeth's reign,

however, conformed to this pattern. The "prodigy houses," as
Summerson calls them, erected in the last three decades of the
sixteenth century were intended for a very different purpose and
consequently took a different form. Houses like Holdenby and
Wollaton Hall were not designed to meet the needs of the house-
holds living in them, but for the reception of Elizabeth and her
court and as an expression of their owners' sense of their own
importance. Splendour and impressiveness rather than utility
were what they aimed at and frequently achieved. Summerson
says of Sir Christopher Hatton's house at Holdenby, "Hatton
hardly used his new house, nor did he build it for use."[3] An extreme consequence of this desire to make the great house striking and dramatic is still to be seen in such a hybrid creation as
Wollaton Hall, built for Sir Francis Willoughby between 1580
and 1588 by Robert Smythson, "architector and surveyor."
Basically Italian in design, Wollaton is adorned "with any
amount of gaudy Netherlandish ornament."[4] Pevsner speaks of
its spectacular qualities and singles out "showiness" as its
main characteristic, while Summerson, who does full justice
to the skill with which the design has been executed, nevertheless feels compelled to describe it as "an extravaganza," an
"exceedingly pretentious palace" and "an inflated bauble, an
architectural symbol rather than a house."[5] These judgments
are in striking agreement with Ben Jonson's attack on ostentatious mansions built for show in his poem To Penshurst.

As a piece of architecture Wollaton Hall is something of a
sport; its design did not influence subsequent work; but in its
conscious and deliberate striving after effect to the exclusion
of other considerations it is a clear pointer to the future. The
decisive change which ultimately altered the whole style and
character of the large country house came with the rise of the
professional architect during the third decade of the seventeenth
century. The Banqueting House at Whitehall, the first purely
classical building to be erected in this country, was finished
in 1622. Inigo Jones, who designed it, had a knowledge and understanding of Italian aims and methods such as no previous
designer had had; and the result was a building with a new kind
of beauty of its own, relying for its effect on form, proportion,
symmetry, and definition of line. The example thus set soon
began to affect the design of the large country house and after
the Restoration it became the dominant mode.

In some ways the change was for the good. Many of the
great houses built during the later seventeenth and early eighteenth centuries are the expression of a genuine concern for
beauty of form. But in some cases the complete break with the
native tradition did result in functionalism being sacrificed to
stateliness. As Gotch points out, much of the house was devoted to state functions and was intended for occasional use only.
The family lived in what was left over, while the servants were
banished to the basement or to a detached wing.[6] The great hall
declined in importance; in Hardwick Hall, completed in 1597,
it is already placed on the axis of the main entrance and runs
across the house, not along it, and at Aston Hall near Birming-
ham, finished in 1635, it has become a vestibule. The large
house came to run the risk attendant on any kind of building
concerned primarily with effect — that the search for the grand
and the imposing, when it is not anchored by an equal attention
to more functional considerations, may easily result in the
grandiose. In the medium-sized Queen Anne house, built to be
lived in, the architectural revolution produced something that
is wholly admirable; its effects as seen in Chatsworth, Blenheim or Castle Howard are more questionable.

The change was not, of course, entirely the result of the
rise of the architect and of a widespread interest in architecture.
It was made possible and helped on by social changes, and by
developments in the economy of the great house itself. The decline in "housekeeping" which took place in the early seventeenth century meant that the great hall was no longer necessary as a communal dining-room. There was a marked tendency
for the great man to make much more use of intermediary of-
ficials in his dealings with tenants and servants, and in this
way to cut himself off from direct contact with the humbler day-
to-day activities of his estate.[7] Most important of all, however,
the seventeenth century saw an important alteration in the whole
relationship of the great landowner to his country home. Down
to the time of the Civil Wars it was the centre of his life and
there his main activities were concentrated. Family papers
like the Memoirs of the Verney Family give a vivid picture of
how full and absorbing that life could be, not only for the country gentleman himself busy with building, with settling disputes among tenants, with obtaining adequate water supplies and
so on, but also for his wife and daughters occupied with the

management of the house, with preserving fruit, and with the laying in of provisions against the winter. G. M. Trevelyan points out the advantages of this confinement to rural society during the reigns of the first two Stuarts:

> for there both the ladies and the gentlemen found the duties and realities of life thick around them, in daily contact with other classes. As yet they had not been attracted to an isolated life of fashion in London, and the country house was still the scene, not merely of relaxation, but of business.[8]

Even under Charles I, however, the change Trevelyan talks about was in fact beginning. While a household like that of the Verneys was still the general rule, a certain number of country families began to feel the lure of the town and the court. David Mathew actually takes the Crofts who lived at Saxham, and of whom Carew wrote, as the representative instance of a country family with court connexions. He writes:

> Sir Henry Crofts and his wife both came from the middle ranks of the gentry but with Court connections. The younger daughter had been in the Queen's household, apparently soon after Buckingham's murder; the son also held a post about her person. The elder Crofts remained in the country, although not too far from Newmarket. They did not purchase or rent a house in London or Middlesex like the true courtiers.[9]

In this case the split between the older generation who remained in the country and the younger generation who gravitated to the court is clearly marked. After 1660 the process was accelerated to such an extent that the Earl of Rochester could say "that when he came to Brentford the devill entred into him and never left him till he came into the country again to Alderbury or Woodstock."[10] He felt himself to have two distinct personalities, one for the country and another for the town and court, and he had no doubt which was the better. His relations with his tenants seem to have been good, he took his responsibilities as a country gentleman seriously, but it is plain that his home at Alderbury was not the centre of his life, and that he could not

be a father to tenants and servants from whom he was separated
by long periods of absence. In fact even in the country Rochester
seems to have been a split personality. He would retreat to his
Lodge at Woodstock and spend months "wholly employed in
study," but then his friends from London would arrive and study
would give way to debauchery.[11] At one moment one is aware of
a continuity between his way of life and that followed by men like
Sir Robert Sidney or Lord Falkland in the earlier part of the
century, at the next one feels a vivid sense of contrast between
the activities with which Buckingham, Buckhurst and the rest
were entertained at Woodstock, and the way in which poets and
philosophers were entertained at Penshurst and Great Tew.
Rochester built no new house, but it is plain that his country
home, though not yet a place of relaxation involving neither
duty nor responsibility, was well on the way to becoming so.

The final stage in this process is reached in the early eighteenth century with such figures as James Brydges, Duke of
Chandos, who was long identified with the Timon of Pope's
Epistle to Burlington. Chandos, although he came of a good
family, was essentially a self-made man, and though he is now
remembered as the owner of Cannons, his main interest was
in the City. Cannons for him was something with which he could
impress his friends and acquaintances and a place where he
could take his leisure. So much of a showplace was it that as
early as 1724 visitors were being allowed to see it and escorted
over it on the payment of a fee.[12] Chandos's most recent biog-
raphers say of him:

> Chandos is better remembered today as the builder of
> an almost legendary Cannons, as the patron of Handel,
> and as Pope's victim, than for his service to the coun-
> try as paymaster of the troops abroad, or for his in-
> fluence in the City and in the early fortunes of what
> now is called industrial and imperialist development.
> Yet in his view the creation of Cannons was a small
> issue compared with his incessant zeal to promote the
> affairs of the South Sea, the East India, and the Africa
> companies, the York Buildings, and the Sun Life Insur-
> ance Companies. His interest in things such as soap-
> and glass-making, the coal industry, English mining,
> the water-supply of London and the slave-trade was

equalled only by his detailed study of estate management. And if we may gauge his interest by his correspondence, he was actually more absorbed in mining
ventures and building speculations at Bath and Bridg-
water than by the erection of his own great mansion.[13]

F. W. Bateson has since shown in his edition of the Moral
Essays that Timon was not intended by Pope as a caricature
of Chandos, but the fact that the identification was made and
was widely accepted would seem to be sufficient justification
for taking Cannons as the type of house that Pope was attacking.
The contrast between it and the Penshurst Ben Jonson wrote of
is startling. There is no indication that Cannons or its master
served any function at all in the life of the surrounding countryside. Nor does Chandos's interest in the arts, other, perhaps,
than the art of music, appear to have been very deep or very
discriminating. He was a generous patron, but he seems to
have collected pictures and objets d'art generally (often buying
them on a dealer's advice without ever having seen them) rather
because it was the fashionable thing to do than because he genuinely enjoyed them. In much the same way he filled his gardens
with exotic trees and birds from as far away as the West Indies
and the Gold Coast. In his hands the great house was well on
the way to becoming a museum and the garden to becoming a
zoo. In 1747, only twenty-four years after its completion and
less than three years after Chandos's death, the demolition of
Cannons was begun. Once its owner was dead the house ceased
to have any purpose or meaning.

III

To Penshurst is the poem which established the tradition;
and like so much of Jonson's work it springs from the union
between his deep interest in classical literature and his lively
critical observation of the life of his day. The literary model
for it was provided by Martial's epigram, Baiana nostri villa,
Basse, Faustini (Book III, No. LVIII). Not only is there literal
translation from the Latin ("The painted partrich" for picta
perdix), but the two poems follow a similar line of development.
Both poets begin with a description of the house, stressing its

unostentatious solidity and usefulness; both go on to paint the
fertility of the estate with its cattle, its poultry, and its fish;
and both follow this with a passage devoted to country hospitality. Even the cheerful, ungrudging waiter who enjoys serving
his master's guests is to be found in Martial's epigram before
he appears in Ben Jonson's poem. Yet despite this structural
similarity Jonson's is incomparably the fuller and richer poem.
The whole view of life on which it rests is broader and more
complete than that of the Latin model, the texture of the verse
is more closely woven. In part this difference can be accounted
for by the fact that both poets write with their eye on the object.
It is not Martial's fault that, compared with the spaciousness
and dignity of the home of the Sidneys, the Baian villa appears
cluttered and rather draggle-tailed (avidi secuntur vilicae si-
num porci). But there is more to it than a mere difference in
the places described. Where Martial's poem rests on a simple
contrast between the crude but solid comforts of the farm and
the sophisticated hollowness (famem mundam) of the suburban
villa, Jonson sees Penshurst in a bigger and more interesting
context. To Penshurst is a product of the same interests and
preoccupations which led to the writing of the great satirical
comedies, Volpone and The Alchemist, and is, in its own lesser
way, the counterpart to those works. In the comedies Jonson,
as L. C. Knights has shown, attacks the vices of the time in the
name of traditional morality. To money values, which he regards as unnatural and perverted, Jonson opposes human values.
But in the comedies the values Jonson believes in and upholds
are implicit rather than explicit and fully stated; in To Penshurst, on the other hand, the reverse is the case. The poem is,
to my way of thinking, the fullest statement we have of that
traditional piety which is the basis of his satire. The contrast
in it is not a contrast between town and country, but between
the right use of wealth and the wrong, between good human relationships and bad ones, between the house as a place to live
in, the centre of an organic whole made up of man and nature,
and the house as an expression of individual pride, an imposi-
tion on the community and a powerful threat to an established
way of life.

Ben Jonson was not the first to see Penshurst in this way.
It is generally accepted that when Sir Philip Sidney described
Kalander's house in the Arcadia it was in fact his own home

that he was thinking of. His description is worth quoting because he also recognizes that the house expresses a certain attitude to life, and because it may well have been in Jonson's mind when he wrote To Penshurst:

> They perceived he was not willing to open him-
> selfe further, and therefore without further question-
> ing brought him to the house: about which they might
> see (with fitte consideration both of the ayre, the
> prospect, and the nature of the ground) all such
> necessarie additions to a great house, as might well
> shewe, Kalander knew that provision is the foundation
> of hospitalitie, and thrift the fewell of magnificence.
> The house it selfe was built of faire and strong stone,
> not affecting so much any extraordinarie kind of fine-
> nes, as an honorable representing of a firme state-
> lines. The lightes, doores and staires, rather directed
> to the use of the guest, then to the eyes of the Artificer:
> and yet as the one cheefly heeded, so the other not
> neglected; each place handsome without curiositie,
> and homely without lothsomnes: not so daintie as not
> to be trode on, nor yet slubberd up with good felow-
> shippe: all more lasting then beautifull, but that the
> consideration of the exceeding lastingnesse made the
> eye beleeve it was exceeding beautifull. The servants
> not so many in number, as cleanlie in apparell, and
> serviceable in behaviour, testifying even in their
> countenaunces, that their maister tooke aswell care
> to be served, as of them that did serve.[14]

Kalander's house is meant to be lived in, it is not a show-piece; and it is this opposition between the useful and the ostentatious that provides a backbone for the whole body of poetry from Ben Jonson to Pope that I am considering. The same basic idea is already there in Martial's epigram where he praises the Baian villa because its grounds are not laid out with useless beds of myrtle (non otiosis ordinata myrtetis), but it was part of Jonson's whole way of thinking and in his poem he expands and enriches it. He sees Penshurst in the way that Sidney sees it as a place that has grown up to meet human needs. It is built of "the countrey stone," has arisen, as it were, out of the earth it stands on. Its strength is in essentials, in primary things:

> Thou art not, PENSHVRST, built to envious show,
>   Of touch or marble; nor canst boast a row
> Of polish'd pillars, or a roofe of gold:
>   Thou hast no lantherne, whereof tales are told;
> Or stayre, or courts; but stand'st an ancient pile,
>   And these grudg'd at, art reverenc'd the while.
> Thou ioy'st in better markes, of soyle, of ayre,
>   Of wood, of water: therein thou art fair.[15]

In these opening lines Jonson establishes an attitude to the house, and, by contrast, to the newer and more elaborate mansions which were going up at the time, that is maintained throughout the poem and is triumphantly stated again in the last four lines:

> Now, PENSHVRST, they that will proportion thee
>   With other edifices, when they see
> Those proud, ambitious heaps, and nothing else,
>   May say, their lords have built, but thy lord dwells.

These opening lines do more, however, than state a preference; they lead on to what is the main theme of the poem, namely, the function of the house in the community as the centre of a complex web of relationships which makes up the fabric of civilized living. When Jonson writes, "And these grudg'd at, art reverenc'd the while," he links the house with the people of the surrounding countryside. Penshurst has a place in men's lives, it satisfies emotional as well as practical needs, it stands for something. It is the embodiment of a natural bond between lord and tenant. The building of fine new houses very often meant the arbitrary raising of rents and the disruption of all links between landlord and tenant except that of hard cash. Jonson makes the point in a way that reminds one that he was also the author of Volpone:

> And though thy walls be of the countrey stone,
>   They're built with no mans ruine, no mans grone,
> There's none that dwell about them, wish them downe;
>   But all come in, the farmer, and the clowne:

> And no one empty-handed, to salute
> Thy lord, and lady, though they have no sute.

The tenants of the Sidneys are not exploited; the relationship is a reciprocal one of duties and responsibilities on both sides, freely and gladly entered into. The tenants come because they want to, not because they must. Nor does the function of the great house end at the boundaries of the estate; the tradition of "housekeeping" is kept up and links Penshurst with the life of the country as a whole. Hospitality is extended as readily and ungrudgingly to the poet as to the King. The house by providing them with a common meeting ground enables all classes to feel themselves members of the whole.

The house can play this rôle in the life of the community because it is sound at the core, because the family who live in it have been properly brought up. The last section of the poem is devoted to a short but telling picture of family life, with a stress on the way in which the children learn by the example of their parents to recognize their place in the scheme of things, and their duties to God as well as to man. The bonds between tenant and lord are an extension, as it were, of the bonds between child and parent.

The great house and its inmates are the heart of a living organism which includes more than man. The estate matters as much as the people who live on it. Part of Jonson's poem is therefore devoted to the relation between man and nature. Herford and Simpson in their introduction to The Poems seem to me not to understand Jonson's view of nature. They demand that he should have treated it in the way the romantics did. They give him credit for a few "fresh and individual notes" in this poem and in Sir Robert Wroth, but then go on to say:

> But these flashes of vivid experience are rare, and sometimes give place to decorative embellishments in the style of pseudo-classic Pastoral; — Pan and Bacchus feasting under the Kentish beeches of Penshurst, or the fish and fowl eager for the honour of furnishing the table of the Sidneys:

> The painted partrich lyes in every field,
> And for thy messe, is willing to be kill'd.[16]

THE COUNTRY HOUSE POEM

The passages in question are far from mere decorative embellishment, they are Jonson's way of making it clear that just as there is a reciprocal relationship between man and man, so also there is a give and take between man and nature, between the great house and the great estate. But like Marvell in <u>Appleton House</u> Jonson distinguishes between primitive nature, "a rude heap together hurl'd," and nature subjected by man and "in more decent Order tame." It is the latter he refers to throughout. Man and this ordered nature are interdependent; each sustains the other, and without the other would degenerate into mere savagery. "The fish and fowl eager for the honour of furnishing the table of the Sidneys" are silly only when detached from the poem to which they belong. Within the poem they have their place as the consciousness, so to speak, of a humanized nature.

This whole conception of man and nature working together in a harmonious way receives its simplest and most effective expression when Jonson writes:

> Then hath thy orchard fruit, thy garden flowers,
>> Fresh as the ayre, and new as are the houres.
> The earely cherry, with the later plum,
>> Fig, grape, and quince, each in his time doth come:
> The blushing apricot, and woolly peach
>> Hang on thy walls, that every child may reach.

The things of nature, like everything else connected with Penshurst, find their proper end and pleasure in being put to use. It is Jonson's sense of the interdependence of the parts on one another which gives his poem its close-knit quality; it enables him to write of nature in terms appropriate to man, and of man in terms appropriate to nature:

> Some bring a capon, some a rurall cake,
>> Some nuts, some apples; some that thinke they make
> The better cheeses, bring 'hem; or else send
>> By their ripe daughters, whom they would commend
> This way to husbands; and whose baskets beare
>> An embleme of themselves, in plum, or peare.

413

To Penshurst then presents in concrete terms a whole and consistent view of life in which not only man's relation to man, but also to God on the one side and to nature on the other are given due place. It is not merely a complimentary poem about a house and a family, it is a poem about a way of life, which is embodied in the house and expresses itself through it.

Sir Robert Wroth is a much more classical poem than To Penshurst in the sense that its direct debt to Latin poetry is greater. The first half (ll. 1-46) follows in its general development and in much of its detail (with suitable substitutions of English activities for inappropriate Roman ones) the first thirty-six lines of Horace's Epode II, Beatus ille, while the final section (ll. 67-end) owes much to the end of Virgil's second Georgic and to the concluding lines of Juvenal's tenth Satire. The house as such hardly appears in the poem at all, and there is nothing whatever about its architecture. The contrast in this case is not between the useful, comfortable house and the showy one, but between the contented, traditional life of the country and the anxious, acquisitive life of the town and court. Even country life is idealized to the extent that the positive side of Jonson's picture is given over entirely to country sports and relaxations rather than to daily business. There is in fact a conscious equation of life at Durance with the world of the golden age:

> Such, and no other was that age, of old,
>   Which boasts t'have had the head of gold.

This idealization is not, however, carried out merely for its own sake. It serves the larger purpose of the poem by setting off the other theme of it, Jonson's vigorous attack on everything opposed to the kind of life led by Sir Robert Wroth. Jonson is fully aware of the way in which court and town were beginning to attract the country gentleman away from his proper sphere. He begins his poem by praising Sir Robert Wroth for resisting the attraction:

> How blest art thou, canst love the countrey, WROTH,
>   Whether by choice, or fate, or both;
> And though so neere the citie, and the court,
>   Art tane with neithers vice nor sport:
>   .   .   .   .

THE COUNTRY HOUSE POEM

> But canst, at home, in thy securer rest,
> Live, with vn-bought provision blest.

The new acquisitive life of the town is castigated in terms that
are very reminiscent of Volpone, not only in their detail, but
in the way in which man's inhumanity to man is seen as the
fruit of overweening pride. The vigour and assurance of the
attack is pointed by the firm, hard, confident rhythm:

> Let this man sweat, and wrangle at the barre,
> For every price, in every iarre,
> And change possessions, oftner with his breath,
> Then either money, warre, or death!
> Let him, then hardest sires, more disinherit,
> And each where boast it as his merit,
> To blow vp orphanes, widdowes, and their states;
> And thinke his power doth equall Fates.

But despite the general range of the satire, and despite the
lack of references to architecture, the poem is a country house
poem in the sense that Jonson's satire rests on his concrete
apprehension of life in the great house as it was actually lived.
At the very centre of the poem is a lively picture of an unin-
hibited mixing of classes in winter festivities in the great hall
at Durance. The full force of the passage comes out when it
is remembered that Sir Robert Wroth's wife was Lady Mary
Sidney, daughter of the master of Penshurst, and niece of Sir
Philip Sidney:

> The rout of rurall folke come thronging in,
> (Their rudeness then is thought no sinne)
> Thy noblest spouse affords them welcome grace;
> And the great Heroes, of her race,
> Sit mixt with losse of state, or reverence
> Freedome doth with degree dispense.

It is precisely because there is a general acceptance of the idea
of degree, with all that it entails, that degree can be dispensed
with. The eighteenth-century nobleman, less sure of his own
position, could not risk a lowering of class barriers in this way. His
house and the whole conduct of it were designed to keep them up.

These two poems, the one concerned specifically with the house as such, the other with the more general issue of the opposition between the traditional life of the country and the new life and values of the town, provided the broad general patterns for the other poems that I wish to consider.

IV

Thomas Carew's To Saxham is an altogether slighter piece of work than either of Jonson's poems. It is essentially a finished and delicate piece of compliment which makes it quite clear that Carew knew Jonson's poems well without thoroughly understanding them. The winter setting derives from Sir Robert Wroth; the idea of the birds, beasts and fishes offering themselves as a sacrifice to the table goes back to To Penhurst. But in this case the kind of criticism that Herford and Simpson make of To Penhurst would be fully justified, because when Carew writes,

> The scalie herd, more pleasure tooke,
> Bath'd in thy dish, then in the brooke,

the picture is a piece of sheer decoration unrelated to any fundamental conception of an interplay between man and nature such as that which informs To Penshurst. In Carew's poem no contrast is drawn between town and country, the architecture of Saxham is not mentioned, there is no religious framework, no view of society as a whole. The place never really emerges from the poem at all, nor is there anything of that sense of constant activity which Jonson conveys so well. In fact it would seem that when Carew wrote To Saxham he had not appreciated the true significance of either of Jonson's poems, his eye had been caught rather by certain surface qualities. To this statement one qualification must, however, be made. The poetry becomes firmer, more direct, more serious when he writes of the hospitality which the Crofts continued to extend to all and sundry in the Elizabethan manner:

> Those chearful beames send forth their light,
> To all that wander in the night,

> And seeme to becken from aloofe
> The weary Pilgrim to thy roofe;
> Where if refresh't, he will away,
> Hee's fairly welcome, or if stay
> Farre more, which he shall hearty find,
> Both from the Master, and the Hinde.
> The stranger's welcome, each man there
> Stamp'd on his chearfull brow doth weare;
> Nor doth this welcome, or his cheere
> Grow lesse, 'cause he staies longer here.17

Here Carew has realized, and conveyed through the verse, one function of the house in the life of the community, but, for the rest, the poem is an elegant piece of compliment and nothing more. It cannot be said to put forward any coherent view of life or society.

To my friend G. N. from Wrest is a very different matter. Here Carew gets beyond the superficial aspects of Jonson's poems, penetrates to their significance, to the firmly held values on which they rest, and makes those values his own. In this poem the octosyllabics of To Saxham are replaced by the heavier couplets of To Penshurst, and the change in metre corresponds to a change in attitude, to a growth in seriousness.

Carew, when he wrote this poem, had just returned from Charles I's expedition to Berwick in May and June 1639. The English army had experienced very bad weather, and Carew was in a mood to appreciate the difference between nature in the raw and the humanized landscape of Bedfordshire. The poem opens with a striking contrast between the Border country, which he sees as sterile and inhuman, and the rich fertility of the home of the De Greys. To emphasize the point Wrest is actually depicted in terms appropriate to a court beauty:

> Here steep'd in balmie dew, the pregnant Earth
> Sends from her teeming womb a flowrie birth,
> And cherisht with the warme Suns quickning heate,
> Her porous bosome doth rich odours sweate;
> Whose perfumes through the Ambient ayre diffuse
> Such native Aromatiques, as we use
> No forraigne Gums, nor essence fetcht from farre,
> No Volatile spirits, nor compounds that are

> Adulterate, but at Natures cheape expence
> With farre more genuine sweetes refresh the sense.

The stress on the native, home-grown quality of the scented
flowers that surround the house, together with the implied criticism of what is fashionable and exotic, serves to knit this opening into the main body of the poem. The theme of Carew's poem,
like the theme of To Penshurst, is the value of traditional ways
of living and of building, and the place of the great house in the
life of the community. The description of the house shows that
Carew knew Jonson's poem well; it also shows that with Jonson
to guide him he could observe and think for himself:

> Such pure and uncompounded beauties, blesse
> This Mansion with an usefull comeliness,
> Devoide of Art, for here the Architect
> Did not with curious skill a Pile erect
> Of carved Marble, Touch, or Porpherie,
> But built a house for hospitalitie;
> No sumptuous Chimney-peece of shining stone
> Invites the strangers eye to gaze upon,
> And coldly entertaines his sight, but cleare
> And cheerful flames, cherish and warme him here:
> No Dorique, nor Corinthian Pillars grace
> With Imagery this structures naked face,
> The Lord and Lady of this place delight
> Rather to be in act, then seeme in sight;
> In stead of Statues to adorne their wall
> They throng with living men, their merry Hall,
> Where at large Tables fill'd with wholsome meates
> The servant, Tennant and kind neighbour eates.

Between the first decade of the century when Ben Jonson
wrote To Penshurst and 1639 when Carew wrote this, the revolution in English domestic architecture had begun. Inigo Jones
had been at work; and Carew had almost certainly seen houses
adorned with "Dorique and Corinthian Pillars" in this country
as well as during the course of his travels in Italy. Indeed the
use of the classical "orders" had come in during the reign of
Elizabeth as a purely decorative device of no practical use
whatever. One would expect him as a courtier to have approved

of the new style, but with Ben Jonson and his own good sense to guide him he does not. Instead he approves of the house that belongs to the countryside it stands in and that serves a social purpose. In his eyes also sound human relationships matter more than elaborate decoration. He delights in the mingling of classes in the great hall, where, although there is a certain segregation of the different classes at different tables, the group still remains a group. His poem, like Ben Jonson's, is based on the perception that it is "use," the functional quality of the house that makes for beauty. The phrase "usefull comelinesse, Devoide of Art" is a guide to his attitude, and the whole argument of the poem is clinched by the lines that follow the description of the feast:

> Nor thinke, because our Piramids, and high
> Exalted Turrets threaten not the skie,
> That therefore Wrest of narrownesse complaines
> Or streightned Walls, for she more numerous traines
> Of Noble guests daily receives, and those
> Can with farre more convenience dispose
> Then prouder Piles, where the vaine builder spent
> More cost in outward gay Embellishment
> Than reall use; which was the sole designe
> Of our contriver, who made things not fine
> But fit for use.

These are lines that both Jonson and Pope would have approved of not only for the general attitude they express, but still more for the way in which Carew through his pointed allusion to the Tower of Babel traces the motive behind elaborate and costly building back to human vanity and pride.

Carew's insistence on "use" extends even to his treatment of the mythological deities whom he handles with a rugged independence in reducing them to their prime significance. Instead of being surrounded by statues of Ceres and Bacchus the house contains good store of the things those deities symbolize:

> We offer not in Emblemes to the eyes,
> But to the taste those usefull Deities.
> We presse the juycie God, and quaffe his blood,
> And grinde the Yeallow Goddesse into food.

419

Throughout the poem there is, as in Ben Jonson's poems, a realization of the interdependence of man and nature. Carew does not reject art; he rejects only the art that conflicts with nature; the art that co-operates with nature to improve and order he welcomes. The poem that results is not a piece of surface imitation by way of compliment, as To Saxham is, but a celebration of the fertile intercourse between man and man and between man and nature, which centres on the great house and finds its fullest expression through it.

V

Herrick is a poet who has suffered from the readiness with which so much of his work lends itself to inclusion in anthologies. Almost invariably he is represented by the "love poems" which are not so much love poems as light elegant trifles on dress and jewels. The part of his poetry which can be "explained" by reference to the years he spent as a jeweller's apprentice has had more attention than it deserves, while some of his more solid achievement has been unduly neglected. Dr. Leavis describes Herrick's manner as "trivially charming."[18] There is no more to be said on the evidence of the poem Dr. Leavis chooses to analyse, but the words are quite inadequate as a description of A Panegerick to Sir Lewis Pemberton which is Herrick's main contribution to the genre of the country house poem. With Ben Jonson to guide him, Herrick can be serious about serious matters, has a wider range of reference, a fuller awareness of the life of the times than Dr. Leavis credits him with, and shows dramatic powers that are far from contemptible.

A Country-Life: To His Brother Mr. Thomas Herrick is not about a country house. Herrick's brother was a farmer, not a country gentleman. Yet the poem is of some interest because, as Moorman points out, while it goes back ultimately to Horace's Beatus ille, and while references to Horace's work in general abound in it, the starting-point for it was Sir Robert Wroth.[19] The poem is very early (Moorman dates it 1610-13), yet even so Herrick has already managed to capture something of Jonson's manner. It is there not merely in the use he makes of Jonson's metre and in the broad general contrast between town and country which is his theme, but far more significantly in the weighty, confident, ethical tone of the opening:

> Thrice, and above, blest (my soule's halfe) are thou
> In thy both Last, and Better Vow:
> Could'st leave the City, for exchange, to see
> The Countrie's sweet simplicity:
> And it to know, and practice; with intent
> To grow the sooner innocent:
> By studying to know vertue; and to aime
> More at her nature, then her name:
> The last is but the least; the first doth tell
> Wayes lesse to live, then to live well.[20]

The characteristic manner of Ben Jonson is stamped on those last six lines; they might well be his.

As yet, however, Herrick cannot keep it up. Like Carew in To Saxham he knows and admires Jonson's work without having thoroughly understood it. After the Jonsonian strength of the first thirty lines or so, the poem falls away. The farmer's life becomes a peg for pretty fancies, and, while there are some playful touches of metaphysical wit in Herrick's picture of the merchant's cares and anxieties, the poem as it develops loses all pretensions to seriousness.

The failure of this early essay in the Jonsonian manner serves to underline the achievement of A Panegerick to Sir Lewis Pemberton. Here the metre is once again that of Sir Robert Wroth, but in its main outlines and in much of its detail the poem follows To Penshurst. There is a direct concern here with the house and what it stands for. Herrick is not interested in architecture as such, but when he writes of "the worn Threshold, Porch, Hall Parlour, Kitchin," he says enough to show that the house was built on the old traditional pattern. More significant still, the house fulfills the traditional functions. Like Penshurst it is not built for show. The first place Herrick turns his attention to is the kitchen,

> Where laden spits, warp't with large Ribbs of Beefe,
> Not represent, but give reliefe
> To the lanke-Stranger, and the sowre Swain;
> Where both may feed, and come againe.

This sets the key for much that follows. There is a boisterous gusto in Herrick's picture of the "housekeeping" at Sir Lewis Pemberton's which surpasses anything of the kind in the other poems I am concerned with. The grudging servant who is hinted at by Martial, mentioned by Ben Jonson, and who thereafter becomes a stock figure in this kind of poem, is nowhere else so fully imagined and so dramatically presented as here. Herrick catches not only his idiom, but even the sour, snarling tone of his voice:

> No commer to thy Roofe his Guest-rite wants;
> Or staying there, is scourg'd with taunts
> Of some rough Groom, who (yirkt with corns) sayes, Sir,
> Y'ave dipt too long i' th' Vinegar;
> And with our Broth and bread, and bits; Sir, friend,
> Y'ave fared well, pray make an end;
> Two dayes, y'ave larded here; a third, yee know,
> Makes guests and fish smell strong; pray go
> You to some other chimney, and there take
> Essay of other giblets; make
> You merry at anothers hearth; y'are here
> Welcome as thunder to our beere.

The scene is dramatic, the language vigorous, richly and forcefully colloquial; we hear the groom as well as see him. The manner of this is not "trivially charming," it has affinities with the manner of Jonson's comedies.

Nor will Dr. Leavis's phrase do for the rest of the poem either. Although Herrick delights in painting the lavish hospitality of the place he can also judge it and see its effect on those who share it. It is marked by a rough equality and serves to bind men together. The guests share Sir Lewis's good manners as well as his good fare; they pay a willing tribute of respect to the lord and lady of the house by not overstepping the bounds of decorum:

> No scurrile jest; no open Sceane is laid
> Here, for to make the face affraid.

The great house is a positive civilizing influence, and the nature of its influence is symbolized in Sir Lewis himself taking the lead in a "House-dance."

THE COUNTRY HOUSE POEM

In the last part of Herrick's poem there is a remarkable understanding of the way in which the value and significance of the house in the life of the community as a whole, depend in the last analysis on the kind of life lived by the family who inhabit it. There is a fine strength in the lines where Herrick states his conviction that the true foundations of the house are the goodness and greatness of its owners. The house will continue so long as it satisfies the needs of the community, and its capacity to do that depends ultimately on the moral insight and the sense of responsibility of the family. Herrick makes it quite clear that he was fully alive to many of the changes that were threatening the old way of life he so much approved of.

> Comliness agrees
> With those thy primitive decrees,
> To give subsistance to thy house, and proofe,
> What Genii support thy roofe,
> Goodnes and Greatnes; not the oaken Piles;
> For these and marbles have their whiles
> To last, but not their ever: Vertues hand
> It is, which builds, 'gainst Fate to stand.
> Such is thy house, whose firme foundations trust
> Is more in thee, then in her dust,
> Or depth; . . . .
> . . . .
>
> Safe stand thy Walls, and Thee, and so both will,
> Since neithers height was rais'd by th' ill
> Of others; since no Stud, no Stone, no Piece,
> Was rear'd up by the Poore-mans fleece:
> No Widowes Tenement was rackt to guild
> Or fret thy Seeling, or to build
> A Sweating-Closset, to anoint the silke-
> Soft-skin, or bath in Asses' milke:
> No Orphan's pittance, left him, serv'd to set
> The pillars up of lasting Jet,
> For which their cryes might beat against thine eares,
> Or in the dampe Jet read their Teares.
> No Planke from Hallowed Altar, do's appeale
> To yond' Star-chamber, or do's seale
> A curse to Thee, or Thine; but all things even

> Make for thy peace, and pace to heaven.
> Go on directly so, as just men may
>   A thousand times, more sweare, then say,
> This is that Princely Pemberton, who can
>   Teach man to keepe a God in man:
> And when wise Poets shall search out to see
>   Good men, They find them all in Thee.

By the time this conclusion is reached the poem has become something much more than a panegyric on an individual. It has developed into a full statement of a view of life that takes into account the social, moral and religious sanctions on which that view of life rests. It demonstrates admirably the strength that Herrick could draw from a tradition of poetry that was closely bound up with a way of life that he knew from personal experience; and it shows the utter inadequacy both of Dr. Leavis's "trivially charming," and of the hackneyed "delicate filigree-work," as descriptions of Herrick's poetry in general.

VI

The final stage in the story of this particular kind of poem is reached with Marvell's Upon Appleton House, to my Lord Fairfax, which begins as a country house poem though it then grows into something new and different. The first ten stanzas are a complete and pregnant summary of the attitudes towards the great house that I have been tracing so far. Quickly and wittily Marvell places Appleton House in relation to seventeenth-century developments in architecture, to nature, to the social scene, and to the moral and religious preoccupations of the age.

Marvell was fortunate in his subject. Fairfax first went to live at Nunappleton after his marriage in 1637, and the life he and his young wife led there is described by M. A. Gibb as follows:

> The Fairfaxes were popular with their neighbours; since the days of Elizabeth they had been noted for keeping a good table. Strong ties of friendship bound them with the Slingsbys of Scriven, the Vavasours of Hazelwood, the Ingrams of Templenewsam, and their

424

cousins, the Bellasis, were regular visitors at Nunappleton.[21]

At the time when Marvell lived there (1651-1653) the old house
had been replaced by a new one which was completed about the
time of Fairfax's retirement from active politics in 1649. The
fullest description of this new house and of the general's attitude to it is given by G. R. Markham, who writes:

> On entering it, Lord Fairfax wrote the following
> lines "Upon the New-built House at Nunappleton": —
>
>> Think not, O man! that dwells herein,
>> This house's a stay, but as an inn
>> Which for convenience fitly stands
>> In way to one not made with hands;
>> But if a time here thou take rest,
>> Yet think eternity the best.

> It was a picturesque brick mansion with stone copings
> and a high steep roof, and consisted of a centre and
> two wings at right angles, forming three sides of a
> square facing to the north. The great hall or gallery
> occupied the centre, between the two wings. It was
> fifty yards long, and was adorned with thirty shields
> in wood, painted with the arms of the family. In the
> other rooms there were chimney pieces of delicate
> marble of various colours, and many fine portraits on
> the walls. The central part of the house was surmount-
> ed by a cupola, and clustering chimneys rose over the
> two wings.[22]

From this it would seem that though the house was new, its design was in the main traditional. The shape conformed to the E
plan so familiar in the sixteenth century, and the roof remained
high-pitched.

Even more important for Marvell's poem than either the
house or the conduct of the household was the character of the
man who lived in it. Fairfax, with his strong sense of moral
responsibility and his firm refusal to follow the temptations of
ambition, is as good an example of the country gentleman of

the early seventeenth century at his best as it is possible to find. He was interested in poetry, he was something of a bibliophile and something of an antiquary. He was not a Sir Philip Sidney, but he shared many of the qualities of the true courtier, the Renaissance gentleman, of whom Sidney was the type.

In Marvell's poem it is the presence of Fairfax that gives Nunappleton House its character, just as in the companion piece, Upon the Hill and Grove at Bill-borow, the hill acquires its personality from Fairfax again. It is not an ambitious house because its owner is not ambitious:

> For he did, with his utmost Skill,
> Ambition weed, but Conscience till.   (st. XLV)[23]

The first thing Marvell seizes on is the native origin of the house and the fact that its creation has involved no spoliation of nature, no excessive and pointless exercise of human ingenuity. Contemporary movements in taste and architecture are brilliantly criticized in the condensed wit of the opening stanza:

> Within this sober Frame expect
> Work of no Forrain Architect;
> That unto Caves the Quarries drew,
> And Forrests did to Pastures hew;
> Who of his great Design in pain
> Did for a Model vault his Brain,
> Whose Columnes should so high be rais'd
> To arch the Brows that on them gaz'd.   (st. I)

What buildings Marvell was thinking of when he wrote these lines I do not know, but he conveys superbly both the straining after effect that is to be found in such a later work as Blenheim, and the strain such an edifice puts on the spectator who seeks to take it in.

From this powerful opening Marvell goes on to relate buildings rapidly and effectively to human needs and to human vices. From the natural world he draws the conclusion that the true end of building is use. Of all the creatures, misguided man alone builds from motives of pride and ostentation. Like Carew before him, Marvell drives the point home by a witty reference to the Tower of Babel. Birds, beasts, tortoises build to meet their needs:

> But He, superfluously spread,
> Demands more room alive then dead.
> And in his hollow Palace goes
> Where Winds as he themselves may lose.
> What need of all this Marble Crust
> T'impark the wanton Mote of Dust,
> That thinks by Breadth the World t'unite
> Though the first Builders fail'd in Height?
>
> But all things are composed here
> Like Nature, orderly and near.   (sts. III and IV)

For Marvell here, as so often throughout his work, the natural and the orderly are one and the same. It is human pride that disturbs the beauty created by the interaction of man and nature on one another. The natural, the humble and the sober are all seen as belonging to the older social order which Fairfax and his house embodied. It is the character of the man that matters and gives the house its meaning. A great man can confer dignity and grandeur on a simple house, but a magnificent house only serves to emphasize the insignificance of an owner who has no claim to greatness except his house. The contrast between the truly great man with his unquestioning acceptance of the obligations imposed on him by his position, and the upstart who is also something of a snob, is well brought out by Marvell in a passage which leads up to an explicit statement of the idea of "use":

> So Honour better Lowness bears,
> Then That unwonted Greatness wears.
> Height with a certain Grace does bend,
> But low Things clownishly ascend.
> And yet what needs there here Excuse,
> Where ev'ry Thing does answer Use?
> Where neatness nothing can condemn,
> Nor Pride invent what to contemn?   (st. VIII)

Marvell's criticism of new styles in architecture and new developments in society does not end here. Like Carew in his poem about Wrest, he praises Nunappleton because it dispenses with statuary figures in relief and with elaborate furniture in favour of ministering to the needs of the poor and of establishing good human relationships:

> A Stately Frontispiece of Poor
> Adorns without the open Door:
> Nor less the Rooms within commends
> Daily new Furniture of Friends.   (st. IX)

Fairfax's acceptance of his duties as a landowner and his rejection of pride and ambition, which enables him to fulfil those duties so well, both go back ultimately to his view of the nature and meaning of life, which is religious. It is no accident that Marvell closes this first section of his poem with some lines derived from Fairfax's own little poem Upon the New-built House at Appleton which I quoted earlier:

> The House was built upon the Place
> Only as for a Mark of Grace;
> And for an Inn to entertain
> Its Lord a while, but not remain.   (st. IX)

In the traditional scheme of things on which Marvell draws so heavily, property, like life itself, was a trust, a loan from God, not a perpetual possession.

From this point onwards Marvell turns to other things. The greater part of his poem is outside my scope, but it does include a full and striking definition of what he means by "nature." The nature Marvell writes of in such a powerful and evocative way is emphatically not wild, untamed nature — that he describes in st. LXXXXVI as

> But a rude heap together hurl'd,
> All negligently overthrown,
> Gulfes, Deserts, Precipices, Stone — ;

but nature humanized and made to serve man. The grounds of Nunappleton House are this kind of nature; and for this reason he makes Fairfax's daughter the genius of the place.

VII

With Marvell the tradition I have been following so far comes to an end. From this time onwards the pattern established by To Penshurst ceases to be used. The change corresponds with the change that came over English poetry generally. From the middle of the seventeenth century the poet became less dependent on the patron; and, while the country house became grander than before, and even continued as a cultural centre for another century, it no longer occupied that focal position in the life of the nation which it had held during the first half of the seventeenth century. Increasingly it became a backwater outside the main current of political, social and intellectual life which centred on London.

Dryden, who so consciously identified himself with the rising commercial class and the town, wrote no poem about the country house. His nearest approach to it was in his Epistle, To my honour'd Kinsman, John Driden, of Chesterton. This begins, in a manner that reminds one that Dryden translated Horace's second Epode, with the lines:

> How Blessed is He, who leads a Country Life,
> Unvex'd with anxious Cares, and void of Strife.24

But although the poem begins like this, and although Dryden praises his cousin for his hospitality, there is no true understanding of country life or feeling for it. Dryden's poem is something utterly different from any previous English poem that has its roots in Horace. Praise of the country soon turns into praise of the single life; this in turn gives way to general satire on physicians. Finally Dryden finds his real theme, a consideration of the country squire's position, not in the countryside, but in the political and economic life of the nation:

> Well born, and Wealthy; wanting no Support,
> You steer betwixt the Country and the Court:
> Nor gratifie whate'er the Great desire,
> Nor grudging give, what Publick Needs require.
> Part must be left, a Fund when Foes invade;
> And Part employ'd to roll the Watry Trade.

Dryden's cousin lived in the country, was active as a Justice of the Peace and engaged in country sports, but it is plain after this that the serious business of his life was carried on at Westminster not in the country. Yet although Dryden records the fact, he does not seem to appreciate its significance as part of a quiet social revolution. There is hardly a hint in his poem that he is in any way aware of the values which the country house and the estate had embodied for poets of the preceding generation. When his poem is compared with To Penshurst, or with any of its progeny, a certain deficiency in his capacity to look at the life of his own age critically makes itself felt. He does not seem to realize that the quiet social revolution had brought losses as well as gains. There is something almost complacent in his too ready acceptance of the world he lived in. Strong though his poetry is, it lacks the particular strength that comes from a steady concern with the moral significance of things.

This steady concern with moral significance, which I miss in Dryden's poetry, is very much there in Pope, who also inherited far more than Dryden did of that outlook on life which we think of as belonging to the early seventeenth century. Consequently when Pope writes about the great house he does so in a way that has affinities with the manner of the poets I have discussed already. The point is almost made by F. W. Bateson in the Introduction to his edition of the Epistles to Several Persons, where he seeks to define what Pope understood by "virtue":

> for Pope "virtue" did not mean quite what it means to us. The most specific reference, though it does not amount to a definition, is in one of the later Imitations of Horace:
>
> > Here, Wisdom calls: "Seek Virtue first! be bold!
> > "As Gold to Silver, Virtue is to Gold."
> > There, London's voice: "Get Mony, Mony still!
> > "And then let Virtue follow, if she will."
>
> Here Pope seems to be saying that the opposite of the pursuit of virtue is the pursuit of money. And therefore presumably, if London symbolizes money, virtue must be symbolized by the country. God made the

country, in fact, man made the town. Virtue, on this interpretation, is a class-concept, the system of values of the "landed interest," the "Country Party." Vice is therefore the social philosophy of the urban capitalists, the rising middle classes who, with their champions in Parliament and at Court, were already a threat to the supremacy of the squirearchy.

It is significant at any rate that Burlington, Bathurst, and Cobham were all three prominent members of the landed aristocracy.[25]

If the notion of virtue as a class-concept were left out, this statement would apply equally well to Ben Jonson's Sir Robert Wroth. "Class-concept," as Bateson uses it, implies class antagonism, and I do not believe that Pope thought in terms of class antagonism any more than Jonson did. For both of them their thinking about social issues is controlled by the idea of the co-operative, interdependent society. The enemies of this society are individuals, not classes -- those who disregard the needs and claims of their fellow human beings. The man who does this is guilty of the sin of pride. In Ben Jonson's words he has come to "thinke his power doth equall Fates." There is nothing in Pope's Epistle to Burlington to show that Timon and Villario are nouveaux riches who have settled in the country, and not members of the hereditary aristocracy.

Once it is recognized that Pope's criticism of society is fundamentally moral, much of Bateson's main criticism of the Epistle to Burlington falls to the ground. He writes (p. xxvi):

> In the end, then, instead of being an "ethic epistle"
> on the vice of prodigality To Burlington turned out
> to be something of a hotchpotch, one-third philosophy,
> one-third gardening, and one-third architectural compliment.

Pope's main target throughout the epistle is not the vice of prodigality, but the vice from which prodigality springs, and which throughout his work he sees as the chief source of human misery, the vice of pride. Pope himself had no doubts about what he was attacking. In the letter prefixed to the third edition of the poem he speaks of the public excitement the poem had aroused and the attacks he had been exposed to; he then goes on:

> I will leave my Betters in the quiet Possession of their
> Idols, their Groves, and their High-Places; and change
> my Subject from their Pride to their Meanness, from
> their Vanities to their Miseries.[26]

The language Pope uses is the plainest possible indication
of his attitude; the poem is an attack on those who follow false
gods and put the satisfaction of their own pride and vanity before the needs of the community.

The criterion that Pope uses to determine whether a particular activity is a manifestation of pride and vanity or not, is
the same as that used by Ben Jonson and his followers; the determining factor is whether this activity is useful or not. After
the opening lines in which he satirizes the fashion of buying
pictures and antiques on the advice of others, Pope turns to
Burlington with the words:

> You show us, Rome was glorious, not profuse,
> And pompous buildings once were things of use.

The lines are one of the keys to the poem. Instance after instance follows of those who have overlooked the main end of
building and have gone off after strange gods. "Villario's ten-
year toil" was a search for distraction; Timon's library intended for anything but reading; his chapel, its furniture, even the
sermon preached in it, designed to lull the thoughts and distract
them from religious activity. This monstrous perversion of
things from their proper end and use, and the motive for it,
are superbly condensed into two lines:

> And now the Chapel's silver bell you hear,
> That summons you to all the Pride of Pray'r.

In the same way that pride perverts the relationship of man to
God, so also it perverts the relationship of man to man. Among
the great man's duties is that of dispensing hospitality. Timon
carries this duty out; but as a sop to his pride, not as a duty.
As a result, instead of binding his guests closer to him, he
arouses their animosity:

> Treated, caress'd, and tir'd, I take my leave,
> Sick of his civil Pride from Morn to Eve.

Even the poor, Timon feeds out of vanity, not out of any sense of community.

And finally it is this same motive of pride which perverts, or as Pope puts it, inverts, the whole relationship of man to nature. Instead of co-operating with nature and putting it to its proper use, the Timons and the rest do violence to it:

> The suff'ring eye inverted Nature sees,
> Trees cut to Statues, Statues thick as trees.

Pope's whole view of the way in which art and nature can cooperate under the guidance of good sense is very close to Carew's description of the same process in his poem about Wrest. Furthermore phrase after phrase in Pope's poem recalls the work of the poets of the early seventeenth century, not, I think, because Pope was recollecting what they had written, but because he shared the same outlook, because his insight was of the same kind. Take, for example, some of the lines with which he introduces Timon's Villa:

> At Timon's Villa let us pass a day,
> Where all cry out, "What sums are thrown away!"
> So proud, so grand, of that stupendous air,
> Soft and Agreeable come never there.
> Greatness, with Timon, dwells in such a draught
> As brings all Brobdignag before your thought.
>
> To compass this, his building is a Town,
> His pond an Ocean, his parterre a Down:
> Who but must laugh, the Master when he sees,
> A puny insect, shiv'ring at a breeze!
> Lo, what huge heaps of littleness around!
> The whole, a labour'd Quarry above ground.

In reading these lines one cannot help recalling Marvell's lines quoted earlier: "Within this sober Frame expect . . ." etc.

Pope's conception of what the great house should be was, of course, different from that of Ben Jonson and his successors,

in the purely architectural sense. Where they set up the traditional Elizabethan house in opposition to the baroque, Pope set
up the classical designs of Palladio. But underneath this surface
difference he is wholly in agreement with them that the right
and proper end of building is use, not show; and that the proper
aim of the individual should be the subordination of himself to
the service of the community, not exploitation of the community
for his own personal ends. His poem is given over largely to
attack, but it ends with a positive statement which sums up very
well most of the points I have been trying to make, for here he
places the great man and his house in relation to the society and
to the natural world of which he is part:

> Who then shall grace, or who improve the Soil?
> Who plants like Bathurst, or who builds like Boyle.
> 'Tis Use along that sanctifies Expence,
> And Splendour borrows all her rays from Sense.
> His Father's Acres who enjoys in peace,
> Or makes his Neighbours glad, if he encrease;
> Whose chearful Tenants bless their yearly toil,
> Yet to their Lord owe more than to the soil;
> Whose ample Lawns are not asham'd to feed
> The milky heifer and deserving steed;
> Whose rising Forests, not for pride or show,
> But future Buildings, future Navies grow:
> Let his plantations stretch from down to down,
> First shade a Country, and then raise a Town.

Seen against the background of the country house poem,
Pope's Epistle to Burlington is not "a hotchpotch, one-third
philosophy, one-third gardening, one-third architectural compliment." Behind the gardening and the architecture, and hold-
ing them together in a coherent whole, is Pope's attack on
human pride and his conception of the true society. The weakness of the poem is the "one-third philosophy." After his penetrating exposure of the elements in human nature that are
inimical to his idea of the true society, there is something
facile, despite the wonderful lines in which Pope expresses his
faith, in the way in which he clings to the theory of a "Ballance
of things":

434

> Yet hence the Poor are cloath'd, the Hungry fed;
> Health to himself, and to his Infants bread
> The Lab'rer bears: What his hard Heart denies,
> His charitable Vanity supplies.
> Another age shall see the golden Ear
> Imbrown the Slope, and nod on the Parterre,
> Deep Harvests bury all his pride has plann'd,
> And laughing Ceres re-assume the land.

There is something lacking in the moralist who assumes that the very vice he is attacking has its place in the proper working of things. History supplied the answer to Pope here. In so far as Timon's Villa is Cannons, "laughing Ceres" only reassumed the land for a short time when the house was pulled down, and then gave way to the bricks and mortar of Edgware. The kind of society that Pope approves of was already no more than a ghost when he wrote his poem.

NOTES

1 See John Summerson, Architecture in Britain 1530 to 1830, London, 1953, pp. 25-29.

2 J. A. Gotch, The English Home from Charles I to George IV, London, n.d., p. 5.

3 Summerson, op. cit., p. 38.

4 Nikolaus Pevsner, The Buildings of England — Nottinghamshire, Penguin Books, 1951, p. 209.

5 Summerson, op. cit., pp. 31, 33 and 41.

6 Gotch, op. cit., pp. 5 and 6.

7 For a detailed picture of this process see Gladys Scott Thomson, Life in a Noble Household, 1641-1700, London, 1937, chaps. VI-IX.

8 G. M. Trevelyan, England under the Stuarts, London, 1925, p. 6.

9 David Mathew, The Age of Charles I, London, 1951, p. 286.

10 Aubrey's "Brief Lives", ed. A. Clark, Oxford, 1898, II, p. 304. (I owe this reference to Professor V. de S. Pinto.)

11 See V. de S. Pinto, Rochester, London, 1935, p. 169.

12 See C. H. Collins Baker and Muriel I. Baker, The Life and Circumstances of James Brydges, First Duke of Chandos, Oxford, 1949, p. 181.

13 Ibid. , Introduction, p. xii.

14 The Complete Works of Sir Philip Sidney, ed. A. Feuillerat, C. U. P. , 1939, I, p. 15.

15 This and all subsequent quotations from Jonson's poems are taken from Ben Jonson, ed. Herford and Simpson, VIII, Oxford, 1947.

16 Herford and Simpson, Ben Jonson, II, Oxford, 1925, p. 369.

17 The text of this and subsequent quotations from Carew's poetry is taken from The Poems of Thomas Carew, ed. Rhodes Dunlap, Oxford, 1949.

18 F. R. Leavis, Revaluation, London, 1936, p. 36.

19 F. W. Moorman, Robert Herrick, London, 1910, pp. 31-33.

20 This and subsequent quotations from Herrick's poetry are taken from The Poems of Robert Herrick, London, 1902. (World's Classics edition).

21 M. A. Gibb, The Lord General: A Life of Thomas Fairfax, London, 1938, pp. 16-17.

22 C. R. Markham, A Life of the Great Lord Fairfax, London 1870, pp. 365-66.

23 This and subsequent quotations from Marvell's poetry are taken from The Poems and Letters of Andrew Marvell, ed. H. M. Margoliouth, Oxford, 1927, I.

24 This and subsequent quotations from Dryden are taken from The Poems of John Dryden, ed. John Sargeaunt, Oxford, 1925.

25 Epistles to Several Persons, ed. F. W. Bateson, London,

1951, p. xxxix. This edition is the source of subsequent quotations from Pope.

26 Bateson, op. cit. , p. 128.

POPE'S TO BATHURST AND THE MANDEVILLIAN STATE

Paul J. Alpers

I

"The idea of the entire Essay [To Bathurst] is borrowed from Mandeville," said W. J. Courthope, referring to Pope's apparent use of the paradox expressed in the sub-title of The Fable of the Bees -- "private vices, public benefits." Courthope regretted this influence, for "Mandeville was a low-spirited materialist," while "Pope himself was not deficient in generous instincts and noble ideas."[1] Courthope's mistake -- leaving aside the name-calling -- was to assume that Pope agrees with Mandeville. On the contrary, To Bathurst indicates a fundamental opposition to Mandeville which has been overlooked only because Pope's friend and editor Warburton magnified the poet's pretensions to systematic philosophy. To Bathurst is not a "moral essay" (which was Warburton's title, not Pope's), but a Horatian epistle -- a brilliant satiric poem and not a curio from the Age of Reason. It is worth more attention than it has received simply because the type and range of social observation are unique in Pope's poetry: he has more of the novelist's interests in this poem than in any other. In his response to realities harsher than those of Grub Street and high society, one can see the rationale of the cataclysmic denunciations which climaxed his career as a satirist.

The Fable of the Bees is important in understanding To Bathurst, not because of a direct influence on Pope, but because it used contemporary ethical assumptions and dispositions in such a way as to challenge every Augustan writer on man in society. Mandeville shocked his time by challenging rigoristic ethical concepts and the notion that the health of the state is established by, or can be evaluated in the same way as, the moral health of the individuals who comprise it. In ethics, Mandeville attacked rigorism by pushing it to its extreme.

Reprinted from English Literary History, Vol. 25 (1958), pp. 23-42, by permission of author and publisher.

POPE'S TO BATHURST

Professor Kaye summarizes his position:

> The conception of virtue propounded by Mandeville
> proclaimed, first, that no action was really virtuous
> if inspired by selfish emotion; and this assumption,
> since Mandeville considered all natural emotion funda-
> mentally selfish, implied the ascetic position that no
> action was virtuous if done from natural impulse. Sec-
> ondly, Mandeville's definition of virtue declared that
> no action was meritorious unless the motive that in-
> spired it was a "rational" one. As Mandeville inter-
> preted "rational" to imply an antithesis to emotion
> and self-regard, both aspects of his ethical code — the
> ascetic and the rationalistic — alike condemned as
> vicious all action whose dominant motive was natural
> impulse and self-regarding bias.[2]

Mandeville, on investigating the psychology of motivation, found
that every man acts selfishly, and that therefore no human action is virtuous. His ethical theories thus stimulated writers
like Hume and Adam Smith to formulate a utilitarian scheme of
ethics.

Mandeville's blasphemy in social theory was his argument
that not only can some compensatory social benefit result from
vice, but that vice and luxury are necessary to a flourishing
state. "This opinion was in opposition not only to all the more
ascetic codes of morality, but in contradiction to what might
be called the classic economic attitude, which set forth the
ideal of a Spartan state, exalted the simpler agricultural pursuits, and denounced luxury as the degenerator of peoples and
impoverisher of nations."[3] Mandeville connects his ethical and
economic views imperfectly: his theory of society accepts a
quite conventional definition of virtue and still asserts that vice
is a public benefit. The following passage from "A Search into
the Nature of Society" shows the pertinence of Mandeville's
writings to the Epistle to Bathurst. It admits Pope's ethical
assumptions, but, by defining wealth as the luxury of corrupt
aristocrats, it denies the public utility of the Man of Ross:

> It is certain that the fewer Desires a Man has and the
> less he covets, the more easy he is to himself; the

439

ALPERS

more active he is to supply his own Wants, and the
less he requires to be waited upon, the more he will
be beloved and the less trouble he is in a Family; the
more he loves Peace and Concord, the more Charity
he has for his Neighbour, and the more he shines in
real Virtue, there is no doubt but that in proportion
he is acceptable to God and Man. But let us be Just,
what Benefit can these things be of, or what earthly
Good can they do, to promote the Wealth, the Glory
and worldly Greatness of Nations? It is the sensual
Courtier that sets no Limits to his Luxury; the Fickle
Strumpet that invents new Fashions every Week; the
haughty Dutchess that in Equipage, Entertainments,
and all her Behaviour would imitate a Princess; the
profuse Rake and lavish Heir, that scatter about their
Money without Wit or Judgment, buy every thing they
see, and either destroy or give it away the next Day,
the Covetous and perjur'd Villain that squeez'd an
immense Treasure from the Tears of Widows and
Orphans, and left the Prodigals the Money to spend:
It is these that are the Prey and proper Food of a
full grown Leviathan; or in other words, such is the
calamitous Condition of Human Affairs that we stand
in need of the Plagues and Monsters I named to have
all the Variety of Labour perform'd, which the Skill
of Men is capable of inventing in order to procure an
honest Livelihood to the vast Multitudes of working
poor, that are required to make a large Society: And
it is folly to imagine that Great and Wealthy Nations
can subsist, and be at once Powerful and Polite without.[4]

Mandeville is what we may call a political realist: this passage, though it intends to shock, is a responsible economic
statement that luxury is necessary both to provide labor at
home and to stimulate trade abroad. Mandeville tends to establish an economically powerful state as an end in itself, or, to
put it another way, to define a state's health solely by economic
criteria. Pope stands for the "classical economic attitude," if
not in its Spartan aspects, at least in its insistence that the state
has a moral existence. Every time Pope treats contemporary

society, he in effect opposes The Fable of the Bees. In To Bathurst, Pope comes to grips with the contemporary situation in such a way as to make it impossible for him to reply to Mandeville by means of a vision, like that at the end of To Burlington, of what a state ought to be.

To Bathurst is a more realistic poem than To Burlington because it puts under considerable pressure the literal possibility of making England a second Rome. The most immediate result is a sharper definition of Pope's quasi-Mandevillian economic theory. In what Bateson calls "the earliest statement of [his] optimistic ethics," Pope remarked to Spence, "As to the general design of Providence, the two extremes of vice may serve (like two opposite biases) to keep up the balance of things."[5] This seems Mandevillian enough, at least to the extent of asserting that partial evil can be universal good at the level of human society. Spence's notes on Pope's table talk in May, 1730 — when the poet was most excited about the grand scheme of his Ethic Epistles -- show Pope still entertaining Mandeville's paradox, "private vices, public benefits." Bateson remarks:

> The theory of a "Ballance of things," . . . is implicit
> in the whole argument of the Essay on Man, and Spence's
> notes show Pope feeling his way, as it were, to the
> illustration of this theory in the socio-economic sphere.
> One epistle . . . is to be devoted to the vice of prodi-
> gality and the social function it unconsciously performs.
> "Prodigality scatters abroad money that may turn out
> to be useful in other hands." Another epistle . . . will
> deal with avarice. . . . "Avarice lays up money that
> in other hands would be hurtful." Ethically the moral
> in either case is that of a golden mean, "The middle
> the point for Virtue."[6]

The definition of virtue, however, introduces some confusion: the balance between avarice and prodigality is not any sort of economic harmony, but the virtuous man's temperate use of riches. The miser and the prodigal, seen in this light, are not social forces but moral grotesques, whose ridiculous example should teach man the mean between two extremes.

To Burlington defines the proper use of riches by the marvellous identification of that virtue with good taste, and, conversely, of prodigality with bad taste. The aesthetic and moral responses are, as Professor Brower has shown, identical: the role of a cultivated aristocrat is defined by a poem which only the cultivated aristocrat can understand.[7] The description of Timon's villa is as much a statement of faith in certain ideals (rather, perhaps, faith in a certain way of responding to life) as the literal statement of faith, the vision at the end. The point to emphasize here is that this poem is directed to the individual; it exhorts the aristocrat to persevere in the complex Roman ideal which the poem has defined and exemplified:

> You too proceed! make falling Arts your care,
> Erect new wonders, and the old repair,
> Jones and Palladio to themselves restore,
> And be whate'er Vitruvius was before:
> Till Kings call forth th' Idea's of your mind,
> Proud to accomplish what such hands design'd,
> Bid Harbors open, public Ways extend,
> Bid Temples, worthier of the God, ascend;
> Bid the broad Arch the dang'rous Flood contain,
> The Mole projected break the roaring Main;
> Back to his bounds their subject Sea command,
> And roll obedient Rivers thro' the Land;
> These Honours, Peace to happy Britain brings,
> These are Imperial Works, and worthy Kings.   (191)

The crucial line for our purposes is "Till kings call forth th' Idea's of your mind." In context, this is neither a condition nor a prediction, but the statement of a natural fact, the moment of ripeness when a civilization will bloom and flourish. But Pope is assuming that there will be social order, and that it will be attained by the proper, the natural functioning of the aristocracy. It is the precise opposite of Mandeville's thesis. The health and glory of society are established by the aesthetic and moral sense of individuals who have transcended the domination of a ruling passion, who in no fruitful way can be said to be selfish.

These points are strikingly illustrated by the use Pope makes of Mandeville's paradox:

> Treated, caress'd, and tir'd, I take my leave,
> Sick of his civil Pride from Morn to Eve;

> I curse such lavish cost, and little skill,
> And swear no Day was ever past so ill.
>
> Yet hence the Poor are cloath'd, the Hungry fed;
> Health to himself, and to his Infants bread
> The Lab'rer bears: What his hard Heart denies,
> His charitable Vanity supplies.
>
> Another age shall see the golden Ear
> Imbrown the Slope, and nod on the Parterre,
> Deep Harvests bury all his pride has plann'd,
> And laughing Ceres re-assume the land.   (165)

It is necessary to quote the pertinent couplets in context, for they provide the transition between the day at Timon's villa and the magnificent vision of the future age of Britain. There is genuine pathos in Timon's pitiful insignificance: the very selfishness which makes him waste vast sums on himself counteracts his niggardliness. Pope's note to this passage says:

> The Moral of the whole, where PROVIDENCE is justified in giving Wealth to those who squander it in this manner. A bad Taste employs more hands and diffuses Expence more than a good one.

The note seems to concur with Mandeville's economics. But Mandeville is interested in the prodigal only as a dispenser of wealth. He would never say, "What his hard Heart denies / His charitable Vanity supplies" — not because he considers social utility a certificate of moral worth (he explicitly does not), but because Pope's line assumes that the proper way to distribute wealth is through charity. The good man stands outside the clock-work universe; in his social cosmos, the virtuous nobleman is the watchmaker.

In deciding to trust Pope the poet and moralist rather than Pope the schematizer, one is supported by the tone of the passage and by Pope's rhetorical posture. It is not in God's eye alone that Timon's partial evil is seen to be a universal good. Pope and Burlington, standing at the center of the poem, see this too. The sensibility which understands the ludicrous pathos of Timon's beneficence is that which comprehends the vision which follows. Pope is not committed to Mandeville's paradox as a final explanation of social order.

There is, therefore, a great difference between this passage and the analogous passage in To Bathurst, to which Pope refers the reader in the note quoted above:

> "Extremes in Nature equal good produce,
> "Extremes in Man concur to gen'ral use."
> Ask we what makes one keep, and one bestow?
> That POW'R who bids the Ocean ebb and flow,
> Bids seed-time, harvest, equal course maintain,
> Thro' reconcil'd extremes of drought and rain,
> Builds Life on Death, on Change Duration founds,
> And gives th' eternal wheels to know their rounds.
>
>   Riches, like insects, when conceal'd they lie,
> Wait but for wings, and in their season, fly.
> Who sees pale Mammon pine amidst his store,
> Sees but a backward steward for the Poor;
> This year a Reservoir, to keep and spare,
> The next a Fountain, spouting thro' his Heir,
> In lavish streams to quench a Country's thirst,
> And men and dogs shall drink him 'till they burst.
>
>   (163, 161)

Nature remains constant, but man no longer participates in its processes. The picture of harmony which, as in To Burlington, hangs as a pendant to the quasi-philosophical statement, has as its hero, not the virtuous aristocrat, but the miser and the prodigal, who serve their function when they are stripped of all human attributes and become a reservoir and a fountain. Pope can no longer relegate Mandeville's paradox to a footnote; in order to assert natural order in the real world of To Bathurst, he must resort to the amoral mechanics of The Fable of the Bees.

But the poet, by the very operation of his sensibility, is no more committed to Mandevillian harmony than he was in To Burlington. Pope has his vision of Nature, and he sees that the balance of economic forces is not a harmony, but a violent oscillation. The country is either starved or bloated, and the final couplet (with its implications of chaos as men and dogs rush to the streams) looks back to and anticipates couplets which, in this context, produce fairly grim overtones:

> Could France or Rome divert our brave designs,
> With all their brandies or with all their wines?
> What could they more than Knights and Squires confound,
> Or water all the Quorum ten miles round?   (39, 51)

> While the gaunt mastiff growling at the gate,
> Affrights the beggar whom he longs to eat. (197, 195)

The comparison of riches to insects, damaging enough in itself, is an ironic echo of Proverbs, xxiii. 5: "Wilt thou set thine eyes upon that which is not? for riches certainly make themselves wings; they fly away as an eagle toward heaven." Pope's ideal of society is the one stated at the end of To Burlington; he is driven into his uneasy position in To Bathurst precisely because the sensibility which is glorified in the earlier poem is operating on a wider range of social phenomena.

II

If Elwin and Courthope, unconsciously following Warburton's lead, are excessively philosophical in their interpretations of Pope's epistle, it is possible for the modern commentator to be, one might say, too poetical. G. Wilson Knight implies that Pope is arguing for some sort of primitivism in To Bathurst:

> Pope's emphasis on vital direction rather than any
> moral absolute or set of absolutes determines his
> human analysis. He sees wealth . . . doing the devil's
> work. His sense of the concretely vital is used to ex-
> pose the appalling dangers inherent in the ever more
> abstract tendencies of finance, . . . and the essential
> intangibility of the most dangerous vices being shown
> to work in double harness with the growing intangibility
> of wealth. Pope's positive emphasis is simple and
> concrete.[8]

Professor Knight makes Pope sound a bit too much like D. H. Lawrence. He quotes, presumably as the key couplet of the poem:

> What Riches give us let us then enquire,
> Meat, Fire, and Cloaths. What more? Meat,
> Cloaths, and Fire.   (81, 79)

This seems to me to miss the point of the poem, or rather to
miss the general point that Pope is defending a complex civilization which he can still consider a possible model for human
society, and of which he finds certain palpable manifestations
in books, buildings, and virtuous men. Certainly Pope uses
Nature — concrete, harmonious, and vital — as a moral touchstone, as much in To Bathurst as in To Burlington. But Pope
and the aristocrat he addresses now face a problem which was
previously avoided: how do the ideals expressed in To Burlington make themselves felt in a mercantile society whose center
is London, a society in which the Puritan bourgeoisie is rapidly
rising and the body of the aristocracy is hopelessly corrupt?

The first eighty lines of the poem are a prologue to the con-
frontation of contemporary society. Like its predecessor, To
Bathurst opens with the poet wittily addressing the cultivated
aristocrat. The two men stand securely at the moral center of
the poem, as they conduct a mock-argument about the role of
riches in the universe. Starting from this point, Pope, in what
seems a rather aimless examination of avarice, brings about
a significant change of tone. We no longer have the comic control, operating through a fantastic conceit and with the pathetic
overtones already noted in To Burlington, of:

> Astride his cheese Sir Morgan might we meet,
> And Worldly crying coals from street to street,
> (Whom with a wig so wild, and mien so maz'd,
> Pity mistakes for some poor tradesman craz'd).

>   (49, 61)

Or the marvellous absurd pathos of:

> Shall then Uxorio, if the stakes he sweep,
> Bear home six Whores, and make his Lady weep?

>   (59, 71)

Instead there is the grotesque reality:

> What can they give? to dying Hopkins Heirs;
> To Chartres, Vigour; Japhet, Nose and Ears?
> Can they, in gems bid pallid Hippia glow,
> In Fulvia's buckle ease the throbs below,
> Or heal, old Narses, thy obscener ail,
> With all th' embroid'ry plaister'd at thy tail? (87, 85)

Pope is not espousing the Mandevillian view that man's only natural wants are "Meat, Cloaths, and Fire."[9] The wealth which causes corruption is soon more sharply defined as wealth abused:

> They might (were Harpax not too wise to spend)
> Give Harpax self the blessing of a Friend. (93, 91)

And in analyzing the miser, Pope soon turns to his public behavior: "Perhaps you think the Poor might have their part?" (101, 99).

The easy play of aristocratic wit has been severely disturbed through moral commitments made in its very operation. The shift of tone in the comic analysis of avarice is made by means of the images which wit proposes to itself. Pope, significantly treating corruption in government in the "prefatory matter" of the poem, ironically invokes a golden age of barter:

> Oh! that such bulky Bribes as all might see,
> Still, as of old, incumber'd Villainy!
> In vain may Heroes fight, and Patriots rave;
> If secret Gold saps on from knave to knave.
> Could France or Rome divert our brave designs,
> With all their brandies or with all their wines?
> What could they more than Knights and Squires confound,
> Or water all the Quorum ten miles round?
> A Statesman's slumbers how this speech would spoil!
> "Sir, Spain has sent a thousand jars of oil;
> "Huge bales of British cloth blockade the door;
> "A hundred oxen at your levee roar." (35, 49)

As the comic idea develops, Pope's view shifts from a mythical world to contemporary London:

447

> Blest paper-credit! last and best supply!
> That lends Corruption lighter wings to fly!
> Gold imp'd by thee, can compass hardest things,
> Can pocket States, can fetch or carry Kings;
> A single leaf shall waft an Army o'er,
> Or ship off Senates to a distant Shore;
> A leaf, like Sibyl's, scatter to and fro
> Our fates and fortunes, as the winds shall blow:
> Pregnant with thousands flits the Scrap unseen,
> And silent sells a King or buys a Queen.   (69, 39)

Both passages might be called mock-heroic. The first, however, renders corrupt senators ineffectual -- as they are when seen sub specie aeternitatis. The second passage is much more deeply ironic, for in its mock exaltation of paper currency, it describes its actual operation in the world.[10] Surely Pope does not say that tangible oxen are better for man than intangible paper; he does say that the flitting leaves give knavery unlimited power, and in the scraps of paper he can use the dangerous instrument of corrupt senators as a symbol of their moral worthlessness. The poetic problem posed by this realism is indicated by the fact that, in order to attack corruption by greed, Pope has assumed the guise of the politician, whose praise of paper credit is real. This ironic strategy and the degree of involvement it implies are notably absent in To Burlington.

In his survey of the contemporary world dominated by avarice (lines 79-152), Pope runs rapidly through a gallery of usurers, aristocrats, and directors of the South Sea Company and the corrupt Charitable Corporation. He concludes with brief portraits of Peter Walter, Gage and Lady Mary Herbert, and Sir John Blunt — all of whom, by hoping literally to buy thrones, carry modern statesmanship to its logical extreme. Blunt's mad vision, the climax of this section, takes the mock-heroic irony of the "Blest paper-credit!" passage one step further. In the earlier lines, Pope's ironic evaluation corresponds to literal fact, and his posing as a politician is merely a device; the poet himself remains outside, in a position to evaluate and describe. Here the satirist's vision and that of the maddest miser of them all become identical:

> "At length Corruption, like a gen'ral flood,

> "(So long by watchful Ministers withstood)
> "Shall deluge all; and Av'rice creeping on,
> "Spread like a low-born mist, and blot the Sun;
> "Statesman and Patriot ply alike the stocks,
> "Peeress and Butler share alike the Box,
> "And Judges job, and Bishops bite the town,
> "And mighty Dukes pack cards for half a crown.
> "See Britain sunk in lucre's sordid charms,
> "And France revenged of ANNE's and EDWARD's arms"!

(137, 135)

Pope's praise is deeply and terribly ironic precisely because it is not facetious:

> 'Twas no Court-badge, great Scriv'ner! fir'd thy brain,
> Nor lordly Luxury, nor City Gain:
> No, 'twas thy righteous end, asham'd to see
> Senates degen'rate, Patriots disagree,
> And nobly wishing Party-rage to cease,
> To buy both sides, and give thy Country peace.

(147, 145)

This is not superficial sarcasm. The rich irony of the passage comes from the moral framework established by what has preceded it (Pope brings to a climax his punning on "Senate" and "Patriot") and from the resonance of words like "righteous" and "peace."

Now let us return to the philosophical core of the poem, which was quoted on page 444. Although one can hardly claim for this poem the dialectical progression attained in the Epilogue to the Satires, Pope's vision of "That POW'R who bids the Ocean ebb and flow" can be seen as the poet's reaction to his own involvement in the vision of Sir John Blunt. Pope, in restating a theory of divine supervision of wealth in human affairs, speaks now, not so much with the voice of the cultivated aristocrat, but in the prophetic tones of the public hero, the defender of truth. But we have already noted that, in illustrating the balance of powers, Pope shows no confidence that the harmony of the universe is reproduced in contemporary society. Prophetic

449

tones, then, will express not ultimate confidence, but the virtuous man's horrified reaction to the world around him. Pope does not successfully define this attitude in To Bathurst. But he does put himself in a position to speak heroically, and what we must observe now is that he does so by examining the Mandevillian reconciliation of avarice and prodigality, as they are represented by Old Cotta and his son.

These two portraits (the first full-length portraits in the poem) quite contradict the sanguine scheme which Pope drew up for the Ethic Epistles. The miser and the prodigal do not store up and distribute wealth; rather, they destroy it. Old Cotta does not "lay up money that in other hands would be hurtful"; nor does his son "scatter abroad money that may turn out to be useful in other hands." The miser withholds money which should be used for charity and for the support and cheerful entertainment of his tenants. His son pours out money which disappears in the bottomless pit of the State:

> Yet no mean motive this profusion draws,
> His oxen perish in his country's cause;
> 'Tis GEORGE and LIBERTY that crowns the cup,
> And Zeal for that great House which eats him up.
> The woods recede around the naked seat,
> The Sylvans groan — no matter — for the Fleet:
> Next goes his Wool — to clothe our valiant bands,
> Last, for his Country's love, he sells his Lands.
> To town he comes, completes the nation's hope,
> And heads the bold Train-bands, and burns a Pope.
> And shall not Britain now reward his toils,
> Britain, that pays her Patriots with her Spoils?
> In vain at Court the Bankrupt pleads his cause,
> His thankless Country leaves him to her Laws.   (205)

This is primarily a portrayal of the Whig squire, but it is noteworthy that no reference to Britain admits an innocent interpretation: the last line, for example, is quite pointless without an ironic reflection on contemporary justice.[11] Britain, in its present condition, will ill repay the devotion of any patriot. The quality of Young Cotta's patriotism, therefore, is an evaluation of patria itself.

In undercutting the economic theory of compensation of

extremes, and in attacking luxury -- that is, in insisting on non-
economic, moral criteria to judge the state and the distribution
of wealth -- Pope adumbrates his opposition to Mandeville. But
the portrait of Young Cotta is not a full-scale attack on the corrupt state. There is, in these two portraits, the same comic
pathos we have observed before -- a delicate, rather Shavian,
pity which implies a broad and secure moral sense observing
the comic phenomena. At the end of the portrait of Young Cotta,
this higher consciousness -- the poet's sensibility -- is brought
face to face with its true foe, by the recognition that the patriotic Whig squire is as helpless in the grip of a corrupted England
as he is in the eye of a moral Providence.

Pope attacks Mandeville's paradox with criteria of personal
morality -- hence his use of the portrait. To adequately show
that private virtues are public virtues, he must oppose to the
corrupt state the statesman, the higher human power who can
reconcile the extremes represented by the Cottas. Pope makes
a step towards accepting this challenge in the exhortation to
Bathurst:

> To balance Fortune by a just expence,
> Join with Œconomy, Magnificence;
> With splendour, charity; with plenty, health;
> Oh teach us, BATHURST! yet unspoil'd by wealth!
> That secret rare, between th' extremes to move
> Of mad Good-nature, and of mean Self-love.   (223)

This is the major statement in the poem of the Roman, aristocratic ideal. It is firmly committed to the insights and ironic
tones that have preceded it: social harmony, the proper use of
wealth, must be achieved by virtuous noblemen who, not being
enslaved by money, can control it. In their social universe,
they are gods: they "ease, or emulate, the care of Heav'n"
(230). Indeed, in this world, they must correct some of the inevitable mistakes of Providence:

> Whose measure full o'erflows on human race,
> Mend Fortune's fault, and justify her grace.   (231)

The awareness of man's responsibility for man's problems --
along with the sense of his potential glory -- provokes the

violent image in the next two couplets:

> Wealth in the gross is death, but life diffus'd;
> As Poison heals, in just proportion us'd:
> In heaps, like Ambergrise, a stink it lies,
> But well-dispers'd, is Incense to the Skies.   (233)[12]

Pope then raises a question which he cannot avoid: what can the virtuous individual do in a corrupt world? After two rhetorical questions which imply that no Lord "knows a cheerful noon / Without a Fiddler, Flatt'rer, or Buffoon," Pope asks:

> Who copies Your's, or OXFORD's better part,
> To ease th' oppress'd, and raise the sinking heart?
> Where-e'er he shines, oh Fortune, gild the scene,
> And Angels guard him in the golden Mean!
> There, English Bounty yet a-while may stand,
> And Honour linger ere it leaves the land.   (243)

Compare To Burlington, lines 177-180:

> Who then shall grace, or who improve the Soil?
> Who plants like Bathurst, or who builds like Boyle.
> 'Tis Use alone that sanctifies Expence,
> And Splendour borrows all her rays from Sense.

In the England of Pope's vision, Bathurst and Boyle represent the aristocracy; they lead and shape society. In To Bathurst the lord and the poet are the pained observers of a corrupt aristocracy and a middle class driven mad by gold. The men who are at the center of the ideal society stand on the fringes of the Augustan world.

III

To Bathurst is explicitly political, but its aim is no more to propose a plan of political action than it is to repose confidence in a postulated order of nature. Rather Pope must define an attitude which maintains the dignity of the conclusion of To Burlington. The satirist seeks a way of expressing moral

concern -- the responsibility felt for an ideal which is threatened
by fools and knaves. The pathetic echo of Vergil ("And Honour
linger ere it leaves the land")[13] seems a sign that Pope is ready
to take his stance as the public hero. The satirist in this role
"invites us to join . . . 'the invisible church of good men' everywhere, 'few though they may be — for whom things matter.' And
he never lets us forget that we are at war; there is an enemy."[14]
But open war is never declared in To Bathurst, although Pope
has put himself in a position where he must attack not individuals, but bodies of men -- the aristocracy, the middle class, the
government. There is no way to prove that, in such a position,
Pope must develop Miltonic tones in his Horatian poems. But we
shall see that there is a failure of rhetorical self-definition in
To Bathurst; and this argues that the true ending of the poem is
in Pope's last major works, Dunciad IV and the Epilogue to the
Satires, in both of which the poet as vates is involved in the
politics and warfare of satire.

We have seen that Pope uses the portrait as a means of
criticizing, by standards of personal morality, certain attitudes
which dominate public life. But there are limits to the portrait
as a weapon, and Pope's choosing to conclude the poem with five
"characters" seems to me a failure of design. The portraits of
Villiers, Cutler, and even Sir Balaam show not the social horror of a nation mad for money, but the moral corruption of the
individual who is dominated by gold. If this seems a sufficient
achievement for the poem as Professor Knight characterizes
it, we should note that in the longest of these portraits, Pope
goes beyond individual analysis and the problems of personal
morality. By making the Man of Ross an exemplary hero and
Sir Balaam the representative of a whole class, Pope attempts
to face the problem he has previously established: he and Bathurst are outnumbered and, morally and literally, do not hold
the reins of government. But his use of the portrait makes the
poet's statement oblique. He does not define his emotional and
moral reaction to the public horror of Vice's enslaving England
in her golden chains.

To rouse the watchmen of the public weal, the satirist must
speak heroically and in his own voice. The incompatibility between prophetic invective and the method of portraiture becomes
evident when Pope uses the relatively humble Man of Ross to
berate the lords who have forsaken their social responsibilities.

The strategy is clear — to find an example striking enough in itself to rebuke the nobility. But the sensationalism which characterizes this portrait underlines the fact that Pope is trying to pass off a freak as a hero. The disparity between the strength of his attack and his positive commitment emerges in the concluding couplet:

> Blush, Grandeur, blush! proud Courts, withdraw
>   your blaze!
> Ye little Stars! hide your diminish'd rays.   (281)

It is difficult to agree with Professor Mack that this echo of Paradise Lost is mock-heroic — "a way of qualifying an attitude, of genuinely 'heroicizing' [the] Man of Ross . . . yet undercutting [him] with a more inclusive attitude."[15] The only more inclusive attitude available is the aristocratic ideal which the Man of Ross presumably embodies. Pope's difficulty is that expanding the Miltonic couplet, in the interest of poetic decorum, would bring him very close to attacking not only the corrupt nobility, but aristocracy itself. Pope is a bit uneasy about the Man of Ross: he is not willing to commit himself to Men of Ross, a class of country squires (like Fielding's Allworthy) which could supply new moral strength to England. The hero is rara avis, and this fact practically concedes victory to Mandeville; we can defend Pope only by saying that this portrait is the poorest section of the poem.

On the other hand, the concluding narrative of Sir Balaam's career is superb, and it is ungrateful, perhaps, to speak harshly of it. We are concerned, however, with the highest poetic stakes, the satiric sublime which Pope does attain in his finest poems; in To Bathurst it is clear that, having abandoned the heroic note after the Man of Ross, the poet has regained rhetorical control only by attenuation. By the end of the poem, the epistolary relationship with Bathurst has broken down; Pope is no longer speaking to a fellow aristocrat. More important, Pope introduces an entirely new, and rather jaunty, tone and pace. He imposes a pseudo-conclusion on us: our impression that the portrait of Sir Balaam is a true ending for the poem is only due to the length of the narrative and the sudden shift to an unusual style.

The source of the foreign strain is highly important: it

seems to me undeniable that Pope has made a brilliant adaptation of Swift's poetic style. The genre itself – the progress of
a soul -- though unique in Pope, is typical of Swift. Equally
characteristic are the vulgar imagery and the use of asyndeton.
Most important, Pope parodies the Book of Job by Swift's method of vulgarizing myth – setting the gods down on earth to cir-
culate in human society. The matter-of-fact narrative reduces
social fact, mythological events, and symbolic behavior to a
common level, and gives a wonderful inevitability to Sir Balaam's rise and fall:

> My Lady falls to play; so bad her chance,
> He must repair it; takes a bribe from France;
> The House impeach him; Coningsby harangues;
> The Court forsake him, and Sir Balaam hangs:
> Wife, son, and daughter, Satan, are thy own,
> His wealth, yet dearer, forfeit to the Crown:
> The Devil and the King divide the prize,
> And sad Sir Balaam curses God and dies.   (395)

But if Pope achieves ironic depths that are beyond Swift, he
also sacrifices a good deal. In saying that the King gets a dear-
er prize than the Devil does, he gives a grim account of Sir
Balaam's notion of evil, but he has pretty well cut himself off
from giving his own version of the powers of darkness: Satan
has been so thoroughly identified with money that he has ceased
to exist as himself. The point of the splendid irony in the last
line is that Sir Balaam has been damned long since, that not
only is his cursing God a meaningless gesture, but that he is
incapable of cursing God. And then one wonders just what is
the relationship of Providence and Pope to Sir Balaam. The
petty world of London is so morally ineffectual that it cannot
shake the order of the universe. The Deity and his prophet are
indifferent.
  Pope has reached a point where dissection of a personality
is ineffectual. Sir Balaam is a dunce, and one of the two major
shortcomings of To Bathurst is its failure in moral Realpolitik.
To find out what happens when fools and knaves outnumber virtuous men, we must turn, first, to the Epistle to Dr. Arbuthnot
and ultimately to the fourth book of The Dunciad. The other
shortcoming is an inadequate treatment of the corruption by

avarice of a political and social ideal: for this, we must go to
the Epilogue to the Satires. Yet to point out these deficiencies
in To Bathurst is really to indicate the stature of the poem, and
its unique range of observation helps us to understand that Pope's
late prophetic tones are not merely the result of personal iras-
cibility. No doubt Pope was gloomier in 1740 than when he wrote
The Rape of the Lock. But his melancholy has a significant relation to the role he conceived for the satirist when, resuming
serious poetry in the 1730's, he stooped to truth and moralized
his song. Courthope cites, in a footnote to the ironic praise of
paper credit, the following passage from Adam Smith:

> The gold and silver money which circulates in any coun-
> try may very properly be compared to a highway, which,
> while it circulates and carries to market all the grass
> and corn of the country, itself produces not a single
> pile of either. The judicious operations of banking, by
> providing (if I may be allowed so violent a metaphor)
> a sort of waggon-way through the air, enable the coun-
> try to convert, as it were, a great part of its highways
> into pastures and cornfields, and thereby to increase
> very considerably the annual produce of its land and
> labour.

Smith welcomes paper credit, it stirs the economist in him.
He and Mandeville (who was in some respects his master) are
modern in their tendency to split the political and the moral
imagination. Pope will not accept this separation. He is the
last English poet for whom a political ideal as a pertinent critique of contemporary society is central and vital. The prophetic
strains with which he defends this ideal show him to be the legitimate heir of Spenser and Milton.

NOTES

1 The Works of Alexander Pope, ed. Whitwell Elwin and W.
   J. Courthope (London, 1881), III, 121, 127.

2 F. B. Kaye, "The Influence of Bernard Mandeville," SP,
   XIX (1922), 90. Reprinted in Studies in the Literature of
   the Augustan Age: Essays Collected in Honor of Arthur

Ellicott Case, ed. Richard C. Boys (Ann Arbor, 1952),
p. 157. Hereafter cited as Case Essays.

3   Kaye, 104 (p. 171 in Case Essays).

4   The Fable of the Bees, ed. F. B. Kaye (Oxford, 1924), I,
355. Hereafter cited as Fable.

5   Epistles to Several Persons (Moral Essays), ed. F. W.
Bateson (London, 1951), p. 148. This is volume III-ii of
the Twickenham edition. All quotations are from this volume, and a word should be said about Bateson's text of
To Bathurst. All the readily available editions of Pope
(e.g. Everyman's Library, The Modern Library, and Professor Sherburn's The Best of Pope) are based on Elwin
and Courthope, which in turn is based on Warburton's text.
Warburton gives the poem the form of a dialogue between
Pope and Bathurst. He made this innovation after Pope's
death, so there is no question that Professor Bateson is
right to reject it. But he also rejects two more of Warburton's changes, which were made before Pope's death and
thus had his approval. Warburton transposed lines 37-38
and 65-78 of Pope's text (which had appeared in ten editions
between 1732 and 1743) to become, respectively, lines
33-34 and 35-48 in the "death-bed edition" of 1744, in Elwin and Courthope, and in the modern editions just mentioned. Professor Bateson gives two reasons for restoring
Pope's text (pp. 74-77). The first is that Warburton's revisions were made in late 1743 and early 1744, when Pope,
sick and dying, gave his friend "virtually a textual carte
blanche" (pp. 10-11). Furthermore, Warburton's transposi-
tions, made in the name of logic, produce serious poetic
flaws. The most striking, which seems to me to provide
nearly "objective" proof, is the awkward transition:

> Oh filthy check on all industrious skill,
> To spoil the nation's last great trade, Quadrille!
>   Since then, my Lord, on such a World we fall,
> What say you? "Say? Why take it, Gold and all."

It is inconceivable, I think, that Pope would have let this
stand had he been in good health (in the original version the

transitional couplet follows the passage beginning "Blest
paper-credit!" -- quoted on p. 448 of this essay.) There is no
doubt, I think, that we should accept Bateson's text as
Pope's.

Since this text is available only in the Twickenham
edition, I give two line references for every quotation. The
first is that of Bateson's text, the second (in italics) that
of Warburton's. In some cases the lineations are identical
and only one reference is given.

6   P. xxiv. We should note that Mandeville, using only economic criteria, considers prodigality a "virtue" and avarice a
"vice."

7   Reuben A. Brower, The Fields of Light (New York, 1951),
pp. 138-163.

8   Laureate of Peace (New York, 1955), p. 66. To my knowledge, Knight's commentary, brief as it is, is the only
recent attempt to characterize To Bathurst as a poem, and
not merely as a political document.

9   "If once we depart from calling every thing Luxury that is
not absolutely necessary to keep a Man alive, then there
is no Luxury at all; for if the wants of Men are innumerable, then what ought to supply them has no bounds; what
is call'd superfluous to some degree of People, will be
thought requisite to those of higher Quality; and neither
the World nor the Skill of Man can produce any thing so
curious or extravagant, but some most Gracious Sovereign
or other, if it either eases or diverts him, will reckon it
among the Necessaries of Life; not meaning every Body's
Life, but that of his Sacred Person" (Fable, I, 108). Pope,
on the other hand, insists that there is always "natural"
behavior for man, no matter how highly developed is his
economic organization.

10   Pope added an elaborate footnote with contemporary instances of the facts alleged in this passage.

11   In line 208 there is an echo (noted by Mack, but not by
Bateson) of Psalms, lxix. 9: "For the zeal of thine house
hath eaten me up"; the irony is directed at both Young
Cotta and the "house," the state. See Maynard Mack,

" 'Wit and Poetry and Pope': Some Observations on his Imagery," in Pope and his Contemporaries, ed. James L. Clifford and Louis A. Landa (Oxford, 1949), p. 29.

12 Compare Mandeville: "I look upon Avarice and Prodigality in the Society as I do upon two contrary Poisons in Physick, of which it is certain that the noxious Qualities being by mutual Mischief corrected in both, they may assist each other, and often make a good Medicine between them" (Fable, I, 106). Pope, as it were, insists that a physician be in attendance.

13 "extrema per illos / Justitia excedens terris vestigia fecit" (Georgics, II. 473).

14 Maynard Mack, "The Muse of Satire," The Yale Review, XLI (1951), 91. Reprinted in Case Essays, p. 230. Professor Mack is quoting Professor Bredvold.

15 " 'Wit and Poetry and Pope,'" p. 37. Cf. Paradise Lost, IV. 34: "at whose sight all the Stars / Hide thir diminisht heads."

IV. HORATIAN POEMS

POPE AND ADDISON

Norman Ault

I. HOSTILITIES

Quod Te Roma legit, Rumpitur Invidia!

If meaner Gildon draws his venal Quill,
I wish the Man a Dinner, And stand still:
If Dennis rails and raves in furious Pet,
I'll answer Dennis when he's out of Debt.
'Tis Hunger and not Malice makes them Print; 5
And who'd wage War with Bedlam or the Mint?
But were there One whom better Stars conspire
To form a Bard, and raise his Genius higher;
Blest with each Talent, and each Art to please,
And Born to Write, Converse and live at Ease; 10
Should such a One, too fond to Reign Alone,
Bear like the Turk, no Brother on the Throne:
View him with Jealous, yet with Scornful Eyes,
And Hate for Arts, which caus'd himself to Rise;
Damn with faint Praise, Assent with Civil Leer, 15
And without Sneering, teach the Rest to Sneer;
Willing to wound, but yet afraid to Strike,
Just hint a Fault, and Hesitate Dislike;
Alike reserv'd to Censure, or Commend,
A timerous Foe, and a suspicious Friend; 20
Fearing e'en Fools; by Flatterers besieg'd,
And so obliging, that he ne'er oblig'd:
Who when two wits on Rival Themes contest
Approves of Both, yet likes the worst the best;
Like Cato, gives his little Senate Laws, 25
And sits attentive to his own Applause;

Reprinted from Norman Ault, New Light on Pope, Methuen & Co.: London, 1949, pp. 101-127, by permission of the publisher and of Oona Ault. This article appeared earlier in Review of English Studies, Vol. 17 (1941), pp. 228-251.

> While Wits and Templars every Sentence raise,
> And Wonder with a Foolish face of Praise:
> Who but must Grieve, if such a One there Be,
> Who would not Weep, if Addison were He?   30

(Welbeck: Harley Papers)

Great must have been the provocation, one would have thought, or scarcely human the malignity, that prompted the writing of these searing lines of Pope's. But for two hundred years little attention was paid to any possible provocation, with the result that a legend of Pope's treachery to his friends, as exemplified chiefly by these verses, was handed down from generation to generation of readers. It has likewise been too frequently forgotten that Pope spoke just as publicly with quite another voice in his Epistle to Mr. Addison, Occasioned by his Dialogues on Medals, where, after describing the antics of mere antiquarians, he proceeds thus:

> . . . Theirs is the Vanity, the Learning thine:
> Touch'd by thy hand, again Rome's glories shine;
> Her Gods, and god-like Heroes rise to view,
> And all her faded garlands bloom a-new.
> Nor blush, these studies thy regard engage;
> These pleas'd the Fathers of poetic rage;
> The verse and sculpture bore an equal part,
> And Art reflected images to Art.
>   Oh when shall Britain, conscious of her claim,
> Stand emulous of Greek and Roman fame?
> In living medals see her wars enroll'd,
> And vanquish'd realms supply recording gold?
> Here, rising bold, the Patriot's honest face;
> There Warriors frowning in historic brass?
> Then future ages with delight shall see
> How Plato's, Bacon's, Newton's looks agree;
> Or in fair series laurell'd Bards be shown,
> A Virgil there, and here an Addison.

With the publication of these two pieces, Pope himself would seem to have raised, and challenged, the question: Which is the more blameworthy, to have written both — or to have inspired both? This question, as hinted above, has generally been answered in one way. But although present opinion, deriving in great measure from the two recent biographies of the poet previously mentioned,[1] leans towards another answer, the problem is still far from being settled. One more endeavour to trace the history of what are generally known as the "Atticus" lines, and their relation to the Epistle to Addison, may therefore be attempted; especially as the familiar facts are to be reexamined in the light of much new evidence.

As early as 1709, Pope published a translation of parts of the twelfth and sixteenth books of the Iliad.[2] But this translation had been handed about in manuscript still earlier, and had been seen by — amongst others — his old friend, Sir William Trumbull, who wrote enthusiastically on April 9, 1708, urging him, but without success, to translate the whole work. Some five years later, during which time he had turned four other fragments of Homer (three of them from the Odyssey) into English verse, Addison succeeded where Trumbull had failed. This generally neglected truth about the beginnings of Pope's great undertaking was explicitly and unmistakably told, once and for all, in its "Preface" in 1715, without a breath of correction or denial from any one concerned. The statement runs:

> Mr. Addison was the first whose Advice determin'd me to undertake this Task, who was pleas'd to write to me upon that Occasion in such Terms as I cannot repeat without Vanity.

Pope also later printed two letters — whose authenticity has not been disproved — written by Addison soon after the project had been decided upon, showing the older man's warm interest in it and conveying his good wishes for its success.[3] As these are dated respectively October 26 and November 2, 1713, and as Bishop Kennett noted in his diary about this time (Dr. Johnson dates the entry, November 2) that Swift was busily enlisting subscribers for "Mr. Pope (a papist) who had begun a translation of Homer into English verse . . . [which] the author shall not begin to print till I have a thousand guineas for him"[4]; it is also certain that the long and arduous undertaking was well started before the close of 1713. News of the project spread; and before long a kind of opposition party of Whig complexion

465

began slowly to take shape. Within a fortnight of the signing of the agreement between Pope and Bernard Lintot, the bookseller, on March 23, 1714, the first attack in print on Pope and the Iliad project appeared in an anonymous "play" entitled, A New Rehearsal, or Bays the Younger. This was a slashing criticism, cast in dialogue form, of the works of Rowe and Pope, by Charles Gildon, a minor author, dramatist, and compiler of miscellanies, who, besides damning The Rape of the Lock, then recently published, made an apparently unprovoked attack on its author, in which his claim to a knowledge of Greek and ability to translate Homer were unmercifully ridiculed. Gildon's attack was published on April 6, 1714,[5] and was followed within four days by another, this time an anonymous epigram much advertised in the newspapers by its title, Advice to Mr. Pope, On his intended Translation of Homer's Iliads[6]; and in this Pope is taunted with making more money out of the Iliad than ever Homer did, with the very successful subscription of the translation then going forward: "First take the gold — then charm the list'-ning Ear." Next month saw the republication of his Proposals for a Translation of Homer's Iliads, this time accompanied by "a List of those who have already Subscrib'd"[7]; and on June 8, 1714, Gay writes to Swift that "Book I" is already completed.[8] On August 10, advertisements[9] of "the 5th Edition" of Oldmixon's miscellany again prominently name the Advice to Mr. Pope on his intended Translation of Homer among the principal attractions of the book.

These attacks, however, were but affairs of outposts, preliminaries to the main battle which seems to have begun when the newspapers joined in at the end of the year. On December 10, 1714, for example, Philip Horneck published in The High-German Doctor a long bantering account of a fictitious interview with Lintot, in which, after the bookseller carefully explains the delay in publishing The Iliad ("We have been Nine Months Debating about the first Word of the Book, whether we should express Μηνιν by the English Word Rage, or Wrath"), the dialogue proceeds to ridicule the whole undertaking, its subscribers as well as its publisher, its poet's religion as well as his lack of classical scholarship. It may have been this attack which induced Pope to announce on December 25,[10] and during the next two weeks, that the translation of the first four books of the Iliad, which was to have been published "by the Beginning of

May next . . . shall be deliver'd two Months sooner than the
Time promis'd." And it is this announcement, doubtless, that
explains why so many of Pope's enemies chose to concentrate
their activities on this particular month of March, 1715; for
besides the well-known major attacks by the pseudonymous
"Mr. Preston"[11] (March 5), by Burnet and Duckett[12] (March 7),
and by the unknown Author of A Complete Key to . . . The What
D'ye Call It (April 2 or earlier), there were Burnet's further
attack in The Grumbler (March 10, or 17)[13] and another instal-
ment from Horneck's pen[14] (March 15). Indeed, these last two
gentlemen were peculiarly persistent, and returned to the attack
from time to time, Horneck[15] once again on April 23 and Burnet[16] on May 6, not to mention some slighter things; in addition
to which there should also be noted a reissue of Gildon's New Rehearsal, probably on May 14 (as will be shown later), and a
"Second Edition" of Homerides on May 30. Then on June 4,[17]
Pope having postponed publication in March to circumvent his
enemies, the first volume of The Iliad, containing the first four
"Books," at last appeared to a waiting world.

Unfortunately that is not the whole story. Four days later
a rival translation, entitled The first book of Homer's Iliad,
was published with Addison's approbation and praise.

How much of this persecution of Pope was due to Addison's
instigation and active participation will probably never be known.
Several of his friends have testified to the fact that he did not
like the young poet. For instance, Burnet wrote to his friend
Duckett the following year (June 1, 1716): "I have [often] seen
Addison caressing Pope, whom at the same Time he hates worse
than Belzeebub and by whom he has been more than once lampooned."[18] Also it was no secret that most of Pope's enemies at
this time were Addison's friends or partisans – fellow-frequent-
ers of that haunt of the Whigs, Button's coffee-house. Indeed
there is indubitable proof that Addison was implicated to some
extent both in the general attempt to discredit Pope and his
great translation (the very work which, as already shown, he
himself had persuaded Pope to undertake), and also in the rival
publication put forward in Tickell's name. For, as regards the
first, besides much masterly use of a pre-Nelsonian blind eye
to the manifest activities of his friends, there are Burnet's letters[19] still surviving to prove that Addison had a hand in the
revision of Homerides for the press; and, as regards the second,

there is his own admission to Pope, that he had had Tickell's translation in his hands to "look over."[20] It should also be noted that Thomas Tickell, who was then probably Addison's most intimate friend, and, later, his literary executor, was thought by many of Pope's contemporaries — not all of them his friends — to be little more than Addison's stalking-horse in this affair; and from Pope's remarks it is apparent that he too inclined to the same opinion from time to time. And he was so far justified, that, whether the idea of a competitive translation originated with Addison, as some said,[21] or with a suggestion of the rival bookseller, Tonson, as others opine,[22] Addison was, to all intents and purposes, its literary sponsor. Nevertheless, it was Tickell who signed the agreement with Tonson (the publisher of several of his earlier works) to translate the whole Iliad; for the document has recently been discovered[23] bearing his signature, and the date, May 31, 1714, which is two months later than the date of Pope's agreement with Lintot. It is likewise certain that Pope's translation was well on its way before that of his rival, which is said to have been written at Oxford in the summer of 1714.[24] And then, when Tickell's "Book I" was finished, instead of proceeding as usual to publication without reference to Pope's undertaking, as might have been expected of an innocent poem, the interested parties seem to have held it for months ready for immediate issue, as though playing a grim kind of cat and mouse game with Pope's volume.

The attacks on Pope did not entirely cease with the publication of the rival translations, even though Tickell had announced that he would not proceed with his version. Addison — with the Buttonian crowd as chorus — appears to have been more outspoken than ever in his praise of Tickell's translation and his preference of it to Pope's, and he sent copies of it to his friends signifying his approval.[25] Lintot, commenting on "Mr Tickles Book" in a letter to Pope,[26] dated June 10, 1715, reports that "the malice & juggle at Buttons" is, next to politics, "the talk of the town." And on July 8, 1715, Gay wrote to Pope, who was then in the country hard at work on the next volume of The Iliad:

> I have just set down Sir Samuel Garth at the Opera.
> He bid me tell you, that every body is pleas'd with your
> Translation, but a few at Button's; and that Sir Rich-
> ard Steele told him, that Mr. Addison said Tickel's

translation was the best that ever was in any language
. . . I am inform'd that at Button's your character is
made very free with as to morals, &c. and Mr. A[ddi-
son] says, that your translation and Tickel's are both
very well done, but that the latter has more of Homer.[27]

Such, then, is a summary of the state of affairs to which
Pope alludes in the famous satire on Addison above quoted. But
in addition to all these specific and verifiable actions and reac-
tions, there are the less demonstrable but not less real effects
of the mutual misunderstanding which persistently dogged the
association of the two men, and which can only be explained by
the fundamental incompatibility of their temperaments. The
grave reserve, conscious "correctness," and slightly patronizing manner of the older man and the brilliance, irritability, and
high-spirited indiscretions of the younger — almost every characteristic facet of either personality must have been an all too
frequent cause of offence to the other. What if the beginning of
all the trouble between them -- the incident which settled their
attitude to each other for ever — had no more importance than
a boyish quip at a pretence of modesty by a grown man of the
world?

Addison's poem, A Letter from Italy, was addressed to
Lord Halifax in 1701; but it was not published till 1704, in Tonson's Poetical Miscellanies: The Fifth Part, where it was given
pride of place as the opening poem, and where, about the same
time or a little later, it was seen by young Pope. The boy, who
was then only "sixteen or seventeen years of age," and still unknown to Addison, was himself busy on a translation (as he
called it) of Chaucer's Merchant's Tale, entitled January and
May; and, on reading Addison's poem, was apparently struck
by the difference between the slightly grandiose air of the poet,
especially in the lengthy descriptive passages, and the verbal
humility of his closing lines. For although admittedly "fired
with the name" of Nassau the poet rather ingloriously ends:

> I bridle in my struggling Muse with Pain,
> That longs to launch into a bolder strain.[28]
> But I've already troubled you too long,
> Nor dare attempt a more advent'rous Song.
> My humble Verse demands a softer Theme,

> A painted Meadow or a purling Stream,
> Unfit for Heroes; whom Immortal Lays,
> And lines like Virgil's, or like yours shou'd praise.

And the boy, who, it appears, was then writing about (but not "describing") January's "spacious garden," demurely slips in a couplet, the real significance of which seems hitherto to have been overlooked, because he later[29] changed the epithet in his allusion to Addison, from "the boldest Bard" to "the gentlest Bard," with the consequence that his little jest at the diminuendo from Addison's "bolder Strain" to his "softer Theme" disappeared. What Pope originally wrote about January's garden, and what Addison originally read, was —

> . . . this charming Place —
> A Place to tire the rambling Wits of France
> In long Descriptions, and exceed Romance;
> Enough to shame the boldest Bard that sings
> Of painted Meadows, and of purling Springs.

Pope's January and May was published (with the Pastorals and an Episode from the Iliad, together making his first appearance in print) in Poetical Miscellanies: The Sixth Part, 1709, some three weeks before he was twenty-one. Was it, one wonders, this little sparkle of youthful high spirits which the lofty-minded Addison remembered, when, two and a half years later, he sat down to review An Essay on Criticism in The Spectator for December 20, 1711? For Addison's article, which is supposed to have first made them acquainted, was afterwards remembered by the young poet not so much for the praise that concluded it (which could not but please him), as for the snub with which it began. The review opens with these words: "There is nothing which more denotes a great Mind, than the Abhorrence of Envy and Detraction"; and, after expatiating on that theme at some length, continues as follows:

> In our own Country a Man seldom sets up for a
> Poet, without attacking the Reputation of all his Broth-
> ers in the Art . . . But how much more noble is the
> Fame that is built on Candour and Ingenuity, according

to those beautiful Lines of Sir <u>John Denham</u>, in his
Poem on <u>Fletcher's</u> Works!

> But whither am I stray'd? I need not raise
> Trophies to thee from other Mens Dispraise:
> Nor is thy Fame on lesser Ruins built,
> Nor needs thy juster Title the foul Guilt
> Of Eastern Kings, who, to secure their Reign,
> Must have their Brothers, Sons, and Kindred slain.

> I am sorry to find that an Author, who is very justly
> esteemed among the best Judges, has admitted some
> Stroaks of this Nature into a very fine Poem. . .

The title of the poem is thereupon untactfully misquoted as
<u>The Art of Criticism</u>. Pope, as it happened, did not see this
number of <u>The Spectator</u> until December 29; and thinking his
friend Steele was the author, he wrote to him the next day[30]
and thanked him for his praise of the poem, and also for his
"candour and frankness" in pointing out "the error I have been
guilty of in speaking too freely of my brother moderns." Pope
then went on to say that if a second edition should be called for,
he would "strike out all such strokes which you shall be so kind
as to point out to me." (It is noticeable that he does not admit
knowledge of the "errors.") Steele replied on January 20, 1712,
that the paper was written, not by himself, but "by one w[th]
whome I will make you acquainted"[31]; — that is, by Addison;
and in that way, it seems, Pope and Addison at last met. The
acquaintance, however, did not really prosper; and it soon becomes apparent that the criticism, which the touchy young poet
was ready (when convinced) to accept from a friend who obviously wished him well, he was not prepared to take from a stranger
whose attitude to him was so markedly different from Steele's,
and who — Pope soon came to believe — had a personal reason
for his censure. Thus it was that, before the year was out, Pope
had written some indignant lines directly rebutting Addison's
charge, and even made them the "curtain" of his next major
work, <u>The Temple of Fame</u>. This reply to Addison seems also
to have escaped comment hitherto, probably because — although
the poem had been written and sent to Steele, some time before
November 12, 1712[32] — its publication was for various reasons

delayed until February 1, 1715,[33] so that The Rape of the Lock, Windsor Forest, and the Ode for Musick had appeared in the meantime and obscured the connection. No more than ten lines of the close of The Temple of Fame can be given here, in which it will be noticed that while they are a general repudiation of Addison's strictures, in the third couplet in particular Pope makes an effective use of the third line of the six his critic had reprovingly quoted from Denham.

> Nor Fame I slight, nor for her Favours call;
> She comes unlook'd for, if she comes at all:
> But if the Purchase costs so dear a Price,
> As soothing Folly, or exalting Vice . . .
> Or if no Basis bear my rising Name,
> But the fall'n Ruins of Another's Fame:
> Then teach me, Heaven! to scorn the guilty Bays;
> Drive from my Breast that wretched Lust of Praise;
> Unblemish'd let me live, or die unknown,
> Oh grant an honest Fame, or grant me none!

Only a denial of the charge as yet, while the man who made it is allowed to go scot free. Counter-attack did not come till later, when to injury (not very serious, perhaps, except for its after effects on a sensitive young poet) Addison had added something very like treachery in his relations with Pope about the Iliad, and had, moreover, given Pope greater cause to suspect him of jealousy, than could ever have been found in the Essay on Criticism to suspect Pope. Then it was, and only then, that Pope was exasperated enough to retort Addison's censure upon Addison himself in the satire with which this chapter opens, where, to add to its sting, he subtly paraphrased the root idea of the verses Addison had quoted at him, in a couplet of franker statement, presently to be noted. Furthermore, their mutual misunderstanding (if misunderstanding by this time has not become too mild a term) had led Pope to suspect that sinister motives lay behind Addison's attempt to dissuade him from making any alterations in the first version of The Rape of the Lock — alterations which, when once carried out, made the poem the supreme masterpiece of its kind. Neither can Addison be said — nor can Pope have thought him — to have behaved quite straightforwardly in the matter of Pope's championship of Cato[34] against

Dennis's criticisms; and there were other things of the kind, of which space forbids mention. And it is against this background of strained relations, mutual friction, and sense of injury, that the ancient story of Pope's alleged treachery must once again be discussed.

It has always been recognized that the gravamen of the charge rests in the main on the date of the undated satire. Was it written and shown to Addison in his lifetime, as man to man and poet to poet? or was it an attack on a dead friend no longer able to defend himself?

Now one of the most obvious truths about Pope's literary habits is that, for various reasons -- aesthetic, political, personal, or what not -- he frequently delayed the publication of his pieces, oftentimes for many years, so that with the majority of them the date of printing is no guide at all to the date of composition. That fact is indisputable. Nevertheless, as Addison died on June 17, 1719, and as neither the satire nor the epistle was published during his life, Pope's enemies (amongst whom may strangely be numbered some of his editors) have often asserted that the satire, if not the epistle also, was written after its subject's death. No material evidence supports their contention. All they could point to were the supposed dates of publication, and a late anonymous attack on Pope (one of the first repercussions of The Dunciad) in Mist's Weekly Journal of June 8, 1728. In the course of this amazing and lengthy diatribe, which purports to sketch Pope's literary life and works, and accuses him of various misdemeanours while so doing, the author, who signs himself "W. A.," makes the absurd statement that Pope's rise "from an humble Obscurity," his fame, friends, and social success, not omitting his acquaintance with "the whole Body of our Nobility," were all owing to Addison who had "strongly supported" him from the first. The writer then goes on to relate how Addison, not approving of Pope's translation of the Iliad, "employ'd a younger Muse[35] in an Undertaking of this Kind, which he supervis'd himself," and which "the World allow'd" was in consequence every way better than Pope's. He says also, that, notwithstanding Pope's natural chagrin at this "Judgment of Mankind," he hid his real feelings, and sought to retain Addison's friendship. The narrative naïvely continues thus:

He therefore continued his Assiduity to his generous
Benefactor, making . . . Poems to his Fame, as a
certain Dissertation upon Medals can testify. . . .
But no sooner was his Body lifeless, . . . but the
Author, whose Works are now in Question, reviving
his Resentments at the Expence of all Gratitude and
Decency, libelled the Memory of his departed Friend,
traduced him in a sharp Invective, and what was still
more heinous, he made the Scandal publick.

That, in effect, is the tale which continued for so long to
hold the general ear, and those its foundations. And after it had
been judicially confirmed in 1778 by the learned Blackstone —
who summarized the case on the facts as then known, and adju-
dicated in favour of Addison[36] — the legend became gospel. Unfortunately, Pope's own account of the genesis of the satire —
as recorded by Spence — had, until recently, contained two or
three apparently irreconcilable statements, and so failed to
command belief. Now, however, thanks partly to the discovery
of Spence's original punctuation,[37] and partly to some other
new evidence, those impossibilities are reduced to mere difficulties.

The opening words of Pope's account, as printed in the
Anecdotes, ran: "Gildon wrote a thing about Wycherley, in which
he had abused . . ." Now, with those first six words corrected
according to the manuscript,[38] the relevant passage reads:

Gildon wrote a thing (about Wycherley?) in which
he had abused both me and my relations very grossly.
Lord Warwick[39] himself told me, one day, . . . that
Addison had encouraged Gildon to publish those scan-
dals, and had given him ten guineas after they were
published. The next day, while I was heated with what
I had heard, I wrote a letter to Mr. Addison, to let
him know, that I was not unacquainted with this behaviour
of his; that if I was to speak severely of him in return for
it, . . . it should be something in the following manner.
I then subjoined the first sketch of what has since been
called my satire on Addison. He used me very civilly ever
after; and never did me any injustice, that I know of, from
that time to his death, which was about three years after.[40]

Happily, Pope's account can be substantiated by the independent testimony of several of his contemporaries (inimical as well as friendly) at least as regards the existence of the poem before Addison's death. Pope's friend, Lord Oxford, wrote in his copy of the Epistle to Arbuthnot, 1734, now in the Bodleian, a note to line 209, saying: "The Assertion of some anonymous authors that Mr. P. writ this Character after the Gentlemans death, was utterly untrue; it having been sent him several years before, and then shown to Mr Secretary Craggs, & yᵉ present Earl of Burlington . . ." Similarly, a bitter enemy, Lady Mary Wortley Montagu (for it was long after the famous quarrel), speaking to Spence of these lines, said emphatically, "Yes, that satire was written in Addison's life time."[41] And, on another occasion, Dr. Trapp, who apparently was no more than an acquaintance of Pope's, though a close friend of Tickell's at Oxford, informed Spence, with much surprise that there should be any doubt about it, that "many people, and he himself for one, had seen it in Addison's life-time."[42] To these witnesses should be added the corroborative testimony of Bishop Warburton,[43] and — if it is not the same voice — Pope's biographer, Ruffhead[44]; besides which there is also Pope's letter to Craggs of July 15, 1715,[45] not yet proved apocryphal, which contains a prose counterpart — echo or anticipation — of portions of the poem. Lastly, but not least important, is the inference to be drawn from Addison's warning to Lady Mary (either on her return to England not long before his death, or in the two or three months before her departure on August 1, 1716), when, speaking of Pope, he said: "Leave him as soon as you can, he will certainly play you some devilish trick else: he has an appetite to satire."[46] As no sustained piece of satire by Pope had then been published — except the early lines, To the Author of Successio, in 1712, and, perhaps one should add, the anonymous prose Narrative of Dr. Robert Norris, in 1713 — his "appetite to satire" could not have been very evident at that time; and Addison seems to have spoken too feelingly not to have spoken from personal experience. Not even Addison, who (as shown above) had condoned — and, in one instance, revised — his friends' attacks on Pope, could have pumped up such vicarious indignation, either about a boy's ridicule of Settle in the former piece, written when Pope was only fourteen years old; or about the genuine fun with which Pope overwhelmed Dennis and his criticisms of Addison's own play, Cato, in the latter.

With all this evidence available -- if not all made use of —
to rebut the charge of treachery against Pope, and establish
both the early date and Addison's knowledge of the satire, too
much importance has recently been attached to a page in Pope's
autograph among the Homer MSS. , containing some half-dozen
sketches of couplets.[47] For this page, long known to students,
and printed as early as 1776,[48] is not "the 'Atticus' portrait in
early embryo," as has been stated,[49] any more than it is the
origin of the Epilogue to the Satires, Dialogue II, which likewise enshrines one of the couplets; or the first sketch of an
Epigram on Moore-Smythe (then about thirteen years old!),
which makes use of another; or a projected revision of the Essay on Criticism, because yet another couplet is a re-writing
of two lines in that poem. The truth is, the page is nothing but
a number of attempts at more or less disconnected couplets,
all of them on the subject of wit, and all except one mentioning
it. Thus while at least three of the couplets were used in other
poems of Pope's, only one was, after some remodelling, inserted in the satire. This couplet, as Pope first sketched it
here, ran as follows:

> But our Great Turks in wit must reign alone
> & ill can bear a Brother on ye Throne.

But the idea in this version of the couplet — sole point of contact
with the "Atticus" portrait though it is — had at that time already
acquired something of a history in Pope's hands, so that "embryo" seems hardly the mot juste for it; for, as we have seen,[50]
it had been etched on Pope's memory by Addison's acid use of
Denham's lines to censure him in 1711. It also reappears in
Pope's translation from Statius (which, though dated 1703, was
not published until May 20, 1712), where, speaking of the two
brothers who shared a throne by alternate occupation, he tells
how they were each consumed with envy of the other,

> And impotent Desire to reign alone,
> That scorns the dull reversion of a throne.   (ll. 180-1)

Moreover, the same idea yet once again reappears in his translation of the first book of the Iliad (completed on or before June 8, 1714)[51] in the line:

What King can bear a rival in his sway?   (l. 383)

So that, even if the statement, "the writing on this leaf must date about July 1715,"[52] had been proved to be true — which it probably is — its alleged "significance with regard to the origin of the portrait"[53] would still be of no importance; because all that would have been established thereby, would be, not that Pope began to write the character of Atticus at that date, but only that he was continuing earlier attempts to shape the same idea into a more telling couplet than that which Addison had quoted against him, apparently for future use against some unspecified person.

Similarly, difficulties are raised by the most recent attempts to identify the particular attack by Gildon, to which Pope referred in his conversation with Spence, and is supposed to refer in the much-discussed epithet "venal" of the first line of the satire: "If meaner Gildon draws his venal Quill." This attack has been thought to be that delivered in Gildon's anonymous Memoirs of . . . Wycherley, 1718,[54] and much ingenuity was exercised to reconcile it with Pope's statement — but in vain. A later suggestion,[55] however, is that the abuse, which Addison paid Gildon to print, was the anonymous libel, entitled, A True Character of Mr Pope and his Writings, 1716 — a suggestion that raises more problems than it solves. For not only did Pope at different times think that different people wrote it (for example, he gives it to Dennis in an autograph note in his own copy of A True Character, now in the British Museum[56]; to Gildon in one place in The Dunciad,[57] and to Dennis and Gildon jointly in another[58]); but Professor Sherburn and Professor Case favour each a different candidate for its authorship, and — as Pope himself asked — "Who shall decide when Doctors disagree?" The date of the pamphlet, A True Character, also raises insuperable obstacles; because, as it was published on May 31, 1716,[59] it would follow that Pope's warning letter to Addison, and the "subjoined" poem also, must have been written and sent after that date. But so late a date for the letter squares neither with Pope's statement nor the known facts. Addison had already begun to make amends to Pope by praising

477

his Iliad in The Freeholder as early as May 7, 1716; and this change of face and policy had become a matter of gossip amongst his "little Senate" before the end of May; for on June 1, Burnet wrote to tell his country friend, Duckett, that Addison and his "gang" had "dropt their resentment" against Pope.[60] It is incredible that Addison, arbiter of morals and pattern of propriety for so long, should have extended a conciliatory hand to Pope on May 7, and then later in the self-same month paid Gildon (if the pamphlet is his) to publish that furious abuse of him; and quite as unlikely that Pope should have written complaining of Addison's hostile attitude to his Iliad weeks after the older man had at last begun publicly to write in its praise.[61]

The truth is that no printed attack yet suggested agrees with Pope's account and the known facts, not to mention other evidence (for the most part overlooked hitherto) which seems to point to yet another publication. On April 6, 1714, as already mentioned, Charles Gildon published an anonymous "play" called A New Rehearsal, or Bays the Younger, which contains what seems to have been a quite gratuitous attack on Pope and his friend Rowe, the playwright, and which, in consequence, is probably the original cause of Pope's subsequent resentment against its author. Amongst other things, Pope is grossly caricatured in the play as "Sawny Dapper," an absurd little poet who is held up to ridicule for his pretentious claim to a knowledge of Greek and an ability to translate Homer. Pope is also — by the mouth of that caricature — made to confess that he himself had actually written Wycherley's panegyric, To my friend, Mr. Pope, on his Pastorals.[62] Here is offence enough, one might suppose, for any reprisals; and, incidentally, here is also a probable explanation of the curious way in which Wycherley's name (mentioned also elsewhere in the play) has been caught up into the Pope-Gildon-Addison imbroglio in Spence's report of Pope's conversation.

A New Rehearsal not only fills the part as regards subject-matter and author, but its appropriate date of publication and its mention of Wycherley together remove the sole obstacle which some have found to the acceptance of Pope's account of the "Atticus" lines. Only in one small detail does its identification with Gildon's "thing" seem to fall a little short of Pope's description, and that is, that it does not contain any very obvious abuse of Pope's relations. There is, however, one small

scrap of dialogue (on pages 40-41) which looks like a covert
sneer at the social status of the Pope family, insomuch that it
touches on the way "Sawny Dapper" has managed to "raise himself" by his poetry above his earlier circumstances. But even
if that cannot be counted "gross abuse" the discrepancy could
easily be explained by the simple fact that Gildon made two or
three attacks on Pope within three or four years, in at least
one of which he had abused the elder Mr. Pope. It is very probable, therefore, that when describing these events to Spence,
after an interval of some twenty busy years, Pope simply forgot
for the moment, either which particular "thing" of Gildon's had
ridiculed his father, or the date of its publication. All the other
evidence available, together with the absence of any probable —
or even possible -- alternative publication by Gildon before or
during 1715, suggests that this was the abuse of which Pope
complained.

But with all the New Rehearsal's provocation of Pope, it is
questionable whether, in 1715, Gildon would have achieved dis-
honourable mention in this immortal rebuke of Addison, if he
had only been content to be the first of the pamphleteers to
damn Pope's great translation before it was written; but the offending pamphlet was reissued with a new title-page,[63] once,
if not twice, during that critical summer of 1715. How could
all the persecution of the preceding twelve months not be recalled to Pope's mind when he heard the gossip of the youthful
Lord Warwick (not the staidest or most reliable of young men
about town)? And if the gossip was true only so far as it mirrored Addison's antipathy to Pope, and if money had ever been
known to pass from Addison, the leader of the Whig literary
party, to Gildon, an occasional writer for the Whig party, for
services rendered (no matter the service) — it is conceivable
that Pope, at such a juncture, "heated" as he says, "with what
I had heard," genuinely accepted the whole miserable story at
its face value, in spite of what to-day seems its inherent im-
probability, and acted accordingly. Such a natural course of
events could explain Pope's statement — if explanation were
needed; and that such a course of events was also probable may
be seen in a begging letter in the British Museum,[64] which was
sent to Addison by Gildon but written by an amanuensis because
of his increasing blindness. This document reveals Gildon actually appealing to Addison's "native generosity" for what seems

to have been occasional, if not habitual, "Releif, which Justice
requires to my Sufferins," but whether it was solicited from his
private purse or party funds is uncertain. For although this letter was not written until four years later -- actually, February
2, 1719 -- it does at least indicate the way in which some previous "Releif" or payment might have coincided more or less
with the publication of A New Rehearsal, or some other pamphlet attacking Pope, and might all unmaliciously have been thus
misrepresented by young Warwick's gossip.

Yet another indication of Gildon's venality in this affair is
supplied by Pope's notorious lampoon on Curll, the piratical
publisher, A Full and True Account of a . . . Revenge by Poison, On the Body of Mr. Edmund Curll, in which Gildon is asserted to have received extra payment expressly to abuse Pope
in this very pamphlet, A New Rehearsal.[65] Pope's lampoon was
published at the end of March, 1716, not improbably about the
time that he dispatched the warning letter, with the "subjoined"
satire, to Addison. If, therefore, in March 1716 Pope could
state in prose that Gildon's pen had been purchasable two years
previously, it follows that the much discussed phrase, "his
venal pen," could have appeared in a poetical allusion to the
same incident, written, so it seems, only a little earlier than
the prose, namely, in "the first sketch on my satire on Addison." As a matter of fact, it actually does appear in the Welbeck
transcript given above, which is apparently the earliest surviving version of the satire.

But although in Pope's account of the satire Gildon alone
is singled out for blame (apart, that is, from Addison), in the
satire itself John Dennis, the critic, stands pilloried beside
him, and consequently demands a word at this place. The story
of the famous quarrel between Pope and the old critic has been
recently retold more than once[66]; and there is now no doubt that
Pope's rapier was ever ready to answer Dennis's bludgeon,
though thrust and blow cannot to-day be always related to each
other with certainty. Thus Pope's lamentable thrust at his old
enemy's poverty may be nothing more than a part-payment of
old scores -- a return for blows of a much greater brutality.
But, seeing that the occasion of the satire was primarily the
translation of The Iliad and Addison's dubious activities in connection with it, and that Gildon's crime was connected with the
same sorry business, it is reasonable to suppose that Dennis --

the only other person named in the early versions – had likewise
sinned in some way against Pope's great translation. No attack
by Dennis on that work, however, has been found earlier than
the True Character of Mr. Pope, above mentioned, in which he
almost certainly had a hand, and in which, after making some
derogatory remarks about Pope's Iliad, he (or another) promises to publish proofs of them at some future date. To this
statement, Pope, in his copy of A True Character, has added
a marginal note in his own hand, recognizing Dennis's authorship in these words: "As he did ye next y^r in his Remarks on
Homer." It is, therefore, a not unlikely conjecture that Dennis,
who seems to have regarded each major poetical work of Pope's
as a personal affront,[67] and who was as big a bully in speech
as in print, had given vent to some typical Dennisian "remark"
about The Iliad by word of mouth ("If Dennis raves and rails in
furious Pet"); and that Pope heard of it in due course, and
straightway popped him into the imperishable amber of his
verse alongside Gildon, harmless there to rail and rave forever.

It is, however, just possible, perhaps, that the allusion to
Dennis was added to "the first sketch" at some date after May
31, 1716; that is, after the publication of A True Character.
The suggestion is quite warrantable; for if there is one thing
beyond question, it is that Pope touched and retouched his portrait of Addison from time to time in tireless revision. Consequently, any alterations or additions could have been indistin-
guishably incorporated in the poem at any stage between "the
first sketch" of 1715 and the first printed text of 1722. Indeed,
the four contemporary manuscript texts known to the writer
differ not only from each other but from the printed texts also.
For instance, it seems certain[68] that the version at the head of
this chapter – the Harleian transcript at Welbeck Abbey[69] –
preserves what is probably the oldest surviving text, if not actually "the first sketch" sent to Addison; while, on the other
hand, the Longleat manuscript, which is in Pope's autograph,
just as certainly represents his latest revision of the poem in
its original short form of thirty lines. But revision by no means
ceased with publication, and the subsequent developments of the
Addison portrait must be noted in passing. After at least four
appearances in print between 1722 and 1726, each differing from
the others, the poem was suddenly expanded (by additions not

materially affecting the Addison portrait) to sixty-eight lines
in "The Last Volume" of the Swift-Pope Miscellanies, 1727[-8],
where it was printed and acknowledged — though only indirectly —
by Pope for the first time. The poem again received considerable modifications and interpolations when it came to be inserted in the Epistle to Arbuthnot in 1734, in which place "Atticus"
was first substituted for "Addison" (or "A——n") in the last
line of the previous texts. Later still, the "Miscellanies" version was further corrected on its appearance in the 1742 edition,
and was thus the last text to pass through Pope's hands.

II. ARMISTICE

Turning now to the more pleasing aspect of the Pope-Addi-
son relationship, the first remarkable fact to be noted is that
Pope's encomium of Addison, quoted above,[70] has been far too
frequently excluded from previous discussions of the problem,
to the consequent distortion, if not actual misrepresentation,
of the truth. And even when admitted, the uncertainty about the
occasion and date of the epistle itself has made possible, if not
encouraged, the most extraordinary statements about them,
from those of Mist's Mr. "W. A." down to, and conspicuously
including, the remarks of Elwin and Courthope.[71] Thus, as the
troubled year, 1715, is one of the dates ascribed to the epistle,
and as it would appear highly improbable that the satire and
the eulogy derive from the same period, like two sides of the
same medal, it is obvious that the "Atticus" aspect of the problem cannot be settled without first reaching some reasonable
solution of the difficulties presented by the epistle.

This, at the outset, is made easier by the discovery of an
early text hitherto unrecorded and unknown. Addison's Works,
in which this epistle has been thought to have first appeared in
print, was published on October 2, 1721.[72] But it now seems
certain that the poem had been previously published in an edition
(probably pirated) of Pope's Works, "Printed by T. J. for the
Company," and dated 1720. A copy of this little-known book is
now to be found both in the Bodleian and the British Museum,
and in both copies the Epistle occupies the last two leaves; and
as these leaves have consecutive pagination and signatures with
the rest of the book, and display the same printer's ornament

there can be no question that they belong to, and were issued
with, these copies. Mr. R. H. Griffith, however, lists a copy[73]
lacking these leaves; which would seem to suggest that there
were two issues of the book in the same year, one with and one
without the Epistle to Addison.

Pope himself made different statements at different times
about the date of the epistle:

(i) In the "Appendix" of all the editions and issues of the
"Variorum" Dunciad in 1729, Pope included a page of which
the heading and first few lines run thus:

"A LIST OF ALL OUR AUTHOR'S GENUINE WORKS.
The Works of Mr. Alexander Pope . . . 1717. This Edition contains whatsoever is his, except these few
following, which have been written since that time.
Inscription to Dr. Parnel's Poems; To the . . . Earl
of Oxford . . .
Verses on Mr. Addison's Treatise of Medals, first
printed after his death in Mr. Tickel's Edition of
his Works.
Epitaphs: On the . . ."

(ii) Six years later, in various editions of his Works in
1735, Pope added a note to the Epistle to Addison, stating:
"This was written in 1715, at which time Mr. Addison intended
to publish his Book of Medals. It was some time before he was
Secretary of State."

(iii) To the foregoing note, Pope, in 1739, and in later editions, appended the further statement: ". . . but not printed
till Mr. Tickel's Editions of his works in 1720, at which time
the Verses on Mr. Craggs which conclude this Epistle were
added."

(iv) The editions of The Works which first saw the expanded note (No. iii, above), saw also a new note appended to the
Epistle to Jervas, which reads: "This Epistle, and the two following [to Miss Blount], were written some years before the
rest (i. e. before the Epistles to Addison, Craggs, Oxford,
and Arbuthnot, and the Ethic Epistles], and originally printed
in 1717." Thus, as the Epistle to Jervas could not possibly have
been written before 1713, and almost certainly not until the
close of the year, "some years" should mean that the Epistle

to Addison must be later than 1715.

As with other poems of Pope's which present the same problem of variously ascribed dates, the solution would seem to be found in his methods of composition, which allowed longer or shorter periods of time to elapse, not only between the first draft and the corrected version, but also — as he frequently pointed out — between the writing of different parts of the same poem (such as Windsor Forest, The Rape of the Lock, The Dunciad, and the Epistle to Arbuthnot — to name only the best-known examples). It is probable, therefore, that Pope was not intentionally untruthful or misleading in his varying statements about this poem, simply because when he made them he was thinking chiefly of one or other of the separate parts, of which it seems to have been composed.

Thus the first half of the Epistle to Addison[74] which is not even in epistolary form since it is not addressed to any one, and which has no mention of, or allusion to, Addison, might well have been first sketched out as an impersonal poem on classical antiquities with special reference to coins and medals, as early as the stated year, 1715. Indeed, its beginnings not improbably date a little earlier, for the following reasons. First, it was during 1713 and 1714 — that is, contemporaneously with the commencement of the work on his translation of Homer — that Pope's interests took so decided a bent towards antiquarianism. This is clearly demonstrated by the Epistle to Jervas, written towards the end of 1713, and Martinus Scriblerus, discussed, projected, and to some extent drafted at the meetings of the "Scriblerus Club" in the first half of 1714; both of which have much in common in subject and phrase with the Epistle to Addison, and especially the section under discussion. Secondly, while it is difficult — in the light of the foregoing pages — to imagine any friendly intercourse between Pope and Addison for some months before and after the publication of the first volume of The Iliad (or, in other words, at any time during the troubled year 1715), their previous relations, though never very cordial, are known to have been amicable enough for ordinary social intercourse; and they used to meet freely and frequently in the popular coffee-houses and elsewhere. In the summer of 1713 Addison took over temporary control of The Guardian while Steele was away electioneering[75]; Pope was contributing to the paper at that time and must have seen the

"Essay" on Medals which Addison wrote and included in the
issue of July 1. It may, therefore, have been this essay which
quickened, if indeed it did not awaken, Pope's interest in these
relics of the antique world; and with this subject occupying both
their minds in 1713-14, that would appear to be the most likely
time for Addison to have shown Pope the manuscript of his Dialogue on Medals, which had been begun as far back as 1702, and
which Pope unquestionably saw before it was printed in 1721.
Again, it would seem to be about this time that Addison spoke
to Pope of publishing his Dialogues, though the actual publication may have been planned for 1715, as Pope states. What
looks like a hint at this project of Addison's (hitherto discounted
as another of Pope's misstatements), has recently been found in
a book entitled, The Knowledge of Medals . . . Written by a
Nobleman of France. Made English by an Eminent Hand. The
Second Edition. To which is added, An Essay concerning The
Error in Distributing Modern Medals. By Joseph Addison, Esq.,
1715, where a reprint of Addison's "Guardian" essay, which
occupies its last pages, ends with the following note:

> An Eminent Writer assures us, that Mr. Addison
> has not a little applied himself to the Study of Medals;
> the Mystical Meaning of whose Reverses he has ex-
> plain'd in a Work well worthy to be made Publick, and
> which it is hoped he will soon oblige the World with.

This book, The Knowledge of Medals, which was originally published in 1697, republished on February 22, 1714,[76] and again,
with Addison's essay included for the first time, on August 6,
1715,[77] is further evidence that an interest in classical antiquities was growing more general as the new century progressed.
It is not, therefore, surprising to find that this section of the
Epistle to Addison does not entirely derive either from that
author's Dialogues or his Essay on Medals; as is shown by the
fact that Pope includes much detail not found in either. (For
instance, in lines 26-30, of the six or more verifiable coins
alluded to by Pope, only the first one, bearing the inscription
"Judaea Capta" is mentioned by Addison.)
  The next section of the Epistle (lines 45-62) is that in which
Addison is addressed and perhaps excessively praised — lines,
therefore, which could not possibly have been written by Pope,

either during the time when Addison was disparaging his translation of the Iliad and promoting that of his rival, Tickell, or
until sufficient time afterwards had elapsed for the resultant
soreness in Pope's mind to have healed: for even in the winter
of 1716-17, he was still feeling resentful enough to allude to
the Addison-Tickell conspiracy in Sandys's Ghost. Hence,
agreeably to the poet's assertion in The Dunciad, 1729, this
encomiastic section of the epistle (not to mention the conclusion)
was in all probability not written after the publication of The
Works of Mr. Alexander Pope on June 3, 1717[78]; another reason
being, that, had the epistle been so near completion earlier, it
was too important a poem to have escaped inclusion in that magnificent volume. At the other extreme, as these lines were obviously written before Addison's death, they cannot be later
than June 1719.

The final section of the poem (lines 63-72) is devoted to
somebody else entirely — Mr. "Secretary" Craggs. This seemingly strange conclusion of an epistle to Addison appears hitherto to have been generally accepted by readers in the belief
that Pope was somehow commemorating the deaths of two
friends in the same poem. But even that unsatisfactory explanation is no longer tenable; because, since the discovery of the
above-mentioned early text, it is certain that at least Craggs
was not dead when these lines were first printed; and, seeing
that Pope addresses Addison, in line 63, not as one evoking a
recently disembodied spirit, but as one man to another -- "Then
shall thy Craggs (and let me call him mine)" -- it is quite as
certain that Addison also was alive when it was written. The
"intrusion" of Craggs into this epistle can at last be explained
by the facts that Addison was not only alive when these lines
were penned, but was actively planning a collected edition of
his Works with Tickell's assistance; and that he had not only
arranged for it by June 4, 1719, but had actually written its
"Dedication," in which he "publicly bequeathes" his "writings"
to his and Pope's mutual friend, Craggs. Unquestionably, Pope
must have learnt this from one or other of them; whereupon he
composed this conclusion to be added to the epistle (already in
existence and possibly intended to accompany the Dialogues) in
the knowledge that that treatise, as part of Addison's Works,
would now first appear in print under Craggs's aegis. (The
accident that, in 1727, Pope found it possible, by a small

alteration introducing the word "wept," to convert the last six lines into an epitaph on Craggs, has, of course, nothing to do with the date of the original lines.)

The last stage in the composition of the Epistle to Addison was not reached until 1726, when a further six lines were added near the beginning (lines 5-10); and these are the only lines it is safe to say Addison never saw. It thus appears at last possible that Pope's various statements about the date of the epistle can be clarified to this extent: that although, when applied to the poem as a whole, they are obviously contradictory, they are, to a great extent and all unexpectedly, correct when applied to its various parts. Thus, the first part was written not later than 1715 (statement No. ii, above); the second part was written between 1717 and 1719 (No. i); the third part was literally added in 1720 to the epistle already written (No. iii); and, lastly, the poem as a whole was in fact first printed in 1720 as claimed, though "Mr. Tickel's Edition" was not published until 1721 (No. iii).

When all the foregoing facts concerning Pope's two poems, the satire and the epistle, are considered, it will be seen that his account to Spence of the early history of the satire, could have been, and probably was, on the whole and in intention, true -- bating, perhaps, some natural lapses of memory about events then nearly twenty years old.[79] Certainly nothing has been found seriously to contradict it; and certainly it is nearer to the truth than is the tradition of his treacherous and unprovoked attack on Addison, which obtained for some two hundred years. That the satire was Pope's reaction to Addison's dubious attitude and activities in the long-drawn-out "Battle of the Iliad" cannot now seriously be contested on the known evidence, or that it was sketched out at some time between June 1715 and May 1716; that is, after the publication of the rival Addison-sponsored translation and before Addison's initial attempt to propitiate Pope in The Freeholder. Between those two dates the order of events is unfortunately sparsely documented; but it would appear that after Pope's accumulated resentment had found relief in a satirical sketch of Addison's character, he put it on one side for a time, and nothing more happened, until he heard "one day" from Lord Warwick that Addison had in effect hired Gildon to attack him. Whether the report was true, and whether the "thing" in which the attack was made can now

be identified, have strictly no bearing on the argument. The
important point about Warwick's gossip is that Pope believed
it, and, incensed beyond measure, promptly sent Addison the
first sketch of the satire with an accompanying letter warning
him of what "he could an he would." But whatever the particular course of events may have been between June 1715 and the
following May, the evidence is indisputable that Addison, for
some unrevealed reason that greatly puzzled his friends at Button's, suddenly changed his attitude towards Pope -- the first
effects of which are seen in his public praise of Pope's translation on May 17, 1716, and, not less significantly, in Burnet's
surprise at his volte-face. Thereafter, until he died "about
three years after," Addison used Pope "very civilly" -- according to Pope's own statement to Spence.

But what Pope failed to mention in his account is that, for
his part, he met Addison's attempts at conciliation more than
half way, and not only withheld the satire from immediate publication, but, when the last soreness had passed away, at some
date between June 1717 and June 1719, wrote in lavish praise
of his quondam enemy, in a "full-dress" epistle to him, which
he allowed to be published in 1720.

Later still, three and a half years after Addison's death,
Pope's satirical lines on him crept anonymously into print in
The St. James's Journal for December 15, 1722, and apparently aroused no attention or comment whatever. In the Journal
the satire was introduced in the postscript of a letter about
other matters, in these words: "P. S. The following Lines have
been in good Reputation here, and are now submitted to Publick
Censure." The letter itself is dated "Button's, 12 Decemb. 1722"
and is signed "Dorimant." On this evidence alone it has been
suggested that "Dorimant" is one of Pope's pseudonyms; this
signature, however, was a popular one at the time and for long
afterwards; it is found in the newspapers from 1722 to 1730,
appended to numerous letters and articles with which there is
not the least evidence or reason to suppose that Pope had any
connection. It is not known who was responsible for that first
publication of the satire; but for some months previously the
poem was being handed about in manuscript, to judge from
Bishop Atterbury's letter to Pope (February 26, 1722)[80] asking
for a copy of it; and from the fact that the transcript found
among Lord Oxford's papers at Welbeck -- which, as previously

stated, differs from the printed version – is endorsed in the
Earl's autograph "1722." This private circulation clearly shows
that the poem could have been sent to the Journal without its
author's knowledge or consent; it likewise explains how Curll –
who was certainly responsible for the next three reprints of it,
and who was the first to reveal its author's name -- could have
obtained his copy, which also differs not a little from both the
Welbeck manuscript and the first printed text.

Lastly may be mentioned the fact that Pope never publicly
acknowledged or printed the satire until the longer text was
authoritatively published by him in "The Last Volume" of his
and Swift's Miscellanies, as mentioned above; in the Preface
of which he owned it for the first time (though only by implication) in a sort of semi-apology to Addison, thus:

> In regard to two Persons only, we wish our Rail-
> lery, though ever so tender, or Resentment, though
> ever so just, had not been indulged. We speak of Sir
> John Vanbrugh . . . , and of Mr. Addison, whose Name
> deserves all Respect from every Lover of Learning.

There remains Pope's last reference to Addison, which also
should be noted in this connection, both because of its importance as the utterance of his latter years, and because it unal-
terably sets the balance of generosity heavily in his favour. It
is found in the Epistle to Augustus, 1737, where, after speaking
of the poets of "Charles's days," he proceeds to contrast with
them those of his own time, beginning with Addison:

> And in our [days] (excuse some Courtly stains)
> No whiter page than Addison remains.
> He, from the taste obscene reclaims our Youth,
> And sets the Passions on the side of Truth;
> Forms the soft bosom with the gentlest art,
> And pours each human Virtue in the heart.

From all of which it will perhaps appear, that – apart from the
later poems, the Satires, Moral Essays, and so forth – where
the genre not only permits but postulates a freedom of reference – it is not always necessary either to condemn Pope's irritability when on occasion he seems to attack some one with

rhyme but without reason, or to allude to the inferiority complex of a cripple psychology to explain or excuse it. In such cases, as the following chapters abundantly prove, research has generally revealed that what may appear an unjustifiable attack was really of the nature of reprisal or punishment for injuries received, or believed to have been received. And though this settling of old scores in the lusty Old Testament manner may not be the loftiest morality conceivable, it is at least a step in the right direction. For so, Pope may begin to lose some of that diabolic malignity with which popular legend still reproaches him, and at the end of two centuries of misrepresentation come to be recognized as tolerably human after all.

NOTES

1 Namely by Edith Sitwell, 1930; and G. Sherburn, 1934.

2 Poetical Miscellanies: The Sixth Part, 1709, pp. 301-23.

3 Letters, 4to, 1737, pp. 99f.

4 Ball, II, pp. 414-15.

5 According to The Evening Post.

6 Published in Poems and Translations. By Several Hands. (Ed. J. Oldmixon), 1714. The piece was in fact written by John Hughes, but it is probable that Pope did not know who wrote it until many years later.

7 Advertised in The Evening Post, from April 3, to April 10, 1714.

8 Ball, II, p. 145.

9 In The Post Boy.

10 In The Evening Post.

11 In an imitation of Pope's recently published "Temple of Fame," called Aesop at the Bear Garden, 1715.

12 In Homerides . . . By Sir Iliad Doggrell, 1715.

13 According to subsequent references; but these two numbers have not yet been located.

14 In The High-German Doctor.

15 Ibid.

16 In The Grumbler.

17 See The Evening Post.

18 In Add. 36772. Printed by D. Nichol Smith in Letters of
    Thomas Burnet to George Duckett, 1712-1722 (Roxburghe
    Club), p. 99. No such lampoon is known to Pope scholars,
    except the "Atticus" lines, then unprinted.

19 Ibid. , p. 81.

20 Spence, p. 147.

21 See excerpt from Mist's Weekly Journal below, pp. 473-4.

22 See Thomas Tickell and the Eighteenth Century Poets, R.
    E. Tickell, p. 36.

23 Ibid. , p. 39.

24 Ibid. , p. 42.

25 See Burnet, p. 92.

26 Add. 4807, f. 96 v.

27 Correspondence, I, 1735 (ii), p. 102.

28 Not to interrupt the argument, the reader might like to be
    reminded in a footnote of Dr. Johnson's remarks on this
    couplet of Addison's: — "To bridle a goddess is no very
    delicate idea; but why must she be bridled? because she
    longs to launch; an act which was never hindered by a
    bridle: and whither will she launch? into a nobler strain.
    She is in the first line a horse, in the second a boat, and
    the care of the poet is to keep his horse or his boat from
    singing." Johnson, II, p. 406.

29 In The Works, 1717.

30 EC, VI, p. 388.

31 Add. 4807, f. 159 v.

32 Correspondence I, 1735 (ii), p. 33.

33 Griffith, I, i, p. 39.

34 In writing and publishing The Narrative of Dr. Robert Norris, 1713; see Pope's Prose, I, pp. xxviii ff.

35 Meaning Thomas Tickell, though he was actually two years older than Pope, having been born in 1686; Pope in 1688.

36 Biographia Britannica, I, 2nd Edn, 1778, pp. 56-8.

37 See "Pope, Addison, and the 'Atticus' Lines," by A. E. Case, in Modern Philology, November 1935, pp. 187 ff.

38 Egerton, 1960.

39 Addison's prospective step-son.

40 Spence, pp. 148-9.

41 Ibid., p. 237.

42 Ibid., p. 149.

43 Warburton, IV, pp. 26 ff.

44 Ruffhead, pp. 192 ff.

45 Letters, 4to, 1737, pp. 117 ff.

46 Spence, p. 237.

47 Add. 4807, f. 118 v.

48 Additions, I, p. 56.

49 Sherburn, p. 146.

50 See ante, pp. 470-1.

51 See ante, p. 466.

52 Sherburn, p. 146.

53 G. Sherburn in Philological Quarterly, XXI, ii, pp. 215 f.

54 Sherburn, pp. 147 f.

55 Case, pp. 191 ff.

56 B. M., 1421, g. 6 (5), p. 16. See also below, p. 481.

57 In "Testimonies of Authors," Sutherland, p. 25.

58 Ibid., p. 42.

59 According to The Flying Post.

60 Burnet, p. 99.

61 Since this paragraph was written, Mr. Sherburn has changed his mind, and, without citing any evidence to solve the above-mentioned difficulties attaching to Mr. Case's conjecture, now thinks A True Character is "still a good suggestion." Philological Quarterly, XXI, ii, p. 215.

62 Poetical Miscellanies: The Sixth Part, 1709, p. 253.

63 Remarks on Mr. Rowe's Tragedy of the Lady Jane Gray. The Remarks, amounting to no more than a dozen pages which are prefixed to this reissue of A New Rehearsal, was published on May 14, 1715, according to The Post Boy; and a "Second Edition" was announced as "just publish'd" in The Weekly Packet, July 2, 1715.

64 Egerton, 1971, ff. 33-4.

65 Pope's Prose, I, p. 263.

66 Sherburn, Chap. IV; Pope's Prose, I, pp. xi-xxxiii. See also Ault, "The End of Dennis," New Light on Pope (London, 1949), pp. 286 ff.

67 Dennis wrote: Reflections Critical and Satyrical upon . . . An Essay upon Criticism; Remarks upon Mr. Pope's Rape of the Lock; Two Letters concerning Windsor Forest, and the Temple of Fame; and Remarks upon Mr. Pope's Translation of Homer.

68 As will be shown in the forthcoming volume of Pope's Miscellaneous Poems ("The Twickenham Edition," Vol. VI).

69 Recorded and printed for the first time in an article by the present writer in the R. E. S. , XVII, October 1941 (pp. 428-51), in which much of this chapter appeared.

70 See ante, p. 464.

71 EC, III, p. 201.

72 The date was announced in The Post Boy, September 26-28, 1721.

73 Griffith, I, i, p. 95.

74 That is, lines 1-44, omitting the passage (ll. 5-10) first added in 1726.

75 Pope's <u>Prose</u>, I, pp. xx, xxvii.

76 According to <u>The Evening Post</u>.

77 According to <u>The Post Boy</u>.

78 Announced in <u>The Daily Courant</u>.

79 The account occurs in the section dated 1734-36.

80 <u>Letters</u>, 4to, 1737, p. 220.

POPE AS TEXTUAL CRITIC:
A BIBLIOGRAPHICAL STUDY OF HIS HORATIAN TEXT[1]

Lillian Bloom

In his definitive edition of Pope's Imitations of Horace, John Butt acknowledges that "the text of Horace which Pope habitually used" is unknown to him. He does, however, state with certainty (and unfortunately upon but a single piece of internal evidence) that Bentley's edition of Horace, the most famous and most widely used of its day, was consciously "avoided" by Pope when the latter set up his own Latin text to accompany his translations.[2]

With that the matter rested until Bonamy Dobrée, wandering about the shelves of the Brotherton Collection in the Library of Leeds University, found by chance a book which was entitled Pope's Horace. According to Mr. Dobrée "this is a small 8vo Elzevir Horace published at Leyden in 1629 (the second title gives 1628), edited by Heinsius, in a binding which appears to be one of the 17th century. The third fly-leaf bears the name A. Pope, which to the inexpert eye looks like Pope's signature. On the fourth flyleaf, written so as to resemble print, there stands: -- Ex libris ALEXANDRI POPEI. Pret. 15s."[3] There remains little doubt in Mr. Dobrée's mind that this particular edition of Horace belonged to Pope. And in that conclusion the English scholar seems justified. Mr. Dobrée, however, ends his article on a qualifying and cautious note: ". . . whether this is the text he habitually used is, of course, another matter. There are no marks or remarks of any kind throughout the volume."[4]

So much then for the scholarship which has been gathered about this one problem. The matter is admittedly a minor one when viewed against the entire body of scholarship and criticism centering about the greatest of the neo-classical poets. At the same time this fact does not mitigate the complexity of the problem or its solution. The latter depends in part upon the objective

Reprinted from Journal of English and Germanic Philology, Vol. 47 (1948), pp. 150-155, by permission of author and publisher.

analysis of a rather subjective issue: Pope's attitude and reaction to Bentley and the latter's edition of Horace. In this respect, too, distinction must be made between Pope's evaluation of Bentley as a man on the one hand and as an editor of the Roman satirist on the other. Once this distinction is understood, it becomes clear that Mr. Butt dismissed Pope's use of Bentley too quickly and too easily. Moreover, it is necessary to discover to just which editions of Horace, Pope, had access. When this last matter is determined, one must then proceed to a word-for-word, line-by-line examination of the several texts involved. Finally, by the comparative study of this evidence, one may with a certain amount of justification decide upon the text or texts which Pope "habitually used" in establishing his own Horatian text.

Pope's objection to Bentley as a scholar and as a person was primarily a philosophical one. Like the other humanists of the early eighteenth century, Pope defined all learning, whether speculative or practical, as useful knowledge which functioned for and was made subservient to the good of all mankind. This learning was grounded upon a recognition of human needs and a fine sense of discrimination which aimed at the poise and social development of man. But Bentley was a pedant, and pedantry failed to achieve the view and scope of humanistic learning.[5]

To this attitude then may be traced Pope's hostility towards the scholar and pedant, Bentley. But at the same time Pope himself was a keener and more sensitive Latinist than present day scholars are ready to acknowledge. For this reason, therefore, it would have been impossible for him to disregard Bentley and his work completely. We know, even if only from the satirical portrait in The Dunciad, that Pope was familiar with many of Bentley's textual discoveries and contributions,[6] and even Mr. Butt admits Pope's use of Bentley's edition of Horace for one of the satires.[7] On the basis of this information, it is not presumptuous to modify Mr. Butt's original remark as to Pope's complete repudiation of Bentley as an Horatian editor. Instead one can argue that Pope recognized with objectivity and candor the evidence that Bentley added much to the text of Horace; that he challenged many of the inflexible and arbitrary standards of a mediocre vulgate; but that he added with over-zealous enthusiasm many more bad readings to his original text than he eliminated. If Pope recognized this fact, then it is also logical to suppose that instead of completely ignoring the text of Bentley, he used it with extreme caution and discrimination, weighing each emendation and variant reading before he adopted it.

But if Pope used Bentley's text with selective care, there were still other Horatian editions to which he had free access, indeed which he had in his own library. Mr. Dobrée has already pointed out the Elzevir edition which preserves conservatively the standard readings of the vulgate. To this text and Bentley's must be added still more. Pope had in his library the ever popular Desprez edition prepared for the use of the Dauphin;[8] the somewhat erratic edition by Alexander Cunningham, a work which not only borrowed freely of Bentley's emendations, but which also added many new readings of its own;[9] and a critique of Bentley's edition by Cunningham which is largely a verbose and vitriolic commentary on Bentley's earlier work on Horace.[10]

By the minute comparison of these four editions, the Heinsius, the Bentley, the Desprez and the Cunningham texts, the evidence points to a conclusion which must weaken the current belief that Pope's knowledge of the classics was relatively superficial and lacking in penetration. Pope used the Elzevir edition prepared by Heinsius as his basic text. He varied nothing except the punctuation when he wished it to be more in accord with the sense and mood of his own translation. But at the same time he read along in Bentley and acquired for his own purposes those Bentley readings which he thought to be valid emendations. However, Pope was not a professional scholar and, therefore, it is logical to suppose that his trust in his own powers of classical erudition was not absolute. Thus, his selection of Bentley's emendations would be based on the one hand upon the latter's own evidence of manuscript authority, and on the other upon Cunningham's criticism and acceptance of each new Bentley reading as it came up. Under such conditions Pope's Horatian text emerges finally as an eclectic text, based largely on the vulgate readings preserved by Heinsius and occasionally emended by the most substantial of the Bentley variants.

This conclusion can best be proved by the specimen analysis of two or three of the satires and epistles in the three editions involved. For example, in The First Satire of the Second Book of Horace, Pope's Horatian text follows the edition of Heinsius exactly. In four lines, however, Pope alters single words so that they no longer agree with the Elzevir text.

1. Pantolabum Scurram, Nomentanumve nepotem?[11]
   Pantolabum scurram, Nomentanumque nepotem;[12]
2. Grande malum Turius, si quid se judice certes;[13]
   Grande malum Turius, si quis se judice certet.[14]
3. Cederet, introrsum turpis; num Laelius, & qui[15]
   Cederet, introrsum turpis? num Laelius, aut qui[16]
4. Equidem nihil hinc diffindere possum.[17]
   Equidem nihil hic diffindere possum.[18]

These four changes stem from a single source; they are all emendations which appeared for the first time in Bentley's radical edition of 1711.

1. Pantolabum scurram, Nomentanumve nepotem?[19]
2. Grande malum Turius, si quid se judice certes.[20]
3. Cederet, introrsum turpis; num Laelius, & qui[21]
4. Equidem nihil hinc diffingere possum.[22]

By the same method of collation it becomes evident that Pope could not possibly have used either Desprez or Cunningham as a basic text because of the large number of discrepancies which exist between his own text and the other two texts respectively.[23] At the same time it should be pointed out that Pope, except in one particular instance,[24] has not in this satire or in any other ever borrowed a reading from Bentley which had not been approved and accepted by Cunningham.[25]

In The Second Satire of the Second Book of Horace, Paraphrased, the identical situation holds true. Pope carefully follows the Elzevir text word for word to turn aside at three scattered points in order to adopt those variants which were first introduced by Bentley.

1. Utrum imitabitur? hac urget lupus, hac canis, aiunt[26]
   Utrum imitabitur? hac urget lupus, hac canis, angit[27]
2. Mundus erit qui non offendat sordibus, atque[28]
   Mundus erit, qui non offendet sordibus, atque[29]
3. At mihi seu longum post tempus venerat hospes[30]
   At mihi cum longum post tempus venerat hospes,[31]

As in the previous satire, it is Bentley who furnishes Pope with these particular variants.

1. Utrum imitabitur? hac urguet lupus, hac canis, aiunt[32]
2. Mundus erit, qua non offendat sordibus, atque[33]
3. Ac mihi seu longum post tempus venerat hospes,[34]

From the citations given above it becomes obvious that rarely did Pope ever diverge from Heinsius more than three or four times in a single satire. For example, Pope, when setting up the Latin text for the first satire of the second book, used only four out of eleven possible Bentley emendations; and for the second satire of the second book Pope borrowed only three of Bentley's sixteen new readings. However, in the case of The First Epistle of the First Book of Horace, Pope went to Bentley's edition for eight out of fourteen emendations. Thus Pope, while reproducing the Heinsius text in large part, turns aside in the following instances:

1. Est quâdam prodire tenus, si non datur ultra[35]
   Est quodam prodire tenus, si non datur ultra.[36]
2.   Haec Janus summus ab imo
   Prodocet[37]
                       Haec Ianus summus ab imo
   Perdocet:[38]
3.   Est animus tibi, sunt mores, est lingua, fidesque
   Si quadringentis sex, septem millia desint,
   Plebs eris.[39]
   Si quadringentis sex septem millia desunt,
   Est animus tibi, sunt mores, & lingua, fidesque:
   Plebs eris.[40]
4. Liberum & erectum, praesens hortatur, & aptat?[41]
   Liberum & erectum, praesens hortatur, & optat?[42]
5. Bellua multorum est capitum, nam quid sequar aut
       quem?[43]
   Bellua multorum es capitum. nam quid sequar aut
       quem[44]
6.   Si curtatus inaequali tonsore capillos
   Occurro, rides;[45]
   Si curtatus inaequali tonsore capillos
   Occurri; rides:[46]

7. De te pendentis, te suspicientis, Amici[47]
   De te pendentis te respicientis amici[48]

A quick glance at Bentley's edition is enough to assure one that each of these departures from Heinsius is peculiar to and originates directly from the eighteenth-century English scholar.

1. Est quadam prodire tenus, si non datur ultra.[49]
2.   haec Janus summus ab imo
   Prodocet:[50]
3. Est animus tibi, sunt mores, est lingua fidesque:
   Sed quadringentis sex septem millia desint;
   Plebs eris.[51]
4. Liberum & erectum, praesens hortatur & aptat?[52]
5. Belua multorum est capitum. nam quid sequar,
              aut quem?[63]
6. Si curatus inaequali tonsore capillos
   Occurro:[54]
7. De te pendentis, te suspicientis amici[55]

This same procedure and method is followed in each of the satires and epistles for which Pope sets up a Latin text. For example, in both An Imitation of the Sixth Satire of the Second Book and The First Epistle of the Second Book of Horace, Imitated, Pope departs from Heinsius to take up five different Bentley readings in each work.[56] Yet even to this method Pope was not slavish. Indeed, the Latin text for The Second Epistle of the Second Book of Horace, Imitated, which borrows only one of Bentley's sixteen possible emendations,[57] is interesting for the further light which it throws on Pope's editorial independence. In the following lines:

Tu me inter strepitus nocturnos atque diurnos
Vis me canere, & contacta sequi vestigia vatum?[58]

Pope has used a reading which varies from both Heinsius and Bentley.

Tu me inter strepitus nocturnos, atque diurnos
Vis canere, & contracta sequi vestigia vatum?[59]

> Tu me inter strepitus nocturnos atque diurnos
> Vis canere, & non tacta sequi vestigia vatum?[60]

Once again, however, the source for this particular reading is
Bentley — this time indirectly. The latter's non tacta was a new
reading, and in order to defend it, Bentley found it necessary
to list and to attack all earlier readings. Among these was contacta which, with its implications of literary imitation, Pope
found particularly pertinent to his own and the neo-classical
theory of poetic creation.

> How shall I rhime in this eternal Roar?
> How match the bards whom none e'er match'd before?[61]

And finally in The Seventh Epistle of the First Book of Horace, Imitated in the Manner of Dr. Swift, Pope borrows two
Bentley emendations,[62] only to change one in favor of the Heinsius reading in a later edition. In the 1739 edition of this satire
Pope's Latin version read:

> Forte per angustam tenuis nitedula rimam

and agreed with Bentley's reading of nitedula rather than Heinsius's and the vulgate's vulpecula. In the 1740 octavo, however,
Pope changed his original reading and returned to that of his
basic text. One cannot state the reason for this change with absolute certainty. Nevertheless, it is fairly reasonable to suppose that Pope was motivated by the desire for caution; for
Pope, who was willing to accept a Bentley emendation on good
manuscript authority, was naturally hesitant and even sceptical
when it came to an original conjecture.

This then is the evidence for the conclusion that Pope's
Latin text was an eclectic one. Heinsius's edition served as the
constant base for Pope's own. When, however, he felt that
Bentley had unusually strong manuscript support, he turned
aside from the readings of the Dutch scholar and followed instead those offered by Bentley.[63] If this tentative solution to the
bibliographical problem of Pope's Horatian text is the correct
one, then it is easy to understand why the particular edition
which Pope "habitually used" never came to light, for it is not
one single text, but two — with a third used as a constant check.

NOTES

1 For the subject of this paper and for several of the details of information contained within, I am indebted to Professor Maynard Mack, Yale University.

2 Alexander Pope, Imitations of Horace (edited by John Butt), New York, Oxford University Press, 1942, p. xliii. Mr. Butt's original statement should be quoted in its entirety. "The most famous editor of Horace in Pope's time was Bentley, but except in Sober Advice Pope never followed Bentley's text. Indeed he avoided it. Having accidentally printed one of Bentley's conjectures in the seventh epistle of the first book — nitedula in l. 29 -- he substituted the old reading volpecula, when revising the poem for the next edition."

3 Bonamy Dobrée, "Pope's Horace," The Times Literary Supplement (Saturday, August 12, 1939), p. 479. Mr. Dobrée's note further describes the book as follows:

> Pasted in below the signature, and crossed out, there is a scrap of paper written over on the other side, and torn at the left hand bottom edge, so making the last line doubtful. On this is written: — / Alexander Pope / Poeta Anglus / floruit / M D C C X L / H. M. / Optimo viro / Gulielmus Glocest. Episc. / amicitiae causa / . . . casta (?) posuit / Warburton gave away this copy, for on the second fly-leaf is written: — / M. S. Smith / C. C. C. Oxon / dedit dono vir illust: mus / Gul. Episc. Gloc. 1778

4 Ibid. (Mr. Dobrée's note was written in answer to Mr. Butt's statement which was first made in the English edition of the Imitations of Horace, published by Methuen & Co., Ltd. in 1939.)

5 See Pope's own satirical portrait of Bentley in The Dunciad, Bk. IV, l. 203 ff. See also D. Mallet, Of Verbal Criticism: An Epistle to Mr. Pope, London, 1713. This latter poetic essay discusses Bentley's scholarly efforts, particularly his editions of Horace and Milton, in the light in which they appeared to Pope.

6   The Dunciad, Bk. IV, l. 203 ff.

7   See above, footnote 2.

8   Louis Desprez, Q. Horatii Flacci, Opera, Amsterdam, 1695.

9   Alexander Cunningham, Q. Horatii Flacci, Poemata, London, 1721.

10 Alexander Cunningham, Animadversiones in Ricardi Bentleii notas et emendationes ad Q. Horat. Flacem, The Hague, T. Johnson [i. e. , a piracy], 1721. All three of these works, cited in footnotes 8, 9, 10, are at present resting in an English private library. The Desprez and Cunningham editions of Horace's poetry contain Pope's signature on the fly-leaf.

11 Pope, Sat. II. i. 22. All citations from Pope's Horatian text are taken from Butt's edition of Pope's Imitations of Horace. (In all the following quotations the italics are mine.)

12 Daniel Heinsius, Quintus Horatius Flaccus, (Elzevir Press), Leyden, 1629. Sat. II. i. 22.

13 Pope, Sat. II. i. 49.

14 Heinsius, Sat. II. i. 49.

15 Pope, Sat. II. i. 65.

16 Heinsius, Sat. II. i. 65.

17 Pope, Sat. II. i. 79.

18 Heinsius, Sat. II. i. 79.

19 Richard Bentley, Q. Horatius Flaccus, Cambridge, 1711. Sat. II. i. 22.

20 Ibid. , Sat. II. i. 49.

21 Ibid. , Sat. II. i. 65.

22 Ibid. , Sat. II. i. 79. It is to be noted that in this same line Pope disregards Bentley's change of diffindere to diffingere on the grounds of insufficient manuscript authority. Bentley's change of hic to hinc was, however, based on the best of manuscript support, and it is an emendation which is

accepted by many of our contemporary textual critics today.

23 Not only does Pope's text vary from Desprez's in the case of the emendations discussed above and those listed throughout the paper, but it varies in approximately 29 other instances as well. Pope's text differs from Cunningham's in approximately 156 readings.

Epistle	No. of Variants in Desprez	In Cunningham
I. i.	3	15
I. vi.	2	12
I. vii.	3	9
II. i.	3	37
II. ii.	7	34
Satires		
II. i.	5	16
II. ii.	4	21
II. vi.	2	12

24 In Ep. I. i. 105. Cunningham retains the vulgate reading of respicientis, while Pope accepts Bentley's reading of suspicientis (Ep. I. i. 102).

25 Pope's dependence upon Cunningham as a check for the acceptability of Bentley's reading is well illustrated in the line cited in footnotes 17, 18, 22. Cunningham accepts the reading of hinc for hic but ignores the change of diffindere to diffingere. Thus the line in Cunningham's edition

Equidem nihil hinc diffindere possum

is the same as it appears in Pope's text.

26 Pope, Sat. II. ii. 46.

27 Heinsius, Sat. II. ii. 64.

28 Pope, Sat. II. ii. 47.

29 Heinsius, Sat. II. ii. 65.

30 Pope, Sat. II. ii. 99.

31 Heinsius, Sat. II. ii. 118.

32 Bentley, Sat. II. ii. 64.

33 Ibid. , Sat. II. ii. 65.

34 Ibid. , Sat. II. ii. 118.

35 Pope, Ep. I. i. 32.

36 Heinsius, Ep. I. i. 32.

37 Pope, Ep. I. i. 51-52.

38 Heinsius, Ep. I. i. 54-55.

39 Pope, Ep. I. i. 54-55.

40 Heinsius, Ep. I. i. 57-59.

41 Pope, Ep. I. i. 66.

42 Heinsius, Ep. I. i. 69.

43 Pope, Ep. I. i. 73.

44 Heinsius, Ep. I. i. 76.

45 Pope, Ep. I. i. 91-92.

46 Heinsius, Ep. I. i. 94-95.

47 Pope, Ep. I. i. 102.

48 Heinsius, Ep. I. i. 105.

49 Bentley, Ep. I. i. 32.

50 Ibid. , Ep. I. i. 54-55.

51 Ibid. , Ep. I. i. 57-59.

52 Ibid. , Ep. I. i. 69.

53 Ibid. , Ep. I. i. 76.

54 Ibid. , Ep. I. i. 94-95.

55 Ibid. , Ep. I. i. 105.

56 Pope, Sat. II. vi.   Heinsius, Sat. II. vi.
    l. 4. nil   l. 4. nihil
    l. 10. quae   l. 10. qua
    l. 70. uvescit   l. 70. humescit

l. 78. si quis nam   l. 78. nam si quis
l. 83. ille   l. 83. illi
(See the corresponding lines in Bentley's text.)

Pope, Ep. II. i.	Heinsius, Ep. II. i.
l. 18. hoc	l. 18. hic
l. 150. ire domos impune minax	l. 150. ire minax impune domos
l. 155. redacti	l. 155. reducti
l. 213. magus	l. 213. magnus
l. 270. quicquid	l. 270. quidquid

(See the corresponding lines in Bentley's text.)

57   Pope, Ep. II. ii. 158. & aere est; Heinsius, Ep. II. ii. 158. & aere.

58   Pope, Ep. II. ii. 79-80.

59   Heinsius, Ep. II. ii. 79-80.

60   Bentley, Ep. II. ii. 79-80.

61   Pope, The Second Epistle of the Second Book of Horace, Imitated. ll. 114-115.

62   Pope, Ep. I. vii. 22. paratus; Heinsius, Ep. I. vii. 22. paratum.
Pope, Ep. I. vii. 29. nitedula; Heinsius, Ep. I. vii. 29. vulpecula.

63   It is to be noted that Pope accepted only a single original Bentley conjecture. See Pope, Ep. I. i. 73. est. (Cf. Bentley Ep. I. i. 76. for the same reading.) This is to be compared with the reading of Heinsius, Ep. I. i. 76. es.

POPE'S POETICAL MANUSCRIPTS

John Butt

The editor of Pope's poems is supported and comforted in his difficult task by the knowledge that his author would have approved the enterprise. Though he may exhibit tastelessness and folly, though he may set commas and points exactly right, though he may "explain a thing till all men doubt it," he may nevertheless reflect that he would escape the painful prominence of a fly in the amber of The Dunciad, because he is contributing, however humbly, to maintain his author's classic position. Pope never doubted that he was a classic. As early as his thirtieth birthday, he showed his concern for his text and his canon by publishing The Works of Mr. Alexander Pope in magnificent quarto and folio, adorned with a portrait of the author and with head- and tail-pieces by Gribelin, and recommended by the verse addresses of Wycherley, Parnell, the Countess of Winchilsea, the Duke of Buckingham, and others. He was building a monument, where all the writings by which he hoped to be remembered are decently exhibited.

As the years went by, he took even greater pains to present his poems as a modern classic should appear. When the second volume of The Works was published eighteen years later in 1735, it was found to contain notes explanatory and critical. Some of his poems had been accompanied by explanatory notes on first publication — the Epistle to Arbuthnot is a striking example; but it was a new departure, and an eloquent testimony to the classical position he had already attained, that he decided to print the variant readings in texts of poems no more than two years old. He seems to have taken this step on the advice of Jonathan Richardson the younger, who records in rambling phraseology:

As for his Essay on Man, as I was witness to the whole conduct of it in writing, and actually have his

Reprinted from Proceedings of the British Academy, Vol. 40, pp. 23-39, by permission of the author.

> original MSS. for it from the first scratches of the four
> books, to the several finished copies (of his own neat
> and elegant writing these last) all which, with the MS.
> of his Essay on Criticism, and several of his other
> works, he gave me himself for the pains I took in col-
> lating the whole with the printed editions, at his re-
> quest, on my having proposed to him the 'making an
> edition of his works in the manner of Boileau's' . . . .[1]

The number of recorded variants is modest, and all are derived
from printed texts; but in his edition of 1736 Pope decided to
gratify his readers with some variants rejected from his manuscripts. These too were doubtless collected by Richardson under Pope's direction. The Bodleian autograph of the Essay on
Criticism and the Washington University autograph of Windsor
Forest both bear directions for transcribing passages which
collation reveals to have been omitted from the printed text,
and in the Berg collection of the New York Public Library is a
copy of The Dunciad which Richardson seems to have used for
transcribing variants from that poem too.

Richardson might be regarded as Pope's first editor, or,
if that term seems too bold to describe the self-effacing manner in which he performed a menial task, Pope's first editorial
assistant. He was to give way to a more powerful personality,
William Warburton. It was Warburton who completed the apotheosis of the classic. When the revised Dunciad was published
in 1743, it was prefaced by an "Advertisement to the Reader"
signed "W. W." which began as follows:

> I have long had a design of giving some sort of
> Notes on the Works of this Poet. Before I had the hap-
> piness of his acquaintance, I had written a Commentary
> on his Essay on Man, and have since finished another
> on the Essay on Criticism. There was one already on
> the Dunciad, which had met with general approbation:
> but I still thought some additions were wanting (of a
> more serious kind) to the humorous Notes of Scriblerus
> and even to those written by Mr. Cleland, Dr. Arbuth-
> not, and others. I had lately the pleasure to pass some
> months with the Author in the Country, where I pre-
> vailed upon him to do what I had long desired, and

favour me with his explanation of several passages in
his Works. . . .[2]

That extract gives the impression, and was perhaps designed to give the impression, that Pope had surrendered himself to an editor even before his death, that he had already
matriculated as one of the Ancients; and the impression is confirmed by the note on the verso of the title-page facing this
preface,

Speedily will be publish'd,
In the same Paper, and Character, to be bound up with this,
The ESSAY on MAN, /The ESSAY on CRITICISM, /And the rest of
the Author's ORIGINAL POEMS, /With the COMMENTARIES and
NOTES of / W. WARBURTON, A. M.

"You must be the vainest man alive," said Lord Marchmont to
Pope on this occasion; "You must want to show posterity what
a quantity of dullness you can carry down on your back without
sinking under the load."
But there, irrespective of its quality, is the type of apparatus which Pope believed he ought to carry: notes on the date
of a poem's composition, explanatory comments upon obscure
allusions, parallel passages from earlier writers — for there
too Pope has given the lead to his editors -- and variant readings.
During the past 200 years Pope's lead has been followed
by numerous editors. A few obscure allusions to men and things
still await explanation; but I think it may now be said that we
have an ample harvest of parallels from former writers, that
all printed variants have been collected, and, incidentally, that
the canon offers little further scope for argument. But in one
particular his editors have shown some reluctance in following
his lead. They have paid little attention to his manuscripts.
Warburton, it is true, added a few readings, in his haphazard
way, to those collected by Pope and Richardson, and Elwin and
Courthope added many more, though without recording all, or
attempting to list the manuscripts which came to their notice;
but the Twickenham editors have excluded manuscript readings
on policy. I believe we were right. Of some of the shorter
poems, the text could not be established without recourse to
manuscript authority; but if we had attempted an adequate

treatment of the more extensive manuscripts, we should have
had no space for other commentary.

But the work needs doing, and it largely remains to be
done. The first step must be a census of existing manuscripts,
a task which might have been accomplished without much trouble in the late seventies of the last century when Elwin and
Courthope were at work, but which has since become considerably more difficult owing to dispersals. The first major dispersal took place on 30 July 1889 at the Nassau Lees sale. A copy
of the sale catalogue in the Bodleian Library records the prices
which the manuscripts fetched and the prices which Bodley was
prepared to bid. The total recorded is £123. 10s. , a modest
sum we may now think to pay for the autographs of Sapho to
Phaon, the Essay on Criticism, Windsor Forest, the Essay on
Man, and for five manuscripts of the first three Moral Essays.
Of these, Bodley acquired the Essay on Criticism for £20. 10s. ;
the remainder are now in the United States.

But this is not all. Some forty-eight poems survive in
Pope's hand, totalling fifty-five manuscripts altogether.[3] Several of these have come to light in recent years, and we may
therefore suppose that the tally is not yet complete. Of many
important poems no manuscript is known to survive. Elwin and
Courthope had access to a manuscript of The Dunciad, but I do
not know what has become of it; and no manuscript has been
traced of The Rape of the Lock, Eloisa to Abelard, the Imitations of Horace, and the Epilogue to the Satires. Even so, the
number of survivors is very remarkable indeed. How fortunate
should we be if we could claim that even one poem had survived
in the handwriting of Spenser or Donne or Dryden.

There is considerable difference between the manuscripts
of the early and the manuscripts of the later poems. Of the
early poems no rough draft is extant. Each survives only in a
fair copy made to permit the poem to be submitted to friends
for advice, or when it was preparing for press. The exception
is the manuscript of the "imitation" of Rochester called "Of
Silence," now in the William Andrews Clark Memorial Library
of the University of California at Los Angeles.[4] When Pope
first published this poem in 1712 he declared that it had been
"written some years since," and later he claimed that it had
been "done at fourteen years old," that is to say, in 1702. The
manuscript is undated, but the hand is certainly early, and I

suspect that the Clark version is indeed the original text of
1702. If my guess is right, this is the earliest text we possess
of any of Pope's poems. It is, as we might expect, substantially
different from the printed text. If this is the version which Pope
had before him when he revised the poem for publication in 1712,
it shows that only seventeen of the original 48 lines reached the
standard which he then demanded. A comparison of the opening
stanzas, describing the origins of Silence in witty terminology,
readily indicates the kind of revision required.

> Silence! thou primitive parent even to thought
> Thy work er'e Nature was begun was wroght
> Behind, and just behind, thy Elder Brother thought.

> Yet o're that mighty nothing thou didst reign
> (Before rude Chaos broke thy easy chain)
> And held'st o're chaos self a short liv'd Sway again.

> Great breathing space! er'e time commenc'd wth Earth,
> Er'e fruitfull Thought conceivd Creations Birth
> Or Midwife word gave aid and spake the Infant forth.

So reads the manuscript. Even without the poet's revised version before us, it is not difficult to see where improvements
might be made. The opening line is halting in its rhythm, and
we should expect from the mature Pope something a little less
clumsy and flabby than lines 2 and 3. We might also object,
with reason, that Silence cannot be both primitive parent and
elder brother to Thought, that Thought should not be antecedent
to Chaos in the second stanza, but is more justly described in
the third stanza as conceiving Creation's birth. In brief, the
order of events at the Creation is confused in the manuscript
version, and the phrasing needs some tightening. The printed
version condenses the three stanzas to two: its attack is more
commanding, and it offers a more coherently witty account of
the Creation:

> Silence! Cœval with Eternity;
> Thou wert e're Nature's self began to be,
> 'Twas one vast Nothing, All, and All slept fast in thee.

> Thine was the Sway, e'er Heav'n was form'd or Earth,
> E'er fruitful Thought conceiv'd Creation's birth,
> Or Midwife Word gave Aid, and spoke the Infant forth.

But while we admire the improvements made at the age of twenty-four, we should also notice that the last two lines of the fourteen-year-old poet needed no correction. To those of us who are inclined to cast doubt upon the accounts of Pope's precocity this manuscript should prove reassuring. The Ode on Solitude, which he claimed to have written at about twelve years old, is first discovered in a manuscript nine years later. Even if we believe his statement about the date of composition of that his earliest poem, we may wonder how closely the verses of 1709 resembled the verses of 1700. But here in the Clark manuscript, and only here, we can see and admire what the fourteen-year-old could do.

The most beautiful of the early fair copies is the manuscript of the Pastorals, now in the possession of Mr. Arthur A. Houghton, Jr. The verso of the title-page bears a note in Pope's later hand stating that this was the copy which passed through the hands of Congreve, Walsh, Garth, Halifax, Wharton, Dorchester, Buckingham, and others. Since we know, from other evidence, that Congreve showed Tonson, the bookseller, a manuscript of one of the Pastorals in 1706,[5] it is perhaps not too bold to assume that that was the year in which this manuscript was prepared. It has been most carefully designed and executed, partly with a distinguished group of readers in view, partly with an eye to the appearance of the poem in print. Who can doubt that a man capable of such calligraphy would insist on comparable workmanship from his printer? This manuscript was found to require too much correction before the poem was fit for press, and another which has not survived must have served as printer's copy. We cannot therefore be certain how Pope treated his printer on that occasion. But this is precisely what the Bodleian manuscript of the Essay on Criticism enables us to judge. This manuscript is scarcely less beautiful in its current hand than the Houghton manuscript in its mimicry of print, and Pope has been equally concerned to visualize the poem's printed appearance. The marginal notes confirm that this was the reason for his care. "End the first page here," he writes, and the printer obeys; "Leave the space of a line blank here," and the printer follows his direction. Indeed the printer's calculations still stand in the margins, and serve to indicate that Pope corrected the proofs sheet by sheet as the printer finished them.[6]

But though he gave precise directions for the printer to follow, he does not appear to have exacted unswerving obedience. Unless we are to suppose that Pope changed his mind at proof stage about accidentals, it would seem that the printer was not scrupulous in preserving the spelling, punctuation, and use both of capitals and italic in an unmistakably clear copy. Two slight, but significant, examples can be observed in ll. 709-12, which read in the manuscript:

> But soon by Impious Arms from <u>Latium</u> chas'd,
> Their <u>ancient Bounds</u> the banishd <u>Muses</u> pasd;
> Thence <u>Arts</u> o'er all the <u>Northern World</u> advance,
> But Critic Learning flourishd most in <u>France</u>.

For Pope's comma after "advance" the printer set a semi-colon, and printed the words "Critic Learning" in italic. The distinction is tiny; but if a preference is to be expressed, it must in each case be for the poet's manuscript. The structure of the second couplet reflects the structure of its predecessor; thus the comma after "chas'd" points to a comma after "advance." It will be noticed, furthermore, that the relation of "Arts" to the "Northern World" is repeated in the relation of "Critic Learning" to "France." The recognition of the relationship is assisted by the choice of type, the italic of "Northern World" being balanced by the italic of "France," leaving roman with initial capitals for "Arts" and "Critic Learning." That is how Pope has arranged for the reader's understanding to be assisted by his visual impression; but the printer has spoiled the poet's effect. From this and other examples I think we may deduce that, in spite of his interest in layout and the appearance of his page, Pope took little care to set commas and points exactly right when his printer had set them wrong; and his editor may reflect that though he has in the Bodleian manuscript a perfect copy to follow in accidentals, he has little hope of preserving the poet's intentions in every detail when he has merely the first printed edition before him, and still less hope when he is following a copy more remote from the poet's manuscript.

I suspect that these early holographs were preserved in the first instance on sentimental grounds. Manuscripts on which so much care had been lavished both by the penman and his friendly critics would not lightly be thrown away. Later he came to recognize their value as a record of the early textual history of his poems. As such he handed them over to Richardson, and as such they still remain. Only one of them has yet been made accessible, the Washington University manuscript of Windsor Forest, which Professor Robert M. Schmitz has edited with the care it deserves.[7] In that volume a photograph of each sheet of manuscript is faced by a transcription and a record of all variants. Thus in one poem at least we are enabled to trace all recorded stages of development and correction, and, incidentally, to discover that the emendations show Pope breaking almost every one of the seven stylistic rules of versification which he had laid down in letters to Cromwell and Walsh a few years earlier. We must hope that Professor Schmitz's excellent lead will be followed in treating the remaining manuscripts of importance.

But more complex than these fair copies are the manuscript drafts of later poems. Swift had seen "Paper-sparing Pope" at work, and he admirably describes the origin of these scraps in a poem probably written while he was staying at Twickenham in 1727:

> Now Backs of Letters, though design'd
> For those who more will need 'em,
> Are filled with Hints, and interlin'd,
> Himself can hardly read 'em.
>
> Each Atom by some other struck,
> All Turns and Motion tries;
> Till in a Lump together stuck,
> Behold a Poem rise![8]

Swift was describing the composition of The Dunciad; yet so far as "Backs of Letters" are concerned, what he says applies equally well to the Homer manuscripts, now in the British Museum, which were handed over to Thomas Dancastle to transcribe for press. One fair copy, however, seems rarely to have been enough. Mr. Callan has recently shown us[9] that at least one more transcript must have intervened between Dancastle's fair copy and printer's proof. This is no more than we ought to expect. In a note on the first Dialogue of the Epilogue to the Satires, Warton reports that he often heard Dodsley say that he was employed by the author to copy them fairly:

> Every line [Warton continues] was then written twice over; a clean transcript was then delivered to Mr. Pope, and when he afterward sent it to Mr. Dodsley to be printed, he found every line had been written twice over a second time.[10]

But Warton should not have inferred that these two Dialogues "were more diligently laboured, and more frequently corrected than any of our author's compositions." The two Huntington Library manuscripts of the Epistle to Bathurst betray comparable diligence, and the manuscripts of the Essay on Man and the Epistle to Arbuthnot show the poet labouring untiringly in correction.

In a pioneering essay on "Pope at Work,"[11] published eight years ago, Professor George Sherburn used the two manuscripts of the Essay on Man to demonstrate the emergence of verse paragraphs from rudimentary digests in prose. He showed too with what patient labour Pope sorted and arranged his paragraphs, and what subsequent use he made in later poems of material discarded from the Essay. Professor Sherburn also drew some illustrations for his argument from the manuscript of the Epistle to Dr. Arbuthnot. It is partly because I venture to differ from some of his conclusions respecting that manuscript that I propose to deal with it now in some detail, and partly because it serves more conveniently than the Essay on Man as a gloss upon Swift's stanza:

> Each Atom by some other struck,
>   All Turns and Motion tries;
> Till in a Lump together stuck,
>   Behold a Poem rise!

The manuscript, in the Pierpont Morgan Library, New York, is a teasing collection of fragments. The most substantial portion is a draft of 260 lines, written on both sides of the outer half of four sheets of paper. This practice of writing on the outer half only was adopted by Pope to permit himself the use of the inner half for additions and corrections. The Morgan manuscript was not intended as a final version, therefore; but it may be taken to show that the atoms had begun to cohere, and that the poem, though not yet perfected, was nevertheless complete. All the same, the Morgan version is 150 lines shorter than the poem as we read it today, and we shall see later what significance the additional lines hold.

The paper on which this draft is written is no longer entire. One sheet is torn at the top and another at the bottom, involving the loss of certainly a few lines. But I believe that Pope himself did the tearing, and that we therefore possess all — or almost all — that he intended to preserve. My evidence for this conjecture is that he has numbered the lines of verse throughout, and has counted as line 1 the first verse on a sheet whose top has been removed. I assert that Pope did the numbering, though I must own that it is rash to identify a poet's numerals when we cannot always be positive about his letters. However, the lines of verse in his drafts are very frequently numbered, and the numerals in this manuscript correspond closely with those in others. Furthermore, the numerator shows that he possessed an authoritative knowledge of the manuscript, for he threads his way through the most perplexing mazes and rarely makes a mistake in assessing the number of lines missing in the manuscript and represented there by an "&c."

Pope therefore did the numbering, and it was he, then, who tore off a slice from the first sheet sufficient for seven lines of verse, or for a title and some four lines. My surmise is that he was discontented with the draft title, or with the first lines, or with both, and that he left as a possible opening the following passage:

> And of myself too something must I say?
> Take then this Verse, the Triffle of a Day;
> And if it lives, it lives but to commend,
> The Man of Friendship, but no boasting Friend,
> The Man of Courage, but not prone to fight,
> The Man of Learning, yet too wise to write.

It is not a good opening — indeed it is cancelled in the manuscript

— but it is a possible opening, and Pope evidently so regarded it until a better could be found.

But who was this "Man of Friendship, but no boasting Friend," this "Man of Courage, but not prone to fight," this "Man of Learning, yet too wise to write"? Not Arbuthnot, I fancy; for though he was "A Man of Learning," he was not too wise to write: in fact he was a prolific writer. And where, we might ask, is the expected reference to Arbuthnot's medical skill? Not here, certainly; and we look in vain through the rest of the draft for such well-loved lines as

> Friend to my Life, which did not you prolong,
> The World had wanted many an idle Song

and

> To second, ARBUTHNOT! thy Art and Care,
> And teach, the Being you preserv'd, to bear.

They had not yet been written at the time of this draft. Whom then do the opening lines describe, and to whom therefore was the epistle originally addressed? A later couplet seems to provide the answer:

> Think you, these People's Anger is a curse?
> Ah Cleland! their Repentance is a worse.

We know Cleland as the reputed author of a "Letter to the Publisher" prefixed to The Dunciad, but we know little more of him. If, as Professor Sutherland suspects, he was the Major Cleland whose regiment was badly cut up at Almanza, he is suitably addressed as a man of courage, and we may agree that though an army officer should be ready to fight, he should not be prone to it. That he was a Man of Friendship and a Man of Learning, yet too wise to write — or to write often — that "Letter to the Publisher" of The Dunciad would amply show, if we could be certain that Cleland had indeed written it and not merely lent his name to what Pope had himself composed. Two years later, in 1731, Cleland had written — or lent his name — to a letter to the Daily Post Boy defending Pope from the attacks then being made upon the Epistle to Burlington. It was therefore

highly appropriate that Pope should address an epistle in defence of satire to the man who had recently defended him from
his enemies or lent his name to that defence. Recently, for I
shall bring some evidence to show that this draft was written
early in 1732, three years before the publication of the Epistle
to Dr. Arbuthnot, and therefore shortly after Cleland's letter
to the Post Boy.

After the opening address the poem continues:

> Why did I write? What sin to me unknown
> Dipt me in Ink? my Parents, or my own?

and from that point proceeds as we know it, in a draft which
required little correction, celebrating the friends who had encouraged him, incorporating the prologue to the Atticus lines,
and the famous character itself.

At this point the poet's severest difficulties began. The
original draft is much over-written; but it is still possible to
discern what had at first satisfied him:

> I sigh; & curse in bitterness of woe
> The Fame that made one worthy Man my foe:
> Friendships from Youth I sought, & seek it still;
> Fame, like the Wind, may breath where-e're it will.
> What tho' my Name stand rubrick on ye walls
> Or plaister'd Posts, with Claps in Capitals?
> Who says I rule the ragged Race y^t write?
> I keep like Asian monarchs from their sight;
> On play or Poem never hold debate
> But leave to Bub the whole Parnassian state.

The manuscript shows that Pope discerned here some opportunities for expansion. It was impossible to resist a description of Bubb Dodington amongst the poets he patronized, and
accordingly a first sketch of the character of Bufo is squeezed
into the margin at this point. But earlier the curse upon that
Fame which had made Atticus his foe was expanded into the
lines:

> Cursd be y^t Verse, how well so ere it flow
> That e're shall make one worthy man my foe

> Give ye good scandal, or ye Guiltless fear
> Or make ye softeyd Virgin shed a Tear.
> But he who hurts a harmless Neighbour's peace
> Insults faln worth or Beauty in distress,
> The woman's fool who Scandal helps about,
> Who writes ye Libel, or who copies out,
> The Fop whose Pride &c.

"&c." denoting a passage already composed elsewhere and ready for transference unchanged to a position in a fair copy. In these lines we recognize an early version of the prologue to the character of Sporus, still at this time unwritten. The passage was to stay there in the margin until a better place was found for it, one less confusing to the present issue.

What was the issue? Unlike Bubb, the poet avoids the ragged race that write. Instead he cultivates a quiet life at Twickenham:

> A quiet Prince I slumber on my seat
> I plant, I saunter, chatter, drink, & eat
> Whole years have [past, since I have] writ or read
> Or kn[own if Dennis were alive or] dead?

Yet even here he cannot be suffered to remain in peace: the gossips speculate on what he is writing:

> 'I saw him walk with Swift — Indeed? no doubt
> (Cries honest U[pto]n) something will come out:

I need not quote the remainder of a familiar passage which stands at this place in something like its final form.

But further troubles lie in wait for the poet:

> Yet worse — vile Poets rise before ye Light
> And walk like Margrets Ghost at dead of night.
> No Walls can guard me, & no Shades can hide
> They thrid my Thickets, thro' my Grot they glide.

Then follows, in mounting irritation, the well-known list of importunate scribblers who pester him, the "Parson mad or steepd in Beer," the "Irish Poetess," the "rhyming Peer," the

"Clerk ordaind his Fathers soul to cross," and the rest of them.
And then, when the poet can bear it no longer, he cries at the
climax of his resentment:

> Shut, shut the door, good John! fatigud I said
> Tye up the Knocker, say I'm sick, Im dead.

This climax is reached at the head of a new sheet of paper,
which is to be found not in the Morgan Library but a few thousand miles away at the Huntington Library in California. This
Huntington manuscript has been regarded as a second autograph
manuscript of the poem; but I think it may more easily be interpreted as a continuation of the Morgan draft, especially since
Pope's numeration of the lines is continuous.

The Huntington draft then resumes the list of importunate
writers: Welsted who sends a message, "You know his Grace,
and I'm a Stranger, Ask him for a Place"; the playwright who
wants his tragedy revised, the author who dedicates in high
heroic prose, the flatterers who to his person pay their court --
"I cough like Horace, and am thick and short". . . .

> But Friend! this Shape wch you & Curl admire
> Came not from Ammon's Son, but from my Sire.

This provides the transition to the last verse paragraph on the
Huntington sheet:

> Of gentle blood; part shed in Honor's Cause
> (While yet in Albion Honor had applause)
> The Good man sprung: his Fortune's all his own
> Well-got, obligd to few, in debt to none.
> Unlearn'd, his Morals never taught by Art;
> One Language, but that Language of the Heart:
> By Genius honest, & by Nature wise;
> Healthy, by Temp'rance & by Exercise:

These lines describe the elder Pope, and we recognize them
as coming near the end of the poem. But there is no more to
be found in California: the manuscript breaks off on a line numbered 254 and with a catchword "who." We hurry back to New
York for the conclusion, and there we find it in the Morgan

manuscript on a sheet containing a mere six lines:

> Who knew no Lawsuit, no domestick Strife,
> Religious Contest, or mad Party-Life:
> Whose Life, tho long, to Sickness was unknown;
> Whose Death was instant, & without a groan:
> Oh grant me thus to live, & thus to dye!
> Who sprung from Kings shall not be blest as I.

There the poem ends in its earliest draft. A rule is drawn below it, and the total number of lines (260) recorded. And if we have any remaining doubt whether two sheets now separated by 3,000 miles were once contiguous, there on the last Morgan sheet is a tell-tale blot from a correction Pope had hurriedly added to the Huntington fragment.

The draft was finished, but much remained to be done before it could be sent to a copyist, part of whose work — with the poet's further correction — survives bound up in the Morgan manuscript. Paragraphs were to be shifted; and of these the most important was that bold removal of the climax ("Shut, shut the door, good John") to replace the unsatisfactory opening lines. It stood, as I mentioned, at the head of a fresh sheet. Pope altered the place of this sheet, numbered it "1," and wrote "Incipit" at the head; at the same time I think it probable that he tore off the top of what had been the first sheet, and cancelled the original beginning of the poem. Certain consequential changes were also made. The list of scribblers who preceded the climax were then associated with the group which followed it, and as a memorandum of this change Pope bracketed these lines, endorsing them with the note "all this before in initio."

And there was other work to be done. Transitions were to be improved. Personal allusions were to be generalized into Theophrastan types: thus Bubb becomes first Bubo and then Bufo, Welsted becomes Pitholeon, and the Irish poetess, too easily identified as Mrs. Sykins or Mrs. Barber, acquaintances of Swift, becomes a maudlin poetess merely. And there was to be many a happy revision in phraseology. Yet the poem stands in this early draft already recognizable, and we might have said complete if we did not recollect some prominent absentees. Where is Arbuthnot? Where is Sappho? Where is the poet rocking the cradle of declining age? Where is Queensberry weeping over Gay's urn? And where, above all, is Sporus?

The cradle of declining age was already lying on Pope's desk. We know that those beautiful lines describing the poet at his mother's deathbed were in existence in September 1731, for in that month Pope sent a copy of them in a letter to Aaron Hill. Another transcript lies among the Morgan fragments, waiting to be tagged on to the account of the elder Pope with which we have seen the earlier draft concluded. It was a happy stroke of genius to use this picture of filial devotion both to supplement what he had said of his other parent's death and to give a quiet domestic close to a poem, which was now to open in unbearable domestic irritation, and in which victory had been gained at great personal cost.

Arbuthnot's absence in the early draft I have already accounted for. He replaced Cleland, and we happen to know when. The earliest reference to the Epistle in Pope's correspondence is a letter written to Arbuthnot in August 1734. There Pope tells his friend:

> I determine to address to you one of my Epistles, written by piecemeal many years, & wch I have now made haste to put together; wherein the Question is stated, what were, & are my Motives of writing, the objections to them, & my answers.[12]

The draft as we have it, therefore, was in being before August 1734, and we may presume to correct Pope and say that though it had been written by piecemeal many years, it was before August of that year that most of the pieces had been put together.

Other evidence supports this. Amongst the important absentees in the Morgan draft, we noticed Sappho and Sporus, Lady Mary Wortley Montagu and Lord Hervey. It was in March 1733 that that blest pair of Sirens had collaborated in some Verses to an Imitator of Horace, and it was in the following August that Hervey wrote his Epistle to a Doctor of Divinity. The Advertisement prefixed to the first edition of the Epistle to Arbuthnot informs the reader that these lampoons upon his Person, Morals, and Family had stimulated Pope to draw together what he had already written. But the Morgan draft contains no allusion to either of these offenders. It is difficult to resist the conclusion that this draft was in being before the offence was given. Though Sappho appears nowhere in the Morgan manuscript, Sporus is found lurking in one of the fragments. The character exists not as a first draft but as a much corrected fair copy, and if time permitted it would be instructive to show the poet characteristically permitting his atoms to try all turns and motion in this narrow space. I must content myself with pointing out that the fragment is headed "Blockheads in his stead." This is the cue to the position which the new character is to occupy in the poem, and it is interesting to observe that those words form the last line, the amended last line, of the passage about the Fop which Pope had earlier found some difficulty in fitting into the draft. I infer that the Fop was already in place before Sporus was written, and that Sporus is therefore a very late addition.

But if the draft was in being before Hervey and Lady Mary gave offence, it was in being before March 1733, and we must begin to question whether indeed this early version of the Epistle to Arbuthnot was not written before the first Imitation of Horace published the previous month, and not some eighteen months after it, as we have hitherto supposed. Again there is evidence to support this conjecture. Where are the lines on Gay's death and on Queensberry weeping over his urn? They are not in the Morgan draft. Gay died early in December 1732, and Pope wrote a draft of his epitaph during the next few months, for he sent a version of it to Swift on 16 February 1733, at the very same time as the first Imitation of Horace was published. Are we then to place the Morgan draft if not before Gay's death, at any rate before the epitaph was written and the first Imitation of Horace published? I think we may, and I feel reassured in this conclusion on finding in the margin of the draft as a possible variant the line:

But something said of Chartres, is too bold.

Something too bold had been said of Chartres in the Epistle to Bathurst published on 16 January 1733. Pope is evidently trying to find a place in this draft for his comment; but in the end he was to fit it, not into the Epistle to Cleland/Arbuthnot, but into the Imitation of Horace. This therefore serves to thrust back the Morgan draft into 1732, and opens up the engaging possibility that the Epistle to Cleland/Arbuthnot was begun early in the year, when Pope was smarting under the assaults made upon The Epistle to Burlington. But though this is conjecture, it is supported by the address of this version to Cleland, who had so recently published a defence of that poem in the Daily Post-Boy.

From this manuscript, then, we may deduce that a shorter version of the poem was in existence nearly three years before publication, that this shorter version was addressed not to Arbuthnot but to Cleland, and that the famous opening lines were then designed as a climactic outburst. Whether my conclusions are acceptable in every detail I must allow others to decide. But I think there can be no doubt that this is the sort of information which a study of the manuscripts will reveal, in addition to what they may tell us of Pope's stylistic intentions (as Professor Schmitz has shown) and in addition to what we may learn from studies like Professor Sherburn's about the emergence of verse from prose and about the contamination of one poem with another. If only they can be made more widely accessible in photographic facsimile, we may hope for results as fruitful as those which followed the publication of the manuscript of Milton's minor poems in the library of Trinity College, Cambridge.

APPENDIX

The following is a list of autograph manuscripts, with present locations, in approximate order of composition:

1. Upon Silence in Imitation of a Modern Poem on Nothing. William Andrews Clark Memorial Library, University of California at Los Angeles. [?1702.]

2. A Paraphrase on Thomas a Kempis. W. H. Robinson Ltd., 1938 [after 1700].

3. Epigram. Occasion'd by Ozell's Translation of Boileau's Lutrin. Bodleian Library, Oxford. 1708.

4. Verse Letter to Cromwell. Bodleian Library, Oxford. 1708.

5. Argus. Bodleian Library, Oxford. 1709.

6. Ode on Solitude. Bodleian Library, Oxford. 1709.

7. Pastorals. Arthur A. Houghton, Jr. [1706-9.]

8. Sapho to Phaon. Pierpont Morgan Library, New York. [1707-12.]

9. Rondeau. Bodleian Library, Oxford. 1710.
10. An Essay on Criticism. Bodleian Library, Oxford. 1711.
11. Windsor Forest. Washington University, St. Louis. 1712.
12. The Happy Life of a Country Parson. The Marquess of Bath. [?1713.]
13. Scriblerian Invitations. The Marquess of Bath. 1714.
14. To Eustace Budgell, Esq, On his Translation of the Characters of Theophrastus. The Duke of Devonshire. 1714.
15. To a Lady with The Temple of Fame. W. H. Robinson Ltd., 1953. 1715.
16. The Iliad of Homer. British Museum.
17. A Character of Addison. The Marquess of Bath. [c. 1715.]
18. Epistle to Mr. Jervas. British Museum (Add. MS. 4807). 1715.
19. Sandys's Ghost. The Marquess of Bath. [c. 1716-17.]
20. The Court Ballad. British Museum (Stowe MS. 973). 1716-17.
21. A Hymn Written in Windsor Forest. Mapledurham. 1717.
22. Lines to Lord Bathurst. Boston Public Library, Mass. 1718.
23-25. Epitaphs on the Stanton Harcourt Lovers. 3 manuscripts: Mapledurham; Pierpont Morgan Library, New York. 1718.
26. Epistle to Robert Earl of Oxford. The Marquess of Bath. 1721.
27. Epitaph on the Honble Simon Harcourt. The Marquess of Bath. 1722.
28-30. To Mrs. M. B. on her Birth-day. 3 manuscripts: The Marquess of Bath; Mapledurham; British Museum (Stowe MS. 964). 1723.
31. Epitaph on Lady Kneller. D. F. Hyde. 1725.
32. Presentation Verses to Nathaniel Pigott. Harvard College Library. 1726.
33. The Capon's Tale. Pierpont Morgan Library, New York. [c. 1726.]
34. Epigram. ("When other Ladies to the Groves go down"). British Museum (Stowe MS. 755). 1730.

35. Epitaph on Mr. Elijah Fenton. The Duke of Portland. 1730.

36. Epistle to the Right Honourable Richard Earl of Burlington. Pierpont Morgan Library, New York. 1731.

37-38. On the Countess of Burlington cutting Paper. 2 manuscripts: The Duke of Devonshire; The Marquess of Bath. 1732.

39. Horace, Satyr 4. Lib. 1. Paraphrased. The Duke of Devonshire. 1732.

40. The Six Maidens. The Marquess of Bath. 1732.

41-42. An Epistle to the Right Honourable Allen Lord Bathurst. 2 manuscripts: Huntington Library, San Marino. 1732.

43-44. An Essay on Man. 2 manuscripts: Harvard College Library; Pierpont Morgan Library, New York. 1732.

45. To the Earl of Burlington, asking who writ the Libels against him. The Duke of Devonshire. 1733.

46. A Character intended for An Essay on Man. Yale University Library. 1733.

47. Epigrams Occasioned by Cibber's Verses in Praise of Nash. The Marquess of Bath. [c. 1734.]

48. An Epistle to Dr. Arbuthnot. Huntington Library, San Marino; Pierpont Morgan Library, New York. 1732-4.

49. Epigram, on One who made long Epitaphs. British Museum (Egerton MS. 1947). 1736.

50. Horace His Ode to Venus. The Marquess of Bath. 1736.

51. The Ninth Ode of the Fourth Book of Horace. British Museum (C. 28. e. 17). [c. 1737.]

52. Epigram on a Picture of Queen Caroline. The Duke of Devonshire. 1737.

53. Lines on Ministers. British Museum (Egerton MS. 1950). [c. 1738.]

54. Epigram on Cibber. Pierpont Morgan Library, New York. 1742.

55. Fragment of Brutus, an Epic. British Museum (Egerton MS. 1950). 1743.

NOTES

1   The Works of Alexander Pope, ed. W. Elwin (London, 1871), ii. 261.

2   The Dunciad, ed. J. Sutherland (London, 1943), p. 251.

3 A list is given in the Appendix.

4 The extract is printed here by permission of the Director.

5 G. Sherburn, The Early Career of Alexander Pope (Oxford, 1934), p. 51.

6 The use of this manuscript as printer's copy is dealt with by Dr. Percy Simpson in Proof-Reading in the Sixteenth, Seventeenth, and Eighteenth Centuries (Oxford, 1935), pp. 99-104.

7 Robert M. Schmitz, Pope's Windsor Forest 1712. A Study of the Washington University Holograph (St. Louis, 1952).

8 "Dr. Sw— to Mr. P—e," The Poems of Jonathan Swift, ed. H. Williams (Oxford, 1937), p. 406.

9 "Pope's Iliad: A New Document," The Review of English Studies, N.S. iv (1953), p. 114.

10 The Works of Alexander Pope, ed. J. Warton (London, 1822), iv. 294.

11 Essays on the Eighteenth Century Presented to David Nichol Smith (Oxford, 1945), pp. 49-64.

12 Imitations of Horace, ed. J. Butt (London, 1939), p. xxi.

PATTERNS OF IMAGERY IN POPE'S ARBUTHNOT

Elias F. Mengel, Jr.

In his " 'Wit and Poetry and Pope': Some Observations on his Imagery" Maynard Mack speaks of Pope's wide variety of patterns "that help supply the kind of unity which he is popularly not supposed to have."[1] An Epistle to Dr. Arbuthnot offers striking illustration of this conception: analysis reveals patterns of images running throughout, each one discrete yet all so related as to give to the whole a metaphoric value which helps to tie the poem together. I do not mean to suggest that Arbuthnot has no other kind of unity apart from that given to it by these patterns of imagery, or that this imagery functions autonomously.[2]

Five main images emerge, all connected in a kind of evolution: animal-filth-disease-persecution-virtuous man. The animal image yields the filth, the noxious element out of which disease arises, disease turns into persecution, and persecution reveals the virtuous man.

The animal image comprises all references to animals, worms, and insects in the poem, that is, to any sentient being below man. The basis of this image seems to lie in the association of the poetasters with "low Grubstreet." To Pope these men write and act without thinking, in automatic response to certain stimuli: they are like trained hawks, "May Dunce by Dunce be whistled off my hands!" (254),[3] or like frogs that live on flies, wordcatchers that live on syllables (166). Furthermore, like spiders (89), they live in their own filth, so that disease flourishes in Grubstreet. From there in swarms and packs the creatures descend on Pope, carrying their infection with them. Pestered as he is by these flatterers and foes, he cannot keep from slapping in self-defense. Thus Pope justifies satire from a man of peace. It is not spiteful or inhumane to slap a mosquito or beat off a mad dog. He suffers fools with the greatest patience and restraint, but, stung beyond endurance,

Reprinted from Publications of the Modern Language Association, Vol. 69 (1954), pp. 184-197, by permission of author and publisher.

he is forced to cry out. And when he finally does lash out, there is something heroic in his flapping fools and whipping scoundrels regardless of their rank. However, he is far from bellicose: he keeps apart from the warfare of the wits. It is by stressing this proud aloofness ("I kept, like <u>Asian</u> Monarchs, from their sight," 220) that Pope can make the transition to his final picture of himself as <u>vir bonus</u>, full of love, nursing his aged mother and asking <u>Heaven's</u> blessing for his friend. This is the culminating image of this <u>apologia</u> for his life and art in that it represents the furthest remove from the popular conception of the satirist as a malevolent man.

The drama of the poem begins with a wry and casual tone, leads up gradually to a high pitch of indignation in the Sporus portrait, and closes on the even higher plane of serenity, all passion spent. Within this rhetorical sequence Pope's patterns of imagery work in such a way as to direct the movement. By skilfully playing off one against the other the comic and serious sides of these images, by making minor fluctuations between the comic and the serious, Pope controls the tone of his poem and brings about a gradual movement from gay to grave. It is to these smaller waves within the large one that G. Wilson Knight must refer when he writes of <u>Arbuthnot</u> that "its emotions swell and subside, with a very careful and skilful undulatory movement, whose balance repays attention."[4]

In the second line of the poem, the disease image, "I'm sick, I'm dead," is of course comic exaggeration: Pope is not at home to the poetasters. "The Dog-star rages" of the following line suggests (when read in connection with the sixth line, "They rave, recite, and madden round the land") the maddening heat of dog days (as well as the custom in Juvenal's time of rehearsing poetry in August).[5] The mere juxtaposition of "rave, recite, and madden" produces a comic metaphor: the rimesters in their fine frenzy of creation are mad dogs rushing about the land. Likewise, the correlation of Bedlam and Parnassus implies a mock-heroic metaphor in the connection of lunacy with the classical <u>furor poeticus</u> of the divinely inspired. Moreover, a further reference to the animal image is suggested in the following lines:

What Walls can guard me, or what Shades can hide?

> They pierce my Thickets, thro' my Grot they glide,
> By land, by water, they renew the charge,
> They stop the Chariot, and they board the Barge. (7-10)

Here the mock-heroic play is obvious: the fortress in a state of
siege is nothing but thickets and a grot; and the Chariot and
Barge, a carriage and a boat. Yet, in addition, Pope's diction
suggests a mad swarm of insects descending on the villa, the
sudden swoop of hornets or a plague of locusts. This reading
seems to receive further support from the verb "fly" in line
21, "All fly to Twit'nam. . . ."

The dominant wry tone of the first twenty-six lines now
takes on a note of pathos in the next lines, but it is pathos controlled by a carryover of the preceding comic mood:

> Friend to my Life, (which did not you prolong,
> The World had wanted many an idle Song)
> What Drop or Nostrum can this Plague remove?
> Or which must end me, A Fool's Wrath or Love?

(27-30)

The plague of Pope's congenital ill health is now added to the
plague of poetasters, and when Pope now speaks of these pestif-
erous creatures, his hyperbolic fears ("which must end me,"
"I'm sped," "they read me dead," 30-32) take on a serious
meaning. The persecution image in the next lines is again predominantly comic (we have the mock-heroic picture of the martyr on the rack), but in the comedy there is submerged a serious reference to Pope as martyr, which has been carried over
from the pathos of the previous lines:

> Seiz'd and ty'd down to judge, how wretched I!
> Who can't be silent, and who will not lye;
> To laugh, were want of Goodness and of Grace,
> And to be grave, exceeds all Pow'r of Face.
> I sit with sad Civility, I read
> With honest anguish, and an aking head.   (33-38)[6]

The four anecdotes or exempla that follow in rapid succession dramatize the relentless importunity which forces Pope

"to speak, or burst." Since he can't be silent and he will not lie, his patience explodes into disgust when in the last and climactic anecdote the poetaster proposes a shady deal:

> ". . . your Int'rest, Sir, with <u>Lintot</u>."
> <u>Lintot</u>, dull rogue! will think your <u>price</u> too much.
> "Not Sir, if you revise it, and retouch."
> All my demurrs but double his attacks,
> At last he whispers "Do, and we go snacks."
> Glad of a quarrel, strait I clap the door,
> Sir, let me see your works and you no more.   (62-68)

In the argument with Arbuthnot which follows Pope sets up another dramatic situation in which another kind of pressure causes a spontaneous explosion of contempt. He makes the cautious Arbuthnot say:

> "Good friend forbear! you deal in dang'rous things,
> "I'd never name Queens, Ministers, or Kings;
> "Keep close to Ears, and those let Asses prick,
> "Tis nothing"

There is an ignoble suggestion in this advice to keep close to ears which gives Pope the cue to rise to lofty scorn. Thus he interrupts Arbuthnot (here his <u>adversarius</u>) in an unrestrained attack upon all the foolish:

> -- Nothing? if they bite and kick?
> Out with it, <u>Dunciad</u>! let the secret pass,
> That Secret to each Fool, that he's an Ass.   (75-80)

This indignation supports the disgust of the animal and filth images that follow:

> You think this cruel? take it for a rule,
> No creature smarts so little as a Fool.   (83-84)

> Who shames a Scribler? break one cobweb thro',
> He spins the slight, self-pleasing thread anew;
> Destroy his Fib, or Sophistry; in vain,
> The Creature's at his dirty work again.   (89-92)[7]

But now Pope undercuts this scorn by Arbuthnot's interruption, in which he makes witty reference to Pope's extreme shortness, a mockery of his former heroics:

> "Hold! for God-sake — you'll offend:
> "No Names — be calm — learn Prudence of a Friend:
> "I too could write, and I am twice as tall,
> "But Foes like these!"

Pope, however, again ignores the counsel and continues his scornful attack (explicitly a scorn of these creatures and implicitly a scorn of hedging):

> One Flatt'rer's worse than all;
> Of all mad Creatures, if the Learn'd are right,
> It is the Slaver kills, and not the Bite.   (104-106)

The mode is once again predominantly comic in the description of the ridiculous homage which his suitors pay Pope:

> There are, who to my Person pay their court,
> I cough like Horace, and tho' lean, am short,
> Ammon's great Son one shoulder had too high,
> Such Ovid's nose, and "Sir! you have an Eye — "
> Go on, obliging Creatures, make me see
> All that disgrac'd my Betters, met in me:
> Say for my comfort, languishing in bed,
> "Just so immortal Maro held his head:"
> And when I die, be sure you let me know
> Great Homer dy'd three thousand years ago. (115-124)

Although this is probably the most comic passage in the poem, still there is a serious heroic suggestion here in that these suitors (to be sure for the most absurd reasons) do class him with the highest poets and even couple him with Alexander the Great. This same tension between self-depreciation and self-glorification is carried over in the mock-heroics of the couplet that follows:

> Why did I write? what sin to me unknown
> Dipt me in Ink, my Parents', or my own?   (125-126)

PATTERNS OF IMAGERY IN ARBUTHNOT

Pope's cry that his talent is a cursed inheritance or judgment on his guilty self is mock anguish. It is tongue-in-cheek, yet the Biblical reference (St. John IX. 2) carries with it a suggestion of solemnity: "And his disciples asked him, saying, Master, who did sin, this man, or his parents, that he was born blind?" This serious heroic element is confirmed if, as a secondary reading, the phrase "dipt me in ink" is taken to be an allusion to Achilles, whose parent dipped him in the Styx to make him invulnerable.

From this predominantly humorous passage Pope turns to pathos, the transition effected by the serious suggestion of Pope as the great poet. The fact that he has just been poking fun at himself, especially at his physical shortcomings ("I cough . . . and tho' lean, am short"; ". . . one shoulder had too high"; ". . . languishing in bed"), enables him to make a serious and moving reference to his ill health without seeming maudlin:

> The Muse but serv'd to ease some Friend, not Wife,
> To help me thro' this long Disease, my Life,
> To second, ARBUTHNOT! thy Art and Care,
> And teach, the Being you perserv'd, to bear. (131-134)

This direct and open bid for sympathy has been earned by all the controlled allusions to his illness which have gone before.

When the disease image next appears, it is again connected with animals and filth, and builds on the former references:

> I ne'er with Wits or Witlings past my days,
> To spread about the Itch of Verse and Praise;
> Nor like a Puppy daggled thro' the Town,
> To fetch and carry Sing-song up and down;
> Nor at Rehearsals sweat, and mouth'd, and cry'd,
> With Handkerchief and Orange at my side:
> But sick of Fops, and Poetry, and Prate,
> To Bufo left the whole Castalian State.   (223-230)

"To spread about the Itch" possibly suggests a loathsome disease.[8] But the disgust of this first couplet is balanced by the comedy of the animal image in the second: the foppish wit both in his actions and his poetry seems as mechanical and senseless as the puppy in its proud retrieving of the trainer's stick. A

suggestion of disgust is perhaps kept here in the filth image
"daggle," to walk in a slovenly way through mire. In the third
couplet the ridiculous affectations of playwrights at rehearsals,
"sweat, and mouth'd, and cry'd," call to mind the deliriums
of the sick. Finally, "sick of" is now much more than simply
a hyperbolic "weary of": it carries with it all the disgust which
the association of animals, filth and disease has built up since
the sham "say I'm sick" of the opening.

The comedy of this passage leads into the absurd picture
of Bufo that follows:

> Proud, as Apollo on his forked hill,
> Sate full-blown Bufo, puff'd by ev'ry quill;
> Fed with soft Dedication all day long,
> Horace and he went hand in hand in song.   (231-234)

This Bufo (toad), trying to be a Horace-Maecenas, calls to mind
the silly old frog that tries to be an ox in Aesop.

The disgust which has been gradually built up from the opening lines by the interrelated patterns of animals and filth now
finally bursts forth, untempered by comic admixture, in the
scorn of the Sporus portrait:

> Let Sporus tremble -- "What? that Thing of silk,
> "Sporus, that mere white Curd of Ass's milk?
> "Satire or Sense alas! can Sporus feel?
> "Who breaks a Butterfly upon a Wheel?"
> Yet let me flap this Bug with gilded wings,
> This painted Child of Dirt that stinks and stings;
> Whose Buzz the Witty and the Fair annoys,
> Yet Wit ne'er tastes, and Beauty ne'er enjoys,
> So well-bred Spaniels civilly delight
> In mumbling of the Game they dare not bite.
> Eternal Smiles his Emptiness betray,
> As shallow streams run dimpling all the way.
> Whether in florid Impotence he speaks,
> And, as the Prompter breathes, the Puppet squeaks;
> Or at the Ear of Eve, familiar Toad,
> Half Froth, half Venom, spits himself abroad,
> In Puns, or Politicks, or Tales, or Lyes,
> Or Spite, or Smut, or Rymes, or Blasphemies.

> His Wit all see-saw between <u>that</u> and <u>this</u>,
> Now high, now low, now Master up, now Miss,
> And he himself one vile Antithesis.
> Amphibious Thing! that acting either Part,
> The trifling Head, or the corrupted Heart!
> Fop at the Toilet, Flatt'rer at the Board,
> Now trips a Lady, and now struts a Lord.
> <u>Eve's</u> Tempter thus the Rabbins have exprest,
> A Cherub's face, a Reptile all the rest;
> Beauty that shocks you, Parts that none will trust,
> Wit that can creep, and Pride that licks the dust.

                                        (305-333)

In this greatest concentration of animal images in the poem one notes a climactic progression, an accumulation of disgust. In the beginning Sporus is beneath contempt as almost non-existent, but by the end of the portrait he is a filthy, abhorrent creature. To Arbuthnot he is simply a thing of silk, a mere white curd of ass's milk, a butterfly. But to Pope he is a gilded bug that stinks and stings, or a fawning spaniel, a hunter taught to cringe from killing. Then, all beauty and delicacy gone, he becomes an ugly, filth-spitting toad, an importunate, malicious toady like Satan "close at the eare of <u>Eve</u>," and finally a snake, Satan on his belly in the dirt. In this gradual building up of loathing, the Sporus portrait recapitulates the movement of the animal-filth connection of which it is both the end and the climax.[9]

Upon reaching this pitch of feeling Pope drops for good his mask of irony and shows himself the solemn and righteous man. Now he can speak of himself in the third person and in an exalted mode:

> Not Fortune's Worshipper, nor Fashion's Fool,
> Not Lucre's Madman, nor Ambition's Tool,
> Not proud, nor servile, be one Poet's praise
> That, if he pleas'd, he pleas'd by manly ways.

                                        (334-337)

"But why insult the Poor, affront the Great?"

> A Knave's a Knave, to me, in ev'ry State,
> Alike my scorn, if he succeed or fail,
> Sporus at Court, or Japhet in a Jayl.　　(360-363)

The remainder of the poem gradually refines away the scorn that emanates from the Sporus passage by stressing Pope's patience and piety. The keynote of this last movement is sounded in the following couplet:

> Yet soft by Nature, more a Dupe than Wit,
> Sapho can tell you how this Man was bit.　　(368-369)

Far from being mean and spiteful, this dreaded satirist is even gullible. Furthermore, he suffers meekly for Virtue's sake the foulest slanders:

> Full ten years slander'd, did he once reply?
> Three thousand Suns went down on Welsted's Lye.
>
> (374-375)

> Let the Two Curls of Town and Court, abuse
> His Father, Mother, Body, Soul, and Muse.
>
> (380-381)

In the wistful description of his father's life which follows, Pope not only demonstrates a proper filial devotion, but also announces his own ideal life, the life of peace on a few paternal acres:

> Stranger to Civil and Religious Rage,
> The good Man walk'd innoxious thro' his Age. . . .
> By Nature honest, by Experience wise,
> Healthy by Temp'rance and by Exercise:
> His Life, tho' long, to sickness past unknown,
> His Death was instant, and without a groan.
>
> (394-395, 400-403)

Here in the implied contrast between his father's Arcadian life and that which he himself is doomed to lead we have the climax of the disease and persecution images. The father, in the noiseless tenor of his way, knew nothing of the plagues from which the son is suffering. His was a life of wholesome simplicity and peace, whereas Pope's existence is full of anguished groans. Sick himself, he is made worse by his sick civilization.

Finally, the love and yearning of this passage is brought to an even higher pitch in the prayer-like close, the climax of the good man image and thus of the poem itself. Here with the heightened style the interjection "O" is natural, the low "death-bed" is raised to the "Bed of Death," and the last word is "Heav'n":

> O Friend! may each Domestick Bliss be thine!
> Be no unpleasing Melancholy mine:
> Me, let the tender Office long engage
> To rock the Cradle of reposing Age,
> With lenient Arts extend a Mother's breath,
> Make Languor smile, and smooth the Bed of Death, . . .
> Whether that Blessing be deny'd, or giv'n,
> Thus far was right, the rest belongs to Heav'n.

(406-411, 418-419)

NOTES

1　In Pope and His Contemporaries, Essays Presented to George Sherburn, ed. James L. Clifford and Louis A. Landa (Oxford, 1949), p. 33.

2　For an analysis of the rhetorical (oratorical) unity of Arbuthnot the reader is referred to Elder Olson, "Rhetoric and the Appreciation of Pope," MP, XXXVII (1939-40), 13-35.

3　The OED cites Burton's Anatomy of Melancholy II. ii. iii. 317, "As a long-winged Hawke when he is first whistled off the fist, mounts aloft."

4　"The Vital Flame: An Essay on Pope," in The Burning Oracle (Oxford, 1939), p. 188.

5　The Twickenham Edition of the Poems of Alexander Pope:

Vol. IV, Imitations of Horace, ed. John Butt (London, 1939), p. 96, n. 3.

6 Pope makes the same casual connection between persecution and satire later in the following couplet (where "guiltless is hyperbolic and "smile" an understatement):

> Poor guiltless I! and can I chuse but smile,
> When ev'ry Coxcomb knows me by my Style? (281-282)

7 It is tempting to see a scatological suggestion in the "dirty work" of the spider, especially when one notes that in Swift's Battle of the Books the bee calls the proud spider's cobweb castle "excrement and venom." And there is an obvious scatological metaphor later in Arbuthnot:

> Just writes to make his barrenness appear,
> And strains from hard-bound brains eight lines a-year.

> (181-182)

8 I am indebted to Professor George Sherburn for pointing out that "the Itch of Verse" suggests Juvenal 7:52, cacoethes scribendi, an incurable itch to write, a phrase often quoted jocosely by writers and critics of Pope's day.

9 Cf. 1. 170, "Of hairs, or straws, or dirt, or grubs, or worms." Here, too, the local progression points to the general movement.

POPE, THE BYZANTINE EMPRESS,
AND WALPOLE'S WHORE

James M. Osborn

Critics of Pope's poetry have uniformly praised the force and subtlety of his two dialogues published in 1738 and afterwards designated "The Epilogue to the Satires." These critics have bestowed the highest encomiums on the concluding passage of Dialogue I, Pope's description of Vice Triumphant, who, once enthroned in power, receives obsequious flattery from all sides, except only from Pope himself. Joseph Warton, in his 1797 edition of Pope,[1] wrote: "This is perhaps the noblest passage in all his works, without any exception whatever." Pope's next editor, W. L. Bowles, asserted: "More dignified and impressive numbers, more lofty indignation, more animated appeals, and more rich personifications never adorned the page of the Satiric Muse."[2] W. J. Courthope similarly praised "the splendid picture of the Triumph of Vice . . . the highest pitch of indignation,"[3] and the most recent editor, John Butt, terms it "one of the grandest passages of his later poetry."[4] The force of Pope's lines is incontestable:

> Vice is undone, if she forgets her Birth,
> And stoops from Angels to the Dregs of Earth:
> But 'tis the Fall degrades her to a Whore;
> Let Greatness own her, and she's mean no more:
> Her Birth, her Beauty, Crowds and Courts confess,
> Chaste Matrons praise her, and grave Bishops bless:
> In golden Chains the willing World she draws,
> And hers the Gospel is, and hers the Laws:
> Mounts the Tribunal, lifts her scarlet head,
> And sees pale Virtue carted in her stead!
> Lo! at the Wheels of her Triumphal Car,
> Old England's Genius, rough with many a Scar,
> Dragg'd in the Dust! his Arms hang idly round,

Reprinted from Review of English Studies, New Series, Vol. 6 (1955), pp. 372-382, by permission of author and publisher.

His Flag inverted trails along the ground!
Our Youth, all liv'ry'd o'er with foreign Gold,
Before her dance; behind her crawl the Old!
See thronging Millions to the Pagod run,
And offer Country, Parent, Wife, or Son!
Hear her black Trumpet thro' the Land proclaim,
That 'Not to be corrupted is the Shame.'
In Soldier, Churchman, Patriot, Man in Pow'r,
'Tis Av'rice all, Ambition is no more!
See, all our Nobles begging to be Slaves!
See, all our Fools aspiring to be Knaves!
The Wit of Cheats, the Courage of a Whore,
Are what ten thousand envy and adore.
All, all look up, with reverential Awe,
On Crimes that scape, or triumph o'er the Law:
While Truth, Worth, Wisdom, daily they decry —
'Nothing is Sacred now but Villany.'

Yet may this verse (if such a Verse remain)
Show there was one who held it in disdain.

All Pope's editors and critics have accepted the portrait
of Vice as being an abstract personification. As such it makes
a fitting conclusion to the satire — Pope artfully rises from
particulars to the universal in a crescendo of indignation against
the iniquities of his age. But at this point the careful reader
finds himself puzzled. Pope usually wrote on more than one
level of meaning with overtones of allusion and analogy. Is this
passage an exception, containing no more than a stock literary
allusion to the Whore of Babylon?

The only one of Pope's editors to point a parallel to this
apologue was William Warburton, Pope's intimate friend and
literary executor. In the 1751 edition of Pope's Works Warburton stated: "The Poet, in this whole passage, would be understood to allude to a very extraordinary story told by Procopius
in his Secret History: the sum of which is as follows."[5] Warburton then recounted in a footnote three pages long the story
of the prostitute Theodora who became the wife of the Emperor
Justinian, and once in power received slavish adoration from
the multitude. Warburton's phrasing here is evasive, and his
parade of erudition is pedantic; such qualities, combined with

his pomposity, made him a favourite butt for the wit of later commentators. Gibbon remarked sardonically, when writing of Theodora in The Decline and Fall, "Without Warburton's critical telescope, I should never have seen, in the general picture of triumphant vice, any personal allusion to Theodora."[6] Courthope added a century later: "The idea of personifying the corruption of Walpole's age as a prostitute was sufficiently obvious without the abstruse aid of Procopius."[7]

Though Warburton has properly been fair game for his successors, many of his specific suggestions, including this one, cannot be dismissed lightly. Instead, it may be more profitable to inquire whether Pope had read Procopius and whether there is any evidence that Pope did indeed have the Theodora parallel in mind. Here one of the unpublished jottings in the manuscripts of Pope's modest Boswell, Joseph Spence, sheds a glimmer of light. During a conversation in March 1743, Pope recommended to Spence Cousin's Histoire de Constantinople (8 vols., Paris, 1672-4) as being "very convenient, to save one the drudgery of reading through all the Byzantine historians."[8] Cousin's translation of Procopius's Secret History appears in vol. ii, and the passage describing Theodora's triumph (pp. 150-1) reads as follows:

Il n'y a point de crime dont ne soit capable celui qui s'est une fois depouillé des sentimens de l'honneur, & qui ne se soucie plus d'être en exécration aux gens-de-bien. Quand il s'est une fois armé le front d'impudence, il n'y a plus d'infamie où il fasse difficulté de se plonger. Pas un Magistrat ne témoigna de l'indignation de cette honte de l'Etat. Ils étoient prêts de l'adorer comme une divinité. Aucun Prélat ne parut en avoir de la douleur. Ils allérent la saluer comme leur Impératice. Le peuple qui avoit été le spectateur de ses bouffoneries & de sa prostitution, se prosterna aussi-tôt à ses piés, comme un esclave aux piés de sa souveraine. Il n'y eut point de soldat qui se fâchat de courre toutes sortes de hazars pour la défense de ses intérêts. Enfin personne, de quelque condition qu'elle fût, ne s'opposa à cette monstrueuse élévation. Tout le monde s'accorda d'un commun consentement à cette sujetion infame. Il semble que la fortune affecte de faire admirer l'empire

> qu'elle exerce dans le monde, & de montrer qu'elle
> ne se soûmet ni aux régles de la bien-séance, ni au
> jugement de la raison. Elle éléve certaines personnes
> à des grandeurs prodigieuses, où selon toutes les ap-
> parances, elles ne devoient jamais parvenir, & elle
> se moque des obstacles qui pouvoient empêcher leur
> avancement. En-un-mot elle se vante que tout lui
> céde & lui obéit.

The parallels in situation, in phraseology (some indicated by editorial italics), and in moral tone suggest that Warburton knew what he was talking about. It is difficult to believe that these parallels are merely coincidental.[9]

That Warburton should have been aware of the Theodora analogue is not surprising, considering that he singled out the quality of "elegant and satiric ambiguity" as being a special feature of the poem. Later critics have similarly remarked Pope's powers for "the ironic and the oblique," in Warton's phrase, but were unwilling to pursue Warburton's hint. Court-hope in 1881 was particularly impressed with Pope's powers as demonstrated in this very poem, saying: "This satire requires to be read very carefully, as almost every phrase has a double allusion, and the marvellous skill of the workmanship is only appreciated when the irony is thoroughly understood." Courthope's footnote ridiculing Warburton seems to have blinded him to the possibilities in the parallel to the Empress Theodora.

But there is a problem beyond the Theodora analogy in the Vice Triumphant passage, a problem of "double allusion," to recall Courthope's phrase. Here again Warburton and Spence supply the key to the matter. In a memorandum of a conversation with Pope in 1756, Spence recorded that Phryne in the Epistle to Bathurst (1732, ll. 119-20) was a gibe at "Miss Skerrett." Warburton then added the information, "The note on Justinian and Leonora meant at her." Because Spence jotted down the wrong name (Leonora for Theodora) the significance of the remark has been overlooked. It means that Warburton's long note was an elaborate irony on the parallel between the careers of Theodora, the prostitute who, on her marriage to Justinian, became Empress of Byzantium, and Molly Skerrett, long the mistress of Sir Robert Walpole, who became "First Lady" of the British Empire when Sir Robert married her in 1738.

But do the events of Molly Skerrett's marriage fit in with the circumstances of Pope's poem? First a glance at Pope's position in politics in 1738-9 is necessary. For more than a decade opposition to the long rule of Sir Robert Walpole had been led by Lord Bolingbroke, who was, as we know, Pope's "Guide, Philosopher, and Friend." From this position of intimacy with Bolingbroke, Pope gradually took an increasing part in the strategy of the opposition leaders; his villa at Twickenham, within ten miles of Richmond and Kew, served as a gossip-centre and later as a meeting-place for opposition policy sessions.[10] By 1737, in the Epistle to Augustus, Pope even dared to point the rapier of ironic ridicule against the King himself. With this poem and others that followed Pope deliberately performed a political service to the Patriots, as the opposition party centring upon the Prince of Wales were called. Though Pope was debarred by his religion from official participation in government, he was, in Sherburn's phrase, "an important agent" of the Patriots. Indeed, Pope later hinted in his verses to Lady Shirley that he was threatened with prosecution by the House of Lords.

The leading theme of the Patriots, ever since The Craftsman had begun to hammer away at it, was corruption. The Patriots assailed the corrupt morals of the court, corruption in commerce (frauds in the South Sea Company, the Charitable Corporation, and the Derwentwater Commission, which Walpole protected against investigation), corruption of national courage (in facing Spain and other nations) and Walpole's cynically corrupt practices in buying votes and elections. Pope stressed this theme consistently with such phrases as "Corruption, like a gen'ral flood . . . Shall deluge all" (Epistle to Bathurst, 135-7). Similar phrases, "the corrupted Heart" (i. e. Lord Hervey: Epistle to Arbuthnot, 327), "Times corrupt" (Epistle to Augustus, 251) and "corrupted Peers" (Ep. I, bk. i. 99) became increasingly frequent in Pope's poems, as did more generalized references to "Vice" in many manifestations. That the Patriots were successful in establishing this attitude is shown by an incident in 1737 when their idea of a Patriot King, namely Frederick the Prince of Wales, attended a performance of Addison's Cato. As reported by Lord Hervey, the audience greeted the Prince with warm applause when he entered the theatre; later, "where vice prevails, and impious men bear sway, the post of honour is a private station" — there was another loud huzza, with a great clap, in the latter part of which applause the Prince himself joined in the face of the whole audience."[11]

An unmatched opportunity for writers of the opposition to dramatize corruption in high places came in spring 1738, at a time when Bolingbroke was in France. Walpole's popularity had already been weakened by the events of the previous year — the struggle to prevent an increase in the Prince of Wales's pension, the Licensing Bill to control the theatres, and flagrant bribing of members of Parliament. Early in 1738 Sir Robert's supine attitude toward supposed Spanish insults to British ships caused widespread grumbling. Then, on 3 March, Walpole publicly announced his marriage to Molly Skerrett, his mistress of many years' standing, known to have borne him two children before the recent death of the first Lady Walpole.

Though Molly Skerrett undoubtedly was personally attractive and possessed many merits, there is no question that the marriage shocked a good many of the squirearchy and country party. The diary of Sir John Percival, first Earl of Egmont, records the situation:

> Last Friday Sir Robert Walpole declared his marriage to Mrs. Skerrit by whom he had two daughters during his late lady's lifetime. She was the same day introduced to Court and received with great marks of distinction by his Majesty and the Princess Amelia. The Duchesses of Newcastle and Richmond contended earnestly which of them should have the dishonourable honour of presenting her to the King, but at length Mrs. Walpole, Horace Walpole's wife, did the office, as the nearest relation, and to shew that Sir Robert marrying his whore was by consent of his family. Thus a stay-maker's daughter carried the bell from two duchesses.[12]

The extremes of partisanship are crystallized in some verses which the Earl transcribed several days later:

> I can't conceive why in decline of life
> Sir Robert should betroth a second wife;

> Can you suppose he feels an amorous rage,
> Thus swell'd with fat, and thus excis'd by age?
> He surely don't, but wonder not, my friends,
> The knight in this pursues his constant ends.
> He, long inured to plunder and defraud,
> Unmoved by virtue, and by shame un-aw'd,
> Perverts to private use a public whore,
> That he may rob the public, one way more,
> The only way he never rob'd before.[13]

This was the situation when Pope published One Thousand Seven Hundred and Thirty Eight. A Dialogue Something like Horace. The copyright was registered on 12 May, and the poem was available to the public within the next few days. The poem was "more popular than the bookseller had anticipated" and went through three issues, totalling perhaps 4,000 copies, a large initial sale for such a publication.[14] How many readers saw a parallel between the description of Vice Enthroned and the influential position of the second Lady Walpole we have no way of knowing. The situation was delicate, for Walpole was still the most powerful man in Britain, and his new wife was the apple of his eye. Pope's talent for irony stood him in good stead.

Two weeks later, on 4 June, the situation was suddenly changed. On that day, only three months after being made an honest woman, the second Lady Walpole died "of a Miscarriage succeeded by a Fever."[15] When alive Molly Skerrett had been a convenient symbol of corruption at the head of the state; now Molly dead became the subject of widespread commiseration. Walpole's devotion to her had been manifest, and his genuine grief now aroused general sympathy even among persons who hated his policies. Pope's response to the event is unrecorded, for both good taste and political prudence recommended silence. From his viewpoint the usefulness of the Vice-Theodora-Molly analogy had expired with Molly's last breath.

Pope's subsequent references to Walpole are properly cautious. Dialogue II, published on 18 July, sheds little light on the parallel. The poem mentions Walpole twice, but with guarded care Pope distinguished between the man and the politician:

> Sure, if I spare the Minister, no rules
> Of Honour bind me, not to maul his Tools. (146-7)

The other reference reads as follows:

> . . . Sir ROBERT's mighty dull,
> Has never made a Friend in private life,
> And was, besides, a Tyrant to his Wife. (133-5)

Pope introduced these lines by a direct statement that they are a "lye," i.e. irony. But we may doubt whether the grieving Prime Minister found balm in this left-handed gesture acknowledging that Pope recognized his affection for Molly Skerrett. (The publication date, within six weeks of her funeral, leaves no doubt that Molly and not Walpole's first wife was intended, though Pope's editors have missed the point.) Pope maintained the irony when he wrote on 31 July to his friend and legal adviser, William Fortescue, who years earlier had introduced him to Walpole's table on several occasions,[16] "You see I have made him [Walpole] a second compliment in print in my second Dialogue, and he ought to take it for no small one, since in it I couple him with Lord Bol[ingbroke]. As he shows a right sense of this, I may make him a third, in my third Dialogue."[17]

The third dialogue never was finished, but is preserved as the fragment known under the title "One Thousand Seven Hundred and Forty." Doubtless Pope sketched out parts of it at various times before that year. A short verse paragraph is devoted to Sir Robert Walpole, beginning with the couplet:

> Rise, rise, great W[alpole] fated to appear,
> Spite of thyself a glorious minister!

It ends with an allusion to Molly Skerrett:

> At length to B[ritain] kind, as to thy [whore]
> Espouse the nation, you [debauched before].[18]

This couplet is significant as further evidence of Pope's treatment of Molly Skerrett. From his first allusion to her in 1732 under the name of Phryne, the notorious courtesan of Athens, Pope's attitude was consistent with the Theodora parallel.

Now to approach the "Vice Triumphant" passage from another angle — what may be called the "theme" of these Dialogues. Pope's chief point in both poems is the dilemma of the satirist, forced to choose between the advantages and disadvantages of writing personal particulars or abstract generalizations. In the words of his latest editor, "Pope's theme [was] his conviction that general satire is useless, and that living examples must be made if any reform is to be effected."[19] Indeed, Pope emphasized the problem by writing the poems in dialogue form, one speaker, a straw man first labelled "A" but later identified as a "Friend," arguing for generalized and innocuous subject matter, while "B," who later when the mask is dropped becomes Pope himself, argues for personal invective. In Dialogue II Pope even repeats several specific names from Dialogue I to demonstrate the superiority of his position over that advocated by the anonymous (and somewhat pusillanimous) "Friend."

Pope's practice in the poem follows his precept: he named the persons satirized much more specifically than in any of his earlier Horatian imitations. In most cases their names were unmistakable, with few letters lacking, but many names were written out in full. One of them, Dr. Conyers Middleton of Cambridge, recorded surprise at finding his name there "at it's full length."[20] Moreover, Pope supplied footnotes (printed posthumously in Warburton's 1751 edition) explaining the targets of his satiric shafts. As Warton remarked, "Pope has himself given more notes and illustrations on these Dialogues than on any other of his poems."[21] In Dialogue I the first 134 lines carry twenty-four notes by Pope, an average of one for every six lines. Yet the last thirty-six lines, the passage personifying Vice Triumphant, was left bare of any note from the poet's hand. In the light of Pope's "theme" it puts no strain on the imagination to see the Vice Triumphant passage as a double allusion to be passed by unrecognized by the general public but caviare to the cognoscenti.

Contemporary evidence that Pope's reference to Molly was recognized is found in another poem inspired by Sir Robert Walpole's second marriage. Published some time after Molly Skerrett's death, this satire bore the title The Rival Wives; or, The Greeting of Clarissa and Skirra in the Elysian Shades.[22] This poetical dialogue between the ghost of Catherine Shorter, the first Lady Walpole (died 20 August 1737), and that of Molly

Skerrett, is competent but undistinguished. The subject follows the party-line of the Patriots, namely to bemoan the decline of Britain's strength at home and her prestige abroad due to the softening of national character consequent on corruption in high places.

For our purpose the chief interest lies in certain parallels between this poem and Pope's personification of Vice Triumphant. The Rival Wives appeared approximately six weeks after Pope's Dialogue I, and the following lines are addressed to the recently deceased Molly Skerrett:

> The World by Fortune blinded, made their Court
> To You, who'd lately been their Game and Sport.
> Hence view the vain Delusions of Mankind,
> How Riches dazzle, and how Titles blind!
> If Great ne'er stick at Vice — Who dare defame?
> The vicious Poor alone can merit Shame.
> L[or]ds with Impunity each Moment cheat,
> For what low petty Rogue their Fate would meet;
> And what our Ancestors would deem a Crime,
> Is grown a Virtue by the Course of Time.   (p. 6)

It is difficult to believe that contemporary readers would have failed to notice how closely this passage resembles Pope's lines 141-4:

> Vice is undone, if she forgets her Birth,
> And stoops from Angels to the Dregs of Earth:
> But 'tis the Fall degrades her to a Whore:
> Let Greatness own her, and she's mean no more.

This idea recurs several times in The Rival Wives, e.g. on p. 13:

> Vice if successful, loses strait its Name?
> If unsuccessful, meets with certain Shame.

So, too, a direct parallel occurs in the picture of fulsome flattery paid by court sycophants to the new Lady Walpole. Pope's couplet reads:

BYZANTINE EMPRESS AND WALPOLE'S WHORE

> Her Birth, her Beauty, Crowds and Courts confess,
> Chaste Matrons praise her, and grave Bishops bless.

(145-6)

Compare it with this passage from page 11 of The Rival Wives:

> A Reverend Lawn with Scrapes his Homage pays,
> Though Conscience gives the Lye to all he says.
> One strait finds out you're born of noble Birth,
> And that your Beauty charms all Men on Earth:
> While in your Anti-chamber humbly wait
> Ladies of Rank, Condition, and Estate.
> All Scandal silenc'd; rich and virtuous grown,
> You claim a Rank now equal to their own.

In the midst of his personification Pope alluded to the low level to which Britain's prestige supposedly had sunk in consequence of Walpole's peace-at-any-price foreign policy:

> Lo! at the Wheels of her Triumphal Car,
> Old England's Genius, rough with many a Scar,
> Dragg'd in the Dust! his Arms hang idly round,
> His Flag inverted trails along the ground!   (151-4)

Similarly in The Rival Wives, Molly Skerrett's influence over Walpole is blamed for causing such national shame:

> And when a flagrant Blunder I espy,
> 'SKIRRA! thy Love occasioned this' I'll cry.
> See where the once fam'd Empress of the Main,
> By Pirates robb'd, from Vengeance does refrain;
> Sees Europe's Scum defy her falling Pow'r,
> Her ruling FLAG insulted, mock'd and tore . . .
> Thus Britain's sunk in Sloth and Lux'ry drown'd,
> The Scorn and Dupe of all the Nations round.   (pp. 15-16)

How much can we deduce from these parallels — and even parallels to parallels? The evidence is predominantly circumstantial; but it is abundant, and it is consistent. Though there are gaps in our knowledge, no facts casting doubt on the double

549

allusion to Theodora and Molly Skerrett have appeared. Clearly Molly Skerrett loomed large in the public eye in the spring of 1738. Equally clear is the case that some Englishmen saw similarities between phases of her career and Pope's portrait of Vice Triumphant. Moreover, readers in 1738 who were familiar with opposition propaganda would recognize that the term Greatness, especially when italicized, alluded to Walpole.[23] This is not to suggest that any contemporary reader was so literal-minded as to believe that the second Lady Walpole played a black trumpet or rode in a chariot.

In the absence of positive evidence against the double-allusion theory, negative arguments of importance should be considered briefly. The first question requiring an answer is, Does the chronology fit Pope's habits of composition? His usual custom was to keep the draft of a satire in embryonic form for a lengthy gestation period and then publish when convenience or occasion prompted. In the case of Dialogue I, only the last thirty-eight lines would have required recasting, once the announcement of Sir Robert Walpole's second marriage provided the occasion. Ten weeks elapsed before the publication -- long enough for Pope to have developed the double parallel. Indeed, the only datable circumstance connected with the conclusion of the poem is Pope's letter of 28 April to Ralph Allen asking permission to use Allen's name, a mere fortnight before the satire reached the public.

Present-day Pope scholarship must face the positive evidence in Warburton's statement to Spence in 1756, evidence that is in no way diminished in value because it has heretofore been overlooked. Equally significant is the fact that all the bits of this jigsaw puzzle now fit together — all are consistent with the double allusion to Empress Theodora and Empress Molly. Hence, Pope's vivid lines on Vice Enthroned, which have long been acknowledged to be one of the noblest passages in English poetry, become even more remarkable when read with the double allusion in mind. Pope's skill at the multiple keyboard of Horatian "elegant ambiguity" may be valued even more highly than his saeva indignatio.

NOTES

1 iv. 317.

2 Works of Alexander Pope (London, 1806), iv. 334.

3 Pope's Works, ed. W. Elwin and W. J. Courthope (London, 1881), iii. 453.

4 Twickenham Edition of the Poems of Alexander Pope (London, 1939), iv. p. xxxix.

5 iv. 314-16.

6 Ed. J. B. Bury (London, 1901), iv. 215.

7 Op. cit. , iii. 471.

8 Full details will be given in my forthcoming edition of Spence's Anecdotes.

9 Pope may have used the 1685 Amsterdam reprint of the Paris edition, from which I have quoted. He may also have seen the 1674 English translation of the Secret History, but verbal parallels are lacking.

10 Evidence in the Stuart Papers suggests that about this time Pope was also intriguing with friends of the Pretender; see G. H. Jones, "The Jacobites, Charles Molloy, and Commonsense," R. E. S., N. S. iv (1953), 144-7.

11 Lord Hervey, Some Materials Towards a Memoir of the Reign of King George II, ed. Romney Sedgwick (London, 1931), iii. 839.

12 The Diary of the first Earl of Egmont, ed. R. A. Roberts (London, 1923), iii. 839 (Hist. MSS. Comm. 16th Report)

13 Ibid. , ii. 469, 471.

14 R. H. Griffith, Alexander Pope, a Bibliography (Austin, Texas) i, part ii (1927), 383.

15 Gent. Mag. (1738), p. 324. The fatal miscarriage probably indicates a pregnancy of more than three months, suggesting that the discovery that Molly was again with child may have prompted Walpole's decision to legalize his connexion with her.

16 Alluded to in Dialogue I, 29-30: "Seen him [Walpole] have I, but in his happier hour of Social Pleasure . . . ," &c.

17 Pope's Works, ed. Elwin and Courthope, ix (London, 1886), 142.

18 The blanks were filled in by J. W. Croker, whose ingenuity has passed unchallenged.

19 Ed. cit. , p. xxxix.

20 Ibid. , p. 303.

21 The Works of Alexander Pope, ed. Joseph Warton (London, 1797), iv. 298.

22 Printed ostensibly by W. Lloyd, otherwise unknown except for the Rival Wives answer'd; or, Skirra to Clarissa; publ. early in August 1738 (Gent. Mag. (1738), p. 440).

23 This suggestion I owe to Professor Robert Rogers.

THE "ROMANTICISM" OF POPE'S HORACE

G. K. Hunter

Pope was known in his own day as the English Horace, but this alignment has its difficulties, as he himself indicated:

> But Horace, Sir, was delicate, was nice;
> Bubo observes, he lash'd no sort of Vice:
> Horace would say, Sir Billy serv'd the Crown,
> Blunt could do Bus'ness, H-ggins knew the Town,
> In Sappho touch the Failings of the Sex,
> In rev'rend Bishops note some small Neglects,
> And own, the Spaniard did a waggish thing,
> Who cropt our Ears, and sent them to the King.
> His sly, polite, insinuating stile
> Could please at Court, and make AUGUSTUS smile:
> An artful Manager, that crept between
> His Friend and Shame, and was a kind of Screen.

("Epilogue to the Satires," Dialogue I, 11-22)[1]

Here he seems to align himself with Persius (from whom — following Dryden's words — the lines are adapted), which should indicate to us that the facile antithesis between the "Epilogue and Johnson's London as, respectively, English Horace and English Juvenal is insufficient to describe Pope's relation to these ancient norms of satire. Pope, it is true, is urbane, polished and polite, and to this extent "Horatian" rather than "Juvenalian," but this characterisation applies to the surface only; when we compare the centres from which their satires are directed, Pope can be seen to be quite unHoratian, even in poems which advertise their ancestry as "Imitations of Horace."

The ways in which the Imitations differ from their originals are often obvious and part of the design, which is (as Johnson says) "to accommodate . . . sentiments of an old author

Reprinted from Essays in Criticism, Vol. 10 (1960), pp. 390-414, by permission of author and publisher.

to recent facts, or familiar images"; what I am analysing in the following pages are not these changes, however, but the structural alterations and shifts of emphasis which the author uses but does not expose — the subtle (and often, I suppose, unconscious) manipulations by which the original is taken out of the background of assumptions it accepted rather than stated. When Pope's Imitation of the First Satire of the Second Book is looked at from this point of view we can see that the theory of satire it presents (beneath the veil of epistolary casualness) is not preserved by Pope in anything like its original form. When we enumerate and tabulate the divergences between the two poems we can see that in fact another theory of satire has been fitted inside the skin of Horace's poem, a theory which depends far more on the sensibility of the individual author and is far more concerned with the gap between individual ideals and social realities than Horace ever was. The changes move Horace's point of view to a position which is certainly less "Augustan" — public, assured, serene, socially oriented — and to that extent (if the polarity be allowed to have meaning) may be said to be more Romantic. In using the word I take "Romanticism" to have the meanings analysed by René Wellek in Comparative Literature I (1949) and to involve primarily a substitution of the order of the individual mind for the Order of the external world (social, natural, and eventually Divine) as a basis for belief and action, a substitution of subjective evaluation for the traditional acceptance of received values, objectively justified. Pope does not, of course, rest his outlook on any fully Romantic "shaping spirit of imagination," but his criticism of society is different from that of a superficially similar Stoic "retiredness," for it aims not at apatheia but at a good society to be achieved through the pathos of the individual sensibility,

the strong Antipathy of Good to Bad

— and if this is not Romantic I do not know what to call it. Whatever we call it, however, we should notice that it is radically distinct from that Fancy's Maze which Pope himself set in antithesis to the Truth of such poems as the Imitations, and which critics have usually labelled "Pre-Romantic." For the "Romanticism" of the Imitation is not fanciful; it deals seriously with what Pope is calling Truth — factual evaluations about real life.

THE "ROMANTICISM" OF POPE'S HORACE

The antithesis I propose, between the classically objective manner and the Romantically subjective attitude behind it, cannot
be assimilated to the other one.

In the poem we are discussing this general change can only
be studied as the sum of its particular instances, but the method
of close analysis is easier to follow in this poem than in the
other Imitations, since this remains closest to the text of its
original. At the beginning of the poem Horace is defending himself for writing satire by a conversation with the famous jurist
Trebatius. As far as the hope of improving society goes, it
appears, the satirist's task is a thankless one, and the jurist
when asked for advice tells Horace in one pithy word to give it
up (Quiescas). "But I can't sleep," says Horace. "Then," replies Trebatius, "either woo sleep by exercise or write a less
troublesome kind of verse — praise Caesar."

Pope begins with the same situation, but straight away we
see a change of emphasis:

> There are (I scarce can think it, but am told)
> There are to whom my Satire seems too bold,
> Scarce to wise Peter complaisant enough,
> And something said of Chartres much too rough.
> The Lines are weak, another's pleas'd to say,
> Lord Fanny spins a thousand such a Day.
> Tim'rous by Nature, of the Rich in awe,
> I come to Council learned in the law.   (1-8)

Here, the local allusions, the long qualifying clause leading up
to "I," and the self-characterisation in the added parenthesis in
line one, all shift attention away from the situation and serve
to concentrate it instead on the personality of the author. Of the
same kind, and even more significant, is the change of emphasis in the lines which follow. Horace says that he writes because
he is unable to sleep; no cause of the inability is given; we are
left to suppose that we are dealing with a gently ironic excuse,
or at most with a private weakness. Pope, however, is unable
to sleep for a definite stated reason:

> I nod in Company, I wake at Night,
> Fools rush into my Head, and so I write.   (13-14)

555

Pope is forced to write satire because of the folly of the world he lives in; the philosophy of satire implicit here is quite un-Horatian; it is in fact much nearer the world of Juvenal's <u>facit indignatio versum</u>, or his <u>Quam difficile est non scribere satiram</u> which Dryden renders in a manner already half-way towards Pope:

> Such fulsome objects meeting everywhere,
> 'T is hard to write, but harder to forbear.   (42-3)

That Dryden's translation of Juvenal's first satire is in Pope's mind as he imitates Horace would seem to be indicated by the close imitation of Dryden's

> But when Lucilius brandishes his pen,
> And flashes in the face of guilty men   (251-2)

in his own

> . . . when I point the Pen,
> Brand the bold Front of shameless, guilty Men,
>
> (105-6)

The tone of Pope is without the savage indignation; the surface is smooth and self-deprecatingly ironic; but the social mode of the satire, the relationship of the satirist to his society is Juvenalian.

In Horace the personal battle is one which seems to arise by chance. He genuinely desires to live at peace:

> O Pater et Rex
> Jupiter! ut pereat positum rubigine telum,
> Nec quisquam noceat cupido mihi pacis!   (42-4)

but in Pope the battle between the satirist and society is basic and unceasing. He translates the lines above clearly enough but places his rendering in the context of a political analogy which alters the meaning:

> Save but our <u>Army</u>! and let <u>Jove</u> incrust

> Swords, Pikes, and Guns, with everlasting Rust!
> Peace is my dear Delight — not Fleury's more: (73-5)

The personal wish becomes contaminated by the complex ironies of the political situation (see the next line: "But touch me,
and no Minister so sore") and we are led to think, "He's about
as sincere as a politician." In fact the whole effort for a ces-
sation of hostilities appears in Pope only as an attempt to secure tactical advantages. Horace says that the sheathed sword
is the correct wear for a man who is not threatened; Pope
renders this by

> Satire's my Weapon, but I'm too discreet
> To run a Muck, and tilt at all I meet;   (69-70)

It would be natural enough, he implies, for the satirist to seek
to tilt against everyone, but there is a tactical advantage in
discretion.

Horace's whole defence of satire is lightly ironic in tone,
but concealed deprecatingly behind the irony one can see two
main lines of argument. For one thing, satire is a natural
activity, as natural as the bull's horns or the wolf's jaw. Such
a defence, however, might leave the satirist still exposed to
legal and proper punishment; against this Horace has to use
another line of argument, and this he derives from the personality and practice of Lucilius, within whose shadow he claims
to be working. Lucilius hated fools and knaves and attacked
them in his satire, but the best men of his day (Scipio and
Laelius) did not object to this; similarly, Horace has his noble
friends, and his satire does not offend them. A natural bent
for satire cannot be a vice if the best men patronise it.

Pope translates all this, mainly line for line and sometimes word for word (this is the closest of his Imitations), yet
by a series of subtle adjustments he transfers the defence of
his satire to another basis. For Pope, the description of satire
as a natural and harmless human activity, which occupies the
greatest space in Horace and sets the (mildly ironic) tone of
the poem, is almost irrelevant. He alters whatever he can
without departing too grossly from his original. Thus Horace
tells us in ll. 47-60 that each natural kind uses what power it
has: the judge threatens, the witch poisons, bulls use their

horns, wolves their jaws, and none can be diverted to other
modes of attack; so Horace the satirist, whether he be dying,
wealthy, poor, in Rome or in exile, will continue to exercise
his characteristic mode — the power to satirise. Pope changes
much of this in his rendering: by using passives for actives he
turns the power that the witch Canidia wields into one for which
she must be feared; the author becomes identified with the victim rather than parallel to the witch in his obsession. It is true
that the Horatian argument still stands, but in a form so atten-
uated that it has to be sought for before it can be found. In Horace the argument moves forward by a series of one-line parallel
phrases till we come to the satirist himself:

> Cervius iratus leges minitatur et urnam;
> Canidia Albuti, quibus est inimica, Venenum;
> Grande malum Turius, si quid se judice certes;
> Ut, quo quisque valet, suspectus terreat, utque
> Imperet hoc natura potens; sic collige mecum.
> Dente lupus, cornu taurus petit; unde, nisi intus
> Monstratum? (47-53)

The placing of the sic collige mecum keeps the relationship of
first, second and third persons clear in our minds. In Pope,
however, this phrase is not translated, and by postponing the
reintroduction of the first person he makes the relationships
more vague. The procession of the usual victims — Sappho,
Walters, Chartres, etc. — is sufficiently lengthy and complex
(natura potens being omitted) for us to feel when we come to
the climax:

> Then learned Sir! (to cut the Matter short)
> What-e'er my Fate . . . I will Rhyme and Print
>
> (91-100)

that the connection of the writer with the activities of Sappho,
etc., must be the obvious one that he will rhyme ("and Print")
against them. Pope has meticulously preserved the letter of
Horace's defence, but has conveyed another spirit inside it:

> Slander or Poyson, dread from Delia's Rage,

> Hard Words or Hanging, if your Judge be <u>Page</u>,
> From furious <u>Sappho</u> scarce a milder Fate,
> <u>P-x'd by her Love, or libell'd by her Hate</u>:
> Its proper Pow'r to hurt, each Creature feels,
> Bulls aim their horns, and Asses lift their heels,
> 'Tis a Bear's Talent not to kick, but hug,
> <u>And no man wonders he's not stung by Pug</u>:
> So drink with <u>Waters</u> or with <u>Chartres</u> eat,
> They'll never poison you, they'll only cheat.
>   <u>Then learned Sir! (to cut the Matter short)</u>
> What-e'er my Fate, <u>or well or ill at Court</u>,
> Whether old Age, with faint, but chearful Ray,
> Attends to gild the Evening of my Day,
> Or Death's black Wing already be display'd
> To wrap me in the Universal Shade;
> <u>Whether the darken'd Room to muse invite</u>,
> <u>Or whiten'd Wall provoke the Skew'r to write</u>,
> In Durance, Exile, Bedlam, or the Mint,
> Like <u>Lee</u> or <u>Budgell</u>, I will Rhyme <u>and Print</u>   (81-100)

Horace's "sly, polite, insinuating style" relies principally on charm to convey an impression of the author's sanity and centrality of outlook. His graceful irony and mocking self-deprecation communicates authority by not needing to make the direct claim; one can understand why he has long been a favourite author in English Public Schools. Pope's methods are more worried and more obtrusive; he finds it hard not to assume the superiority that his wit entitles him to. Horace is content to present satire as a harmless taste, like a taste for dancing, horseriding or boxing:

> quot capitum vivunt, totidem studiorum
> Millia: me pedibus delectat claudere verba,
> Lucili ritu, . . .   (27-9)

Pope actually renders all these words, but by widely separating the general observation (<u>quot capitum</u> . . . <u>Millia</u>) from the application to his own case he considerably weakens its relevance as an explanation of his own satire:

Each Mortal has his Pleasure: <u>None deny</u>

> Scarsdale his Bottle, Darty his Ham-Pye;
> Ridotta sips and dances, till she see
> The doubling Lustres dance as fast as she;
> F—— loves the Senate, Hockley-Hole his Brother
> Like in all else, as one Egg to another.
> I love to pour out all myself, as plain
> As downright Shippen, or as old Montagne.   (45-52)

Here, as at the beginning of the satire, we can see Pope turning
Horace's claim that satire is harmlessly natural into a defence
of it as socially necessary. By caricaturing the activities of
others and stressing the virtue of his own activities he makes
the residual parallelism less important than the distinction.

The same changes bear on Pope's rendering of Horace's
second line of argument — that he follows Lucilius in his taste
for satire and in having the protection of the great men of the
time. The relation of this second defence to the first, described
above, is delicately but effectively tampered with.

Horace's argument (ll. 24-34) may be divided into four
stages:

(a) everybody pursues different objects;
(b) I choose to follow Lucilius in writing satire;
(c) Lucilius put his whole personality into his books;
(d) they have real integrity, and that is why I choose
to follow him in literary warfare.

As presented by Horace, b is related to a as particular illustration to general rule: Horace's satire is yet another example of
the variety of human pursuits — this relationship being empha-
sised by the antithetical placing of "Millia: me." On the other
hand, c is not a direct consequence of b, but develops the idea
of nostrum melioris utroque, which Pope does not translate.

In Pope, the same arguments appear in the same order;
however, as I have already indicated, a is more isolated from
b than in Horace. In mere terms of punctuation we should notice
that the only major pause in the passage occurs after a (at the
end of l. 50), whereas in Horace the major pause comes after
b (at the end of l. 29). Not only in Pope's punctuation, but also
in his sense, b finds its closest tie with c and d in a process
of argument which might be paraphrased: these old writers told

everything; they had real integrity. I too tell everything, and
if this reveals my faults, at least it proves my integrity at the
same time; I intend to use this to publish the present age. If
we wish to fit a into this framework, we find it easiest to assume that Ridotta, F[ox], etc., are what the satirist sees — his
justification for being a satirist — and this view is strengthened
by the fact that Pope consistently degrades the examples he
takes over. Ridotta not only dances but also sips, and there is
some doubt whether the doubling of the lustres is more due to
giddiness or alcohol; in translating the innocent lines,

> Castor gaudet equis; OVO PROGNATUS EODEM
> Pugnis: . . .   (26-7)

Pope has infused all the contempt he can into ovo, and ignored
its perfectly legitimate original meaning.

Pope is concerned, in fact, with a different kind of defence,
based on his sense of personal integrity. This he elicits from
the text of Horace by avoiding the complicated description of
Lucilius's methods and reintroducing himself as quickly as possible as the focal figure:

> I love to pour out all myself, as plain
> As downright Shippen, or as old Montagne.
> In them, as certain to be lov'd as seen,
> The Soul stood forth, nor kept a Thought within;
> In me what Spots (for Spots I have) appear, . . . (51-5)

Shippen and Montaigne, who here replace Lucilius, are unlike
Lucilius in that there are two of them, dissimilar to one another and both only vaguely related to Pope and his practice; all
this keeps them from overshadowing Pope. Their qualities are
only analogous, not at all explanatory; in consequence, there
is no need for a sequor hunc (i.e. Lucilius) to justify the reintroduction of the author, as we find it in the original:

> . . . me pedibus delectat claudere verba
> Lucili ritu, nostrum melioris utroque.
> Ille, velut fidis arcana sodalibus olim
> Credebat libris; neque si male gesserat, usquam
> Decurrens alio, neque si bene: aquo fit ut omnis

> Votiva pateat veluti descripta tabella
> Vita senis; sequor hunc, . . .   (28-34)

The serious use of past example to justify present satiric
writing has in fact disappeared. If Pope had been really anxious
to "imitate" Horace's use of Lucilius he could easily have found
a modern parallel in Dryden (as Rochester had done in his "Allusion to Horace, the 10th Satyre of the 1st Book"); that there
was no lack of Popian anticipation in Dryden's career, the "parallel" attached to the Dunciad makes obvious. But Pope wishes
to define the satirist as an individual engaged in a personal
moral struggle, whose integrity depends indeed on the fact that
it is a struggle of individual persons. Hence he chooses not to
appear as the follower of another satirist, for that would reduce the personal tension. What Horace attributes to Lucilius,
Pope blatantly arrogates to himself; the change might be taken
as simply indicative of pride, but in fact it is necessary to the
whole philosophy of satire that Pope is presenting. If there is
pride here it is the proper pride of the satirist, which finds its
most famous expression in:

> Yes, I am proud; I must be proud to see
> Men not afraid of God, afraid of me.

> ("Epilogue to the Satires," Dialogue II, 208-9)

Horace praises Lucilius for his integrity as a person, his
refusal to dress up his writings, their religious fidelity to his
personal opinions. Pope gives himself the same praise, but
for different reasons. It is not as a man that he is claiming
virtue, but in terms of his office as a satirist, so that Lucilius's
integrity becomes impartiality (this impartial glass) and the
failings of the man are mentioned only because they guarantee
the office and the satire. The fact that the old man's writings
exposed his life is a good in itself for Horace (he wasn't a dishonest person, and his saturae give an uncensored and uninhib-
ited picture of life), but in Pope the self-exposure is only one
stage in the process of writing satire:

> In this impartial Glass, my Muse intends
> Fair to expose myself, my Foes, my Friends;

THE "ROMANTICISM" OF POPE'S HORACE

> Publish the present Age, but where my Text
> Is Vice too high, reserve it for the next . . .   (57-60)

This development of the theme of personal integrity (or impartiality) leads Pope from his text towards his unHoratian but central defence of the satirist who is seen set up against or even above an overt social order,

> Safe from the Bar, the Pulpit, and the Throne,
> Yet touch'd and sham'd by Ridicule alone.
>
> ("Epilogue," Dialogue II, 210-11)

This is the centre of Pope's defence of satire, as certainly in this Imitation as in the second dialogue of the "Epilogue to the Satires." The last fifty lines of the Imitation make the point again and again, and it is significant, I think, that Pope treats his original much more freely here than anywhere else in the poem. In a letter to Swift dated 16 February 1732/3 Pope speaks of ". . . a Parody from Horace, writ in two mornings . . . in truth my own single motive was about a score of lines towards the latter end, which you will find out" (Sherburn, III, 348); it is difficult for the reader of today to find exactly which "score of lines" is intended, but obviously ll. 105-40 is the general area of reference, and this is just the passage in which the un-Horatian virtue of embattled satiric independence is most clearly celebrated.

For Horace the satirist stands in the shadow of his patrons; their approval is a guarantee of his integrity (the gap between Greatness and Goodness is not a subject he is prepared to exploit; they applaud when he attacks either Metellus, their adversary, or the morally vicious Lupus, for their virtue is untouched — enhanced even -- by the attack.) Pope is no less proud of his aristocratic connections:

> Envy must own, I live among the Great, . . .   (133)

but he is even more proud of his own independence:

> No Pimp of Pleasure, and no Spy of State, . . .   (134)

Horace also treasures his independence, but it is with him a more humble and less strident condition. He expects maiorum . . . quis amicus to allow him his satiric tastes, but knows very well that tact, good humour and genuine humility are a condition of this. He declares that he is (or rather that Lucilius was)

> Scilicet UNI AEQUUS VIRTUTI ATQUE EJUS
> AMICIS.   (70)

but this is not for him a banner in any warfare against the Establishment (the capitals are Pope's), since Goodness and Greatness are not conceived as incompatible or even as opposed. The office of satirist is not allowed to take the poet outside the social obligations of friendship and dependence; the Primores populi who are said to be among his victims are lay-figures, especially when seen against the passionately apprehended courtiers of Pope's imagination. Pope, on the other hand, is concerned to stress the independence of even his "great" friends from any kind of Establishment:

> . . . the best Companions . . .
> Chiefs, out of war, and Statesmen, out of place.
>
> (125-6)

where Horace has only

> ubi se a Vulgo et Scena, in Secreta remorant . . .
>
> (71)

-- that is, Scipio and Laelius do not have to become enemies of the Establishment in Horace in order to achieve friendship with satirists. It is worth nothing that Pope is the host in his retreat, whereas Lucilius was only a playmate to these relaxing statesmen. For Pope the integrity of satire is best guaranteed by the isolation of the satirist, by his sensibility to wrong wherever it occurs, and by his fearless independence of speech:

THE "ROMANTICISM" OF POPE'S HORACE

> Scriblers or Peers, alike are Mob to me.   (140)

Pope does not ask patrons to approve only when others are attacked; he expects their greatness to emerge in their tolerance
of virtuous and independent criticism even when they themselves
are the objects of it; the satirist has a public function to perform, and friendship must find room for its demands; here,
where the official critics are most liable to fail, satiric ruth-
lessness is most necessary:

> Can there be wanting to defend Her Cause,
> Lights of the Church, or Guardians of the Laws?

(Clearly this is a type of question expecting the answer, "Yes".)

> Could pension'd Boileau lash in honest Strain
> Flatt'rers and Bigots ev'n in Louis' Reign?
> Could Laureate Dryden Pimp and Fry'r engage,
> Yet neither Charles nor James be in a Rage?
> And I not strip the Gilding off a Knave,
> Unplac'd, un-pension'd, no Man's Heir, or Slave?
> I will, or perish in the gen'rous Cause.
> Hear this, and tremble! you, who 'scape the Laws.

>   (109-18)

Horace identifies himself largely with the social order (though
he always keeps a final layer of irony in reserve): virtue for
him is really built into the system. The praise he gives to
Augustus is therefore genuine and serious. Pope, however, invariably renders Latin encomium of the Emperor by English
mock-encomium; the whole "Epistle to Augustus" is, of course,
built on this basis. The present poem treats Trebatius's serious advice to write poems in praise of the sovereign and his
prowess in war as follows:

> Or if you needs must write, write CAESAR's Praise:
> You'll gain at least a Knighthood, or the Bays.
>   P. What? like Sir Richard, rumbling, rough and fierce,
> With ARMS, and GEORGE, and BRUNSWICK crowd
>   the Verse?

> Rend with tremendous Sound your ears asunder,
> With Gun, Drum, Trumpet, Blunderbuss & Thunder?
> Or nobly wild, with Budgell's Fire and Force,
> Paint Angels trembling round his falling Horse?

And his fortitude and justice as follows:

> Then all your Muse's softer Art display,
> Let Carolina smooth the tuneful Lay,
> Lull with Amelia's liquid Name the Nine,
> And sweetly flow through all the Royal Line.   (21-32)

What in Horace were things — real wars and real valour — are rendered in Pope by merely flattering images and sounds: heroic becomes mock-heroic; Virgil is reduced to Blackmore; the obviousness of the noisy rhetorical effects is used to indicate the shallowness of the poetic attitudes.

The Law is again something that Horace acknowledges as above him and, relating back to Caesar as it does, something whose rightness has a divine sanction. The difference in Pope's attitude is nicely illustrated by the changes at the end of the poem. Trebatius tells Horace that a satirist is in danger; the Sacred Laws condemn mala carmina. With light irony Horace turns the charge away from himself by reinterpreting mala carmina as "badly-written verses," for there he knows he is not liable. In Pope, the irony (as usual) is turned away from the poet towards the framework of institutions; the laws are liable to condemn satires, not because the laws are right, but because of malpractice and the obscurantism of legal method:

> F. Your Plea is good. But still I say, beware!
> Laws are explain'd by Men — so have a care.
> It stands on record, that in Richard's Times
> A Man was hang'd for very honest Rhymes.
> Consult the Statute: quart. I think it is,
> Edwardi Sext. or prim. & quint. Eliz: . . .   (143-8)

As elsewhere, we see the satirist set against and above "the Bar, the Pulpit, and the Throne," and these being pinpointed poetically by the harsh and crabbed legal diction. The social system which Pope, unlike Horace, cannot quite accept,

requires for its own health that the satirist should be free of
everything but his own sensibility.

The Horatian "Augustanism" of this satire is, in fact, a
fine classical façade behind which, as so often in the period,
there shelters a life far from poised, equable and objective.
The façade is a fair sign of what the English Augustans desired,
but not of what they were. We find throughout the Imitations a
desire for peace, calm, solidarity, tradition, but no serene
assurance of support from these things. Instead the main support for Pope's point of view would seem to be the injured
Byronic sensibility of the individual. Byron, of course, uses
his sense of isolation to dramatise himself, and gives us no
reason to think about the good society; Pope, on the other hand,
is concerned to dramatise himself in relation to the good society. It is true also that the line Dryden-Pope-Byron represents
a gradual descent from the standpoint of public conscience, but
it is a false antithesis which lumps Dryden and Pope together
and sets them against the Romantic attitude in Byron (cf. J. D.
Jump in Pelican History of English Literature, V 254), since
Pope shares attitudes with Byron as well as with Dryden. I
think Pope still genuinely believed, as the Romantics hardly did,
that the traditional social order, like the "kinds" in poetry,
was divinely decreed or metaphysically justified -- hence the
care he lavished on the classical façade. At the same time,
however, if his deviations from Horace may be considered adequate evidence, he believed that the Frame of Order should not
be accepted passively; it requires its martyrs and witnesses
to demonstrate against any betrayal of standards, wherever
this is found, in the Establishment or out of it; and for Pope
the basis of this witness must always be the individual sensibility of the poet, which gives him access to truths which are concealed from others by the disorders of real life. To pursue the
Augustan virtues in the age of George II is, in fact, to set up
a contrast of ideals and realities very like that of the Romantics.
Pope certainly did not believe in any kind of individualistic,
historically conditioned or relativist ethic; yet he did see the
individual sensibility as the only place where genuine moral or
critical judgments could be made. His belief in objective standards of right and wrong, descending in coherent and unmodified
traditions from the classical world into his own age, included
an awareness that these standards (or rules), "discovered, not

devised," only come alive when the individual rediscovers them for himself, and then re-embodies them in something like "that unequalled fire and rapture which is so forcible in Homer." For Pope, in short, poetic objectivity depends on the quality of the poet's subjective response, which carries him from particular to general:

> God loves from Whole to Parts: but human soul
> Must rise from Individual to the Whole.

> (Essay on Man, IV. 361-2)

His Augustanism functioned in perspectives which have come to seem the exclusive property of the Romantic poets.

NOTE

1 My texts, of both Pope, and Horace, are taken from Professor Butt's "Twickenham" edition. I have tried to indicate passages in Pope's Imitation for which I find no warrant in the original by underscoring.

POPE AND THE SATIRIC ADVERSARY

John M. Aden

> Quisquis es, o modo quem ex adverso dicere feci.
>
> Persius, Satire I

A little used and less noted device of Pope's formal satire is the adversarius, or interlocutor of the satiric dialogue. Though neither Pope nor his Roman predecessors made extensive use of the device, its advantages proved considerable, especially in the rhetorical design of the satire, and especially for Pope, who capitalized these advantages beyond the example of his models. The dialogue permits an enlivening of the satiric discourse, a diversification of style, tone, and statement; promotes dramatic immediacy; and affords at least the appearance of objectivity. Where the interlocutor is friendly, the poet benefits by the presence of a second satirist on the scene. Where he is antagonistic, he furnishes concrete evidence of the satirist's provocation and specific justification of his contention, difficile est satiram non scribere. When corruption is added to antagonism, the adversary provides the satirist an especially effective means of establishing the ethical proof so important to his rhetorical purposes, enhancing, by the contrast he makes, the image of the satirist as vir bonus, manifestly superior to the dull, vicious, or naive fellow contending with him.

Some account of the use of this formula in the Roman satura will help to further its definition and provide a context in which Pope's performance can be measured and appreciated.[1] Horace, who used it more than any other, used it little. Of his eighteen satires (sermones), only five, or something less than a third, are dialogues between Horace and a specific, participating interlocutor or adversary: II.i (Trebatius), II.iii (Damasippus), II.iv (Catius), II.vii (Davus), and II.viii (Fundanius). Satire II.v is a dialogue, to be sure, but between Ulysses and Tiresias,

Reprinted from Studies in English Literature, Vol. 2 (1962), pp. 267-286, by permission of author and publisher.

and the satirist is not involved except as creator of the fictional conversation. The fact that with one exception (I. ix. Ibam forte via Sacra) Horace employed no dialogue (and hence no adversary) until his second book is interesting, suggesting as it does his own late recognition of the possibilities of the form. Even I. ix is not fundamentally a dialogue, but rather the report of a dialogue between the persecuted satirist and a bore who has cornered him. The dramatic immediacy of the piece is undercut by its narrative frame in the imperfect tense. But Horace had caught the idea, and continued to experiment with it in the second book.

In II. i he conceives, in Trebatius, a brilliant example of the friendly adversary, in this case a close-mouthed, discreet, and somewhat cynical professional advisor, who, though opposing the satirist, does so for his own good. In II. iii he hits upon the device of using a more vulnerable adversary. Damasippus, the chap who had found salvation in Stoicism and wanted Horace to benefit by the same. But, as happens in almost all Horace's remaining examples, the dialogue machinery barely manages to sustain itself, for Damasippus dominates the discourse and delivers a long Stoic lecture repeated from his master Stertinius. Much the same thing happens in II. iv, for example, where Catius, the Epicurean, is allowed to dominate the satire with an extended monologue on the gastronomic niceties of the day. In II. vii the dialogue is with Davus, Horace's slave, who is given his master's permission to speak out on the occasion of the Saturnalia. Here the interlocutor more nearly approximates the hostility implied in the term adversary, but the pattern of interior monologue emerging from the conversational frame recurs and perseveres in II. viii, where Fundanius, a friendly adversary (if an adversary at all, in any real sense of the word), reports to Horace the absurdities of a dinner party (cena) given by Nasidienus Rufus. Dialogue has only token existence, Horace merely leading his friend out to tell about the banquet, for which purpose he takes only nine of the ninety-five lines of the poem.

Of Horace's examples, thus, only three present a clear-cut adversary, those involving Trebatius, Damasippus, and Davus; and of these only Davus is overtly hostile. Damasippus turns the charge of madness against Horace only in his last brief speech, and Trebatius is friend and mentor, who opposes the satirist out of concern for his welfare (or, as it may be, out of his cynical indifference to the satirist's crusade). Furthermore, Horace's practice furnishes only one example (II. i) of a genuinely sustained dialogue, his formula tending toward the monologic structure most characteristic of Roman satire. Horace's normal procedure is by means of brief opening dialogue to trigger a protracted monologue on the part of the adversary, whom, when he has overextended himself, Horace trips up or rebuffs in a tidy and quickly dispatched resumption of dialogue.

Juvenal is even less disposed than Horace to dialogue structure. Of his sixteen satires, only two (or about an eighth) involve the presence of a second person on the satiric scene — the Third and the Ninth — and of these the former scarcely qualifies as a dialogue. Juvenal's temperament, so much more positive than Horace's, was not the kind to tolerate much experimentation with ironic modes and techniques. Even III, as I have said, is not a true dialogue, though two persons are involved, for the satirist merely reports what his friend Umbricius said to him on the occasion of his leaving the ignoble strife of Rome. Once Umbricius's speech begins, at line 21, the satire reverts to a monologue of 300 lines. Satire IX is a genuine dialogue, the satirist speaking four times and at intervals throughout the poem, but it does not involve an adversary, for Naevolus is a suppliant, seeking a shoulder to cry on and a way out of his predicament.

Persius is the only one of the three great Roman satirists to employ an adversary between whom and the satirist there exists genuine tension or opposition, and he is the only one to make his adversary notably naive or intellectually corrupt. Persius, it is plain, is much more strongly disposed toward dialogue than either Horace or Juvenal, for though only two of his six satires exhibit a definite participating adversary (I and III), nearly all of them strain in that direction, making greater use of what I may call a nonce or purely rhetorical adversary than either his predecessor or his successor.

In I Persius pits himself against a defender of the effete and decadent literary taste of the day, a fellow who by his protests in behalf of the new mode and against the manly and satiric bent of the old, furnishes the satirist the targets against which to let fly his arrows of disdain and rebuke. At the same time, the adversary affords the satirist manifest proof to his

audience that he (the satirist) is not merely shadow-boxing
when he registers his complaints against the corrupt modern:
ecce homo. Satire I is a sustained dialogue, with the satirist
matching speech for speech his adversary, and the tone of annoyance and disapproval is pronounced throughout. In Satire III,
however, Persius also regresses in the direction of monologue,
dominating the discourse with the young derelict who is his adversary and eventually delivering a lecture to the slugabed,
who is permitted to speak only long enough to reveal his indis-
position to get up of a morning and force himself into any worth-
while activity.

Persius strengthens the image and function of both roles
in the dialogue, that of the satirist in terms of his more nearly
equal participation in the conversation and his more caustic
attitude and speech, and that of the adversary in terms of his
more noticeable antagonism or culpability. In these respects
Pope more nearly resembles him than he does either Horace,
whom he ostensibly imitates, or Juvenal, with whom he has
very little in common at all. Like Persius, Pope keeps dialogue
distinct, consistently sets the interlocutor at odds with himself
(if sometimes only apparently so), makes capital of the corrupt adversary, manifests a spirit of impatience or contempt,
and speaks with a bitter tongue. But he learned much from
Horace too, especially in the uses of the friendly adversary
and in the strategy of irony. Only occasionally does he rise to
the genus grande of Juvenalian style, though when he does it
is powerful indeed. But in respect to dialogue Juvenal had
nothing to contribute.

Quantitatively, Pope's use of the dialogue-adversary technique is about par with the Roman. Exclusive of the odes (IV. i
and ix) and the Ethic Epistles, and including those poems
"Something like Horace," Pope's Horatian poems – which is to
say, his formal verse satires – number thirteen. Of these,
four, or about one third, employ dialogue with participating
adversary: The First Satire of the Second Book of Horace,
Imitated (Feb. 1732/3), An Epistle from Mr. Pope to Dr. Arbuthnot (Jan. 1734/5), and the two dialogues of the Epilogue to
the Satires (May and July, 1738).

Pope's first dialogue was an imitation of Horace, composed
in "two mornings,"[2] when he was confined in early 1732/3 with
a fever: ". . . Lord Bolingbroke, who came to see me, happened

to take up a Horace that lay on the table; and in turning it over, dipped on the first satire of the second book, which begins Sunt quibus in satirâ, &c. He observed, how well that would hit my case, if I were to imitate it in English."[3] The adversary Pope imitated in that satire was Trebatius, "one of the most considerable lawyers of his time,"[4] a terse and unillusioned advisor to the satirist, whose problem was what to do about the complaints leveled against his satire. To the satirist's "quid faciam," Trebatius replies with professional brevity: "Quiescas." He is even less vocal to Horace's next question. You mean give up all verse? asks Horace. "Aio." If Horace is sleepless, let him oil himself, swim thrice across the Tiber, and meet the night with plentiful wine. If he must write, let him celebrate Caesar. When Trebatius adds, "multa laborum / praemia laturus," it is hard to say whether he is venturing a sly joke or speaking quite soberly. Upon Horace's observation that it is not easy to gain the ear of Caesar, Trebatius remarks that even so it is better to try than to go about offending Pantolabus and Nomentanus or exciting hostility generally. To Horace's insistence that he is provoked and that, come what may, he must write, Trebatius counters, perhaps with a show of sardonic humor, My boy, you will die young! Some great one will deal you a killing frost. When Horace appeals to the example of Lucilius, Trebatius merely reminds him that there are laws against libel. But, pleads Horace, if the verses be good, if Caesar approve, if the provocation be just and the satirist blameless? Why then, concludes Trebatius, "Solventur risu tabulae, tu missus abibis."

Trebatius is a good lawyer, wise in the ways of the world, and perhaps uncommonly close-mouthed for his profession. His contribution to the dialogue is, unlike that of most of Horace's interlocutors, slight, amounting to about seventeen of the satire's eighty-six verses. His remarks are not devoid of humor of a wry kind, but they are never playful, and their humor arises more from the chance of what is said than from any design on the part of the speaker to be witty. Trebatius is a kind of cynical eiron, a foil to the alazoneia of the eager satirist. He is one of Horace's subtlest adversaries, serving not only in the end to "authorize" Horace's satire, but in the course of the poem to intensify its indictment by juxtaposing to Horace's idealistic principle his own expedient one.

In his adaptation Pope retains the cautionary character of

Trebatius, but puts the adversary more in key with himself: witty, sympathetic, and, at heart, as much satirically inclined as the satirist. Pope's Fortescue[5] is more personable and lively than Trebatius, and a somewhat more talkative advisor. He speaks some thirty-four and a half of Pope's 156 verses, or something over a fourth of the whole. The difference is not great, but one is sensible of it. The real change, however, is in the personality and attitude of the speaker.

Fortescue begins almost as tersely as Trebatius (as much as the difference in languages would allow), pronouncing to the Roman's Quiescas, "I'd write no more." But then, unlike Trebatius, he warms to the problem and becomes witty in his answers where the Roman was matter-of-fact. If Pope is sleepless and if fools rush into his head, he could nevertheless do nothing worse than to write:

> Why, if the Nights seem tedious — take a Wife;
> Or rather truly, if your Point be Rest,
> Lettuce and Cowslip Wine; Probatum est.
> But talk with Celsus, Celsus will advise
> Hartshorn, or something that shall close your Eyes.[6]

By comparison with Trebatius's essentially sober advice, this is a tissue of witticism and bawdy, and refuses to take the question of the satirist (quid faciam?) quite seriously, perhaps because it recognizes that the satirist himself is not quite serious. It jests on the use of wives for sleeplessness, and, almost certainly, on the poet's obvious lack of qualification for that remedy. It then wittily turns on that jest and breaks another upon it — that, on second thought, a wife may not be the best remedy for restlessness after all. A sleeping potion then! Professor Butt reminds us of the anaphrodisiac properties of lettuce and of the likelihood of whimsicality in the prescription of hartshorn, a stimulant rather than a soporific.[7]

When he comes to Trebatius's advice, Write of Caesar, at which the Roman may have winked in multa laborum / praemia laturus, Fortescue spells out the ludicrous possibilities: "You'll gain at least a Knighthood, or the Bays." In the time of a Walpole and a Cibber, neither of these rewards could be taken seriously (even if Pope were not a Catholic) and in suggesting them Fortescue is given another function Horace did not confer

upon Trebatius, viz. , that of fellow satirist. While he pretends
to counsel discretion, Fortescue joins in the game and helps to
score the "enemy," not only here, but in his next suggestion:

> Then all your Muse's softer Art display,
> Let Carolina smooth the tuneful Lay,
> Lull with Amelia's liquid Name the Nine,
> And sweetly flow through all the Royal Line.

A vein of irony and ridicule runs through this advice, which is
all but open in its contempt for the royal household. Such audacity was scarcely available to Horace, even had he been inclined
to it. As for Trebatius, he was incapable of it, either by temperament or by policy.

Even when he tries to be earnest, Fortescue cannot resist
slyness: "Better be Cibber, I'll maintain it still, / Than ridicule all Taste, blaspheme Quadrille" (37-38). Here he alludes
to Pope's Epistle to Burlington and Epistle to Bathurst, which,
he suggests, obviously with tongue in cheek, it is better to
forego and follow instead the insipid panegyrism of Laureate
Cibber. By now, too, it becomes apparent that Fortescue is
consistently naming the names he advises his friend to avoid.
He continues to do so in his next comment, which is, at the
same time, the most nearly serious statement he makes in the
entire dialogue:

> A hundred smart in Timon and in Balaam:
> The fewer still you name, you wound the more;
> Bond is but one, but Harpax is a Score.   (42-44)

Nor should it escape notice that in the reference to Timon,
Fortescue is obliquely countering the charge that by that character the poet meant the Duke of Chandos. Fortescue is adversary in name only; he is in reality the poet's ally, and we see
him progress from Pope's counsellor to his advocate to his
fellow satirist.

When Pope, like Horace, says, "I will Rhyme and Print"
(Horace had said only scribam),[8] Fortescue almost translates
Trebatius: "Alas, young Man! your Days can ne'r be long," but
then he lapses into his facetious mood again: "In Flow'r of Age
you perish for a Song." Where Trebatius let the jest, if it were

a jest, go with "O puer," Fortescue, having said "young man," instantly perceives that he speaks to a friend nearly forty-five years old, and so corrects himself with a witty play on the cliché "flower of youth," and perhaps a pleasantry at his friend's expense as well. Unlike Trebatius, he will specify the potential enemies and continue his contribution to the satire he pretends to decry: "Plums, and Directors, Shylock and his wife, / Will club their Testers, now, to take your Life!" To Pope's plea about provocation, virtue, and friendship with the great, Fortescue explains: "Your Plea is good. But still I say, beware! Laws are explain'd by Men — so have a care." Trebatius had merely called attention to the existence of the law. Fortescue remembers the jurists, who, he would seem to say, are more crucial to the issue than the laws. He continues:

> It stands on record, that in Richard's Time
> A Man was hang'd for very honest Rhymes.
> Consult the Statute: quart. I think it is,
> Edwardi Sext. or prim. & quint. Eliz:
> See Libels, Satires — here you have it — read. (145-149)

Several things are noteworthy about this. For one thing, Fortescue gives us a glimpse of himself as a professional man in a way that Trebatius does not. He knows the cases, the statutes at least he can make a good show at ransacking his memory and his books. He is, in other words, more real than Trebatius because more circumstantial in his self-display. And Fortescue displays his legal skill, his rhetorical subtlety in word play, as in the case of honest, which, though it seems to concede the point of criminal frankness associated with satire, at the same time asserts the ideas of virtue, uprightness, and sincerity. But even more important in the economy of the poem is the suggestion which this speech affords of the setting which Miss Randolph reminds us lurks somewhere in the background of the typical satura, though Horace's poem seems to lack it.[9] The advantage in Pope's case is considerable, placing as it does the satirist and his respected interlocutor on a familiar, easy, and dignified footing. Fortescue has a book in hand, opens it to the appropriate places, hands it to his friend to read for himself. From this arises a distinct impression of scene — the only one in the poem, though it reaches back at once and gathers in the rest of the dialogue — and the reassurances, both dramatic and ethical, which that promotes. It is as if poet and friend are come together in the friend's chambers or study, talk with the intimacy and frankness of witty companions, handle the books that surround them, and enjoy a problem and a jest together. The effect is to make seem private, and hence more candid, what is, in actuality, quite public.

The poet will leave this scene with good advice, but with something more important even than that. Fortescue's last speech, dismissing the case, is in Trebatius's low key, but adds a significant point. To Horace's proposal of a hypothetically justified case of satire, Trebatius says only that the satirist might expect to have a case against him dismissed. Fortescue tells his poet, "you may then proceed."[10] He does more than exonerate the satirist; he gives him his blessing to continue his work.

Pope has heightened and complicated the adversary he borrowed from Horace. His Fortescue enlivens the dialogue with his own wit, contributes more or less openly to the satire he purports to warn against, defines himself as a personality, provides an effective suggestion of setting, and, at the last, renders an opinion that doesn't just get the satirist off, but that encourages him to get on — with his work. Horace pits himself against a stubborn adversary and wrings from him a concession at best; Pope recruits a partisan, who shares his ideals, adds the force of his reputation and wit into the bargain, and sanctions his perseverance in the cause. Pope's adversary has, without sacrificing any of the tensional value of Horace's become a powerful ally. Like Arbuthnot, Fortescue stands revealed, despite his pose, "To Virtue only and Her Friends, a Friend."

I include the Epistle to Arbuthnot among the poems employing an adversary because, even though as originally published no adversary was identified, I believe a case can be made for Warburton's procedure in giving some of the speeches to Arbuthnot in the 1751 edition of the Works.[11] Normally, it is true, the epistle, as a form, does not employ an interlocutor, that presumably being a contradiction in terms. According to Acron, epistulis ad absentes loquimur, sermone cum praesentibus.[12] None of Horace's Epistles admits a participating adversary, though they often create, within the framework of the epistle,

what I have called a <u>nonce</u> adversary, for the purpose of rhetorical question and <u>answer</u>.[13] In Pope such a nonce adversary
is very common, and what no doubt began as such in Pope's
original wrestling with the poem may have given way to the introduction of his correspondent as, in effect, a present or participating adversary. What more likely happened is that Pope
felt the attraction of both forms, the epistle and the dialogue,
and admitted a confusion of form into his poem. Not that the result is damaging, for I cannot agree with Professor Butt that
the shift to dialogue is "a change for the worse," though it admittedly introduces a contradiction in technical point of view
that is somewhat troublesome. Theoretically, an epistle, being
a monologue, cannot be a dialogue. The fact remains that Pope
seems to have made it not only possible, but successful.

Partly, one supposes, by virtue of Pope's hesitancy in the
decision, partly by virtue of the quantitatively small part assigned the adversary (Arbuthnot speaks only thirteen and one
half of the poem's 419 verses), Pope's second interlocutor does
not achieve the reality status of his first, remaining on the
whole, rather like Trebatius, a disembodied voice. But he is
not left entirely so, for he alludes at least to his height ("I too
could write, and I am twice as tall") and thus achieves some
status as an image. The relative shadowiness of figure is amply
compensated for, however, by the adversary's trenchancy and
audacity, which are quite enough to bring him alive and to distinguish him from the abstracter nonce adversary. Pope must
have realized all along the value of having Arbuthnot on the
scene, having his own say rather than merely serving as a
puppet for Pope's ventriloquism, for the former is precisely
the impression the speeches eventually assigned to Arbuthnot
make, that of a present interlocutor, reasoning, sympathizing,
and ultimately collaborating with the poet.

When the adversary speaks, he does so as the anxious
friend, solicitous of the satirist's well-being. He exhibits none
of Fortescue's facetiousness or playfulness, but when he lends
himself, like Fortescue, to the very cause he decries, he does
so with an edge not found in the speech of the earlier adversary.
His first remark is in reply to the satirist's question whether,
like Midas's Queen, he must not speak out:

"Good friend forbear! you deal in dang'rous things,

POPE AND THE SATIRIC ADVERSARY

>"I'd never name Queens, Ministers, or Kings;
>"Keep close to Ears, and those let Asses prick,
>"Tis nothing" . . .   (75-78)

The advice is good, and it is urged sincerely, but it has a sting
too and a daring innuendo — "Keep close to Ears, and those let
Asses prick." One recalls that it was "Midas, a sacred Person
and a King," who had the ass's ears, and he realizes that it is
unnecessary to await an Epistle to Augustus to see a satirist
bite his thumb at a George Augustus. The satirist is shrewd
enough in this instance, however, to let a great and respected
public figure and friend do the biting for him. "Tis nothing,"
incidentally, is finely ambiguous and teasing, and ought not to
go unnoticed.

The adversary's next interruption is a warning against the
use of personal names and a reminder that the satirist is physically vulnerable to retaliation:

>   . . . "Hold! for God-sake — you'll offend:
>"No Names — be calm — learn Prudence of a Friend:
>"I too could write, and I am twice as tall,
>"But Foes like these!". . .   (101-104)[14]

Again good advice followed by the advisor's own stroke, scarcely disguised, for the foes are the names Pope has just mentioned: Colly, Henley, Moor [James Moore-Smythe], Phillips,
and Sapho; and "like these" admits of indefinite construction
along unflattering lines. When he advises prudence, moreover,
Arbuthnot is doing what every friendly adversary does, that is,
more than he reckons; for he is not only counselling wisdom,
but in so doing, providing a mark by which the satirist's superiority to convenience may be measured.

When Sporus is mentioned the adversary cannot suppress
his contempt, and his advice to let Sporus alone is itself an
attack upon him: "What? that Thing of silk, / Sporus, that
mere white Curd of Ass's milk? / Satire or Sense alas! can
Sporus feel? / Who breaks a butterfly upon a Wheel?" By
means of his adversary Pope can have it both ways, can express
the feeling that Hervey is beneath contempt and yet pile on him
all the same, all the while gaining the sanction of an Arbuthnot.

Two further interjections by the adversary are quite brief,

and function merely to provide the needed questions: "But why insult the Poor, affront the Great?" (v. 360), enabling the poet to proclaim "A Knave's a Knave, to me, in ev'ry State"; and a final question, "What Fortune, pray?" (v. 390), enabling the poet to distinguish the means of his family from the ill-gotten gains of others.

Whether the concluding couplet of the poem belongs to Arbuthnot or to Pope must remain a conjecture. Warburton assigned it to Arbuthnot, and it is certainly more effective as his than as Pope's, but lacking quotation marks in any of the editions Pope sponsored, they cannot with the same confidence be assigned to him. As Arbuthnot's they would show the adversary persuaded by the satirist's argument and in effect, like Fortescue, endorsing it, proclaiming, moreover, that ultimate judgment of the poet belongs to Heaven, not to his enemies: "Whether that Blessing be deny'd, or giv'n, / Thus far was right, the rest belongs to Heaven."[15]

In some respects Pope's second adversary retains the character and functions of his first: both are friendly adversaries, opposing the satirist for his own good; both participate in the satire while ostensibly opposing it; and both (if the last couplet of the Epistle does belong to Arbuthnot) pronounce an exoneration of the satirist. But in other respects Arbuthnot differs from Fortescue, and one is left with the impression of unique personality in Pope's friendly adversaries. Gone now is the facetiousness of Fortescue, his witty jibes at the common foe, his easy rapport with the satirist, and in its place is a bluntness, a sarcasm, and a fierceness matching that of the satirist himself. This is partly the effect, as I have suggested, of his being Arbuthnot rather than Fortescue. But it must be acknowledged an effect too of a reflex in Pope's technique with the friendly adversary, for what has happened is that the adversary has changed character along with the satirist. The friendly adversary in Pope is partly an alter ego. What really changes is the satirist, and the adversary is accommodated to the change. Pope is now more tart, more indignant — more himself and less Horatian — than he was in the Imitation, and the adversary reflects this shift in point of view. In both poems the adversary works with and for the poet, but how he does so is dictated partly by his identity as a person, partly by the satirist's peculiar disposition in each poem. As far as this affects the Epistle to Arbuthnot, it may provide additional explanation of the reduced scale of the adversary's participation. Pope is rather too heated on this occasion to allow his adversary much intervention. When he does admit him, though, he has him lay about to good and solid effect.

Pope's final, and consummate, experiment with the adversary occurs in the two dialogues of the Epilogue to the Satires, both composed and published in the spring and summer of 1738. In these poems he makes the adversary a genuinely hostile figure, introduces a new dimension of irony, and translates the interlocutor into a symbol of the whole satiric indictment.

Dialogue I (originally titled One Thousand Seven Hundred and Thirty Eight. A Dialogue Something like Horace) is essentially an ironic structure in which Pope permits a corrupt adversary to dissuade (or seem to dissuade) him from a defense of satire and to talk (or seem to talk) him into an ostensible defense of Vice. The relation of the poet to the adversary is thus unique in this poem, both with respect to Pope's earlier and his later practice. In the Imitation (Satire II. i) Pope, following Horace, contended with his adversary, who, unlike Horace's, did not really want to dissuade the satirist anyway. In the Arbuthnot, though the adversary was more earnest in his efforts to dissuade, he was at the same time more ready to give vent to strong satire himself. In the second dialogue of the Epilogue, satirist and adversary are at genuine sixes and sevens.

The difference is made to arise, properly enough, from the character conferred upon the several adversaries. In the earlier defenses the adversary was actually friendly to the poet, intelligent, and, if shrewd, nonetheless honest. In Dialogue I the adversary, who is not on Pope's side at all, but a true adversary, a symbol of Pope's hostile public and a spokesman for its corrupt principles, is neither friendly, intelligent, nor honest. He is instead somewhat foppish (a Sir Courtly Wit) and presumptuous,[16] a good deal vicious, and not a little stupid: an epitome of the corruption he speaks for. Such a creature has the traits of a true alazon, blandly unaware of his knack for self-exposure. What more natural, then, than for the satirist to slip into the role of eiron, let this fellow extend himself and feel that he is triumphing, while all along the ground is shifting under him and depriving him of footing. No need to argue with a dunce when you can damn him with feigned praise.

The dialogue's effectiveness is ultimately the product of Pope's portrayal and manipulation of this vulnerable adversary. For Pope not only wins the argument, but through the personification of vice and folly in his adversary makes dramatically real the threat to virtue which he proclaims. Part of the "willing World" drawn in "golden Chains" at the wheels of Vice's "Triumphal Car" is the adversary himself, both a victim and a counterpart in the real world of the Vice symbolized in the metaphoric world of the poem. In him the audience may view Vice "her own image, and the very age and body of the time his form and pressure."

The shift to a negatively functioning adversary is marked by several external tokens. The adversary is designated by the conventional rubric "Fr." [Friend], thus generalizing him on the one hand, leaving him undiscriminated from the crowd of timeservers he speaks for, and dissociating him from the poet's acquaintance on the other.[17] Also, contrary to earlier procedure, the adversary is permitted to speak first, a gambit which not only shows him as aggressor but which reveals his character and mentality, both of which maneuver him into a position of immediate vulnerability. Finally, the promotion of the adversary's speaking part is sharply increased over previous examples,[18] the reason being the satirist's desire to let the fellow damn himself, as he does, with astonishing thoroughness.

The self-indictment begins at once. By opening the dialogue with an echo of Damasippus's rebuke of Horace (Satire II.iii — 1-4), the adversary displays a fashionable familiarity with Horace but no sense of the awkwardness of the comparison which he invites by it. For Damasippus is, after all, a zealot, a mere spouter of Stoic doctrine, and he proves in the end, with the Stoicism he dumps so facilely on Horace, the butt of Horace's ridicule. The adversary's play on Damasippus's lines is made, too, at the expense of strict accuracy regarding the frequency of Pope's publication. In a note to these opening lines Pope says that they were "meant to give a handle to that which follows in the character of an impertinent Censurer," and there is every reason to suppose that he meant this comment to include such revelations of opaqueness and factual unreliability as we have noted already, or such others in this immediate context as the Friend's revealing comment that, when Pope does publish, "the

582

Court see nothing in't." Damasippus had not designated the
Court as the judge of Horace's performance, but had said only
nil dignum sermone canas: you make no poem worth heeding.
If his standard was a fanatical Stoicism, it was at least better
than that of Pope's adversary.

But these lines about the Court deserve further comment
for the exceptional economy of Pope's technique is nowhere better demonstrated. By the remark the adversary intends no more
than that the Court is unimpressed with what the poet has published, but the way he says it and the implications flowing from
it are extremely damaging to him and to the opposition he represents. For what the Court does not approve is, among other
things, the Epistle to Augustus, with its reflections on the King
and on the times, a disapproval, therefore, scarcely either
candid or moral. But when the adversary words it, "the Court
see nothing in't," he suggests yet another interpretation, viz.,
that the Court is not intelligent enough to see what it is that the
poet is doing. In their dullness they are left wondering what
this poet is writing about.

The Friend continues in this vein, complaining next (of all
things!) of the poet's correctness and of his moral bias (which
he disallows to Wit), both of which he describes, along with the
charge of stealing from Horace, as "Decay of Parts." In such
wise does he betray his own and the Court's inverted values.
Nor does he enhance the image of his morals and wit by his
shallow and palpable attempts at flattering the poet, "who once
with Rapture writ."

In the same speech (Pope hasn't spoken yet: why should
he?), the adversary confidently commends Horace for all the
wrong reasons,[19] for his "sly, polite, insinuating stile," which,
he notes, "Could please at Court, and make Augustus smile."
He suggests that the satirist follow suit, and recommends
specifically the consolation of Sir Robert's "Groat." To the
poet's protest that to do so would cost him his laughter, the
adversary makes no difficulty of suggesting that he indulge his
satiric bent on "Scripture," "Honesty," Patriotism, harmless
themes, which "all Lord Chamberlains allow." He may, in fact,
vent his satire on any but "Fools or Foes," a suspicious and,
one would think, embarrassing set of categories to defend.
When the poet ironically yields to this High Argument and bids
adieu to Satire, the Friend, who does not recognize when he is

well off (the satirist has just consented to lay his satire by), holds out the consolatory suggestion that the poet might still attack those disgraced, already down and out, once again bidding him only spare those in place. All this, it should be noted, is tossed off in a brisk, dancing pace that bespeaks the glib self-assuredness of the "well Whipt Cream of Courtly Sense."

Damaging as it is, however, the adversary's corrupt morality is not perhaps his most vulnerable point. What may be worse, though it is no doubt a symptom of the former, is his mental ineptitude, his touch of stupidity and dullness. He is not only a vicious man, but something of a dunce too, and perhaps Pope wants us to suppose that the two have a way of going together. Here, at any rate, is a spokesman who can accuse the satirist of stealing from Horace (vv. 7 ff.) and then turn around in the next breath and praise Horace and distinguish his manner from that of the satirist (vv. 11 ff.); who in his reply (vv. 37 ff.) to the satirist's remarks on Walpole can himself inadvertently slander the minister; who immediately on the heels of the blunder can put himself in the extremely awkward position of acknowledging the virtue of Lyttleton and of Fleury and of condemning Hervey (Lord Fanny: vv. 45-52); who can express a doctrine so crass (vv. 53-62) that even Vice would blush to own it; and who, finally, can unintentionally damn the very Court he is defending ("There, where no Passion, Pride, or Shame transport," etc., vv. 97-104).

Pope's adversary is still participating in his satire, but unwittingly now, and for that reason all the more effectively. The Friend in Dialogue I, like the personae of Swift's satires, is so convinced of his own and his country's normalcy and of the rightness of their vision that he is incapable of recognizing, or even of conceiving, such a thing as self-incrimination, to say nothing of acknowledging public wrong and ruin. Pope's adversary fulfills the parable: "Out of thine own mouth will I judge thee, wicked Courtier."

Against this corrupt symbol, to whom he stands as positive foil, looms the satirist who is the object of his vicious and clumsy blandishments — the vir bonus, but more than that, vir ingeniosus as well: a man who can draw the line between Walpole's good and his evil (vv. 27-36); who is witty enough to play the ironist with his adversary, pretending to give up satire (along with "Distinction . . . Warmth, and Truth") and agree

to praise folly; who pretends even to come to the defense of
Vice and to safeguard against common use that the dignity of
which is rightfully the Court's alone, and who thus shames the
nation's leadership, which would destroy, not redeem, its
country.

The adversary of the second Dialogue, like his noble kinsman in I, is, with slight differences of emphasis, also a self-
deceived, morally corrupt _persona_. The difference in the two
is to be felt largely in the manner of their exposure. Where in
Dialogue I the adversary exposes himself through his stupidity
and moral confusion, that in II is tripped up or squarely answered by the poet, who opposes him at every turn, with the
exception of two or three momentary instances of ironic pose.
The folly of the Friend in II lies more in simple heedlessness
and argumentative incaution than in outright stupidity, though
he is by no means as mentally alert as he needs to be in order
to engage Pope. This defect of carelessness, with its hint of
mental sluggishness, is comically exposed near the outset of
the poem. In the political vein of his predecessor, the Friend
suggests to the satirist that he "Spare . . . the Person, and
expose the Vice," with which the poet pretends to comply, only
to suck in the adversary. "Ye Statesmen, Priests . . . Ye
Tradesmen vile . . . Ye Rev'rend Atheists!" cries the satirist,
whereupon the Friend breaks in: "Scandal! Name them, Who? /
P. Why that's the thing you bid me not to do." Upon the poet's
subsequent allusion to the "pois'ning Dame," the Friend interrupts again:

> Fr. You mean — P. I don't. — Fr.
> You do.
> P. See! now I keep the Secret, and not you.
> The bribing Statesman — Fr. Hold! too high you go.
> P. The Brib'd Elector — Fr. There you stoop too low.
> P. I fain wou'd please you, if I knew with what:
> Tell me, which Knave is lawful Game, which not?

Obviously the Court will have to field a better man than this
if it expects to discredit the satirist. The fact that it apparently
cannot is not the least of the satirist's proofs against it. Its
representative, at any rate, has so far managed only to botch
the job; he has revealed the slow wit and inconsistency of his

ilk and has proved quite handily the satirist's contention that
general satire is ineffective.

If not as obviously depraved as his brother in Dialogue I,
the adversary in II nevertheless shares his double standard
and, like him, dramatizes the evil the poem decries. He would
have the satirist do his victims at least the favor of a dash for
anonymity (v. 11). He has, as we have seen, his own taste for
scandal, which ironically vitiates his complaints against the
satirist. He would spare the man trying to make his way in the
world ("You hurt a man that's rising in the Trade," v. 35). He
would divert satire to the dead and low-life (Jonathan Wild,
v. 54). His whole argument tends, in other words, to the worldly comfort of no satire.

But while he is on the one hand a temporizer with vice, on
the other he functions as the agent of the poet's strictly argumentative needs, raising the right questions to occasion the
satirist's defense of his satire. That he raises them for the
wrong reasons is but an added effect of the poet's art. If you
must satirize, he asks, why must you use names? Why do you
return over and over to the same victims? Do you complain of
those in power because your friends are out? What is it to you
anyway? he asks, his crassness mingling now with the poet's
most quiet need. Pope continues to have it both ways. He wanted these questions, needed them, and he met them with strength
and wit; but at the same time he got them posed by a fellow
basically unprincipled, who, in putting them, inadvertently
contributed to the satire himself. But by nothing does Pope
more finely discriminate between himself and his adversary
(and his adversary's constituency) than by the Friend's objection to the satirist's simile of the Westphaly hogs: "This filthy
Simile, this beastly Line, / Quite turns my Stomach . . ."
(vv. 181-182). The adversary's is a morality that can stomach
vice, but not the image of it.

Against this temporizing figure is balanced once again the
image of the poet, standing for the right, with his "strong Antipathy of Good to bad" and his sense of "Affront," which should
be the adversary's too. After the poet's great peroration in defense of satire ("O sacred Weapon!" vv. 212-253), the adversary is understandably shaken and draws back in a nervous and
feeble attempt to divert the satirist' indignation: "Alas! alas!
pray end what you began, / And write next winter more Essays

on Man," that is, general, philosophic, personally innocuous satire. The satirist doesn't even bother to notice.

The Friend of Dialogue II has served the satirist as provoker of the quarrel, proposer of vicious conduct, exemplar of hypocrisy and slow-wittedness, stubborn asker of questions the poet wants and needs anyway, and therefore provider of various opportunity for the satirist to display his candor and defend his satire. He has served as commender of moral laissez-faire and relativism, exhibitor of delicacy in the face of honest scatology but stomach enough for flattery, prodder into the noblest apology for satire on record, and betrayer of the intimidation which must always mark the corrupt in the presence of aroused virtue. From him, as from his immediate predecessor and, in a different way, the friendly adversaries of the earlier dialogues, Pope has extracted the last full measure of collaboration. That in itself may be one reason, among others, why Pope did not compose other dialogues in the few years remaining to him. He had done about all that could be done with it. He had taken a device scarcely defined in Roman usage — hardly known to Juvenal at all, experimented with ingeniously but tentatively by Horace, and only somewhat narrowed in focus by Persius — and made of it a brilliant and versatile accessory of the satiric strategy. He diversified and intensified Horace's precedent in the use of the friendly adversary, and elaborated and extended Persius's in the use of the hostile one. He outstrips the field in the fusion of irony and virulence, in the creation of dramatic tension, and in the integration of the adversary into the total satiric economy.

NOTES

1   Cf. Mary Claire Randolph, "The Structural Design of the Formal Verse Satire," PQ, XXI (1942), 368-384.

2   Letter to Swift, 16 February 1732/3, in The Correspondence of Alexander Pope, ed. George Sherburn (Oxford, 1956), III, 348. Also Letter to Richardson, III, 350; and Letter to Caryll, III, 353.

3   Joseph Spence, Anecdotes, ed. S. W. Singer (London, 1822), p. 297. For the reasons why it "would hit my case," see Robert W. Rogers, The Major Satires of Alexander

Pope. ISLL, XL (Urbana, 1955), pp. 66 ff.

4 Pope to Fortescue, [18 February 1732/3], Correspondence, ed. cit., III, 351. C. Trebatius Testa was friend and correspondent of Cicero.

5 Fortescue was not designated in any of Pope's editions, which carried only the initial L for the adversary. Warburton is responsible for the designation of Fortescue, in 1751. See Correspondence, III, 351n. Warburton was not without a kind of authority, however. In a letter to Fortescue (see above, n. 4) Pope wrote: ". . . have you seen my imitation of Horace? I fancy it will make you smile; but though, when I first began it, I thought of you; before I came to end it, I considered it might be too ludicrous to a man of your situation and grave acquaintance, to make you Trebatius. . . ." Cf. also the note on the MS. reading of "Hollins," Fortescue's doctor, for Celsus (verse 19), in the Elwin-Courthope edition of Pope's Works, IX, 133.

6 Pope is quoted throughout from the Twickenham Edition of the Imitations of Horace, ed. John Butt (London, 1939). The lines quoted above are vv. 16-20. Such citations hereafter appear in the text in parentheses.

7 John Butt, ed. Imitations of Horace, notes pp. 5-6.

8 For Pope's particular adaptations of Horace, see J. W. Tupper, "A Study of Pope's Imitations of Horace," PMLA, XV (1900), 181-215.

9 See Randolph, "Formal Verse Satire," p. 372.

10 Italics mine.

11 Butt, ed. cit., summarizes the changes made in the text by Warburton, pp. 93-94. Although Butt allows that the "change from epistle to dialogue may be the work of Pope," he regards it as "a change for the worse," and restores the poem to its earlier epistolary form. Professor Robert W. Rogers (Major Satires, pp. 70-71) traces in detail the piecemeal career of the poem's composition, from which it becomes clear that there is a sufficient confusion surrounding the origins, manuscripts, and texts of the poem to warrant an open mind on the subject of the form. See

also Pope's letter to Arbuthnot, 25 August 1734, in Correspondence, III, 428.

The arguments against dialogue structure boil down to the fact that (1) the poem is entitled an "epistle," (2) in none of the MSS. or texts supervised by Pope is an interlocutor designated by rubric. In favor of dialogue structure (or, more properly, of mixed structure) may be urged (1) the presence of quotation marks at every point later identified by Warburton as Arbuthnot's interjection (that there are quotation marks elsewhere in the poem is no hindrance, for they are all clearly associated with some identified speaker), (2) the correlation of the speeches later assigned to Arbuthnot with his advice to Pope in the letter of 17 July 1734 (see Correspondence, III, 417, and Pope's replies III, 419-420, 423-424, 428, 431), and (3) the "lead-in" to the first speech assigned to Arbuthnot. Pope has just said, vv. 73-74, "And is not mine, my Friend, a sorer case, / When ev'ry Coxcomb perks them in my face?" when the reply follows (vv. 75 ff.). Since there can be no doubt that the "Friend" of verse 73 is Arbuthnot, there can hardly be any doubt that the speech beginning v. 75 is Arbuthnot's. This identification is in all likelihood sustained in the "Friend" mentioned in the second speech, v. 102. None of the other three speeches assigned to Arbuthnot carry such an identifying vocative, but since all other quotations in the poem are assigned to some specified speaker (in the nonce category), there is reason to give these to the Friend who has spoken, in the same vein, twice before.

12 Quoted in the Loeb edition of Horace's Satires, Epistles and Ars Poetica, ed. H. Rushton Fairclough (Harvard, 1955), p. xxi.

13 Cf. Horace's "Si quis nunc quaerat 'quo res haec pertinet?'" (I. ii. 23), "Nunc aliquis dicat mihi: 'quid tu?'" (I. iii. 19), "ecce, / Crispinus minimo me provocat . . ." (I. iv. 13-14). The nonce adversary is in fact the most common form, either in epistolary or satiric writing, and is apparently the basis of Miss Randolph's generalization about the adversarius in formal verse satire.

14 Cf. Arbuthnot's letter to Pope, 17 July 1734, and Pope's reply, 26 July 1734 (Correspondence, III, 417, 419-420).

15 Part of the difficulty surrounding the interpretation of this couplet stems no doubt from the fact that the final paragraph of the Epistle, like other parts of it, was one of the pieces of earlier vintage brought together to form the "Bill of Complaint" published 2 January 1734-5 as An Epistle to Dr. Arbuthnot. A version of these verses was written as early as 3 September 1731 and included in a letter to Aaron Hill (Correspondence, III, 226-227). This version may also be consulted in Butt, ed. cit., p. 127n.

16 In Pope's own note [1751] the adversary is characterized as "an impertinent Censurer." See Butt, ed. cit., p. 297.

17 In the first edition (1738) adversary and satirist were designated respectively A and B. Fr. (F.) and P are substituted in 1740. (The same is true of Dialogue II.)

18 40.7% of the whole number of verses. Fortescue spoke some 22% of the lines in his poem, Arbuthnot 3.1% of those in his. The adversary of Dialogue II speaks about 8.23% of the verses in the poem.

19 The reasons are wrong in terms of Pope's values. It is possible of course that Pope might concur in the notion that Horace was guilty of these faults. Cf. the lines from Dryden's translation of Persius's Satire I. 116-118, quoted in Butt, ed. cit., p. 299n. It should be remarked that in them Persius's description of Horace seems intended for a compliment.

V. HOMER, SHAKESPEARE, AND THE LETTERS

POPE'S ILIAD: A NEW DOCUMENT

Norman Callan

There has recently come to light in Paris a collection of the proofsheets of the first eight books of Pope's Iliad,[1] bound as a single volume and corrected by Pope himself.[2] The volume comprises the complete text of the translation of Books I-VIII of Homer's Iliad, together with the Observations and ancillary matter contained in volumes i and ii of the edition.[3] There are some mistakes in the binding of the ancillary matter, but not much significance can be attached to this beyond saying that whoever bound up these proofs was either careless or else unfamiliar with the order of the edition.[4] The size of the paper used was apparently the same as that in the edition, but the pages have been heavily cropped to fit the binding, with the result that some of the marginal corrections have been mutilated.

The pagination presents certain peculiarities. In Books I-IV it corresponds with that of the first volume of the edition: that is to say, the text of the translation begins on "page one," and the notes again on a fresh "page one," for each book. In Books V-VIII the pagination of the proofs runs consecutively from 322 to 640, that of the edition from 1 to 306.

On the inside of the front cover of the volume is the following manuscript note, presumably written by the donor himself:

> Ce livre a un avantage inappréciable, et qui croîtra de siecle en siecle; c'est celuy d'etre un assemblage de feuilles corrigées de la main même de Pope; on y trouve, entre autres variantes, quelques leçons primitives qui n'ont jamais vu le jour, puisque l'edition n'a point été tirée sur ces leçons primitive imprimées, mais sur les corrections de l'auteur; et comme ces corrections sont démontrées être de la main même de Pope, tout cela est infiniment curieux

Reprinted from Review of English Studies, New Series, Vol. 4 (1953), pp. 109-121, by permission of author and publisher.

à considerer. Voyez entre autres exemples les deux
premiers vers de la page 358, L. V; Le quatrieme
vers de la page 366, même livre; les vers 606, et
647, encore du même livre; et une infinité d'autres
variantes manuscrites, et autographes de Poppe.
Sivry est en quelque sorte confus de se trouver fortuitement en possession d'une perle isolée, qu'il ne
sait avec quoy assortir. Il croit remplir les intentions
de Pope lui meme, en suppliant Monseigneur le Marquis de Paulmy, de mettre cette rareté a sa vraie
place; c'est a dire parmi les autres raretés de sa
Bibliotheque. C'est un hommage qu'il le prie d-accepter.

17 fevrier 1777

Across the heading of the first page of Names of Subscribers has been written the name I. N. Chevert in a hand that suggests a period earlier than that of de Sivry's note.

The manuscript corrections are very numerous throughout
the entire volume. They fall into two distinct classes: (a) those
which are strictly proof-corrections, that is to say rectifica-
tions of printer's errors, and (b) author's corrections, ranging
from emendations of a single word to cancellations and revisions of quite long passages. Those belonging to class (a) are,
of course, plentiful all the way through: those belonging to
class (b) are to be found only in the last four books — that is to
say, the books contained in the second volume of the edition.

Apart from one or two clear exceptions, it seems beyond
all reasonable doubt that the revision was carried out by Pope
himself.[5] Of these exceptions the most interesting are the
notes written on a blank half-page at the end of Book V:[6]

Leave this Space for a Copper Plate.[7]

? if a printers Ornament will not do well enough here
Such a one as ends a Book in <u>Trivia</u>.

To Mr Lintot
        Mr Pope is not at home — There are very
few Erratas in this sheet.

POPE'S ILIAD: A NEW DOCUMENT

I believe the Common Printers Ornament will not please.
Y^r Svt. C. Jervas

The first two notes are in the same handwriting, which differs
from that of Jervas's note to Lintot. At the foot of page 513
the same hand seems to have written the terse injunction "more
Coppy," and it is probable that this note and the first two on
page 445 are all from Lintot himself. Jervas's hand seems to
have been responsible for one or two small corrections: at line
448 in Book VII there is a cancelled marginal query "Atridae"
(for "Atrides" in the text), which looks like his; and at the penultimate line of Book VIII there is a similarly queried but un-
cancelled note "o'er their heaps of corn." This has been incorporated into the text in Pope's hand to replace the weaker "fed
with strength'ning Corn." Jervas could hardly have chosen a
more likely passage in which to signalize his share in the translation.[8]

As an example of proof-correcting in the early eighteenth
century the volume is of considerable bibliographical interest.
Pope, as one would expect from his manuscripts, is precise
in his reading and economical in his methods of correction. In
the "Essay on Homer" (Book I), we find him putting the printer
right about hyphens: "concer-/ning" is corrected to "concern-
/ing," and "contrac-/ting" to "contract-/ing." In the "Geo-
graphical Table" which follows Book II he has trouble with
diphthongs — e.g. "P˄thia/h," "P˄thiotis/h." This difficulty
persists in editions printed during Pope's lifetime, and may
have been due to his own uncertain spelling of Greek names.
There is an example — the only one I have noted — of his use of
Greek script in Observation xlv of Book VI. He begins by setting the compositor right rather laboriously letter by letter:
Σ ἠληυψ ἀ βλψτφσἡ Αρτεμι–|δοβλντος is marked in the text and
marginally corrected ϵδϑ|ο|ϟ|ϐ. Then he seems to lose patience
and writes the words out in full, correctly spelled, but omitting
the accents. Line-numbering goes wrong (as it was still apt to
do in the editions) at line 460 of Book VII: Pope's marginal
comment has unfortunately been mutilated by the cropping of
the page, but his manuscript numbering continues for the next
forty lines. His method with typographical faults can be seen
from such marginal comments as "in the common letter" (for
"Roman"), and "the letter set awry here" (for a dropped letter).

The corrections as a whole give the impression of a man who worked rapidly and knew just what was required.

From this brief account we may now turn to one or two points of interest which the discovery of the volume raises.

The most tantalizing question is that of the volume's provenance. In spite of the fact that he speaks of "fulfilling Pope's intentions," both the date of his note and the fact that he came by the volume fortuitement make it unlikely that de Sivry was personally acquainted with Pope. One tempting speculation is that it may have some connexion with Anne Dacier, the savante who had been so tart on Pope's "Preface," and with whom Pope is said to have corresponded: but guesses of this kind will have to await the findings of Mme. Le Gal.[9] In the meantime there are other questions.

One of these concerns whatever help is to be had in solving that perennial mystery "the affair of the rival translators." As reconstructed by Professor Sherburn the story of the publication of Pope's first volume is briefly this.[10] The book had been promised for May 1715; when, however, Tickell appeared as a rival translator, Pope issued an advertisement advancing the date of his own publication by two months. In this way, Professor Sherburn supposes, he hoped to bluff Tickell into publishing first, and thus have the chance of correcting any faults in his own work by the light of his rival's superior learning. But Tickell was the better poker-player — or at least he was in a stronger position to "see" his opponent, and as a result Pope's translation hung fire until he was eventually forced to publish on 6 June, a month after the date originally promised. Tickell's version followed within a week.

This interpretation of the facts, although so persuasive because apparently so typical of Pope's activities, has always seemed to me open to question. I cannot understand what advantage Pope would have gained by the schoolboy trick of letting his opponents have first knock on a good wicket, simply for the sake of seeing how many runs he would have to make. It is true that if he could have had a preview of Tickell's version he might have been able to put right one or two doubtful passages in his own rendering of Book I,[11] though even here he could hardly have done much without obvious plagiarism. But what of Books II, III, and IV? Were the errors of Book I to have been rectified with the help of Tickell's rendering, and those of the remaining books left to look after themselves? It would have been all too easy for his enemies to spot what had happened and take advantage of it. Pope's best course was surely to publish first, thereby making the most of the public's uncloyed expectation. He knew that his volume was likely to be an altogether more substantial affair than Tickell's, and it may be that by advancing his own date of publication he hoped to stampede the opposition into print before they had time to reinforce their somewhat meagre counterstroke. But whatever the reasons, it has always seemed to me more probable than not that the Post Boy advertisement was genuine, and that Pope intended to publish in March if he could.

For this view two facts which I have already mentioned in connexion with the Arsenal volume now seem to offer some support. The first is the complete absence of any tinkering by Pope with the printed text of the first four books. This is a surprising state of affairs, when we compare the evidence of very copious tinkering to be found in the next four. If, however, the printing of the translation had been pressed forward so as to be ready two months ahead of schedule, the explanation would be clear enough.

That something of this kind may have happened seems to be indicated by the second fact — the curious way the pages of the first four books are numbered, both in the proofs and in the edition. In all of them, as has already been said, the pagination of both text and Observations begins at 1, an arrangement which would seem to imply that text and notes were set up separately, and perhaps at considerable intervals of time. I would suggest that what may have happened was that the text of the translation was already being printed in January, but that, because Broome's contributions from Eustathius were not forthcoming, the printing of the notes was delayed, perhaps for quite a long time, and had to be done eventually as an entirely separate job. Pope's letter to Broome of 29 January lends some weight to this suggestion. "I could be glad," he writes, "if you have done any part, that I had the papers by the first opportunity sent to Lintot, the first volume being now in the press."[12] This, if Pope has not cooked the date, seems to imply that Broome was a very long way behindhand, and if so it would afford another possible reason for the absence of tinkering with the text in the proofs. As we shall see later, there are one or two instances in the second volume where the information contained in a note seems to have been the cause of a radical alteration in Pope's rendering.[13] If Broome's notes had been ready in time it is not unlikely that we should have found something similar happening in the first volume. If, on the other hand, by the time the Observations were available, the text of the translation was already in its final printed form, the absence of any such happenings would be explained. Lastly, in the way of supplementary evidence, it may be worth noting that the presence of frequent discrepancies in the first volume between the catch-lines of the Observations and the form of words in the text tallies with just such a situation.[14]

The facts offered here are perhaps open to other interpretations: they do, however, suggest (to me at any rate) that Pope's proclaimed intention of publishing in March may have been perfectly genuine, and not a matter of bluff at all.[15]

But historical detection, however absorbing, is not as important as the light which a document may throw on the working of a poet's mind, and it is in this respect that the proofs are likely to be of greatest value. We may regret that Dr. Johnson, who first discovered the fascination of comparing Pope's manuscript version[16] with the printed text, and was only able to restrain his flow of instances by reflecting that he was not writing solely for philosophers and poets, should never have set eyes on the Arsenal volume. Johnson presupposed an "intermediate copy";[17] but now "Transcripts on transcripts, proofs upon proofs arise," and the first thing that emerges from a study of several passages is that his supposition, though sound, is inadequate. Pope's friend Thomas Dancastle transcribed the Iliad for the press;[18] and presumably the proofs now yield us a complete copy of this transcription.[19] But that the version which he transcribed was not always the one to be found in the Homer MS. is strikingly illustrated by the following instance:

Homer MS., f. 84 v.

> Prostrate before the sacred shrine they fall
> With lifted hands and loud for mercy call.
>   ye shining Veil displays
> ~~The Veil~~, the Priestess self . . . ~~conveys~~

~~Then placed at Pallas feet~~
    on Minervas   s
Placed ~~at ye goddess~~ Knees & thus she pray~~d~~
~~Hear sacred Pallas~~   ~~Goddess divine thou ever dredful Maid~~
~~O Goddess most divine! redoubted~~   ~~Divinest Goddess~~
Goddess of Goddesses! ~~O Pallas aid~~   ~~Venerable Maid~~
                              Oh dredful Maid
             ~~Minerva~~   ~~Aid~~
Troys safe defence   victorious Pallas aid   Oh dredful Maid
              ~~unconquerd~~
                    thou ever dredful Maid

Proofs, VI. 374 ff.

        uplifted and imploring eyes,
With Hands ~~before the sacred Shrine they fall~~
They fill the Dome with supplicating cries
~~With Hands advanc'd, and loud for Mercy call~~:
        then
The Priestess ~~self~~ the shining Veil displays
Plac'd on Minerva's Knees, and thus she prays,
Oh awful Goddess! ever-dreadful
~~Goddess of Goddesses! Oh dreadful Maid~~
Troy's strong Defence, unconquer'd Pallas aid.

It is a beguiling but unlikely theory that Pope left his long-suf-
fering amanuensis to take his pick of the alternatives offered
in the manuscript: more probably he indicated his choice in
whatever communication accompanied the foul papers. The re-
duplication of "with hands" in the first line of this passage
offers scope for speculation. Had Dancastle for once slipped
up or had Pope forgotten to cancel the earlier version? Perhaps
Pope was using these two words as a mnemonic for the final
form, which was lurking in the back of his mind, but had not
fully crystallized.
    Whatever may have happened in this particular instance,
we have in the excerpt as a whole a remarkable example of
Pope "perfecting his utterance."[20] One wonders whether his
concern over the invocation of Pallas arose from a desire to
avoid an effect like that of the ill-fated O Sophonisba! Sophonisba O!: certainly it was not due to overmuch pondering on

Homer's text, for most of his attempts have little or nothing to do with the Greek.[21] Nevertheless, in this case at least, Homer comes to his assistance. "Troy's strong Defence" is not only an immense improvement on anything earlier, it is a pretty close rendering of the Greek *ῥυσίπτολι* — so close, indeed, that the cynical might wonder whether it was Pope's own. For the student of Pope the poet, however, as distinct from Pope the classical scholar, the remarkable thing about this passage, and about so many others in which we see the same process at work, is the immeasurable superiority of the final version over everything that has led up to it. One gets the impression that the ultimate formulation, so compact and assured, must have always existed subliminally in Pope's mind, and that the false starts are mere literary doodling until it rises to full consciousness. Obviously this is not quite what happened; but it certainly describes the effect on the reader of the finished product.

As might be expected of the author (or part-author) of the Peri Bathous, one of Pope's chief concerns was to avoid flatness. Usually this appears, if at all, in his first drafts and has been raised to a sufficient elevation by the time the proofstage has been reached. Yet even here he is on the alert:

Proofs, v. 399 ff.

> Next rushing to the Dardan Spoil, detains
> The heav'nly Coursers with the flowing Manes.
> These in proud Triumph to the Fleet convey'd
> ~~These order'd to the Fleet, are sent aboard~~
> No longer now a Trojan Lord obey'd.
> ~~And change their Trojan for a Grecian Lord~~.

Pope wanted to heighten both the magnificence of Diomede's exploit and the pathos of the coursers bereaved of their Trojan master: but if we turn to his first attempts, other things emerge which are of credit to Pope as an honest translator. The Homer MS. has the same version as the unrevised proof at this point, but below this version stands the cancelled couplet:

> ~~Then gives comād to send the steeds aboard~~
> ~~& change their Trojan for a Grecian L~~d

Obviously this is not only flat, but a trifle absurd, since Diomede would have given no command about changing masters
after the change had already been effected. For all that it is
much closer to the Greek δῶκε δε Δηϊπύλῳ...νηυσὶν ἔπι
γλαφυρῇσιν ἐλαυνέμεν. It preserves, too, what is certainly an
intentional antithesis in the Homeric line between Τρώων and
Ἀχαιούς.[22] Thus, whether we approve of them or not, the considerations which led Pope to his final version are clear enough;
and it is pleasing to find that an insufficient understanding of
the Greek was not among them.

Somewhat different considerations seem to have been at
work in the following passage from the same book:

Homer MS., f. 56 r.

From Meges force ye swift Pedaeus fled	his Consort's care to prove
Antenor's ~~Son whom fair Theano bred~~	Yet not too mean Theano's
~~And reard as~~ offspring from a forein bed	Theanos him
Yet fair Theano, to approve Her faith, had nurst her wth a Mothers love	She ~~kindly~~ nursd ~~kept well~~ with a Y^e stranger mother's love

Proofs, v. 91 ff.

> From Meges' Force the swift Pedaeus fled,
> Antenor's Offspring from a foreign Bed,
>   Spouse Theano heav'nly fair
> Whose gen'rous ~~Consort, Theano the fair~~
> Nurs'd the young Stranger with a Mother's Care.

The proof version has been reached by means of patching from
the MS., the only innovations being "gen'rous" in the third
line and "young" in the fourth. As usual the MS. shows Pope a
good deal nearer the actual Greek than in his final version.
Most of his marginal alternatives are clearly attempts at rendering χαριζομένη πόσεϊ ᾧ, attempts which he finally compres-
ses into the single epithet "gen'rous."[23] The rather obscure
"Yet not too mean" suggests that in his first draft he is trying

to include antiquarian information in his rendering. This is a trick which Pope was not above borrowing from Chapman; but whereas Chapman's interpolations are usually concerned with ethical points, Pope's are often snippets of information culled from Eustathius or Dionysius Halicarnassus by his industrious friends. In this instance, however, he wisely leaves the matter to a long note.[24] The rendering must now have seemed satisfactory; but, unfortunately, in solving the problem of how to turn χαριζομένη πόσεϊ ᾧ he failed to notice that he had been forced to stress <u>Theano</u> wrong, and so in the proof he has to alter the phrasing once more. The result, though it passes muster, and may even have seemed preferable to Pope, since it manages to suggest a connexion between the Greek δῖα and the notion of deity, is not so strong as the earlier version. It does, however, illustrate clearly Pope's remarkable alertness in matters of detail.

Another instance of such alertness, though for a different reason, appears in Book VIII:[25]

<u>Proofs</u>, VIII. 550 f.

all-conscious Eyes the
He whose <s>broad Eyes the subject</s> World behold,
Eternal Thunderer
The <s>Majesty of Gods</s> &c.

Pope's first rendering seems a pretty close approximation to the Greek, and it is not easy to see why he should have wanted to change it until one recalls that he had used almost exactly the same form of words to cover a similar situation some five hundred lines earlier:

Thence his broad Eye the subject World surveys . . .[26]

Presumably Pope had forgotten this until he saw his revises, and he made the alteration accordingly. What will perhaps seem odd to anyone who knows the Greek better than he knows Pope is that he should have chosen to make the alteration in the second passage rather than the first; for it is in the later passage of Homer that the words εὐρύοπα ("broad Eyes") and ὑπὸ ποσσὶ ("subject") occur; but this again is one of Pope's

little habits. Where the more or less conventional attributes
of gods and heroes are concerned he seems to keep a stock
supply of lines and phrases which he uses with the arbitrariness
of a Humpty Dumpty — or indeed of a Homer. Thus one may
sometimes think that he has completely misunderstood a line
of Homer, only to come across it satisfactorily rendered a
good way farther on. It may be that this arose from his custom
of getting passages of Homer by heart before translating them,
with the result that frequently recurring lines sometimes became misplaced. This, in a translator, though undoubtedly a
sin, seems to me a very venial one. Indeed in some ways it
reflects credit on Pope, for he not only recognizes the scene
instinctively, but instinctively uses the appropriate Homeric
phrases. No doubt there are people who would have preferred
him to keep an eye on the passage he was supposed to be translating. Perhaps they are right. Here at any rate it may be
conceded that Pope's emendation, if not strictly accurate, conveys very adequately the effect of the passage. That is a conclusion to which one continually recurs in the study of this
translation.

On the whole, when the proofs are taken in conjunction
with the Homer MS., the light they throw on Pope's knowledge
of Greek is in his favour. There is one passage, however,
where for once he seems to deserve the charges of contemp-
tuousness and irresponsibility brought against him by "Hesiod"
Cooke.[27] On most occasions when the meaning of Homer is in
dispute Pope manages to avoid taking sides. This he does by
combining in his rendering the sense of as many interpretations as he can.[28] One could hardly call it an heroic method,
but Pope uses it quite openly and with considerable skill. It is
therefore somewhat disconcerting when the "history" of a passage shows him not only making a stand of his own, but a stand
on ground which is decidedly unfirm. The occasion is the famous speech of Agamemnon dissuading his brother from taking
up Hector's challenge:[29]

$$τούτῳ \ δὲ \ πρόμου \ ἄλλου \ ἀναστήσουσιν \ Ἀχαιοί.$$
$$εἴ \ περ \ ἀδειής \ τ' \ ἐστὶ \ καὶ \ εἰ \ μόθου \ ἔστ' \ ἀκόρητος,$$
$$φημί \ μιν \ ἀσπασίως \ γόνυ \ κάμψειν, \ αἴ \ κε \ φύγῃσι$$
$$δηίου \ ἐκ \ πολέμοιο \ καὶ \ αἰνῆς \ δηϊοτῆτος.$$

603

In the edition Pope renders this:[30]

> The mightiest Warrior of th' Achaian Name,
> Tho' bold, and burning with Desire for Fame;
> Content, the doubtful Honour might foregoe,
> So great the Danger, and so brave the Foe . . .

on which Gilbert Wakefield (whose attitude to Pope's Iliad sometimes reminds one of Bentley's to Paradise Lost) comments:

> Our poet here is enveloped in a cloud of darkness
> raised by himself. He has totally mistaken a passage,
> which is perfectly plain to any man, who has but a
> moderate knowledge of the original: nor has any one
> of his predecessors in English translation represented
> the sense amiss.[31]

There is some truth in this: Chapman, Hobbes, and Ogilby
all make these lines refer to Hector and not to the Greek champion — though Hobbes represents the sense amiss in other respects. On the other hand, Joshua Barnes in his Latin gloss,[32]
and Mme. Dacier, whom Pope seems to have followed, are
decidedly ambiguous:

> Les Grecs auront soin de choisir un autre ad-
> versaire à Hector, et quelque intrepide et quelque
> infatigable qu'il puisse estre dans les combats, je
> vous responds que s'il peut échapper au danger où
> il s'expose, il se reposera volontiers de ses grands
> travaux.[33]

Pope, in fact, hardly deserves such massive censure: grammatically his version is possible, and in a note on the passage
he makes both his knowledge of the alternative rendering and
his reason for preferring his own perfectly clear:

> It cannot with Certainty be concluded from the
> Words of Homer, who is the Person to whom Agamem-
> non applies the last Lines of this Speech; the Interpret-
> ers leave it as undetermin'd in their Translations as
> it is in the Original. Some would have it understood of

> Hector, that the Greeks would send such an Antagonist
> against him, from whose Hands Hector might be glad
> to escape. But this Interpretation seems contrary to
> the plain Design of Agamemnon's Discourse, which
> only aims to deter his Brother from so rash an Under-
> taking as engaging with Hector. So that instead of
> dropping any Expression which might depreciate the
> Power or Courage of this Hero, he endeavours rather
> to represent him as the most formidable of Men, and
> dreadful even to Achilles.[34]

So far so good: Pope is entitled to his opinion, even if he holds
it rather perversely in the face of the accepted interpretation.
But that he is not altogether disingenuous appears from an
inspection of the "history" of the passage:

Homer MS., f. 97 v.

        our   some powerful
Greece in ~~thy~~ Cause shall arm ~~a stronger~~ Hand
    ~~shall~~
~~Greece can produce some Chief his Match in Might~~
Bold as he is insatiate of ye Fight
He tempts a danger that ~~transcends~~ his might
      sure if Heaven   may match
And ~~if ye our~~ ye ventrous Champion spares
The great delivrance will deserve his Prayers.

In his first steps Pope is as "undetermin'd" as the best of
them; and, moreover, it is evident from the last line that he
had been "led astray by Hobbes":

> Some other we'll oppose to Hector's might,
> That, haughty as he is, shall make him stoop,
> And thank the Gods if safe he come from fight.[35]

That he rectified the mistake in time is no doubt creditable,
but his note continues in rather the unctuous tone of the reformed rake denouncing vice:

> The Phrase of γόνυ κάμψειν , which is literally

605

> to bend the Knee means (according to Eustathius) to
> rest, to sit down, καθεσθῆναι, and is used so by
> Æschylus in Prometheo. Those Interpreters were
> greatly mistaken who imagin'd it signify'd to kneel
> down, to thank the Gods for escaping from such a
> Combate. . . .[36]

This rather startling change of front must have come about,
I think, as a result of information supplied by Broome before
the copy went to press. The repercussions are to be seen in
the unrevised version of the proofs, where he deserts Hobbes
for Barnes and Dacier:

> Greece in our Cause shall arm some pow'rful Hand.
> Bold as he is, insatiate of the Fight,
> He tempts a Danger that may match his Might.
> What Chief soe'er from hence in Safety goes
> Shall bless the welcome Hour that brings Repose.

By this time he has dropped the idea of "stooping in prayer,"
but he is still uncertain what to do with the phrase αἴ κε φύγῃσι,
and so falls back on the ambiguous Latin gloss si effugerit.
That he was uncertain to the last may be inferred from
the fact that in the proofs his final version is written between
the printed lines, but the latter have not been cancelled. Poor
Pope, was he hoping for yet another chance to revise?

In the end, however, he comes out boldly in favour of the
interpretation that the doubtful words "signify not to escape out
of the Combat (as the Translators take it) but to avoid entring
into it."[37] In doing this Pope is being faithful to Homer according to his lights. For him Homer's supreme characteristic is
that he does nothing "from want of Choice but from an Insight
into Nature."[38] Where Pope is faced with conflicting interpretations (as he supposes) the one which seems to illustrate this
insight best is the one he prefers.[39] It may not be altogether
the method of a scholar; but equally it does not convict Pope of
being either a charlatan or an ignoramus.

In quoting from the Arsenal volume I have used mainly passages which have undergone extensive revision because this
seemed the most compendious way of illustrating the material
available. Briefer revisions are often no less interesting, and,

of course, far more numerous. In fact, if these proofs did nothing more than confirm our impression of the immense labour that went into Pope's Iliad they would be valuable. They do more than this, however, for they illustrate Pope's methods, both as a poet and as a translator, and perhaps, as I have suggested, throw some light on historical problems hitherto obscure.

NOTES

1 The Iliad of Homer. Translated by Mr. Pope, London, 1715 (vol. i), 1716 (vol. ii), &c. This is referred to as "the edition" throughout the following pages. Vol. i covers Homer's Iliad, I-IV, vol. ii covers V-VIII.

2 The book, which is in the Bibliothèque de l'Arsenal, was discovered by Mme. Simonne Le Gal when engaged in collecting materials for a bibliographical study of Poinsinet de Sivry, who presented it to the library in 1777. It is thanks to Mme. Le Gal's kindness and that of the Curator of the Bibliothèque de l'Arsenal that I have been able to examine these proofs and to give the brief account of them which follows.

3 The reproduction of the Farnese bust and the maps in vol. i, and the map of Troy and the Errata page in vol. ii are wanting.

4 Probably careless; for the most likely person to have done this would be Pope himself. He made a collection of the manuscript of the translation and another of the pamphlets attacking it. That he should have preserved the proofs in the same way seems at least possible.

5 An expert's opinion is awaited; but the following points would seem to settle the matter. (i) The handwriting closely resembles that of the Malet MS. of Pope's "Homer" and of other known Pope manuscripts. (ii) Many of the corrections are of a kind which only the author could have made. (iii) De Sivry's statement is quite definite (for what it may be worth); and Jervas's note to Lintot (on this page) implies that Pope himself would have corrected the proofs had

he been "at home." (iv) The economical style of the corrections suggests Pope.

6 Proofs, p. 445.

7 The edition has no colophon here: only a ruling and the catchword.

8 This is the famous "moonlight scene." It is full of painters' terms, and bears obvious relations to Rembrandt's The Night Watch. That Jervas should have helped Pope with it would not be at all unlikely.

9 She has now propounded some possibilities in Le Bulletin du Bibliophile, No. 1, 1952.

10 The Early Career of Alexander Pope (Oxford, 1934), pp. 125 ff.

11 Actually Pope did something rather like this when he altered the opening lines of Book I to a version nearer Tickell's for the second edition. But this was in 1720, when Pope could afford to be generous.

12 The Works of Alexander Pope, edited by Elwin and Courthope (London, 1871-89), viii. 124. This edition is referred to hereafter as E-C.

13 See below, p. 117.

14 The question of whether Broome was responsible for the Observations, and not merely for the references to Eustathius, does not affect the argument and cannot be pursued here. Pope may have sent him his Observations in draft form, using an early version of his text for the catchlines, and by the time Broome had done his part there may have been no time left for revisions.

15 One is still left with the problem of why the publication was so long delayed. I can only surmise that Broome's notes may have been very late indeed. There may also be some truth in the story of the printed sheets that were such an unconscionable time a-drying (E-C, vi. 227).

16 B. M. MSS. Add. 4807-9. Usually called the "Homer MS." All references are to Add. 4807.

17 Lives, ed. G. B. Hill (Oxford, 1905), iii. 119.

18 E-C, ix. 489.

19 Several leaves of the transcription are preserved in MS. Add. 4809: Pope has used the backs for his version of the Odyssey.

20 See Sherburn, "Pope at Work," in Essays on the Eighteenth Century Presented to David Nichol Smith (Oxford, 1945), p. 62.

21 Cf. Homer, Iliad, vi. 305: πότνι᾽ Ἀθηναίη, ῥυσίπτολι δῖα θεάων . One odd inconsistency in this passage is Pope's treatment of the word πέπλον which he here renders "veil." At line 113 and again at 340 he translated it as "carpet," which he revised in the proof to "mantle." This is eclecticism indeed. All three meanings are possible, but hardly when applied to the same object.

22 Cf. Homer, Iliad, v. 323 f.:

καλλίτριχας ἵππους
ἐξέλασε Τρώων μετ᾽ ἐϋκνήμιδας Ἀχαιούς

23 This is the kind of thing a reader who does not know either the Greek or the MS. is apt to miss in thinking the adjective a mere conventional expletive.

24 Book V, Obs. X. On Theano, and the social status of bastards in antiquity. This is one occasion where the information in a note may have altered a rendering in the text (see pp. 597-8 above). At least part of this note was probably written after the translation of Book VIII had been completed.

25 Homer, Iliad, VIII. 443 f.:

αὐτὸς δὲ χρύσειου ἐπὶ θρόνου εὐρύοπα Ζεὺς
ἕζετο, τῷ δ᾽ ὑπὸ ποσσὶ μέγας πελεμίζετ᾽ Ὄλυμπος.

26 Pope, Iliad, VIII. 65; cf. Homer, Iliad, VIII. 51 f.:

αὐτὸς δ᾽ ἐν κορυφῇσι καθέζετο κύδεϊ γαίων
εἰσορόων Τρώων τε πόλιν καὶ νῆας Ἀχαιῶν.

27 The Battel of the Poets (1729):

> When was I known basely to court the Schools,
> And not to rail at dull methodic Fools,
> Who dare not venture from their Depth to wade? . . .
> A Genius form'd like mine will soar at all,
> And boldly follow where subscriptions call.
> My gentle Touch from Homer clear'd the Rust,
> And from the Brow of Shakespeare wip'd the Dust.

28 See, for instance, the opening lines of Book I (1st edn.) and Pope's Observations ad loc.

29 Homer, Iliad, VII. 116 ff.

30 Pope, Iliad, VII. 134 ff.

31 Homer's Iliad translated by Alexander Pope . . . with additional notes . . . By Gilbert Wakefield (1796), Book VII, note ad loc.

32 ΟΜΗΡΟΥ ΙΛΙΑΣ κ.τ.λ. (ed. Joshua Barnes, 1711), Book VII, gloss ad loc.: "Licet intrepidusque sit & etiamsi pugnae sit insatiabilis, Existimo eum libenter genu flexurum; si effugerit Ardenti ex bello & gravi pugna."

33 L'Iliade d'Homere traduite en François, . . . par Madame Dacier (1711), vol. ii, p. 96.

34 Pope, Iliad, VII, Obs. XV.

35 Homer's Iliads in English. By Tho. Hobbes (1676), p. 98.

36 Pope, Iliad, VII, Obs. XV.

37 Pope, Iliad, VII, Obs. XV.

38 Ibid. I, Obs. liii.

39 A brief example from the proofs may make this clearer. In the description of Paris' house (VI. 393) he renders the Homeric καλά as "stately," with a cancelled variant "glittering." In the proof "stately" is emended to "pompous" because he wishes to depreciate Paris' character.

THE DEVELOPMENT OF POPE'S ILIAD PREFACE:
A STUDY OF THE MANUSCRIPT

Douglas Knight

Now that Pope has begun to recover something of his proper position as a poet, we are tempted to ask a new question by means of the notorious dictum of the Victorians. Granted that his poetry makes him something other than a "classic of our prose," what of Pope's prose itself? And in particular, what are the qualities which show it to have independent value as opposed to the mere attributive value of any work by a major poet? There is perhaps no better material for answering this question than his Preface to the Iliad translation, which has long been recognized as one of his ablest pieces of criticism, and of which there is a substantially complete first draft, heavily revised, in the Homer manuscripts.[1]

What is possibly most striking in the manuscript is that the concision native to Pope's published prose as well as poetry is not consistently present. Pope shows here, for example, a mannerism of which his finished work is free: a constant use of pairs or triplets which amplify an idea but do not really develop it. "The Reach, Extent and Fecundity of his Imagination"; "the most enliven'd Manners and Forms of Homer's Expression"; "Impertinent in themselves, apply'd out of Place, & tediously repeated"[2] — such phrases are altered in the published Preface to bring their diffusely Johnsonian grandeur under control. At times a whole clause will be compressed to a word. Thus Pope first writes of Nestor and Odysseus that they differ in wisdom, "the one prevailing still by hidden Art, the other by open Reason."[3] In the published Preface only the word open is kept, in a sentence which maintains the central distinction between the two characters but with no distracting redundancy of detail.[4]

Other local changes correct an unjustified complexity. Pope originally wrote that the lesser epic poets exceeded "all

Reprinted from Modern Language Quarterly, Vol. 16 (1955), pp. 237-246, by permission of author and publisher.

reasonable Space of Time" in the duration of their compositions, a phrase which calls attention to itself but has no more meaning than the customary "length of Time" which he published in its place.[5] The highfalutin phrase, in turn, is like the spectacular one, often a distraction. In the manuscript Pope remarked of Homer's repetitions that they were "not ungraceful" where he dealt with such exalted speakers as "the first Powers of Earth in high Concerns of State." In the published Preface he speaks more calmly of messages "from Higher Powers to Inferiors in Concerns of State."[6] The alteration frees us from an inflated language and therefore from the necessity of "rising to an occasion" which is not really a climax in the organization of his statement.

With revision of this minute sort we can often say more than that the meaning is clarified; it may be discovered in the course of a rhetorical tightening. By even so trivial a substitution as "Dionysius of Halicarnassus has pointed out many of our Author's beauties" for the original "Dionysius of Halicarnassus has given us many instances of our Author's Beauties,"[7] Pope has done more than free himself from pomposity. He has made precise his statement that the purpose of the critic is to indicate — in the root sense of the word, and as he himself does in his annotation — what the beauties are.

Similarly "a grave man" becomes "a plain man" in support of a developing antithesis: "There is a graceful and dignifyd Simplicity as well as a bald and sordid one, which differ as much from each other as the Air of a Grave Man from that of a Sloven; the former will more easily keep clear from the Extream of Formality, than the latter from that of Negligence. . . ."[8] It is clear that Pope discovered his antithesis as he wrote about it; the clause, "the former will . . . ," does not appear at all in the published Preface, for it is the scaffolding of metaphor but not the thing itself. When added to the conclusion of his paragraph, the one shift of word, from grave to plain, is adequate to sustain both image and antithesis without overstating either.

Beyond its increase in clarity, such revision suggests a characteristic of the general rhetorical development of the Preface. This development, like that of the minute changes, takes place within the amorphous but customarily elaborate detail of a first draft which is seldom the mere suggestion of

things to come but rather the confused and yet elaborated form
of things which are still to be refined and ordered. It is this
refining order which discovers the riches evident at so many
points in the published Preface:

> But after all, it is with great Parts as with great Vir-
> tues, they naturally border on some Imperfection;
> and it is often hard to distinguish exactly where the
> Virtue ends, or the Fault begins. As Prudence may
> sometimes sink to Suspicion, so may a great Judg-
> ment decline to Coldness; and as Magnanimity may
> run up to Profusion or Extravagance, so may a great
> Invention to Redundancy or Wildness. If we look upon
> Homer in this View, we shall perceive the Chief Ob-
> jections against him to proceed from so noble a
> Cause as the excess of this Faculty.[9]

There are two manuscript stages in the achieving of this perspicuity, and in each we can see how Pope's mind moved rapidly over the subject as a whole and then slowed to consider the
precise relationships of its parts.

> We have seen [in inserted above] how distinguishing
> a manner that [great] Faculty appears wch forms the
> [great altered to grand] character of [Ho] our Author
> [appears throughout his work inserted above]. But
> it is with great Parts as with great Virtues, they
> [necessarily] naturally border on some Defect and it
> is [hard] often hard to [dist] know exactly wh[?] the
> Virtue ends or the [Vice] Fault begins. [2 inserted
> above and canceled] [& inserted and canceled] [As
> Magnanimity sometimes [may inserted above] run[s]
> up into Profusion or Extravagance so may [———? in-
> serted above] a great Invention to Redundancy or
> Wildness; and] [1 inserted above and canceled] [as
> altered to As] Prudence [may inserted above] some-
> times sink[s] to suspicion so [does] may a great
> Judgment decline[s] to Coldness, and Magnanimity
> may run up to Profusion or Extravagance so may a
> great Invention to Redundancy or Wildness. If we look
> upon Homer in this View, we shall perceive the chief

> Objections which have been raised agst him to pro-
> ceed from this noble Cause, [of the Vastness] [Fer-
> tility inserted above] of his Invention [& inserted]
> [We shall find many] that —— [?] consequently those
> things [to deserve] which seem the least defensible
> in him, [to be] are such [glorious inserted above]
> Faults as no[ne] one [but altered to less] than Homer
> could have the genius to commit.[10]

As Pope first devises the comparison which is the heart
of this paragraph, he has its various elements in hand but not
its illumination of Homer's latent weakness. His first discovery in the course of writing is that the various aspects of the
comparison between prudence and judgment on the one hand,
magnanimity and invention on the other, can be made steadily
to ascend in their relevance to Homer. He indicates the change
first by numbering the clauses and then by transferring to its
proper rhetorical position at the end the clause which occurred
to him first in the course of composition because it grew directly from his understanding of Homer's potential weakness.

Pope's second discovery in the course of revision is that
the opening and close of the paragraph do not adequately support its central point. Between the draft and the published Preface he eliminates the redundancy in the opening, for which he
substitutes a simple But in the published Preface. At the same
time he modifies the special pleading of the close, which implies a Byronic virtue in the fault gloriously indulged. The
central point of the paragraph is both weakened and distorted
by such a conclusion; as Pope discovers that central point, he
continues to maintain the nobility of Homer's fault, but he no
longer tries to defend its glory.

The governing attitude behind this revision also animates
Pope's discipline of metaphor, as well as of the other chief
qualities in the rhetorical vigor of the Preface. This attitude
can be defined by two related questions: how does a particular
passage contribute to the precise, though complex, understanding of some specific point? And how does it move the whole
piece forward? The questions when applied to metaphor are
really a final test of Pope's skill at revision, for the temptation to retain a brilliant image is for him as for any good poet
enormous.

One of the most conspicuous of these temptations is so
both because it is unusually effective in itself and because it
does not appear in the published Preface at all. While discussing the character of great poetry as a prelude to his analysis
of Homer, Pope originally wrote: "It is the Invention which
distinguishes in different degrees all great Genius's whatsoever; Tis the Mark which Nature setts upon them, the Star
lighted up from their birth, to proclaim them to Mankind."[11]
The very power of such an image is its threat; there is an inevitable jar when we are dropped from it to the necessarily
neutral statement which follows. "The utmost Study and Learning, all the Stretch of human Art and Industry . . . can never
attain to this."[12]

The care demanded, if Pope is to retain an image and
avoid such discordancy, is best illustrated by the most extended metaphoric passage which he permits to appear in the published Preface.

Methinks I see these different Followers of Homer,
some sweating and straining after him by violent
Leaps and Bounds, the certain Signs of false Mettle;
others slowly and servilely creeping in his Train;
while the Poet himself is all the time proceeding with
an unaffected and equal Majesty before them.[13]

Here every aspect of the image of a king's processional is
subdued, kept muted and implicit by the fact that each of its
terms is also a completely appropriate term for the literary
relationship being described. If we include the one phrase canceled in the manuscript, however, the whole image becomes
apparent and explicit: "an equal Pace of Majesty before them."[14]
The removal of Pace seems to imply that Pope found it too
overt for his purposes. As so often in his poetry, he keeps the
image just below the surface of discourse, so that it advances
the argument by relating its various aspects to one whole,
while it does not obtrude itself enough to distract from the
purpose served by that whole. Where in the poetry, however,
the function of a submerged image is both logical and alogical,
here one might rather describe it as the epitome of logic, the
compression of a relationship of ideas into the briefest compass
possible without destroying the significance of the parts. The

Janus-like quality of the passage, at the same time, prevents
either image or idea from dominating over the other; instead
they function as mutual solvents, so that both the individual
dangers of faulty imitation and the general preëminence of
Homer are equally apparent.

II

In every such modification of the style there is a quality
of exploration — exploration which is simultaneously a discovery
of the way in which something should be said and of what it is
most important to say. It is not surprising, then, that this
same quality should animate Pope's actual development of his
subject in the course of revision.

The Iliad Preface is perhaps best known for its recognition
of the qualities in Homer — Pope calls them Invention and Fire —
which have often been thought alien to the poetic interests of
the English Augustans. It should no longer be necessary to
labor the point that the best of them were as aware as Sidney
or Coleridge that a work of art exists only by virtue of its
imaginative order. A central concern with Homer's imaginative power, however, is by no means so clearly present in
Pope's first draft as it is in the printed version. The manuscript as a whole is, indeed, cluttered with references to traditional as well as contemporary scholarly opinion. Madame
Dacier's obligations to Duport and Eustathius, Longinus on
Homer's Imagination and Boileau on his descriptive power,
Rapin on the supposed superiority of Virgil to Homer,[15] all
find their way into the draft but not into the published Preface.
Such references give the clear impression of a mind fairly
well saturated with "reading in the field," but still in the process of bringing to light its own governing insight.

This does not mean that anything so simple as an ascend-
ance of personal opinion is allowed to take place as these references vanish in the course of revision. Rather there is a
discovery that Dacier and La Motte, like Rapin, Boileau, and
Scaliger, are on the periphery of Pope's concern with the
heroic tradition rather than at its center. The quarrel of the
Ancients and Moderns, in which the first two figure so prominently, is important to Pope as a student of Homer. But his

excisions indicate that he is far from thinking it important to a general critical examination of the Iliad.

Pope's concern with Homer as a poet rather than as a battleground for clashing views about the rise or decline of society inevitably makes him suspicious of that Quarrel. In all versions of the Preface he avoids the direct issues of human progress and the ideal state about which so much of the war revolved; but one of the longest canceled passages in the revision indicates that he originally took a much more explicit stand on these issues than the published Preface shows. After remarking on "this disparity of Customs [and Manners] in different Ages [and Countries]," he continues,

> This will also acquit Homer from the [Accusation] Charge agst him [on account of] for the Grossness of his Heroes Manners and Sentiments. Mons. de la Motte has drawn up [this] the Accusation at large, the Substance whereof is, that they are boasting, abusive, cruel, and impious. He is indeed so just as to excuse Homer [on] the last of these [Articles] Points on account of the nature of the heathen religion wch seemed to require no other Piety than that of frequent Sacrifices and ceremonies. As to their Abusiveness, he affirms that Great Men differ from the Vulgar in their manner of expressing their Passions; but I must have leave to [dissent from him and to] think that in violent Passions (such as that [those] of Achilles and Agamemnon) the great are as subject as any others to these Sallies. . . .[16]

Considered merely as statement, this is like a later and also canceled criticism of La Motte's "Iliad in miniature"; refutation of the detail of La Motte's attitude is so insistent that it becomes an end in itself for the duration of the passage. And the rhetorical result of such argumentation, of course, is a full stop in the onward movement of the section as a whole. In the published Preface the passage becomes "seeming Defects will be found upon Examination to proceed wholly from the nature of the Times he liv'd in. Such are his grosser Representations of the Gods, and the vicious and imperfect Manners of his Heroes. . . ."[17] Homer rather than La Motte is maintained at the center of discussion; we are led to consider the brutality of certain aspects of life in the Iliad, while we are freed from having to consider irrelevant though cogently stated criticisms of that life.

In much the same way Pope frees us from a good deal of merely factual information. A summary of Renaissance editions and translations of the Iliad, for instance, is the most extended example of material which was incorporated in the first draft because it was a product of Pope's study of his subject.[18] As we have seen, however, the manuscript represents among other things a discovery that his discussion of Homer was to be something quite different from a record of his study. This seeming s crifice of factuality is actually the negative aspect of a positive discussion of Homer's poetic quality which comes more and more to animate the Preface.

This is by no means to imply that Pope always sacrifices the particular in developing the Preface toward its general end. In discussing the servility of Homeric imitators, the revision is all the other way; in the first draft we are given a mere list of the chief events imitated by others:

> in every Episode or single part they have copied him
> to servility, even to a Man. If he has Funeral Games,
> they must have them celebrated at any rate: [If he sends
> his Hero to the Shades, theirs must go after him:] If he
> gives a regular Catalogue of the Army, they draw up
> their Forces in the same Order: If his Hero recounts
> his Adventures in a foreign Court, they [insert above:
> constantly] use the self same method to shorten the
> Duration of the action: and if he concludes his Poem
> just upon the Death of the Hero's Antagonist, not a
> Writer after him dares proceed a Step farther.[19]

In the published Preface the passage has become damningly and almost wittily specific, and the canceled clause of the draft has been recast to support the wit:

> they have follow'd him in every Episode and Part of
> Story. If he has given a regular Catalogue of an Army,
> they all draw up their Forces in the same Order. If
> he has funeral Games for Patroclus, Virgil has the

> same for Anchises, and Statius (rather than omit them)
> destroys the Unity of his Action for those of Arche-
> morus. If Ulysses visit the Shades, the Aeneas of
> Virgil and Scipio of Silius are sent after him. . . .20

Like the suppression of a dozen details of fact, this development of the danger of close imitation has its end in a presentation of the true character of Homer — or of any good poet. Pope
becomes more specific about the writers who fail in invention
just as he becomes less so about the quarrel of Ancients and
Moderns; in each case he puts the primary emphasis of the
Preface on the questions of poetry which are most important
both for Homer and for himself.

At the same time, however, he extends the discipline of
his subject so that it includes himself. The first draft is studded with personal reference, almost all of which is suppressed
in the published Preface. There are two aspects of this personal quality, the first what one might call personal scholarship,
and the second outright comment on Pope's own position as a
translator-poet.

The personal scholarship expresses itself in analyses of
Homer's practice which Pope can support only by his own un-
aided judgment. "To throw his Language more out of Prose,
Homer seems to have invented his Compound-Epithets,"21
he remarks in the draft. By changing invented to affected he
avoids a statement which no one could make with authority,
and leaves a sound critical remark unmarred. Similarly, in
the discussion of Homer's gods he endorses strongly in the
manuscript the supposition that they do not appear in Greek
writing before Homer.22 By muting this opinion in the published Preface, he protects himself against a pretense of an-
thropological knowledge which could not be sustained, while at
the same time he establishes at the center of discussion the
aspect of his point which is significant for Homer's poetry.

> For we find those Authors who have been offended at
> the literal Notion of the Gods, constantly laying their
> Accusation against Homer as the undoubted Inventor
> of them. But whatever cause there might be to blame
> his Machines in a Philosophical or Religious View,

they are so perfect in the Poetick, that . . . his Gods
continue to this Day the Gods of Poetry.[23]

Direct personal reference in the first draft is suppressed
for a different reason, and with a different result. It is a distraction from the chief subject of the Preface which will not
merely distort but actually at certain moments replace that
subject. If Pope keeps himself in the reader's eye — even by
such brief remarks as "I must give some account of my Management," or "I could sooner pardon. . . ," "I shall not envy . . ." — he has kept him from Homer.[24]
The most extended passage of personal discussion in the
first draft deals, as one might expect, with Pope's view of his
own task as a translator:

[Having now shown in what I suppose the Excellence
of Homer to consist, what Notion I have of the Characters and Beauties of him, and next what Methods
I have taken in my Attempt to imitate them; if I have
established the former rightly, and deduced the latter
consequently, my Design is just, whatever the Execution. And whoever thinks me to have faild in that, will
use me fairly if he [alternate canceled version: That
must be submitted to ye world, and I shall think myself fairly used by any who] will give as good reasons
that my Execution is wrong as I have done that my
Design is right.] [alternate version, also canceled:
It will be expected I shall do [should add] a Paragraph
in my own Person. I confess I now tire of such a Work
[illegible clause]. I will tell ye reader my very thought
of my own task [two words illegible] & think myself
utterly incapable of doing].[25]

One's objection to the variant forms of such a confession
is that they are exclusively concerned with the translator.
Any progress in the Preface as a whole is interrupted, since
for the moment we are allowed to consider only the apprehension and weariness which Pope finds in himself at the end of
so long a task. The excision of the passage makes clear this
weakness; for its removal brings together two legitimate discussions of the relation of the translation to its original.[26]

POPE'S ILIAD PREFACE

Here as with every other aspect of the subject of his Preface,
Pope's changes make clear the fact that, as he wrote, it became steadily a more single subject for him. He began by a
verbal excursion through the various aspects of his own information and attitudes; but he finished by a sacrifice of them to
the abiding question of the nature of Homer's greatness.

Pope's discovery of his true subject as he works his way
in the draft through the varieties of information about Homer
is a constant parallel to his discovery of its proper style.
There results in both cases a "placing" of the Preface, a removal of it from relatively commonplace statement to an order
which satisfies simultaneously the demands of rhetoric and art.
A central attitude to Homer, on the one hand, is developed with
a maximum both of individual vigor and general implication;
while, on the other hand, these qualities are achieved in such
a way that the Preface comes to be coherent and exciting within
itself. Pope discovers, in style as in statement, the individual
"example" which will both participate in the whole and be itself
alive. He absorbs the complexity of his subject and the multiple
possibilities of his rhetoric into an order which gives them
clarity without distorting them into mere simplicity.

III

Such an achievement with these two aspects of the Preface,
the two chief materials from which it is built, inevitably implies the creation of a consistent relationship between the Preface and its reader. And this relationship in turn is compounded
from that established, on the one hand, with the Preface itself,
the implied mind from which our understanding comes, and on
the other hand, with Homer, the subject around which our understanding is ordered. As a work of criticism which is also
a work of art, the Preface must maintain the excitement of
both relationships.

The demands of this dual task are perhaps nowhere better
seen than in the opening sentences, where the primary relationship between what the reader reads and what he reads about
must be established.

The Glory of the greatest Invention in the world is

621

> universally allowed to Homer. There is scarce a
> Science in which we do not find him skilld even before
> Mankind had a Notion that such a Science was in being.
> All the Springs of [Polite Learning] Poetry were first
> open'd by him, thro the amazing Strength of this Faculty.
> As to Poetry, we owe [insert above: to him] the very
> Beginning Form and Spirit [?] of it, a Consideration
> which those who compare him with Virgil ought to have
> always in their eye: on the contrary by ye whole Course
> of the Parallels [which have been] drawn [?] by Scaliger
> and others, one might imagine they had never so much
> as heard that Homer lived the first. The Praise of
> Judgment Virgil has [disputed] justly contested with
> him, and other Authors may have their Pretensions
> as to other particulars, but his Invention stands yet
> unrivalld by any Man.[27]

Immediately striking in such a passage is the associative and
therefore personal arrangement of ideas which marks their
first occurrence to Pope. Invention in its widest sense dominates his mind, for as soon as he mentions the word it leads
him to speak of qualities in Homer which are not primarily
poetic. The canceled words Polite Learning at the start of the
third sentence reveal this overly general attitude to us — and
obviously reveal it to Pope as well. He substitutes Poetry,
starts to discuss it in the following sentence, and is almost
immediately betrayed into a pronouncement on the vexed critical problem of how to do justice to both Homer and Virgil.
Only when he returns to Virgil himself from a castigation of
the critics, does he return to the subject appropriate to his
opening.

The real center of these rambling speculations, however,
is revealed in the two sentences which open the published
Preface.

> HOMER is universally allow'd to have had the greatest
> Invention of any Writer whatever. The Praise of Judg-
> ment Virgil has justly contested with him, and others
> may have their Pretensions as to particular Excellen-
> cies; but his Invention remains yet unrival'd.[28]

Beyond the obvious gain in coherence and concision, there is
in this final form of the opening a definition both of Pope's and
the reader's relation to Homer. The reader in particular is
guaranteed two things: first, that he will be introduced to the
most central aspects of the subject; and second, that he will
not be dominated by the whims, vagaries, and personal inclina-
tions of his author. Pope may be concerned about the injustice
done Homer by Scaliger, but the reader will not meet that concern until it becomes in the course of discussion the most important point for him to consider.[29]

The mask which Pope puts on as the speaker of the Preface
is not that of mere impersonality, however, but that of the person who points out while he almost never points to himself. We
are aware of him as someone who asks us to look; but we are
equally aware that what we see, though it is seen through a
persona, is organized so as to be equally significant to all the
individuals who look at it. The voice of the Preface is as a
result the voice of a community which includes Homer, the
speaker, and ourselves. Pope speaks to us about Homer, but
at the same time he speaks for us and Homer equally.

The developing coherence of style and subject matter in
the course of revision gives the sharpest emphasis to this relationship. Above all, Pope creates for the Preface a speaking
voice which is both interpretive and oracular; this voice describes Homer's greatness with individual vigor but in stylistic
terms which place it beyond the range of mere individual opinion. And by means of this voice he develops as the heart of his
subject an analysis of the aspects of Homer which are as persistent as poetry itself — which, in fact, define its basic nature.
The finished Preface presents as a complex whole the strong
sense of a continuing relation between Homer and a community
of readers, and an equally strong sense of the self-contained
and absolute nature of great poetry.

NOTES

1 The Homer manuscripts are in the British Museum, Add.
   MSS 4807-09. The Iliad occupies the first two of these
   three volumes.

2 Homer MSS, I, 5^v, 6^r, and 9^r.

3 Homer MSS, I, 4^V.

4 Iliad of Homer, translated by Mr. Pope (London, 1715),
  I, C1^V in the Quarto issue: "the main Characters of Ulysses
  and Nestor consist in Wisdom, and they are distinct in
  this; the Wisdom of one is artificial and various, of the
  other natural, open, and regular."

5 MSS, I, 3^V; Iliad, I, B3^V.

6 MSS, I, 13^r; Iliad, I, F1^r.

7 MSS, I, 7^r; Iliad, I, D1^r.

8 MSS, I, 12^r; Iliad, I, E3^r and 3^V: "There is a graceful and
  dignify'd Simplicity, as well as a bald and sordid one,
  which differ as much from each other as the Air of a plain
  Man from that of a Sloven: 'Tis one thing to be tricked up,
  and another not to be dress'd at all. Simplicity is the Mean
  between Ostentation and Rusticity."

9 Iliad, I, D2^r and 2^V.

10 MSS, I, 7^V and 8^r. In reproducing passages of the first
   draft I have bracketed all alterations; and I have explained
   the nature of the alterations in each case, except for the
   straightforward cancellations which are bracketed without
   comment.

11 MSS, I, 2^r; only the first clause of the passage is published.

12 Ibid.; this is altered in the published Preface, Iliad, I,
   B1^r and 1^V, to read: "The utmost Stretch of human Study,
   Learning, and Industry, which masters every thing be-
   sides, can never attain to this."

13 Iliad, I, E3^r.

14 MSS, I, 11^V.

15 MSS, I, 14^V, 10^r, 5^V, and 9^V.

16 MSS, I, 8^V.

17 Iliad, I, D3^r.

18 MSS, I, 14^r and 14^V.

19 Ibid., I, 3^V.

20 Iliad, I, B3^V-B4^r.

21 MSS, I, 6^r; Iliad, I, C3^V.

22 MSS, I, 4^r: "If Homer were not the first who introduced the Deities (as Herodotus imagines) into the Religion of Greece, he was undoubtedly the first who brought them into Poetry; and formed that machinery which makes its greatest Importance and Dignity. For neither are there any Traces of this in those Workes which can be supposed as ancient, or near as ancient; nor is any such thing hinted by those authors who have preserved to us the Accounts of them. . . ."

23 Iliad, I, B4^V-C1^r.

24 MSS, I, 12^V, 11^V.

25 Ibid. , I, 13^V.

26 Iliad, I, F1^V-F2^r: "Few Readers have the Ear to be Judges of it, but those who have will see I have endeavour'd at this Beauty [of relating sound and sense].
    "Upon the whole, I must confess my self utterly incapable of doing Justice to Homer. I attempt him in no other Hope but that . . . of giving a more tolerable Copy of him than any entire Translation in Verse has yet done."

27 MSS, I, 2^r.

28 Iliad, I, B1^r.

29 Ibid. , I, E1^r.

THE "ARSENAL" PROOF SHEETS OF
POPE'S ILIAD: A THIRD REPORT

R. M. Schmitz

A bound volume of proof sheets for Books I-VIII of Pope's
Iliad, discovered about six years ago by Mme. Simonne Le Gal
in the Bibliothèque de l'Arsenal, turns out on bibliographical
examination to be a more curious document than the first two
accounts of it have indicated. The first report, by Mme. Le
Gal,[1] vaguely hinted at some confusion by noting that the second
part was much more interesting than the first. Mr. Norman
Callan, when he published the second report,[2] sidestepped a
basic confusion in the "Arsenal" sheets by giving what was
actually two reports in one. The latter part of his article dealt
with the revising techniques of Pope and drew material from
the many revisions which Pope had written into the proofs for
Books V-VIII. The former part, noting that the proofs for Books
I-IV contained no revisions, argued the troublesome problem
of Pope's and Tickell's competing translations on the grounds
of this negative evidence.

Behind Mr. Callan's observations on the proofs for Books
I-IV lie the facts that Pope discovered in December of 1714 that
Thomas Tickell would publish a competing translation of Book
I, and that Pope subsequently inserted an advertisement in The
Post-Boy advancing his own publication date by two months,
from May 1 to March 1. The last fact Professor Sherburn interprets as the opening step in a bit of literary chicanery by
which Pope "hoped to bluff Tickell into publishing first, and
thus have the chance of correcting any faults in his own work
by the light of his rival's superior learning."[3] In opposition to
this view, Mr. Callan notes the complete absence of revision
in the first half of the "Arsenal" volume and takes this to mean
that Pope's "proclaimed intention of publishing in March may
have been perfectly genuine, and not a matter of bluff at all."[4]

Throughout this part of his report Mr. Callan declared

Reprinted from Modern Language Notes, Vol. 74 (1959), pp. 486-489, by
permission of author and publisher.

himself startled by the "surprising state of affairs" . . . "the complete absence of tinkering" in the first four books and "the very copious tinkering" in the second four. He found further difficulties when he compared the pagination of the proof sheets with that of "the edition," stating:

> In Books I-IV it corresponds with that of the first volume of the edition: that is to say, the text of the translation begins on "page one," and the notes again on a fresh "page one" for each book. In Books V-VIII the pagination of the proofs runs consecutively from 322 to 640, that of the edition from 1 to 306.[5]

In these remarks Mr. Callan is trapped by two false assumptions. The first is that the "Arsenal" volume is all of one piece. The second is that "the edition" — the one used by Mr. Callan for comparison with the proofs — was the only issue of Pope's Iliad during the years 1715 and 1716.

We may begin to see some light by listing below the issues of Volumes I and II as numbered and dated in the Griffith bibliography:[6]

(1) Vol. I Quarto (No. 39), subscription edition, June 6, 1715.
(2) Vol. I Folio (Nos. 41, 42), trade edition, June 10-15, 1715.
(3) Vol. II Quarto (No. 47), subscription edition, March 22, 1716.
(4) Vol. II Folio (Nos. 49, 50), trade edition, March 22, 1716.

The two halves of the "Arsenal" volume are of markedly different format, and, though heavily clipped, the volume still displays page numbers and signatures to prove that it contains not the proofs for (1) and (3) as Mr. Callan's observations require, nor for (2) and (4) which represent his printed "edition," but rather the proofs for (2) and (3).

Furthermore, the first page of the "Arsenal" volume, i. e. Names of Subscribers, has at the right lower corner the manuscript notation "4⁰ B. L. 15," which I take to be Lintot's memorandum that the work in hand was being recast from the first

Quarto (1). This observation is confirmed at every point where
format and errors in recasting can give evidence, and it is
most certainly confirmed at the bottom of the first page 55
where the paragraph headed "Errata in the Essay," giving page
citations to the Quarto (1), is left intact except in altered page
numbers to fit the Folio (2). In other words, the first half of
the "Arsenal" volume represents proof for the trade edition
(2) with the text of which Pope was not likely to and did not
"tinker."

Pope did, however, read and correct the Folio proof with
great care, and provided his printer with more than enough to
do. Besides supplying a dropped line and correcting a false
catchword, Pope corrected capitalization, spelling, hyphena-
tion, pointing, spacing, alignment, and false and broken letters – at 126 places. To make all the corrections – and the
printer did make 107 of them – called for the opening up and
reclosing of 84 page formes. This sort of thing – with perhaps
an afterthought or two by Pope – was seriously delaying Lintot
in getting out his trade edition – the one from which he, not
Pope, would get the profits. At all events, Lintot's nerves were
pretty well frayed when he wrote to Pope on June 10: "Pray de-
tain me not from publishing my Own Book. . . . I designed to
publish Monday sevennight pray interrupt me not by an Errata.
I doubt not the sale of Homer if you do not disappoint me by
delaying the Publication."[7]

As for the second half of the "Arsenal" volume, it is, as
before indicated, the proof to the subscription Quarto (3) of
Volume II, and with such proof Pope would and did "tinker" a
great deal, indulging his insatiable appetite for revising and
polishing the text. But how the two kinds of proof came to be
thrown together is anyone's guess. A student of Pope's personal
papers will, however, recognize in the "Arsenal" volume the
kind of accidental conflation which occurred more than once in
the dispersal of Pope's papers after his death. All we know
about the provenience gives no answer to the question how the
papers were thrown together. The proofs came fortuitement
into the hands of the Parisian man-of-all-letters Louis Poin-
cinet de Sivry who in 1777 presented them to Antoine-René
d'Argenson, Marquis de Paulmy and founder of the Bibliothèque
de l'Arsenal.[8]

THE "ARSENAL" PROOF SHEETS

NOTES

1 "En Marge de l'exposition du 'Livre Anglais'; l'Homère de Pope," Bulletin du Bibliophile et du Bibliothécaire, N. S. I (1952), 49-54.

2 "Pope's Iliad: a New Document," RES, N. S. IV (1953), 109-121.

3 Quoted from Callan, p. 112. See George Sherburn, The Early Career of Alexander Pope (Oxford, 1934), pp. 125 ff.

4 Callan, pp. 113-14.

5 Callan, p. 109.

6 Alexander Pope, a Bibliography, Vol. I, pt. i (Austin, Texas, 1922), pp. 40-50.

7 The Correspondence of Alexander Pope, ed. George Sherburn (Oxford, 1956), I, 295. Lintot did not actually issue his edition until June 30, ten days after the "Monday seven-night" of the letter. This date, somewhat advanced over Griffith's June 10-15, is based on an advertisement in The Post-Boy for June 25-28 stating that the trade edition would be issued "Thursday next," i. e. June 30.
    Professor Sherburn has been kind enough to transcribe for me a number of advertisements which strongly support the idea that the subscription Quartos and trade Folios of Volume II through VI were not, as Professor Griffith indicates, simultaneous, but were separated by a week or ten days. Perhaps the delays were due, in part at least, to Pope's continuing the practice of giving detailed attention to the Folio proofs.

8 A note written into the "Arsenal" volume and dated February 17, 1777, reads: "Sivry est en quelque sort confus de se trouver fortuitement en possession d'une Perle isolée, qu'il ne sait avec quoy assortir. Il croit remplir les intentions de Pope lui même, en suppliant Monseigneur le Marquis de Paulmy, de mettre cette rareté a sa vraie place; c'est a dire parmi les autres raretés de sa Biblio-thèque."

"THE DULL DUTY OF AN EDITOR"

James R. Sutherland

There was nothing accidental in the celebrated quarrel between Pope and Lewis Theobald, unless it is to be considered
an accident that Pope ever got himself involved in the business
of editing. Once he had stooped to textual truth and intermitted
his song, the clash with Theobald was inevitable. The two men
approached literature from different directions. They met, it
is true, over the Works of Shakespeare; but they looked for,
and found, different things there. Theobald (or so Pope believed)
was that sort of reader who "sees hairs and pores, examines
bit by bit," whereas Pope himself was the apotheosis of the
common reader. Over all Pope's editing there lingers the easy
grace of the amateur; he was one of the "gentlemen," and Theobald -- with far more at stake -- one of the "players." It is often
assumed that Pope knew Theobald to be a better editor than
himself, and that his satire of the man can safely be attributed
to this knowledge, and to the annoyance it caused him. But this
is perhaps to judge the issue from a modern standpoint: it is
at least doubtful if Pope considered Theobald a good editor at
all. These two editors interpreted their duty to Shakespeare
very differently; they had not even begun to agree about what
it was that an editor has to do. Theobald's views on editing
were set forth clearly in the Preface to his edition of Shakespeare:

> The Science of Criticism, as far as it affects an Editor,
> seems to be reduced to these three classes; the Emen-
> dation of corrupt Passages; the Explanation of obscure
> and difficult ones; and an Inquiry into the Beauties and
> Defects of Composition.

No doubt Theobald was listing those three editorial tasks in
what he conceived to be their order of importance; for he went

Reprinted from Review of English Studies, Vol. 21 (1945), pp. 202-215,
by permission of author and publisher.

on to tell the reader that his own attention has been "principally confin'd to the two former Parts," and that though he had offered some specimens of the third kind of criticism these were "but occasional, and for the sake only of perfecting the two other Parts, which were the proper Objects of the Editor's Labour." He added, with a sneer: "The third lies open for every willing Undertaker; and I shall be pleas'd to see it the Employment of a masterly Pen": a sneer, because in the War of the Dunces the word "undertaker" had been freely used by Pope's enemies in referring to his work as translator of Homer and editor of Shakespeare.

Opposite this, we may place a brilliant note of Pope's, written when he was only twenty-seven, and therefore dating from a time before he had become an editor himself:

> It is something strange that of all the Commentators upon Homer, there is hardly one whose principal Design is to illustrate the Poetical Beauties of the Author. They are voluminous in explaining those Sciences which he made but subservient to his Poetry, and sparing only upon that Art which constitutes his Character. This has been occasion'd by the Ostentation of Men who had more Reading than Taste, and were fonder of shewing their Variety of Learning in all Kinds, than their single Understanding in Poetry. Hence it comes to pass that their Remarks are rather Philosophical, Historical, Geographical, Allegorical, or in short rather any thing than Critical and Poetical. Even the Grammarians, tho' their whole Business and Use be only to render the Words of an Author intelligible, are strangely touch'd with the Pride of doing something more than they ought. The grand Ambition of one sort of Scholars is to encrease the Number of Various Lections; which they have done to such a degree of obscure Diligence, that we now begin to value the first Editions of Books as more correct, because they have been least corrected. The prevailing Passion of others is to discover New Meanings in an Author, whom they will cause to appear mysterious purely for the Vanity of being thought to unravel him . . . For Reading is so much dearer to them than

631

> Sense, that they will discard it at any time to make
> way for a Criticism . . .[1]

Here already we have what was to be Pope's settled attitude
towards the commentators upon dead poets; and if we allow for
the fact that in his <u>Homer</u> Pope is not himself an editor, but a
translator who has obliged his subscribers with a commentary
on his author, we have a statement setting forth his views on
editorial commentary. Commentators (he finds) persist in commenting upon everything except the poetry; they concentrate
upon matters which are either irrelevant or of secondary importance; they have more learning than taste, and they make
use of their reading to propose unnecessary corrections or to
invent difficulties so that they may display their erudition.

> So spins the silk-worm small its slender store,
> And labours till it clouds itself all o'er.

From this attitude Pope never departed. More and more firmly
he held to the antithesis which he was to express in his <u>Epistle</u>
<u>to Dr. Arbuthnot</u> between the Theobalds with their "pains, read-
ing, study," and the Popes with their "spirit, taste, and sense";[2]
between the minute but short-sighted critic, and the enlightened
reader who understands "how parts relate to parts, or they to
whole."[3]

To all this we might apply the caution uttered by Scriblerus
on another occasion: "Fair and softly, good poet!" For if we
must have editors, then they must be expected to submit willingly to a good deal of that drudgery which Pope despised, or affected to despise; otherwise they are unlikely to perform their
tasks adequately. When he consented to edit Shakespeare, Pope
soon found himself facing problems of text and explanation which
would not yield to even the finest "spirit, taste, and sense,"
but which afterwards yielded on more than one occasion to
Theobald's reading and study. For an editor of Shakespeare
there was certainly ample scope to illustrate "the poetical
beauties of the author," but in his own edition Pope contented
himself with drawing attention to what he called "the most shining passages" by the use of commas in the margin, or, occasionally, of a star to distinguish a whole scene.[4] He had not,
however, changed his mind about the importance of remarking

upon an author's excellencies; that was, he still insisted,[5] "the better half of criticism."

What Pope thought about editors and editing — or what, at any rate, he was prepared to say about them — may be further pieced together from scattered passages in his poems and letters and from the Preface to his edition of Shakespeare. But for his liveliest and most complete criticism of contemporary scholarship we must turn to the Dunciad, and not merely to the poem itself but to the elaborate accretion of Prolegomena, Testimonies of Authors, Errata, Appendices, Indices, and Notes which he deliberately allowed to silt up round the poem. It may be questioned whether many readers to-day give more than a passing glance to the prose sections of the Dunciad; but they are all very much part of Pope's joke, and to ignore the critical apparatus is to miss a good part of his satirical intention.

When the Dunciad first appeared anonymously in May 1728, it was burdened with only a short preface ("The Publisher to the Reader"), and a few brief explanatory notes. About a month later, however, Pope was writing to Swift to say that the poem was going to be reprinted "in all pomp . . . It will be attended with Proeme, Prolegomena, Testimonia Scriptorum, Index Authorum and Notes Variorum." In short, it was to burlesque the more pompous aspects of contemporary scholarship. Swift was invited to contribute to the notes in the manner of "dry raillery, upon the style and way of commenting of trivial critics," or by collecting "the parallel passages of the ancients."[6] What share Pope's friends had in compiling the notes to the Dunciad it is impossible now to determine; but though they may have contributed something, the greater part of the commentary was almost certainly the work of Pope himself.

The "Advertisement" and "A Letter to the Publisher" contain little to our purpose; the fun begins with "Testimonies of Authors, Concerning our Poet and his Works." Pope's main purpose in this section was to do for the general public what he was continually doing in those private letters which he afterwards made public — to set himself in as favourable a light as possible. While including attacks upon himself and his works, he more than counterbalanced any unfavourable impression those might create by inserting a large number of commendations from the most prominent men of letters of the day. But the "Testimonies" had also a playful reference to the contemporary practice of prefacing the works of modern authors with a section of commendations by other literary men.

The section that follows, "Martinus Scriblerus of the Poem," is a direct burlesque of the pedantic critic. While Pope is again serving a practical purpose here by giving a description of the scope and nature of his poem, he is also, by his references to Aristotle and Eustathius, and his solemn discussion of epic action, ridiculing the pedantic commentator.

It is in the notes, however, that he launches his main attack on modern editing — on verbal criticism in general, and on its modern exponent, Lewis Theobald,[7] in particular. Theobald, it should be remembered, was made King of the Dunces not because he was Pope's most persistent or most malicious enemy, but because in 1726 he had published his <u>Shakespeare Restored</u> — or, to give it its full title,

> Shakespear restored: Or, A Specimen of the Many
> Errors, As well Committed, as Unamended, By
> Mr. Pope in his Late Edition of this Poet.

Whatever the merits of this work, there can be no doubt that it lived up to the second part of its title at least: Theobald may not have succeeded in demonstrating that he was himself the heaven-sent editor of Shakespeare, but he had shown that Pope certainly was not. Had Pope chosen to have it out with Theobald in prose, he could frequently have turned the tables on him, for Theobald's zeal often outran his editorial discretion. But Pope must have realized that on only too many occasions there was no sound answer to be made to Theobald's strictures, and that merely to defend his own editing would leave Theobald in possession of the field. The best policy here was to attack, and the best method of attack was ridicule — a ridicule so devastating that his critic would be hopelessly discredited. In this Pope very nearly succeeded. The editorial Humpty-Dumpty undoubtedly had a great fall; and it is only in modern times that he has been put together again.

In the poem, therefore, Pope is more concerned to render Theobald everlastingly ridiculous than to state his case against contemporary editors and editing. But he does state that case in his notes, where he proceeds to develop his own settled

convictions about the sort of literary scholarship which Theobald represented, and which -- for one reason or another, but
chiefly because he had little taste for it, and was not good at it
himself -- he always resisted. The banter in Pope's prose commentary is often superb; but as note succeeds note it becomes
clear that the banter is based on certain firm convictions which
he held about the scholarship of his own day.

In the eyes of his contemporaries — and, indeed, in his
own eyes — Theobald had established an undoubted claim to
attention by being the first critic to apply Bentley's method of
verbal criticism to the text of an English author. His Shakespeare Restored was, he claimed,

> . . . the first Essay of literal Criticism upon any
> Author in the ENGLISH Tongue. The Alteration of a
> Letter, when it restores Sense to a corrupted Passage,
> in a learned Language, is an Atchievement that brings
> Honour to the Critick who advances it: And Dr. BENT-
> LEY will be remember'd to Posterity for his Per-
> formances of this Sort.[8]

It is not surprising that Pope should devote a good deal of space
to examining or ridiculing the pretensions of verbal criticism.
He pounces on this theme in the opening note to Book I, where,
in a comment signed "Theobald," he gravely discusses the
correct spelling of Dunciad.

> Ought it not rather to be spelled Dunceiad, as the
> Etymology evidently demands? Dunce with an e,
> therefore Dunceiad with an e. That accurate and punc-
> tual Man of Letters, the Restorer of Shakespeare,
> constantly observes the preservation of this very
> Letter e, in spelling the Name of his beloved Author,
> and not like his common careless Editors, with the
> omission of one, nay sometimes of two ee's ([as
> Shak'spear] which is utterly unpardonable . . .

This is followed by the remark of Theobald quoted above, that
the alteration of a letter brings honour to the critic. By opening his commentary with a pedantic discussion which does
nothing to illustrate "the poetical beauties of the author," Pope

is adroitly suggesting the irrelevance and triviality of so much verbal criticism. But this is only the first shot, and he recurs again and again to the same theme. Emendations in the text of the poem are gravely proposed by Scriblerus, and a whole section, "Virgilius Restauratus," is devoted to satirizing Bentley's emendations in the text of Horace and other classical authors. Pope's cleverest retort to Shakespeare Restored comes in the long note to III. 274, where he inserts a series of emendations to Double Falshood. Theobald, it will be remembered, had offered this play to the public as the work of Shakespeare, and Pope jumped at the opportunity which this afforded of turning the tables on Theobald. ". . . I am infinitely concern'd," Scriblerus is made to observe, ". . . that so many Errors have escaped the learned Editor"; and he proceeds to supply a number of conjectural emendations, which, however ludicrous, have an air of plausibility, which generally involve no more than "the alteration of a letter," and which are presented in what is a fair parody of Theobald's style. Of a passage in Act I, Sc. i:

> I have his letters of a modern date,
> Wherein by Julio, good Camillo's son
> (Who, as he says, shall follow hard upon,
> And whom I with the growing hour expect)
> He doth sollicit the return of gold, . . .

Scriblerus remarks:

> This place is corrupted: the epithet good is a meer
> insignificant expletive, but the alteration of that single
> word restores a clear light to the whole context, thus,

> I have his letters of a modern date,
> Wherein, by July (by Camillo's son,
> Who, as he saith, shall follow hard upon,
> And whom I with the growing hours expect) . . .

Again, in Act IV, Sc. ii:

> To oaths no more give credit,
> To tears, to vows; false both!

> False Grammar I'm sure. <u>Both</u> can relate but to <u>two</u>
> things: And see! how easy a change sets it right!

>   To tears, to vows, false <u>troth</u> —

> I could shew you that very word troth in <u>Shakespear</u>
> a hundred times . . .

Here Pope has hit Theobald's editorial manner perfectly. There
is more wit hidden away among the <u>Dunciad</u> notes than is generally realized to-day.

The readiness of Theobald, in what Pope felt to be his rage
for conjectural emendation, to set aside the readings of his
text was not unnaturally a fruitful theme for the annotator of
the <u>Dunciad</u>. By suggesting that Theobald had an overweening
confidence in his own private judgment, Pope was, of course,
indirectly defending his own failures to emend in his edition of
Shakespeare. But here again, though the satire is certainly
<u>ad hoc</u>, it also represents a reasoned conviction. In the open-
ing note to Book II he makes a shrewd exposure of the dangers
of conjectural emendation:

> Two things there are, upon which all verbal Criticism
> is founded and supported: The first, that the Author
> could never fail to use the very best word, on every
> occasion: The second, that the Critick cannot chuse
> but know, which it is. This being granted, whenever
> any doth not fully content us, we take upon us to con-
> clude, first that the author could never have us'd it,
> And secondly, that he must have used That very one
> which we conjecture in its stead.

Beside this sarcastic note one may set Pope's claim in the
Preface to his Shakespeare to have "discharged the dull duty
of an editor . . . with a religious horror of all innovation,[9]
and without any indulgence to my private sense or conjecture."
Pope did, in fact, make a large number of emendations, and
some of those were made on the assumption that "an author
could never fail to use the best word on every occasion" — the
best word being often no better than the word that Shakespeare
might have used if he had been writing in 1720. On the other

hand, he could fairly claim that he was not using his "private sense or conjecture"; he was usually emending what seemed to him, owing to his lack of familiarity with Elizabethan English, a manifest printer's error, the sort of error that Lintott's compositor might have made in setting up The Rape of the Lock. By the standards of the early eighteenth century Pope was a conservative editor; and he probably resisted the temptation to astonish the world with a conjectural emendation far more often than did Theobald.

Yet if he was inclined as an editor to shun innovation, he was quite capable on a suitable occasion of laughing at a superstitious reverence of manuscript or textual authority in someone else. Thomas Hearne, the antiquary, is disposed of in a sarcastic note:10 his fault is that he will not sufficiently use his editorial discretion, but everywhere displays a servile reverence for manuscript "authority." "I shall follow the Manuscript," says Scriblerus, ". . . mov'd thereto by Authority, at all times with Criticks equal if not superior to Reason. In which method of proceeding, I can never enough praise my very good Friend, the exact Mr. Tho. Hearne; who, if any word occur which to him and all mankind is evidently wrong, yet keeps he it in the Text with due reverence, and only remarks in the Margin, sic M. S. In like manner we shall not amend this error in the Title itself [the spelling of Dunceiad as Dunciad], but only note it obiter, to evince to the learned world that it was not our fault, nor any effect of our own Ignorance or Inattention."

No doubt Hearne deserved some at least of Pope's ridicule. Yet it is equally true that Pope was scarcely capable of doing justice to scholars like Hearne, or, for that matter, Theobald. And the reason for this, which is by no means wholly to his discredit, is also the main explanation of his deficiencies as a scholar: Pope was intensely, even passionately, interested in literature, he was not interested in what he would have considered mere reading. It was one of his complaints about Theobald that he dimmed his eyes and stuffed his head "with all such reading as was never read."11 In so doing, Theobald was (to Pope) serving the goddess of Dullness; it may have been so, but he was also equipping himself to be an editor of Shakespeare. It was this sort of specialized reading that Pope could not bring himself to undertake. He might by the turn of events find himself editing Shakespeare for Jacob Tonson; but he was first and foremost a poet and a man of wit, and he was not going to dim his own eyes by burrowing in antiquated and out-of-the-way books that Shakespeare might conceivably have read. His satirical account of the contents of Theobald's library[12] is enough to show his attitude to the miscellaneous and recondite reading of his contemporary. When he had been faced with the task of annotating his Homer he had viewed with dismay the prospect of reading through the long line of commentators. Again it was more than he could bring himself to do, and he had appealed to his friend Parnell:

> The minute I lost you, Eustathius with nine hundred pages, and nine thousand contractions of the Greek character, arose to my view! Spondanus with all his auxiliaries, in number a thousand pages (value three shillings), and Dacier's three volumes, Barnes's two, Valterie's three, Cuperus, half in Greek, Leo Allatius, three parts in Greek, Scaliger, Macrobius, and (worse than them all) Aulus Gellius! All these rushed upon my soul at once, and whelmed me under a fit of the headache.[13]

When Parnell failed, he prevailed upon Broome to dredge in Eustathius for him, and extract anything that he thought of value. In returning thanks to Broome for those labours (24 March 1720) he remarked that while he himself had "the flowery walks of imagination to expatiate in," Broome had "drudged in only removing the loads, and clearing rubbish, heaped together by the negligence no less than by the industry of past pedants, whose very taste was generally so wrong, that they toiled most on what was least worth."[14] We may note again Pope's emphasis on taste as opposed to mere learning.

It was also part of Pope's complaint about Theobald and others of his kind that they were more interested in their own reputation than that of their author. The author tended to be no more than a means for the editor to display his erudition.

> There, dim in clouds, the poreing Scholiasts mark,
> Wits, who like Owls see only in the dark.[15]

639

To that Pope added the following note:

> These few lines exactly describe the right verbal
> Critick: He is to his Author as a Quack to his Patients,
> the more they suffer and complain, the better he is
> pleas'd; like the famous Doctor of that sort, who put
> up in his bills, He delighted in matters of difficulty.

Years later, when he wrote The New Dunciad, Pope returned
to the same charge — this time against Bentley, who is made
to remark:

> For me, what Virgil, Pliny may deny,
> Manilius or Solinus shall supply:
> For Attic phrase in Plato let them seek,
> I poach in Suidas for unlicens'd Greek . . .16

"Some critics," Pope explains, "having had it in their choice
to comment either on Virgil or Manilius, Pliny or Solinus,
have chosen the worse author, the more freely to display their
critical capacity." And in an earlier note Scriblerus had remarked:

> Herein shall we imitate the laudable Spirit of those,
> who have . . . delighted to comment on the Fragments
> of dark and uncouth Authors, preferred Ennius to
> Virgil, and chosen to turn the dark Lanthorn of Lyco-
> phron, rather than to trim the everlasting Lamp of
> Homer.17

To Pope and his fellow wits the scholar who devoted his time
to the elucidation of some crabbed author of the past had lost
all sense of proportion. He had lost sight of literary values
altogether; he was not interested in what was good or bad, but
only in what was obscure.

In the criticism of Theobald (who seems to have been in
private life a modest enough man) there is undeniably a constant tendency to emphasis and self-advertisement; his commentary on Shakespeare was from the first coloured by his
anxiety to draw attention to Pope's errors and omissions, and
later by his pardonable desire to demonstrate his own competence.

In consequence, he frequently showed a sad lack of self-control, and only too often he allowed himself to run riot in parallel passages and irrelevant erudition. Several of Pope's notes in the Dunciad are successful parodies of Theobald's garrulous commentary in Shakespeare Restored; others are intended to expose his rather arrogant manner of insisting on the ignorance or carelessness of his predecessors. Few editors, on the other hand, have been less ostentatious than Pope, a creative writer condescending to criticism, but always sympathizing with his own kind.

> Let it suffice, O Pallas! that every noble ancient,
> Greek or Roman, hath suffer'd the impertinent cor-
> rection of every Dutch, German, and Switz School-
> master! . . . When these men have ceas'd to rail,
> let them not begin to do worse, to comment! let them
> not conjecture into nonsense, correct out of all cor-
> rectness, and restore into obscurity and confusion.
> Miserable fate! which can befall only the sprightliest
> Wits that have written, and befall them only from such
> dull ones as could never write![18]

The dull ones who could never write: among those Pope, of course, included Theobald. Somebody, he tells us (and the somebody is probably Pope himself) made the following epi-gram on Theobald's annotations of Shakespeare as they kept appearing in the public journals:

> 'Tis generous, Tibald! in thee and thy brothers,
> To help us thus to read the works of others:
> Never for this can just return be shown;
> For who will help us e'er to read thy own?[19]

Pope's attitude to the "mere scholar" may be clarified if we recall the attitude of most cultured people of his generation to the virtuoso, the collector of moss, beetles, butterflies, and what not.

> Yet by some object ev'ry brain is stirr'd;
> The dull may waken to a Humming-bird;
> The most recluse, discreetly open'd, find

> Congenial matter in the Cockle-kind;
> The mind, in Metaphysics at a loss,
> May wander in a wilderness of Moss . . .[20]

So the goddess of Dullness tells her votaries. Addison had been more explicit:

> It is, methinks the Mark of a little Genius to be wholly
> conversant among Insects, Reptiles, Animalcules,
> and those trifling Rarities, that furnish out the Apart-
> ment of a Virtuoso.[21]

So, too, with the antiquarians, the collectors of statues and coins. They also suffered from a sort of monomania; their minds did not range philosophically, but were confined to a narrow and partial scrutiny of one small corner of human knowledge. Sir Isaac Newton, we are told, "though he scarce ever spoke ill of any man, could hardly avoid showing his contempt for your virtuoso collectors and antiquarians. Speaking of Lord Pembroke once, he said, 'let him have but a stone doll and he is satisfied. I can't imagine the utility of such studies: all their pursuits are below nature.'"[22] To Pope and his friends a Theobald, poring over his books and noting the different occasions on which Shakespeare used some obsolete word, was a sort of literary virtuoso "conversant among Insects, Reptiles, and Animalcules." He was not so much a reader as a collector.

Yet in this unnatural struggle between learning and taste Pope was to find more than once that learning might prove the stronger. That he was uneasily conscious of not having read sufficiently the books that Shakespeare probably knew may perhaps be deduced from the evident annoyance that one particular discovery of Theobald's caused him. In annotating a passage in Troilus and Cressida, V. v:

> the dreadful Sagittary
> Appals our numbers . . .

Pope had referred his readers to Teucer, the archer in Homer. In a letter to Matthew Concanen, which appeared in Mist's Journal, 16 March 1728,[23] Theobald was able to show that "this passage contains a piece of private history, which, perhaps,

Mr. Pope never met with, unless he consulted the old Chronicle, containing the Three Destructions of Troy, printed by Caxton in 1471, and Wynken de Werde in 1503; from which Book, as I shall hereafter shew, our Poet obtained this circumstance." Theobald thereupon quotes a short passage about "a mervayllouse beste that was called Sagittarye" which slew many of the Greeks with his bow. So much did Theobald's correction prey upon Pope's mind that after referring to it contemptuously in his note to I. 129, he returned to the same point at I. 162, and again at I. 166 and 212. Finally, as if that were not enough to ridicule Theobald's suggestion, he printed as an appendix, "A copy of CAXTON's Preface to his Translation of Virgil," apparently relying on Caxton's antiquated English to move the reader to derisive laughter. But Theobald was right; it was indeed a notable victory for mere learning, and Pope would have done better to leave ill alone.

This ridicule of Theobald-cum-Caxton suggests another defect in Pope's editorial equipment. If Theobald and Hearne took perhaps a pedantic delight in mere antiquity, Pope had all the prejudice of the polite writer in favour of the up-to-date. He had the Augustan distaste for the uncouth, and a not entirely adult tendency to laugh at the homely language of his forefathers.[24] A scholar like Hearne, therefore, who shows an almost naive enjoyment of the antiquated, was easy game. He is honoured with three couplets[25] in the Dunciad:

> But who is he, in closet close y-pent,
> Of sober face, with learned dust besprent? . . .

and Pope's notes on the passage are illuminating.

> Most rightly are ancient words here imployed in speaking of such who greatly delight in the same: We may say not only rightly, but wisely, yea excellently, inasmuch as for the like practise the like praise is given to Hopkins and Sternhold by Mr. Herne himself . . .

And again, after quoting Hearne's praise of "the old English Saxon tongue," Scriblerus remarks:

> I do herein agree with Mr. H. Little is it of avail to

643

> object that such words are become <u>unintelligible</u>.
> Since they are <u>Truly English</u>, Men <u>ought</u> to under-
> stand them; and such as are for <u>Uniformity</u> should
> think all alterations in a Language, <u>strange</u>, <u>abom-
> inable</u>, and <u>unwarrantable</u>.

Those sarcastic notes are in accord with almost all Pope's
pronouncements about the language of earlier days. In his celebrated <u>Guardian</u> essay (No. 40) he had laughed at Philips's use
in his <u>Pastorals</u> of such antiquated terms as "welladay" and
"whilome." In "The Art of Sinking," Ch. IX, he had ridiculed
those writers whose imitation consists in "copying the Blemishes, or Imperfections of celebrated Authors," and who, in
imitating Milton, reproduce with the utmost exactness such
archaisms as "nathless," "paynim," "emprize," and so on.
In the Preface to his <u>Iliad</u> he had, it is true, ventured to assert — though with no great air of conviction — that "perhaps
the mixture of some . . . old words after the manner of Milton,
if done without too much affectation, might not have an ill effect in a version of this particular work, which most of any
other seems to require a venerable, antique cast." But when
he used antique words himself it was usually for comic effect,
as in his burlesque imitations of Chaucer and Spenser.

This prejudice (the word is hardly too strong) against the
language of former times was bound to interrupt Pope's enjoyment of Shakespeare; and he must often have longed to eliminate or to modernize some archaic turn of speech in his author.
In this matter his friend and predecessor as an editor of Shakespeare was better fitted for his task. Nicholas Rowe was so far
from deploring the archaic element in Shakespeare that after
his own edition had been published he went so far as to write
his own <u>Jane Shore</u> "in imitation of Shakespeare's style." Rowe,
it is true, was careful not to go too far, but he went further
than Pope approved. "It was mighty simple in Rowe," he once
remarked, "to write a play now, professedly in Shakespeare's
style, that is, professedly in the style of a bad age."[26] Pope
cannot be suspected of malice here; he liked Rowe, and Rowe
had been dead for many years when the remark was made. The
style of the Elizabethans was to Pope — as to most of his contemporaries — quite simply a bad style; we had advanced since
Shakespeare's day.[27] As an editor, therefore, he must sometimes

have been distressed by Shakespeare's obsolete or out-of-the-
way expressions. That he did frequently modernize Shakespeare's English is only what we might have expected.

There is plenty of evidence, too, that Pope was also affected by a malady most incident to Shakespeare's editors — the
desire to expunge from his page everything that he considered
unworthy of his author. But here it should be remembered that
he was exposed to far greater temptation than Theobald; he was
the victim of his own excellent taste. Writing, after all, was
Pope's business, and he had a constant itch to improve not only
his own but other men's work, to bring a phrase to the final
perfection of which it was capable. He had been doing this all
his life, with Wycherley, with Parnell, with the Duke of Buckingham, with Broome and Fenton; the thing had become a habit.
When he turned to the editing of Shakespeare, he approached
his task, as Professor Nichol Smith has said, "in the spirit of
a literary executor."[28] Here again the Dunciad throws some
light on what Pope really thought about an editor's obligations
to reproduce faithfully and completely his author's text. In his
address to the goddess of Dullness Theobald is allowed to boast:

> Here studious I unlucky moderns save,
> Nor sleeps one error in its father's grave,
> Old puns restore, lost blunders nicely seek . . .[29]

To leave his meaning in no doubt, Pope adds a note:

> As where he laboured to prove Shakespear guilty of
> terrible Anacronisms, or low Conundrums, which
> Time had cover'd . . .

The implication here seems to be that if an editor stumbles
upon an anachronism or a low conundrum in his author he is
to keep quiet about it for the sake of his author's reputation.
Amica veritas, sed magis amicus Plato. If time has buried
some wretched pun, why dig it up again? The editor's business
is to display his author in the best possible light, and if his
imperfections can be covered or removed or explained away,
so much the better. It was this laudable desire to prevent Shakespeare from dishonouring himself that led Pope to relegate
whole passages "which are excessively bad"[30] to the foot of the

page and print them in smaller type. And then Theobald, like
some unlucky cur, had come nosing about among this garbage
and dug it up again.

It has been customary to represent Pope as writhing in
agony at the attacks of Theobald and others, and retaliating with
malice and venom upon those who had gibed at him or exposed
his defects. That the publication of Shakespeare Restored must
have annoyed him deeply is obvious enough; but an unprejudiced
reading of the Dunciad will hardly bear out the contention that
Theobald had goaded him to helpless rage. Indeed, Pope's satire on Theobald is far too telling and far too light-hearted to be
the work of a man who has lost his temper. Theobald's thrusts
had undoubtedly gone home, but they had not fallen on any part
where a wound could be fatal. By his own standards Pope had
certainly not scamped his work for Tonson; he had taken real
pains with his edition of Shakespeare, and had discharged his
duty, as he said himself, with more labour than he expected
thanks. But editing, after all, was only a secondary matter with
Pope. Looking back on what he may sometimes have thought to
be wasted years, Pope could write:

> Hibernian Politicks, O Swift, thy fate,
> And Pope's whole years to comment and translate.[31]

To this he added a note:

> The Author here seems to lament that he was so long
> imployed in translating and commenting. He began the
> Iliad in 1713 and finish'd it in 1719. The Edition of
> Shakespear, which he undertook merely because he
> thought no body else would, took up nearly two years
> more in the drudgery of comparing Impressions, rec-
> tifying the Scenary, &c. and the translation of half the
> Odyssey employ'd him from that time to 1725.

No doubt this is rather too off-hand; but Pope having none of
Theobald's burning enthusiasm for emendation was not much
tempted to show his paces as an editor. His real business was
poetry. Editing, on the contrary, came first with Theobald;
he was a second-rate writer, but he had high hopes of being
remembered as a first-class scholar.

"THE DULL DUTY OF AN EDITOR"

Writing of the effect on Pope of Shakespeare Restored, Johnson remarks:

> From this time Pope became an enemy to editors, collaters, commentators, and verbal criticks, and hoped to persuade the world that he miscarried in this undertaking only by having a mind too great for such minute employment.[32]

I do not seek to set aside that judgment, but it has been my aim to suggest that it might with some advantage be modified. Pope's attitude to collators and commentators goes back to days long before Theobald had become a particular source of annoyance to him; it was indeed an attitude that he shared with the other wits of the day. He certainly retaliated upon Theobald, and with devastating effect; but he was also expressing the natural antipathy of the man of letters for the scholar. A natural antipathy, since the wits are seldom scholars, and the scholars are rarely wits. At best such a contest is like the encounter of the expert swordsman and the retiarius with his net and trident: one of them will win, but it is a pity they should ever be matched.

NOTES

1 The Iliad of Homer. Translated by Mr. Pope . . . 1715 (fol.), vol. i, p. 3.

2 Op. cit., ll. 159-60. See D. Nichol Smith, Shakespeare in the Eighteenth Century, 1928, who adds (p. 47) that not till Johnson did any critic combine the two qualifications.

3 The Dunciad, IV, 235.

4 See John Butt, "Pope's Taste in Shakespeare," Shakespeare Association Pamphlet, 1935.

5 In the Preface to his edition of Shakespeare.

6 Pope to Swift, 28 June 1728.

7 And Theobald's master, Richard Bentley. But Bentley figures more prominently in the Dunciad of 1743.

8 Op. cit., p. 193.

9 Cf. Pope's note to the Iliad quoted above, in which he claims that we are now beginning "to value the first Editions of Books as more correct, because they have been least corrected."

10 I. i.

11 The Dunciad, I. 166. When Cibber became hero, in 1743, this line had to be removed to IV. 250.

12 The Dunciad (1729), I. 111 ff.; (1743 — Cibber's library), I. 127 ff.

13 The Works of Pope, ed. W. Elwin and W. J. Courthope, 1871-89, vol. vii, p. 451 ff.

14 Ibid., vol. viii, p. 44.

15 The Dunciad III. 187-8 (1729); III. 191-2 (1743).

16 The Dunciad (1743), IV. 225 ff.

17 The Dunciad, IV. 6 n.

18 Added in 1735 at II. 179; (1743: II. 187).

19 I. 164 (1729); I. 177 (1743).

20 The Dunciad (1743), IV. 445 ff.

21 The Tatler, No. 216.

22 J. Spence, Anecdotes . . . , ed. S. W. Singer, 1820, p. 325.

23 Reprinted by J. Nichols, Literary Illustrations, vol. ii, pp. 203 f.

24 Cf. his letter to Humfrey Wanley, Works, ed. cit., vol. x, p. 115. Gay shared his enjoyment of this form of humour. See his "Proeme to the Courteous Reader" in The Shepherd's Week.

25 III. 181 ff. (1729); III. 185 ff. (1743).

26 J. Spence, Anecdotes, ed. cit., p. 174.

27 See "Shakespeare's Imitators in the Eighteenth Century," Modern Language Review, vol. xxviii, No. 1, Jan. 1933, pp. 24 ff.

28 *Shakespeare in the Eighteenth Century*, 1928, p. 34. "What
has an executor to do with a series of papers that are not
quite ready for the press? He is disloyal to the memory
of his friend if he perpetuates the little blemishes which
his friend would undoubtedly have removed; and if he hits
on a happy little alteration which he is convinced his friend
would have at once adopted, a rearrangement of words, or
the omission of a clumsy or obscure phrase, he may not
be the trusty friend that he was expected to be if he stays
his hand."

29 I. 143 ff. (1729). In 1743 these lines had to be omitted, as
having no reference to Cibber.

30 The Preface to Pope's *Shakespeare*.

31 These lines first appeared in 1736 at III. 327-8 (1743: III.
331-2); they were substituted for an earlier version of the
couplet.

32 *Lives of the Poets*, ed. G. B. Hill, III, 138-9.

THE IMPORTANCE OF POPE'S LETTERS

D. F. Bond

One by one the obstacles to a full and sympathetic understanding of Pope are disappearing before the labors of a corps
of twentieth-century scholars. Thanks to the pioneer work of
R. H. Griffith, the bibliography of Pope has been brought, at
least provisionally, into an orderly framework. The co-operative efforts of the Twickenham editors have provided an authentic historical context in which the poems may at last be read
without misunderstanding and prejudice. And now, with this
magnificent new edition[1] of the correspondence, students will
no longer have to depend on the chaotic, incomplete, and un-
sympathetic edition of Elwin and Courthope for Pope's letters.

The present edition brings together well over fifteen hundred letters of Pope, together with nearly five hundred addressed to him, and over a hundred and fifty others which throw
light on Pope's activities — a total of over two thousand letters,
arranged for the first time in one chronological sequence and
edited, it hardly needs saying, with unrivaled erudition and
sympathetic understanding by the most eminent Pope scholar
now living. Professor Sherburn has not been able to print every
extant letter — occasionally he has to refer to a letter as "not
available for publication" — but his edition must be well-nigh
complete, drawing as it does from a wide variety of sources —
libraries, family archives, private owners, and dealers — on
both sides of the Atlantic. The result, crowning a lifetime of
research, surely constitutes one of the major works of humanistic scholarship produced in our time.

The new collection increases by about a third the total of
letters in the Elwin-Courthope edition and includes notable additions to the correspondence with William Fortescue, Hugh
Bethel, Ralph Allen, and Bishop Warburton. But, of course,
it is not primarily in numbers that the present edition excels;

Reprinted from Modern Philology, Vol. 56 (1958), pp. 55-59, by permission of the author and of The University of Chicago Press. Copyright
1958 by The University of Chicago.

in its high standards of accuracy, its wealth of illustrative material, and, above all, its approach to its subject, it is so far superior to its nineteenth-century predecessor that the two can hardly be mentioned together. The chief importance of the correspondence, Elwin thought, lay in its relation to the morality of Pope," and he could only conclude gloomily that "we have to decide whether [Pope's] letters are not many of them fraudulent, and the circumstances attending their publication a series of ignominious plots, infamous false accusations, and impudent lies" (I, xxvii). As every reader of the Early Career knows, Professor Sherburn can refute Victorian suspicions of eighteenth-century manners without falling into the opposite error of condoning everything which Pope did. Consequently, while not indorsing Elwin's view of the "dry and frigid generalities" of the letters, he can permit himself to view them as "self-consciously noble and polished" and temperately characterize them as "serious, carefully written examples of moral — and political — eloquence" (I, x).

The complicated story of Pope's own publication of his correspondence, disentangled by Griffith and others, is here given in a somewhat overbrief summary, followed by a list of editions (1726-42) of the letters which supplements and in some cases corrects Griffith's bibliography. Although some readers may regret the decision not to provide a fully critical edition of Pope's texts as "not sufficiently rewarding," any one who has attempted to work through the confusions inherent in the variant issues of a large part of the correspondence will prefer this edition to the alternative of waiting for a possible text of absolute finality, if such a text is indeed in this matter a possibility. Only about a tenth of the letters here printed were published by Pope; and, of those, about a third exist in Pope's autograph or in contemporary and trustworthy transcripts. By comparing the originals of these with Pope's texts, the editor is able to show, revealingly enough, the kind of changes and omissions which Pope felt necessary and desirable. In printing from Pope's autographs he also enables the reader in many cases to note the omissions which Elwin made of indecorous passages. A characteristic example occurs in the letter to Caryll of January 9, 1713/4 (I, 207).

In printing the letters Professor Sherburn adopts a convenient system of symbols to indicate (1) letters not hitherto

included in collections, (2) those which rest only on the authority of Pope's editions, (3) those suspected as conflations or
fabrications, and (4) those published by Pope but now available
from a more authentic source. The user of the edition is thus
able at a glance to formulate some judgment as to the validity
of the text in question. Another helpful device is the headline
on each page giving the names of writer and recipient of each
letter, as well as the date. Useful, too, are the chronological
summaries of Pope's activities placed at the beginning of each
year, with an appraisal of the significance of the letters surviving from that year. The footnotes, including a number from
Pope himself and from Elwin-Courthope, are placed properly
at the bottom of the page and are admirably precise and illuminating.[2]

Because of Pope's position in the literature of his day and
because of his friendships and quarrels, an edition of his correspondence becomes an encyclopedia of information on eighteenth-century ideas and personalities. Its chief value, nevertheless, lies in the light which it throws upon Pope himself.
"If Pope was as great a poet," his latest editor justly remarks,
"as we have been led to believe, his mind is worth study, and
his personal qualities can be more directly seen in his letters
than elsewhere" (I, x). Some indication of the riches which
this collection has to offer may be gathered from a glance at
the Index, occupying the greater part of Volume V, with the
longest entry "Alexander Pope" covering over fifty columns.[3]
This entry is divided into eight sections: "Biographical Data";
"Works"; "Letters"; "Villa, Gardens, and Grotto"; "Rambles
and Visits"; "Character"; "Reading"; and "Portraits." The
materials indexed here, it is safe to say, afford the fullest
guide in existence to Pope's biography and will be of obvious
utility to generations of future researchers. Particular attention should be paid to the section on "Character" (pp. 180-89),
a kind of omnium-gatherum of extraordinary range, from
"Pope's Good Deeds" to "Observations on Wit." The number
of persons, places, and topics included in the Index as a whole
will prove to be both interesting and informative. The present
edition does not attempt to index every proper name occurring
in the letters, notably in the correspondence with Bolingbroke,
where the pages are wearisomely studded with allusions to
historical figures; and occasionally there is no identification

made of a name, e.g., Sir John Shelley, on whom the Elwin-Courthope edition is informative. The reader must be cautioned, too, that the Index, valuable as it is, is far from complete and if one finds no entry under, say, "Machiavelli," this cannot be taken as an indication that there is no reference to this figure in the correspondence.

Elwin, it will be remembered, thought a chronological arrangement of Pope's letters neither desirable nor possible — undesirable because "a unity of subject often runs through his intercourse with particular persons," and impossible because so many of the letters are undated. Professor Sherburn obviates the first of these objections by means of a most valuable "Alphabetical List of Correspondences" (V, 21-48), enabling his readers thus to follow straight through Pope's letters to and from a single correspondent without difficulty. As to the other point, many of the letters are, of course, impossible to locate chronologically, and often a conjectural date is acknowledged as "a wild guess." But it is immeasurably better to have provisional dates assigned than to lump the letters together without dates at all. The present arrangement provides a tentative sequence for the correspondence and is not likely to mislead. The contrast with the tangled and unsatisfactory grouping of letters in Elwin-Courthope is constantly apparent. Here the full evidence is supplied, and the reader may try his ingenuity in dating by means of the clues supplied in the footnotes.[4]

The accuracy of the texts cannot readily be appraised without access to the manuscripts from which many of the letters are printed. One might guess that in the letter to Caryll (II, 37) the word in the sixth sentence is "unseasonable" (Elwin's reading) rather than "unreasonable," and that at II, 43 (l. 13), Pope wrote "fewer spirits to support such a state than I used to have formerly." In Fenton's letter to Broome (III, 37) a possible reading in the third paragraph is: "The war is carried on against him furiously in pictures and libels; and I hear of nobody but Savage and Cleland who have yet drawn their pens in his defence." The following corrections should be made in a second edition (I exclude errors of punctuation):

I, 63 (to Cromwell), l. 6: revolving years; p. 64, l. 21: with what he tells us; p. 151, l. 8 f. b.: have yet met with; p. 248, l. 22: shall go to supper; p. 258, l. 5: stood an end; p. 270, l. 8: historical, grammatical; p. 297 (to Broome), l. 2:

acknowledgments; p. 321 (to Broome), l. 2: acknowledgments; p. 322, l. 12: neighbour; p. 366, l. 22: presented children; p. 393 (first letter), last line: make ten; p. 399, last line of prose: was also; p. 401, l. 22: stags-eyes; p. 422, l. 13: You see here that I give you; p. 474, l. 18: and that there is; p. 486, l. 6 f. b.: throughly sensible; p. 519 (second letter), l. 3: scarcely; p. 520, l. 18: restless, and agreeable.

II, 29 (to Hughes), l. 8: and most faithful; p. 46 (from Jabez Hughes), l. 10: who had always; l. 20: waved; p. 119, l. 8: know that I am; l. 18: for this matter; p. 182 (to Broome), l. 8: at any time; p. 204, next to last line: mutual; p. 205 (to Broome), last line: at verse 188 to 200; p. 207, l. 18: begin with the alteration; p. 208, l. 6 f. b.: to an end; p. 214 (to Broome), l. 10: circumstances; p. 231 (letter of April 24), l. 11: you could come; p. 244, next to last line: apprehensions; p. 263 (first letter), next to last line: Twitnam; p. 266, l. 8 f. b.: Nicols; p. 271, l. 15: in a week more; p. 338 (to Broome), l. 5: your own sake; p. 389, l. 11 f. b.: brings me my own note; p. 429 (to Broome), l. 2: have been hurried; p. 431, last line: noisy foolish falsehoods; p. 432, l. 17: than ever I knew him; p. 456 (to Knight), l. 4: as well else have; p. 457, l. 3: yet have; p. 465, l. 5: early on Sunday morning; l. 6: at London; p. 513, l. 10: to the Downs; p. 519 (Thomas Cooke to Pope), l. 1: I had this day; p. 520, l. 24: from what I have heard.

III, 138 (to Gay), l. 6: all good and happiness; p. 139, l. 5: informations; p. 142 (to Gay), l. 8: physicians to one another; l. 9: It was a remedy; p. 143, l. 5: of our ancestors; p. 228, l. 3 f. b.: walls; p. 229, l. 27: without pomp or affectation; p. 230, last line: whose speaking; p. 231 (to Richardson), next to last line: services; p. 299, l. 7 f. b.: will contrive to meet; p. 313, l. 3: state of stupidity; l. 13: a sound nap till towards Christmas; p. 331, l. 6: indeed reasons; l. 12: particularised; p. 352 (second letter), l. 1: I am as much; p. 378, last line: than usual; p. 379, l. 25: and give you the reasons; p. 484 (Mallet to Pope), l. 12: à l'Angloise; p. 496, last line: the interposition of some dark body; p. 497, l. 3: be the more.

IV, 38, last line: consequences; p. 111 (Hill to Pope), l. 2: Lord B——ke's; l. 7: distance; p. 120 (Hill to Pope), l. 15: great unhappiness; p. 168, l. 5: more than a recompence; p. 198, l. 4 f. b.: till; p. 199, l. 10 f. b.: and I now feel; p. 208, l. 5: by post; p. 244, l. 13 f. b.: Collection; p. 266, l. 8 f. b.:

translated it into; p. 294 (first letter), next to last line: is not
now prefixed; p. 307 (Mrs. Whiteaway to Orrery), l. 7: sending
it you; p. 423, l. 4: I thought I had a right; l. 15: obliged; l. 20:
respect which you avow; p. 478 (second letter), l. 1: agreeable;
p. 511 (second letter), l. 2: which I pray God to continue; p.
512, l. 5: by half a spoonful; p. 523, l. 5: say of him.

In the line from the Aeneid quoted in the letter to Caryll
(I, 122), infensi ("hostile, enraged") is in fact the correct reading in Virgil and not an error of Caryll's scribe. In the two
letters to Steele (I, 146-47, 149-50) there are more substantive
variants in the Spectator printing than are here recorded. At
II, 229, there is a slight error in note 2. Elwin (VII, 403) does
not emend the text of Pope's letter to Bolingbroke as stated
here; his reading is "Notwithstanding you tell me the Oracles.
. . ." In Arbuthnot's letter of July 17, 1734 (III, 416), the reading have appears in editions 1737-42. Of the letter to Louis
Racine (IV, 415-16) a different version was published in May,
1754, in the Scots Magazine (XVI, 231-32). There are a few
errors in references.[5]

The Post-Man was not a Tory newspaper (I, 71); it is, in
fact, listed among the "Whig Papers" in the Examiner of April
24, 1712. The Feast of St. Peter is incorrectly named (I, 116).
Lucy Aikin's name is, as often, misspelled (I, 139; V, 50), as
is that of William Oldisworth at I, 373. The Colonel Frowde
mentioned in Gay's letter to Caryll (I, 288) was the uncle, not
the brother, of Philip Frowde, the dramatist and author of The
Fall of Saguntum. J. B. Rousseau (I. 385) was born in 1671,
not 1670, and Sir Richard Hoare (I, 394) died on January 5,
1718/9, not 1718. The DNB gives the date November 2 for the
birth of Prince George William (I, 451). According to Elwin,
to whom we are referred (II, 367, n. 1), Edward Caryll married in June, 1729, not "early in 1730." Bishop Atterbury (II,
169) embarked on board the "Aldborough" on Tuesday, June 18,
and arrived in Calais on the following Friday, June 21, according to the Political State of Great Britain (XXV, 672). Were
the civilities which Jervas speaks of (I, 244) only "efforts to
control the pens of the 'Little Senate' "? This seems less than
fair to Addison: the date is August 20, 1714, and Jervas specifically mentions the likelihood of Addison's good offices on
Pope's part "at Court." The Lord Cornwallis mentioned in the
letter to Broome (I, 270) is the fourth Baron Cornwallis (1675-

1722); in the Index he is confused with his son (of the same
Christian name), who at this time was only fourteen. (The
other references, II, 365, 396; III, 498, are correctly to the
son, later the first Earl Cornwallis [1700-1762].)

It is misleading to say (II, 56) that The Persian and Turk-
ish Tales compleat were translated in two volumes by Ambrose
Philips and William King, since Philips and King were responsible for separate and evidently rival versions. The two volumes which Dr. Atterbury found so "Monsterous" were apparently the translation by "the late Learned Dr. King, and several
other Hands," published by W. Mears and J. Brown in two volumes on August 18, 1714 (advertisements in the Post Boy of
August 17 and 19). The translation by Ambrose Philips was
published by Tonson in three volumes, appearing successively
on July 6, 1714; August 21, 1714; and February 11, 1714/15.
(The Mears-Brown version is dedicated to Lady Theodosia
Blye, Baroness of Clifton; the three volumes of Philips' translation are dedicated to the Countesses of Godolphin, Sunderland,
and Dorset, respectively.) The advertisement by Mears and
Brown in the Post Boy of August 19 ("Yesterday was publish'd")
announces that "This Translation is much better done and printed on finer Paper than that said to be done by Mr. Phillips,
which will not be compleat, when a 2d Vol. is publish'd." Tonson, on the other hand, advertises in the Daily Courant and the
Spectator of Wednesday, August 18, the forthcoming second
volume of Philips' translation on the following Saturday, with
a comment on the rival version:

> N. B. To prevent Gentlemen's being mistaken,
> who have already bought the first Vol. this is to inform
> them, that the Edition of the Persian and Turkish Tales,
> which is this Day Published in two Vols. is not Trans-
> lated by the same Hand, but by an unknown Hand.

Atterbury's reference (II, 108) to the poem in praise of
hogs, "every Verse of Which begins with a P," is clearly to the
Pugna porcorum of Johann Placentius (1642), reprinted in the
Latin jest book of 1648, Nugae venales (Gentleman's Magazine,
November, 1776, pp. 511-12, and February, 1777, p. 70).
Pope's allusion (II, 369) to the Tatler's joke concerning being
"dull by design" perhaps deserves comment. Steele had concluded

THE IMPORTANCE OF POPE'S LETTERS

Tatler, No. 38, by saying: "It is to be noted, That when any Part of this Paper appears dull, there is a design in it," a statement frequently quoted against Mr. Bickerstaff -- e. g. , in the Examiner of July 12, 1711, and in Defoe's Review of August 18, 1711. Addison in turn promised to give over the Spectator when it should grow dull (No. 10), and Steele prophesied in the same journal (No. 19) that he would "sometimes be dull" in order to gratify the envy of his detractors. The jest -- it is referred to again in Spectator, No. 338 — was long a popular one: Fielding alludes to it in 1752 in the first number of the Covent-Garden Journal.

But the question of how much to annotate can never be answered to everyone's satisfaction. With letters from such a variety of correspondents and covering so wide a field of interests, an editor of Pope's correspondence might easily be tempted to swell the commentary to Scriblerian proportions. As they stand, the notes are succinct and illuminating, constantly enlivened with those strokes of wit and irony which have characterized the writing of Professor Sherburn over the years. One can think of no more helpful and delightful companion to the letters.

A particular problem arises in connection with the Latin quotations which occur so frequently in eighteenth-century correspondence. When Pope writes to Jonathan Richardson (II, 177), "Homo sum, humani nihil alienum puto," will the present-day reader be enlightened or insulted by a footnote? Elwin usually passed over such things without comment, perhaps taking them for granted as a part of a Victorian reader's background. Professor Sherburn usually gives the source but leaves the Latin or Greek untranslated — surely an unrealistic procedure at the present time. Some of the Latin tags — like the Virgilian auri sacra fames (II, 257) or the Horatian Jus et Norma loquendi (II, 218) are left unnoticed. Virgil's olim meminisse is identified at II, 364, but left without a note at IV, 81. Two familiar lines from Martial are left unidentified (II, 388; III, 260), and there are other Latin quotations which possibly call for identification.[6] Similarly with the English quotations. Milton's "last Infirmity of noble Minds" (I, 213) is left unnoticed, as are the quotations from Paradise Lost at II, 50, 165, 317. Biblical quotations are usually identified, often with a reference to the Latin version, but not uniformly. Shakespeare's "our life rounded with a sleep" (I, 186, 202) is evidently taken as recognizable by every reader, but the lines cited by Aaron Hill (II, 35), though they come from Hamlet, are surely too unfamiliar to be left without identification. The line, " 'Tis Expectation makes a Blessing dear" (I, 347), which Pope calls a "famous Verse," takes on added interest when we learn that he is quoting from Suckling's "Against Fruition" (it is in Bartlett's Familiar Quotations). Other English passages which should perhaps be identified are the comparison of life to piquet (I, 233), the two lines about Dryden (I, 255), and Sir William Temple's observation on the loss of friends (IV, 12).

Many more questions might be raised concerning annotation. But they would serve only to indicate the richness and variety of the materials assembled in these volumes and the problems which the editor has had to face and which he has for the most part triumphantly solved. It is hard to think of any other eighteenth-century correspondence, not excepting that of Walpole, which offers greater substance for anyone interested in the literature of the "indispensable century." These letters, covering forty years and involving nearly two hundred correspondents, not only will be read with renewed interest and delight in their new format but will furnish abundant materials for a generation of research. It is the edition which has been long awaited and for which both editor and publishers may be warmly congratulated.

NOTES

1 The Correspondence of Alexander Pope. Edited by George Sherburn. 5 vols. Oxford: Clarendon Press, 1956. Pp. xli + 524; 533; 519; 526; 234.

2 For annotation of the letters, the Elwin-Courthope edition will still, in spite of inaccuracies, merit consultation. Elwin occasionally prints supplementary letters not included here, e. g., the letter of Broome to Pitt of March 24, 1741/2 (E-C, VIII, 183-85), and he frequently provides biographical and historical information, sometimes of value, which has not been carried over into the present edition. On Edward Blount, to take but one example, Elwin tells us more about his daughters (II, 296; E-C, VI, 383)

and quotes from a contemporary newspaper the date and circumstances of his death (II, 319; E-C, VI, 386). Elwin's evidence as to dating of letters "from the post-mark" (III, 116; E-C, VIII, 161) or from a marginal annotation (III, 330; E-C, IX, 499) and his marking certain others as "Extracts" (Faulkner to Orrery, IV, 280; E-C, VIII, 428; Mrs. Whiteaway to Orrery, IV, 307; E-C, VIII, 461) might have been reproduced more consistently. At other times he supplies details about the letters which seem worth preserving, as when he tells us (E-C, VIII, 35) that Pope's letter to Broome of February 10, 1714/5 (I, 276) "is franked by Addison," an interesting point in view of the relations between Pope and Addison in 1715.

3   In the initial summary (V, 139) of the entries under Pope's name the page numbers are all wrong, doubtless because of last-minute additions at the beginning of this volume.

4   For the letter to Gay (I, 195) here assigned to October 23, 1713, Professor Sherburn abandons his former view of 1712 (Early Career, p. 75) and reverts to Elwin's conjecture of 1713. The arguments in favor of 1712 still seem entirely convincing.

5   I, 338 n.: Virgil's Eclogues i, 79. II, 75 n.: Dennis' Original Letters, I, 286. II, 130: E-C, VIII, 57. II, 212: Essay on Criticism, l. 525. II, 480: Addison's Cato, v. 1.10. III, 303: Horace's Odes i. 32. 2-3. IV, 148 n.: Pope to Lord Orrery, October 19 [1738].

6   The couplet in Lady Mary's letter (I, 514) which looks at first sight like Silius Italicus is identified by my colleague, Professor Edward L. Bassett, as from Seneca, Apocolocyntosis vii. 2. 11-12.

VI. THE DUNCIAD

THE DUNCIAD

R. H. Griffith

In the stream of Pope's own mental life, The Dunciad is
not a digression, but is of the integral texture of it, which was
the same from first to last. The Dunciad continues, on the
reverse side, the doctrine of the Essay on criticism. A couplet from the Essay (ll. 264-65) might have served as the motto
or text for The Dunciad:

> Neglect the rules each verbal critic lays,
> For not to know some trifles, is a praise.

The crime of a man is to expend energy upon things that do not
advantage mankind. Dryden had stated the obverse, the true
doctrine (State of innocence, sig. b 1, verso): "They wholly
mistake the Nature of Criticism, who think its business is
principally to find fault. Criticism, as it was first instituted
by Aristotle, was meant a Standard of Judging well. The chief-
est part of which is to observe those Excellencies which should
delight a reasonable Reader. If the Design, the Conduct, the
Thoughts, and the Expressions of a POEM, be generally such
as proceed from a true Genius of Poetry, the Critique [critic]
ought to pass his judgment in favor of the Author. 'Tis malicious and unmanly to snarl at the lapses of a Pen, from which
Virgil himself stands not exempted." From 1715 to 1727 journals multiplied rapidly; and the publication of ill-founded opinions and benighted criticisms multiplied more rapidly. Why,
Welsted and A. Philips were being acclaimed the great poets
of England! To this was added the mountainous accretion of
verbal criticisms and, worse, criticisms of commas in Theobald's Shakespear restored. A wave of wrong methods, wrong
standards was threatening the extinction of Learning in England.
This Pope "experienced." Thus he saw it. He was mistaken —
doubtless. His was the mistake of all who bemoan the departure

Reprinted by permission from Philological Quarterly, Vol. 24 (1945),
pp. 155-157.

of "the good old days." He could perceive the passing away of the good and helpful in the old order; but the good and helpful in what was to come was not yet manifest. The ideal of Theobald and Bentley, perhaps not clearly perceived by themselves, a diminishing tolerance of error, an increasing demand for precision, is a method or tool or attitude of mind necessary to a growing understanding of the structure of things. Four years after Pope's death Hartley stated (too narrowly, in his turn), "Criticism . . . may be defined the Art of restoring the corrupted Passages of Authors, and ascertaining their genuine Sense, and Method of Reasoning" (Observ. man, I, 356). Pope entered manhood condemning the waste of energy; he departed life doing the same thing.

We can go further and learn more if we look at The Dunciad and Pope's whole work and Pope himself in his place in a larger framework.

A sufficient number of things, gestated in the womb of time, emerged and became working forces in men's minds around about the year 1540 to make that time the beginning of the Modern World in England. Among all of them the presiding idea was that an individual's will should not be subjected to the will of a group or another individual imposed upon it. The idea has made its progress in stages. In religion, the English church freed itself from Rome and became the Church of England and from 1540 a party contention was that it had allowed too little freedom of individual judgment. In state organization, from the middle of the period (1603) a further struggle was to evade having "Divine Right" perpetuate the hierarchical set-up in the political machinery. By 1720-30 the checks-and-balance "institution" of King-Parliament-Church was a halting place; but soon dissent was dissatisfied and vigorously at work. The period from 1660 to 1780 nurtured the demand for popular government and led to The Revolutions. That from 1780 to 1900 was spent in getting manhood suffrage ("freedom" of the individual) and trying to make it work.

The period from 1540 to 1660 was the age of gentlemen, and control was in the hands of royalty, nobles, and gentry. Estates were the mark of them, and education was planned for their needs and tastes. Their needs were to learn, not how to do things, but how to give instructions to their laborers or their agents and overseers over workmen; and how to do the governing

664

of the commonalty. Their tastes were to be developed through college generation after college generation to determine what were the excellences in the arts. The humanities were the nobleman's reading; and the Greeks and Latins had produced most of the reading worthy his attention. The professions — priests, lawyers, physicians, teachers, literary men — were cadets in his house or his upperclass servants, catering to his needs and pleasures, and were both supported and guided by patronage.

Dryden and Pope were of the next period, 1660-1780, and both were educated into, and adopted as their own, the scale of excellences of the preceding period (1540-1660). They were aware of forces stirring beneath their mental feet that threatened change, even breakdown of the established order. They desired orderliness, wanted standards. Dryden's was among the large group of minds that wish to be told what to believe. In beliefs he moved, slowly perhaps but surely, to the Tory party, the Roman Catholic Church, the Rules in art, even if in practice he sometimes followed afar off. In Pope's day (Pope and Perrault's Ancients and moderns were born in the same year) subterranean forces had broken the surface and had become perceptible, though interpretation of them lay in the future. Newspapers, journals, pamphlets, "novels," theaters were drawing a livelihood from the public, a public but lately become literate. And that little-thinking public was to be the judge of what is excellence! (The Drama's Laws the Drama's Patrons give.) Pope (Order is Heaven's first law . . . And who but wishes to invert the laws / Of Order, sins against th' Eternal Cause), Pope, champion from 1711 to 1744 of the aristocratic way, Pope could not imagine order achievable in any but a hierarchical system, with the best and most authoritative of proven excellence at the top. Order was now being ignored from below. What good the disturbance was engendering in its womb, Pope was unaware of. To him there was the threat of Anarchy flooding in, a new Dark Ages to engulf England.

Many, far too many readers have thought of The Dunciad as merely a personal brawl, in which Pope engaged his (numerous!) enemies in a knock-down, drag-out fight. What he really has done, is what a great poet necessarily does. He has taken an experience actually lived through and felt intensely, and placed it in a framework wherein its meaningfulness transcends its individual importance. The result he named The Dunciad.

THE DUNCIAD, BOOK IV

George Sherburn

The last poem that Pope wrote was probably the fourth
Book of the Dunciad, and for a poet whose art was always
marked by control, a last poem should be at least among his
best. Yet Joseph Warton and others have thought this Book an
"unhappy" addition to the poem; and in recent years, when commentators have agreed in preferring the 1729 version of the
Dunciad to that of 1743, there has been danger that we may casually seem to undervalue the merits of Book IV — which, unlike
Books I-III, is obviously not in competition with an earlier version. It may be permissible, consequently, to examine again
the diverse complexity of the Book in such detail as will enable
us at least to see its true nature.

First, we may consider its intellectual quality. If the reader is one of those who think intellectual poetry a contradiction
in terms, he clearly need read no further here; for to the present writer it seems true that to read Book IV without regarding
it as an intellectual pronouncement is to miss the greater part
of its power. Pope, as Warton remarked with high praise,
"chose to be the poet of reason," and the statement is true,
even if it is necessary to realize that reason was a word of
varying implications in Pope's day.

Professor Sutherland has called attention to the fact[1] that
two hundred lines of this Book derive from Pope's project for
a poetical essay on education, and certainly education in at
least lines 138-336 is a featured topic. Pope covers the whole
field from the time when the boy-senator is flogged for dull
memory work ill done to the glorious moment when the finished
fop returns from the "educational" grand tour. The schools,
Pope alleges, padlock the mind rather than open it; and the
university wastes time on logic and metaphysics, subjects so
pedantic and impractical as to make it easy for the student to

Reprinted from Texas Studies in Literature and Language, Vol. 24 (1944),
pp. 174-190, by permission of the publisher and of the estate of George
Sherburn.

be unaware of "Civil Duties" and to believe contentedly in the doctrine so dear to Dulness —

The Right Divine of Kings to govern wrong!

The passage devoted to the universities is memorable for the eloquent and dramatic episode (lines 203-74) involving Pope's old enemy Richard Bentley, who died, aged eighty, about four months after the lines appeared in print. Though perhaps the most personal of all the satire in Book IV, these lines are typical of the development away from mere personality to a wider meaning. Pope, it is clear, had slight grounds for a personal hatred of Bentley: his dislike was consistently for the slashing dryasdust scholarship the man exemplified. Depiction of personal traits, however, is marked in this passage -- in Bentley's tempestuous academic career, his love of port, his brusque, awful manner as well as in the manipulations of his hat; but, what is far more important, Bentley is made chiefly the effective symbol of the fact that

The critic Eye, that microscope of Wit,
Sees hairs and pores, examines bit by bit —

and, thus microscopically focused, will never comprehend larger and nobler issues. Pope is still blind to the real if humble uses of technical literary scholarship, but its dangers he perceives and expresses with immortal trenchancy. His sense of the seriousness of these dangers transcends and dignifies his prolonged animus against Bentley. The satire here is not intellectual merely because it is about scholarship: it is creditably based on respectable intellectual principles.

In keeping with his usual method of arranging sequences of episodes in contrasting moods or tones, Pope passes from the friends of Aristotle (Bentley and the other dons) to the travelled fops and virtuosi, and then reverts to more intellectual matters in his condemnation of free-thinkers. His fashionable travellers are castigated for their vapidity, and they illustrate the failings inherent in the "Cibberian forehead," as Bentley and Dr. Clarke illustrate the "Cimmerian gloom" of dark intellectuality (line 532). Pope's travellers and virtuosi tend to be obscurely pseudonymous. Paridel, Annius, Pollio, and Mummius are all uncertainly identified or not at all. The point again is that here finally the poet is more concerned with fashionable follies than with individual fools. The elegant specialists, or virtuosi, are to Pope the sort of men who, if they do not imagine reason given them "but to study flies," certainly

> See Nature in some partial narrow shape,
> And let the Author of the Whole escape:
> Learn but to trifle; or, who most observe,
> To wonder at their Maker, not to serve.

Thus they answer the wishes of Dulness, who hopes to see literary learning, awareness of civil duties, and the investigation of nature, all extinguished by a devotion to miscellaneous and unmeaning factual detail or by intricate and ultimately perplexing logical complexities. Such is the burden of Pope's satiric comment on education.

His remarks about free-thinkers must surprise those who insist that the author of the Essay on Man was himself at heart a deist. One is, of course, tempted to explain his attacks (lines 459-516) on "rationalizing divines" (as Fielding loved to call them) and on other heterodox or skeptical persons as due to the influence of his new adviser, Warburton. But, at least briefly, in the earlier forms of the Dunciad, before he knew Warburton, Pope had paid his respects to Anthony Collins, Toland, Tindal, and Woolston,[2] and the evidence is fairly conclusive that he was early eager in his scorn of free-thinkers. Here in Dunciad IV he attacks not merely such men as Tindal and Thomas Gordon ("Silenus"), but he is glancing at more important personages. One is, presumably, Dr. Samuel Clarke, who promoted argument over the divine attributes and also expounded the theological ideas of Sir Isaac Newton. Writing in a period when the empiricism of Locke made attacks on "high priori" metaphysics fashionable, Pope naturally fell into the confusions of his day. Clarke had been blamed for the alleged heterodoxy of Queen Caroline, and while it is improbable that his "reasoning downward" made him "doubt of God," more people than Pope and Bolingbroke believed him a doubter. His method of reasoning was quite contrary to the spirit of Locke's work. Pope evidently preferred this new empiricism; for he has his "gloomy clerk" say scornfully:

Let others creep by timid steps, and slow,
On plain Experience lay foundations low,
By common sense to common knowledge bred,
And last, to Nature's Cause thro' Nature led.
All-seeing in thy mists, we want no guide,
Mother of Arrogance, and Source of Pride!
We nobly take the high Priori Road,
And reason downward, till we doubt of God:
Make Nature still incroach upon his plan;
And shove him off as far as e'er we can:
Thrust some Mechanic Cause into his place;
Or bind in Matter, or diffuse in Space,
Or, at one bound o'er-leaping all his laws,
Make God Man's Image, Man the final Cause,
Find Virtue local, all Relation scorn,
See all in Self, and but for self be born:
Of nought so certain as our Reason still,
Of nought so doubtful as of Soul and Will.

Dr. Clarke, however, was also an experimental scientist, and his position (if indeed it is surely intended for his) is somewhat misrepresented. Since Bolingbroke and Warburton both apparently disliked Clarke's metaphysics, it is impossible to determine if either or both here influenced Pope; but it is obvious that the poet intended to be on the side of the angels and at the same time to shun metaphysical or "misty" thinking.

A famous passage from Shaftesbury's Characteristics also meets Pope's disapprobation here. Other passages from the work had given inspiration for parts of the Essay on Man; but in Dunciad IV the "sweet enthusiasm" of Theocles ("The Moralists"), which identified Nature with Deity, is reprehended in one couplet (487-8) and in a long footnote doubtless partly due to Warburton. The passage might seem a further defense against the charge of Spinozism or fatalism made against the Essay on Man, but in any case it is an attack on fashionable heterodoxy or deism.[3] Probably Shaftesbury's "extravagancy" and Platonic apriorism annoyed Pope — and Bolingbroke, who also silently borrowed from Characteristics — more than did many specific doctrinal statements.

Throughout this part of Dunciad IV Pope is, of course, making an anti-rational appeal to common sense as an antidote

669

to the metaphysics of rationalizing divines or deists. He opposes also all limited "microscopic" technical study as well as the follies of travellers and elegant virtuosi. Both "folly's cup" and "wisdom's grave disguise" are scourged. Education fails because the pupil is made

> First slave to Words, then vassal to a Name,
> Then dupe to Party; child and man the same;
> Bounded by Nature, narrow'd still by Art,
> A trifling head, and a contracted heart.

What Pope commends is the humanly sympathetic and "open" mind actuated by judgment and common sense: what he disapproves are metaphysics, the superficial follies of the wealthy, and the microscopic scholarship of men such as Bentley, Kuster, Burman, and Wasse. These scholars are mentioned by name, as are leading free-thinkers or theologians of the time. Concerning the virtuosi Pope is pseudonymously coy; but clearly his gallery of dunces is well filled and includes a rich assortment of all kinds. Poets and painters get off easily in this Book, and although Italian opera is ridiculed, we have in lines 65-70 the most famous and most timely compliment ever paid to Handel.[4]

So much for the intellectual content of the poem; its imaginative quality may be considered in two aspects — the structure of the Book as a whole and the specific quality of individual images.

The structural pattern of Book IV seems at first sight more original, less in the heroic tradition, than were the devices of the earlier Books. Book I derived from MacFlecknoe and other sources; Book II, echoing the funeral games for Anchises (Aeneid V), and Book III, drawing from the prophetic visions of Aeneid VI and Paradise Lost XI and XII, seem perhaps more normal for a mock epic. Book IV presents a grand drawing-room, appropriate for a royal birthday, at which titles or orders of merit are bestowed by the Queen of Dulness. The scene is chiefly that of such a drawing-room, but it unfolds in a slightly confusing dreamlike fashion into an academic meeting for the conferring of degrees. This latter aspect of the scene intrigued both Pope and Warburton, not merely because the Dunciad was a satire on pedantry, but because in 1741 both Pope and Warburton had been proposed for the LL. D. at Oxford, and since the grace was not voted for Warburton, Pope declined it for himself. They were both unusually "degree-conscious" at the time the poem was finished.

Book IV has been thought confused in structure; but there were special reasons why its pattern of action was easily grasped in the early 'forties. Henry Fielding in two or three very popular farces had shown royal levees crammed with incongruous episodes that followed each other kaleidoscopically much as do the passages of Book IV. And it may be added that in these plays and elsewhere in the 'thirties Fielding perhaps did more to ripen Cibber's fame in satire and make him eligible for the laureateship of Dulness than anyone else — Cibber himself excepted. When Cibber wrote his famous Letter to Mr. Pope, Inquiring into the MOTIVES that might induce him in his Satyrical Works, to be so frequently fond of Mr. Cibber's Name (1742), he might more appropriately have addressed his inquiry to Fielding[5] if his concern in the matter was, so to speak, disinterested; but Cibber in 1742 foresaw an attack by Pope in the making, and what Pope said at that moment mattered more than what Fielding had been incessantly saying for ten years.

As models for his projected Book IV Fielding furnished Pope two or three scenes from royal drawing-rooms. In the Author's Farce (1730) he had scored with an uproarious scene from the drawing-room of Queen Nonsense, and in 1736 Pasquin showed as rival queens Common Sense and Ignorance, and the drawing-room of Queen Ignorance was as confused and delightfully heterogeneous as a bear-garden. In his Historical Register for 1736 an episode in Act III shows "Apollo in a great chair, surrounded by attendants" and casting the parts à la Cibber for Shakespeare's King John. Probably not Fielding's (and certainly not Hesiod Cooke's) was a piece of similar structure, called The Battle of the Poets; or, The Contention for the Laurel, which was very briefly inserted in the second act of Tom Thumb just before Cibber was made laureate. A scene with a foolish king or a mock queen or goddess enthroned makes an admirable focal point about which farcical episode may loosely revolve. These plays by Fielding were enormously popular, and they almost certainly gave form to the new Book of the Dunciad. Doubtless authors other than Fielding anticipated Pope in the use of this scene, but no other author at the time had prepared Pope's public for the device as had Henry Fielding.

Not merely the structure of these farcical drawing-rooms but also the individual episodes in them bear some relation to Book IV. In the Author's Farce Fielding is ridiculing the irrational theater of his day, and he introduces many more types of amusement than Pope presents; but he introduces types and persons notable in the Dunciad, such as Pantomime (whose capers resemble those of Mad Mathesis), Novel (Eliza Haywood), Orator Henley, Count Ugly (Heidegger), and Opera. Fielding's contest for the bays in this farce is won by Opera. Sir Farcical Comic in the first form of the play thereupon sings his lament, and thus puts Nonsense to sleep, much as in Dunciad II the reading contest had been soporific. The song is one of Fielding's neatest absurdities concerning Cibber. In a preface to the Provok'd Husband (1728) Cibber had murdered the king's English in several ways that Fielding never forgot.6 Among other things he had misspelled paraphernalia. Hence when the disappointed Sir Farcical (i.e., Cibber) sings Nonsense to sleep, it is with the reproachful lines:

> Can my Goddess then forget
> Paraphonalia
> Paraphonalia
> Can she the Crown on another Head set,
> Than of her Paraphonalia?

The action throughout this puppet-show episode is thoroughly farcical and confusedly noisy; but the visible action made the shifting "turns" easier to grasp than they would be in a non-dramatic poem.

In Pasquin (1736) Fielding is still dealing in "Dunciad" material. Theology, law, and physic, all fail Queen Common Sense, and presently she is told that

> Queen Ignorance is landed in your realm,
> With a vast power from Italy and France
> Of singers, fiddlers, tumblers, and rope-dancers.

Eventually Common Sense is killed by her Priest, and Ignorance settles herself to rule with the plaudits of the Royal Society, Grub-street, the learned professions, Harlequin, and the opera; but they are all frightened off stage by the sudden appearance of the mere ghost of Common Sense. The thinking, again, seems much influenced by the 1729 Dunciad, and possibly it is prophetic in some respects of Dunciad IV.

At any rate the structural pattern of this last Dunciad had been made familiar to the world of fashion by Fielding's popular farces. The pictorial effect of a spurious goddess enthroned with symbolic attendants grouped grotesquely and statuesquely near by and with different groups of "subjects" passing in (satiric) review before the goddess would not perplex the imaginations of those who had been among the "fashionable mobs" who had attended the little theater in the Haymarket before the crisis of 1737. The episodic unfolding of Fielding's farces and Pope's Book IV are also somewhat similar, and, finally, both writers were satirists with a particular fondness for the low "Cibberian forehead."[7]

It is probable that Pope, who habitually composed in episodic fragments, may have written parts of Book IV before he adopted the royal drawing-room as a device for loose unification. We have his remark to Spence about "an Essay on Education; part of which I have inserted in the Dunciad,"[8] and at the point (line 138) where the inserted section begins, there is some wavering in the transitions. After the stage is set, Opera in the first abrupt episode petitions for the silencing of Handel. There follows a curious passage (73-80) that states Pope's strong and sincere concept of the positive attractive power of dulness for the many who instinctively swarm about the goddess "conglob'd" like bees "about their dusky Queen." These "naturally dull," a footnote explains, are followed by the involuntarily dull, and by a third group that are accidentally or temporarily dull. By the time we reach line 101 the movement of these attendants has clarified and become in some sort processional —

There march'd the bard and blockhead, side by side.

And the stately stride of Montalto (Hanmer) is succeeded by the more vigorous march of Bentley (lines 203ff.), who in turn gives way to the travelled fops (line 275). These successive groups, we are told in line 136, are

Each eager to present the first Address.

But in the section on education that immediately follows no petitions are presented. We have the early petition of Opera, and thereafter none until the lac'd Governor naturally ends his presentation of his foppish young traveller and the imported mistress (lines 282-335) with a request for acceptance and protection. Annius follows at once with a petition for aid in his numismatical "cheating," and he is opposed by Mummius. So likewise the petition of the expert in carnations is opposed by the lover of butterflies. On the whole, one must conclude, the poet is preoccupied with description of the grotesque and miscellaneous court rather than with a rehearsal of petitions: he seeks diversity of episode fully as much as he does structural unity of the whole. This tendency, in spite of all the learned have said, is quite typical of English neo-classicism, and in this as in most of Pope's poems episodes follow loosely in diverse and contrasting moods, just as in a suite by Purcell or Handel an allegro is followed by an andante or a courante by a rigadoon.

In all these contrasting episodes is apparent a rich variety in the nature of individual images, a variety which is the immediate and chief source of appeal in the poem. At the start of any consideration of these it must be recognized that it is erroneous to think that Pope is deficient in concrete, highly specific imagery. His theory is not that of "general effects secured through general details," though that may have been the method of Sir Joshua Reynolds and other reputable theorists. Pope's most significant comment on the matter is found in the note to his Iliad, Book VI, line 595 (1716), concerning the farewell of Hector to his infant son Astyanax:

> There never was a finer Piece of Painting than this. Hector extends his Arms to embrace his Child; the Child affrighted at the glittering of his Helmet and the shaking of the Plume, shrinks backward to the Breast of his Nurse; Hector unbraces his Helmet, lays it on the Ground, takes the Infant in his Arms, lifts him towards Heaven, and offers a Prayer for him to the Gods: then returns him to the Mother Andromache, who receives him with a Smile of Pleasure, but at the same instant the Fears for her Husband make her burst into Tears. All these are but small Circumstances,

but so artfully chosen, that every Reader immediately
feels the force of them, and represents the whole in
the utmost Liveliness to his Imagination. This alone
might be a Confutation of that false Criticism some
have fallen into, who affirm that a Poet ought only to
collect the great and noble Particulars in his Paintings.
But it is in the Images of Things as in the Characters
of Persons; where a small Action, or even a small
Circumstance of an Action, lets us more into the
Knowledge and Comprehension of them, than the material and principal Parts themselves. As we find this
in a History, so we do in a Picture, where sometimes
a small Motion or Turning of a Finger will express the
Character and Action of the Figure more than all the
other Parts of the Design. Longinus indeed blames an
Author's insisting too much on trivial Circumstances;
but in the same Place extols Homer as "the Poet who
best knew how to make use of important and beautiful
Circumstances, and to avoid the mean and superfluous
ones." There is a vast difference betwixt a small Circumstance and a trivial one, and the smallest become
important if they are well chosen, and not confused.

Himself a painter, Pope knew the value of a vivid phrase;
he recognizes clearly the imaginative power of the highly specific, "small" detail. It is true that in Dunciad IV many minute
details do not now come truly to life without the aid of annotation. Editors have done much, but the topical nature of satire
still causes the casual reader perplexity.

> A Feather shooting from another's head,
> Extracts his brain, and Principle is fled —

is a curious way of suggesting that the plume worn by Knights
of the Garter takes from the members of that order all principle
except "Homage to a King." Similarly Pope's terse manner of
saying (lines 533-6) that Self-conceit is a mirror which shows
us to ourselves subjectively transformed into "Patriot, Chief,
or Saint" — or what we will — requires study. The poem abounds
in difficult details drawn from specialized techniques such as
then belonged, for example, to the amateur of carnations:

> Soft on the paper ruff its leaves I spread,
> Bright with the gilded button tipt its head.

Professor Sutherland has been admirably illuminating on these
lines, but the "gilded button" is perhaps still somewhat too
much involved in the mystery of the florist's hot-beds. Other
instances of Pope's technical "learning" may be found in the
various details (e. g. , lines 549-65) that come from culinary
arts. In many such passages Pope's imagery seems as "far-
fetched" and specialized as that of his great predecessor — and
in some sense master -- John Donne.

This is a point to realize. Pope may be deficient in the
conventional images of poetry — those drawn from nature or
from such inspiring universals as love or death — but from first
to last his satires are full of images that might occur to a modern realistic painter or poet. The French cook, "a Priest succinct in amice white," would be merely a perfect "Dutch piece"
if Pope had not added the symbolism that elevates the gourmet's
cult to a religious level, by means of the amice, the "copious
Sacrifice," and the dubious devotion due

> To three essential Partridges in one.

Pope recurs repeatedly to food-metaphors; a good example is
lines 227-32 of Bentley's speech:

> For Attic Phrase in Plato let them seek,
> I poach in Suidas for unlicens'd Greek.
> In ancient Sense if any needs will deal,
> Be sure I give them Fragments, not a Meal;
> What Gellius or Stobaeus hash'd before,
> Or chew'd by blind old Scholiasts o'er and o'er.

These lines are typical of the vivifying use to which Pope can
put metaphors in debasing intellectual matters that meet his
contempt. Frequently his technical images are purely descriptive rather than (as in Bentley's speech) prejudicial. Take, for
example, the intellectually apt couplet:

> Like buoys, that never sink into the flood,
> On Learning's surface we but lie and nod.

This is fair evidence of observation on the part of a poet whose sea-faring included only voyages on the Thames and one crossing to the Isle of Wight. We may be less content with his ingenuity in meaning when he writes

> See! still thy own, the heavy Canon roll,
> And Metaphysic smokes involved the Pole.

He may mean simply that the heavy artillery (of metaphysics) is always on the side of Dulness; but from his footnotes one must assume that he expects some Canon of Christ Church, Oxford, to feel that the smoke encircles a paranomasiac poll!
　　Less ingenious but more biting is such a picture as that of the complete exquisite, Paridel --

> Stretch'd on the rack of a too easy chair;

or the picture of the "bowzy Sire," Thomas Gordon, less elegant in its informality. He

> shook from out his Pipe the seeds of fire;
> Then snapt his box, and strok'd his belly down:
> Rosy and rev'rend, tho' without a Gown.
> Bland and familiar to the throne he came,
> Led up the Youth, and call'd the Goddess Dame.

In these somewhat "homely" images Pope is at his best when dealing with mankind; but he is not limited, and describes the crafty Annius in rural terms:

> Soft, as the wily Fox is seen to creep,
> Where bask on sunny banks the simple sheep,
> Walk round and round, now prying here, now there;
> So he; but pious, whisper'd first his pray'r.

The poet brings to all this sort of thing a firm hand and an unerring line -- to borrow his own graphic phrase -- but he does not altogether limit himself to "Dutch" realism. The grand tour of his fop leads to a satiric gilding of the Italian lily that advertises the poet's skill in metrics and in lush detail of artificial loveliness. The fop was guided

> To happy Convents, bosom'd deep in vines,
> Where slumber Abbots, purple as their wines:
> To Isles of fragrance, lilly-silver'd vales,
> Diffusing languor in the panting gales:
> To lands of singing, or of dancing slaves,
> Love-whisp'ring woods, and lute-resounding waves.

Such imagery is pleasing but perhaps obvious. To see that Pope's imagination is operating subtly throughout the poem one may wisely consider the appropriate physical movements that vivify and characterize the dull as they pass the throne of the goddess. Opera, the first, is

> a Harlot form soft sliding by,
> With mincing step, small voice, and languid eye
>
> . . . .
>
> By singing Peers up-held on either hand,
> She tripp'd and laugh'd, too pretty much to stand.

Compare this with Sir Thomas Hanmer, the long-since Speaker of the House of Commons, come to present to Dulness his edition of Shakespeare:

> There mov'd Montalto with superior air;
> His stretch'd-out arm display'd a Volume fair;
> Courtiers and Patriots in two ranks divide,
> Thro' both he pass'd, and bow'd from side to side:
> But as in graceful act, with awful eye
> Compos'd he stood, bold Benson thrust him by:
> On two unequal crutches propt he came,
> Milton's on this, on that one Johnston's name.
> The decent Knight retir'd with sober rage,
> Withdrew his hand, and clos'd the pompous page.

After Sir Thomas

> crowds on crowds around the Goddess press,
> Each eager to present the first Address.

And among these were the university dons led by Richard Bentley:

678

THE DUNCIAD, BOOK IV

> Before them march'd that awful Aristarch;
> Plow'd was his front with many a deep Remark:
> His Hat, which never vail'd to human pride,
> Walker with rev'rence took, and lay'd aside.
> Low bow'd the rest: He, kingly, did but nod;
> So upright Quakers please both Man and God.

After Bentley's address, not decently waiting its termination,

> In flow'd at once a gay embroider'd race,
> And titt'ring push'd the Pedants off the place . . . .

This marks a decline in vigorous movement, a decline that
appropriately leads to the universal yawn. Paridel's relaxation
is followed by the bowzy snoring of Silenus (Gordon): the diminuendo is now (line 493) marked, but throughout the Book the
movement of the actors on Pope's stage is living and appropriate. He sees them move, and makes them visible to us.

Beauty is not the province of satire; and Pope's poem is
not rich in pretty or alluring detail: realism, vigor, incisive-
ness are what we expect here -- and find. The best couplet
about the fop, for example, comes when, newly exported from
the university, he begins his travels:

> Intrepid then, o'er seas and lands he flew:
> Europe he saw, and Europe saw him too.

In Italy and France he

> Try'd all hors-d'oeuvres, all liqueurs defin'd,
> Judicious drank, and greatly-daring din'd.

Obviously still in 1742 Pope has a perfect mastery of satiric
epithet! The poet is altogether impartial: he castigates the
pedant as neatly as he does the fop. Among the jewels in Bentley's speech to Dulness come, reset from Theobald's words
in the earlier form of Book I, the following lines:

> For thee we dim the eyes, and stuff the head
> With all such reading as was never read:
> For thee explain a thing till all men doubt it,

679

And write about it, Goddess, and about it:
So spins the silk-worm small its slender store,
And labours till it clouds itself all o'er.

One sees here again the steady aim and the sure fire, the
language of real life controlled and for its purpose perfect.

And so it seems permissible to borrow Dryden's words
from a better occasion and cry out, "Here is God's plenty."
There is not the Chaucerian humanity, but there is a humanity
that Chaucer would understand and approve, and there is a
richness of expressive detail drawn from the most extreme
vocations, both aristocratic and proletarian, such as Pope
achieved practically nowhere else in the same degree. And
Pope's sense of intellectual values, expressed many times in
his career, he here restates with a solemn sincerity and a
relative lack of personal animus that is fitting in a final poetic
achievement. This solemnity is seen in the opening lines and
in the famous conclusion. Even critics who insist that true
poetry must be either sublime or pathetic, and who consequently give Pope a low rating, are reconciled to the dignity, sweep,
and profound emotion embodied in these last lines. They have
been repeatedly praised for their true Longinian sublimity. It
is well to remember that in the opinion of Longinus sublimity
came from the mind. Book IV of the Dunciad is so crammed
with extremely diverse imagery that Joseph Warton, for example, thought it "one of the most motley compositions, that,
perhaps, is anywhere to be found in the works of so exact a
writer as Pope."9

But to leave the poem at that is a gross undervaluation both
of Pope's organizing design — whether from Fielding or not —
and, above all, of the basic integrity of his sense of intellectual
values. Pope has a just prejudice against the dunce as an intellectual vacuum as well as against the dunce "with loads of
learned lumber in his head." The fourth Book is not a contradiction of the first three Books: it is a richer and more imaginative restatement of the values announced in 1728 and 1729.
For once Bowles was right about a poem by Pope when he wrote
at the end of his introduction to Book IV:

In polished and pointed satire, in richness of versification and imagery, and in the happy introduction of

characters, episodes, figures, and every sort of
poetical ornament, adapted to the subject, this book
yields, in my opinion, to none of Pope's writings of
the same kind.10

NOTES

1 The Poems of Alexander Pope (Twickenham ed.), V (1943),
   xxxi. Unless otherwise specified all textual quotations
   from the Dunciad are from this edition, by Professor
   James R. Sutherland.

2 Ed. cit., V, 144-5, 174-5.

3 One must suspect from a curious footnote to the Essay on
   Man, Ep. II, 1. 165ff., as found in the quarto edition of
   1743, p. 16, that Pope was somewhat confused in his attitude towards Characteristics. Relevant also is the note
   to Dunciad IV, 244, and of course one finds much in Paul
   Vater's Pope und Shaftesbury (Halle, 1897).

4 The great composer was, when Pope wrote these lines,
   bankrupt and in Ireland — producing among other things
   Messiah. He so appreciated Pope's praise that in his next
   opera (Semele, 1743) he inserted in Congreve's libretto the
   famous aria, "Where'er you walk" — set to the words of
   Pope's Summer, lines 73-6.

5 Practically all of Fielding's attacks on Cibber are treated
   in Houghton W. Taylor's "Fielding upon Cibber," MP,
   XXIX (1931), 73-90.

6 Cibber's "To the Reader," where most of his blunders
   occur, is dated January 27, 1727/8, but the printed version appeared in time for Pope to make last-minute inser-
   tions from it in his "Peri Bathous," which was on sale
   March 8. The newspapers seized upon the errors before
   that date, but Pope must have responded instantly to this
   preface; Fielding responded perpetually.

7 It has been thought (W. L. Cross, History of Henry Fielding,
   I, 132-4) that Pope and Fielding were not friendly; but there
   seems to be no reason for such an assumption apart from
   the attacks of the Grub-street Journal on Fielding's plays.

681

These had nothing to do with Pope. Richard Russell, editor of the Journal, was a friend of Jeremy Collier, and early in his Journal he had announced his intention of continuing Collier's war upon theatrical immorality and profaneness. This aim easily embroiled Russell with Fielding. Pope and Fielding were both friends of Ralph Allen and of the Earl of Chesterfield, and, in an unpublished letter to Allen, Pope mentions Fielding as at least an acquaintance. A copy of Joseph Andrews still exists that Pope had bound up in his favorite red morocco and gave to Ann Arbuthnot. Fielding in turn filled his writings with high compliments to Pope. Ten weeks after the New Dunciad appeared in 1742 Fielding and William Young ("Parson Adams") published a translation of Plutus the God of Riches, the footnotes of which attacked Theobald in a way that must have delighted Pope. In choosing their dunces and their friends Pope and Fielding were accidentally or consciously "of a mind."

8   Spence, Anecdotes (ed. Singer, 1820), p. 315.

9   Warton, Essay on the Genius and Writings of Pope (Fifth edition, 1806), II, 369.

10   Pope's Works (ed. William Lisle Bowles, 1806), V, 258.

POPE'S SOCIAL SATIRE: BELLES-LETTRES AND BUSINESS

Hugo M. Reichard

    The modern redemption of the Dunciad has been in part a
demonstration that the poem deals with extant dunceness more
than with forgotten dunces.[1] By way of extending the demonstration, I wish to show how luminously Pope associates the spread
of bad books with the dynamics of a commercialized society.
While dealing of course with other problems too, the Dunciad
and its pendants treat a notable aspect of the issue which pervades and unifies most of his mature satire — the antinomy of
mercenary and humane values. Repeatedly between 1728 and
1743 Pope contemplates the predicament of a nation that is
"sunk in lucre's sordid charms" and of men who are "alike in
nothing but one lust of gold."[2] He protests the corrupt practices
of politicians like Walpole, the extravagance of aristocrats like
Timon, and the acquisitive enterprise of business men like
Balaam. As far afield as the great Parisian banquet of the Dunciad (IV. 549-564) Maynard Mack has sensitively detected Pope's
animus toward a "money culture."[3] Since it underlies his general outlook of gloom,[4] this animus is even behind the sighs
for a "sinking land" which appear briefly amid the spacious
optimism of the Essay on Man (IV. 265-266). A similarity between two of Pope's finest symbols marks the special place of
the Dunciad within his vision of evil: in the Epilogue to the
Satires the goddess Vice rules an avaricious world by means
of "golden chains" (I. 147-148, 161-162); and Dulness, the deity
of the Dunciad, fixes society to a bimetallic standard of "lead
and gold" (IV. 13-16).
    The premise of the Dunciad is Pope's belief that art is a
cultural value of the first order and that the artist takes rank
among a nation's most distinguished persons. In his own way
a gifted poet is as useful to the state as the lawgiver; even in
the lesser genre of satire he is entrusted with a sacred instrument.[5] It is this esteem for literature which quickens Pope's

Reprinted from Publications of the Modern Language Association, Vol.
67 (1952), pp. 420-434, by permission of author and publisher.

abhorrence of men who write poorly. Yet neither the love nor the hate gets out of hand. Nowhere does he say that modern authors are in fact the legislators of mankind, or that vile authors in particular have brought on the ruin of nations. In his opinion, to anticipate, most writers are accessories rather than principals of the society about them; and a society gets almost exactly the writers that its leaders are worthy of. As a young poet, in the Essay on Criticism, Pope correlated the declines of Roman arts and empire (vss. 683-692); in his prime he views Grub Street as a function of unfortunate contemporary changes.

The groups that Pope holds accountable for the degradation of literature are those represented, almost proportionally, at the heroic games which fill the second book of the Dunciad. They include the nobility (vss. 191-220, i. e., 30 lines), the government (vss. 269-358, i. e., 90), and the publishers (vss. 31-190, i. e., 160); they also include, if only implicitly, by large proxies, an indiscriminate public that consumes the stuff for which unscrupulous politicians, publishers, writers (vss. 221-268), and critics (vss. 365-418) are variously responsible. If these four groups do not themselves write trash, they preside over the process.

Pope, who complains often of the bungling of aristocrats in government, deplores likewise their inadequacy as patrons of the arts. Ideally the nobleman would be endowed and trained after the fashion commemorated in the epitaph "On Charles Earl of Dorset":

> Dorset, the grace of courts, the Muse's pride,
> Patron of arts, and judge of nature, died:
> The scourge of pride, though sanctified or great,
> Of fops in learning, and of knaves in state.

Aristocrats formed on that model would rightly take precedence as arbiters of character and taste; from them, rather than nobodies, the world would take its judgments of men and books.[6] Unfortunately, however, blood will no longer tell of intelligence and sensibility. If he is only a "fop, whose pride affects a patron's name,"[7] a person of quality is unlikely to carry on the humanist tradition of a Dorset. In the hands of gentlemen who are wretched critics and writers, as well as stupid enthusiasts

for operatic and theatrical gibberish,[8] patronage has deterior-
ated into a sorry and infrequent transaction. To patrons of this
stamp dunces flock, and dunces they always entertain and sometimes remunerate. Both the games and the triumph of Dulness
attract those

> Who pay her homage in her sons, the Great;
> Who, false to Phoebus, bow the knee to Baal;
> Or, impious, preach his word without a call.
> Patrons, who sneak from living worth to dead,
> Withhold the pension, and set up the head;
> Or vest dull Flatt'ry in the sacred Gown;
> Or give from fool to fool the Laurel crown.
> And (last and worst) with all the cant of wit,
> Without the soul, the Muse's Hypocrite.
>   There marched the bard and blockhead, side by side,
> Who rhym'd for hire, and patroniz'd for pride.[9]

On the rare occasions when the new-model patron distributes
small sums as well as broad smiles, he singles out his outstanding flatterers and pimps.[10]

If the aquatic games of Dulness are any sign, the subven-
tions of the government are even more mischievous and extensive than is the patronage of the aristocracy. In the Epistle to
Augustus King Charles II is pointedly remembered as a mon-
arch under whom "the willing muses were debauch'd at Court"
(vss. 139-154), and George II is ironically addressed as a
"great patron of mankind" who is just as apt to mend his country with arts as with morals and laws (vss. 1-6). George Augustus is promptly installed in the Dunciad as the sovereign
dunce of the land (I. 6). Appropriately, the ministers of an
"Augustus born to bring Saturnian times" (III. 320) confine their
favors to their supporters, so that Cibber holds the laureateship while Swift languishes in Ireland and Gay dies in neglect.[11]
There is a market at Court, not for truth, but for panegyric,
bawdry, and blasphemy.[12] There is even a larger market for
polemic writing in defense of the government and denigration
of its opponents:

> Here strip, my children! here at once leap in,
> Here prove who best can dash through thick and thin,

> And who the most in love of dirt excel,
> Or dark dexterity of groping well.
> Who flings most filth, and wide pollutes around
> The stream, be his the Weekly Journals bound.[13]

In certain cases the rewards for controversial writers extend
beyond keepsakes to honors, places, and pensions.[14] Evidently,
if a man prefers to write propaganda for the government instead of puffs for the rich, he can turn from the private patron
to the state.

Apart from politics and patronage the writer has a third
recourse: by way of theatre-managers and publishers, with
whom we deal shortly, he can peddle his wares to the middle
class -- a vast and unleavened audience for books and plays. In
the theatre spectators demand farce and sex, costume and
spectacle:

> There still remains to mortify a Wit,
> The many-headed Monster of the Pit:
> A sense-less, worth-less, and unhonour'd crowd;
> Who to disturb their betters mighty proud,
> Clatt'ring their sticks, before ten lines are spoke,
> Call for the Farce, the Bear, or the Black-joke.
> What dear delight to Britons Farce affords!
> Ever the taste of Mobs, but now of Lords;
> (Taste, that eternal wanderer, which flies
> From heads to ears, and now from ears to eyes.)
> The Play stands still; damn action and discourse,
> Back fly the scenes, and enter foot and horse;
> Pageants on pageants, in long order drawn,
> Peers, Heralds, Bishops, Ermin, Gold, and Lawn.[15]

A theatre of this sort obviously appeals to the lowest common
denominator of taste in a fashion that adumbrates some productions of the stage today and many of the movies, radio, and
television.

Reading matter, as the phrase goes, is similarly in demand. If he cannot find employment as a script-writer, the
hack can turn from the stage to the press, which Pope finds
busily creating prototypes of the tabloid newspaper and the slick
magazine, pulp fiction and the comic book, editorial-page verse

and best-selling novels. It is from the press that

> Miscellanies spring, the weekly boast
> Of Curl's chaste press, and Lintot's rubric post;
> Hence hymning Tyburn's elegiac lines,
> Hence Journals, Medleys, Merc'ries, Magazines:
> Sepulchral Lyes, our holy walls to grace,
> And New-year Odes, and all the Grub-street race.[16]

Since the public buys up printed materials rapidly for reading or wrapping, scribblers can eke out a living by torturing sense and metric, idiom and metaphor, fact and fiction. They find customers for all manner of abominations, from bombast and plagiarism to pornography.[17]

The general public for such books and plays is composed of many elements. One supposes that it includes apprentices and artisans; certainly it includes women and domestics.[18] But most notable of all are the tradesmen and merchants of the City. In general, Citizens and Dulness are intimately associated. The goddess likes Guildhall almost as much as Grub Street itself, and is especially close to those successful Citizens who become sheriffs and mayors.[19] More specifically, in Pope's view, the business man responds only to literary sludge. His understanding of a thoughtful hero like Cato is slight; and his homage to a talented poet like Butler, posthumous. Time was when he kept his own aviary of City swans like Settle, in whose voice municipal holidays lived one day more.[20] But the Citizen no longer needs to have his literature made to his measure; what he wants he finds plentiful now on the open market, thanks to the laws of supply and demand. Even butchers attend and enjoy the performances of Orator Henley in the pulpit or Colley Cibber on the stage.[21]

If this mass audience keeps seedy men of letters gainfully employed at times, it nevertheless gives Pope pause. Its taste is not only an eyesore but also a contagion, bringing to one dead level every mind. By default of the aristocracy, the middle class has become the jury of literary excellence. When plays are designed for tradesmen and servants, it is barbarian as well as indecorous that, according to the third Moral Essay, "peeress and butler share alike the box" (vs. 140), laughing, gaping, and clapping in unison. A nation has abandoned or

truncated its scale of values when "one Poetic Itch / Has seiz'd
the Court and City, Poor and Rich," and when farce — the staple
of the illiterate — has become the delicacy of the nobility.[22] For
butchers alone to relish Cibber would perhaps be sufficiently
regrettable; it is an outrage, Pope means to say in the Dunciad,
that dukes join butchers in applauding the man (I. 223). Aristocrats are new and distinguished addicts to the "charms, that
smite the simple heart / Not touched by Nature, and not reached
by Art" (III. 229-230). The thematic movement of the Dunciad —
how Dulness progresses from "booths, to theatre, to Court"
(III. 200-300) — is the poetic reflection of the historical process
by which ascendancy passed from landed gentlemen to business
men. It is, furthermore, no incidental reflection on Pope's
part. The translator of Homer is unlikely to have picked at random the very proposition which opens his epic:

> The Mighty Mother, and her Son who brings
> The Smithfield Muses to the Ear of Kings,
> I sing.

By way of underscoring the point of these crucial lines, Pope
subjoins a lucid, resolute note: "Smithfield is the place where
Bartholomew Fair was kept, whose shews, machines, and
dramatical entertainments, formerly agreeable only to the
taste of the rabble, were . . . brought . . . to be the reigning
pleasures of the court and town." On account of a revolution in
taste as well as politics and economics, the Dunciad closes in
spiritual darkness and chaos. As middle-class theatre-goers
and book-buyers replace aristocratic patrons in paying the
piper and calling the tune, "art after art goes out, and all is
night" (IV. 640). The bourgeois Balaam has succeeded Lord
Dorset; and the nadir, rather than nature, has become the norm
of taste.

Literature is now brought into the market place where,
like other commodities, books and ideas are turned over
shrewdly rather than philosophically. The middlemen between
the consumers and producers of this literature are the theatre-
managers and the stationers. The managers, to begin with,
are of course exhibited in the Dunciad in the person of Cibber.
He is a modern Midas of the theatre: when one recalls that
Midas of old combined a knack for turning things into gold with

a flair for rating Pan's music over Apollo's, one appreciates the dual capacity in which "our Midas sits Lord Chancellor of plays" (III. 324). Cibber's bimetallism — his golden tact and leaden taste — seals him of the tribe of Dulness, the goddess who is of "business the directing soul" (I. 169).

Publishers display much the same endowments as managers. They also supply and influence what the market demands. From Curll's "chaste press" pour bawdry and obscenities; from Lintot's, along with much else, colored title pages that look ahead to the spectral charms of modern book jackets (I. 39-40). The contests in which stationers engage at the games of Dulness reveal more than the resourceful competitiveness of the trade. They disclose besides the nature and quality of the articles which are handled. Alive to the usefulness of an established author's name, stationers dredge up and publish discarded scraps, piratical editions, plagiarisms, or forgeries of his work. For such enterprises they are on occasion brought to court and pilloried.[23] But they are not confined to gross and actionable practices in the making of books. From buxom authoresses they accept, in addition to private favors, scandal chronicles and pornography.[24] And from gaunt authors, to whom we now turn, they sweat reams of vendible copy.[25] Their code is deplored in the Dunciad in a dictum that mixes and contrasts the ideal and the real: "Glory, and gain, the industrious tribe provoke" (II. 33).

The drudges who concoct popular and profitable literature for the publishers are forerunners of the free lance, the staff writer, and even more opulent kinds of modern men of letters. In the Dunciad Pope can perform a classical vivisection of the authorial hired hand because he can get at that member of our society directly and unceremoniously. He sees and reports so much because he examines the specimen early, before the industrial revolution replaced the quill with the typewriter and, by an improvement of status and stipends, translated the literary demimonde into the literary profession.

Pope finds in the popular writer an ugly complication of inherited and acquired disabilities. Morally, to waive such matters as cursing, gambling, and drinking, the hack refuses the tasks that are left to an author by the great authors before him, and applies himself instead to the chores set by his employers. He forges and plagiarizes, prevaricates and libels, flatters and blasphemes. He turns out oriental tales and topical novels, broad farces and bedroom comedies, as the vogues come and go.[26] His versatility is blemished only by his talent, knowledge, and craftsmanship; he may be either badly educated or poorly trained, and is often congenitally unfitted for a calling to which he is led by chance or misjudgment, by vanity or madness.[27] To be sure, one need not agree completely with all that Pope says of scribblers. When the Dunciad concedes the average hack even "less human genius than God gives an ape" (I. 282), Pope is doubtless going a little too far.

It is his distinction, nevertheless, shared by too few subsequent artists, that he reacts strenuously to the unlovely writing that forms the most enormous part of modern literature. If his choice of proper names were much faultier than it is, if he had mistaken a dozen Defoes for dunces, he might continue to claim that "the poem was not made for these authors, but these authors for the poem."[28] For the Dunciad is a defense of good books against sacrilege to which later generations have become desensitized, and an illuminating account of the processes which have surrendered literature to "the Pindars and the Miltons of a Curl" (III. 164). If it is intended to apply to the whole of Pope's satire, the opinion that "the great topic of his ridicule is poverty"[29] is utter nonsense, inasmuch as he is primarily concerned with affluence — with the abuse of wealth by persons of quality. If it is intended to apply to the literary satire alone, the statement is still nonsense, since the stressed topic of the war with the dunces is dunceness.[30] The indigence of the hack is at once less important to Pope than mediocrity or incompetence, and also meaningful in its proper place in a way that Johnson curiously fails to grasp.

The context of Pope's allusions to authorial poverty is a capacious scrutiny of the psyche and bearings of the commercialized man of letters. As he makes his examination, Pope provides a stimulating diagnosis of the impulses and vagaries which make people take pen in hand to earn a living. He notes among other things the competitiveness and sensitivity that are found in the lowest species of the genus irritabile vatum as well as in an Atticus. But the heart of his account lies in the formulation and treatment of the "four guardian virtues" of the writing profession.[31]

The first of these is "Fortitude, that knows no fears / Of

hisses, blows, or want, or loss of ears." Here is indeed an
unextinguished hearth of potboilers. It is, however, for the
second and third of the professional virtues that Pope has suffered most misunderstanding:

> Calm Temperance, whose blessings those partake
> Who hunger, and who thirst for scribling sake:
> Prudence, whose glass presents th'approaching jayl.

One suspects that the statement and illustration of these drab
matters were particularly in Johnson's mind when he declared:
"The great topic of his [Pope's] ridicule is poverty: the crimes
with which he reproaches his antagonists are their debts, their
habitation in the Mint, and their want of a dinner. He seems
to be of an opinion, not very uncommon in the world, that to
want money is to want everything." It has to be granted, even
insisted, that Pope is interested not only in the infra-literary
output of hack writers but also in their sub-standard income.
One need not deny, furthermore, that he appreciates and incidentally exploits the pejorative as well as comic overtones
of a hollow purse. No more often than Boileau, Dryden, or
Byron does Pope decline to marshal arguments ad hominem
or, in particular, to enlist the prejudices of the snob. In the
Dunciad, nevertheless, rags implicate morals more than caste.
　　The modern popular writer, with his royalties and contracts, will hardly recognize his primitive ancestor in Grub
Street, working for a pittance, carrying his worldly goods on
his back, and living from hand to mouth.[32] A hack who is animated by inter-office memoranda is several income-brackets
removed from the malnutrition of a "meagre, muse-rid mope,
adust and thin, / In a dun night-gown of his own loose skin,"
whose inspiration wells up from the bottom of his stomach.[33]
Ill clad as well as fed, the aboriginal hack may wear the same
threadbare suit for five or six years. His housing, when he
has any, may be a drafty, unheated garret in the red-light
district.[34] The worst is not yet. Inasmuch as freedom of the
press is still very much circumscribed, his scurrilities may
lodge him in the pillory; and since his wages are low and unsteady, his bills may oblige him either to elude the bailiffs or
to rot in a debtor's prison.[35] In old age, finally, he may have
to descend from amusing the barely literate in print to diverting

the wholly illiterate in person; so the ghost of old Settle wails
in the Dunciad:

> Yet lo! in me what authors have to brag on!
> Reduc'd at last to hiss in my own dragon . . .
> Like the vile straw that's blown about the streets,
> The needy Poet sticks to all he meets,
> Coach'd, carted, trod upon, now loose, now fast,
> And carry'd off in some Dog's tail at last. (III. 285-292)

If one may take as a criterion Johnson's longer and graver account of Savage's tribulations ("toil, envy, want, the garret,
and the gaol"), Pope's descriptions of literary temperance and
prudence must be pronounced accurate.

The main affirmative meaning of Pope's treatment of poverty in the fourth estate requires some preliminary negatives.
Unless I have missed many allusions to the topic in combing
the canon, want of sixpence or supper does not figure in the
poems so often as Johnson fancied; it receives far less notice,
to get back to Pope's first principles, than want of rhyme or
reason. Again, it is no rare opinion that to want funds is to
want everything; but Pope does not hold it. Though Johnson
remains in most ways the finest critic that Pope has ever inherited, it must be said that at times — for example, in slashing at some of the Moral Essays, all the Imitations, and all
the political satire — he shows a dramatic predilection for
playing Ahab to Pope's white whale. With the Dunciad (if not
the hump) he seems to identify some of the exasperations of
his early drudgery. At any rate Johnson's vision is in some
way clouded when he takes Pope for an advocate rather than an
adversary of the notion that ready cash is all. Pope would have
certainly subscribed to the judgments of the Idler that the eighteenth century was "an age of commerce and computation"
(No. 38), a time "in which commerce has kindled an universal
emulation of wealth, and in which money receives all the honours which are the proper right of knowledge and of virtue"
(No. 73). For Pope reports with indignation that wealth "seems
at present to be the favourite, nay, the only, mistress of mankind, to which all their endeavours are directed, through all
the paths of corruption and luxury."[36] The mature satires are
meditations on just this crisis of values, in which people of

wealth and quality are acutely engaged in abusing both their distinctions.

Pope does not of course think that men without wealth and quality are generally more virtuous: with the large exception of the scribblers, he does not notice such have-nots much in his satire; and when he uses them incidentally as foils, he makes them almost always analogues rather than antitypes of his butts from the upper classes. Since he believes in degree and subordination, one is scarcely surprised to find him complaining that the rich and great are becoming as bad as the poor and lowly — the parson, for example, like the cobbler, and the statesman like the huckster. But neither the chain of being nor his own scale of living keeps Pope from recognizing integrity and talent where he finds them. He discriminates rigorously between a "man of wealth" and a "man of worth," and he faithfully constructs his compliments and strictures on the principle that, not money, but moral "worth makes the man, and want of it the fellow."[37] Consider the humblest hero of the satires, the Man of Ross who significantly finds an annual surplus of £500 on his hands. The very point of telling the story of the Man of Ross is that the poet knows of good people among the poor, to whom this commoner gives all his time and much of his modest income, while men of high rank and large fortune give almost nothing. A central article in Pope's impeachment of the aristocracy is that, alike as patrons of the arts and as landlords in the provinces, noblemen have become indifferent to worth and want in the lower orders of society.[38] How badly Johnson misapprehended Pope's attitude toward destitute writers becomes plain when one considers that a man is not likely to be vexed by the scarcity or stupidity of patrons unless he is concerned for the number of artists who stand in need of intelligent, generous patronage.

Nor is the literary market any more automatic and absolute a stigma in Pope's eyes than is literary indigence. It is one of the sources of his strength as a social critic that he has an Antaean foothold in earthly economics. Very sensibly, he believes in the desirability of a secure, minimum income.[39] He understands of course that, in order to eat, a writer has to work out some sort of arrangement with publishers, theatre-managers, and the public. Even Shakespeare, he observes in the Epistle to Augustus, set his pen to paper for gain rather than glory (vss. 69-72). Pope's criticism of literary commercialism is judiciously qualified because it is not the jeering of an outsider at a market from which he has abstained or been excluded; on the contrary he is sometimes said to be the first business man among English poets, as well as the finest satirist. After giving up "ten years to comment and translate," he is unashamed of the proceeds:

> (thanks to Homer) since I live and thrive,
> Indebted to no Prince or Peer alive.[40]

The reason that Pope is unashamed of his profitable ventures on the literary market is that he is proud of the distinguished work he had to sell, and proud besides of the independence and integrity he had left. But not every author who brings his wares to market offers something genuinely worth buying; nor does every author have the fibre to pass intact through adversity and success, pressures and temptations.

One grubby tenement is exhibited in the Dunciad as the common "cave of poverty and poetry" (I. 33-34), not because Pope wishes to sneer, as Johnson charges, but because he is rendering a useful truth. He is saying that sometimes incompetence impoverishes the artist, and that often poverty corrupts the man. Of hacks in distress he thinks "it is not charity to encourage them in the way they follow, but to get 'em out of it: For men are not bunglers because they are poor, but they are poor because they are bunglers."[41] Though one wishes that literary rewards and punishments were meted out so scrupulously by publishers, critics, and readers, one can hardly query the kernel of fact in Pope's overstatement. There is still more fact and applicability to his appraisal of poverty as a cause, rather than an effect. When he guides us through his cave of poverty and poetry, he talks sense as well as sarcasm; if he does not for a moment think that poverty (or anything else) justifies bad verse, he certainly believes that poverty can drive a man to it:

> I must not here omit a Reflection, which will occur
> perpetually through this Poem, and cannot but greatly
> endear the Author to every attentive Observer of it:
> I mean that Candour and Humanity which every where

> appears in him, to those unhappy Objects of the Ridi-
> cule of all mankind, the bad Poets. He here imputes
> all scandalous rhimes, scurrilous weekly papers,
> lying news, base flatteries, wretched elegies, songs
> and verses . . . not so much to Malice or Servility
> as to Dulness; and not so much to Dulness, as to
> Necessity; And thus at the very commencement of his
> Satyr, makes an Apology for all that are to be satyr-
> ized.[42]

Similarly, when he touches on the sad fact that a cold winter
and an empty coal scuttle can bring a man to scribble the most
revolting indecencies and lies, he subscribes to the tough-
minded view that want is a powerful stimulus of mischief, but
he teases the soft-hearted idea that want is also a firm claim
to amnesty: "Our indulgent Poet, whenever he has spoken of
any dirty or low work, constantly puts us in mind of the Poverty of the offenders, as the only extenuation of such practices.
Let any one but remark, when a Thief, a Pickpocket, a Highwayman or a Knight of the Post is spoken of, how much our
hatred to those characters is lessen'd, if they add, a needy
Thief, a poor Pickpocket, a hungry Highwayman, a starving
Knight of the Post, &c."[43] Because Pope is too adamantly
loyal to the sanctity of belles-lettres to extend clemency to in-
digent botchers and vandals, one need not imagine that he is
unable to comprehend their plight and compulsions. Understanding need not abort satire, and satire need not negate understanding. The penury of literary offenders may be the spur of
their crimes without becoming the shield.

Here is the firmest facet of Pope's multiple intention in
allowing the destitution of his dunces to show. To the effort one
would have expected Johnson, who can speak in the Adventurer
of "the crimes to which poverty incites" (No. 131), to respond
immediately and cordially. After reporting (to select one further passage from dozens) that Savage sometimes slept "on a
bulk, in a cellar, or in a glass-house, among thieves and beg-
gars," Johnson concludes: "It cannot but be imagined that such
necessities might sometimes force him upon disreputable practices."[44] Though Pope's theme that poverty corrupts is no
novel text, it is one of those truths of which men need more
often to be reminded than informed. The "temperance" and

"prudence" of the seedy men of letters to be found in the Dunciad contain vastly more earnest than jest; they bear in upon us the truth that material privation and insecurity warp the moral and intellectual development of human beings. In one of its aspects the Dunciad is a tonic deterrent against fathering virtues on necessity.[45]

To the principal aspect of the Dunciad, however, we return in the last of Dulness's cardinal virtues. If modern popular writers have felt their withers unwrung by the spur of poverty, they fall well within the jurisdiction of

> Poetic Justice, with her lifted scale
> Where, in nice balance, truth with gold she weighs,
> And solid pudding against empty praise.

Behind the printed claptrap that stuffs our newsstands and bookshops, our mailboxes and minds, labors the man with the "venal quill."[46] At one rate or another he is for hire: in the words of the Epistle to Augustus, "But fill their purse, our poet's work is done, / Alike to them, by pathos or by pun" (vss. 294-295). Ignoring the counsel to keep his piece awhile and lick the lump into some shape — and of course the yet sounder advice to hold his peace forever — the mercenary author persists in dispatching his art without pause or hesitation.[47] As the upshot of the Dunciad shows, his pen is mightier than the word because it returns all to darkness. The significance of his handwriting is the evangel of the Dunciad, which transmits across two centuries an awareness and defiance of the degradation of culture.

Vitally and fully belles-lettres participate in the inner tragedy of the "sinking land." In the world of Pope's satires the studious head is wagged by the calculating tail, as the producer sits in his box office and the publisher in his circulation department. Apollo's journeymen take their appointed stations in a society where patronage is dying out, ministries of propaganda are coming on, and Arnold's philistines are taking over.

In a sense the able writer, represented in the poet who surveys the life about him and who strenuously defends the values of the good society, is the hero as well as the main character of Pope's cycle of satires. But the bad writer is in no sense whatsoever the grand villain. While literary dulness is a crime, it is not so heinous (because not so far-reaching) as other crimes which alarm Pope. Relatively, in the scale of evil beings hacks are small fry:

> Yet like the Papists is the Poets state,
> Poor and disarm'd, and hardly worth your hate.

> Yet Sir, reflect, the mischief is not great;
> These Madmen never hurt the Church or State.[48]

The gradation of offenses, to be sure, must not be mistaken for the absolution of even lesser sins. Large or small, evil remains evil to Pope and receives no quarter:

> "But why insult the Poor, affront the Great?"
> A Knave's a Knave, to me, in ev'ry State,
> Alike my scorn, if he succeed or fail,
> Sporus at Court, or Japhet in a Jayl,
> A hireling Scribler, or a hireling Peer,
> Knight of the Post corrupt, or of the Shire.[49]

Three books of the Dunciad make it unnecessary to prove that Pope does not pass over literary abominations for the sake of arraigning worse social and political turpitude. Like Dorset he contrives to scourge both fops in learning and knaves in state.

While the indictment is sweeping, it is at the same time judiciously weighted. The reason why he designates the fourth book of the poem "the Greater Dunciad, not so indeed in size, but in subject,"[50] is that there his text is vice too high to be equated for a moment with the misdemeanors of the literary slums. It is not alone the adulteration of national taste which dictates the "removal of the imperial seat of Dulness from the City to the polite world."[51] Other and more powerful processes are also at work. From the beginning of the first book to the end of the last the sovereign dunce of the land is of course Augustus rather than Cibber. The most potent and successful despoilers of the land are not the hireling scribblers but the hireling peers, not the ministerial tools but the ministerial knaves of state, not needy cheats like Jonathan Wild (or for that matter Iscariot Hackney) but opulent dignitaries like the director

Blunt and the ubiquitous Sir Robert Walpole.[52] The dazzling triumph of Vice which closes the first part of the Epilogue to the Satires is celebrated, not among the dregs of the nation, but among the very best people exclusively:

> Vice is undone, if she forgets her Birth,
> And stoops from Angels to the Dregs of Earth:
> But 'tis the Fall degrades her to a Whore;
> Let Greatness own her, and she's mean no more . . .
> Hear her black Trumpet thro' the Land proclaim,
> That "Not to be corrupted is the Shame."
> In Soldier, Churchman, Patriot, Man in Pow'r,
> 'Tis Av'rice all, Ambition is no more!
> See, all our Nobles begging to be Slaves!
> See, all our Fools aspiring to be Knaves!

(vss. 141-164)

Since the two great deities of the sinking land are sisters every way, the supreme conquest of Dulness is likewise effected in the "three estates" of first importance, rather than the fourth.[53]

Yet the literary jungle is very much made in the image of the great world of Pope's satires. Grub Street is radically fastened to, and fashioned like, the higher quarters of the society. The hack and the duke, the banker and the statesman all live by the same bimetallism of lead and gold, and all thrash about in the same darkness and disorder. The scribbler who frets his fingers for half a crown is the gauche kinsman of speculators and politicians who manipulate thousands.[54] If the Dunciad notices one Midas who sits Lord Chancellor of plays (III. 324), the Epistle to Dr. Arbuthnot observes the greater Midas who occupies the throne (vss. 69-82). Variously stationed in council chambers, drawing rooms, and studies, men who are dull, venal, and vicious proceed effectually "to blot out order, and extinguish light."[55] In the cataclysm which overtakes the world within Pope's satires, belles-lettres suffer the common fate of all humane values.

NOTES

1   Major contributions to the redemption have been made by
Robert K. Root, The Poetical Career of Alexander Pope
(Princeton, 1938), pp. 125-155, 215-226; George Sherburn,
"The Dunciad, Book IV," Studies in English (Austin, Texas,
1945), pp. 174-190; and Reginald H. Griffith, review of
James Sutherland, ed. The Dunciad, in PQ, XXIV (1945),
152-157.

2   Moral Essay III, vs. 143; Imit. of Hor. , Ep. I. i. , vs. 124.
My citations from the Dunciad, the Imitations, and the
Essay on Man are to The Poems of Alexander Pope, ed.
John Butt, Maynard Mack, and James Sutherland (London,
1939-50), Vols. III. i, IV, and V. Citations from the Moral
Essays and other poems not yet published in the Twicken-
ham edition are to Works of Alexander Pope, ed. Whitwell
Elwin and William J. Courthope (London, 1871-89). Finally,
the Dunciad is cited in the 1743 (or "B") version, unless
otherwise specified.

3   " 'Wit and Poetry and Pope': Some Observations on His
Imagery," in Pope and His Contemporaries, ed. James L.
Clifford and L. A. Landa (Oxford, 1949), p. 30.

4   For a stimulating account of Pope's gloom, with an emphasis different from mine, see Louis I. Bredvold, "The
Gloom of the Tory Satirists," in Pope and His Contemporaries, pp. 1-19.

5   Essay on Man III. 283-286, IV. 263-266; Imit. of Hor. ,
Ep. II. i. , vss. 203-204; Epil. to the Sats. , Dial. II, vss.
212-215.

6   Epistle to Dr. Arbuthnot, vss. 135-146.

7   Ibid. , vs. 291.

8   For examples of such aristocratic efforts and enthusiasms
see Moral Essay IV, vss. 133-140; Imit. of Hor. , Ep. II. i. ,
vss. 105-106, 310-311; Epistle to Dr. Arbuthnot, vss. 16,
149, 243-244, 279-280, 322-323; Epil. to the Sats. , Dial.
I, vss. 45-50, 68-72; Dial. II, vss. 160-161, 168-227;
Dunciad II. 379-382 and IV. 45-50, 94-118, 541-548, 567-
568.

9 Dunciad IV. 92-102. See also II. 25-26 and Moral Essay
   III, vss. 237-248.

10 Dunciad II. 191-220; Epistle to Dr. Arbuthnot, vss. 231-266;
    Second Satire of Donne, vss. 25-26.

11 Dunciad, I. 6, 299-318; III. 319-338; IV. 181-188.

12 Imit. of Hor., Ep. II. i., vss. 13-14, 209-212, 368-369;
    Sat. II. i., vss. 21-32. Fourth Satire of Donne, vss. 102-
    107; Moral Essay I, vss. 139-140; Moral Essay II, vss.
    181-192; Epil. to the Sats., Dial. II, vss. 220-231.

13 Dunciad II. 269-358 (vss. 275-280 are quoted); see also
    I. 205-214; Epistle to Dr. Arbuthnot, vs. 251; Epil. to the
    Sats., Dial. II, vss. 140-156.

14 Dunciad I. 304, III. 179-184, 323, IV. 98; Imit. of Hor., Ep.
    II. i., vss. 370-379.

15 Imit. of Hor., Ep. II. i., vss. 290-337 (vss. 304-317 are
    quoted); see also Dunciad I. 69-72, II. 221-230, III. 228-272,
    307-316.

16 Dunciad I. 37-44.

17 Ibid., II. 31-190, 221-418.

18 Moral Essay III, vs. 140; Imit. of Hor., Ep. II. i, vss.
    172-173.

19 Dunciad I. 263-264, 269-270; Imit. of Hor., Ep. I. vi, vs. 43.

20 "Epilogue to Mr. Rowe's Jane Shore," vss. 39-44; Dunciad
    I. 85-104, III. 277-282, IV. 127-134.

21 Epistle to Dr. Arbuthnot, vs. 98; Dunciad I. 223, 326,
    III. 209.

22 Imit. of Hor., Ep. II. i, vss. 169-170 (italics mine) and
    310-313.

23 Dunciad II. 3-4, 51-52, 69-72, 78, 101-102, 113-116,
    121-140, 151-156.

24 Ibid., I. 39-40, II. 157-190, with Pope's notes to vs. 157.

25 Ibid., II. 78; Epistle to Dr. Arbuthnot, vss. 63, 180.

26 Dunciad I. 127-134, II. 45-50, 115-140, 191-220, 269-358; Epistle to Dr. Arbuthnot, vss. 51-54, 103-124, 179-184, 239-240, 338, 374-387; Imit. of Hor. , Ep. II. i, vss. 209-212.

27 Imit. of Hor. , Ep. II. i, vss. 169-170, 179-190, 406-407; Ep. II. ii, vss. 70-71, 135-146; Sat. II. i, vss. 99-100; Second Satire of Donne, vss. 27-28; Epistle to Dr. Arbuthnot, vss. 1-6, 19-22, 151-156, 223-228; Dunciad I. 123-126, 279-281, and (A) III. 159 n.

28 Dunciad, ed. cit. , p. 205 ("The Publisher to the Reader").

29 Samuel Johnson, Lives of the Poets, ed. G. B. Hill (Oxford, 1905), III, 204.

30 The stress is exemplified by Dunciad I. 37-44, 55-78, 93-106, 115-134, 169-190, 273-286; II. 221-268; III. 135-212, 227-272; IV. 21-44, 627-640.

31 Ibid. , I. 45-54.

32 Imit. of Hor. , Ep. II. i, vss. 198, 302-303; Epistle to Dr. Arbuthnot, vss. 62-63, 180; Second Satire of Donne, vss. 13-20, 25-26; Dunciad II. 78.

33 Dunciad II. 37-42; see also I. 35-36, 48, 115-120, 185-186; Epistle to Dr. Arbuthnot, vss. 13-14, 44, 131, 151-156.

34 Dunciad II. 22-23, 27-30, 279-282, 420, III. 37-40; Epistle to Dr. Arbuthnot, vss. 41-42.

35 Dunciad I. 48, 295, II. 61, 117-118, 147-150, 420-428, III. 34; Epistle to Dr. Arbuthnot, vss. 13, 43, 156; Imit. of Hor. , Sat. II. i, vs. 99.

36 Pope to Caryll, 27 Sept. 1732; Elwin-Courthope, VI, 234.

37 Imit. of Hor. , Ep. I. vi, vss. 81-82; Ep. II. ii, vss. 226-229; Sat. II. vi, vss. 145-148; Moral Essays III, vss. 17-20; Essay on Man IV. 193-205.

38 Moral Essay III, vss. 229-282; Moral Essay IV, vss. 169-184; Epistle to Dr. Arbuthnot, vss. 231-266; Second Satire of Donne, vss. 113-124; Imit. of Hor. , Sat. II. ii, vss. 111-122; Dunciad III. 330, IV. 132.

39 Moral Essay III, vss. 77-81; Essay on Man IV. 79-80; Imit. of Hor. , Ep. I. vii, vss. 69-70; Ep. II. ii, vs. 295.

40 Dunciad III. 332; Imit. of Hor. , Ep. II. ii, vss. 68-69.

41 Dunciad, ed. cit. , p. 15 ("A Letter to the Publisher," by "William Cleland"). Cf. Second Satire of Donne, vss. 13-14.

42 Pope's note to Dunciad (A), I. 41. The note is substantially unchanged at (B), I. 34. Italics mine.

43 Pope's note to Dunciad (A), II. 270 or (substantially un- changed) (B), II. 282.

44 Lives, ed. Hill, II, 399.

45 Editors of the Dunciad should perhaps put into their pro- legomena this (and only this) pensée of Oscar Wilde: "Wealthy people are, as a class, better than impoverished people, more moral, more intellectual, more well be- haved. There is only one class in the community that thinks more about money than the rich, and that is the poor. The poor can think of nothing else. That is the misery of being poor" (Plays, Prose Writings, and Poems, Everyman ed. , p. 265). Before accepting the passage as an epigraph, Pope himself would doubtless have undermined "moral" with the qualifier "in petty affairs," for his rich knaves and dunces do not disgrace themselves by picking pockets.

46 Dunciad I. 52-54, II. 207-208, IV. 101-102; Epistle to Dr. Arbuthnot, vss. 48, 113-114, 131, 151, 364; Imit. of Hor. , Ep. II. i, vs. 192.

47 Epistle to Dr. Arbuthnot, vss. 33-46; cf. Imit. of Hor. , Ep. I. i, vss. 77-84. See also Dunciad III. 157-164.

48 Second Satire of Donne, vss. 11-12; Imit. of Hor. , Ep. II. i, vss. 189-190.

49 Epistle to Dr. Arbuthnot, vss. 360-365.

50 Dunciad IV, initial note by Pope.

51 Dunciad, ed. cit. , p. 51 ("Martinus Scriblerus of the Poem"). See also III. 299-300.

52 Epil. to the Sats. , Dial. II, vss. 38-51, 140-156; Moral

Essay III, vss. 135-150; Imit. of Hor. , Sat. II. i, vss. 71-72; Dunciad IV. 492-626.

53 Dunciad IV. 599-604.

54 Epistle to Dr. Arbuthnot, vs. 180; Imit. of Hor. , Ep. I. i, vs. 86; Epil. to the Sats. , Dial. I, vs. 14; Dial. II, vs. 49.

55 Dunciad I. 28, 311-314, IV. 1-44, 581-582, 605-656; Moral Essay III, vss. 11-12, 137-138.

LIGHT AND NATURE: A READING OF THE DUNCIAD

Thomas R. Edwards, Jr.

I

Although the simple joke at the heart of the Dunciad is the same joke Pope uses in the Rape of the Lock — if you describe small, bad people with the language you ordinarily use to describe the largest and best people the human mind can conceive of, the result will be disastrous to the former — still it is obvious that in the Dunciad the effect of the joke has changed.[1] Take, for example, this passage, with its startling reversal of the normal process of purity yielding to decay:

> Thro' Lud's fam'd gates, along the well-known Fleet,
> Rolls the black troop, and over-shades the street,
> 'Till show'rs of Sermons, Characters, Essays,
> In circling fleeces whiten all the ways:
> So clouds replenish'd from some bog below,
> Mount in dark volumes, and descend in snow.
>
> (II, 359-364)

The simile demands a complex response, combining revulsion at the Dunces' corruption ("bog"), wonder at their stupid but stubborn perseverance (it must be hard to make even fake snow from such dirty material), pleasure in the poetic power that can bring a kind of beauty out of such ugliness, and amusement that the comparison is used at all. This last feeling differs, however, from the amusement evoked by epic parody in the Rape of the Lock; while the Dunciad has a beauty of its own, it is far from the almost childlike pleasure in small, glittering things expressed by the earlier poem. Pope's use of incongruity is becoming less simply comic — laughter at clouds being replenished from bogs will be just a little nervous.

Reprinted from Philological Quarterly, Vol. 39 (1960), pp. 437-463, by permission of author and publisher.

LIGHT AND NATURE: THE DUNCIAD

Uncomfortable juxtapositions of the conventionally pleasant and the ugly run through the poem. The remarkably profuse imagery comparing men to animals elaborately relates the world of the Dunces to the lower orders of creation; and although in part we feel superior to the Dunces because we are human, reasonable, and so forth, we have at the same time to concede them a certain mindless but disturbingly potent vitality. Pope has other ways of suggesting that to be a Dunce is to have given up all meaningful ties with ordinary nature, thus ceasing to be human. The world of Dulness is full of monstrous distortion — in Book I (81-84), for example, the goddess proudly views her "wild creation" of "momentary monsters," who are elsewhere compared to statues and machines. If they retain a semblance of humanity, some deformity or other will mark them as Dulness' own, as in the case of the "meagre, muse-rid mope, adust and thin" (II, 37), Defoe earless in the pillory (II, 147), or the Virtuoso who is "canker'd as his Coins" (IV, 349); if they still look fully human, they are much embarrassed (IV, 525-528). Perhaps the richest vein of distortion runs in the allusions to monstrous births and perverse familial relations, for Dulness is the "Mighty Mother," and her maternity implies a dreadful change in the normal processes of fruition and growth:

> Here she beholds the Chaos dark and deep,
> Where nameless Somethings in their causes sleep,
> 'Till genial Jacob, or a warm Third day,
> Call forth each mass, a Poem, or a Play:
> How hints, like spawn, scarce quick in embryo lie,
> How new-born nonsense first is taught to cry . . . .[2]

> (I, 55-60)

The reference is to literary deformity, to be sure, but the imagery invites a response that seems too strong for the reference — Pope asks us to react to bad writing as powerfully as we react to departures from natural birth and growth.

The most famous and most often deplored kind of ugliness in the Dunciad is of course the obscenity, the way in which Pope dwells upon the excretory processes and debased sexuality. The delicate sexual innuendoes of the Rape of the Lock

705

give way to vigorous expressions of interest in the obscene and
all its details:

> Renew'd by ordure's sympathetic force,
> As oil'd with magic juices for the course,
> Vig'rous he rises; from th' effluvia strong
> Imbibes new life, and scours and stinks along;
> Re-passes Lintot, vindicates the race,
> Nor heeds the brown dishonours of his face.

(II, 103-108)

The elegant irony of "sympathetic," the mouth-filling Latinate
diction (e.g., "vindicate" in the sense of "lay claim to"), and
the neat epic parody in "brown dishonours"[3] combine in a deceptive sonority of movement that makes the bite of "scours
and stinks" and "brown" especially impolite. Pope's artistry
struggles with our revulsion and subdues it, and the result is
richly poetic, but "comedy" is not precisely the word for what
happens. Though we must probably laugh at Curll in order to
avoid some more painful response, the vision of a human being
drawing sustenance from filth cannot simply seem amusing.
The struggle between tonal dignity and conceptual ugliness
produces a degree of imaginative violence that would have torn
the Rape of the Lock to pieces; in this new poetic context violent personal feeling seems to be making decorous public discourse almost impossible.

The rhetorical situation that lies behind such uses of ugliness seems an elaborate one. Everyone knows that Pope was
a relentless hater, and there has always been a strong suspicion (to put it mildly) that the Dunciad represents only its author's personal animosity toward most of the Augustan literary
world. Yet the poem seems much more impressive than a
product of mere spite should. Its violence may in fact be seen
as dramatic rhetoric of a rich and powerful sort — Pope is
"guaranteeing" the moral validity of his hatred by refusing to
disguise or gloss it over in any decorous way. It is as though
he were saying: "Half measures won't do; the honest man eventually finds that stupidity and vanity are intolerable, and he
must speak out strongly against them even if social decorum
be violated." The voice that speaks in the Dunciad is that of

the compulsive truth-teller; when we know that it is Pope who has adopted this role, that the master of the barbed needle has had to take up the pole-ax, matters seem desperate.

The style of the Dunciad cannot of course be accounted for by so crude a label as "ugliness." On the one hand, we are to take the deformed, depraved world of Grub-street as an image of the actual world we ourselves inhabit, or of what it may become if dullness prevails. At the same time, however, Pope keeps reminding us that Grub-street may be a special and limited world surrounded by saner, more pleasant realms of order. The surface of negative ugliness is balanced by various modes of positive assertion that work beneath it.

This doubleness, as has often been remarked, appears in the texture of the verse:

> So, (fam'd like thee for turbulence and horns,)
> Eridanus his humble fountain scorns,
> Thro' half the heav'ns he pours th' exalted urn;
> His rapid waters in their passage burn.   (II, 181-184)

The beautiful elevation and movement of the last line modulates the disgust we may feel for the action and for the further obscene suggestion in "burn" (which Scriblerus carefully underlines in a note). It is as though Pope could not help writing beautifully, whatever the occasion. As Dr. Leavis says, the beauty of such a passage "is inseparable from the whole habit of versification. . . . When Pope is preoccupied with the metrical structure, the weight, and the pattern of his couplets, he is bringing to bear on his 'materials' habits of thought and feeling, and habits of ordering thought and feeling. The habits are those of a great and ardent representative of Augustan civilization."[4] This is surely true; and we might add that Pope's habits serve a rhetorical purpose of which he must have been aware. The ability to find beauty in ugliness, without obscuring the fact that it is ugly, is expressive of the highest form of civilized intelligence, and it triumphantly asserts Pope's superiority, in sensibility and moral soundness, to his victims. Dunces make ugliness from beauty, and the difference between their activity and the contrary activity dramatized in the verse itself marks the distinction between anarchy and order.

This undercurrent of positive values takes a number of

forms. Pope plays off Grub-street ugliness against the heroic
dignity of classical epic, the artfully beautiful innocence of
pastoral, the rich fertility of actual nature, and the moral seriousness of the classical and Christian traditions in general.
Such contrasts both underline the squalor of the Dunces' world
and enhance the gravity of their offense, which is in effect an
attempt to subvert human and natural order.

II

The contrast between the ugliness of Dulness and the beautiful dignity of human reason seems to be the primary theme
of the Dunciad. It can be seen, I have suggested, as a stylistic
principle operating in isolated passages — as, for example,
when an obscene image is balanced by "classical" tone or rhythm. It operates, however, in larger ways as well, and indeed
lends to the complete four-book version of 1743 a kind of unity
that has not been fully appreciated, as a study of a central symbolic contrast may help to show.

The prominence of darkness in the Dunciad has been pointed
out, most satisfactorily perhaps by G. Wilson Knight, but the
extent to which the opposition between darkness and light pervades and directs the poem has not received the attention it
should have.[5] The key passage is of course the famous conclusion, in which Pope suddenly abandons the elaborate fictions
of mock epic to turn his eyes upon the cosmos. At line 627 of
Book IV (Pope provides a row of asterisks to mark the division)
the Dunces vanish entirely as the poet turns his attention from
the puny creatures of Dulness to the larger and more general
implications of the intellectual and moral disorder he has been
criticizing. Parody and vituperation yield to an intensely felt
depiction of the death of reason and humanistic value, expressed
in a way that recalls the Christian treatment of doomsday. The
reader is no longer an unimplicated observer and evaluator, as
Pope adopts direct address and the present tense in an effort
to involve us personally in his sudden revelation of what nonsense ultimately leads to. A certain dramatic neatness is lost
by transferring this prophetic speech from Settle, who spoke
it as the conclusion of the earlier three-book versions, to the
anonymous narrator, but there is a compensating gain in

dramatic seriousness. When Settle says it we tend not to believe him — it seems the product of a Dunce's deranged imagination; but when it is spoken by the narrator himself, and so backed by all the resources of feeling that have informed the poem, we must consider it at face value.[6]

The most striking thing about this conclusion is the remarkable richness of meaning that gets attached to the idea of "light," though the word itself appears only once. The advancing power of Dulness puts an end to the arts and sciences, man's means of expressing his superiority to the lower orders of creation, and the basic metaphor involves putting out various kinds of light. First "fancy," the least valuable intellectual faculty to the Augustan way of thinking but nevertheless a useful one, is blotted out: "Before her, <u>Fancy's</u> gilded clouds decay, / And all her varying Rain-bows die away" (631-632).[7] "Gilded" suggests solidity of a sort, and "decay" thus takes on a degree of metaphorical vitality. Though the clouds and rainbows consist of vapor, they do shine, transforming light into color and pattern, and the hint of animation in "varying" makes "die," like "decay," more than a dead metaphor. "Wit" likewise is overcome: "<u>Wit</u> shoots in vain its momentary fires, / The meteor drops, and in a flash expires" (633-634). Wit, like fancy, is only momentary — its value is limited — but its destruction is also a blow to reasonable order.[8] As a meteor it casts a temporary but brilliant light; yet with the advent of Dulness it expires "in a flash," a last flare-up of light before permanent extinction.

But more important than fancy or wit, "<u>Art</u> after <u>Art</u> goes out, and all is Night." At the approach of this "dread <u>Medusa</u>" the very stars fade. Another mythological allusion focusses attention on the "going out" of the Arts:

> As Argus' eyes by Hermes' wand opprest,
> Clos'd one by one to everlasting rest;
> Thus at her felt approach, and secret might,
> <u>Art</u> after <u>Art</u> goes out, and all is Night.　　(637-640)

Though there are many arts, they all relate to a single "body" — civilization — which they inform and guide; the approach of the goddess is "felt" and "secret" not only because she is veiled in fog and gloom but also because she heightens her

invisibility by blinding her enemy, as Hermes blinded Argus
when rescuing Io. Truth flees to her original cavern (the well
from which Democritus claimed to have drawn her), going out
of light; philosophy, which by leaning on Heaven kept close to
the source of physical and spiritual light, now shrinks away
to the dim study of second causes; the other sciences gaze upon
the approaching darkness and go mad.

The end is utter blackness. "Light dies before thy uncreat-
ing word": the light of Genesis[9] and the Word which St. John
says was in the beginning are both obliterated by this new and
blasphemous un-Creation. Dulness can destroy the bases of
order as God established them and as man has kept them up,
and the destruction of order equals the destruction of reality as
man knows it:

> Thy hand, great Anarch! lets the curtain fall;
> And Universal Darkness buries All.

The universal drama is over — the curtain shuts out the light,
and darkness buries not just literature and culture, but all
creation.

The emphasis on light in this conclusion strongly suggests
that the image has more than local significance; and a seeming-
ly-flat couplet may provide a bridge to the rest of the poem.
When Dulness reigns supreme:

> Nor public flame, nor private, dares to shine;
> Nor human Spark is left, nor Glimpse divine!

> (IV, 651-652)

The italics are Pope's, and the significant fact that these are
the only adjectives so emphasized in the poem seems to me to
imply a hierarchy of definitions which makes it possible to
understand more fully the function of "light" in the whole poem.

The light of private intellectual activity, such fleeting illumination as is cast by wit and fancy, does not stand very high
in the Augustan scale of values, as a glance at the opening lines
of Religio Laici or The Hind and the Panther will remind us.
The extinction of "public flame" is more serious — the Augustans' deep concern for maintaining an intelligible community

of ideas and beliefs depends on the arts and the links with tradition they provide. But Dulness goes even further: the onslaught of darkness which obliterates every "human spark," public and private, also obscures the "glimpse divine," the imperfect but enriching vision of a higher light achieved through religious devotion. The uses of light and darkness in the body of the poem may come into better focus if we bear this scale in mind.

Dulness herself, the chief figure in the 1743 version, is characteristically enveloped in mists or clouds, and Cibber's prayer to her -- "And lest we err by Wit's wild dancing light, / Secure us kindly in our native night" (I, 175-176) — shows why: wit and light are the same, and so the true Dunce prefers his <u>native</u> night and the foetal security it affords him. Intelligence is painful, and from his point of view the best alternative to the dancing, dazzling illumination of wit is not steady light but total darkness. Dulness represents the power of passive, mindless maternity and repose, the emblems of which are darkness and sleep.

Her aura of mist and vapor in part magnifies ("A veil of fogs dilates her awful face" [I, 262] — she is majestic and terrifying because we cannot see her true size and shape clearly)[10] and in part ridicules her; she herself cannot see through the veil and so is cut off from reality and understanding. A remarkable series of "massing" and "blotting out" images shows how she and her children seek to extend the blessings of darkness to others:

> Thro' Lud's fam'd gates, along the well-known Fleet
> Rolls the black troop, and overshades the street.
>
> (II, 359-360)

> As thick as bees o'er vernal blossoms fly,
> As thick as eggs at Ward in Pillory.   (III, 33-34)

> Prompt at the call, around the Goddess roll
> Broad hats, and hoods, and caps, a sable shoal:
> Thick and more thick the black blockade extends.
>
> (IV, 189-191)

711

> Then thick as Locusts black'ning all the ground.
>
> (IV, 397)

(For other such passages, see I, 309, 313; III, 85, 125; IV, 247.) Each passage has local satiric significance in relation to the developing action, but each also contributes to a larger meaning: Dunces obscure light, and even their most trivial action may demonstrate this symbolic characteristic.

The conflict of Dulness with light is of course generally waged on a more explicit level. When Cibber tries to burn his books, for example, the goddess extinguishes the fire to preserve the bad writing. The episode (I, 257-260) expresses not only her love for the books but also her aversion to light — it wakes her up (sleep being the ideal state), and so she puts it out. Similarly, she rewards her favorites by concealing them in clouds, as she herself is concealed: " 'Twixt Prince and People close the Curtain draw, / Shade him from Light, and cover him from Law" (I, 313-314).[11] The concealment works both ways: Cibber is hidden, and things are hidden from him. We may take "Law" with "Light" as referring to the divine authority behind nature ("save him from knowing how things really are") or by itself, in the sense of <u>human</u> authority ("save him from the police, who would surely be after him if they knew what he is up to").

The light imagery develops a significant expressive link between the "ugliness" discussed earlier and the poem's positive meaning. Much of the obscenity, for example, associates the Dunces' love of filth with a love of darkness and concealment. The association can be seen most clearly in the cloacal revelry of the diving contest in Book III; if light is an enemy, then darkness and dirt are friends, and all sorts of filth will seem congenial to the Dunce. The references to animals, many of which are commonly associated with darkness, dirt, submersion, or burrowing, work to a similar effect. Some of the vituperation takes on a kind of rhetorical dignity from such imagery: it is easy enough to call one's enemies animals or filth-lovers, but when the aspersions fit into a larger, almost philosophical, expressive pattern, our sense of personal malice is undercut.

Though the Dunces themselves cast light of a sort, their

712

illumination differs significantly from the radiances of intelligible order:

> All eyes direct their rays
> On him, and crowds turn Coxcombs as they gaze.
> His Peers shine round him with reflected grace,
> New edge their dulness, and new bronze their face.
> So from the Sun's broad beam, in shallow urns
> Heav'ns twinkling Sparks draw light, and point their horns.

(II, 7-12)

"Shine" is the clue (compare I, 100, 103, 142, 219-220; II, 1-2;
IV, 411-412, 570). Their light is harsh and glaring; and they
shine not with their own brilliance, like the sun, but with light
reflected from other sources. Their immoderate and indecorous
radiance blinds rather than illuminates. Like mirrors, they remain cold themselves but are able to seem bright and warm by
stealing light from other sources — and they deceive themselves
as well as others:

> Kind Self-conceit to some her glass applies,
> Which no one looks in with another's eyes;
> But as the Flatt'rer or Dependant paint,
> Beholds himself a Patriot, Chief, or Saint.
> On others Int'rest her gay liv'ry flings,
> Int'rest, that waves on Party-colour'd wings:
> Turn'd to the Sun, she casts a thousand dyes,
> And, as she turns, the colours fall or rise.

(IV, 533-540)

Pope here recalls Belinda's sylphs with exquisite local effect,
but behind the effect stands the sharp criticism carried by the
whole light and dark pattern.

False seeing of various sorts is in fact one of Dulness'
most powerful weapons, as she demonstrates in the "heroic"
games. She forms a poet out of "well-body'd air" for which her
children compete, but when the victorious Curll tries to claim
his prize: "A shapeless shade, it melted from his sight, / Like
forms in clouds, or visions in the night" (II, 111-112). The

"fancy-cloud-decay" cluster (see note 7) is here put to a comic use, but the prediction of the poem's conclusion carries omi-nous overtones. Dulness' power to make something of nothing anticipates her final annihilation of everything. It is only a short step to the "re-creation" of the universe into garishly ugly parodies of its proper form:

> She, tinsel'd o'er in robes of varying hues,
> With self-applause her wild creation views;
> Sees momentary monsters rise and fall,
> And with her own fools-colours gilds them all.

(I, 81-84)

The cosmic grotesquery of Cibber's version (III, 231-272) and the final extinction of order fulfil this pattern, as Dulness be-comes a blaspheming disrupter of the divinely-wrought patterns of reality. Out of local jokes emerges the completion of the "private-public-divine" hierarchy.

Light, which we have been treating as imagery, comes in the Dunciad to carry the consistency and intensity of meaning ordinarily called "symbolic." Pope seems to draw upon respon-ses to the light-darkness dualism that are instinctive — "arche-typal" — and not just social and satirically useful. Light is the means by which we orient ourselves to our surroundings and direct our actions, in contrast to darkness, in which we know neither what we are doing nor where we are. Pope's imagery brings various common metaphors to mind — "see the light," "bright as day," and many others — and the latent content of feeling in such comparisons of mystery to understanding en-larges our imaginative response. The symbol also evokes the richness of concept and feeling "light" carries in religious and scientific discourse. It is no coincidence that the August-ans generally seem to have agreed that sight, though in some ways the most abstract of the senses and the least understood, was nevertheless the most immediate in its psychological effect and the most costly to lose — an agreement in which we ourselves probably share.12

We bring a sense of these public symbolic values to the particular uses of light in the Dunciad, and the feelings they evoke support Pope's special attitudes at every step of the way.

LIGHT AND NATURE: THE DUNCIAD

There are all kinds of light, and the "private-public-divine" hierarchy can be taken as a paradigm of the poem's whole rhetorical structure. It can be read as a personal attack on the poet's enemies, as a defense of an ethical ideal against immoral stupidity, or as a warning of a threat to the divine order of reality. Human order, Pope argues, with a famous tradition behind him, is an image of a more exalted order, and an attack on one menaces the other.[13] We proceed up the ladder analogically. Behind the topical, satiric exterior lies the symbolic, and behind the symbolic the "mythic" — the cosmic over-meaning, almost incredible out of context, asserted so powerfully by the conclusion. This structure of layers establishes a beautiful rhetorical ease. If Dunces are filthy beasts, for instance, both filth and bestiality can assume new meaning in another perspective. The variety of feeling evoked by "light" and "darkness" allows Pope to move at will through several levels of discourse (private, public, divine), knowing that his images are intelligible in all three vocabularies. This process of analogical translation can of course begin from different points. Lines like "This brazen Brightness, to the 'Squire so dear, / This polish'd Hardness, that reflects the Peer" (I, 219-220) express a very different kind of feeling from

> Thence a new world to Nature's laws unknown,
> Breaks out refulgent, with a heav'n its own:
> Another Cynthia her new journey runs,
> And other planets circle other suns.   (III, 241-244)

If the Dunciad were only a malicious satire, the latter passage would be absurdly hyperbolic; if it were only serious and philosophical, the former lines would show a wretched breach of decorum. If we try to limit our interpretation to any one level, we soon run into something in the language that frustrates our aim by pointing unmistakably to some other level. The complexity resists simplification — the full richness of Pope's technique will escape us unless we can respond to comedy and seriousness at one and the same time.

715

III

The organizing image of light thus expresses Pope's sense of a positive moral order that stands behind and criticizes the "darkness" of human folly. Light is of course only one of a number of metaphors for this order that appear in the Dunciad — rising and falling, waking and sleeping, organic growth and decay are others that will be touched on in this section — but they all reveal Pope's grasp of a moral and natural order which he assumes his readers understand and share with him. The creation of beauty and coherence out of ugliness and confusion is one of the great Augustan achievements, and the Dunciad is probably the last great poem in English to have such a shared vision of order as its main structural principle.[14]

Yet there seems to be an attitude in the poem working against this "Augustan" quality. De Quincey nearly put his finger on the problem when he said that the last lines confused him: "Do [present times] and their pursuits lead to [the victory of anarchy] as a possibility, or as a contingency upon certain habits which we have it in our power to erase (in which case this vision of dulness has a practical warning), or is it a mere necessity, one amongst the many changes attached to the cycles of human destiny, or which chance brings round with the revolutions of its wheel? All this Pope could not determine."[15] Is the vision a prophecy, or a warning of a state that could come about if the world failed to grow more reasonable? There can be no simple answer, but Pope's final position seems to involve a certain degree of pessimism pulling against the positive meanings.

Pope seems to have had two opposed ideas in his mind about the relation of order to anarchy, two myths about man's role in nature. The first, supporting the positive attitudes expressed in his poems, is essentially the classical concept of a Golden Age: that in the beginning the state of nature was perfect and peaceful, a time when man lived in complete harmony with nature and his fellow creatures in a kind of Arcadia. This pastoral myth, upon which depend the "official" meanings of Windsor Forest, the Essay on Man, and the Epistle to Burlington, dramatizes the human desire to believe that experience is ultimately orderly, that the nature of reality is hierarchical design, and that deviations from rational conduct are corrigible.

It makes satire possible, for it justifies the belief that folly and wickedness are unnatural and that norms exist toward which moral education can work. In terms of our key image, it asserts that natural reality is "light," and that darkness represents a dangerous aberration from natural perfection.

The opposing view is the one made notorious by Hobbes: the state of nature, so far as men can tell, is a state of disorder and conflict; human beings attain the light of dignity and reason only with difficulty and are in constant danger of lapsing back into darkness and anarchy. (Hobbes, it is interesting to note, was supposed to have been afraid of the dark.)[16] We need not postulate any direct influence here — about all we know of Pope's view of Hobbes is that he thought him a good reasoner and a bad translator of Homer[17] — but it seems clear that the hypothesis of man's essential goodness and nature's inherent congruence to human ideas does not fully satisfy Pope. We may for convenience adopt a modern term and call this second view "entropic," for it implies that the tendency of nature is steadily to seek lower levels of organization.[18] At any rate, we find in the <u>Dunciad</u> some suggestions that nature is not entirely hostile to <u>Dulness</u>, that light may <u>not</u> be the ultimate reality, that the public structure of values <u>Pope</u> appeals to with such seeming confidence is in danger of collapsing.

We find, for example, that Dulness' "ancient right" dates from "eldest time," and that she is the daughter of "eternal Night" (I, 9-12).[19] Much is made of the long tradition that stands behind the Dunces (I, 95 ff.), and while Pope is making fun of them by comparing them to bad writers of the past, they nevertheless take on a disturbing dignity from being part of a long historical series. In Cibber's version (Book III), the portion of the globe under the influence of reason is said to be pitifully small, and we may feel that the language expresses feelings that are too serious for the dramatic fiction ascribing the speech to Settle. The claims of Dulness to universal domination are not easy to refute.

The characteristic physical movement in the <u>Dunciad</u> is downwards. There are numerous references to diving and sinking of various sorts. For example, in the throes of composition, Cibber

    gnaw'd his pen, then dash'd it on the ground

> Sinking from thought to thought, a vast profound!
> Plung'd for his sense, but found no bottom there.

> > (I, 117-119)

His nonsense resembles "running Lead" that slips down through
the cracks in his head (I, 123-124), and his wits, like lead bul-
lets, manage to fly briefly but soon fall to earth (I, 181). The
great diving contest forms the climax of the heroic games (II,
269-346), and earlier Cibber considers a nobly selfless gesture:
"Shall I, like Curtius, desp'rate in my zeal, / O'er head and
ears plunge for the Commonweal?" (I, 209-210) Numerous
other downward motions occur:

> As to soft gales top-heavy pines bend low
> Their heads, and lift them as they cease to blow:
> Thus oft they rear, and oft the head decline.

> > (II, 391-393)

> Happier thy fortunes! like a rolling stone,
> Thy giddy dulness still shall lumber on.

> > (III, 293-294)

> The gath'ring number, as it moves along,
> Involves a vast unvoluntary throng,
> Who gently drawn, and struggling less and less,
> Roll in her Vortex, and her pow'r confess.

> > (IV, 81-84)

(See also I, 327; II, 363, 405; IV, 291, 471.) Dulness works like
a force of nature, with an all-engulfing gravitational pull that
cannot be resisted. Everything moves downward toward stasis
and inertia, a curve completed by the falling curtain and universal burial of the final couplet. William Empson says that
"the idea behind MacFlecknoe and the Dunciad [is] that there
is an ominous mystery in the way the lowest and most absurd
things make an exact parallel with the highest."[20] This ominous quality is enhanced by the tendency of high things to slide

downwards and become their low counterparts, despite all the efforts of moral intelligence to keep things separated into their proper levels. Hierarchy collapses into sameness, light yields to darkness, as entropy continues.

In satiric terms, the downward movement attacks the "sinking" Pope had ridiculed in the Peri Bathous, but in the Dunciad he has more on his mind than bad writers' love for the bathetic. The sinking of the Dunces leads to repose and sleep, to a kind of peace Pope does not simply despise:

> Know, Eusden thirsts no more for sack or praise;
> He sleeps among the dull of ancient days;
> Safe, where no Critics damn, no duns molest,
> Where wretched Withers, Ward, and Gildon rest.
>
> (I, 293-296)

> No noise, no stir, no motion can'st thou make,
> Th' unconscious stream sleeps o'er thee like a lake.
>
> (II, 303-304)

> But in her Temple's last recess inclos'd,
> On Dulness' lap th' Anointed head repos'd.
> Him close she curtains round with Vapours blue,
> And soft besprinkles with Cimmerian dew.   (III, 1-4)

The satiric edge never withdraws, and yet there is also a tenderness in the tone and even a kind of yearning. Darkness may bring a welcome end to the complexities of day; sleep and intelligence are in a sense antitheses, but the latter may often yearn poignantly for the former. As Pope remarked early in his career, with bitter truthfulness, dullness is "the safe Opiate of the Mind, / The last kind Refuge weary Wit can find."[21]

The Dunces are thus in a way to be envied — untroubled by the cares and responsibilities of the reasonable man, they can yield happily to the tendency of life to run downhill toward darkness, sameness, and sleep. Pope puts into Bentley's mouth a couplet compactly expressing the general aim of Dulness: "With the same Cement, ever sure to bind, / We bring to one dead

level ev'ry mind" (IV, 267-268). And he later makes Thomas
Gordon, a Whig journalist, redefine the process: "Now to thy
gentle shadow all are shrunk, / All melted down, in Pension,
or in Punk!" (IV, 509-510) The aim of Dulness is sameness,
the utter absence of differentiation and so of order, as though
the maternal Anarch were a ghastly, literal parody of the metaphor ascribed to Spinoza: "The purpose of Nature is to make
men uniform, as children of a common mother."[22] In such a
state intelligence has no place, for there are no qualitative
differences to be discriminated. Order consists of organization
and structure, "degree," and these Dulness melts down and
levels off.

There are indications that the poet himself does not feel
entirely secure as he contemplates the challenge of Dulness.
Among the chimeras with which she fills Cibber's head at the
beginning of Book III, along with "the Statesman's Scheme, /
The air-built Castle, and the golden Dream," we find the "Poet's
vision of eternal Fame." The irony includes Pope himself, it
seems, a supposition which is confirmed at the beginning of
Book IV:

> Yet, yet a moment, one dim Ray of Light
> Indulge, dread Chaos, and eternal Night!
> Of darkness visible so much be lent,
> As half to shew, half veil the deep Intent.
> Ye Pow'rs! whose Mysteries restor'd I sing,
> To whom Time bears me on his rapid wing,
> Suspend a while your Force inertly strong,
> Then take at once the Poet and the Song.   (1-8)

"This astonishing poetry," which "triumphantly . . . enlists
Milton into an Augustan sublime,"[23] daringly introduces the
poet into his mock-poem, demanding a response which a casual
reading of the Dunciad might not have prepared one for. The
speaker's comfortable superiority to his subject for a moment
vanishes as he recognizes his own subjection to time's destructive power. Such recognition lends a resonance of seriousness
to the occasional mention of literary entropy, "Prose swell'd
to verse, verse loit'ring into prose" (I, 274):

> How Prologues into Prefaces decay,

LIGHT AND NATURE: THE DUNCIAD

And these to Notes are fritter'd quite away.

(I, 277-278)

"Leave not a foot of verse, a foot of stone,
A Page, a Grave, that they can call their own."

(IV, 127-128)

"Turn what they will to Verse, their toil is vain,
Critics like me shall make it Prose again."

(IV, 213-214)

The ring of sadness is more than a satiric device. The decay
of literature mirrors the decay of nature: verse loiters into
prose just as order lapses into chaos, light into darkness.
Fame turns out to be doubly elusive — not only does the poet
die, but he finds little likelihood that his work will long survive him. Both the poet and the song must yield to dullness,
darkness, and death.

A powerful vision of dissolution dominates the Fourth
Book. As the "Argument" says: "The Progress and Effects [of
Dulness' final yawn] on all Orders of men, and the Consummation of all, in the Restoration of Night and Chaos, conclude the
Poem." As it was in the beginning, henceforth now and forever
shall be, un-world without end! The poem sings of Dulness'
"Mysteries restor'd" (IV, 5), the return to the "Saturnian days
of Lead and Gold" which, rather than the truly Golden Age of
pastoral myth, comprised the original state of nature. The
goddess is revealed finally as the deity of "Night Primaeval,
and of Chaos old" (IV, 630): "Lo! thy dread Empire, CHAOS!
is restor'd" (IV, 653). The origin of created order, to which
it must return, is the eternal darkness of chaos. (It hardly
seems necessary to comment on how solidly Milton stands behind the Dunciad.)[24] The critical intelligence that made the
poem possible must bow before the irresistible onslaught of
nature — a nature no longer seen as a synonym for light and
order but as a label for a ceaseless mutability destroying all
that makes life dignified or even possible.

This "tragic" dimension of the Dunciad depends on the

Fourth Book and also upon the resonances which the more consistently serious imaginative design of that Book strikes in what had been written earlier. The "sublimity" noted by Dr. Leavis is concentrated most thickly in the invocation to Book IV and the conclusion, and it is such passages as these, when Pope uses Miltonic resources most openly, that bring the underlying seriousness of the other books most fully to life.[25] The poem in three books is more tidy as narrative than the final version, just as the original Rape of the Lock is neater and more "exquisite" than the great poem Pope made from it; but without the Fourth Book, and its open appeal for deep feeling and something like the "degree of horror" by which Burke was to identify the sublime, it is hard to see how the Dunciad could have avoided at least a measure of the oblivion that overtook its long-forgotten poetic offspring.[26]

It would of course be easy to overstate the case. The "tragic" sublimity of the Dunciad does not overcome its positive, "Augustan" meaning, or at least not wholly. The threatened inevitable decay of order, the triumph of entropy, never quite becomes a certainty. The tension between positive ideals and the recognition that reality poses some disturbing challenges to those ideals does not snap, for even the expressions of sublime terror and disgust remain within the bounds of Pope's Augustan style. He can make beauty out of fright, just as he can out of ugliness; the "habits of thought and feeling" embodied in the texture of his verse are sufficiently strong to control and direct his vision of disorder. We may put it that in the Dunciad Pope's "Augustanism" meets its sharpest challenge from the actual world and triumphs — but the struggle, like Shakespeare's in the last plays, exhausted the medium of expression, and Augustan sensibility was never to triumph so finely again.

NOTES

1   This article deals with the 1743 version of the poem in four books; all quotations are taken from The Dunciad, ed. James Sutherland, 2nd ed. (London and New Haven, 1953).

2   For other instances of this kind of distortion, see I, 69-70,

121-126, 311-316; III, 313-314.

3 Compare "the long-contended Honours of her Head" (<u>Rape</u> <u>of the Lock</u> IV, 140) and the discussion of the formula by Geoffrey Tillotson, <u>On the Poetry of Pope</u>, 2nd ed. (Oxford, 1950), pp. 154-155.

4 F. R. Leavis, <u>The Common Pursuit</u> (London, 1952), p. 90.

5 See G. Wilson Knight, <u>Laureate of Peace</u> (London, 1954), pp. 57-58. Rebecca Price Parkin, <u>The Poetic Workmanship of Alexander Pope</u> (Minneapolis, 1955), pp. 116-123, considers the light imagery from a different point of view than mine.

6 Alwyn Berland, "Some Techniques of Fiction in Poetry," <u>Essays in Criticism</u>, IV (1954), 379, argues, perhaps too ingeniously, that at the end of the <u>Dunciad</u> "it is not the author who speaks, not any single <u>character</u>. . . . It is the <u>world</u> itself, the 'character' about to be possessed by the fictional Dulness."

7 There is an image-cluster here of which Pope was remarkably fond: see for example <u>Essay on Criticism</u> 492-493; <u>Rape of the Lock</u> II, 60; <u>Essay on Man</u> II, 284-285; <u>Ep. to Burlington</u> 147; <u>Dunciad</u> I, 80-84, II, 112, III, 10. For a discussion of this imagery see Thomas R. Edwards, Jr., "The Colors of Fancy: An Image Cluster in Pope," <u>MLN</u>, LXXXIII (1958), 485-489.

8 When the poem was exclusively about bad writers, it was <u>wit</u> that was finally engulfed in darkness: "<u>Let there be</u> <u>darkness</u>! (the dread pow'r shall say) / All shall be darkness, as it ne'er were Day; / To their first Chaos Wit's vain works shall fall, / And universal Dulness cover all!" All the 1728 editions have this reading (see Sutherland ed., pp. 192-193); Pope made the major revisions for the first Variorum edition (1729), but their full significance does not clearly emerge until we see the passage in the context of the 1743 version.

9 Longinus used Genesis 1.3 to demonstrate the "sublime" (<u>On the Sublime</u>, IX, 9); Pope's readers could have come to the association of Genesis and sublimity through

723

Boileau's "famous illustration" based on the Longinean account. (See Samuel H. Monk, The Sublime: A Study of Critical Theories in XVIII-Century England [New York, 1935], p. 31.)

10 Compare "As things seem large which we through mists descry, / Dulness is ever apt to magnify" (Essay on Criticism 392-393). The Dunciad as a whole shows Pope reconsidering the confident association of light and nature that runs through the Essay.

11 Compare III, 3-4, IV, 355-358.

12 Marjorie Nicolson, Newton Demands the Muse (Princeton, 1946), p. 52, quotes Locke, Berkeley, and Addison on sight as the most important sense.

13 The undeniable shrillness that occasionally creeps into the Dunciad may in part be due to uncertainty about the validity of the old analogies; for their break-down in the eighteenth century, see Earl R. Wasserman, "Nature Moralized: the Divine Analogy in the Eighteenth Century," ELH, XX (1953), 39-76.

14 The Vanity of Human Wishes is a possible exception, but Johnson's vision of positive order seems more personal and stoic, less confident of public coherence; its hortatory rhetoric seems to expect an audience which initially disagrees with its point of view.

15 Thomas De Quincey, "Pope," in Works (Edinburgh, 1863), XV, 134.

16 For the story, and Aubrey's efforts to refute it, see D. G. James, The Life of Reason (London, 1949), p. 7.

17 Joseph Spence, Observations, Anecdotes, and Characters of Books and Men, 2nd ed. (London, 1858), pp. 150, 158.

18 For a pertinent discussion of "entropy," see Norbert Wiener, The Human Use of Human Beings, 2nd ed. (New York, 1954), p. 12 et passim.

19 Pope's Lines on Dulness (1707) end with the ominous remark that "Wit, which most to scorn it does pretend, / With Dulness first began, in Dulness last must end."

(Minor Poems, ed. Norman Ault and John Butt [London and New Haven, 1954], p. 53.)

20 The Structure of Complex Words (London, 1951), p. 92.

21 Lines on Dulness (Minor Poems, p. 53). See also lines 16-24 of Pope's imitation of Rochester, On Silence (c. 1704?), Minor Poems, p. 18.

22 A. O. Lovejoy, Essays in the History of Ideas (Baltimore, 1948), p. 80.

23 Leavis, The Common Pursuit, p. 91.

24 See Aubrey Williams, Pope's "Dunciad" (Baton Rouge, 1955), p. 139, for Paradise Lost II, 980-986, as a key to Pope's emphasis on original darkness. (All italics in this paragraph are mine.)

25 F. R. Leavis, Revaluation (London, 1936), p. 90; The Common Pursuit, p. 91. Monk, The Sublime, p. 67, describes the eighteenth-century vogue of the sublime as a movement away from the idea that art reflects divine harmony and order.

26 See Richmond P. Bond, "IAD: a Progeny of the Dunciad," PMLA, XLIV (1929), 1099-1105, for a discussion of eighteenth-century imitations of the poem.

THE DUNCIAD AND THE PLOT OF SATIRE

Alvin B. Kernan

> And, whereas the mind of Man, when he gives the Spur
> and Bridle to his Thoughts, doth never stop, but nat-
> urally sallies out into both extreams of High and Low,
> of Good and Evil; His first flight of Fancy, commonly
> transports Him to Idea's of what is most Perfect, fin-
> ished, and exalted; till having soared out of his own
> Reach and Sight, not well perceiving how near the
> Frontiers of Height and Depth, border upon each other;
> With the same Course and Wing, he falls down plum
> into the lowest Bottom of Things; like one who travels
> the East into the West; or like a strait Line drawn by
> its own Length into a Circle.

(A Tale of a Tub, Section VIII)

The greatest satirists have always taken for their subject
not petty vice and simple-minded foolishness at rest, but vice
and foolishness confidently asserting some such brave purpose
as the creation of an earthly paradise, the construction of perpetual motion machines, or the banishment of trouble and pain.
The most consistent subject of satire has always been some
variety of overly optimistic belief in progress which ignores
the hard realities and inevitable complications of life. The self-
deluding nature of such efforts shapes the satiric plot, which
regularly shows vice and foolishness achieving the very opposite of what they intend. Swift offers two examples of this movement, the rise which is a fall, and the straight line curving
back into a circle. We can enlarge these into a general principle
and say that the plot of satire can render the ultimate delusion
and self-defeating nature of foolishness in any number of direc-
tional terms, up which is down, forward which is backward,
out which is in, through which is around.[1] One of these variations

Reprinted from Studies in English Literature, Vol. 2 (1962), pp. 255-266,
by permission of author and publisher.

forms the basic plot of The Dunciad.

Dulness — that quality of mind and being which is the subject of The Dunciad — is not only inertness, the ponderous movement, and the vacant stare; it is busyness, briskness, and pert-
ness as well. The dunces swirl and swarm about the City of
London, engaging in fantastic parodies of epic games, urinating
contests, mud-diving, and noise-making. They race about pur-
suing butterflies, collecting coins, growing flowers. They beat
students savagely, make long speeches, and write endless numbers of bad poems and dreary political pamphlets. Their styles
become substantial, a "mob of metaphors," "motley images,"
and "similes unlike," break out of the printed page to join the
dunces in their "mazy dance" about the town. The mad machinery of spectacular Italian opera spills out into the streets to
swell the hurly-burly to monstrous dimensions:

> All sudden, Gorgons hiss, and Dragons glare,
> And ten-horn'd fiends and Giants rush to war.
> Hell rises, Heav'n descends, and dance on Earth:
> Gods, imps, and monsters, music, rage, and mirth,
> A fire, a jigg, a battle, and a ball,
> 'Till one wide conflagration swallows all.[2]

In all this frenzied, bustling confusion and chaos, critics
have until recently found little evidence of plot. The standard
position has been that Pope's entire efforts were given to the
careful elaboration of a series of portraits of individual dunces,
without much concern for the organization of the entire poem.
But Aubrey Williams in Pope's Dunciad[3] has recently demonstrated in a conclusive fashion that while the poem may lack
a carefully constructed plot in which all episodes are bound
neatly together in a single-line progression, it does in fact
have an "action," a continuing movement from one place and
condition to another. This action, stated in proper epic fashion
at the beginning of the poem, is to bring "the Smithfield Muses
to the ear of Kings." This suggests the corruption of taste and
the translation of vulgarity from the City to the Court, from
the center of commerce to the polite world, and each episode
shows the spread of debased and false artistic standards to
further areas of English life and culture.

But the serious meaning of dulness is expanded and the re-

727

lentlessness of its encroachment on wit intensified, Williams shows, by the introduction of several "progresses" or related actions, which appear not in a schematic but in a random fashion -- random because it is not the nature of dulness to move with the directness and known purpose of the powers in some of the parallels. There are frequent bathetic parallels to The Aeneid and its action, "the Removal of the empire of Troy to Latium." There is a grotesque parody in Book II of the Lord Mayor's Progress, a civic procession in which a newly elected mayor journeyed from the center of the City of Westminster. In Book III there is an inversion of the translatio studii in which Cibber in the underworld is shown not the traditional progress of light and learning from east to west, but the step-by-step engulfment of one great civilization after another by the forces of darkness and dulness. Frequent use of Miltonic language and references to the Satanic quest for new dominions to replace those lost suggest the demonic urge of dulness to enslave man and return the world to its original chaos. Finally, there is an anti-creation, or uncreation, myth running through The Dunciad which inverts the creative acts described in Christian myth. Dulness and duncery proceed to the destruction of light and the world, not with the same directness, but with the same invincible, inevitable power with which the Creating Word moves onward in Christian history from "Fiat lux" to the Last Judgement. These various actions running through the events of the poem serve as metaphors which work, either directly or ironically, to identify and define the true nature of the various specific instances of dulness which are the substance of the poem. But they also mark the steady progress of the empire of Dulness as the dunces carry the Smithfield Muses to the ear of Kings, as darkness, chaos, and sleep spread over all creation.

In certain scenes in The Dunciad the swelling, onward pressure of Dulness becomes visible and audible. For example, at the end of Book I, after Cibber is proclaimed the King of Dunces by his goddess, the news spread outward through the City and voices of praise resound from every corner:

> Then swells the Chapel-royal throat:
> "God save king Cibber!" mounts in ev'ry note.
> Familiar White's, "God save king Colley!" cries;

"God save king Colley!" Drury-lane replies:
To Needham's quick the voice triumphal rode,
But pious Needham dropt the name of God;
Back to the Devil the last echoes roll,
And "Coll!" each Butcher roars at Hockley-hole.

In Book II the dunces progress through the City, and when they reach its limits, the noisiest fools broadcast their nonsense in loud voices to every area in Westminster. At the end of their epic games the assembled multitude of duncery tries desperately to stay awake while "Henley's periods" and "Blackmore's numbers" are read aloud, but sleep spreads irresistibly through them, until all lie stupefied. Book III concludes with the "translatio stultitiae"[4] in which we watch dulness and darkness cover one by one, China, Greece, Rome, and Egypt. The spread of duncery in Book IV is staged in the great rout of men who come forward to announce themselves the true sons of Dulness, in the systematic destruction of the Muses and other personifications of learning, and in the apocalyptic conclusion where darkness moves over the land extinguishing art after art and light after light. No matter how fragmentary and dispersed the immediate activities of the dunces may be, dulness is always expanding powerfully and heavily over civilization.

Below the levels of scene, plot, and action there sometimes exists, at least in the very greatest literature, a verbal groundswell anterior to any particular wave of action and unlocalized in any single shape or substance.[5] This undercurrent generates the specific words, the definite actions, and the events which make up plot. No one verb ever quite expresses this radical movement, but we are closest to it in the particular "verbals" of the poem and in the simpler movements of things and people. Without attempting for the moment to define the basic undercurrent of The Dunciad, I will offer a selection of the kind of verbs which occur most frequently, and then pass on to some of the simpler actions which elaborate the basic verbal quality.

Dulness in the many forms and shapes it assumes, pours, spreads, sluices, creeps, drawls on, stretches, spawns, crawls, meanders, ekes out, flounders on, slips, rolls, extends, waddles, involves, gushes, swells, loiters, decays, slides, wafts, lumbers, blots, o'erflows, trickles. Such words

729

and their variants are omnipresent in The Dunciad, and the
quality of movement they give to dulness appears in more extended form in such lines as the following: The goddess Dulness
looks into the chaos of her poets' minds,

> Where nameless Somethings in their causes sleep,
> 'Till genial Jacob, or a warm Third day,
> Call forth each mass, a Poem, or a Play:
> How hints, like spawn, scarce quick in embryo lie,
> How new-born nonsense first is taught to cry,
> Maggots half-form'd in rhyme exactly meet,
> And learn to crawl upon poetic feet.
> Here one poor word an hundred clenches makes,
> And ductile dulness new meanders takes.   (I, 56-64)

The King of Dunces views his own past productions, "Nonsense
precipitate, like running Lead, / That slip'd thro' Cracks and
Zig-zags of the Head" (I, 123-124). Dulness is to the head of
fools

> like byass to the bowl,
> Which, as more pond'rous, made its aim more true,
> Obliquely wadling to the mark in view.   (I, 170-172)

The dunces play,

> where Fleet-ditch with disemboguing streams
> Rolls the large tribute of dead dogs to Thames,
> The King of dykes! than whom no sluice of mud
> With deeper sable blots the silver flood. (II, 271-274)

Sleep spreads over those assembled to listen to Henley's ora-
tions and Blackmore's endless epics like ripples from a stone
dropped in the water,

> What Dulness dropt among her sons imprest
> Like motion from one circle to the rest;
> So from the mid-most the mutation spreads
> Round and more round, o'er all the sea of heads.

> (II, 407-410)

THE DUNCIAD AND THE PLOT OF SATIRE

"Like a rolling stone," Cibber's

> giddy dulness still shall lumber on,
> Safe in its heaviness, shall never stray,
> But lick up ev'ry blockhead in the way.   (III, 294-296)

Dulness advises her scribbling followers to "spread, my sons, your glory thin or thick, / On passive paper, or on solid brick" (IV, 129-130).

If we add to these words and passages those larger scenes, such as the leisurely wandering advance of the Lord Mayor's party on Westminster, the barbarians flooding out of the north and east on civilization, and the smothering of light after light at the conclusion, we can begin to understand the basic movement of dulness. It is a complex, not a simple, movement, for on first appearance it is heavy, formless, and directionless, a vague slipping, oozing movement, like a sliding sea of mud going in any and all directions. This shapeless pressure is exactly right because it catches the formless and meaninglessness of ignorance and stupidity. But though the spread is without any guiding purpose, it is still relentless and never-ceasing, "obliquely wadling to the mark in view." It flows on and on covering all that it encounters, and in the end it has spread over everything, and all that is rational and useful is buried beneath it.

The "action" observable at the level of the single verb, the limited movement, and the individual scene is exactly duplicated in the overall plot of The Dunciad, which is made up of a very large number of seemingly random events, fantastic scenes, and individual character sketches. But each new event, scene, and portrait shows the ever-widening spread of dulness into the professions, the arts, politics, social life, religion, and all areas of culture. In the end, slipping, floundering, and meandering about, dulness buries London, England, Western Civilization, and the cosmos:

> Lo! thy dread Empire, CHAOS! is restor'd;
> Light dies before thy uncreating word:
> Thy hand, great Anarch! lets the curtain fall;
> And Universal Darkness buries All.   (IV, 653-656)

731

The spread of ignorance and darkness quickens in Book IV.
Dulness holds her court and around her, at the sound of "Fame's
posterior trumpet," throng the innumerable Dunces of England:

> The gath'ring number, as it moves along,
> Involves a vast involuntary throng,
> Who gently drawn, and struggling less and less,
> Roll in her Vortex, and her pow'r confess.   (81-84)

The sons of Dulness come forward one by one to announce their
destruction of sense and art, law and morality. "Night prime-
val" and "Chaos old" move over the land, and "universal Darkness buries All." But Pope has so arranged his poem that this
ultimate expansion is at once a contraction. At the very moment
that dulness becomes everything, everything becomes nothing,
for dulness is finally nothingness, vacuity, matter without form
or idea. This expansion which is a contraction is localized in
the passage quoted just above, where as the number of Dunces
becomes larger and larger, their mass becomes smaller and
smaller as the crowd draws in on Dulness. The vortex is the
figure Pope uses here, and it renders in geometrical terms
the "plot" of the poem. The turbulent outer lip swirls round
and round growing ever larger and engulfing more and more.
It sucks in water and rubbish and whirls them downward through
narrowing circles, which end at last in the pinpoint of nothingness.

This general expanding-contraction is exemplified and
translated to social, moral, and personal terms in the activities and speeches of the various spokesmen of dulness who
parade before their Goddess in the last book. Each one represents the intrusion of dulness on some crucial area of life, and
each boasts the destruction of reason and order in his area.
The brutal teacher, forming minds with whip and precept,
comes first to announce an educational theory which disposes
of all questions and doubts: "When Reason doubtful, like the
Samian letter, / Points . . . two ways, the narrower is the
better" (151-152). Philosophy, history, and classical literature
are dismissed. The curriculum is reduced to the sterile study
of words alone. The ancient and fruitful union of ethics, logic,
and rhetoric — the good man, the clear thinker, and the effective speaker — is dissolved, and in place of the traditional ideal

of the educated man trained to think and express his thoughts in suitable language, the schools produce an empty-headed, noisy kind of dunce charged with examples, tropes, and figures learned by rote:

> We ply the Memory, we load the brain,
> Bind rebel Wit, and double chain on chain,
> Confine the thought, to exercise the breath;
> And keep them in the pale of Words till death. (157-160)

An educational system as confining as this can only narrow its students to fractional men who value smallness to the point where they can believe "a perfect Epigram to be as difficult a performance as an Epic Poem."[6]

The political form taken by dulness is despotism and tyranny, and the dull Goddess longs for the return of "Arbitrary Sway" and a pedant king like James I. Only one principle is necessary for the foundation of the kingdom of dulness, "The Right Divine of Kings to govern wrong." The implication here and elsewhere in The Dunciad is, of course, that tyranny and arbitrary rule have once again conquered England in the persons of the Hanover kings and the corrupt ministry of Walpole and the Whig politicians. Here again the spread of dulness is a contraction, for despotism is a reduction of the traditional personal liberties of Englishmen.

The duncely variety of scholarship and literary study is represented by Pope's old enemy, Richard Bentley, "that awful Aristarch." He and his fellows have taken literature as their province, and looked at in one way their careful study of texts can be viewed as a valid extension of the scientific spirit to literary problems. But in Pope's view these critics only succeed in reducing something once great to something infinitely small. In their hands great poetry turns to prose, and that traditionally moral activity, the reading and explanation of great literature, disintegrates into quibbles over grammar and pronunciation, study of petty textual problems, examination of erudite sources and parallels, speculations on particular readings, and the endless examination of minutiae. Bentley and his followers commit every possible sin against the tradition of humane letters, and in each case they reduce literature to its smallest components:

The critic Eye, that microscope of Wit,
Sees hairs and pores, examines bit by bit:
The body's harmony, the beaming soul,
Are things which Kuster, Burman, Wasse shall see,
When Man's whole frame is obvious to a Flea.

(233-238)

And since in the world of The Dunciad expansion and contraction always go together, the less and less the critics see, the more and more they read and write. "For thee," Dulness, says her critic,

we dim the eyes, and stuff the head
With all such reading as was never read:
For thee explain a thing till all men doubt it,
And write about it, Goddess, and about it.   (249-252)

The triumph of Dulness in education, politics, and letters is repeated in the training of the young gentlemen of fashion, the future governors of the realm. Having been well-educated in duncery at home, the young man undertakes the grand tour, visiting all countries and seeing the ways of all men. But the result of all this "broadening" travel is that he returns "with nothing but a Solo in his head." Having visited all the countries of Europe and seen all the sights — though he and his tutor sought out vice and fashionable ignorance — the young man can remember nothing but an air from a popular opera. He is narrowed even further by his loss of his moral sense. In his exploration of various depravities he has found his moral "freedom" and returns to England with a French whore. Dulness, that always generous goddess, greets him fondly and frees him "from sense of shame."

Pope and The Dunciad have often been criticized for the large number of antiquaries and virtuosi who next appear before Dulness. Such trivial activities as these, it has been argued, have no place in a catalogue of the great and dangerous kinds of ignorance. After all, when you are dealing with world-shaking vices, why stop to berate coin and butterfly collectors? The answer to this charge is, of course, that the triviality of these occupations is precisely what is needed at this point.

Pope is showing a world in which, as dulness spreads, human
intelligence contracts into ever smaller and smaller areas;
what could be better for this purpose than to show the minds
and energies of the well-to-do and potentially intelligent concerned with collecting coins, classifying butterflies and mosses,
cultivating exotic breeds of hothouse flowers, and arranging
seashells? These typical Royal-Society activities represent the
scientific approach to the natural world, and Pope's charge
against science, both the professional and amateur varieties,
is the same as that leveled against the duncely kind of scholarship: it reduces something very large and meaningful to something small and meaningless.

> O! would the Sons of Men once think their Eyes
> And Reason giv'n them but to study Flies!
> See Nature in some partial narrow shape,
> And let the Author of the Whole escape,
> Learn but to trifle; or, who most observe,
> To wonder at their Maker, not to serve.   (453-458)

These are only the more outstanding ways in which world
and man grow ever smaller in Book IV. In general, what we
have here is a bathetic world in which the grand scheme of a
divinely ordered universe is contracted to a mechanical operation, in which religion falls off to elaborate cookery, and in
which all forms of virtue, intelligence, and art are scaled down
to their corresponding, or antithetical, forms of dulness. The
cause of all the specific reductions is an ultimate and general
reduction of all the world to self:

> Make God Man's Image, Man the final Cause,
> Find Virtue local, all Relation scorn,
> See all in Self, and but for self be born:
> Of nought so certain as our Reason still,
> Of nought so doubtful as of Soul and Will.   (478-482)

By making self-interest the moral touchstone, by trusting to
what he alone can see and understand, by turning away from
the literary productions and social values bequeathed by the
past — in short, by pride — man reduces all the world to his own
puny size. Reduction of all to self lies underneath each of the

particular forms and activities of dulness which make up the
body of The Dunciad, Blackmore's long, dull epic poems, the
writing of political pamphlets for hire, the mad excesses of
opera, the greedy willingness of publishers to print slander and
obscenity, the sycophantic birthday odes addressed to the King
by Colley Cibber, and the obliteration of literary and moral
standards. The result is a new and narrower kind of man, the
true subject of Dulness:

> First slave to Words, then vassal to a Name,
> Then dupe to Party; child and man the same;
> Bounded by Nature, narrow'd still by Art,
> A trifling head, and a contracted heart.   (501-504)

The spread of dulness is a contraction of life. This would
seem to be the central irony of The Dunciad and the action which
the plot imitates on many levels. Throughout the poem we are
aware of the shapeless but ceaseless onward movement of Dulness and her sons over the face of the world, and yet as dulness
spreads out and out, it narrows down and down, until at the end
of the poem it is both everything and nothing at once. This ex-
pansion-contraction pattern is central to The Dunciad, and it is
supported by a number of other ironic movements which also
show that while dulness is frighteningly real, it is also an empty illusion, a something which is somehow a nothing. The
dunces are unbelievably solid, heads of bone and foreheads of
brass, and yet they are misty, vague, insubstantial. The light
which they bring to the world in various forms turns out always
to be darkness, and the knowledge they offer turns out to be
ignorance. They rise high in poetry, oratory, and other heroic
activities, only to plunge deeper down into the bathetic. Their
levity becomes gravity, their wakefulness a sleep; their briskness ends in lethargy, and their triumphs in the defeat of all
humanitas.

NOTES

1 William S. Anderson has shown that the individual satires
of Juvenal, which "depend upon a self-contradiction or . . .
paradox," have various forms of the "reflexive" plot.
Satire III, for example, the famous description of Rome

which was the model for Samuel Johnson's London, is spoken by a stout, honest old Roman, Umbricius, who is leaving the city because he can no longer earn a living or endure the indignities forced upon him. Umbricius "takes the Rome of traditional associations — its majesty, justice, wealth, beauty, and honesty — and exposes its self-contradiction . . . the lack of opportunity, the aliens, the fires, the thieves, etc., all of which signify the loss of the traditional Roman qualities and cumulate in a totally negative picture of an uninhabitable city" (p. 88). By the time Umbricius has finished describing the degradation of Rome he has proved that Rome is no longer Rome. And since he is the last of the Romans, his leaving is not a departure from Rome but a departure of Rome from a heap of stones and a mob of people on some hills along the Tiber. "Studies in Book I of Juvenal," Yale Classical Studies, XV (1957), 33-90.

2   III, 235-240. The Dunciad, vol. 5 of The Twickenham Edition, ed. James Sutherland (London, 1943). My references throughout this essay are to The Dunciad (B), the 1743 version of the poem in four books, with Cibber rather than Theobald as King of the Dunces. Even more recent critics who argue stoutly for the integrity of the poem hesitate to say that Book IV, published in 1742 as The New Dunciad, fits very smoothly into the poem as a whole. I have no wish to argue that Pope planned any elaborate connection between the first three books and the last one, but the evidence offered in the following pages does, I believe, suggest that The Dunciad in Four Books of 1743 is, however it came about, much more of a unity than has previously been thought.

3   London, 1955. This book has completely reoriented the study of The Dunciad, showing order, pattern, and scheme where critics once found only a jumble. My own argument about the basic plot of the poem rests solidly on Williams' work.

4   Williams, p. 47.

5   I have in mind here that "action" which Aristotle seems to refer to when he speaks in The Poetics of a play being "an imitation of an action" (6.2), and which he distinguishes

from plot by making the plot the primary mode of imitation. Dramatic poems as well as plays have such actions. Francis Fergusson in The Idea of a Theater and several subsequent articles has argued that the term "action" is better translated as "motive." But present usage makes motive refer primarily to psychic motive, mental drives, and this is the way Fergusson applies the term. I agree that the action or motive of work may be expressed in a character, but it is also, I believe, a more general force at work in all aspects of a play, poem, or novel. Thus, we can expect to find that the particular action of life — that pressure towards a particular fulfillment which is the soul of any living thing — which the writer wishes to imitate can be seen moving in such natural events as a storm at sea or the swing of a clock's pendulum; in the operation of such institutions as a court of law or in the shape of a battle; as well as in the activities by which the characters try to express themselves. Wherever there is movement — in the splashing of rain on the window or the gradual decay of a body — the action has recorded its passage in matter. The motive of a character is often directly opposed to the action of the world in which he finds himself.

6   This statement is attributed to Dr. South by Pope in his note to IV, 174.

THE "NEW WORLD" OF POPE'S DUNCIAD[1]

H. H. Erskine-Hill

I

The Rape of the Lock and the Dunciad of Pope, both properly referred to as mock-heroic poems, are nevertheless very
different from one another. They have also received different
degrees of critical favour. While the Rape of the Lock has been
generally praised, critics have rarely awarded the Dunciad
any but the most qualified approval. It may therefore seem
plausible to suggest that the differences between the two poems
are merely those between a successful and an unsuccessful attempt to write in the mock-heroic mode. The positive standard
is thus taken to be the Rape of the Lock, and it is held that for
a variety of reasons — including the nature of his material and
the different period of composition — Pope failed to make of the
Dunciad a balanced, consistent and unified mock-heroic poem.
The most recent critic to maintain this position is Ian Jack,
who has argued that the Dunciad lacks the "sure observance of
decorum" and "consistent following-out of the mock-heroic
idea" which gave the Rape of the Lock its "superiority." Jack
also finds a fundamental disparity of tone and content between
the first three and the fourth books of the Dunciad.

> . . . it remains almost as true in 1743 as before that
> while the last Book has a wide scope and a serious
> moral purpose, the first three Books are primarily
> concerned with Dulness in literature and are largely
> retaliatory in intention. The result, as Warton pointed
> out, is a "marvellous mixture and jumble of images
> and sentiments, Pantomime and Philosophy" . . . The
> poet who began as a wit attacking bad writers ends by
> trying to persuade us that he is a righteous satirist
> lashing the follies of an age.[2]

Reprinted from Renaissance and Modern Studies, Vol. 6 (1962), pp. 47-67,
by permission of author and publisher.

The authority of a number of earlier critics stands behind this view.[3]

Since Jack argued in this way, Aubrey Williams has shown that the Dunciad is a mock parallel, not merely to a piece (pace Tillotson) but to a whole epic action.[4] Williams holds, nevertheless, that the poem's "heterogeneous satiric materials tend at times to overwhelm and blur the . . . narrative movement" and that the action is not "a completely successful structural device."[5] Recently, R. A. Brower has argued that the finally completed poem is unified, with the exception of parts of Book II, by Pope's use of a flexible and resonant "poetic mode" which could combine nonsense with epic grandeur. He has also brought forward the notion of the Dunciad as "epic fantasia," though without systematically developing this idea.[6] What Williams and Brower have said in defence of the Dunciad must be a part of any adequate reply to Jack. Yet since Williams does not claim full propriety for Pope's handling of the mock-epic action, and since any disparity in content and inconsistency in form cannot entirely be made up for by the flexible and allusive mode of the actual poetry, however appropriate, Jack's case still remains to be answered.

My argument here will be that the Dunciad differs by design from the Rape of the Lock, and that it is therefore a mistake to judge the later mock-heroic poem on the pattern of the earlier. I shall suggest that, approached in this way, the Dunciad of 1743, while not an impeccable poem, makes its highly original effect unmarred by major faults.

II

The Dunciad differs most obviously from the Rape of the Lock in its action. While the earlier poem has an original action of its own, based upon a quarrel in contemporary society, the action of the Dunciad is an allusive parody of that of Virgil's Aeneid. In the Rape of the Lock Pope had to keep the development of the action to the fore in order to maintain his readers' interest; in the Dunciad, since the action follows that of a known story, there is a less urgent need for the readers' attention to be focussed upon successive stages of its development. Within the broad framework of the mock-epic parallel

Pope can afford to be more discursive than he is in the Rape of the Lock; without unduly bewildering the reader he can allow the action to recede into the background, to be recalled when needed by an appropriate allusion. In the Rape of the Lock, allusions are freely made to the Iliad, the Odyssey, the Aeneid, and other classical and modern epics, in order to elevate to an heroic plane an action independent of these poems. The epic allusions in the Dunciad, besides serving to elevate a "low" subject, as in the earlier poem, have an additional function. They are mostly to the Aeneid; they observe very broadly the order of events in the Aeneid; and they serve to inform the reader with what significant degree of fidelity or freedom its action is being parodied. If these differences in Pope's handling of the action in the Dunciad appear justifiable, it may seem less easy to justify the gradual but final submerging of the mock-epic parallel, from about half-way through Book III onwards. Both the greater part of Book III and the whole of Book IV are prophecies, the first by Settle (in place of Anchises), the second by the poet himself; action here broadens out into fantastic vision, and within the scope of this vision much that has no significant epic parallel is allowed a place.

If the action of the Rape of the Lock parallels that of no one particular epic poem, practically every stage of it has a familiar epic "ingredient." Pope has included: the divine warning in a dream, the arming of the epic hero, the sacrifice to the gods, formal warfare, the epic feast, the seizing of a trophy, the intervention of gods hostile to the hero, the visit to the underworld, the statement of the moral (important in Renaissance epic theory) and an example of the less formal, more desperate kind of epic fighting. (Belinda's sail down the Thames seems to echo a specific rather than a conventional heroic episode: Aeneas' voyage to the mouth of the Tiber at the beginning of Aeneid VII.[7] The apotheosis of the lock parallels the tale of the Lock of Berenice, Catullus, LXVI, and recalls Virgil's fifth Eclogue.[8]) By contrast, the action of the much longer Dunciad parallels fewer typically epic events. In Book I, the burning of his books by Cibber-Aeneas, first the conventional epic sacrifice to the gods, is next transmuted into a parallel to the burning of Troy, and finally (though this has not so far as I know been pointed out) to the Trojans' burning ships which, at the desperate appeal of Aeneas, Jupiter sends a

storm to extinguish (Aeneid V). In Book II the parallel is of
course to the conventional heroic games, and many of the specific allusions are to Aeneid V. In Book III the action parallels
the visit of Aeneas to Hades in Aeneid VI. Particular epic allusions are relatively infrequent in Book IV; neither they nor
the discernible action — at once a celebration of the triumph of
Dulness and a kind of mock degree-giving — serve to sustain
the mock-epic parallel of the earlier books. Dulness's final
speech, however, seems to stand in the place of the statement
of the epic moral; and it is of course true that Book IV, as the
fulfilment of Settle-Anchises' prophecy in Book III, is connected
formally with the earlier part of the poem. It is nevertheless
clear that Pope, in the Dunciad, was no longer interested in
creating a complete mock-epic poem like the Rape of the Lock.
All kinds of epic "ingredients" are left out, including the most
obvious of all: the epic battle, which Tassoni, Boileau and
Garth had all given a prominent place in their own poems.

It is notable in the Rape of the Lock that, despite the epic
parallels, epic allusions and epic manner, the poem never
takes one very far from a recognizable, non-epic, human world
— a world which has much in common with the comedies of
Congreve. The milieu of Belinda is never obscured by the
heroic accoutrements in which it is presented. Its beautiful
and stylized image remains precise and clear at the centre of
the poem, surrounded and heightened by the diminished yet
baroque flourishes of the epic machinery and the epic manner.
A good example is the long opening speech of the guardian
sylph, in Belinda's dream. This might have been treated as
an opportunity for a prolonged excursion into fantasy; in fact,
after the necessary information about the sylphs has been conveyed, our attention is directed back, with a heightened feeling
of drama and suspense, to Belinda's world. The only time in
the poem when Pope temporarily leaves behind the familiar and
human is during the underworld scene in Canto IV. Here a
measure of fantasy is consistent with the mock-epic rationale
that the poem follows. It is significant that it is precisely at
this point that the Rape of the Lock comes closest to the Dunciad. The Dunciad once again contrasts with the earlier poem,
for, as Martinus Scriblerus is made to say of the 1729 version,
and it is still truer in 1743, "the Machinary is a continued
chain of Allegories, setting forth the whole power, ministry,

and empire of Dulness . . . ."[9] The whole action of the poem
(the removal of the empire of Dulness from the city to the
court, after which its power is seen to threaten the very world)
may be said to be allegorical rather than real, and the world of
the poem is consequently much farther from the familiar and
human than is that of the Rape of the Lock. Such a "real" setting as there is in the Dunciad is most consistently apparent
in Book II; in general, fragments of the real world are assimilated into the dominant fantastic world of the poem, where
they lend it solidity.

Thus in the Rape of the Lock the parallel-and-contrast
between epic and mock-epic, Homer's world and Belinda's, is
kept continuously in focus, and is a positive part of the poetic
effect. This, more than anything else, constitutes the "consistent following out of the mock-heroic idea" which Jack has
praised. In the Dunciad Pope has largely abandoned this sharp
and continuous contrast, in favour of a dominant allegorical
fantasy. This is exemplified in the different way Pope handles
the supernatural in each poem. The sylphs and spirits in the
Rape of the Lock are Pope's equivalent to the gods in Homer
and Virgil. While their actions influence and sometimes determine the fortunes of the human protagonists, they themselves
are normally invisible to human eyes. This helps to maintain
the clear juxtaposition of the epic world with Belinda's world.
In the Dunciad, the "machinery" consists of one goddess: Dulness. She is Pope's equivalent to Venus, in the Aeneid, and
is the special patroness of Cibber-Aeneas. Pope appears to
be departing from obvious epic precedent, in introducing one
supernatural figure only, and from normal epic practice in
allowing Dulness to be so regularly and continuously visible
amongst her followers. In Book I, indeed, she only appears
at a crucial moment, and with her face veiled in fogs (fogs
which allude to the "shades of night" into which Venus vanishes,
in Aeneid II, and also have satirical point of their own[10]). In
Book II, however, Dulness actually presides over the "heroic"
games, and in Book IV is once more visible among her followers for a whole book. Pope did have some epic precedent for
making Dulness preside at the games. The goddess Thetis is
said to have proposed the prizes for the funeral games of her
son Achilles, as Pope mentions in the Argument to Book II.[11]
The fact remains that neither Homer nor Virgil ever did more

than allude to an event of this kind. Pope therefore gives the impression of departing from mock-epic consistency in his presentation of the goddess Dulness. The result is a blurring of any clear-cut contrast there might have been between the recalled heroic world and the world of the dunces. Instead there is a surprising, perhaps bewildering mingling of the two.

Consistent with the kind of difference already noted between the Rape of the Lock and the Dunciad is the fact that, as Warburton observed, the goddess Dulness is the "principal Agent" of the later poem.[12] Cibber-Aeneas is not sufficiently active. Consistent again is the fact that Pope sometimes puts direct satire, or self-satire, into the mouths of figures like Cibber, Settle and Aristarchus. This drew the particular criticism of Warton as "outrageously unnatural."[13] Altogether it is clear that the Dunciad does indeed differ from the Rape of the Lock in many ways, not all of which have been noted by Jack. It is true to say that if Pope intended to write another consistent and thorough-going mock-epic poem like the Rape of the Lock, then the Dunciad is a failure. Yet a certain consistency has emerged in the ways in which the later differs from the earlier poem, and this may prompt us to look for another kind of artistic coherence in the Dunciad.

III

Let us now approach the poem from a less formal standpoint, and consider the nature of Pope's subject — Dulness, or folly in the context of letters — and what Pope's attitude towards it was. Here a particular line of Pope's thought, as it may be traced from the Art of Sinking in Poetry to the Dunciad, is relevant. In the Art of Sinking, Pope makes fun of the mixed metaphor in the following way:

. . . its principal Beauty is when it gives an Idea just opposite to what it seem'd meant to describe. Thus an ingenious Artist painting the Spring, talks of a Snow of Blossoms, and thereby raises an unexpected Picture of Winter.[14]

Pope's attitude to this example of the art of dunces seems to be one of plain ridicule. Yet the phrase "a <u>Snow</u> of Blossoms," in spite of its obvious irrationality, its obvious untruth, at one level, to "Nature," has a very vivid visual appeal, and a sense of rich profusion. It is striking, perhaps, because it takes us a little beyond the bounds of the observable in nature. Whether such thoughts occurred to Pope, between writing the <u>Art of Sinking</u> and the <u>Dunciad</u>, it is hard to say; but his attitude to the same subject, in a passage from Book I of the <u>Dunciad</u>, certainly seems to have been modified and become more complex:

> There motley Images her fancy strike,
> Figures ill pair'd, and Similies unlike.
> She sees a Mob of Metaphors advance,
> Pleas'd with the madness of the mazy dance:
> How Tragedy and Comedy embrace;
> How Farce and Epic get a jumbled race;
> How Time himself stands still at her command,
> Realms shift their place, and Ocean turns to land.
> Here gay Description AEgypt glads with show'rs,
> Or gives to Zembla fruits, to Barca flow'rs;
> Glitt'ring with ice here hoary hills are seen,
> There painted valleys of eternal green,
> In cold December fragrant chaplets blow,
> And heavy harvests nod beneath the snow.[15]

Pope is here adopting a much more richly ambiguous attitude towards the "world" conjured up by this kind of irrationality in literature. Up to the line "How Farce and Epic get a jumbled race," Pope is inviting laughter at something ludicrously distorted and unnatural. Words like "motley," "Mob," "ill pair'd," "jumbled race," convey the sense of something cheap, low and unruly, and of a repulsive distortion of nature engendered by literary cross-breeding (a famous passage from Horace's <u>De Arte Poetica</u> lies behind Pope's lines).[16] At the same time a note of revelry and exuberance is introduced by "the madness of the mazy dance." This exuberance is seen to have powers of its own, when, in the next two lines, Pope describes how Dulness can halt time, shift realms, turn sea into dry land. This power is ironically recognized, and the irony is sustained and strengthened, as Pope moves on to consider the <u>generosity</u>

of Dulness -- "Here gay Description Aegypt glads with show'rs"
-- and depicts its fertility and munificence. From the phrase
"jumbled race" on, Pope has appeared to be advancing into a
make-believe world; he moves now into the brilliantly strange,
vivid and immediate landscape of the final four lines. As Brower well says, "Although the landscape is decidedly surrealist,
the charm of the images and the musical delight of the verse
lull us (as in the Pastorals) into accepting the absurd and the
impossible."[17] Pope has brought before our eyes a kind of
beauty which involves the blending of such opposites as were
present in the apparently absurd phrase "a Snow of Blossoms";
he is in fact conjuring up and exploring an imagined world of
folly and fantasy, such as might arise from the writing of a
poet who failed to regard, in his work, the "just standard" and
"universal light" of Nature.[18]

In other parts of the Dunciad Pope appears to be working
in a similar way. A particularly explicit example occurs in
Book III, just after the sudden outbreak of scenic portents, in
Settle's prophecy:

> Thence a new world to Nature's laws unknown,
> Breaks out refulgent, with a heav'n its own:
> Another Cynthia her new journey runs,
> And other planets circle other suns.
> The forests dance, the rivers upward rise,
> Whales sport in woods, and dolphins in the skies;
> And last, to give the whole creation grace,
> Lo! one vast Egg produces human race.[19]

While Pope is, at one level, and particularly in the last line,
condemning as a "monstrous absurdity"[20] the fantastic world
of cosmic enchantments which could be presented on the stage
by means of movable scenery, he is clearly fascinated by the
surrealistic strangeness of it all. He does not simply dismiss
it as a monstrous absurdity, but lingers to make it vivid and
immediate to the reader, expanding considerably on the two
lines of the De Arte Poetica which are probably the main source
of the passage.[21] A specific echo from the grandly prophetic
speech of Anchises, to which this speech of Settle is the comic
parallel, would have put the main stress, by contrast, on the
absurdity of the picture. As it is, the general allusion of this

passage to the Messianic Eclogue, and the particular echo of
Virgil's description of the "happy places" in Hades,[22] tend to
qualify rather than show up the absurdity.

Many passages from the Dunciad could be quoted to show
this strange double response of Pope to the idea of a world
given over to, and transformed by, Dulness.[23] The most obvious point about the diving competition in Fleet Ditch is that
it provides an appropriately nasty symbol for the in fact nasty
activities of unscrupulous, scandal-mongering writers. On this
level the effect is that of burlesque, in the modern sense of the
term; the heroic convention of the games is being paralleled
in low and squalid terms and the diction is, for the greater part
of this particular contest, not heroic but also low. Yet, towards
the end of the episode, we suddenly find Pope writing thus of
Smedley's sojourn in the sewer:

> First he relates, how sinking to the chin,
> Smit with his mien, the Mud-nymphs suck'd him in:
> How young Lutetia, softer than the down,
> Nigrina black, and Merdamante brown,
> Vy'd for his love in jetty bow'rs below,
> As Hylas fair was ravish'd long ago.[24]

Pope, in suddenly reverting from burlesque to mock-heroic,
raising and embellishing what the reader has become accustomed to as low and ugly, is once again creating an impression
of fantasy. What we took for the solid, low world of Fleet Ditch
is unexpectedly metamorphosed into a strange new scene in
which the repulsive is increasingly blended with and overcome
by the beautiful. The unpleasant meanings and associations of
the nymphs' names are offset by their melodious sound. By
that point in the passage the allusion to Hylas, confirmed in
the last line, would already be in mind for Pope's contemporary readers. It is the comparison with Hylas, above all, which
introduces into the description of the sewer the all but beautiful
classical element. Sutherland cites Valerius Flaccus' Argo-
nautica as the place where the story of Hylas is told most fully,
but the thirteenth Idyll of Theocritus is more likely to have
been in Pope's mind.[25] In Theocritus, but not in the Latin poet,
three nymphs (Eunica, Malis and Nycheia) draw Hylas down.[26]
Perhaps it was the fact that Theocritus described Hylas being

pulled down into black water, the waters of Fleet Ditch being
of course also black, which prompted Pope to bring the two
scenes into relation.[27] The whole episode in Theocritus is one
of great beauty and pathos; these qualities are thus introduced
into Smedley's adventure, and lend a strange attraction to the
dunce's symbolic exploit.

It should be noted that the following out of a mock-epic
parallel to Aeneid V, by no means demanded that Pope should
so beautify and romanticise one of his nastiest scenes. What
makes the term "fantasy" appropriate here is the unexpectedness (in the immediate context) with which Pope, at Smedley's
reappearance, reverts from a predominantly mock-heroic
mode, and also the immense distance between Smedley and
Fleet Ditch on the one hand, and the myth of Hylas on the other.
One can only conclude that here, as in the other passages discussed, Pope wished to create and explore, for its own sake,
an imagined world of folly, that he saw this "world" as something strange, fascinating and complex, surrealistically awe-
inspiring or beautiful as well as ridiculous and offensive, and
that he was concerned that it should not be presented as wholly
repulsive. The same ambiguity of attitude in Pope, in my view
a virtue in the context of the poem, is powerfully present in the
earlier part of Settle's prophecy in Book III (of which Brower
has perceptively noted that Pope "can respond to the fascination
of Vandalism and of sterile northern purity . . ."[28]) and in the
sensuous loveliness of decadent Europe, visited by the young
nobleman on the grand tour, in Book IV.[29]

IV

May not what has been true of these specific passages also
be true of the Dunciad as a whole? This would mean that, in the
various stages of creating his poem, Pope was doing more than
satirizing Dulness through his mock-epic parallel. To have
done that consistently three things would have been necessary:
first, that the reader should never be allowed to lose sight of
the actual behaviour of fools and dunces in the modern world,
secondly, that he should never be allowed to lose sight of the
heroic background by reference to which the fools and dunces
may be condemned, thirdly that the modern and the epic worlds

should be sharply juxtaposed, brought into close contact with one another yet kept separate, never allowed to blur or mingle. The following out of this method is one of the main strengths of the Rape of the Lock, and a great part of the "sure observance of decorum" praised by Jack. In the Dunciad, however, Pope often lets one or other side of the contrast between heroic and non-heroic recede from the focus of attention, often allows them to shift and blend with one another, in order to gain a further effect. If the passages discussed are at all representative of the nature of the total poem Pope, in the Dunciad, is interested in the imagined world of Dulness and Folly for its own sake, as something complex, disturbing and fascinating to be explored and rendered with a sense of immediacy. He is, on this assumption, not solely concerned with its contrast with a moral and rational epic standard. This hypothesis would account for the many passages in the Dunciad where the immediacy of the strange beauty or sublimity described, the outlandish fantasy, banishes contrast between epic nobility and actual absurdity to the back of the mind. It would account for Pope's double (and deliberately expressed) response to the idea of a world dominated by Dulness — a response which could at once deplore such a world, and yet endow it imaginatively with surrealistic strangeness, grandeur or beauty. In the Rape of the Lock Pope presented the world of Belinda as elegant and beautiful, but since the relative values of that society had merely slipped somewhat out of proportion with one another, no explanation of Pope's treatment of it there is needed. It does not stand for folly, like that of the Dunciad, and Clarissa is as much a part of it as Belinda. The present hypothesis would explain why Pope, in the Dunciad, is exploring and enlarging upon make-believe, pressing farther and farther into an imaginary and irrational world, and rendering its nature with such immediacy in his poetry. It would account for the fact that in the Dunciad the action is allegorical rather than real, and for the fact that the whole world of the poem is farther removed from the familiar and human than is that of the Rape of the Lock.

Indeed, if one postulates that it was Pope's purpose in writing the Dunciad to present and explore the irrational and fantastic world of duncery and folly — the world as a dunce would see it and as a dunce would transform it — then a number of the apparent difficulties in the poem resolve themselves.

In the context of this intention, it is not inappropriate that the
goddess Dulness should be regularly visible amongst her followers. One does not thus expect a consistent reflection of epic
proceeding; and of course the common visibility of Dulness,
like the constant inactivity of Cibber, has its own satiric point.
Nor need it be thought "outrageously unnatural," but consistent
with the improbable world presented, that Pope should sometimes make Cibber, Settle and Aristarchus speak satirical
sense of Dulness and themselves. In this context, above all,
the precise extent to which the mock-epic parallel is prominent
may be seen to serve Pope's purpose. In my view the mock-
epic parallel is present, and successful, as a basic unifying
factor; but Pope deliberately allows it to be halted or overlaid
with fantasy as the poem proceeds, its final submergence significantly coinciding with the final triumph of Dulness in Book
IV. Thus Pope may be said to observe the fantastic decorum
of Dulness, and to make the world he is describing more immediate to the reader by permitting something of its irrationality to enter into the structure of his poem. (My case is perhaps
strengthened here by Kathleen Williams' somewhat similar
analysis of Swift's Tale of a Tub.[30]) To have imposed upon the
subject of the Dunciad a strict and consistent mock-epic order
("the sure observance of decorum" which, in Jack's view, gives
the Rape of the Lock its "superiority") would have been entirely
inappropriate. Instead of seeming immediate and threatening,
the world of Dulness would then have seemed objectified and
under control.

    Considering Warton's main criticism of the Dunciad, re-
stated by Jack, can one really think the poem "a marvellous
mixture and jumble" in any damaging sense? Is not Pope legitimately presenting the whole range of Dulness, from the absurd
to the terrifying; is it not a consistent and appropriate quality
of this fantastic world that the reader should be faced with
numerous subtle and unexpected transitions from the ludicrous
to the solemn and back, from the absurd to the strange and
beautiful? The subject is such that "Pantomime and Philosophy"
can rub shoulders without artistic impropriety. Furthermore,
Jack's assumption that there is a clearcut division in content
and intention between Books I-III and Book IV will not stand
up to investigation. There is much high solemnity in Settle's
prophecy in Book III, his subject there being not merely

"Dulness in literature," but the fortunes of civilization in the
course of the history of the world; Book III thus leads up to
Book IV. Nor is it correct to assume that there is absolutely
no ludicrous element in Book IV. The "bard" and the "blockhead," the "pale Boy-Senator," Aristarchus, Annius, Mummius
and the rest are in the main grimly comic figures. If the 1728
Dunciad was, biographically speaking, "retaliatory in intention,"
and if its three books are substantially unchanged as Books
I-III of the 1743 Dunciad, it does not follow that this part of the
poem is any less serious or moral than Book IV. Dulness at
all its levels, from the absurd to the terrifying, is a proper
subject for moral concern, because it involves pride.[31] All
four books describe the fantastic world of Dulness, a world
which includes both the grotesque and the grand, and to which
attitudes of both ridicule and solemnity, on the part of both
poet and reader, are in turn equally appropriate. Of all poets,
it would be least true of Pope to suggest that one response was
less serious than the other; Pope's concern with his subject
is moral throughout.

V

Is it likely from the historical point of view that Pope
planned the Dunciad in the way I have suggested? The claim
that Book IV is inconsistent with Books I-III has always been
lent plausibility by the fact that Pope wrote it fourteen years
after the earlier part of the poem. If we hold, with Warton,
that the 1728 Dunciad is "clear, consistent, and of a piece,"[32]
and then find this apparent consistency broken by the addition
of Book IV, it is a great temptation to assume that Pope, in
the last years of his life, had somehow lost his grasp of the
Dunciad as a unified, total poem. Yet if Pope, at this stage,
could write a poem like the New Dunciad (which has in itself
been called "the most striking manifestation of his genius"[33])
it is likely that he should have lost his sense of total form and
structure, which had guided him so well in making his additions
to the Rape of the Lock? It is possible for an addition to a work
of art, while destroying the old pattern and unity, so to modify
the existing work as to create a new overall pattern which is
equally satisfactory. I suggest that this is what happened in the

creation of the 1743 Dunciad, and that Pope was probably well
aware of those qualities and tendencies of the 1728 poem which
were going to link up with, and be given new emphasis by, the
long final book. It should be clear that if the 1728 poem is
indeed "clear, consistent, and of a piece," it is certainly not
so in the manner of the Rape of the Lock; and it is just as open
to objection, by anyone who chooses to make the Rape of the
Lock his only positive standard, as is the Dunciad of 1743.[34]
 It may nevertheless seem surprising that Pope — engaged
in writing what he himself proclaimed to be, and what in its
most broad and obvious aspects certainly is, a mock-heroic
poem — should have departed so creatively from the pattern he
had established in the Rape of the Lock. An epic poem observes
certain rules; so therefore must the mock-epic: would the
author of the Essay on Criticism be prepared to deviate from
them in the way I have suggested? In answer we may recall the
following passage:

> If, where the rules not far enough extend,
> (Since rules were made but to promote their end,)
> Some lucky licence answer to the full
> Th'intent proposed, that licence is a rule.
> Thus Pegasus, a nearer way to take,
> May boldly deviate from the common track.
> Great wits sometimes may gloriously offend,
> And rise to faults true critics dare not mend;
> From vulgar bounds with brave disorder part,
> And snatch a grace beyond the reach of art. . . .
> In prospects, thus, some objects please our eyes,
> Which out of nature's common order rise,
> The shapeless rock, or hanging precipice.[35]

The whole passage would seem to be particularly applicable
to the Dunciad, as here discussed.
 One would nevertheless expect Pope to have had some kind
of precedent for what he was doing, some work in mind which
would serve to attract the poem Pope was writing a little way
out of the magnetic field of the absolutely consistent mock-epic.
I believe Pope did have such a precedent. The debt of the Dunciad to Dryden's MacFlecknoe is widely acknowledged; much
less attention has been paid to the relation between the Dunciad

and the work of the two great comic authors who, together with
Swift, are actually mentioned in the "Inscription" of the poem.
Addressing Swift, Pope writes as follows:

> O Thou! whatever title please thine ear,
> Dean, Drapier, Bickerstaff, or Gulliver!
> Whether thou chuse Cervantes' serious air,
> Or laugh and shake in Rabelais' easy chair,
> Or praise the Court, or magnify Mankind,
> Or thy griev'd Country's copper chains unbind;
> From bhy Boetia tho' her Pow'r retires,
> Mourn not, my SWIFT, at ought our Realm acquires,
> Here pleas'd behold her mighty wings out-spread
> To hatch a new Saturnian age of Lead.[36]

To regard life, and to write, in the manner of Cervantes and
of Rabelais are here seen as two possible responses to the
rising power of Dulness in England. Pope recognizes that both
are to be found in Swift. A third comic work that Pope evidently
had in mind when he was writing the <u>Dunciad</u> is the <u>Encomium
Moriae</u> of Erasmus, which is quoted in one of the Scriblerus
footnotes, in the variorum edition of 1729.[37] There is plenty
of evidence that Pope was familiar with the comic works of
these three authors.[38]

    It may seem unlikely that works so obviously different from
the <u>Dunciad</u> as <u>Don Quixote</u>, <u>Gargantua and Pantagruel</u> and <u>In
Praise of Folly</u> should have had any significant effect upon it.
It must be remembered, however, that all four works would be
classed together, in the first half of the eighteenth century,
as works of Ridicule. In his essay <u>Of Poetry</u>, Sir William Temple refers to Rabelais as "Father of the Ridicule," mentions
"the matchless Writer of <u>Don Quixote</u>" in the same connection,
and lists <u>La Secchia Rapita</u>, Scarron's <u>Virgil Travesty</u> and
Butler's <u>Hudibras</u> as examples of "that vein" — the vein of ridicule in verse.[39] Addison divides "Ridicule in Writing" into two
branches, Comedy and Burlesque:

> The first ridicules Persons by drawing them in their
> proper Characters, the other by drawing them quite
> unlike themselves. Burlesque is therefore of two
> kinds, the first represents mean Persons in the

Accoutrements of Heroes; the other describes great
Persons acting and speaking, like the basest among
the people. Don Quixote is an Instance of the first,
and Lucian's gods of the second. It is a Dispute among
the Criticks, whether Burlesque Poetry runs best in
Heroic Verse, like that of The Dispensary, or in Dog-
gerel, like that of Hudibras.[40]

It is significant that Addison can list Don Quixote and The Dispensary under the same branch of ridicule. Clearly works like
Gargantua and Pantagruel, Don Quixote, and the Dunciad, in
spite of their obvious differences, would not be considered
poles apart from one another. The Dunciad was the last and
most splendid in its outcome of a long series of attempts by
Pope to triumph over his antagonists by ridicule. It is worth
noticing that an early attempt of this kind, The Critical Specimen, of 1711, borrows comic ideas from both In Praise of
Folly and Don Quixote.[41] Again, the Dunciad is a satire on false
learning. Warburton said of the History of Martinus Scriblerus,

> Mr. Pope, Dr. Arbuthnot, and Dr. Swift projected to
> write a satire, in conjunction, on the abuses of human
> learning; and to make it the better received, they pro-
> posed to do it in the manner of Cervantes (the original
> author of this species of satire) under the history of
> some feigned adventures.[42]

Pope himself notes the relevance of Don Quixote to mock-heroic,
in his Postscript to the Odyssey, where he speaks of the "use
of pompous expression, for low actions or thoughts" as "the
true sublime of Don Quixote" and "the perfection of the Mock-
Epic."[43] It is clear that In Praise of Folly, Gargantua and
Pantagruel and Don Quixote, as works of ridicule and satires
on false learning, could have been regarded by Pope as part of
the same literary ambience as his own projected Dunciad.
What I wish to argue, finally, is that the three works in
question had the effect of drawing the Dunciad somewhat away
from the pattern of the Rape of the Lock, and of encouraging
Pope's inclination to introduce a strong element of fantasy into
his poem. Erasmus' In Praise of Folly perhaps affected the
Dunciad in the most specific and clearly distinguishable ways.

The figure of Folly in Erasmus may well have given Pope the
idea for the particular way he was to present the goddess Dulness. Folly dominates Erasmus' work as Dulness does Pope's,
and both are regularly visible to human eyes. Dulness is discovered "Close to those walls where Folly holds her throne,"[44]
and Pope speaks of "her own fools-colours."[45] Both are full of
self-love; Folly never speaks but in praise of herself (indeed
the Encomium is her oration) while Dulness is seen much of the
time receiving the homage and praise of her followers. As, in
The Critical Specimen, the "conceited frolicksome Country
Lass" Moria gave Dennis her blessing, so Dulness blesses
Cibber in the Dunciad.[46] If this seems to make light of Pope's
obvious intention to create a comic parallel to the goddess
Venus, it must be remembered that there was a traditional
connection between Venus and Folly. Addison reminded his
readers, in the Spectator, that Venus had been called "the
Laughter-loving Dame,"[47] and Folly herself, in the Encomium,
rhetorically asks:

> Why [is] Venus ever in her prime, but because of her
> affinity with me? Witness that color of her hair, so
> resembling my father [Plutus], from whence she is
> called the golden Venus; and lastly, ever laughing if
> you give any credit to the poets. . . .[48]

Again, while Pope presents the quality of dulness in a more
consistently bad light than Erasmus presents folly, both are
to be found associating these qualities, from time to time, with
some strange kind of attractiveness, vitality or beauty. Erasmus makes Folly describe her birthplace, "the Fortunate Is-
lands," as a place

> where all things grew without plowing or sowing; where
> neither labor, nor old age, nor disease was ever heard
> of; and in whose fields neither daffodil, mallows, onions,
> beans, and such contemptible things would ever grow,
> but, on the contrary, rue, angelica, bugloss, marjor-
> am, trefoils, roses, violets, lilies, and all the gardens
> of Adonis invite both your sight and your smelling.[49]

This passage may be compared with the first passage from the

Dunciad quoted above; both writers are associating with folly
a world made intentionally fantastic, to which normal natural
laws do not apply, but which has a vivid and exotic beauty of
its own. Such passages as this in Erasmus' In Praise of Folly
may well have helped to foster in Pope the deliberately expressed ambiguity of attitude to Dulness that I have indicated.[50]
   Gargantua and Pantagruel and Don Quixote are likely to
have had a much more general, but not less important, effect
on the Dunciad. These works are of interest because their
comedy usually works through the presentation of a world of
moral fantasy. Rabelais might, like Swift in Pope's own time,
have kept the world of men and the world of giants distinct
throughout, satirising one by contrast with the other. Instead
he allows them to mingle and produce unexpected and fantastic
comic effects. For long periods the reader is allowed to forget
that Gargantua and Pantagruel are giants, and Panurge a man;
though the giants are presented as morally virtuous, their
jovial patience with the human folly of Panurge has the effect
of breaking down any black and white contrast between them.
In Don Quixote one sees the real world (the whore, not the fair
lady; the tavern, not the castle) through the eyes of Sancho
Panza, when he is not deluded by his master, and through the
eyes of the minor characters. It is exemplified with a particular sober solidity by the curate and the barber and by the
knight's home. But the world of the story is also partly the
world of Don Quixote's literary imagination, just as the world
of the Dunciad is to a large extent the world of a dunce's imagination. Again and again Cervantes allows the real world to
merge subtly and unexpectedly with the fantastic; Sancho Panza
is by no means a reliable touchstone. The knight and the squire
move through a half-real, half-unreal world, representing,
at different times, different literary genres. The setting and
atmosphere of medieval romance merges into classical pastoral, and again into that of Arabian fable. Thus the world is
often seen through the eyes of the foolish yet idealistic knight,
whose mind was soaked in extravagant fiction of all kinds. It
is this general quality that Don Quixote and the Dunciad have
in common: that of creating a world of folly endowed with an
undeniable and fantastic life of its own, and of exploring this
world, moving deeper and deeper into it, as Pope does in the
Dunciad, while the heroic games are succeeded by the prophecy

of Settle-Anchises, and by the fulfilment of that prophecy. As a recent critic has said of In Praise of Folly, these two works possess a similar "essential communication of an idiosyncratic vision of the world and the creation of a unique structure to display this fantasy."[51] Don Quixote had a considerable influence on English literature in the eighteenth century; it is likely that, together with Gargantua and Pantagruel and In Praise of Folly, it provided Pope with the inspiration to make the Dunciad a very different kind of mock-epic poem from the Rape of the Lock.

NOTES

1 This article might be read as a commentary on the following statements: (i) "The 'Chiefless Armies' doze in an immensely fantastic dream-comedy, and the Navies yawn vastly on an enchanted sea" (F. R. Leavis, Revaluation, 1936, p. 88; of Dunciad iv. 605-18.) (ii) "The Dunciad, like MacFlecknoe, is the ludicrous, grotesque, lifesize shadow cast by a piece of an epic poem, the Rape of the Lock an exquisitely diminished shadow cast by an entire epic, by the august epic form itself" (Geoffrey Tillotson, On the Poetry of Pope, 1938, p. 55.) (iii) ". . . the earlier books are linked imaginatively with the fourth and . . . take their place in the epic fantasia of the Dunciad" (R. A. Brower, Alexander Pope: The Poetry of Allusion, 1959, p. 344).

2 Ian Jack, Augustan Satire, 1952, pp. 133-4, 125-6.

3 See Joseph Warton, Essay on the Genius and Writings of Pope: in two volumes, 1806, ii (first published 1782) 368-77; W. J. Courthope, Works of Alexander Pope, ed. William Elwin and W. J. Courthope, 1871-89, v. 230; The Dunciad, ed. James Sutherland, 1943, intro. pp. xli-ii. F. R. Leavis appears to have no regard for the poem as a whole. Protesting that one cannot do justice to Pope in short extracts, he says: ". . . one must read through not merely the Epistles, but, also as a unit, the fourth book of the Dunciad. . . ." (Revaluation, p. 91.)

4 Aubrey Williams, Pope's Dunciad, 1955.

5 Ibid., p. 25.

6 R. A. Brower, Alexander Pope: The Poetry of Allusion, 1959, pp. 319-52, especially 344.

7 LI. 5-36.

8 Catullus, lxvi. 51-68. Virgil, Eclogues v. 56-66.

9 The Dunciad, ed. James Sutherland, 1943, p. 51. All quotations are from this edition.

10 Aeneid ii. 621. Dryden translated: "Obscure in clouds, and gloomy shades of night" (ii. 841; Poems, ed. James Kinsley, iii. 1113).

11 The Dunciad, p. 295. Odyssey xxiv. 85-92.

12 The Dunciad, p. 269, 1. 1n.

13 Joseph Warton, op. cit., ii. 373-4, 376.

14 Pope, The Art of Sinking in Poetry, ed. E. L. Steeves, 1952, pp. 48-9.

15 The Dunciad, B, i. 65-78.

16 Horace, De Arte Poetica, 1-13.

17 Brower, op. cit., p. 328.

18 Pope, An Essay on Criticism, i. 69, 71. Works, ed. Elwin and Courthope, ii. 37.

19 The Dunciad, B, iii. 241-8.

20 Ibid., A, iii. 233n.

21 Horace, De Arte Poetica, 29-30.

22 Virgil, Aeneid vi. 641. Pope also echoes a line of his imitation of the Messianic Eclogue: Messiah, 26. Works, ed. Elwin and Courthope, i. 311.

23 Apart from those mentioned in the text, see: i. 79-84; ii. 337-346, 387-396; iii. 1-34, 253-272, 333-340; iv. 9-16, 71-84, 189-202, 397-436, 549-564, 605-656, in the B text.

24 The Dunciad, B, ii. 331-6.

25 The Dunciad, p. 140, 1. 312n.

26 Theocritus, Idyll xiii. 36-54.

27 Theocritus, Idyll xiii. 49-50.

28 The Dunciad, B, iii. 67-100; Brower, op. cit., p. 338.

29 The Dunciad, iv. 289-310.

30 Kathleen Williams, Jonathan Swift and the Age of Com-
    promise, 1959, p. 133.

31 A point for which I am indebted to Dr. J. T. Boulton's lec-
    tures on Pope, at Nottingham.

32 Joseph Warton, op. cit., ii. 368.

33 F. R. Leavis, op. cit., p. 91.

34 Warton himself, in criticising the apparent impropriety
    of the hero's opening speech, involves the 1728 as well
    as the 1743 Dunciad. Warton, op. cit., ii. 373-4.

35 Pope, An Essay on Criticism, i. 146-55, 158-60; Works,
    ed. Elwin and Courthope, ii. 42-3.

36 The Dunciad, B, i. 19-28. Huntington Brown, in his Rabe-
    lais in English Literature, 1933, discusses Rabelais in
    connection with Pope, Swift and Arbuthnot. He does not
    consider a possible influence on The Dunciad.

37 The Dunciad, A. ii. 46n. Jack has drawn attention to the
    Encomium Moriae in connection with the wide connotation
    Pope gives the term "Dulness." Augustan Satire, p. 125,
    n. 1. Aubrey Williams has spoken of the wide "satiric
    alliance" in which both the Encomium Moriae and the Dun-
    ciad participate (Pope's Dunciad, p. 84).

38 For Erasmus, see George Sherburn, ed. The Correspon-
    dence of Alexander Pope, 1956, i. 122n. 7 (To Caryll, June
    25th, 1711) and Joseph Warton, ed. The Works of Alexan-
    der Pope, 1797, ix. 460 (The Last Will of Mr. Pope). For
    Rabelais, see Joseph Spence, Anecdotes, ed. S. W. Singer,
    1820, p. 207-8. For Cervantes, see Sherburn, op. cit.,
    i. 10, 477; ii. 23; iv. 212.

39 Sir William Temple, "Of Poetry"; Works, ed. Jonathan
    Swift, 1720, i. 246.

40 The Spectator, No. 249, December 15th, 1711.

41 Attributed to Pope by Norman Ault and John Butt in their edition of Pope's Minor Poems, 1954, p. 80. Prose Works of Alexander Pope, ed. Norman Ault, 1936, i. 1-18.

42 G. A. Aitken, The Life and Works of John Arbuthnot, 1892, p. 307 n. 1.

43 Pope, Postscript to the Odyssey; Works, ed. Joseph Warton, iv. 435.

44 The Dunciad, B, i. 29.

45 Ibid. , B, i. 84.

46 Prose Works of Alexander Pope, i. 12.

47 The Spectator, No. 249, December 15th, 1711.

48 Erasmus, The Praise of Folly, translated by John Wilson, 1668; 1958 edn. , p. 24.

49 Ibid. , pp. 13-14.

50 Other examples are ed. cit. , pp. 7-8, 15-19, 23-25, 27-29.

51 Bernard Harris, Men Like Satyrs, Stratford on Avon Studies, II, ed. J. R. Brown and Bernard Harris, 1960, p. 176.